World Development Report 1996

FROM PLAN TO MARKET

PUBLISHED FOR THE WORLD BANK

OXFORD UNIVERSITY PRESS

Oxford University Press

OXFORD   NEW YORK   TORONTO   DELHI   BOMBAY   CALCUTTA
MADRAS   KARACHI   KUALA LUMPUR   SINGAPORE   HONG KONG
TOKYO   NAIROBI   DAR ES SALAAM   CAPE TOWN   MELBOURNE
AUCKLAND

and associated companies in

3 2280 00620 5967

BERLIN   IBADAN

© 1996 The International Bank for Reconstruction and
Development / The World Bank
1818 H Street, N.W., Washington, D.C. 20433, U.S.A.

Published by Oxford University Press, Inc.
200 Madison Avenue, New York, N.Y. 10016

Oxford is a registered trademark of Oxford University Press.

Manufactured in the United States of America
First printing June 1996

This volume is a product of the staff of the World Bank, and the
judgments made herein do not necessarily reflect the views of its Board
of Executive Directors or the countries they represent. The World Bank
does not guarantee the accuracy of the data included in this publication
and accepts no responsibility whatsoever for any consequence of their
use. The boundaries, colors, denominations, and other information
shown on any map in this volume do not imply on the part of the
World Bank any judgment on the legal status of any territory
or the endorsement or acceptance of such boundaries.

ISBN 0-19-521108-1 clothbound
ISBN 0-19-521107-3 paperback
ISSN 0163-5085

Text printed on recycled paper that conforms to the American Standard
for Permanence of Paper for Printed Library Material Z39.48-1984

Foreword

World Development Report 1996, the nineteenth in this annual series, is devoted to the transition of countries with centrally planned economies—in particular, Central and Eastern Europe, the newly independent states of the former Soviet Union, China, and Vietnam—to a market orientation.

This transition, which affects about one-third of the world's population, has been unavoidable. The world is changing rapidly: massive increases in global trade and private investment in recent years have created enormous potential for growth in jobs, incomes, and living standards through free markets. Yet the state-dominated economic systems of these countries, weighed down by bureaucratic control and inefficiency, largely prevented markets from functioning and were therefore incapable of sustaining improvements in human welfare. Although these systems guaranteed employment and social services, they did so at the cost of productivity, overall living standards, and—importantly—the environment, which has been severely damaged in some countries by distorted prices, inefficient use of natural resources, and antiquated plant.

Necessary as the transition to the market has been, it has not been easy. Some countries have been considerably more successful than others in implementing the key elements of change. Above all, the transition has had and will continue to have a profound impact on people's lives. In some of the countries undergoing transition there has been a short-term drop in living standards; in others human welfare has improved dramatically. Everywhere it has changed the basic economic rules of the game and has irreversibly altered the relationship between people and their political and social, not to mention economic, institutions.

This Report is devoted to exploring the experience of economies in transition, to identifying which approaches work and which do not, and to pinpointing the critical elements of success. It does not overgeneralize. It recognizes that the countries it examines represent a diverse array of national histories, cultures, and political systems; in fact, it explores the linkages between these non-

economic factors and economic outcomes. Yet it makes a number of general points that provide valuable information to all reforming economies and to those who care about them. It drives home the utter necessity of both liberalizing economies through opening trade and market opportunities and stabilizing them through reducing inflation and practicing fiscal discipline—and then of sticking to these policies consistently over time. It discusses the necessity of reforming enterprises and expanding the private sector, while restructuring social safety nets to deal with the social impact of the move to the market. And it makes the vital point that, in the long run, clear property rights and widespread private ownership are needed for markets to perform efficiently and equitably.

The Report also makes a major contribution in discussing the institutions that make a market-based economy work. It describes how public agencies, legal systems, financial institutions, and education and health systems can all enhance the success of market economies. These are the institutions that help set and enforce the rules that allow market transactions to proceed in a climate of confidence, that decrease the opportunities for corruption and crime, that mobilize and allocate resources, and that build human capital. And it discusses the need for transition countries to carry through with measures to integrate themselves further within the global economy. Integration into the institutions of the world trading system is an important way to help these countries nourish and sustain the reforms they have undertaken.

Beyond these essential technical and institutional elements of transition, this Report is about *people*. It is about how people can be protected from the loss of security and income that can accompany transition, how they can be helped to cope with the increased mobility and know-how required of workers in market economies, and how their children must receive the education and health care that will allow them to contribute to the prosperity to which their countries aspire. This brings us back to the very reason for transition in the first place, and the reason why this

Report is needed. It is about how to unleash the enormous talents and energies of these countries' populations, and how to help them achieve their vision for a future of opportunity and well-being for all their citizens. In the end, we will gauge the success of transition not merely by statistical measures of national wealth, investment, or productivity, but also by the quality of life of the people who live in these countries.

James D. Wolfensohn
President
The World Bank

May 31, 1996

This Report has been prepared by a team led by Alan Gelb with principal authors Nicholas Barr, Stijn Claessens, Cheryl Williamson Gray, Peter Harrold, Françoise Le Gall (IMF), John Nellis, Zhen Kun Wang, and Ulrich Zachau. The team was assisted by Annette Brown, Gregory Kisunko, Tatiana Proskuryakova, Sarbajit Sinha, Stoyan Tenev, and Triinu Tombak. Gilles Alfandari and Laszlo Urban also contributed to the Report. Stephanie Flanders was the principal editor. The work was carried out under the general direction of Michael Bruno.

Many others in and outside the World Bank provided helpful comments and contributions (see the Bibliographical Note). The International Economics Department contributed to the data appendix and was responsible for the Selected World Development Indicators. The production staff of the Report included Amy Brooks, Kathryn Kline Dahl, Joyce Gates, Stephanie Gerard, Cathe Kocak, Jeffrey N. Lecksell, Brenda Mejia, Hugh Nees, Beatrice Sito, and Michael Treadway. The design was by the Magazine Group. Rebecca Sugui served as executive assistant to the team, and Daniel Atchison, Elizabeth V. De Lima, and Michael Geller as staff assistants. Maria D. Ameal served as administrative officer.

Preparation of the Report was greatly aided by background papers and by contributions from participants in the consultation meetings. The names of these participants are listed in the Bibliographical Note.

Contents

BOXES

TEXT FIGURES

TEXT TABLES

APPENDIX TABLES

Definitions and Data Notes

Selected terms used in this Report

Corporate governance is the monitoring and control, typically by owners, of the management and performance of an enterprise.

Externalities are costs or benefits resulting from an economic activity or transaction that accrue to persons or entities other than those engaged in it.

Gini coefficients are a standard measure of inequality of income distribution, calculated with reference to the departure of an actual distribution from a state of perfect income equality.

Hard budget constraints are said to exist when managers of state enterprises know that the budgets set for them by central government are fixed and that losses will not be financed out of general revenues or by the central bank.

Informalization is the exit of economic activity from that part of the economy where it is subject to laws, regulation, and taxation and covered in official economic statistics.

Liberalization refers, except where stated otherwise, to economic liberalization: the loosening or elimination of government restrictions on domestic transactions, prices, and markets; on external transactions and the free exchange of domestic currency for foreign and vice versa (*convertibility*); or on free entry of firms into domestic markets.

Market failure is any situation in which markets systematically produce more or less of certain goods or services than is optimal for the society as a whole.

Moral hazard is a situation in which the presence of insurance or the expectation of compensating policy weakens or distorts incentives to prudent behavior.

Privatization is used in its strict sense, that of divestiture by the state of enterprises, land, or other assets, and not in the broader sense of any action that moves an enterprise or an economy in the direction of private ownership or that tends to make the behavior of state enterprises more like that of private entities.

Rent seeking is any manipulation of the law or of government authority in order to generate or appropriate an economic rent. Such rents are earnings from productive factors in excess of the minimum needed to keep that factor at its present use; they can arise through the acquisition of a claim on a resource whose ownership was ambiguous or weakly exercised, or through a change in government policy that creates an artificial scarcity.

Stabilization refers to macroeconomic stabilization, or the control and reduction of inflation and the containing of economy-wide imbalances, such as fiscal deficits, and of external imbalances, such as current account deficits.

Township and village enterprises are a form of enterprise organization unique to China in which local government owns all or most of the enterprise but local individuals hold implicit property rights.

Country groups

For operational and analytical purposes the World Bank's main criterion for classifying economies is gross national product (GNP) per capita. Every economy is classified as either low-income, middle-income (subdivided into lower-middle and upper-middle), or high-income. Other analytical groups, based on regions, exports, and levels of external debt, are also used.

Because GNP per capita changes with time, the country composition of each income group may change from one edition to the next. Once the classification is fixed for any edition, all the historical data presented are based on the same country grouping. The income-based country groupings used in this year's Report are defined as follows.

Low-income economies are those with a GNP per capita of $725 or less in 1994.

Middle-income economies are those with a GNP per capita of more than $725 but less than $8,956 in 1994. A further division, at GNP per capita of $2,895 in 1994, is made between lower-middle-income and upper-middle-income economies.

High-income economies are those with a GNP per capita of $8,956 or more in 1994.

World comprises all economies, including economies with sparse data and those with less than 1 million population; these are not shown separately in the main tables but are presented in Table 1a in the technical notes to the Selected World Development Indicators.

Classification by income does not necessarily reflect development status. (In the Selected World Development Indicators, high-income economies classified as developing by the United Nations or regarded as developing by their authorities are identified by the symbol †.) The use of the term "countries" to refer to economies implies no judgment by the Bank about the legal or other status of a territory.

The table "Classification of economies" at the end of the Selected World Development Indicators lists countries according to income, regional, and analytical classifications.

Other analytical groups

In the text of the Report, for analytical purposes Central and Eastern Europe (CEE) comprises Albania, Bulgaria, Croatia, the Czech Republic, Hungary, the former Yugoslav Republic of (FYR) Macedonia, Poland, Romania, the Slovak Republic, and Slovenia. Bosnia and Herzegovina and the Federal Republic of Yugoslavia are also part of this group but are not discussed in the Report.

The newly independent states (NIS) are Armenia, Azerbaijan, Belarus, Estonia, Georgia, Kazakstan, the Kyrgyz Republic, Latvia, Lithuania, Moldova, Russia, Tajikistan, Turkmenistan, Ukraine, and Uzbekistan.

The set of transition economies used in the analyses consists of the above two groups plus Mongolia, China, and Vietnam.

The text also makes reference to the following country subgroups. The Baltic countries are Estonia, Latvia, and Lithuania. The Visegrad countries are the Czech Republic, Hungary, Poland, and the Slovak Republic. Countries whose economies have been severely affected by regional tensions are Armenia, Azerbaijan, Croatia, Georgia, FYR Macedonia, and Tajikistan.

Membership in the Council for Mutual Economic Assistance (CMEA), the now-dissolved trading system of the former communist bloc, consisted in 1989 of Bulgaria, Cuba, Czechoslovakia, the German Democratic Republic, Hungary, Mongolia, Poland, Romania, the Soviet Union, and Vietnam.

The country members of the Organization for Economic Cooperation and Development (OECD) as of publication are Australia, Austria, Belgium, Canada, the Czech Republic, Denmark, Finland, France, Germany, Greece, Hungary, Iceland, Ireland, Italy, Japan, Luxembourg, Mexico, Netherlands, New Zealand, Norway, Portugal, Spain, Sweden, Switzerland, Turkey, the United Kingdom, and the United States. Data for OECD countries for a particular year apply to the organization's membership in that year.

Data notes

Billion is 1,000 million.

Trillion is 1,000 billion.

Tons are metric tons, equal to 1,000 kilograms, or 2,204.6 pounds.

Dollars are current U.S. dollars unless otherwise specified.

Growth rates for economic data reported in the Selected World Development Indicators are based on constant price data and, unless otherwise noted, have been computed with the use of the least-squares method. See the technical notes to the Selected World Development Indicators for details of this method.

The symbol / in dates, as in "1990/91," means that the period of time may be less than two years but straddles two calendar years and refers to a crop year, a survey year, or a fiscal year.

The symbol .. in tables means not available.

The symbol — in tables means not applicable. (In the Selected World Development Indicators, a blank is used to mean not applicable.)

The number 0 or 0.0 in tables and figures means zero or a quantity less than half the unit shown and not known more precisely.

The cutoff date for all data in the Selected World Development Indicators is April 30, 1996.

Historical data in this Report may differ from those in previous editions because of continual updating as better data become available, because of a change to a new base year for constant price data, or because of changes in country composition in income and analytical groups.

Other economic and demographic terms are defined in the technical notes to the Selected World Development Indicators.

Acronyms and initials

CAP	Common Agricultural Policy (of the European Union)
CEE	Central and Eastern Europe (see "Other analytical groups" above)
CMEA	Council for Mutual Economic Assistance (see "Other analytical groups" above)
EBRD	European Bank for Reconstruction and Development
EU	European Union
FDI	Foreign direct investment
GATT	General Agreement on Tariffs and Trade
GDP	Gross domestic product
GNP	Gross national product
IFC	International Finance Corporation
IMF	International Monetary Fund
NGO	Nongovernmental organization
NIS	Newly independent states (see "Other analytical groups" above)
OECD	Organization for Economic Cooperation and Development (see "Other analytical groups" above)
PPP	Purchasing power parity
TVE	Township and village enterprises (see "Selected terms used in this Report" above)
VAT	Value added tax
WTO	World Trade Organization

Understanding Transition

Between 1917 and 1950 countries containing one-third of the world's population seceded from the market economy and launched an experiment in constructing an alternative economic system. First in the former Russian Empire and Mongolia, then, after World War II, in Central and Eastern Europe and the Baltic states, and subsequently in China, northern Korea, and Vietnam (with offshoots and imitators elsewhere), a massive effort was made to centralize control of production and allocate all resources through state planning. This vast experiment transformed the political and the economic map of the world and set the course of much of the twentieth century. Now its failure has set in motion just as radical a transformation, as these same countries change course, seeking to rebuild markets and reintegrate themselves into the world economy.

The *Communist Manifesto*'s portrayal of the turbulent arrival of capitalism in the nineteenth century seems a curiously apt depiction of today's transition landscape:

> Constant revolutionizing of production, uninterrupted disturbance of all social conditions, everlasting uncertainty and agitation. . . . All fixed, fast-frozen relations, with their train of ancient and venerable prejudices, and opinions, are swept away, all new-formed ones become antiquated before they can ossify. All that is solid melts into air. . . .

The long-term goal of transition is the same as that of economic reforms elsewhere: to build a thriving market economy capable of delivering long-term growth in living standards. What distinguishes transition from reforms in other countries is the systemic change involved: reform must penetrate to the fundamental rules of the game, to the institutions that shape behavior and guide organizations. This makes it a profound social transition as well as an economic one. Similar changes have been needed in

many other countries, and the transition experience is therefore of interest to them as well. But most of their reform programs pale in comparison to the scale and intensity of the transition from plan to market.

This Report steps back from the bewildering array of events and policy changes in twenty-eight countries to ask what we have learned about the ingredients of any successful transition and how these should be pursued. This is a transition still very much in progress; many important questions do not yet have definitive answers. The fact that so much remains to be done, however, makes it all the more important to deduce the key lessons of transition to date.

The legacy of planning

Karl Marx had reasoned that socialism would replace capitalism first in the most industrialized capitalist countries. Indeed, the first part of the twentieth century was a period of considerable social ferment, notably in Europe. But revolutionary socialism took hold in more agrarian states, where economic development and the advancement of industry were concerns as important as equitable distribution. The achievements of the planned system were considerable. They included increased output, industrialization, the provision of basic education, health care, housing, and jobs to entire populations, and a seeming imperviousness to the Great Depression of the 1930s. Incomes were relatively equally distributed, and an extensive, if inefficient, welfare state ensured everyone access to basic goods and services (Table 1). But the system was far less stable than it seemed, for the intrinsic inefficiency of planning was overwhelming. Planners could not get enough information to substitute for that supplied by prices in a market economy. Planning became largely a personalized bargaining process, with connections (*blat* or *guanxi*) an important element. This proved bad for industry, worse for agriculture. Also, the suppression of

Table 1 The starting numbers
(percent except where stated otherwise)

| Indicator | Transition economies | | | | | Comparators | | | |
	CEE	Russia	Other NIS and Mongolia	China[a]	Vietnam[a]	Low-income[b]	India	Middle-income	OECD
Population and income									
Population, 1989 (millions)	122	149	139	1,102	64	1,002	850	1,105	773
GNP per capita, 1990[c] (1990 dollars)									
From *World Bank Atlas*	2,268	4,110	2,141	404	188	320	380	2,220	20,170
At PPP	4,647	6,440	4,660	1,000	..	1,086	1,090	4,289	15,615
Growth rate before transition[d]	1.5	1.9	2.3	4.9	..	3.4	5.8	2.9	3.0
Economic structure									
Urban population as share of total population, 1991	61	74	58	18	19	28	27	62	77
Investment share of GDP, 1989[e]	34	34	31	35	16	21	24	25	22
Industry share of GDP, 1989	51	50	40	48	23	28	29	36	31
Energy use (kilograms of oil equivalent per dollar of GDP)[f]	0.81	0.91	0.71	0.38	..	0.14	0.21	0.41	0.31
Human resources									
Gini coefficient, 1989[g]	26	24	24	30	36	46	34	45	33
Life expectancy at birth, 1989 (years)[g]	71	69	70	70	66	56	60	68	77
Illiteracy rate, 1991	3	2	2	31	12	41	52	17	<5
Monetary and exchange rate indicators									
M2 as percentage of GDP	53	100	75	25	19	33	46	41	78
Black market exchange rate premium, 1989	331	1,828	1,822	..	464	87	12	101	0

.. Not available.
Note: All measures for country groups are averages, weighted by population.
a. All data for China are for 1978, and those for Vietnam for 1986, except where specifically noted otherwise (i.e., for GDP growth, energy use, Gini coefficients, and life expectancy).
b. Excluding China and India.
c. Data are for 1991 for NIS and Mongolia.
d. Average annual real GDP growth rate at market prices; data are for 1980–89 for CEE and comparators, 1980–90 for NIS and Mongolia, 1966–78 for China.
e. Gross domestic investment.
f. At PPP using 1992 dollars; data are for 1990 for CEE; 1992 for NIS, Mongolia, and comparators; 1980 for China (staff estimate).
g. Data are for 1980 for China, 1992 for Vietnam.
Source: IMF and World Bank data; International Currency Analysis, Inc., data.

individual incentives required in their place an intrusive set of controls. At the outset these may have been based on ideological commitment and a dedicated vanguard party, but they frequently degenerated into cults of personality and abuses of position by nomenklatura elites.

The deep inefficiencies of planning became increasingly evident with time. Heavy industries such as machine building and metallurgy were emphasized, while development of consumer goods lagged. After posting high annual growth rates in the 1950s (averaging 10 percent according to official estimates), the Soviet economy decelerated: growth averaged 7 percent per year in the 1960s, 5 percent in the 1970s, and barely 2 percent in the 1980s, and in 1990 it

contracted. This trend occurred despite high investment rates—returns to capital formation began a steady and rapid descent in the mid-1950s (Figure 1). A similar stagnation infected Eastern Europe. As a major oil exporter, the Soviet Union benefited from the price increases of 1973 and 1979, but severe shortages and the deteriorating quality of its manufactured goods relative to those of market economies were clear signs of stagnation (Box 1).

Social indicators began to worsen as well, confirming the troubled state of the system. After World War II health indicators in Russia improved rapidly and began to approach levels in the industrial market economies. In the mid-1960s, however, they began to stagnate, and later

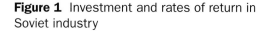

By the 1970s, Soviet investment was yielding little or no return.

Figure 1 Investment and rates of return in Soviet industry

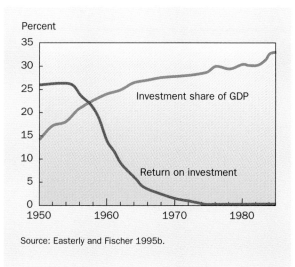

Source: Easterly and Fischer 1995b.

even to reverse: life expectancy fell by two years between 1966 and 1980. This was in marked contrast to the trend in other industrial countries, which experienced increases of some three to four years over a similar period.

Nor were living standards in China's less thoroughly planned economy immune from stagnation. Overall (total factor) productivity declined from 1955 to 1978 despite, or perhaps because of, very high investment in heavy industry. The famines of the Great Leap Forward (1958–60) and the ten disastrous years of Cultural Revolution left Chinese society exhausted by politics and the Communist Party ready for change. Many regions had already begun to experiment with local reforms. Peasants in particular felt that collectivist agricultural policies were harming productivity and living standards. Their views carried weight because the Party had a strong rural base, so that economic improvement became a more urgent goal. The impetus to reform was different again in Vietnam, struggling to recover from forty years of war, and in Mongolia. Unlike China, both had deep links with the Soviet Union and depended on Soviet subsidies. Both needed to break out of isolation.

In response, most of these economies have rejected all or much of central planning and have embarked on a passage—a transition—toward decentralized market mechanisms underpinned by widespread private ownership. Not all follow the same path. Despite common features, the

mass of centrally planned economies was far from monolithic. It was composed of countries with different histories, cultures, and resource endowments. And whereas political change toward multiparty democracy was a prime objective in the post-1989 reforms in Central and Eastern Europe (CEE) and the newly independent states (NIS) of the former Soviet Union, neither China, which initiated economic reforms in 1978, nor Vietnam has experienced a political transition away from governments dominated by the Communist Party. There is thus tremendous variety in the departure points, strategies, and outcomes of transition across countries.

Most of the world's economies, at one time or another, have lifted price controls, opened trade, or privatized state enterprises—with varying degrees of success. But as noted above, transition is different. It is not simply the adoption or modification of a few policies or programs but a passage from one mode of economic organization to a thoroughly different one. The underlying habits and rules of an economic system are often so pervasive and ingrained that they are taken for granted; indeed, the better established they are, the less they are consciously reflected upon. Such institutions as the education system, youth and labor organizations, the organization and supervision of work in firms and on farms, and the availability of information to the public were carefully cultivated to serve the process of bureaucratic allocation and the broader objectives of central planning. Paternalistic and restrictive, these institutions delivered goods and services to meet basic needs while setting severe limits on individ-

Box 1 Falling further behind in world markets

Beginning in the mid-1960s there were unmistakable signs that CEE and the Soviet Union were falling behind the newly industrializing economies in product quality. By 1985 CEE's engineering exports earned less than 30 percent of the average unit value received by all exporters of similar products, and these exports were often twenty years behind in their technology. The quality gap was widest for consumer goods, including electronics, reflecting the scant influence that domestic buyers had on product quality. One study found that by 1990 Soviet cars commanded a mere third of the price of similar Western cars in the Finnish market. As with high energy intensity (Table 1), declining quality reflected the incentives created by the system and its isolation from world markets and foreign direct investment. Even large imports of Western capital goods proved unable to make a major improvement.

ual choice and indoctrinating citizens with antimarket propaganda. Thus, for transition to succeed it must transcend economic engineering, restructure the institutional basis of the social system, and develop civil society—an enormous agenda that will take many years to complete.

The economic challenge of transition is daunting in itself. Planned economies were autarkic: some were bound to each other through the trade links of the Council for Mutual Economic Assistance (CMEA), but none traded extensively with the world at large. Decades of bureaucratic allocation created serious distortions, with some sectors (particularly heavy industry) massively overbuilt and others (light industry and services) severely repressed; perhaps as much as a quarter of the Soviet economy served the military alone. Relative prices diverged greatly from market patterns, and this meant massive explicit or implicit subsidies among sectors. Energy, housing, public transport, and staple foods were extraordinarily cheap, whereas consumer manufactures, if available at all, were often shoddy. Pervasive shortages allowed firms to operate in sellers' markets and reduced incentives to improve quality. With near-complete state ownership, enterprises lacked the defined property rights that spur work effort and profitmaking in market economies. Firms had little reason to use inputs efficiently and strong incentives to hoard both labor and raw materials. Many firms added

negative value; at world prices the costs of their inputs would have exceeded the value of their output. The combination of dominant heavy industry, low energy prices, and wasteful use of inputs caused energy intensity to rise to several times its level in market economies (Table 1) and had harsh environmental impacts (Box 2).

Transition must therefore unleash a complex process of creation, adaptation, and destruction. Queuing gives way to markets. The shortage economy gives way to an economy of vast choice, with repressed sectors and activities growing rapidly and overbuilt sectors contracting or adjusting. Property rights are formally established and distributed, and large amounts of wealth cease to be state owned and controlled. Old institutions and organizations evolve, or are replaced, requiring new skills and attitudes. And the relationship between citizens and the state changes fundamentally, with greater freedom of choice but also much greater economic risk. True, changes of a similar nature may be needed in many economies around the world. But in the transition economies the magnitudes are exponentially greater. For example, transition economies have privatized more than 30,000 large and medium-size enterprises in five years. In the eleven years between 1980 and 1991 the rest of the world privatized fewer than 7,000. Countries will have completed their transition only when their problems and further reforms

Box 2 The environmental legacy of planning

For thirty years or more the planned economies focused on raising output through quantitative production targets, with little regard for costs and with severely underpriced natural resources and capital. Expansion of traditional heavy industries, often using coal as the main source of energy, was a high priority. Industrial development on such a scale has been disastrous for the environment wherever it has occurred. But in the planned economies the pollution effects were intensified by the underpricing, and therefore overuse, of energy and raw material inputs. The system promoted a mindset that saw new investment as the solution to all industrial problems. The philosophy of implementing many small improvements to increase efficiency and product quality—the heart of good industrial management—was almost unknown. Visitors to industrial plants in transition economies invariably see scope for good housekeeping measures to reduce spills, leaks, and waste—good industrial and environmental performance go hand in hand. Even where plants had pollution controls similar to those in estab-

lished market economies, poor maintenance and operating practices meant that they rarely operated at more than a fraction of their design efficiency. Environmental improvement is likely to be a long process involving changes in managerial culture and enforcement of regulations.

The environmental liabilities created by haphazard disposal of wastes are mostly unknown but could be large. Some environmental damage may be irreversible: the destruction of the Aral Sea is an ecological disaster that stemmed from the same desire to raise physical output, in this case of cotton. Pollution of the Black Sea is another serious problem. An issue of particular concern in the NIS is contamination from nuclear waste. Unsafe nuclear reactors and the remnants of the destroyed Chernobyl reactor are additional concerns. Discussion of these issues has stalled because of differences over the severity of the risks and the costs of alternative measures. Limited steps have been implemented to improve controls and safety equipment, operating procedures, and maintenance—but nothing more.

come to resemble those of long-established market economies at similar levels of income.

Taking stock

This *World Development Report* tries to distill the lessons of transition by analyzing two sets of overarching questions in detail. The first set, the subject of Part One, relates to the initial challenges of transition and how these have been tackled by different countries and might be tackled by others.

- Do differences in transition policies and outcomes reflect different reform strategies, or do they reflect primarily country-specific factors such as history, the level of development, or, just as important, the impact of political changes taking place at the same time?

This question deals with the broadest theme of transition. Given the wide range of reform strategies and outcomes across transition countries, it is natural—and important—to ask what accounts for this divergence. The Report's core message is that firm and persistent application of good policy yields large benefits. But the Report shows as well that history and geography matter: that what leaders can accomplish, or even try to accomplish, is strongly shaped by the inherited structure of the economy, by administrative or institutional capacity, and by the ways in which the political system mobilizes and channels public opinion. This interplay between choice and circumstance affects not merely the outcomes of the early stages of transition, described in Chapter 1, but also approaches to other dilemmas that have dogged reformers.

- Are strong liberalization and stabilization policies needed up front, or can other reforms progress equally well without them?

Chapter 2 surveys the range of macroeconomic reforms in transition—liberalized prices and trade regimes, hard budgets, and freedom of entry for new businesses—and discusses the interplay of liberalization, stabilization, and growth. The chapter concludes that both extensive liberalization and determined stabilization are needed for improved productivity and growth and that sustaining these policies requires rapid structural change as well as institutional reform.

- Must a market economy instantly be a private one? Or can privatization take a back seat in the early years of reform?

The proper functioning of markets requires clear incentives, which flow from defined property rights.

Chapter 3 reviews the process of creating an economy dominated by the private sector. It discusses the role of entry by new private business and, in particular, the privatization of state-owned firms, farms, housing, and commercial real estate. It analyzes why quite different approaches to ownership change and divestiture can be associated with positive economic results, and it draws out the policy fundamentals that should prevail. The lessons of transition to date are that new entry is vital, that privatization is important, and that the way it is done matters. But different countries will launch privatization at different moments. Moreover, once adopted, privatization should be seen as the beginning, not the end, of a process of reorganizing the ownership and incentive structure of firms.

- Must there be a gulf between winners and losers from transition? How can social policies ease the pain of transformation while propelling the process forward?

Transition produces winners—the young, the dynamic, the mobile, the connected—but it also imposes costs on visible and vulnerable groups, and in many countries it has been accompanied by a surge in measured poverty. Chapter 4 considers social policy reforms and, in particular, the direct measures to alleviate poverty that need to accompany the shift to market-determined wages, increased labor mobility, and the delinking of social services from enterprises.

The second set of questions considered in the Report looks beyond these early reforms to analyze the longer-term agenda of their consolidation: developing the institutions and policies that will help the new system develop and prosper over time. Each transition country is at a different stage in the reform process, but nearly all have made a decisive break with central planning. They have an even greater challenge ahead, that of consolidating the basis for a thriving market economy. There is no unique blueprint for them to follow; indeed, one of the strengths of the market economy is its variety and adaptability across cultures. Yet essential institutions—legal systems, financial systems, and governments—must be adapted or created. Also, the human capital base that is so essential for long-run growth needs to be strengthened, and countries must carve out for themselves a fully integrated position in the global economy. These issues are taken up in Part Two of the Report.

- How should countries in transition develop and strengthen the rule of law?

Chapter 5 examines why governments need to be strong enough to take the lead in defining the new rules of the game and creating the tools for their enforcement.

But the rule of law cannot be created top-down, by decree. It also requires demand from below, stimulated by the growth of market activities. Building trust in a new system also means demonstrating that politicians and officials will themselves abide by its rules and constraints.

■ How can countries develop effective financial systems?

Countries started their transition with weak, passive banking systems endowed with little capacity to assess credit risk, and with nonexistent capital markets. As Chapter 6 explains, financial sector reform cannot be pursued independently of other reforms, such as macroeconomic stabilization and enterprise reform. However, handling the problems early and decisively can reduce their impact and plant the seeds of a more effective system.

■ How must government restructure itself to meet the needs of a market system?

Chapter 7 considers the problem of achieving fundamental changes in government, both in terms of how it manages spending and revenue collection, and in terms of how it apportions responsibilities among central and local authorities. Both the range and the nature of government's activities must change, with the state more often seeking to facilitate private sector activity than to supplant it.

■ How can countries preserve and adapt their human capital base?

Countries embark on transition with relatively strong endowments of human capital. Yet as discussed in Chapter 8, the inherited health and education systems need extensive reform to increase their effectiveness and flexibility.

■ Why is international integration so vital for transition, and what are the implications for trading partners and capital flows? How can external assistance best support countries in transition?

These topics are considered in Chapter 9. Integration into world markets benefits both the rest of the world and the transition countries themselves, in part by locking in their other reforms. The timing and composition of foreign assistance to transition ought to reflect differences between countries: some face more pressing long-term development needs than others. The challenge for donors is to provide assistance that encourages and facilitates the move to the market rather than substitutes for it.

Chapter 10 distills the key messages of the Report.

The Report's focus is on countries in CEE, the NIS, Mongolia, China, and Vietnam. These countries are now dispersed across a wide reform spectrum, but only one or two of the most advanced reformers are approaching the point at which transition issues are fading into the normal problems of established market economies. The countries examined are far from being the only ones that have had extensively nonmarket economies. A comprehensive list would include Algeria, Cambodia, Cuba, the Lao People's Democratic Republic, Nicaragua, the People's Democratic Republic of Korea, and Tanzania, among others. Many other countries have market or mixed economies resting on weak foundations and have at one time or another adopted parts of the planning model. The process of transition is therefore of interest to a wide-ranging set of countries and peoples.

PART ONE

The Challenge of Transition

COUNTRIES EMBARKED ON TRANSITION FROM VERY different starting points. This part of the Report first considers the patterns and progress of reform, broad outcomes, and the influence of country-specific factors relative to the choice of policies (Chapter 1). The core reforms in transition include liberalizing prices, markets, and new business entry, and implementing programs to regain or preserve price stability. But countries cannot ignore their history and geography, and this legacy, together with political developments, profoundly affects both the relative importance of different market reforms and how policymakers approach them.

Liberalization and stabilization are closely interrelated (Chapter 2). The freeing of markets is the basic enabling reform from which all the potential benefits of transition flow. But market price signals cannot do their work in an environment of severe macroeconomic imbalances and high inflation. Stabilization is thus a vital complement to liberalization in fostering productivity and growth during transition—and beyond.

Creating property rights and incentives and a mostly private economy is a second challenge (Chapter 3). Here, too, initial conditions matter. Some transition countries will have a much more urgent need to privatize than others. But there can be competing objectives and difficulties in creating an effective and popular program.

A third major challenge—vital for social and political as well as economic reasons—is to relieve poverty and address the other ill effects of transition on particular groups (Chapter 4). Many gain from transition, and depending again on the starting point and context for reforms, transition can be accompanied by declining poverty from day one. But the vast adjustments involved in a change of economic system can also have adverse implications for many. The losses they suffer need to be addressed through effective social policies and measures that encourage sustained growth.

CHAPTER 1

Patterns of Reform, Progress, and Outcomes

How can governments approach the array of reforms required in transition? To pose the issue clearly we simplify reality and present two starkly contrasting, stylized approaches. The first is to launch a rapid, all-out program, undertaking as many reforms as possible in the shortest possible time. The second is to change by way of partial and phased reforms.

Each path offers its own distinctive pattern of risks and rewards. But many countries embarked on transition in no position to choose between the two. A country's starting circumstances, both economic and political, greatly affect the range of reform policies and outcomes open to it. Within this range, however, the clear lesson of the past few years' reforms is that, regardless of the starting point, decisive and consistent reform pays off.

Two paths of reform

The all-out approach aims to replace central planning with the rudiments of a market economy in a single burst of reforms. These include rapid price and trade liberalization, accompanied by a determined stabilization program to restore or maintain price stability; a quick move to current account convertibility; the immediate opening of markets to entry by new private businesses; and initiating, at least, a wide range of other changes, such as the privatization of state-owned companies, the demonopolization of industry, and the reform of accounting standards, the tax system, the legal system, the financial sector, and the civil service.

Poland's rapid reform in 1990 and many of the programs launched elsewhere in CEE and, after 1992, in the NIS have approximated this comprehensive model. East Germany's exceptional "instant" transition following unification with West Germany comes closer still (Box 1.1).

The rationale of this approach is well captured by the assertion of President Václav Havel of the Czech Republic that "it is impossible to cross a chasm in two leaps." Reformers wanted to minimize the duration of the inevitable pain and quickly sever the links between the state and the productive system, to guard against backsliding and stagnation.

In line with this reasoning, the ethos of the all-out approach is that wherever rapid change is feasible, it should be attempted. Experience in Poland and elsewhere shows that some changes can indeed occur overnight. Markets can be liberalized, restrictions on small business lifted, and exchange controls abolished—all with the stroke of a pen. Stabilization measures can also be implemented rapidly, even with a simple range of policy instruments. Yet most other reforms are inherently slow. Formal privatization may be accomplished in one or two years, but changing the fundamental governance of large firms almost always takes longer. And developing market-supporting institutions such as legal and financial systems takes years, even decades, because it involves such a fundamental change in skills, organizations, and attitudes. Complexity is not always the only reason reforms may be delayed: politics can also impede the process, as often happens in reforming social programs.

With different reforms moving at different speeds, even the fastest reformers will find that the economy is riddled with inefficiencies at first. Many firms are operating without effective owners; information and legal systems have not yet adapted to market mechanisms; private firms and farms have trouble getting bank credit; governments find it difficult to tax emerging sectors to make up for lost revenues from declining ones.

Box 1.1 East Germany: The instant transition

At the time of unification eastern Germany had a quarter of western Germany's population but contributed a mere tenth of its gross domestic product. Unification provided a market-proven institutional and legal framework and a large contingent of experienced practitioners. It also made available incredibly vast resources—close to $700 billion—to fund both investment and social transfers. However, East-West wage differences needed to offset low productivity in the East soon proved socially and politically infeasible. Wage hikes catapulted eastern German unit labor costs to the highest in the world. The result was mass unemployment, made politically palatable by social transfers that ensured that the living standard of the unemployed was higher than that of employees before unification. But for early retirement and other programs, unemployment would have been over 30 percent.

The former German Democratic Republic is starting to emerge from the trough of adjustment, and the firms that have survived constitute a highly competitive core. But few of the unemployed are likely to find jobs. Transition has relegated an entire generation to the economic sidelines.

Is the solution then a go-slow approach? Not necessarily. Governments need to push through a critical mass of rapid reforms to build credibility and change the behavior of people and firms, locking in these reforms and stimulating new ones. Also, in certain circumstances, reformers need to move quickly to exploit a narrow window of opportunity for dramatic change.

The second model, of piecemeal and phased reform, might start with localized experiments, which are expanded as perceived successes emerge. A few repressed sectors such as agriculture are liberalized up front. After these first steps, markets are slowly but steadily extended to other parts of the economy as the institutional building blocks of a market system are put in place.

This strategy relies on there being scope to reap large productivity gains from the first, partial reforms. These, in turn, raise incomes, so building momentum for further, more difficult reforms in a self-reinforcing process. Gradualist reformers must also be able to sustain the reforms over an extended period and to contain the side effects of liberalizing the economy selectively. Because the market and the plan must coexist for a time, individuals and companies will have a strong incentive to seek economic rents by shifting goods or financial resources from the low-priced, controlled segment of the economy to the high-priced, liberalized segment. The government must be able to keep a tight grip on both the macro- and the micro-economy, supervising those activities still covered by the plan and imposing stiff penalties for noncompliance.

The phased approach—summarized by Deng Xiaoping's phrase, "feeling the stones to cross the river"—is essentially the path followed by China. After the death of Mao Zedong and the denunciation of the Cultural Revolution, China's initial reforms in 1978 opened the door to joint ventures and began to liberalize prices, first at the margin and then more extensively. Most early reforms focused on the rural economy. The household responsibility system, initiated locally to decollectivize agriculture, was extended to other regions. The government raised rural incomes by increasing agricultural producer prices. It then relaxed restrictions on "nonstate" industrial firms (those owned by local governments and collectives) and permitted new entry into a wide range of businesses. New rural township and village enterprises (TVEs) were permitted and encouraged to operate on market principles. The share of output produced by private and nonstate enterprises rose sharply. By 1984 reforms had spread to the urban economy. Local governments were granted greater fiscal autonomy. Management of state enterprises was reformed, as their source of finance moved from the state budget to the banking system. Restrictions were progressively eased on trade and foreign investment, and a variety of institutional reforms were begun, including the re-creation of a central bank. Meanwhile the role of the plan was progressively reduced. Reforms accelerated in 1994 and 1995, particularly with regard to taxes, company law, and foreign trade.

Choices and constraints: Different macroeconomic starting points . . .

The fact that there are two model routes from a planned economy to the market does not mean that all countries are in a position to choose between them. As noted above, to attempt a phased reform, governments need to be fairly sure that its initial effects will be positive, and that they are able to keep control of the economy in its partly liberalized state. Policymakers in most of CEE and the NIS were in no position to deliver either.

First, earlier attempts at partial reform in these countries, including the Soviet Union, had failed to raise efficiency, largely because they were too limited to affect incentives. Perhaps partial measures that shifted authority from planners to enterprise managers, such as those proposed in the 1960s, would have succeeded had they been implemented early and decisively enough, when the productivity crisis was just beginning to emerge. But the several CEE countries that did persistently seek a "third way" between planning and capitalism never found one that led to sustained growth. It is hard to believe that the Soviets would have succeeded where the Hungarians could not.

The second, more important reason why gradualism was not an option in CEE and the Soviet Union was that by the second half of the 1980s the Soviet planned economy was disintegrating from within. In 1986 the Soviet Union launched *glasnost* (political relaxation) and *perestroika* (economic restructuring). *Glasnost* permitted the resurgence of democratic movements and long-repressed nationalism and an outpouring of criticism of the government. *Perestroika* itself involved little reform and was followed by measures to boost investment in the face of shrinking resources. The result was inflation and foreign indebtedness rather than higher productivity. Wages rose sharply relative to official prices, just as they did in Poland and most other CEE countries in the last years of the old regime. With greater enterprise autonomy and continuing subsidies, the Soviet fiscal deficit reached 11 percent of gross domestic product (GDP) by 1988. Bank deposits swelled because there were few goods to buy, creating a monetary overhang.

By 1990 deliveries of inputs were falling well short of planned levels, and black market prices and exchange rates were many times higher than official ones (Table 1). The situation worsened dramatically in 1991, as the deficit soared to an estimated 28 percent of GDP. A monetary reform (involving the freezing and confiscation of financial assets), launched in January 1991, was the last desperate attempt to absorb the monetary overhang without a price explosion. It failed dismally. The planned trade system dissolved. And then the Soviet Union collapsed. The volume of trade among CMEA members and between Soviet republics fell 70 percent. This chaotic environment, combining a disintegrating economy with a rapidly weakening government, allowed no scope for gradual reform. For these countries the all-out approach was the only one available.

. . . And the role of different political heritages

The degree of macroeconomic disequilibrium is not the only factor affecting a country's choice of reform path. Noneconomic factors—politics, history, culture, and geography—can also be very important.

Citizens' attitudes and loyalties toward pretransition regimes varied greatly, depending on how their countries had become socialist. Before the revolutionaries came to power, Russia had been an empire ruled by an autocratic czar, Mongolia had been a theocracy, Vietnam a colony, and China had experienced warlordism following the end of the Qing dynasty in 1912. In these countries, governments dominated by the Communist Party arose mainly from internal political movements and, in China and Vietnam, from nationalist efforts to rout Japanese and French colonizers.

In marked contrast, in the Baltic states and in much of CEE, socialist governments were supported from without and maintained by the Soviet political and military machine in part through repression. Many people deeply resented the Soviet presence, and the legacies of democracy and markets remained strong. Geography is also important: these countries are close to Western Europe, had been exposed to European political norms and culture, and want to join the European Union. The "political breakthrough" after 1989 was therefore particularly strong in these countries. Political reform largely drove their economic reforms, creating a distinctive linkage that might not apply more broadly, to countries in different circumstances. In 1993, widespread support for political breakthroughs in most CEE countries moderated perceptions that the accompanying economic reforms were having an adverse impact (Figure 1.1). Russians surveyed a year later, in contrast, were far more pessimistic about both political and economic progress in their country.

Radical economic reform has proved easier when political change has been rapid and fundamental, as in much of CEE and the Baltic states. Citizens who supported the new political systems in these countries also supported market-oriented economic policies. Traditional bastions of power in the previous systems—the state enterprises and the ministries that ran them—were weakened, and at the outset few interest groups were organized to oppose reform. A window of opportunity—a period of "extraordinary politics"—opened in which far-reaching changes could be initiated with little opposition. But individuals have also made their mark. Most decisive reforms have reflected the vision of one leader or a small and committed group. Similar political breakthroughs occurred in a few countries far from European influence, such as the Kyrgyz Republic and Mongolia, where exceptional political leaders came to power and pushed through decisive reforms. Not all countries, however, had such a strong political breakthrough, and some new states saw other priorities. Ukraine's first independent governments, for example, were preoccupied with asserting a national identity, and reform there accelerated only after severe and prolonged economic decline.

As extraordinary politics becomes ordinary, the path of reform steepens. Political interest groups form, and pressure arises from those who bear the costs of change. As structural and institutional reforms unfold, they involve more decisionmakers and require collaboration from more people; the number of players multiplies and the process gets more complicated. But reform also creates winners and new interest groups with strong pro-market leanings. The public must constantly be reminded of the reasons for change and informed about progress to date. With the notable exception of the Czech Republic, few governments have really been effective in this respect.

Russians remain more gloomy about the future.

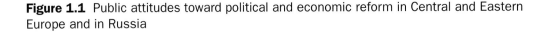

Figure 1.1 Public attitudes toward political and economic reform in Central and Eastern Europe and in Russia

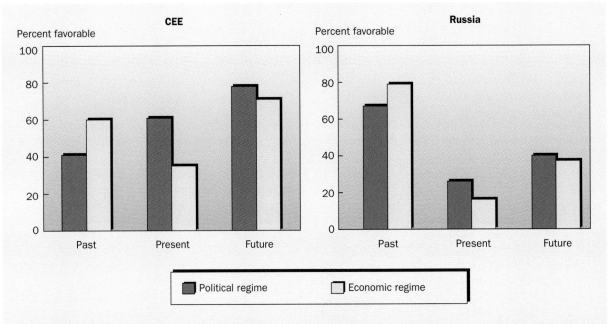

Note: Data are results of opinion surveys, taken in seven CEE countries in 1993 and Russia in 1994, seeking views on past (socialist), present, and expected future (five years hence) regimes. Source: Rose 1995a, 1995b.

Surveys have shown falling approval of the market economy in many countries. But it is not clear how much this reflects views about the reforms themselves and how much it was a reaction to the pain of economic dislocation and adjustment. Both radically reforming governments and less radically reforming governments have been turned out of office. The return to power of former socialists has sometimes slowed reforms, but as yet no replacement government has tried to dismantle the market-oriented approach of its predecessors. Indeed, late-1995 surveys in CEE showed rising popular support for the current—and expanding—market system. In the more advanced reformers the political debate has moved toward entitlement programs, familiar political terrain in long-established market economies. At least in CEE, politics are becoming normal.

This is not to say that economics and politics always develop together harmoniously. If economic outcomes benefit only a few, if the return to growth is too long postponed, and if corruption comes to be seen as endemic, the losers will justifiably react. In many transition economies, for example, managers of state enterprises have used privatization to transform their control rights into property rights, leaving ordinary citizens out in the cold. This has deepened public cynicism about reform and undermined the legitimacy of the postreform economic system. Polls in December 1991 suggested that just over a quarter of Russians disagreed with the proposition that ordinary people would benefit from the introduction of private property. By March 1995 over two-thirds disagreed. Establishing a social consensus will be crucial for the long-term success of transition—cross-country analyses suggest that societies that are very unequal in terms of income or assets tend to be politically and socially less stable and to have lower rates of investment and growth.

Progress and outcomes

How have the varying paths to reform—conditioned as they have been by history, politics, and economic and institutional starting points—been reflected in progress and outcomes to date?

Progress of reform

In assessing progress we look at four broad dimensions: liberalization, property rights and private ownership, institutions, and social policies. First, consider liberalization. The full length of each bar in Figure 1.2 estimates the degree to which the country in question was a market economy in 1995. The measure is approximate and covers three areas: domestic prices and markets, foreign trade and currency convertibility, and openness to new business entry. By 1995 many countries in CEE and the NIS were essentially market economies, with open trade, current account convertibility, and liberal policies toward new entry and private business. A few still retained extensive price and export controls and state trading monopolies—in some cases after announcing reform programs that were not carried through. With more extensive controls on foreign trade and entry, the East Asian countries were less liberalized than the more advanced reformers in CEE and the NIS.

However, a snapshot of one year is far too short a period to capture the economic impact of a process of liberalization. Some countries started their reforms far earlier than others. Therefore the purple segment of each bar shows countries' average level of liberalization in the period 1989–95, recognizing that some countries had freed elements of their economies even before 1989. The CEE countries and the NIS and Mongolia are categorized into four groups by this measure, reflecting both the extent of liberalization and its longevity. The economies of some countries were severely affected by regional tensions, including blockades and in some cases war. These countries are marked by asterisks in Figure 1.2.

With their earlier start, the East Asian countries have been almost as exposed to market forces as the CEE countries, on average, during the last seven years. But within CEE and the NIS wide variations are seen. Since 1989 Russia's economy has had about half the exposure to market forces as the leaders in Group 1 in Figure 1.2, and some other NIS have barely emerged from the planning system.

Another dimension of transition is ownership reform (Figures 1.3 and 1.4). Here, too, there has been great change. In nine countries in CEE and the NIS the private sector now accounts for over half of economic activity. Governments still maintain sizable stakes in many firms classified as private, but with plausible allowances for unmeasured unofficial economies (which Figure 1.3 does not account for), most countries have passed the halfway mark. The shift to a private economy reflects both the entry of new firms (often using old assets from the state sector) and the privatization of state firms. Ownership in China has also diversified substantially toward a wide variety of forms (Chapter 3). Vietnam is the only country in the sample where the state sector's share has risen since

1989, but many enterprises counted as state firms are in fact joint ventures with private (mainly foreign) partners.

Both across countries and across types of assets within countries, large differences are observed in the degree of privatization and the effectiveness of private ownership (Figure 1.4). These differences reflect a variety of country-specific and historical factors, as well as complex political issues that arise as wealth is redistributed. As discussed in Chapter 3, successful transition involves initiating a process of change toward an efficient pattern of ownership. An initial transfer of title is only the beginning of the story.

Institutional reforms are also affected by initial conditions (Box 1.2). Their relative progress across countries is closely associated with the extent and duration of liberalization (Figure 1.5), partly because macroeconomic reforms, as well as ownership reform, tend to create demand for institutional change. Yet even where policy change is rapid, institutional change is slow, and transition will not be complete until institutions effectively underpin markets. There are severe bottlenecks:

- All countries have taken steps to reform the legal framework, but the extent and coherence of reform vary. The reform of judicial institutions and enforcement mechanisms lags far behind, and corruption has become an acute concern in some countries. These are areas of high priority for the future.
- More advanced reformers now have some banks capable of delivering services at least comparable to those available in middle-income countries, but they also have a substantial share of financial assets in poorly functioning banks. Serious conflicts of interest plague many financial systems, and in most countries the scope of market-based finance is limited by poor debt recovery mechanisms. Virtually all countries have many nonperforming loans, which pose a major policy dilemma.
- Most governments have substantially reoriented their roles to meet the needs of a market economy, but in such critical areas as tax administration, public administration, and fiscal decentralization, reforms are still at an early stage in many countries. This has hurt the economy and in some cases has adversely affected regional equity. The power and administrative authority of central governments have diminished in some countries with the considerable, and sometimes chaotic, decentralization of revenues and functions to subnational governments. There is frequent confusion over the roles of the executive, the legislature, and the constitutional courts.

Institutional development is also crucial for sustaining the momentum of reform in the Asian planned economies. China's banks, for example, are less market-based

Countries have liberalized at different speeds and at different times, but the late starters are catching up.

Figure 1.2 Economic liberalization by country

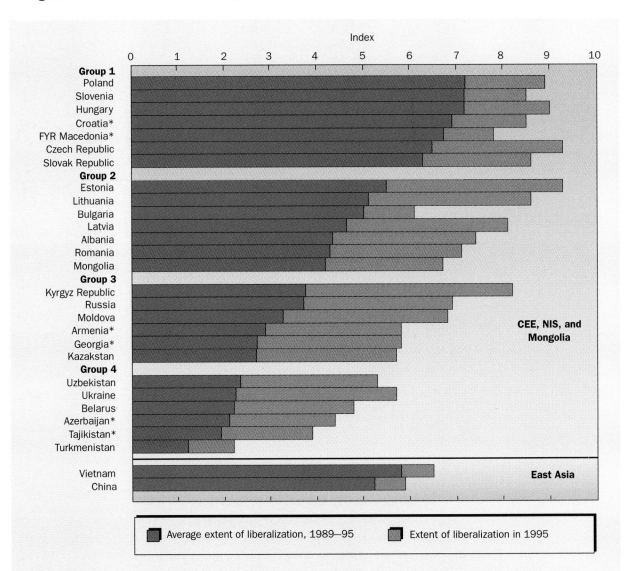

Note: Bars indicate the extent to which policies supporting liberalized markets and entry of new firms prevailed in 1995 and on average over 1989–95. Asterisks indicate economies severely affected by regional tensions between 1989 and 1995. The index is a weighted average of estimates of liberalization of domestic transactions (price liberalization and abolition of state trading monopolies), external transactions (elimination of export controls and taxes, substitution of low to moderate import duties for import quotas and high tariffs, current account convertibility), and entry of new firms (privatization and private sector, or nonstate, development). The weights on these components are 0.3, 0.3, and 0.4, respectively. Initial estimates for the three components were based on comparative information in World Bank and other reports. These were revised following consultation with country specialists as well as experts with a comparative perspective across a number of countries. For the twenty-five countries in CEE and the NIS the transition indicators and accompanying text in EBRD 1994 and 1995 provided a further basis for calibration. Nevertheless, any such index is judgmental and necessarily approximate. See also the De Melo, Denizer, and Gelb background paper.

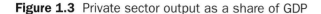

The private sector has grown rapidly.

Figure 1.3 Private sector output as a share of GDP

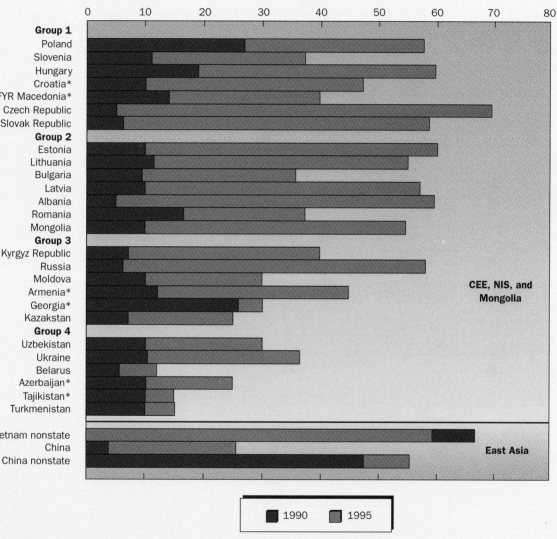

Note: Firms are considered private if less than 50 percent state owned. For Vietnam, the nonstate sector excludes public-private joint ventures. For China, the nonstate sector includes collectives and TVEs as well as private firms; agriculture is considered private in 1995, although land is held through long-term leases. Asterisks indicate economies severely affected by regional tensions between 1989 and 1995. Source: EBRD, IMF, and World Bank data; official data.

than those of CEE, because many loans are still allocated through a central credit plan.

Reforming social policy is politically difficult in all countries and, except for the introduction of unemploy-

ment benefits, has not typically been a prime focus early on. Indeed, where such reform has taken place it has often been reactive, impelled by fiscal shortfalls. Social policy reform is a high priority for the future (Chapters 4 and 8).

Privatization has been uneven.

Figure 1.4 Privatization by type of asset and country group

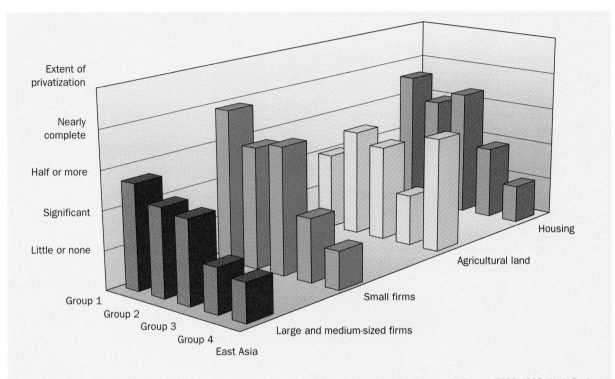

Note: Data are for 1995 and are simple averages of estimates for the countries in each group (see Figure 1.2). Source: EBRD 1995; World Bank staff estimates.

Governments in CEE and the NIS need to develop policies to cope with increased labor mobility, and, frequently, increased poverty within relatively tight budget constraints. Similar considerations apply to the East Asian reformers, which must find ways to respond to an increasingly mobile and industrial rural population that is still outside the formal system of social benefits. China's urban enterprises still bear the burden of pensions, medical care,

Box 1.2 Initial conditions and institutional reforms

Institutional legacies differed from country to country at the outset of transition. Some countries retained a cadre of people with memories of market rules and institutions. Their skills helped to rebuild institutions—for example, Poland had never lost the knowledge of prewar law, and Polish professors had continued their interchanges with Western universities. Similarly, CEE government agencies dealing in international trade developed a familiarity with market-based contract law that proved useful when the time came to reform domestic legislation.

Many new states, however, have had to create market and government institutions from scratch. Some-times the absence of an institutional legacy can actually be an advantage—for example, Slovenia was free to start from a clean slate as it built new institutions such as its central bank, and the experience of the Baltic countries shows that designing new budget or tax laws may be easier while governments are still unencumbered by entrenched entitlements and interest groups. On the other hand, implementing new institutions—whether they be customs agencies, accounting and auditing practices, or treasury and debt management systems—requires large human, technical, and financial resources in all transition countries, and in this regard the new states face a massive additional burden.

Markets fuel demand for new institutions.

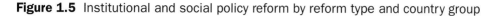

Figure 1.5 Institutional and social policy reform by reform type and country group

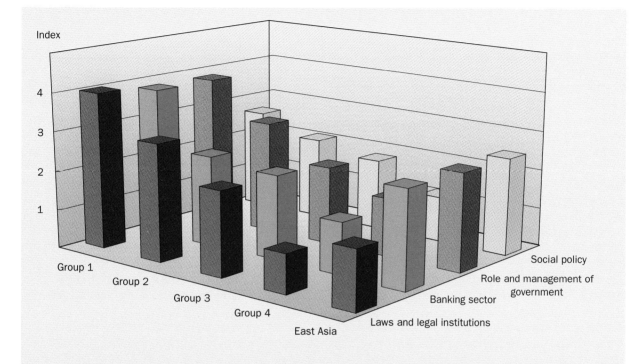

Note: Data are for 1995 and are simple averages for the countries in each group (see Figure 1.2). The *laws and legal institutions index* measures the scope and quality of new legislation and development of judicial institutions: 1, little progress on either; 2, some progress on laws, little on institutions; 3, some progress on both; 4, extensive progress on both. The *banking sector index* measures the independence, skills, and credit allocation practices of the better segment of banks, as well as the functioning of supervision and payments systems: 1, little change; 2, some initial progress; 3, system functioning fairly well but with limitations; 4, system functioning fairly well and with a larger segment of better banks. The *role and management of government index* measures the market orientation of government and the effectiveness of public sector management (see Figure 7.1 for specific indicators): 1, little change; 2, significant reform; 3, substantial reform; 4, advanced reform. The *social policy index* measures progress in pension reform, reduction of subsidies, streamlining and targeting of income transfers, and divestiture of social assets: 1, no reform; 2, limited reform; 3, modest reform; 4, substantial reform. Source: EBRD 1994, 1995; World Bank staff estimates.

and housing—partly because reforms have yet to resolve many difficult problems of the state sector.

Economic and social outcomes

Three features stand out in the range of transitional outcomes to date. The first is the large variance in performance among three sets of countries: the more advanced reformers in CEE and the NIS, the less advanced reformers in this region, and the East Asian reformers. Second, and cutting across these differences, is the clear message that sustained and consistent reform pays off. Third,

addressing the social outcomes of transition requires both economic growth and social policy reform.

In CEE and the NIS, liberalization and stabilization policies have produced the main immediate effects. Other reforms take longer to show results, although it is increasingly clear how important they are to maintaining hard budget constraints and backing up these policies—success depends on the interplay of reforms across a number of areas. Freeing prices rapidly eliminated shortages, and phasing out subsidies to rein in overspending subjected firms to financial discipline and forced some initial restructuring. But freeing prices also caused a burst of very high inflation in all countries except Hungary, where most prices had been liberalized before 1990. CEE and the NIS have seen large declines in output, especially in countries exposed to severe regional tensions (Table 1.1). Yet official data overstate the output decline. They largely fail to include output from informal sectors, whose growth provides a substantial cushion in some countries against declines in formal sector output and employment. Furthermore, some of the lost output consisted of goods no longer wanted (Box 1.3), so that measured output changes are not necessarily good indicators of well-being.

Among advanced reformers, vigorous stabilization programs have paved the way for declining inflation and a resumption of growth as reforms have taken hold. Thousands of new, competitive firms have entered the market. Many state firms have shrunk dramatically, and others have closed altogether. Production has shifted from industry to services, trade has been reoriented toward world markets, and foreign direct investment (FDI) inflows have risen sharply. By 1995 industrial labor productivity was a third higher than prereform levels in Poland and Hungary (Figure 1.6). Poland's growth rate of 7 percent in 1995 was led by the 15 percent growth rate of the private sector; the state sector declined by 3 percent.

The picture was different for the less advanced, or less decisive, reformers in CEE and the NIS, even though the scale of reforms in many of these countries has been large by conventional standards. Adjustment has been much slower, and inflation has remained high, although in most cases it has fallen substantially from earlier levels. But slower adjustment has not meant a smaller drop in output. In fact, output has often fallen by more than in the advanced reformers, and most of these economies are still contracting. These countries have not yet managed to achieve the critical policy mass needed for sustained macroeconomic stability and a resumption of growth (Chapter 2).

In contrast to the CEE countries and the NIS, both China and Vietnam have enjoyed spectacular growth throughout their reform periods (see Table 1.1). Vietnam adjusted to the demise of the CMEA and the loss of Soviet aid—which was not replaced from other sources—without a drop in output (Box 1.4). China's growth (although slightly overstated by official measures) was propelled by exceptionally high saving rates and by large gains in productivity that were partly due to reallocations of labor from lower- to higher-productivity activities. As in CEE and the NIS, much growth in China came from previously repressed sectors, including exports, services, and agriculture.

The social impact of transition has also varied. In CEE and the NIS many people have gained, and imports of high-quality consumer goods have boomed. But the combination of falling output and rising income inequality has led to large increases in poverty and growing insecurity in many countries. Life expectancy has fallen in many, particularly Russia and Ukraine, but has increased in the Group 1 countries (see Table 1.1). Infant mortality rates appear to have declined in many countries, possibly as a consequence of the sharp fall in birthrates in the region.

Table 1.1 GDP growth, inflation, and social indicators during transition

Country or group	Average GDP growth (percent per year)		Average inflation (percent per year)		Change in social indicators, 1989–94[a] (percent)	
	1989–95	1994–95	1989–95	1994–95	Life expectancy	Infant mortality
CEE, NIS, and Mongolia						
Group 1	–1.6	4.3	106.0	18.7	0.7	–1.8
Group 2	–4.2	4.0	149.2	59.0	–0.2	–1.8
Group 3	–9.6	–12.5	466.4	406.8	–4.4	0.9
Group 4	–6.7	–11.4	809.6	1,176.5	–1.6	–1.9
Countries severely affected by regional tensions[b]	–11.7	–7.5	929.7	1,328	0.5	–2.7
Other transition economies						
China	9.4[c]	11.0	8.4[c]	20.6	2.1[c]	–11.1[c]
Vietnam	7.1[d]	7.9	114.8[d]	13.2	1.7[d]	–5.4[d]

.. Not available.

Note: All data for recent years are subject to revision. See Figure 1.2 for the countries in each group.

a. Data do not take into account a possible rise in measured infant mortality rates due to the shift to international methodology in the NIS around 1993. Social indicators are population-weighted.

b. The countries asterisked in Figure 1.2 are taken out of Groups 1–4 and consolidated.

c. Data are for 1978–95.

d. Data are for 1986–95.

Source: IMF and World Bank data.

Box 1.3 Data problems in transition economies

Many statistical systems in the NIS and CEE have not adapted to the new economic system. They often fail to capture the emergence of large "second" economies. Technical weaknesses, compounded by the effects of high inflation, also cause output to be seriously under-reported. A recent revision of Russia's national accounts finds that they had overestimated the cumulative decline in 1990–94 by 12 percentage points. Reassessments of other countries, especially in the NIS, are likely to result in comparable revisions.

In addition, the previous pattern of trade and production in CEE and the NIS was highly inefficient.

New goods (including consumer durable imports, which have boomed) command high quality premia relative to "comparable" old goods, many of which have no market value. Much previous production was directed toward military procurement, which was cut drastically in 1992. These qualitative changes, as well as the end of queuing, which previously absorbed up to four hours a day for many, make it even more difficult to assess the real welfare effects of the output changes that accompany a massive shift in economic regime. Social data have problems, too (see Box 4.1).

Living standards have risen sharply in the growing Asian reformers: the first stages of reform in China lifted almost 200 million people out of absolute poverty, a massive achievement. But the rise in urban-rural differences and increasing regional inequality have now weakened the link between economic growth and poverty reduction. This has led to rising concern about the distribution of gains from reforms (Chapter 4).

Assessment—the interplay of choice and circumstance

To what extent does the divergence of outcomes across CEE and the NIS reflect initial conditions as opposed to policy—the given rather than the chosen? Some countries, typically in CEE, started with more favorable macroeconomic, structural, and institutional conditions. These included lower inflationary pressures, less interdependence with the CMEA system, a more recent history of market economy, and a more favorable location for developing new trade links. Countries also differed in their levels of development, industrialization, and income. The Central Asian countries and Albania, in particular, were less developed and more rural than the others. And some countries achieving independence for the first time needed to construct the basic elements of statehood. Separating the contributions of initial conditions and policies is difficult. Ongoing research on this group of countries suggests that favorable initial conditions do indeed play a significant part in determining cross-country differences in outcomes but that, regardless of the starting point, constancy in reforms has been vital for restoring growth and containing inflation.

Why has China been able to reform in a partial, phased manner and still grow rapidly, whereas even vigorous reformers in CEE and the NIS have suffered large declines in output (but still outperform the slower reformers)? China's favorable initial conditions are the first piece of the puzzle.

Its policymakers did not have to confront some serious obstacles that proved very difficult to turn aside in CEE and the NIS. This is not to imply that China's task was easy. It had to devise and implement a set of market-oriented reforms that gave growth-promoting incentives to farmers and workers while maintaining macroeconomic control and redirecting the interests of the bureaucracy toward supporting reform. These were and remain major achievements. But the transition challenge in China—and policymakers' tools for meeting it—were vastly different.

One way to bring this point home is to compare Russia and China (Table 1.2). When its transition began, Russia's economy was far more developed than China's, with income per capita eight times higher. Over 40 percent of the work force was in industry, and the state's social security system covered virtually the entire population. An elaborate and costly system of sectoral cross-subsidies propped up huge state enterprises and agricultural collectives. The energy sector played a key role in subsidizing both: implicit subsidies from energy production to the rest of the economy amounted to over 11 percent of GDP. A large share of Russian industry added negative value: input costs, valued at world prices, exceeded the value of output. Then trade with the CMEA countries collapsed, prices were liberalized, and demand for military goods declined as cold war tensions receded. The shock to the Russian economy was enormous. Shifting large numbers of people into new firms and formerly repressed sectors (including services) required deep structural adjustment and painful retrenchment in the state sector. Employees and managers exerted enormous pressures to continue subsidies and keep firms afloat, in part because enterprises had traditionally provided so many social services. The pain was intensified by the legacy of decades of planning that had resulted in extreme regional specialization, with many one-company towns. And with price liberalization and the scaling back

Labor productivity is at new highs in some reforming countries, while others are behind the curve.

Figure 1.6 Labor productivity in industry in selected transition economies

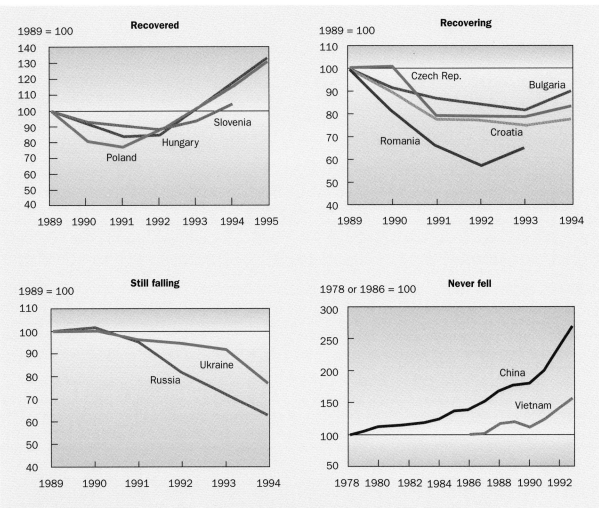

Source: Vienna Institute for Comparative Economic Studies 1995; World Bank data.

of subsidies, agricultural output shrank by nearly one-fourth between 1990 and 1994.

Despite the industrialization efforts of the 1950s and 1960s, China was very poor and largely rural at the start of its reforms. Agriculture employed 71 percent of the work force and was heavily taxed to support industry. Social safety nets extended only to the state sector—about 20 percent of the population. Poor infrastructure and an emphasis on local self-sufficiency led to low regional specialization and large numbers of small and medium-size

firms. The economy was far less centrally planned and administered than the Soviet economy. Local governments had greater power and developed considerable management capacity, preparing them for a more decentralized economy. Chinese industry also received subsidies, but cross-subsidization was less pervasive.

Because the agricultural sector had been so heavily repressed, freeing it up had immediate payoffs. Between 1981 and 1984 agriculture grew on average by 10 percent a year, largely because the shift to family farming im-

Box 1.4 Vietnam: Bold reforms in an East Asian setting

In the mid-1980s Vietnam's economy was growing slowly and suffering from hyperinflation despite massive Soviet assistance. A reform program (*doi moi*) was launched in 1986, starting with limited changes in the rural sector and accelerating in scope and pace in 1989. In a very short time reforms dismantled collectives and returned the land to family farming; liberalized most prices; allowed and encouraged new private businesses in many fields; opened the trade and investment regimes; unified the exchange rate and sharply devalued the currency; cut fiscal deficits and the growth rate of domestic credit; raised interest rates to positive real levels; and—not

least—imposed financial discipline on state enterprises and laid off hundreds of thousands of redundant workers (see Chapter 3). These measures stabilized the economy—inflation fell below 10 percent by 1992—and restored growth, which has averaged 8 percent since 1991. Exports and investment are growing at double-digit rates. Vietnam's transition is not complete. Industrial production remains concentrated in state enterprises, and administrative controls remain pervasive. But its liberalization and stabilization measures were closer to those of Eastern Europe than they were to those of China. Not all East Asian reforms have been phased or gradual.

proved incentives. This allowed for the reallocation of surplus agricultural labor to new rural industries, which generated 100 million new jobs between 1978 and 1994 and encouraged further reform. China thus started transition largely as a peasant agrarian economy and with far greater scope for reallocating labor than Russia.

There were also important differences in financial development at the outset of transition. China's financial system was underdeveloped, with the money stock (M2) equal to only 25 percent of GDP. As markets developed and incomes improved, household savings and bank deposits grew rapidly. This financed growth and buffered the state sector through bank lending at interest rates that

were often below inflation (Chapter 2). Prudent macroeconomic policies were key, holding inflation to modest levels and helping maintain confidence in the currency. Russia's economy, on the other hand, was already highly monetized in 1990, with M2 equal to GDP. The huge monetary overhang from forced saving represented resources already provided to the planned economy. Liberalization of prices and the monetization of fiscal deficits led to hyperinflation, which rendered these savings worthless. By 1994 the Russian money stock had dwindled to only 16 percent of GDP.

Differences in initial conditions and structural characteristics therefore explain a good deal of the divergence of transition outcomes and policies across countries. They do not explain all—the sustained application of market-oriented reform policies, within a broadly "right" macroeconomic environment, has been a crucial ingredient in success. However, the right reform mix must reflect initial conditions and so cannot simply be transplanted between such starkly different countries as China and Russia.

The agenda

The CEE countries and the NIS have not seen the spectacular growth of China and Vietnam, but many have turned the corner and resumed growth, some vigorously. With continued vigilance to sustain hard-won progress and implement further reforms, these countries can join the ranks of the high-growth economies. Other countries in the region have the potential to follow in their path. China and Vietnam, too, will have to push further in many areas, from property rights to institutional development to social policies, to sustain their rapid growth. In every case what matters is the breadth of the policy reforms attempted and the consistency with which they are maintained. The record to date, the challenges ahead, and the lessons these different groups of countries have to learn from one another are explored in detail in the following chapters.

Table 1.2 Russia and China: Two very different countries

Indicator	Russia 1990	Russia 1994	China 1978	China 1994
Sectoral structure of employment (percent of total)				
Industry	42	38	15	18
Agriculture	13	15	71	58
Services	45	47	14	25
Total	100	100	100	100
Employment in the state sector	90	44	19	18
Money and output				
M2 as a percentage of GDP[a]	100	16	25	89
GDP per capita (dollars)				
From *World Bank*				
Atlas	4,110	2,650	404[b]	530
At PPP	6,440	4,610	1,000[b,c]	2,510

a. Data are averages of quarterly ratios.
b. In 1990 dollars.
c. World Bank staff estimate.
Source: IMF, various years (b); World Bank data and staff estimates.

CHAPTER 2

Liberalization, Stabilization, and Growth

Across the transition economies, extensive liberalization and determined stabilization have both been vital for improving economic performance. Liberalization involves freeing prices, trade, and entry from state controls; stabilization means reducing inflation and containing domestic and external imbalances. The two are intricately linked and can and should be initiated early. In the longer term, institutional reforms—establishing clear property rights, sound legal and financial infrastructure, and effective government—will be needed to make markets work efficiently and support growth. But liberalization and stabilization are essential first steps, and they can achieve a great deal even when other key features of an effective market are lacking.

Why is liberalization so important? It decentralizes production and trading decisions to enterprises and households and directly addresses the two fundamental weaknesses of central planning: poor incentives and poor information. Liberalization exposes firms to customer demand, the profit motive, and competition, and it lets relative prices adjust in line with true scarcities. Liberalized markets process information better than central planners, and when goods and services are traded freely, the price mechanism—Adam Smith's invisible hand—matches demand and supply. In most cases the outcome is efficient (market failure is discussed in Chapter 7). Combined with supporting institutions, competitive markets unleash powerful processes to force technological and organizational change. Whereas planned economies experienced low or negative overall productivity growth despite high capital accumulation, at least half of output growth in advanced market economies since World War II has resulted from productivity gains. Creating markets is an investment in a more dynamic system of economic coordination that fosters long-run productivity and output growth. Finally, liberalization, by depoliticizing resource allocation, helps governments cut subsidies to firms and thus facilitates economic stabilization.

Stabilization policy is vital for transition because macroeconomic imbalance denies countries the gains of market reforms. Evidence from a wide range of market economies shows that once annual inflation rises above a threshold level around 40 percent, growth deteriorates dramatically. High inflation obscures relative price incentives and creates uncertainty, inhibiting saving and investment. Therefore price stabilization always complements liberalization as a basis for growth; as shown below, some transition countries have liberalized faster than others, but none has registered sustained growth without containing inflation at moderate levels.

There are some important parallels between Asian and European transition economies in the relationships between liberalization, stabilization, and growth. In all regions growth has largely resulted from the lifting of restrictions on new entry and a surge of previously repressed activities, especially services and export industries (and agriculture in Asia). Freeing prices and trade, reducing subsidies, and containing credit can also revitalize growth in previously dominant sectors, by increasing the competitive and financial pressure on firms to restructure.

However, as outlined in Chapter 1, there are also major differences between countries—in initial conditions, in approaches to macroeconomic reforms, and in outcomes. In China the initial economic structure combined with strong macroeconomic control has so far allowed large growth gains from partial liberalization to translate into high saving and a rapid buildup of financial assets by households. This has helped cushion a state sector that remains a drag on the economy—even though its efficiency may be improving and its relative size is shrinking—and has underwritten the reform process itself. Gradual, partial reforms were not an option for most CEE countries and NIS. There only broad-based liberalization has allowed governments to cut their links with firms enough to bring inflation down to levels that would permit economic recovery. These countries all suffered a large decline at first. But those that liberalized early and comprehensively were able to stabilize the economy sooner and enjoy an earlier, stronger resumption of growth.

Liberalization and growth: A close link

In market economies liberalization usually means eliminating price controls and relaxing trade protection in a few heavily regulated or protected sectors. Liberalizers in transition economies face an unprecedented and more daunting task, that of freeing not only the terms of market transactions but the transactions themselves: abolishing state orders and procurement, state production and trading monopolies, and the centralized allocation of foreign exchange. Liberalization also means freeing entry into production, services, and trade, including the freedom to open a new business, to expand or break up an existing business, and to change product mix, suppliers, customers, or geographical base.

The starting point, speed, and scope of free market reforms have varied greatly among transition economies, as initial conditions and political developments have constrained governments' economic policies and influenced their reform choices (see Chapter 1). Hungary and China began liberalizing gradually in the 1960s and the 1970s, respectively. Vietnam accelerated its liberalization in 1989 after partial reforms had failed to raise growth rates or to stabilize the economy sufficiently. Poland liberalized with one "big bang," freeing 90 percent of prices, eliminating most trade barriers, abolishing state trading monopolies, and making its currency convertible for current transactions all at once in January 1990. Albania, the Baltic countries, the former Czechoslovakia, and the Kyrgyz Republic followed this model of rapid and comprehensive liberalization. Bulgaria initially did the same, but strong interest group pressures for continued protection and state support to enterprises later brought something of a reversal. In Romania price reforms advanced fitfully for three years after half of all prices were freed in 1990, but liberalization has recently accelerated. Russia substantially liberalized prices and imports in January 1992, but extensive export restrictions remained in place until 1995 (remaining export duties are set to be eliminated by mid-1996), and many consumer prices are still subject to local gov-

ernment intervention. Countries have usually been slower to adjust or liberalize housing rents and utility and public transport prices (Box 2.1).

Countries' 1989–95 averages on the liberalization index introduced in Chapter 1 (the purple bar segments in Figure 1.2) provide an aggregate indicator of the combined duration and intensity of liberalization. They assess the medium exposure of each country during 1989–95 to free market forces, including domestic price and trade liberalization, foreign trade liberalization and currency convertibility, and new entry and private sector development. It is worth focusing on liberalization over a period of time, rather than just in 1995, because both past and present reforms influence the behavior of enterprises and households and economic performance today. Of course, progress as measured by this index depends on countries' initial conditions as well as their reform efforts, and countries such as Hungary and Poland have followed different paths but achieved a similar degree of overall liberalization by 1995. Country comparisons reveal that domestic and foreign liberalization usually advance together, with liberalization of entry lagging somewhat. Advanced reformers, however, have proceeded faster on all three fronts: the Visegrad and Baltic countries, which have undertaken the most radical price reforms, have also opened the most to external trade and entry.

East Asia: Partial liberalization succeeds under special circumstances

Apart from small, diamond-rich Botswana, China has been the world's fastest-growing economy since its free market reforms began in 1978. Vietnam, too, has grown rapidly since abandoning pure central planning in 1986, especially after accelerating reforms in 1989. Both have liberalized substantially, but not (particularly China) on a scale or at a speed comparable to the radically reforming CEE countries. As described in Chapter 1, China has been "feeling the stones to cross the river." In contrast to the single bold leap of the CEE reformers, China went through several stages of "combining plan with market" before adopting its current goal: the "socialist market economy" announced in 1992 is the first to contain no reference to either plan or regulation. A specifically Chinese dual-track approach was used for liberalizing prices, external trade, foreign exchange, and the enterprise sector (Box 2.2). This has worked well, on balance, especially in agriculture. But it has not been without significant costs, including forgone benefits from a faster integration into world trade, rampant corruption and rent seeking, and, more recently, growing regional disparities. Partly in recognition of these costs, the government is proposing to unify the country's trade and tax regimes in the near future. Liberalization in Vietnam was broader and faster (Box 1.4). But as in China, significant restrictions remain, especially on trade and entry, and

Box 2.1 Pricing energy and other household essentials—a case for phased liberalization?

In most of CEE and the NIS, as well as in urban China, household energy, rents, and public transport remain the principal products whose prices have not been liberalized and are still far below cost. Rents are often below even maintenance costs. Housing and household energy subsidies amounted to 5 percent of GDP in Russia and 5 to 6 percent in Ukraine in 1995. Although these subsidies have played the role of social buffers, blunting households' sudden exposure to market forces, the potential economy-wide gains from efficient energy pricing are huge. In the NIS they could, according to one estimate, rise over ten years to more than 10 percent of GDP annually.

What combination of energy pricing and compensatory social policies provides the best mix of efficiency and protection for poor households? Efficient energy pricing would require raising household prices sharply. Relative to other prices, for example, household electricity prices would have to rise roughly threefold in Bulgaria, the Czech Republic, and Russia from levels of mid- to late 1995. In Hungary they almost cover economic cost already, and they will be raised further by the end of 1996, to permit foreign investors in the privatized electricity distribution companies an 8 percent return on capital. This example shows that full-cost pricing is

indeed possible, although Hungary's circumstances differ from those in most other countries. A study of energy pricing in Poland suggests that an 80 percent price increase for heat, gas, and electricity—roughly to their economic cost—would, in the short term, cost the average household around 8 percent of its budget.

Ideally, reforms would accelerate price increases in parallel with compensatory payments targeted to the poor, administered through the existing social assistance system. But this may not be feasible in all countries. Lifeline pricing is then often the most practical approach. This involves charging a low, subsidized price for a fixed, modest energy quota and full price for consumption above that level. Lifeline pricing is not perfect, because all consumers (not just the poor) get the subsidy, and because those who use less than the quota have little incentive to reduce consumption. At the margin, however, the bulk of consumers pay a price close to economic cost. Lifeline pricing with a large increase in the above-quota price therefore tends to be more efficient than a smaller, across-the-board increase. Simulations for Poland show that it may also have better distributional effects, even though a modest, fiscally affordable lifeline may still leave some of the poor insufficiently protected.

Box 2.2 China's dual-track price reforms

China's price reforms began in late 1978, implementing a dual-track system in which the share of production subject to state procurement continuously declined, and more and more prices were subjected to varying degrees of market guidance. The reforms began in agriculture and spread slowly, first to consumer goods and later to intermediate goods industries. In each case a free market developed in parallel with the controlled market, where state supply was kept unchanged at the (lower) plan price. Supply in the free market track grew rapidly, so its share in total output rose steadily. Meanwhile the planned price was raised incrementally until it approached the market price. By the end of 1994 this dual-track system had led to the decontrol of more than 90 percent of retail prices and between 80 and 90 percent of agricultural and intermediate product prices, all of which are now market determined. Only a few prices remain fixed or negotiable within a band set by the state.

Although liberalization remained incomplete, dual-track price reforms did improve efficiency, because the price of the marginal unit reflected economic cost and correctly signaled relative scarcity, and because the share of sales at planned prices declined over time. Also, the eventual full liberalization of the small share of output remaining subject to controls proceeded smoothly. Less than 20 percent of food products were still sold at fixed official prices when the last food price controls were removed in 1992, so the final convergence of the two tracks caused minimal disruption to the economy as a whole. But dual-track reforms also were costly to implement—a vast number of people were needed, for example, to administer the rationing and distribution system associated with dual food prices—and required strict enforcement to limit the diversion of price-controlled products to the free market and to rein in corruption, with severe penalties for noncompliance.

difficult reforms of state enterprises and the financial sector have yet to be undertaken (Chapters 3 and 6).

How have free market reforms succeeded in promoting rapid growth in China and Vietnam? Some argue that, in China, gradualism contributed to the reforms' success, as remaining partial controls—based on the continued authority of the Communist Party and enforced through a dense web of local compliance mechanisms—continued to serve a coordinating function, limiting disruptions to production and trade during the phased buildup of market institutions. But the key, in both countries, was the reforms themselves, which spurred growth directly by improving productivity, and indirectly by raising the incomes of large parts of the population and translating them into high saving and investment. The design and sequencing of reforms fit the two countries' economic and political structure and other initial conditions. They began by liberalizing agriculture (land tenure, prices, and procurement), which had previously been heavily taxed. Because most of the work force was in agriculture, better incentives—at the margin prices were flexible, output could be sold freely, and profits accrued to farmers—generated large productivity, output, and income gains, lifting many out of poverty (see Chapter 4). Labor-intensive technology permitted an easy shift to more efficient, family-based production. This in turn freed up a significant share of the labor force to transfer into higher-productivity sectors, especially the new non-state industrial and service sectors that were next in line to be liberalized. The labor force in rural Chinese enterprises increased by 100 million between 1978 and 1994.

China achieved overall (total factor) productivity growth of more than 3 percent a year during 1985–94, exceptional by international standards. An upward bias in recorded GDP growth may exaggerate this figure somewhat, but this high growth in productivity signals that China's growth is relatively intensive—driven by more efficient use of inputs rather than simply more of them—although lower productivity in the still sizable state enterprise sector raises concerns for the future (see below and Chapter 3). Overall, up to one-third of the increase in Chinese output since 1985 can be attributed to greater efficiency. The bulk of the remainder has been due to an unparalleled, growth-promoting investment boom, fueled by income growth which has translated into high rates of household and enterprise saving. Total saving and total investment both averaged close to 40 percent of GDP during 1985–94. This would not have been possible had the government not been able to stabilize the economy by directly curtailing demand during boom periods. In Vietnam, where productivity has grown at comparable rates, increased efficiency accounts for an even larger share of output growth, because investment rates are considerably

lower than in China. Vietnamese output growth has averaged more than 7 percent a year since 1989 and close to 9 percent in 1994 and 1995. In the mid-1980s domestic saving was negative and investment negligible, but both have since increased dramatically.

As noted in Chapter 1, state industries employ only a moderate share of China's labor force. Also, China's overall production structure has never been as distorted as it was in the former Soviet Union, and the defense sector has never been as big. This has allowed China to delay deep state industrial reforms—employment in its state sector grew by 20 million during 1978–94—and still record substantial productivity and output growth. Subsidizing unprofitable state enterprises with increasing amounts of cheap credit has had significant costs in terms of lost efficiency. But thanks to its high national saving, China has so far been able to absorb this cost without fundamentally destabilizing the economy (see below). Without comparable levels of saving, and with Soviet aid drying up in the late 1980s, Vietnam was forced to cut subsidies to enterprises as part of its stabilization program. This triggered cuts in the industrial labor force by one-third during 1988–92 and a brief recession in the state sector, followed by adjustment and improved performance. But industrial restructuring took place without economic and social upheaval. One reason was that Vietnam's enterprises, unlike China's, did not provide extensive social benefits, but another was that the newly liberalized agricultural and private manufacturing and service sectors, which account for 60 percent of GDP and 85 percent of employment, grew rapidly and were able to absorb laid-off public sector workers.

CEE and the NIS: Liberalization boosts recovery from initial output losses

Output has fallen dramatically in European and Central Asian transition economies. Some of the official estimates shown in Figure 2.1 overstate the decline because of statistical weaknesses (see Box 1.3), not least, in many countries, the exclusion of a large and growing unofficial economy (Box 2.3). But the data show a substantial decline even after adjusting for these biases; in Russia, for example, output fell by about 40 percent during 1990–95. Estimates based on electricity demand are also problematic but provide perhaps a lower bound to the output decline; they suggest that GDP fell, on average, by around 16 percent in five CEE countries between 1989 and 1994, and by around 30 percent in eleven NIS. Because of sharp falls in investment, consumption has declined less than output, but there is little doubt that living standards fell in the early stages of reform in most countries, notwithstanding improvements in product quality and the elimination of queues (see Chapter 4).

Output has fallen dramatically across CEE and the NIS.

Figure 2.1 Decline and recovery in GDP in selected transition economies and in comparable historical episodes

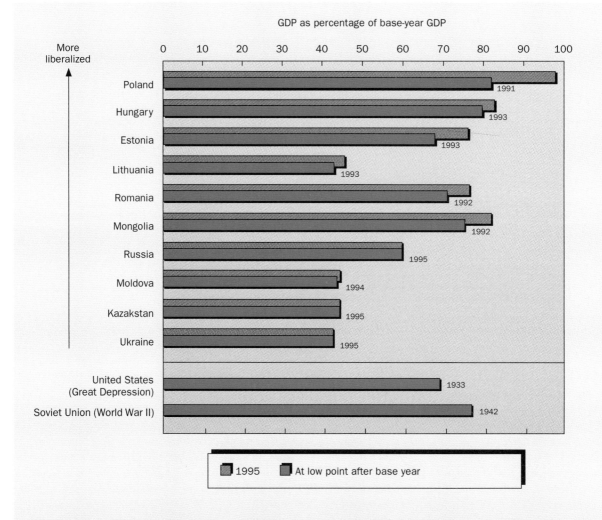

Note: The base year for the transition economies is 1989; historical base years are 1929 for the United States and 1940 for the Soviet Union. Transition economies are listed according to their average liberalization index scores for 1989–95 (see Figure 1.2). Source: Official data.

Total registered employment has also fallen in CEE and the NIS, although there has not been a clear relationship between employment and output declines. Employment has generally fallen more, and unemployment risen faster, in CEE than in the NIS, because in CEE the labor market adjustment has largely come through layoffs and early retirement, whereas in the NIS the response has generally been to cut working hours (see Chapter 4). Between 1989–90 and 1994, for example, registered employment

fell 20 to 25 percent in Bulgaria, Hungary, and Slovenia, but only 7 to 8 percent in Russia and Ukraine.

WHY DID OUTPUT FALL? Some early studies, focusing mainly on CEE, blamed overzealous stabilization for the initial output decline. But the evidence now suggests that it was mainly driven by three factors: demand shifts due to liberalization, the collapse of the CMEA and the Soviet Union, and supply disruptions due to vanishing or absent institutions and distorted incentives.

Box 2.3 Notes from underground: The growth and costs of unofficial economies

Transition has brought marked growth in countries' unofficial economies. Many commercial and even many productive activities go underground to evade high and volatile taxes, circumvent restrictive and often unpredictably changing government controls, and employ workers flexibly and cheaply. Estimates based on electricity consumption suggest that, between 1989 and 1994, the share of unofficial activity in the economy grew, on average, from 18 to 22 percent in a sample of CEE countries and from 12 to 37 percent in a sample of NIS. Surveys in Ukraine confirm a very large unofficial economy.

Unofficial economies tend to be large where political controls have weakened, economic liberalization is lagging, and burdensome regulations and high taxes make the formal environment hostile for the newly developing private sector. Where the informal economy has grown significantly, it has cushioned the output decline and provided an outlet for entrepreneurial talent. But it is mostly a "survival" economy that focuses on short-term objectives, invests little, and loots state assets. Firms waste time and money in their efforts to get around controls and taxes. These efficiency losses, and the difficulty of conducting certain transactions

unofficially, limit its growth. Informalization also lowers government revenues and encourages capital flight. And by its very nature it breeds corruption and undermines the credibility of formal market and government institutions. Thus, a growing informal economy is no substitute for a formal, open private sector, but in fact eventually impedes its development.

Latin America presents striking parallels. There, too, unofficial activities account for between roughly one-fifth and two-thirds of total output. They thrive where political freedoms are many and economic freedoms few. And where informalization has been most extensive (Bolivia, Peru), growth has been slowest. Measures that have helped in Latin America to bring the informal sector back into the economic mainstream are likely to work in the transition economies as well. These include extensive price, trade, and foreign exchange liberalization; tight macroeconomic policies; a sharp reduction of regulatory constraints; and more professional government administration (see Chapters 5 and 7). A combination of carrot and stick—possibly including a one-time, partial tax amnesty—can help reduce the costs of returning to the formal economy.

Liberalization, combined with stabilization, meant the end of the supply-constrained shortage economy, in which even the shoddiest products could always be sold. Now unwanted goods remained on the shelves. Firms and consumers drew down their supply stocks as hoarding became unnecessary—falling inventories contributed about one-third to the output drop in Poland in 1990–91 and over half of the 11 percent drop in the Baltic countries in 1993. In Russia military procurement was cut by 70 percent. Of course, the elimination of unwanted production and excess inventories did not reduce welfare. But all initial cuts in output had second-round effects on spending and demand, which may have doubled the overall effect on output.

The disintegration of the CMEA and the Soviet Union, coupled with trade liberalization, led to a collapse in trade among CEE countries and the NIS. Buyers substituted imports, including consumer durables, from outside the CMEA, while the shift toward world market prices and trade in convertible currencies entailed huge price rises for previously subsidized energy and raw material imports, especially from Russia. According to one rough estimate, Russia's price subsidies to other countries were worth $58 billion in 1990, of which $40 billion

went to the rest of the Soviet Union and $18 billion to other CMEA countries. Ending these subsidies raised the cost of imported production inputs, reducing aggregate supply and output. Many non-NIS countries suffered overall terms-of-trade losses of more than 10 percent of GDP, and even as high as 15 to 20 percent in the case of some highly import-dependent countries. For its part Russia was unable to exploit fully the improvement in its terms of trade because of collapsing trade volumes and its own continued export restraints. The collapse in trade was compounded by the stupendous inefficiency of the initial interstate payment system, which usually took about three months to process transactions.

Finally, in CEE and the NIS, unlike in China, planning institutions had vanished before new market institutions could develop. For example, many countries have discarded the old systems for allocating agricultural credit and distributing farm output, but new wholesale and retail networks and market-based credit systems are not yet in place. The lack of market institutions caused coordination failures throughout the production and trading system—many of them related to limited information and to uncertainty. Inadequate incentives, often linked to deficient property rights, compounded the shortage of modern technology and skills and created formidable obstacles to swiftly redeploying factors of production to emerging sectors. Uncertainty encouraged capital flight by firms and households alike, and many firms became survival-oriented, waiting and hoping for better times rather than restructuring actively. To some extent, such problems are an inevitable result of these countries' dramatic break with the past. But they were exacerbated, in many countries, by inconsistent reform policies—including a lack of policy coordination in the ruble zone (see below). Coordination failures, uncertainty, and distorted incentives constrain the start-up or expansion of profitable activities—even as unprofitable or overbuilt sectors collapse. For example, livestock herds shrank dramatically across the NIS in response to steep increases in fodder prices relative to prices for animal products. But Russian oil production has also fallen—by almost half since 1988—despite a steep increase in the relative price of energy. The main reasons

are an acute shortage of maintenance and upgrade investments and an inadequate legal, institutional, and fiscal framework that discourages management improvements, foreign investors, and new technology.

How has liberalization spurred recovery? Across CEE and the NIS liberalization has been positively associated with growth. In countries where liberalization has been stronger (as measured by average liberalization scores), output losses have on average been smaller (Figure 2.2). And the difference increases over time: relatively stronger liberalization boosted average growth during 1989–95, but it boosted average growth in 1994–95 even more. Two other factors have had a strong impact on recent growth. First, output has tended to increase further since 1989, or decline less, in poorer, more agricultural countries than in richer countries with more overbuilt industrial sectors. Second, each year a country has been adversely affected by regional tensions has added 6.5

Stronger, more sustained liberalization spells a smaller output decline—and a stronger recovery.

Figure 2.2 Liberalization and growth of GDP

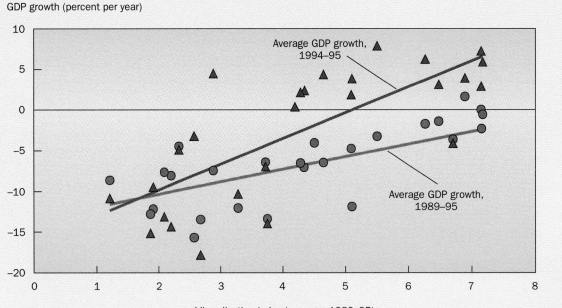

Note: Data are for all twenty-six CEE countries and NIS; results are even stronger if China and Vietnam are included. See Figure 1.2 for details of the liberalization index. Average GDP growth is adjusted to control for the impact of regional tensions in some countries and differences in initial income per capita. Source: De Melo, Denizer, and Gelb, background paper; official data; World Bank staff calculations.

percentage points of GDP, on average, to the annual decline in output since 1989.

Countries have typically returned to growth after three years of sustained liberalization (Figure 2.3). Countries in Groups 1 and 2—those in which liberalization has been more rapid and comprehensive (see Figure 1.2)—experienced an earlier output decline but also an earlier and stronger recovery. Output in countries in the other groups was still falling in 1994–95, but recent reforms have brought a number of them to the threshold of recovery. Ongoing research provides evidence that these patterns of decline and recovery continue to hold even if one controls for differences in countries' initial conditions such as geography, sector structure, or initial macroeconomic imbalance (see Chapter 1).

How can countries judge whether market reforms have paid off overall, given that earlier and more vigorous liberalization has led to an earlier decline but faster medium-term growth? One way is to regard the market system as an asset in which countries invest by liberalizing. Countries have invested different amounts at different times, and these investments have generated initial income (GDP) losses and subsequent income gains of different magnitudes. The value of countries' investments as of the end of 1995 is their total GDP accumulated since 1989 (and discounted back to 1989 to allow for the fact that people value income today more than income tomorrow). Figure 2.4 shows that, on average, liberalization has indeed been a good investment. The least liberalized countries have fared slightly better than moderate reformers. More advanced liberalizers, however, whose cumulative market reforms have now reached a critical mass, have come out far ahead, at least in terms of national income. This does not imply that rapid, all-out liberalization is always possible—or preferable. When choosing how much and how fast to liberalize, governments are constrained by initial conditions, and often the effects of different strategies will be highly uncertain. But as noted in Chapter 1, initial conditions still leave policymakers a fair amount of choice—they influence but by no means predetermine economic performance. The fact that, when these factors are controlled for, liberalization tends to pay off suggests that, on average, policymakers will maximize people's incomes by liberalizing as much as possible within the range left open by country-specific constraints.

New growth comes from letting exports and services expand . . .

Exports and services, two previously repressed activities, have been the major engines of growth in transition economies. Overall, the European transition countries have been strikingly successful at opening their economies and reorienting their exports toward world markets (Table 2.1). Despite early skepticism, many have been able to

Countries that liberalize rapidly and extensively turn around more quickly.

Figure 2.3 Time profiles of output decline and recovery by country group

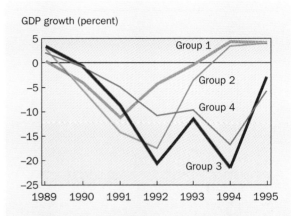

GDP growth (percent)

Note: Countries in CEE and the NIS are grouped by their average liberalization index scores for 1989–95 (see Figure 1.2). Countries severely affected by regional tensions are excluded. Annual growth rates are simple averages for each group. Source: Official data; World Bank staff calculations.

penetrate the "quality barrier" to expanding exports to the West (trade relations with the European Union and integration into world trade institutions are discussed in Chapter 9). Countries have rapidly diversified their exports, and some have begun to reverse the trend of falling unit value for machinery exports—a sign of rising quality. Exports from countries with more open trade regimes, mostly in CEE and the Baltics, declined less with the initial disintegration of the Soviet Union and the CMEA and recovered faster, contributing more to overall output growth (see Table 2.1 and Box 2.4). By contrast, in most NIS, which stuck with state trading arrangements and still impose significant export controls, OECD-oriented exports of manufactures have remained marginal and the contribution of exports to growth has been negligible.

Trade policies in China and Vietnam have combined substantial, although partial, liberalization with active export promotion, with Vietnam relying more on the former and China on the latter. State trading now covers

After seven years, aggressive liberalizers in CEE and the NIS have come out ahead.

Figure 2.4 Liberalization and cumulative GDP

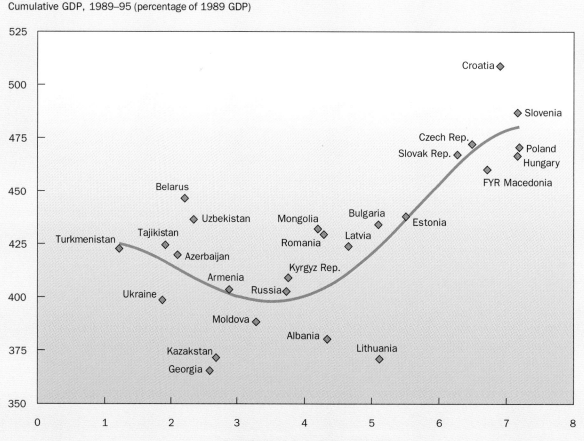

Note: Data are for all twenty-six CEE countries and NIS. See Figure 1.2 for details of the liberalization index. Cumulative GDP is the normalized net present value of total GDP over 1989–95, discounted at 10 percent per year. It is adjusted to control for the impact of regional tensions in some countries and differences in initial income per capita and the abundance of natural energy resources. Results are robust to changes in the discount rate and to the inclusion of China and Vietnam. Source: Official data; World Bank staff calculations.

only a few important products and represents a shrinking share of trade in both countries. Many exports are liberalized completely, and most remaining export controls are not binding, but imports remain subject to significant restrictions, especially in China. Both countries have exempted exporters from import duties on their inputs and created favorable conditions for export-oriented foreign investment—Vietnam mainly through deregulation,

China through the creation of special economic zones, the opening of coastal areas, and preferential tax treatment and access to foreign exchange for exporters.

Although China and Vietnam have liberalized trade less than have the Visegrad and Baltic countries, their overall trade performance has been at least as spectacular. China has sustained export growth of more than 15 percent per year on average since 1978; Vietnamese export

Table 2.1 Trade policy and export performance in CEE and the NIS

	Trade policy			Export performance				
						Average annual contribution of export growth to GDP (percentage points)[c]		
Country group	State trading, 1994	Quantitative restrictions, 1994	Years of current account convertibility by end-1995	Change in share of CMEA or Soviet exports (percent)[a]	Mfg. exports to OECD, 1994 (percent of GDP)[b]	Exports to OECD only, last year before transition to 1994	Total exports, last year before transition to 1994	Total exports, first year of transition to 1994
Group 1	Very small	No	4	−57.2	24.5	2.3	2.1	3.0
Group 2	Very small[d]	No[d]	2	−43.9	18.1	1.4	−3.1	3.7
Group 3	Moderate[e]	Yes[e]	1	−13.6	3.3	0.2	−11.2	0.5
Group 4	Extensive	Yes	0	−14.2	4.4	−0.1	−14.4	0.3
Rg. tensions	Extensive	Yes	0	−20.8	3.7	..	..	..

.. Not available. Mfg., manufacturing. Rg. tensions, group of countries severely affected by regional tensions (see Figure 1.2).
Note: Data are simple averages for each country group (see Figure 1.2).
a. For CEE countries, data are for 1989–94 CMEA exports; for NIS they are for 1990–94 Soviet exports.
b. For Albania, Mongolia, and Slovenia, data are for total exports.
c. The last year before transition was 1989 for Poland, 1990 for the other CEE countries, and 1991 for the NIS.
d. Mongolia was the only Group 2 country with significant state trading and quantitative export controls in 1994.
e. The Kyrgyz Republic was the only Group 3 country that had essentially eliminated export restrictions by 1994.
Source: Kaminski, Wang, and Winters 1996; IMF 1995a; EBRD 1995; World Bank staff calculations.

Box 2.4 Trade policy and performance: Estonia and Ukraine illustrate how close the link

Estonia and Ukraine have pursued diametrically different trade policies. Their trade performance has varied accordingly.

Rapid trade liberalization pays off. Estonia removed virtually all export barriers, eliminated all quantitative import restrictions, kept only a few low import tariffs, and made its new currency fully convertible for current account transactions, all by the end of 1992. Import liberalization introduced world relative prices for tradables. And radical export liberalization—a policy that distinguished Estonia from most other NIS—allowed a rapid reorientation of trade, accelerated adjustment to Western quality standards, and boosted hard-currency export revenues. More than half of Estonia's exports now go to Western Europe, and close to two-thirds of its imports come from there. Export growth contributed 11 percentage points a year to GDP growth during 1992–94. Even if one corrects for Estonia's special advantages—close ties with Finland, proximity to Western Europe, and Baltic Sea ports that have boosted legal and illegal trade—its export performance has been phenomenal.

Slow trade liberalization imposes high costs. Ukraine maintained many price and trade controls until the fall of 1994. State trade—including state procurement and an extensive network of bilateral trade agreements

with other NIS and ex-CMEA countries—remained intact. Administrative controls kept domestic prices below world prices. Tight export controls (including licenses and quotas) sought to prevent producers from selling subsidized goods abroad. Exporters had to surrender foreign exchange earnings at below-market exchange rates. The import regime remained liberal, but domestic buyers lacked foreign exchange to pay for imports. Ukraine's policies proved counterproductive. The intergovernmental agreements failed to stem the trade decline with the other NIS and blocked trade diversification: Western Europe accounted for less than 20 percent of Ukraine's total trade in 1994. Isolation from world markets delayed enterprise adjustment and perpetuated inefficiencies. Exports fell, contributing negatively to output growth during 1992–94, and large trade deficits contributed to a spiraling depreciation of the currency and economic destabilization. Ukraine's reforms in late 1994 included considerable price liberalization and the elimination of most direct export controls, and exports grew in 1995. A nontransparent reference price system continues de facto to restrain exports below a minimum price, encouraging rent seeking and corruption, but as of early 1996 its coverage is limited to a small and declining share of exports.

growth in the shorter period since 1986 has exceeded 25 percent per year. Initial conditions played a significant role in these achievements. China did not suffer a trade shock from dissolution of the CMEA, of which it was not a member, and it was able to draw on its Hong Kong connection and a large expatriate community to help develop its export industries. Vietnam enjoyed an oil export bonanza that partly offset the loss of CMEA markets and cushioned the withdrawal of Soviet transfers and an initial decline in nonoil industries. In addition, both countries were able to exploit their strong comparative advantage in labor-intensive manufactures. Within China and Vietnam (just as across CEE and the NIS), exports have grown faster in those industries and regions with more open trade and foreign investment regimes, and higher exports have been associated with faster output growth. A World Bank study of options for reforming China's trade regime has shown that the remaining export and import restrictions carry high efficiency and welfare costs. These would be reduced by the further liberalization measures proposed in support of China's bid to join the World Trade Organization (WTO).

Some have argued that, whatever the overall speed of liberalization, foreign trade and exchange transactions should be liberalized more slowly than internal markets, to lessen the initial decline in domestic employment and output. Yet there is powerful evidence from transition economies that the benefits of early external liberalization—in parallel with domestic liberalization and stabilization—far outweigh the potential costs. Establishing essentially free trade (except, possibly, a modest and uniform import tariff) early on yields a particularly large return in these countries, for several reasons. First, the legacies of central planning—especially the bias toward autarky and large firms—magnify the efficiency and output gains from competing in world markets, and comparisons of countries' aggregate trade performance bear this out (see above). Firm-level evidence from Bulgaria, Poland, and Russia also shows that trade liberalization has indeed spurred enterprise restructuring and helped make markets competitive. Second, in the early stages of liberalization, producers in most countries have been shielded from foreign competition by heavily undervalued currencies, whether exchange rates are fixed or floating (see below). Undervaluation also created a strong incentive to seek export markets.

By contrast, continued trade controls are likely to yield few benefits for transition countries. Import protection is at best a blunt instrument for alleviating the pain of adjustment, since it cushions entire industries, not just the weakest firms. Entry promotion, retraining programs, and targeted social assistance are likely to be much more effective. Furthermore, unlike these measures, trade controls

need to be enforced against strong incentives for both partners in a voluntary transaction to circumvent them. In transition economies, whose institutional capacity is especially weak, trade controls therefore tend to be relatively ineffective at protecting firms or raising tariff revenues, and instead breed corruption (see Chapters 5 and 7). Finally, worldwide experience has shown that "temporary" protection measures all too often become permanent, and that frequent changes in trade policy are bad for firms that are expanding and developing foreign ties. Both problems have particular relevance to those of the transition countries where political conditions are volatile.

Services have been the second major source of growth in transition economies. One study estimated that reversing the past repression of services in the NIS could increase national income by more than 10 percent and generate around 6 million additional jobs, substantially compensating for declines in other sectors. Service sector output has indeed soared during transition, especially where liberalization is more advanced (Table 2.2). In the leading reformers the initial "service gap" (the shortfall in the service sector share of GDP relative to that in established market economies) has essentially been closed. Spirited entrepreneurs have responded vigorously to improved incentives, often despite serious obstacles, including numerous and frequently changing regulations, slow and often corrupt bureaucracies, and crime, in addition to high taxes and lack of credit. Services have grown less in countries such as Belarus, where reforms are not as advanced.

The adjustment from industry toward services has meant huge shifts in relative prices. In Russia the price of paid services relative to that of goods in the average consumer basket rose fivefold between 1990 and 1994. In parallel, the share of industry in GDP fell 7 percentage points and that of agriculture 9 percentage points, while the share of services increased by 16 percentage points. Industry's share has declined even more sharply in the advanced reformers. This has contributed to an improved environmental record across CEE countries and the NIS, whereas rapid industrial growth has led to deteriorating environmental conditions in the East Asian transition economies (Box 2.5).

Agriculture's share in GDP has fallen somewhat in most transition economies. In CEE and the NIS, agriculture was highly inefficient and, in contrast to East Asia, sustained by subsidies on inputs, credit, and retail prices. The sector has suffered an unnecessarily severe relative price shock—input prices, especially fuels, rose four times as much as output prices—because supply and processing are not yet fully competitive, and governments still intervene to hold down food prices. Further liberalization should allow agricultural producers to retrace some of their lost ground.

Table 2.2 Liberalization and sectoral restructuring

Country group[a]	Average liberalization index, 1989–95[a]	Change in share of GDP, 1989–94 (percentage points)			Share of services in GDP (percent)			Percentage of 1989 services gap filled in 1994
		Agriculture	Industry	Services	Actual, 1989	Normal share[b]	Gap in 1989[b]	
CEE and NIS								
Group 1	6.9	–4	–12	16	42	51	9	173
Group 2	4.7	1	–11	10	35	51	15	68
Group 3	3.4	0	–4	4	33	49	16	25
Group 4	2.0	–2	3	–1	34	49	15	–7
Rg. tensions	3.9	14	–7	–7	41	50	9	–80
China and Vietnam	5.5	–10	5	6	32	41	8	66
Average of all transition economies	4.4	2	–6	5	37	49	13	38

Rg. tensions, group of countries severely affected by regional tensions (see Figure 1.2).
a. See Figure 1.2 for details of the liberalization index and the countries in each group.
b. The "normal" services shares of countries are shares predicted from a regression of sectoral shares on income per capita and population size in a sample of 108 developing and industrial economies. The services "gap" is the difference between the actual and the normal share of services in GDP.
Source: Syrquin and Chenery 1989; official data; World Bank staff calculations.

. . . And from forcing old firms to restructure
Price and trade liberalization and sharp cuts in fiscal and credit subsidies are crucial to forcing firms to adjust and turning the enterprise sector around. Indeed, industrial restructuring has turned out to be highly decentralized in transition economies. Output shifts between subsectors have followed no obvious pattern. Heavy industry, assumed to be the most overbuilt, has not contracted relative to light industry. Branches have not systematically expanded or contracted as their relative competitiveness has improved or

deteriorated with the move toward international prices. Instead, industrial restructuring has involved large changes in output and employment at the firm level. Studies show that enterprise performance varies greatly within an industry, and past profitability often provides little clue as to which firms will thrive and which succumb.

Industries are in flux, with new entry, breakups and mergers, a sharp rise in the number and share of small firms, and new products and processes. Price and trade controls, which affect entire industries, impede this kind

Box 2.5 Transition can help the environment—with the right policies

Transition has reduced environmental damage in most CEE countries and NIS, with pollution dropping as a consequence of the fall in economic activity, especially in industry. There are signs that the recovery in industrial output may not be accompanied by equivalent increases in pollution, because of more effective environmental regulation and improved enforcement. China, in contrast, has grown rapidly. This has resulted in higher pollution and worsening environmental conditions. The environmental performance of most heavy industrial enterprises remains poor, and many new light industries generate water pollution and hazardous wastes, which pose a serious threat. In the most polluted large cities a combination of stricter environmental policies and economic changes seems to have stabilized levels of air pollution—the most immediate environmental threat to human health.

In all transition economies a combination of further market reforms and sound environmental policies can improve environmental performance. First, changes in relative prices should promote more efficient use of energy and natural resources. Second, privatization and reduced state interference in industrial decisions will encourage management to improve the operating performance of existing plant, while replacing old equipment with new plants incorporating cleaner production technologies. Well-designed environmental regulation and investments can contribute to this process. Third, a clear institutional separation of enterprise ownership from environmental regulatory authority should help ensure realistic environmental standards. Fourth, foreign direct investment and international cooperation—such as through the Baltic Sea cleanup programs—can bring in best environmental practices from around the world.

of decentralized enterprise adjustment and market-led differentiation of enterprises by performance. Governments worldwide have tried to pick winners and target support only to viable firms. This is risky business at the best of times; in the volatile environment of transition it is impossible. Even firm-specific, performance-linked credits and subsidies will inevitably assist many nonviable firms. Such support wastes resources and discourages viable firms from adjusting. Moreover, subsidies tend to go to state enterprises. This tilts the playing field against new private entrants, the main source of new jobs.

Experience across CEE and the NIS supports these arguments. Hungary and Poland have sustained strong liberalization and reduced enterprise subsidies, from 7 to 10 percent of GDP in the late 1980s to 2 to 3 percent in the early 1990s. Enterprises there have adjusted, and their performance has improved much more than that of their counterparts in Bulgaria and Russia, where liberalization has been less consistent and budgetary and central bank subsidies to enterprises still averaged 6 to 7 percent of GDP in 1993–94. Chinese state enterprise reforms included decentralized, although partial, liberalization from the beginning; not coincidentally, enterprise productivity and output growth have been higher in the more liberalized regions and sectors, where competition has been stronger, and in the less regulated nonstate segments of the economy (see Chapter 3).

Restructuring of production and output has involved extensive adjustment in labor markets. Although registered unemployment has remained low in some countries, especially in the NIS (see Chapter 4), analysis of economy-wide and sectoral labor flows reveals that total turnover rates (hires plus fires) probably averaged around 20 to 25 percent in the NIS during 1991–93. Such high turnover rates are comparable to those in middle-income developing countries such as Chile and Colombia and exceed those in Canada and the United States. Between 70 and 80 percent of hired and fired workers moved within the same sector rather than to other sectors.

Stabilization: A vital ingredient in transition

Stabilization policy is an essential complement to liberalization in transition. Policies to contain inflation and impose hard budget constraints on firms are necessary for market economies to grow and firms to restructure. But the interaction between macroeconomic policies and other reforms, including liberalization, is greatly affected by initial conditions. In this respect, China is a distinctive case.

China: A cyclical pattern of moderate inflation
Throughout its reform period China experienced moderate inflation, with boom-and-bust cycles in prices and output (Figure 2.5). Each boom has featured rapid credit

China has oscillated between boom and bust.

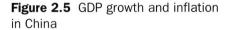

Figure 2.5 GDP growth and inflation in China

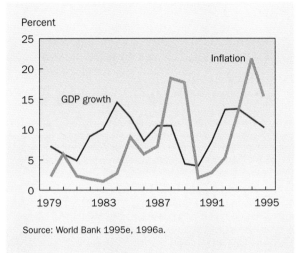

Source: World Bank 1995e, 1996a.

expansion (mainly to finance investment projects) and a sharp rise in inflation. This has been followed by a strengthening of financial policies, especially through direct administrative controls, including ceilings on bank lending, direct prohibitions on investment, and price reregulation. Macroeconomic imbalances widened when reform began in 1978 but were effectively controlled by government policy. The boom cycles have been triggered by reform initiatives. In 1984 enterprise and trade reforms gave increased freedom and expansionary incentives to firms. After a cooling-off period in 1986–87 a new round of trade, price, and wage reforms and the introduction of the contract responsibility system for enterprises (under which multiyear contracts specify the profits and output to be turned over to the state) gave another boost to demand. And in January 1992 reforms designed to encourage investment and enterprise autonomy through locally driven incentives set off another round of inflationary pressures.

This pattern largely reflects the incompleteness of Chinese reforms, especially in the enterprise and financial sectors. With soft budget constraints and with interest rates on bank loans frequently set below inflation, enterprises and powerful local governments have sought to capture the benefits of increased credit in the form of higher local investment, incomes, and employment, expecting that any inflationary costs would be dissipated through the entire economy. Partial price reforms have increased the need for government subsidies, to cover the losses of enterprises whose prices remained fixed at artificially low levels. Meanwhile, fiscal decentralization and difficulties in developing effective tax administration have contributed to large declines in government revenues (Chapter 7). As a result, the government shifted more and more of its fiscal responsibilities to the banking system. The net flow of resources from banks to enterprises has been large, amounting to 7 to 8 percent of GDP in the late 1980s and early 1990s. About half of this was refinanced by the central bank through quasi-fiscal operations. Moreover, bank loans to enterprises and central bank loans to banks have both involved large implicit subsidies (equivalent to around 3 to 4 percent of GDP), in the form of negative real lending rates and noncollection of bad debts (bad enterprise debts are now estimated to account for at least 20 percent of banks' portfolios).

In most other countries such conditions would have led to high inflation. But China has not been like most other countries. This rapidly growing economy has avoided high inflation because of a seemingly insatiable demand for cash and bank deposits by enterprises and households, whose bank deposits increased more than threefold in real terms between 1984 and 1993. The resources raised through money creation—seigniorage—have been exceptional, peaking at almost 11 percent of GDP in 1993 (1 to 2 percent is typical in market economies). In this environment China's central authorities have so far been able to contain inflation by periodically stepping in with administrative controls; these will become less effective as reforms progress.

Demand for money is likely to grow more slowly in China in the future, for three reasons: money balances are already high, close to GDP in 1994; alternatives to bank deposits—equities, enterprise bonds, foreign currency, and real assets—are increasingly available; and capital movements are becoming de facto more open. Bank financing of public sector deficits will then more readily translate into inflation. This adds to the urgency of reducing these deficits—not by administrative fiat but by addressing their structural roots—and expanding the scope for noninflationary deficit financing through domestic bond issues.

Administrative controls still played their part in cooling off an overheated economy in 1994–95. But at the same time central bank credit to the banking system was reduced, and the consolidated public sector deficit has begun falling. To consolidate these gains, China will need to accelerate reforms in the state sector. Improving the effectiveness of indirect instruments of monetary policy requires hardening budget constraints on both enterprises (to increase their interest rate sensitivity) and banks (to strengthen risk considerations in loan decisions and pricing). This will entail deepening reforms in a number of difficult areas that governments in CEE and the NIS have been grappling with, such as bankruptcy and liquidation, layoffs, state bank restructuring, social assets of enterprises, and a social safety net for urban employees (Chapters 3, 4, and 6).

CEE and the NIS: A tortuous path of inflation

Inflation in CEE and the NIS has broadly followed three stages, each corresponding to a phase of reform. The first, during the early months of liberalization, involved the release of the monetary overhang (excess money supply) that had accumulated under central planning. The second, spanning years two and three of liberalization (in some cases longer), has been linked mostly to the speed with which subsidies to enterprises were phased out and prices not previously freed were decontrolled. The third stage, usually reached once inflation has fallen below 40 percent a year, concerns mainly the more advanced reformers and involves exchange rate policy and capital flows. The essence of the inflation story in most CEE countries and NIS is that free market reforms first turned high, repressed inflation into high, open inflation, and then further liberalization and tight financial policies brought inflation down by containing persistent domestic subsidy pressures. This is in stark contrast with the story in China, and somewhat different from that in Vietnam, which experienced high, open inflation already under central planning but since then has sustained sharp cuts in subsidies to enterprises (see Box 1.4).

THE FIRST STAGE: AN INFLATION THAT CAME IN FROM THE COLD. In CEE and the NIS inflation came into the open—suddenly in most countries—and prices soared when they were freed. Money in circulation and in banks exceeded the value of goods and services that firms and households wanted to buy, and this monetary overhang flooded the market, driving up prices. The price stability of the planning system had become untenable, because inflation had been repressed. By late 1991 many black market prices in Russia were five times higher than official prices, the black market exchange rate reached more than forty times the official level, and grain hoarding had become so widespread that supplies for large urban areas were in jeopardy.

This burst of inflation in the first year of liberalization was associated with huge currency depreciations in many economies in CEE and the NIS, regardless of the exchange rate regime. Equilibrium exchange rates are difficult to determine, especially in transition economies, and, in general, when economies with deep inefficiencies open up to world trade some initial depreciation is to be expected. But the data suggest that the initial devaluations in Poland and the former Czechoslovakia were four times larger than what would have been necessary to maintain purchasing power parity for Polish and Czech goods; the Bulgarian lev fell to one-seventh its purchasing power parity (PPP) value, and the Russian ruble to about one-tenth a "normal" level. Capital flight and long-repressed demand for foreign goods placed continued pressure on exchange rates, and this accelerated domestic inflation through rising import prices.

In the NIS the lack of monetary policy coordination in the ruble zone (the common currency area on the territory of the Soviet Union after its disintegration) exacerbated inflation and created severe payments problems for inter-state trade. At the start of 1992 fifteen national banks, act-ing as new central banks, tried to outbid each other in emitting credit, because the proceeds would accrue domestically while the costs, in higher inflation, would be dispersed throughout the ruble zone. The National Bank of Ukraine was especially active in this. In June 1992 the Russian central bank stopped the automatic clearing between bank deposits in other NIS and those in Russia, but then it began to issue large amounts of "technical" credits to many NIS to be used to purchase Russian goods. In Uzbekistan such credits amounted to 60 percent of GDP in 1992. These problems set the stage for the introduction of new currencies throughout the NIS.

THE SECOND STAGE: THE STRUGGLE TO REGAIN CON-TROL. The main culprit in prolonging high inflation was rapid monetary expansion (Table 2.3). Slow reformers permitted rapid growth in the money supply and thereby ended up with the highest inflation rates; the more advanced reformers, by contrast, posted the smallest money supply growth on the way to recording the lowest rates of inflation. In the NIS inflation followed growth in broadly defined money with a rather short lag of four months. In contrast to developments in China, demand for real money balances in the NIS declined, further rais-ing inflation. Households and firms began to adjust to high inflation; in Belarus, for example, the real money stock fell by half in a two-year period.

Generous central bank credits were the main cause of inflationary money supply growth in this stage. Over the three years 1992–94 net domestic credit in Poland roughly tripled in nominal terms, and the money supply roughly tripled in parallel. By contrast, in Russia both grew roughly 150-fold during the same period. Much domestic credit went to support the budget, in response to severe fiscal problems associated with the onset of reforms. For the NIS in particular, transition meant a precipitous fall in government revenues. Receipts from the state enter-prise sector fell sharply, and the new tax administrations proved unable to tax the emerging sectors (Chapter 7). At the same time pressures grew to maintain expenditure at high levels, especially for social purposes. Price liberaliza-tion also exposed the extensive systems of cross-subsidies inherent in the planned economy, shifting all or most of the cost onto the budget. Fiscal deficits were fairly large during 1990–94, averaging 6 to 7 percent of GDP in Bul-garia, Hungary (which had substantial interest payments), and Uzbekistan. They were even higher in Russia, averag-ing 12 percent of GDP.

To ease budget pressures, many governments man-dated that the banking system undertake quasi-fiscal activities, most often by extending highly subsidized cred-its to state enterprises to shore up past patterns of pro-duction and employment. Many enterprises found that their cash balances had been severely devalued, and they demanded additional credits. They received the backing of officials who believed that a shortage of real money bal-ances was largely responsible for the output drop. For example, in Russia in mid-1992 these officials argued that the money supply had to "catch up" with the price increases that had occurred since the beginning of the year. Among slower reformers in CEE and the NIS, credit subsidies from the central bank were often around three times the size of the fiscal deficit.

Table 2.3 Inflation and money supply growth
(percentages per year)

Country group	Average inflation			Growth in money supply, broadly defined[a]		
	1992	1993	1994	1992	1993	1994
CEE and NIS[b]						
Group 1	58	27	19	60	31	28
Group 2	554	169	78	..	110	65
Group 3	1,273	1,163	723	473	276	170
Group 4	829	2,390	1,547	..	1,171	1,112
China and Vietnam	11	9	15	33	25	28

.. Not available.
Note: Data are simple averages for the countries in each group (see Figure 1.2).
a. The definition of the money supply used for each country is the one that most closely approximates M2; its growth is measured from end-year to end-year.
b. Countries severely affected by regional tensions have been excluded.
Source: IMF and World Bank data.

Financing these fiscal and quasi-fiscal deficits in a non-inflationary manner was not easy, and most ended up being funded through seigniorage—put simply, by printing money (Figure 2.6). Inflation, fueled by excessive money supply growth, levied an implicit "inflation tax" on individuals by reducing the real value of their money holdings. This caused huge transfers of income and wealth among households, enterprises, and banks (Box 2.6). Seigniorage averaged more than 16 percent of GDP in Russia during 1992–93, about the same as total central government revenues. In CEE it was more modest, averaging 5 to 6 percent of GDP in Poland and Hungary in 1990–92. Seigniorage in leading reformers has since stabilized at "normal" levels—about 1.5 percent of GDP.

Bringing inflation under control required a sustained reduction in money supply growth. Especially in the NIS, the combination of tightening monetary policy and shrinking money demand meant that, in stark contrast to the Chinese situation, banks could not make net resource transfers to the enterprise sector for any length of time. Monetary rigor had to be supported by sharp cuts in subsidies, especially those provided to enterprises through cheap central bank credits. This, in turn, required sustained liberalization to eliminate the losses due to price controls and other government interventions and to break the close link between enterprises and governments. The experience of successful stabilizers also suggests that positive real interest rates contributed to remonetizing the economy (by raising the demand for money) and stemming currency depreciation. These developments, together with greater central bank independence, bolstered confidence in stabilization programs. By 1993–94 reformers in Group 1—the Czech and Slovak Republics, Hungary, Poland, and Slovenia (see Figure 1.2)—had achieved moderate rates of inflation, averaging 23 percent a year. Annual inflation averaged roughly 120 percent in the Group 2 countries, about 930 percent in Group 3, and almost 2,000 percent in Group 4 (Figure 2.7). Even late or hesitant reformers had begun substantial monetary and fiscal adjustment (for example, Bulgaria's budget deficit was cut by 7 percentage points in 1994). Inflation has now started to come down in all the CEE countries and NIS and remains extreme only in Tajikistan and Turkmenistan, where liberalization was least advanced.

THE THIRD STAGE: INFLATION AS A PRICE OF SUCCESS? Cross-country studies of market and transition economies alike suggest that bringing inflation down from high to moderate levels (around 40 percent a year) is unambiguously good for growth; the direct effects of reducing it further are less clear. Growth resumed in the Czech Republic and Latvia at annual inflation rates of 10 percent and 26 percent, respectively, and in Poland, Estonia, and Lithuania at rates of 42 to 45 percent. However, transition economies have good reasons to try to reduce infla-

Governments running larger deficits rely more on the printing press.

Figure 2.6 Bank and nonbank financing of fiscal deficits

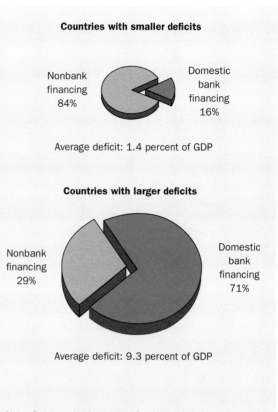

Countries with smaller deficits

Nonbank financing 84%

Domestic bank financing 16%

Average deficit: 1.4 percent of GDP

Countries with larger deficits

Nonbank financing 29%

Domestic bank financing 71%

Average deficit: 9.3 percent of GDP

Note: Data are simple averages for six transition countries with deficit-GDP ratios smaller than 5 percent (Croatia, Estonia, Latvia, Lithuania, Poland, and Slovenia) and eight with ratios greater than 5 percent (Albania, Belarus, Bulgaria, Hungary, Kazakstan, Moldova, Russia, and Slovak Republic). The ratio for each country is the annual average for 1992–94. Source: IMF and World Bank data.

tion below 40 percent. Governments need to build confidence in their currencies (in many cases new ones) and credibility for their policies. Relatively high levels of inflation make this more difficult, by raising the probability that inflation will spiral out of control in the future. Countries should also note that the seigniorage revenues they can now earn at moderate rates of inflation are likely to evaporate as financial systems adjust.

One major obstacle to bringing inflation down further is incomplete price reform. In many transition economies

Box 2.6 Redistribution through inflation: The Russian experience

Inflation in the presence of low nominal interest rates redistributes wealth from savers to borrowers by eroding the real value of savings and debt. In 1992 an enormous inflation tax of 30 percent of GDP was levied on financial assets in Russia (see table). Households lost the equivalent of 12 percent of GDP. Some enterprises also lost, but others gained, as did the financial sector (including the central bank). Large enterprises and financial conglomerates were the main winners.

The inflation tax took a quarter of household income, further depressing consumption. It was also probably regressive, falling on the poor more than on the rich. Moving into dollars or real assets usually involves a transaction of a certain minimum size, which lower-income households can seldom muster—a phenomenon that is well documented in Latin America. Surveys of Russian households confirm that those with higher incomes hold most foreign exchange, and that those with lower incomes in particular express great concern about inflation.

Because inflation wiped out personal savings, it disproportionately affected those who had saved the most. The elderly, increasingly seen selling flowers or family heirlooms on the street, are one such group. But there are others. Under the Soviet system, generous wage and pension benefits had been used to encourage people to move to remote locations—the hope being that after a few years' work they would have enough money to buy a house in central or southern Russia. Most Russians who now live in Vorkuta, in the extreme north, went there to work in the coal mines for exactly that purpose. Now, however, their supposed retirement savings will not even buy airfare back to central Russia, and the people of the city find themselves stranded just when the coal mines are about to close.

Gainers and losers from inflation in Russia
(percentages of GDP)

Category	Losses	Gains	Net gain
Households	12	0	−12
Enterprises	18	16	−2
Financial sector	0	8	+8
Government	0	4	+4
Other NIS	0	2	+2
Total	30	30	0

Note: Data are for the period from February 1992 to January 1993.
Source: Easterly and Vieira da Cunha 1994.

the prices of energy and some services are still far below world levels and will therefore increase substantially in coming years. A recent World Bank study on Russia indicates that prices for housing, transport, and telecommunications (relative to those for manufactured goods) would have to increase roughly sixfold from their 1994 levels just to reach 60 to 75 percent of their relative values in industrial market economies.

Large inflows of foreign capital, including some reversal of capital flight, also frustrate the lowering of inflation, because they add to the money supply and put pressure on prices. This has been a particular problem for more advanced reformers. In a sense it is indeed a price of success, since investors are attracted to the large growth potential and high returns on investment that stem from liberalization and moving to a market economy. But extremely devalued currencies have also been a factor (Latvian prices were around 7 percent of Swedish levels in July 1992). The capital account in CEE went from net outflows of $8 billion in 1991 to net inflows of $13 billion in 1993; inflows also rose sharply in Russia and Vietnam in 1995.

Domestic prices will inevitably have to rise relative to foreign prices, in response to these inflows. But opinion differs over whether advanced reformers should allow this to occur through inflation or through nominal currency appreciation. How long should they allow the inflows to feed through to domestic prices, without adjusting the exchange rate? There is no unambiguous answer. Considerations of the size of the current account deficit and the sustainability of capital inflows aside, transition countries can have strong reasons to keep the exchange rate unchanged. In particular, they may fear that an early exchange rate adjustment will tarnish their hard-won credibility with financial markets and, just as important politically, deprive exporters of the partial shelter of an undervalued currency. The trouble is that most of the alternatives to a nominal appreciation carry other costs. Some countries that have put off changing the exchange rate have tried to limit the inflationary impact of inflows through tight fiscal policy, or by requiring commercial banks to increase reserves. Others have issued bonds in an attempt to mop up surplus cash. Yet such sterilization is expensive, especially in transition economies with underdeveloped capital markets, because the central bank pays far more on the bonds than it receives on its foreign reserves. It also puts upward pressure on interest rates, which can hurt domestic borrowers while actually fueling the problem it is trying to address, by attracting yet more foreign capital. Placing controls on foreign capital flows is no solution: experience in Asia and Latin America suggests that such controls increase the cost of capital in the short term and are ineffective in the long term.

Stabilization pegs—and chronic arrears

Like market economies undergoing adjustment, transition economies have faced a variety of issues related to the design of a stabilization program. The experience of different transition countries has afforded tentative answers to at least some of these dilemmas.

One key question is whether a fixed or a flexible exchange rate is more effective, and less costly, in bringing down inflation. Experience in transition economies shows that inflation has been reduced significantly under both fixed exchange rates (Croatia, the Czech and Slovak Republics, Estonia, Hungary, Poland during most of 1990–91) and flexible arrangements (Albania, Latvia, Moldova, Slovenia, Vietnam). However, studies suggest that although reducing fiscal deficits is crucial for disinflation under both arrangements, a fixed exchange rate can help to bring high inflation down more rapidly and at lower cost to growth. One reason is that the automatic exchange of foreign for local currency by central banks at a fixed rate lets enterprises and households rebuild their real money balances more easily. Also, with flexible rather than fixed exchange rates, domestic authorities have complete discretion over monetary policy, so they have to tighten credit further to make their commitment to stabilization credible. Early in the stabilization process, a fixed rate may thus be a useful policy instrument. Over the medium term the choice of exchange rate regime remains an open question.

Can incomes policies also help restrain inflation? In market economies, incomes policies (for example, penalty taxes on "excess" wages) have a decidedly mixed record at controlling wage increases and promoting price stability. But many analysts consider temporary wage controls an essential component of macroeconomic policy in transition economies, particularly as a substitute for strong owners where unions are powerful, to limit cost-push inflation from rising wages. A study of Poland found that wage controls did inhibit pay increases, although wages beyond the ceiling were paid. By and large, wage controls seem rarely to have been binding during the early stages of price liberalization, and they have not in themselves been sufficient to restrain wages in countries without supporting fiscal and monetary restraint.

When should countries move toward flexible interest rates? As market forces gain strength in transition economies, indirect monetary controls become more effective than direct ones. They do not encourage the growth of informal financial markets, which erodes the share of credit that the authorities control directly, and they help depoliticize the allocation of credit. But the particular problem facing transition economies is that the widespread insolvency of banks and enterprises, together with the legacy of passive creditors and the absence of strong owners, means that a broad spectrum of borrowers will

Figure 2.7 Time profiles of inflation by country group

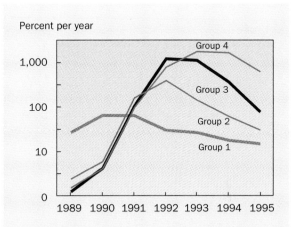

Note: Countries in CEE and the NIS are grouped by their average liberalization index scores for 1989–95 (see Figure 1.2). Countries severely affected by regional tensions are excluded. Annual inflation rates are simple averages for each group. Inflation is plotted on a logarithmic scale. Source: IMF and World Bank data.

want to borrow more, not less, when interest rates rise. This distress borrowing can result in an extended period of very high real interest rates followed by financial crisis. Experience indicates some ways to limit the problem. First, the authorities can enhance the pace and scope of interest rate liberalization by taking steps to increase competition in financial markets as well as to deal with insolvent banks and enterprises. Second, they can exclude unsound banks from credit auctions (as most countries already do). And as in the Kyrgyz Republic and Poland, they can prohibit banks from making new loans to firms in severe difficulty before the start of bank and enterprise restructuring (see Chapters 3 and 6).

How should pervasive arrears be handled? Particularly in transition economies, stabilization policy is complicated by the arrears that enterprises run up with one another, with banks, or with government (in the form of tax and social security arrears). But one lesson of the past few years is that growth in arrears to unsustainable levels is not an inevitable by-product of stabilization. Cross-country experience shows that credible stabilization, including a consistent refusal to inject new credit, is the best way to combat increases in arrears. Where fiscal and monetary policies have been tight—as in the Visegrad countries, the Baltics, and the Kyrgyz Republic—creditors have learned quickly the consequences of not being paid and begin cutting off defaulting debtors. By contrast, irresolute stabilization policies reinforce expectations that government will bail out firms. Complex, centralized programs of netting or clearing arrears tend to fail for precisely this reason, especially when combined with credit injection. Instead of reducing arrears, they weaken financial discipline and encourage more arrears among enterprises, and the resulting high arrears equilibrium further undermines the credibility and effectiveness of macroeconomic stabilization (Box 2.7). Similarly, the secret of Estonia's success in curbing energy arrears (which have plagued many NIS) has been its strictly enforced policy of disconnecting nonpaying enterprises, which has proved a powerful deterrent. By contrast, a reluctance to cut customers off was a key factor behind the buildup of energy arrears in Lithuania,

Moldova, and Ukraine, where energy debts reached between 5 and 8 percent of GDP by early 1995.

As stabilization proceeds and enterprise budgets harden, interenterprise arrears decline and tax arrears rise. Many governments have been unable to enforce tax payment even where legally their claims have top priority, ahead of secured creditors (in Poland and the Czech Republic). Tax arrears (including interest and rescheduled overdue taxes) were estimated at 8 to 10 percent of GDP in Poland and Hungary by the end of 1993 and at almost half that in the Czech and Slovak Republics. In the NIS tax arrears are lower, but rising sharply. To address the problem, government first needs to clear any arrears for which it may itself be responsible. In Russia, for example, two-thirds of the amounts due to enterprises from government were in arrears in mid-1994. Such a stance undermines discipline in the rest of the economy and, as was seen in 1995, can have serious social consequences and fuel political opposition when it prevents workers from being paid. In most transition countries more than 95 percent of taxes due are still being paid, so the integrity

Box 2.7 Government's best response to interenterprise arrears? Strengthen financial discipline

Interenterprise credit typically rises rapidly in the early stages of transition. This partly reflects an adjustment to levels of trade credit common in established market economies. But often interenterprise credit rises further and turns into arrears, as sellers, used to getting paid, continue shipping goods to buyers who have increasing difficulty paying. Afraid that the liquidation of some firms could ripple through the economy in a domino effect and force the liquidation of others, governments often look for measures to reduce exploding interenterprise arrears. But experience shows that interventions can easily backfire and undermine financial discipline.

Kazakstan, Romania, and Russia all implemented a centralized netting out of arrears between firms. In theory such netting can reduce the stock of gross arrears without changing the net position of firms. In practice, however, netting exercises are technically complex. Some firms owe others more than they are owed themselves. The Kazak, Romanian, and Russian programs did not differentiate adequately between enterprises with net credit and those with net debt. Firms were issued new credits sufficient to pay off outstanding debts over and beyond what they were owed themselves. The result was an inflationary net expansion of credit, and the message to enterprises was that both

debtors and careless creditors would be bailed out. Enterprises responded with business as usual, and arrears rose further.

Poland's firm stance on stabilization convinced enterprises that they would not be bailed out, and they became cautious before shipping goods to buyers. Changed expectations reinforced hard budget constraints and eventually stopped the growth of arrears. Poland has also experimented with an alternative method for clearing arrears. Creditors can sell their claims on a secondary market. Because the sale is at a discount, the creditor loses value and learns to be more careful. Buyers of claims can use them to pay for goods and services purchased from the debtor firms. In principle, such markets in secondary debt can help impose financial discipline and reduce arrears without direct government involvement. Their volume and effectiveness in Poland, however, have so far been limited by high transaction costs, by difficulties in resolving disputed claims, by banks' hesitation to sell the bad debt of longstanding customers, and by the legal requirement that debtors consent to the use of claims as payment. Thus, in Poland as elsewhere, conventional debt collection methods—reputation, informal cajoling, debt contract enforcement, foreclosure on collateral, and bankruptcy (Chapter 5)—remain the principal recourse for aggrieved creditors.

of the tax system is not in jeopardy. Heroic efforts to collect taxes from severely distressed firms are unlikely to yield much additional revenue. But tax forgiveness across the board should be avoided since it encourages further increases in arrears. Governments should instead handle tax arrears through case-by-case debt workout schemes. These should be accompanied by improved accounting and auditing, the selective use of bankruptcy, and seizure of commercial receivables and other liquid assets to prevent the problem from recurring. The difficult task, which no country has mastered, is to design a support system that credibly targets subsidies to the most difficult cases, such as distressed enterprises in one-company towns, and keeps subsidies limited, temporary, and fiscally affordable (Chapter 3).

Into the future: What is needed to sustain growth and stability?

Strong liberalization and stabilization help transition economies correct their inherited inefficiencies and macroeconomic imbalances and move to a path of secure and rapid growth. But what can transition economies do to stay on that path?

Lessons from abroad: Get policies right and stick with them . . .

What can transition economies learn from periods of sustained rapid growth elsewhere? One key lesson is that both sound policies and consistency matter. Liberal, pro-competition policies create the potential for enhanced domestic growth, external trade, and access to financing. But countries will only fully exploit this potential by being consistent over time.

Consider postwar Western Europe. Germany's fast recovery and subsequent growth explosion have often been described as an economic miracle—GDP growth averaged 9 percent between 1948 and 1960. Closer examination dispels much of the miracle explanation. Part of the very strong expansion in the initial period was due to catch-up; Germany also benefited from Marshall Plan aid, increased human capital through migration, improvement in the terms of trade, and a strong expansion in foreign markets. But the key to Germany's sustained rapid growth was its consistently market-friendly growth strategy, which included price and trade liberalization, currency reform, tax reductions, and the establishment of strong enabling institutions such as the Bundesbank. Transition economies, like established market economies, benefit from consistent rather than stop-go policies.

Growth averaged 9 percent in Japan during 1948–60, close to 7 percent in Indonesia during 1970–93, and 8 percent (with a rising trend) in the Republic of Korea during 1956–87. In each case growth recovered and surged after a severe economic crisis. In addition to having large agriculture sectors that could serve as a springboard for growth, these countries owed their success mostly to getting the policy basics right. Consistently good macroeconomic management, banking reforms that promoted saving, and a strong focus on education and a suitable skill mix provided the framework for high and rising private investment. And in all the rapidly growing Asian economies favorable trade policies have allowed exports to be a major engine of growth.

. . . And encourage strong saving and investment

As was shown all too clearly under central planning, high investment alone does not guarantee fast growth. The composition and quality of investment, as well as human capital and technological know-how, are also critical. However, sustained rapid growth has been associated with exceptionally high saving and investment rates worldwide. Saving generally averages at least 25 percent of GDP and investment at least 30 percent in fast-growth periods (Figure 2.8). In CEE and the NIS both the rate of capital accumulation and the efficiency of investment are presently inadequate to sustain rapid long-run growth. In CEE in 1994, saving averaged about 15 percent of GDP and investment 17 to 18 percent; average saving and investment rates in the NIS were close to 20 percent. Capital productivity, historically very low in both regions, has recently begun to recover in the leading reformers, but continued improvements will be critical for sustaining growth.

In contrast, saving and investment rates are now approaching a very high plateau in China and are still rising from already respectable levels in Vietnam. Productivity gains will become an increasingly important source of growth in years to come, particularly in China, where saving—and thus investment—rates are likely to decline over the medium term. Given the shrinking scope for improving efficiency through further shifts in resources, achieving these gains will increasingly depend on broadening enterprise and financial sector reforms that boost efficiency at the firm and the industry level. These are likely to include reforms in ownership and allocation of investment. In China, for example, overall productivity in the nonstate sector has been increasing at 4 to 5 percent a year, more than double the rate in the state sector, which continues to absorb the bulk of investment credit. It would be preferable for the government to take the greatest possible advantage of current rapid economic growth to implement difficult but necessary state sector reforms.

What role is there for foreign saving and investment? High investment can be financed externally for some time, but it is funded overwhelmingly by domestic saving in the long run. This is due to a home bias in saving and

Sustained, rapid growth depends on high rates of saving.

Figure 2.8 Saving rates and GDP growth during high-growth periods in selected economies

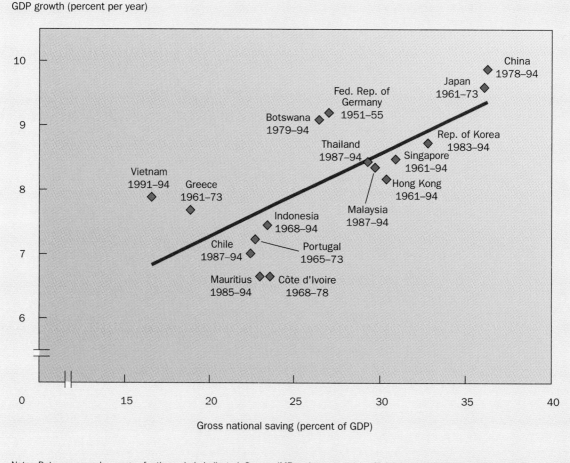

Note: Data are annual averages for the periods indicated. Source: IMF, various years (c); official data; World Bank staff estimates.

investment decisions, limited international capital mobility, the dominant role of retained earnings in funding corporate investment (accounting for the bulk of private investment in industrial countries), and lending constraints imposed by world capital markets. In transition economies, with their weak domestic capital markets and still generally poor credit ratings, promoting domestic saving is especially important. Foreign investment, despite its many benefits, cannot be a substitute for domestic investment.

How can governments promote domestic saving and effective investment? Mitigating economic uncertainty and checking capital flight are critical, and both require most of all ensuring macroeconomic stability. Fiscal reform is crucial: higher public saving, through reduced government deficits and spending, directly increases total saving and means less crowding out of private investment. This is particularly important in those transition economies where government is still large (as in the Visegrad countries; see Chapter 7) or has pursued loose fiscal policies (as in Bulgaria and Tajikistan). A liberal foreign exchange regime and market-determined interest rates are also important, as are sound and stable legal, banking, and government institutions. Progress in these directions, particularly the last, will be difficult for transition economies—even in eastern Germany, where western German institutions have been adopted wholesale, firms single out legal uncertainty and administrative problems as the key obstacles to investment.

Prudent fiscal policies also support growth by preventing the government from running up an unsustainably high debt burden. Most CEE countries and NIS, with the notable exceptions of Bulgaria, Hungary, Poland, and Russia, started with little debt, but many have since run large fiscal deficits, leading to a sharp rise in public indebtedness. The long-term costs of government living beyond its means are well illustrated by Hungary, which has the largest foreign debt per capita among transition countries. Unlike some other heavily indebted reforming countries, Hungary has continued to service its foreign debt without debt reduction or rescheduling. Repayments and interest have largely been financed by more borrowing, both domestically and externally, resulting in rapid growth in the public debt stock. But financing this debt has become hugely expensive. High and rising interest payments increasingly eat into other government spending, because revenues are at a plateau yet budget deficits need to be reduced to keep the debt burden sustainable. The government has therefore decided to use part of the one-off revenues from privatization in 1995 to retire some of its high-interest domestic debt. This may well turn out to be a good investment for the future.

How long will it take to catch up?
Popular wisdom in early postwar Germany was that it would take decades before the average person would own a second pair of shoes. It took five years. When Germany was unified, politicians promised and people hoped that the eastern *Länder* would catch up with their western counterparts in less than five years. By all accounts it will take much longer. So how long might it take for the more advanced CEE and Baltic reformers to reach income levels comparable to those in European market economies? And how long for most of the NIS, China, and Vietnam to join the East Asian newly industrializing economies?

Arithmetic catch-up calculations, with all their limitations, do provide a sobering perspective on the magnitude of the tasks ahead. For China they suggest that it would take five or six years of growth at present rates to reach the current income level in Indonesia and between ten and fif-

teen years to reach that in Thailand. For the Visegrad countries and Slovenia they suggest that it would take about twenty more years at present growth rates to reach the average income level of the EU countries in 1994. Actually catching up with EU average incomes would require much faster growth (around 8 percent a year) or significantly more time (around forty rather than twenty years). Most estimates based on actual conditions in Germany place the catch-up period for eastern Germany at between ten and twenty years; by implication, the catch-up period for the CEE countries and the NIS would be longer, because they lack eastern Germany's favorable initial conditions and rich "big brother." Recent empirical work assesses the prospects for faster CEE catch-up through sustained high growth rates. To make this scenario a reality, CEE countries would need to adopt more market-friendly fiscal policies, including lower marginal tax rates and current government expenditures, an overhaul of government-funded pensions (Chapter 4), and efforts to strengthen government investment—in addition to completing enterprise and financial sector reforms (see Chapters 3 and 6).

The agenda

The clear lesson of transition in both Europe and Asia is that countries that liberalize markets and preserve economic stability are rewarded with resumed or accelerated growth in output and productivity. China's contrasting initial conditions and strong macroeconomic control enabled it to take a more gradual and phased approach to transition. But the main engines of rapid growth in China have been the same as in the successful CEE countries and NIS: rapid entry of new firms, including in the service sector, and growth in exports. China's major challenge for the future is to exploit the large potential efficiency gains from further enterprise and banking reforms and, as the supply of low-cost savings falls with continuing reforms, to enable these funds to be reallocated to more productive sectors. Advanced reformers in CEE and the NIS also have to consolidate their gains, through continued sound macroeconomic policies, and to encourage higher saving and investment by avoiding overregulation and by slimming and reorienting government. Less advanced reformers still face the more urgent task of freeing their economies from the macroeconomic instability and remaining state controls that impede recovery.

CHAPTER 3

Property Rights and Enterprise Reform

At the heart of transition lies a change in incentives, none more important than those for managers of enterprises. Managers in centrally planned economies faced distorted incentives that sooner or later led to poor enterprise performance. Transition requires changes that introduce financial discipline and increase entry of new firms, exit of unviable firms, and competition. These spur needed restructuring, even in state enterprises. Ownership change, preferably to private ownership, in a large share of the economy is also important. Once markets have been liberalized, governments cannot indefinitely control large parts of a dynamic, changing economy. Decentralizing ownership is the best way to increase competition and improve performance.

There are two ways to move to an economy dominated by the private sector: through privatization of existing state assets and through the entry of new private businesses. The two are equally important. New private firms, spurred by liberalization, give quick returns and can accomplish a great deal by themselves; but the mass of state assets in transition economies makes some degree of privatization unavoidable.

The question is not merely how much to privatize, but how and when. Transition economies all experience problems in managing state-owned firms. In some countries, market-oriented reforms short of a massive shift in ownership can bring improvements, even though these may be difficult to sustain over the longer term. In others, rapid and widespread privatization is the only feasible course. All, however, face a dilemma: privatization done incorrectly can produce negative outcomes. Is "bad" privatization then better than none at all? There is no simple answer; it depends on the strength of the state and the capacity of its administrative institutions. The dilemma

does not always arise: smaller assets are easy to privatize, and the outcomes are generally good. But larger transactions are more problematic on both counts, and the trade-offs among the different ends and means of privatizing these assets are intricate and intensely political. Some of the forms of ownership first produced by privatization do not and should not last. The way to think of privatization, therefore, is not as a once-and-for-all transformation, but as the start of a process of reorganizing ownership, shifting over time to respond to the needs of the market economy.

The legacy of central planning

The principal objective of the "socialist firm"—developed in the Soviet Union and later emulated throughout the transition economies—was to meet physical production targets set by central planners. Under central planning, firms did not emphasize profits, quality, variety, or customer service, still less innovation. They were protected from competitive pressures and operated in shortage economies, where everything they produced was snapped up instantly. Managers, most of them production engineers, were judged in terms of output rather than client satisfaction. Financial performance was irrelevant because profits and losses were redistributed among firms. Lacking a bottom line, managers combated frequent input shortages by hoarding labor and inventories. The plan allocated output targets, inputs, and investment. It typically emphasized heavy industry, energy, and investment goods at the expense of consumption goods and services.

For a time the combination of massive investment and ideological commitment forced industrial growth in many centrally planned economies. In the late 1950s, however, evidence of declining Soviet productivity became more apparent (see Figure 1 in the Introduction). Productivity also lagged in China's state enterprises; output growth through the 1960s and 1970s depended on extensive investment. Many countries—Hungary, Poland, the Soviet Union, and Yugoslavia in the past, China and Vietnam still today—tried to improve enterprise performance without resorting to privatization. "Reform socialism" aimed to decentralize decisionmaking to the enterprise level and to create incentives for improved technical and financial performance. Such reforms often yielded temporary improvements in productivity, but the Soviet Union and all the CEE countries eventually suffered reversals. Nor, as discussed below, are Chinese officials today satisfied with the results of their enterprise reform programs. Deeper reforms were required to increase competition, enforce financial discipline, and open capital markets—that is, to fundamentally reorient enterprises and their incentive systems. Thorough reform was also needed in the agricultural sector, which was particularly burdened with inefficient structures and distorted incentives. However, the structure of agriculture and the problems it faced in the planned East Asian economies were quite different from those in CEE and the NIS, as discussed later in this chapter.

The first step: Imposing financial discipline and competition

The first step in transition is to move from the centrally planned regime of transfers and subsidies to one that allows for risk, ensures financial discipline, and creates strong, profit-oriented incentives. This requires opening markets to competition and sharply cutting direct government subsidies. It also requires removing two other cushions: bank credits on easy terms and arrears on payments due to government for taxes, customs duties, and social security (see Chapter 2). Interenterprise arrears are another form of soft finance. Some governments have implemented complex programs for netting and clearing these arrears, but the best advice is to let market forces work out the problem (see Box 2.7).

Financial discipline spurs restructuring— regardless of ownership
Extensive empirical evidence from CEE and elsewhere indicates that most firms, whether state owned or private—or in between, as in the case of China's "nonstate" enterprises (see Box 3.4)—make efforts to restructure if their avenues for rescue close and competition increases. Shrinking subsidies combined with more open markets have universally resulted in labor shedding or falling real wages, or some combination of the two. For example, the largest 150 to 200 firms in the Czech Republic, Hungary, and Poland reduced their work forces by 32, 47, and 33

percent, respectively, between 1989 and 1993 as their sales fell by 40 to 60 percent on average. In addition to layoffs, the more advanced reformers have also seen sales of large amounts of excess inventory and surplus assets. Thousands of trucks sold from state firms, for example, formed the basis of Poland's large private transport fleet. Enterprises subjected to financial discipline show more aggressive collection of receivables, a closer link between profitability and investment, and a reorientation of goals from output targets to profits. Transition forces managers, for the first time, to focus on marketing and product quality.

Whether enterprises actually adjust will thus depend on government policies and, most important, the credibility of government's commitment to reform. Strong and credible macroeconomic stabilizations in the Czech Republic and Poland, for example, stimulated adjustment in many firms. Polish subsidies to enterprises and households shrank rapidly, from more than 16 percent of GDP in 1986 to 5 percent in 1992. Polish managers interviewed in 1990 had little doubt that if they failed to make their firms competitive, the firms would close—and indeed many Polish state enterprises that had existed in 1989 had disappeared by the end of 1995. Banks still had large and rather concentrated bad loan portfolios, but cleanup began in 1993 through a combination of enterprise liquidations, debt sales, and a new bank-led conciliation process (Box 3.1). Tax arrears, however, remain a problem. In Poland, as elsewhere, these have proved the most difficult "subsidy" to eliminate, in part because tax administration is weak (see Chapter 7).

Russian reforms, although extensive, were neither as coherent nor as credible. Total federal subsidies to enterprises (including directed credits) fell from 32 percent of GDP in 1992 to about 6 percent in 1994, but tax arrears and ad hoc tax exemptions increased significantly. Also, local government subsidies to enterprises have increased. Russian firms have begun to adjust, but less than those in Central Europe and in a somewhat different mode. Formal layoffs have been fewer. Employees remain on the books and continue to draw benefits, but they have accepted large cuts in hours and cash compensation and have progressively shifted to informal activities (see Chapter 4).

Governments in the East Asian planned economies approached the problem differently, but even there reforms have sometimes been radical. Vietnam undertook swift and far-reaching state enterprise reforms in 1989. The government eliminated all budget subsidies, cut the number of firms by 5,000 (of which 3,000 were merged into other state firms, but 2,000 actually closed), and exposed some state firms to limited competition from a new private sector. Almost 900,000 workers (a third of the total) were dismissed without any promise of other public sector jobs. In response to this drastic surgery, the

Box 3.1 Innovative approaches to creditor-led restructuring in Hungary and Poland

Who should restructure problem firms in transition economies? In established market economies creditors are important agents of restructuring. Getting creditors to play that role takes financial incentives, adequate information, and strong legal powers in debt collection, debt workout, and liquidation processes.

Poland and Hungary are reforming their banking sectors and implementing creditor-led workout programs to help spur enterprise restructuring. In 1993 Poland adopted a bank-led "conciliation" process that empowers banks to negotiate workout agreements with problem debtors. An agreement reached among creditors holding more than half the value of a firm's outstanding debt is sufficient to bind all creditors. More than 400 such agreements have been successfully negotiated, involving primarily the nine large commercial banks and large state-owned firms.

Hungary took a somewhat different route. Its 1992 bankruptcy law required managers of firms with arrears of ninety days or more to file for reorganization or liquidation. Managers opting for the former retained their jobs and were given first right to present a reorganization plan to creditors. If creditors did not approve it unanimously, the firm was liquidated. The law led to 22,000 filings—17,000 liquidations and 5,000 reorganizations—in 1992 and 1993. The law was amended in late 1993 to eliminate the automatic ninety-day trigger and to reduce the creditor approval requirement to two-thirds of outstanding claims.

The two approaches have much in common. Both require management to put forward a reorganization plan (which should contain both financial and operational conditions) for creditors to negotiate and vote on, and the plan is binding on dissenting creditors if enough of the others approve. Both procedures rely on decentralized negotiations. Although the Hungarian reorganizations begin with a court filing, the courts have relatively little involvement thereafter. The Polish process is out of court, although courts may get involved in approving final agreements or handling appeals.

The new rules have had a significant impact in both countries. Hungarian reorganization cases have been concluded surprisingly quickly, with more than 90 percent of filings in 1992–93 completed during that period. The liquidation cases take much longer; most of those filed in 1992 and 1993 are still pending. Strong firms are more likely to enter and emerge successfully from reorganization, whereas weak firms are more likely to fail in reorganization or to file directly for liquidation. The same is true in Poland: firms entering conciliation have higher average operating profits than firms entering bankruptcy or liquidation. Equally important, both processes have stimulated critical institution building in the banks (particularly their debt workout departments), and the Hungarian scheme has helped build the capacity of the courts and the trustee-liquidator profession.

There is, however, considerable room for improvement. Weak collateral laws (see Chapter 5), poor financial information, and (particularly in Hungary) successive bank recapitalizations have undermined incentives for creditors to use the new procedures to impose strong financial discipline on firms. The reorganization plans that have emerged from the reforms have provided relief from debt service but contain few if any conditions on operational restructuring. Although a good start, it will be some time before the new regimes stimulate as much creditor-led restructuring as their equivalents in established market economies.

---

output of state enterprises rose and revenues from enterprises climbed from 6 to 11 percent of GDP in just three years. State enterprises—a category that includes joint ventures with private foreign or domestic partners—now provide about half of total government revenue. Managers and workers went along with this rapid reform for three reasons: firms retain their after-tax profits, distributing much of it in bonuses and higher wages; most of the dismissed workers were absorbed into the rapidly growing private sector; and state firms had never provided extensive social benefits. In contrast to most CEE countries and the NIS, however, Vietnam's state firms still benefit from a wide array of protective and distortionary measures (exchange controls and land policy, for example) that hin-

der free entry and competition and bias state firms toward capital-intensive production.

China has not taken equally dramatic steps to end the flow of subsidies to state-owned firms, but officials are increasingly concerned with their poor performance relative to the nonstate sector. State enterprises remain important financial and economic actors in China. Although their share of industrial output has declined considerably since the early 1980s, they still accounted for three-quarters of investment and 70 percent of bank credit in 1994. Efforts to improve state enterprise performance have focused on improving corporate governance and management through contracts for managers, new accounting standards, the shifting of supervisory control to the provinces, leasing, corporatization, and the selling of minority shares on domestic and foreign stock exchanges. Hundreds of smaller, unprofitable state enterprises have been closed or merged with other firms. The efficiency of some state enterprises has risen, although by how much is hotly debated. What is not disputed is that the benefits have been largest where enterprises are most exposed to competition and market incentives.

Overall, however, the number of unprofitable state enterprises in China has been growing steadily, because these firms invest too much and earn too little. They face onerous problems of excessive employment, unfunded pensions, and obligations to provide social services they cannot afford. Forty percent of state firms reported losses in 1995, despite paying interest on their borrowings at rates well below inflation. To the extent that they result from increased financial discipline, losses could be a mark of progress. But losses cannot be allowed to continue indefinitely; persistent money-losers must be forced to restructure or close. The frequency with which the government has announced new state enterprise reform programs suggests how difficult reform really is. This is not surprising; a wealth of international experience, from economies as diverse as Japan, New Zealand, Pakistan, and the Republic of Korea, indicates that state enterprise performance can indeed be improved, but improvement is hard to accomplish and even harder to sustain.

In sum, one of the strongest messages to emerge from transition to date is that governments that enforce financial discipline and foster competition will stimulate restructuring in enterprises, regardless of ownership. But many firms get stuck in the early stages. Most adjustments have involved downsizing—of output, employment, and assets. Managers have been survival-oriented; like turnaround managers everywhere, they have focused on sustaining current cash flow. It will take time, and in many cases a clarification and reallocation of property rights, to move from this defensive reaction to a deeper strategic restructuring that involves new and innovative business strategies and investment.

Direct government intervention: Alluring but risky
In addition to—or sometimes instead of—policies to introduce competition and increase financial discipline, some transition governments intervene directly to carry out targeted, top-down programs to restructure enterprises. The problem here is not with the near-universal practice of partial or complete public ownership of certain firms in infrastructure industries with natural monopoly characteristics. Transition economies' interventions in these sectors are generally in line with those in industrial market economies, and indeed in some cases ahead of them: Estonia and Hungary, for example, have sought to exploit the new wave of opportunities for private sector

involvement in infrastructure provision. Rather the concern is with cases where governments extend their reach far beyond infrastructure firms to engage in so-called industrial policy, arguing that transition justifies direct government intervention to give industrial enterprises, public or private, the time, protection, and resources to become competitive.

Advocates claim that without state direction and assistance many high-potential firms and thousands of jobs will be swept away by the imperfect functioning of half-developed markets. In some cases the explicit goal is to improve performance without changing state ownership. For private (usually privatized) firms the typical goal is to select companies with good prospects and improve their chances of survival. Proposed interventions include free or subsidized technical assistance in preparing business plans and bankable projects, management training, loans at below-market interest rates, debt forgiveness, and protection from import competition. Similar policies have been associated with good results in several high-growth Asian economies, and it is natural for officials and observers in depressed transition economies to look longingly at activist measures that might offer hope. However, the countries that have had some success with this approach possess advantages that some CEE countries and most NIS lack: disciplined and well-trained bureaucracies, stable and prudent macroeconomic policies, and a long-standing emphasis on export promotion and international competitiveness. In their absence, a proactive industrial policy runs the risk of continuing the costly subsidization of those firms with political clout while shutting out others with greater potential to succeed.

For some enterprises the objective of government intervention is to restructure and add value, to raise the price they can command upon sale. Few would disagree that the state in transition economies can play a legitimate role in breaking up large state enterprises prior to sale, in assisting enterprises and communities in dealing with "social" assets (schools, clinics, housing, day care centers), and in helping fund severance pay. But going beyond this is likely to be wasteful if not counterproductive. New physical investments under public ownership almost never raise the sale price by the cost of the investment. And a continuation of straight subsidies to cover wage bills and working capital compounds the pain and heightens the severity of the eventual cure.

A number of transition economies have developed what are termed isolation exercises for problem enterprises. A set of poor performers, often the biggest money-losers, are put into a "jail" and examined to determine which are potentially competitive and which merit liquidation. Early experience with jails was not promising. Inmates tended to view their isolation units more as rest homes than as prisons, since they provided both relief from creditors and exceptional resources to meet the wage bill. More-recent isolation exercises, for example in Armenia, the Kyrgyz Republic, the former Yugoslav Republic of (FYR) Macedonia, and Uzbekistan, have tried to overcome these problems by assuring prisoners that governments are indeed committed to their sale or closure, and are not simply using the device to delay the day of reckoning. For example, of twenty-nine firms assigned to the Kyrgyz "restructuring agency," over a twenty-four-month period eight have been liquidated (including a 5,000-employee agricultural machinery plant that the government had regarded as strategic), two have been sold, six more are for sale, eleven are being downsized in hopes of rendering them salable, and two are still in the diagnostic stage. So far the exercise has cost around $20 million, of which half went to cover arrears on energy payments and much of the remainder to provide severance payments for more than 40,000 dismissed workers. Proponents argue that both the information supplied by external consultants and the provision of money to pay for severance costs have been crucial in persuading the Kyrgyz authorities to act. As always, however, the deciding factor is the government's willingness to accept the painful reality that downsizing and closures must occur (Box 3.2).

A 1995 study of the 400 to 500 largest firms in Bulgaria, the Czech and Slovak Republics, and Poland points to the key problem with direct government involvement: the difficulty of picking winners based on past performance. Variation in performance among firms in transition economies is much greater than that in established market economies, and as Chapter 2 noted, neither the past performance of a firm nor its inherited debt structure is a good guide to future viability. Even more than elsewhere, transition governments that try to pick winners are likely to choose poorly.

In sum, avoiding direct government intervention is likely to be the best approach in most cases. Tight, sustained macroeconomic policies can significantly reduce the scale of enterprise losses without direct intervention. They force money-losers to downsize and redundant workers to seek jobs in new private firms. To the extent that governments must subsidize—for political or other reasons—subsidies should be targeted and transparent. The key is to avoid the perception that persistent poor performance is somehow socially justified and entails no painful consequences.

The second step: Creating and allocating property rights

Property rights are at the heart of the incentive structure of market economies. They determine who bears risk and who gains or loses from transactions. In so doing they spur worthwhile investment, encourage careful monitor-

---

Box 3.2 Coal restructuring in Ukraine

Ukraine's coal industry, which employs about 800,000 people, is in deep crisis. Output has fallen by over 40 percent in the past five years. A Ukrainian miner produces an average of 112 tons of coal a year, compared with 250 tons in Russia, 420 tons in Poland, 2,000 tons in the United Kingdom, and 4,000 to 6,000 tons in the United States. Up to half of Ukraine's 250 mines need to be closed in the next decade if the industry is to regain competitiveness. Coal enterprises provide a wide variety of social services, including kindergartens and housing. These are often overstaffed as well: kindergartens, for example, often have one employee for every three children.

Any plan to restructure the coal industry will need to use market incentives, minimize social costs, and have a well-defined role for fiscal support. One approach would involve corporatizing existing mines, excluding those identified as uneconomic, into joint-stock companies as a first step toward privatization or liquidation. Profit-oriented managers rather than the government would decide on the reallocation of investments. Resulting mergers would make it easier for managers to transfer workers from unproductive to productive mines rather than having layoffs at one mine and new hires at another, and thus would allow natural attrition to take care of a substantial part of downsizing. Fiscal support would be needed to fund closing costs, but all new investment would be financed from retained earnings and bank loans. A second element of the plan would involve divesting social assets. Some can be privatized, but others would have to be turned over to municipalities, which, to smooth the transition, would need support, as cost recovery ratios are increased from their present levels of less than 20 percent.

Mine closures can yield significant fiscal savings. A four-year program would require about $250 million to support local governments, $150 million for severance pay, retraining, and temporary employment assistance, and $300 million for closures and environmental costs. But closing uneconomic mines would save $200 million a year, and the benefits of restructuring would be even greater if the remaining mines could reinvest profits to increase productivity. It is cheaper to close uneconomic mines than to cover their losses indefinitely.

ing and supervision, promote work effort, and create a constituency for enforceable contracts. In short, fully specified property rights reward effort and good judgment, thereby assisting economic growth and wealth creation. In addition, a wide distribution of property rights can counteract any concentration of power in the political system and contribute to social stability.

What are property rights?

Property rights include the right to use an asset, to permit or exclude its use by others, to collect the income generated by the asset, and to sell or otherwise dispose of the asset. In market economies these rights are defined in law, usually in great detail (see Chapter 5). Ownership rights to an asset may be split—for example, a widow may have rights to the income from property left by her deceased spouse to her children—but this division is also clearly specified. In transition economies these rights are not at first clearly defined or allocated. Indeed, often such distinctions are not even recognized.

In mature market economies the distribution of property rights across the population and the legal forms through which they are exercised are relatively stable, having evolved over centuries. In most transition economies the initial assignment of property rights is both rapid and partial; it could well be inefficient. Many buildings and plots of land, for example, have been restored to precommunist owners who are neither willing nor able to care for them. Similarly, most former state farms in Russia were privatized as large joint-stock corporations—typically not the most efficient ownership form for agriculture. Thus, for property rights to become fully effective, it is especially important that they be tradable and free to evolve.

Is privatization necessary?

Does it matter whether property is public, private, or something in between? The first obvious test is whether privatization improves performance. An extensive empirical literature (mainly from the 1980s) comparing public and private enterprises in industrial market economies concludes generally, but not uniformly, that private firms exhibit higher productivity and better performance than public enterprises. More recent analyses of performance before and after privatization in industrial and developing countries reach stronger conclusions in favor of private ownership. For example, an analysis of sixty-one privatized companies in eighteen countries (six developing and twelve industrial) showed, in at least two-thirds of the divestitures, postprivatization increases in profitability, sales, operating efficiency, and capital investment—all this, surprisingly, with no evidence of falling employment. In established market economies and middle- to high-income developing economies there is little doubt that private ownership is a significant determinant of economic performance.

Because most privatizations in CEE and the NIS are quite recent, judgments on their impact are just beginning to emerge. The first signs are encouraging in many cases, less so in others. A recent study of Hungarian firms found that new private companies in the sample were quicker than state firms to adjust their labor forces as demand changed. Privatized firms at first resembled state firms, but, encouragingly, after a year or two their behavior looked more like that of new private firms. Enterprise surveys in Poland in 1993 and Russia in 1994 concur that new private firms behave differently from, and better than, state firms, exhibiting more dynamism and generating higher profits. In the Polish survey (and a similar one in Slovenia) privatized firms also outperformed state companies, although this may in part reflect the fact that the better state firms were the first to be privatized.

Other research supports the positive effects of privatization but suggests that these vary by type of private owner. In Russia and Ukraine owners who had bought their small business units at competitive auctions invested more and realized better performance than insiders who had obtained their shops at near-giveaway prices (although even the insider-owned firms did better than state-owned shops). The likely impact of the mode of privatization and of the identity of the new owner is discussed further below.

Poland has been slower to privatize than many other transition economies. Some argue that its 6 percent average annual growth since 1994 shows that privatization is unnecessary. But this assessment is incomplete; what Poland's experience illustrates is rather the importance of determined macroeconomic reforms imposing financial discipline on companies, the emergence of large numbers of new private firms, and managerial expectations of eventual privatization in state firms themselves. Most of Poland's growth has been fueled by expansion of the new private sector, not by well-performing state firms. Also, the turnaround in some Polish state firms in the early 1990s was stimulated in part by managers' belief that privatization was just around the corner. New Zealand's experience (Box 3.3) applies in transition economies: a state with the will to impose a hard budget and expose its enterprises to competition can expect performance in some firms to improve without changing ownership. But the gains from hard budget constraints will be larger and more likely to endure if ownership change accompanies or closely follows these reforms.

Widespread formal privatization of majority stakes in the larger state firms is not presently on China's agenda. Still, much of the Chinese economy has moved away from state ownership, some into private hands but most into intermediate forms of ownership. The nonstate sector has

Box 3.3 Locking in the gains of enterprise reform in New Zealand

In 1986 the government of New Zealand launched a major reform of its poorly performing public corporations. Commercial profitability was set as the main goal; any remaining social objectives had to be agreed by parliament and paid for from the government budget. State-owned firms were placed on the same legal footing as private companies, exposed to competition wherever possible, and required to seek any new financing on commercial capital markets without government guarantees. A new Ministry of State Enterprises shared the ownership function with the Treasury, replacing the involvement of line ministries. Together they appointed each firm's board of directors, drawing almost exclusively from the private sector. The board, in turn, appointed the top management of the firm and set and administered annual performance targets. Managers who achieved their objectives were rewarded; those who did not were subject to sanctions, possibly including dismissal. If the government owners were dissatisfied, they could—and sometimes did—dismiss the board of directors.

Results were impressive. After four years sales, profits, and output per employee had increased in ten of eleven companies examined. Even so, successive governments went on to privatize a number of the companies and contemplated privatizing several others. Why, if the reformed state firms were so successful?

They did so because they recognized the intense difficulty of sustaining reforms over time. In time of crisis governments admit the priority of commercial objectives, impose harder budgets, and grant managers autonomy. But as the crisis fades or a major political claim arises, commitment to managerial autonomy also fades. For example, the postal service was pressured to reopen small, rural post offices, and the electric power company was pushed to buy locally produced coal despite its higher cost. The conclusion of many in New Zealand, both in the firms and in the government, was that privatization was required, not necessarily to improve performance in the short run but to lock in the gains of earlier reforms.

grown much faster than China's state enterprises despite an imprecise property rights framework that is quite alien to Western legal traditions. What accounts for the differences in performance? Box 3.4 offers an answer.

Ownership matters. But the need to privatize is not equally urgent in all settings. Slower privatization is viable (although not necessarily optimal) if the government, or workers themselves, are strong enough to assert control over enterprises and prevent managers from stealing assets, and if saving and growth in the nonstate sector are high. But where governments are weak and enterprise managers strong, or where restructuring needs dwarf available funds, privatization is urgent. Indeed, in these settings the likely and less desirable alternative is "spontaneous" privatization, in which managers purchase assets cheaply or seize them outright, often in collusion with the political elite. In many countries before the privatization process is formalized (such as Hungary and Russia in 1988–91), in several where privatization has been accepted in theory but stalled in practice (Belarus, Bulgaria, Ukraine), and even to some extent in the East Asian transition economies that have eschewed formal privatization, assets or income flows have slipped out of state hands and into private control, if not outright ownership, through a variety of methods. These transfers are often illegal and widely resented. Indeed, in some cases privatization has been delayed less because of political philosophy or uncertainty about the optimal

approach than because continued state ownership preserves the ambiguous property rights that allow profit shifting, tax evasion, and asset looting, largely for the benefit of incumbent managers.

Bulgaria's experience illustrates the point. A coalition government liberalized extensively and early and implemented a determined stabilization program. Swift privatization was anticipated. But a new administration in 1991 diluted the emphasis on reform and blocked adoption of a privatization program until mid-1995. During these four years the Bulgarian state lost much of its capacity to monitor enterprise performance and management. Managers channeled enterprise assets and cash flow to themselves, leaving little to the state but liabilities. Losses of Bulgarian state enterprises, which averaged more than 12 percent of GDP between 1992 and 1994, were covered by loans from an increasingly insolvent banking system. Bulgarian observers concluded that "unclear property rights [are] turning from a legal to a major macroeconomic problem."

Privatizing larger enterprises

Privatizing large and medium-size enterprises has proved far more difficult than originally thought. Policymakers have to weigh complex and often competing goals, satisfy a multitude of competing stakeholders, and cope with the administrative difficulty of privatizing thousands of firms in a relatively short time and without mature, functioning

Box 3.4 China's township and village enterprises

China has developed several halfway forms of industrial enterprise that are neither state owned in the classic sense nor privately owned in the capitalist sense. One important configuration is the township and village enterprise (TVE), owned by local governments and citizens. These mainly produce consumer goods for domestic and international markets. TVEs are generally of two types. The first, owned by the local government, acts like a holding company, reinvesting profits in existing or new ventures as well as in local infrastructure. The second, more recently developed type is much closer to private enterprise in that most are effectively controlled if not formally owned by an individual. Still, they too maintain close fiscal ties to the local government.

The growth and performance of TVEs have been extraordinary. Their share in GDP rose from 13 percent in 1985 to 31 percent in 1994. Output has grown by about 25 percent a year since the mid-1980s; TVEs now account for a third of total industrial growth in China. The nonstate share of industrial output in China climbed from 22 percent in 1978 to a startling 66 percent in 1995. TVEs have created 95 million jobs in the past fifteen years. Capital-labor ratios in collective industry in China are only 25 percent of those in the state sector. Yet labor productivity (output per capita) is close to 80 percent of the level in state enterprises—and rising at more than 10 percent a year. Total factor productivity in TVEs is higher than in the state sector and is growing at 5 percent a year, more than twice the rate in state enterprises.

Several factors explain this remarkable growth and superior record of efficiency:

- *Kinship and implicit property rights.* Strong kinship links among rural Chinese villagers encourage responsibility in entrepreneurs. The sharing of implicit, if fuzzy, property rights leads to a productive combination of risk and reward sharing between entrepreneurs and local governments. Nonetheless, incentives facing TVEs are more like those of private firms in that the residual profits accrue to a limited

group: a traditionally stable local community and, in particular, its government and TVE managers. Studies show the enormous importance of TVE profits in local budgets and the close links between local economic performance and the status, income, and career prospects of local officials.

- *Decentralization plus financial discipline.* The 1984 decentralization of fiscal power in China allowed subnational governments to retain locally generated revenues, creating powerful incentives for the development of local industry. Under this system a nonperforming TVE becomes an unaffordable drain on a limited local budget. In the end persistent moneylosers are closed and the work force is shifted to more profitable lines.

- *Competition.* Studies also show intense competition for investment (including foreign investment) among communities with TVEs. Success in attracting investment is affected by reputation and local economic performance.

- *Market opportunities and rural saving.* A past bias against light industry and services has created vast market opportunities, buttressed by high rural saving and demand following the agricultural reforms of 1978 and by the limited scope for emigration from rural areas.

- *Links with the state enterprise sector.* The large state-owned industrial sector provides a natural source of demand, technology, and raw materials for many TVEs. Foreign investment from Hong Kong and Taiwan (China) plays the same role for many others.

TVEs will continue to grow, but they must also evolve. As their demands for finance increase and extend beyond their communities, and as people become more mobile, the TVEs' limited and implicit property rights will need to be better defined and made more transferable. Aspects of the TVE phenomenon are specific to China, but the experience holds important lessons for other transition economies: the importance of liberal entry, competition, hard budget constraints, and appropriate fiscal incentives for local governments.

---

capital markets. Approaches to privatization abound, from extensive efforts at sales to strategic owners, to insider buyouts, to innovative voucher programs involving the creation of large and powerful new financial intermediaries. These efforts are often complemented by extensive programs of restitution to pretransition owners and by

smaller programs of debt-equity conversion or public offering of shares on newly emerging stock markets.

Each approach to privatization creates tradeoffs among various goals (Table 3.1). Privatizing countries typically want many things: to increase efficiency of asset use by improving corporate governance; to depoliticize firms by

Table 3.1 Tradeoffs among privatization routes for large firms

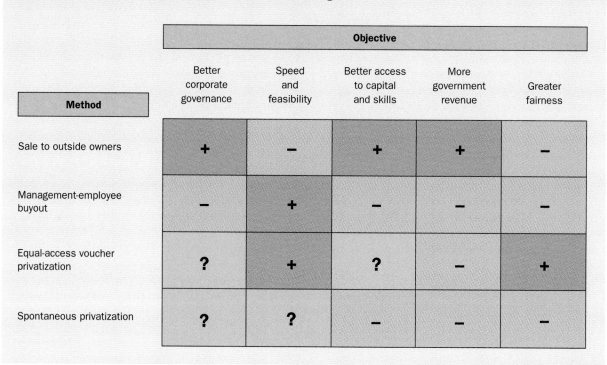

Method	Objective				
	Better corporate governance	Speed and feasibility	Better access to capital and skills	More government revenue	Greater fairness
Sale to outside owners	+	−	+	+	−
Management-employee buyout	−	+	−	−	−
Equal-access voucher privatization	?	+	?	−	+
Spontaneous privatization	?	?	−	−	−

cutting links to the state; to move quickly to create owners who will support further reform; to increase firms' access to capital and expertise; to bolster government revenues; and to ensure a fair distribution of benefits. Within this range countries have different priorities, and some want to proceed more quickly than others. Hungary, with its large foreign debt, has always viewed revenues as critical, the Czechs and the Romanians less so. To Russian reformers a speedy break with the past was paramount, while the Poles have forgone speed and entered into long debates over fairness. The Czechs have consistently stressed privatization's depoliticizing role, while Estonia's privatization program sought out "real" owners capable of bringing new money and management skills to bear.

Table 3.1 presents only a partial view of these tradeoffs. A key additional objective in all transition settings is long-term institution building. Privatization can spur development of such fundamental market institutions as capital markets, legal systems, and business-related professions. By the same token, each approach to privatization sets off a complex process of institutional and ownership change whose long-run results may differ considerably from the shorter-run picture. For example, mass privatization may not produce the best owners in the short run, but it might lead to better corporate governance in the

long run if it promotes the development of capital markets (and subsequent rearrangements of ownership) and of intermediary monitoring institutions for the economy as a whole.

What is effective corporate governance? A primary economic rationale behind privatization is to create owners who are motivated to use resources efficiently. But changes in ownership will not change managerial behavior if the new owners lack the power, incentives, and capability to monitor the managers and ensure that they act in the firm's best interest. Owners must also have the power to change managers, since it often takes a shake-up at the top to spur deep restructuring. For small firms such corporate governance is straightforward: usually the owners are themselves the managers. It is with large firms that the separation of ownership and management creates a need for monitoring. Direct monitoring by shareholders is one way to supervise managers. Another is to sell shares when performance is weak and let falling stock prices discipline managers. In the early stages of transition, direct monitoring is likely to be particularly important, because markets for capital and managerial labor are not sufficiently developed to exert strong competitive pressures on managers.

Political feasibility is a *sine qua non* of any privatization program. There is a profound tension between the need to reward stakeholders—managers, workers, officials in the former branch ministries—and the desire for good economic outcomes that contribute to economic restructuring and institution building and reinforce the benefits of reform in the public eye. Competition among stakeholders has affected the design of most privatization programs. The former Czechoslovakia and the former East Germany, with their centralized power structures and well-developed administrative capacity, could design and implement top-down privatization programs. Poland, Slovenia, and Russia, with more decentralized power structures, well-organized employees (in Poland and Slovenia), and strong managers (in Russia), had no such option. Yet accommodating stakeholder interests is risky and often conflicts with longer-run economic and political goals. Newly privatized entities may fail to restructure because of inappropriate corporate governance. Poorly managed privatization, even if it delivers short-term revenue or performance gains, may be seen as corrupt or highly inequitable, concentrating economic and political power in the hands of a domestic elite or foreign investors rather than expanding an independent and decentralized

middle class. The various routes and illustrative country experiences are outlined below and in Table 3.2.

Sales to outsiders

In the early days of transition most CEE countries hoped to privatize by selling state enterprises case by case as going concerns. This was the best-known model, which had been very successful in established market economies like the United Kingdom and in middle-income developing countries like Chile. Sales to outside "strategic" or "core" investors were also favored because they would bring in revenue and turn the firm over to "real" owners possessing the knowledge and incentives to govern the company efficiently and the capital to restructure it.

Sales to outside investors have largely fulfilled expectations about performance improvements. But they have proved costly and slow, far more difficult to implement than anticipated, and most important, few in number. One reason is the limited amount of domestic capital, combined with the political tensions that can accompany a large dependence on foreign capital. Even where domestic capital is sufficient, insiders (managers and other

Table 3.2 Methods of privatization for medium-size and large enterprises in seven transition economies
(percentages of total)

Country	Sale to outside owners	Management-employee buyout	Equal-access voucher privatization	Restitution	Other[a]	Still in state hands
Czech Republic						
By number[b]	32	0	22[c]	9	28	10
By value[d]	5	0	50	2	3	40
Estonia[e]						
By number	64	30	0	0	2	4
By value	60	12	3	10	0	15
Hungary						
By number	38	7	0	0	33	22
By value	40	2	0	4	12	42
Lithuania						
By number	<1	5	70	0	0	25
By value	<1	5	60	0	0	35
Mongolia						
By number	0	0	70	0	0	30
By value	0	0	55	0	0	45
Poland						
By number	3	14	6	0	23	54
Russia[c]						
By number	0	55	11	0	0	34

Note: Boxed numbers show the dominant method in each country. Data are as of the end of 1995.
a. Includes transfers to municipalities or social insurance organizations, debt-equity swaps, and sales through insolvency proceedings.
b. Number of privatized firms as a share of all formerly state-owned firms. Includes parts of firms restructured prior to privatization.
c. Includes assets sold for cash as part of the voucher privatization program through June 1994.
d. Value of firms privatized as a share of the value of all formerly state-owned firms. Data for Poland and Russia are unavailable.
e. Does not include some infrastructure firms. All management buyouts were part of competitive, open tenders. In thirteen cases citizens could exchange vouchers for minority shares in firms sold to a core investor.
Source: Gray, background paper; World Bank data.

employees) in some countries have been able to block sales. More generally, the process is held back by the sheer magnitude of the job of evaluating and negotiating deals one by one, and then of following up to be sure that the buyers fulfill contract provisions. For example, in Germany it is reported that 20 percent of the thousands of privatization contracts signed by the Treuhandanstalt (the privatization agency) are in dispute.

Placing a value on firms to be offered for sale is particularly problematic. The issue is only partly one of inadequate accounting. Economic and political turbulence often make it impossible to estimate a firm's eventual value. Appraising and assigning responsibility for past environmental damage is also a thorny issue (Box 3.5). Governments that insist on high minimum prices (as has occurred in Hungary and more recently in Ukraine) may find no takers. A final disadvantage of the sales approach is its perceived unfairness. Many ordinary citizens cannot participate and find the process nontransparent and arbitrary, if not corrupt.

These obstacles have been even more debilitating than expected. The German Treuhandanstalt was able to privatize (or liquidate) its 8,500 state enterprises relatively quickly, but at an enormous cost in terms of both skilled personnel and explicit or implicit subsidies to buyers. Among other transition economies, only Hungary and Estonia have privatized a significant share of their state enterprises through direct sales. No other country has even come close to these achievements. In Poland the power of workers to block privatization has slowed progress: five years of effort by various administrations has produced about 200 sales. The conclusion is that sales, although a useful element in the privatization process, cannot in most circumstances be the sole or even the primary method.

A second form of sale to outsiders involves floating shares on public stock exchanges. The infancy of stock exchanges (see Chapter 6) limits this approach in all the transition economies. Furthermore, the method works only for firms with good financial prospects and strong reputations. Even Poland, which has had the most success with this approach, has privatized fewer than thirty firms in this manner. Hungary has had no greater success. Initial public offerings are clearly not the answer to the need for rapid, large-scale privatization, although at the margin they can help develop capital markets and share trading.

Management-employee buyouts

Management-employee buyouts are a widely used alternative to sales, notably in Croatia, Poland, Romania, and Slovenia. Many of the firms privatized through Lithuania's and Mongolia's voucher programs effectively became management-employee buyouts as employees and their families used vouchers and cash to buy major stakes in their own firms. In addition, several voucher-based programs, such as those of Georgia and Russia, gave such large preferences to insiders that most privatized firms were initially owned primarily by managers and employees.

Buyouts are relatively fast and easy to implement, both politically and technically. In theory they might also be

---

Box 3.5 Is environmental liability a serious barrier to privatization?

A prospective investor sizing up an industrial plant in a transition economy wants clear agreement in advance on how responsibility for environmental damage caused by the plant will be allocated. Without such an agreement, the assumption is that the environmental authorities will impose hefty cleanup costs on the company down the line. The Treuhandanstalt's sales procedures included an assessment of environmental liabilities, followed by an agreement on corrective measures, whose cost was taken into account in the final sale price. Other countries, however, lack the skills, financial resources, and even the desire to imitate the German model. Environmental liabilities have usually been ignored. Transferring them with the plant— the philosophy underpinning Czech and Polish legislation—is one solution. But after a sale the new owners may claim, often with some justification, that they were unable to assess environmental liabilities properly because of insufficient time or information, or because regulators have since tightened the relevant standards. The result is often a prolonged period of conflict. In the Czech case it is increasingly clear that the strict transfers of environmental liabilities to companies during the early rounds of voucher privatization will not stick. Discussions are under way to come up with ways for the state and the new owners to share cleanup costs. An alternative approach is for the state to retain responsibility for some or all environmental liabilities, usually defined on the basis of an environmental audit prior to sale. But it can be difficult to make the agreement credible: what prevents the government from later reneging? Setting up a special cleanup fund to discharge the government's commitments might be one way to make them more believable.

better for corporate governance if insiders have better access than outsiders to the information needed to monitor managers. In the early stages of privatization in Slovenia, for example, insiders voluntarily purchased a number of successful firms, which have generally continued to perform quite well.

However, the risks and disadvantages are many, particularly in large-scale buyout programs that include many unprofitable firms in need of restructuring. One disadvantage is that the benefits are unevenly distributed: employees in good firms get valuable assets while those in money-losers get little or nothing of value. Another is that governments typically charge low prices to insiders and thus realize little revenue. Most important, management-employee buyouts may weaken corporate governance, particularly in transition economies, where controls on managers are less developed than in a fully fledged market economy and product and capital markets cannot be counted on to enforce discipline. Insiders are generally unable to bring in new skills and new capital, yet may deter outsiders who can from investing. Managers or employees may simply prevent outsiders from buying shares. Or outsiders may hesitate to invest in firms with significant insider ownership—legally or illegally acquired—because of potential conflicts of interest between inside and outside owners. For example, inside shareholders may vote to pay themselves higher salaries even if doing so reduces profits and share value. The bottom line is that management-employee buyouts can lead to managerial and worker entrenchment that blocks further reform.

Russia's mass privatization program of 1992–94, although it used vouchers, was basically a management-employee buyout program because of its preferential treatment of managers and workers. These insiders could choose between receiving a minority of shares at no cost and purchasing a majority of shares at a large discount. They chose the second option in about 70 percent of cases. These transfers were handled in "closed subscriptions" in advance of open voucher auctions, at which managers and workers could use their vouchers to add to their ownership. In the end insiders acquired about two-thirds of the shares in the 15,000 privatized firms. Outsiders obtained 20 to 30 percent (about 10 to 15 percent each went to investment funds and individual investors), and the rest remained in government hands.

In many respects Russia's mass privatization was a major achievement, particularly in light of the political and economic turmoil that confronted Russian policymakers in the early 1990s. But the program well illustrates the drawbacks of management-employee buyouts and, more broadly, the serious tensions between political feasibility and economic desirability. The extensive preferences given to managers and workers to garner their support,

and the inability to install procedures to protect minority shareholder rights and to promote secondary trading, are now proving costly. Managers control their insider-owned firms with little if any employee-shareholder influence. Some managers have tried, often illegally, to prohibit workers from selling their shares to outsiders. Some have used even less transparent means to block participation by either employees or outsiders or to transfer assets or profits to other firms they control. Given the weakness of laws and institutions, the scarcity of information, and in some cases the laxity of competitive pressures (due in part to the incomplete macroeconomic stabilization before 1995), few if any outside controls existed to thwart such behavior. This is as much a problem of efficiency as of transparency: behavior of privatized Russian firms is so far hard to distinguish from that of state firms.

This kind of insider ownership has not been stable on such a large scale elsewhere in the world and almost certainly will not be in Russia. It is likely eventually to evolve at least in part into ownership by outside investors (banks, investment funds, or other domestic or foreign investors), although an intermediate stage is likely to see increased ownership by managers as they buy up employee shares or divert assets to other companies they own. How long this evolution will take, however, depends largely on the government. If enterprises cannot rely on either open or hidden subsidies to cover their losses, and if price and trade liberalization intensifies competition, some managers will be forced to turn outside for financing. Some evidence indicates that outsiders are finding ways to acquire significant stakes in some privatized firms. A recent survey found that insider ownership in a sample of 142 firms fell from 65 percent in 1993 to 56 percent in 1995—a modest move in the right direction.

On the other hand, lax Russian macroeconomic and competition policies could combine with deficiencies in law enforcement to prolong insider control, further delay restructuring, and permit unfair and fraudulent transactions. In some of the largest and richest firms—in the oil and gas sectors, for example—initial privatizations were particularly murky, and sales of remaining shares have been far from regular. And the "shares for loans" schemes carried out in 1995 generated less revenue than expected and were decidedly opaque. Overall, many Russians resent the way privatization has been conducted, feeling they have received a pittance while some managers—and their high-placed political supporters—gained fortunes. One study estimated that the 19 percent of adult Russians employed in privatized firms obtained 56 percent of equity sold through June 1994; the remaining 81 percent who received only vouchers ended up with 15 percent of the divested assets. Transactions in 1995 almost certainly added to the disparity.

Ukraine presents another case of insider entrenchment. Although generally slow to privatize, the government has implemented some management-employee buyouts. It introduced a voucher privatization program in 1994–95 but has so far failed to carry it through effectively. Macroeconomic reforms have been slower than in Russia, and some firms still have ready access to state subsidies. A recent survey of privatized companies in both countries indicated that Russian insider-owners, facing somewhat greater financial discipline, had taken more steps to improve efficiency and were less hostile to outsiders than their Ukrainian counterparts. These results point once again to the importance of financial discipline in promoting restructuring and ownership change in firms privatized through management-employee buyouts.

Equal-access voucher privatization
A third form of privatization distributes vouchers across the population and attempts to allocate assets approximately evenly among voucher holders. Such programs excel in speed and fairness. But they raise no revenue for the government, and they have unclear implications for corporate governance. Mongolia, Lithuania, and the former Czechoslovakia were the first to implement this form of privatization. Albania, Armenia, Kazakstan, Moldova, Poland, Romania (in its 1995 program), and Ukraine have followed, and Bulgaria is now preparing such a program. Some countries (such as Georgia and Russia) have used vouchers but given strong preference to insiders, as discussed above. A few countries (Estonia and Romania in its 1991 program) have used vouchers to transfer only minority stakes in certain firms. Hungary, FYR Macedonia, and Uzbekistan are among the few privatizing transition economies that have specifically rejected vouchers, arguing that shares given away are perceived by recipients to have no value, and that voucher programs merely delay the arrival of "real" owners.

The Czech Republic's mass privatization program has been the most successful to date. In two successive waves (the first while part of Czechoslovakia), the Czechs transferred more than half the assets of state enterprises into private hands. Citizens were free to invest their vouchers directly in the firms being auctioned. However, to encourage more concentrated ownership and so create incentives for more active corporate governance, the program allowed the free entry of intermediary investment funds to pool vouchers and invest them on the original holders' behalf. More than two-thirds of voucher holders chose to place their vouchers with these competing funds. The ten largest obtained more than 40 percent of all vouchers in both waves (about 72 percent of all vouchers held by such funds), leading to concentrated ownership of the Czech industrial sector in these large funds. This is in

stark contrast to the experience of Mongolia, which forbade the entry of intermediary funds and ended up with heavy insider ownership.

Are the Czech funds active owners, capable of exercising good corporate governance? Although it is too early to judge definitively, some funds are developing both hands-on shareholder monitoring (as practiced in Germany and Japan) and active share trading (more common in the United States) as tools for monitoring managerial performance. These funds are putting representatives on company boards, demanding better financial information, and imposing financial discipline on the firms they own. They are trading large blocks of shares among themselves or selling them to new strategic investors, and a moderately active share market has developed, on the Prague Stock Exchange and in the much larger over-the-counter system. Clearly, however, patterns of ownership in the Czech Republic are still in flux. Some observers hope that the funds, together with banks or in place of them, will become the cornerstone of the financial infrastructure essential for capital allocation and corporate governance in a market economy. Others expect the funds' influence to dwindle rapidly as strategic investors pick up controlling blocks of shares. In either case the goal of institution building appears to be well served by this approach.

The Czech experience illustrates how a well-designed voucher privatization program can overcome many problems. It can depoliticize restructuring, stimulate development of capital markets, and quickly create new stakeholders with an interest in reform. But plenty of obstacles lie along the road from mass privatization to efficient capitalism. Governments need to implement complementary reforms—for example, regarding the supervision of financial intermediaries and the regulation of natural monopolies (Box 3.6). The former Czechoslovakia and Russia allowed free entry of investment funds, whereas Poland and Romania called for the top-down creation by government of a predetermined number of funds. Each approach has its risks. A particularly vexing question is: who monitors the monitors? Supervising financial agents, difficult enough in established market economies, is even more problematic in transition economies, where norms of disclosure and fiduciary responsibility are weak, and watchdog institutions and oversight mechanisms are in their infancy. Policymakers need to think carefully about how to regulate funds to protect individual investors in the funds and other minority shareholders in firms partly owned by the funds.

Privatizing small firms

Small firms have proved much easier to privatize than large ones. Most small firms were engaged in trade and services, activities with simple technology and easy entry.

Box 3.6 Do's and don'ts in privatizing natural monopolies

Privatizing public utilities and infrastructure industries, such as electricity, telecommunications, natural gas, oil pipelines, water supply, ports, airports, and railroads, raises complex issues that do not apply to other industries. These industries are typically large and capital-intensive. They are critical to the functioning of the economy and hence often viewed as strategic. Parts of some of them are natural monopolies in which competition is technically impossible. And for largely political reasons they often charge low, controlled prices that result in financial losses. Privatizing them involves at least four steps:

- Introducing competition by separating the monopoly parts from the competitive parts, allowing new firms to enter the competitive parts, and possibly restructuring the monopoly parts
- Establishing laws and institutions to regulate price and quality in the monopoly parts
- "Commercializing" the enterprises and
- Attracting private sector participation through concession arrangements or privatization (whether sales to strategic investors, mass privatization, or a mixture of both).

Commercialization involves creating enterprises that, although still public, are similar in structure and operation to private enterprises. Enterprises should be removed from the control of ministries and converted into joint-stock companies reporting to a board of directors. Prices should be increased to efficient levels and subsidies reduced and targeted (see Chapter 2). The financial structure of these enterprises should be similar to that of private companies: assets may need to be revalued and debt (initially owed to the government) may need to be added to the balance sheet as a liability.

A growing number of transition economies—most notably the Czech Republic, Estonia, Hungary, and Russia—are joining the worldwide trend toward infrastructure privatization. Others are considering doing so. In the energy sector Hungary has gone the furthest in privatizing through sales. It has adopted a regulatory framework, raised average prices to near world levels, and split companies into smaller entities. It has sold majority stakes in its oil and gas production company and several power generation and gas and power distribution companies to strategic investors. This desire to sell firms for cash, motivated in part by the need to raise revenues, has spurred price and regulatory reforms because prospective buyers need the assurance these reforms provide. Hungary has learned from its 1992 and 1993 attempts to sell electric power and gas distribution companies, which failed because of a lack of proper pricing and regulatory policies.

The Czech Republic and Russia provide an interesting contrast to Hungary's sales approach. They included partial stakes in their large, integrated energy companies (such as 30 percent of the Czech power company and 50 percent of Russian power and gas companies) in their voucher privatizations. These stakes were essentially given away, and so generated no demand for price and regulatory reform. Household energy prices remain low, and neither country has made much progress in developing effective regulatory systems. Any future increases in government-controlled prices will generate huge windfalls for the new owners. Because of their low initial levels of debt, the companies are building large cash surpluses as industrial energy prices approach world levels. In the meantime there is little corporate governance from outside owners, creditors, or government. Although in other ways these voucher privatization programs (particularly the Czech one) were impressive, the government's lack of attention to complementary reforms in the area of natural monopolies is problematic.

None of the major obstacles to privatizing larger entities—high capital requirements, major restructuring needs, and regulatory and governance weaknesses—apply to small firms. Local authorities can take charge of transferring small units, and because they are easier to value, many parties can gain access to enough information for open auctions to succeed. Even where insiders are given strong preference (as in Russia), assets can be quickly transferred to higher-value uses through secondary markets. Governments, however, must resist the temptation to impose artificial limits on property transfers, by setting minimum prices, for example, or by forcing buyers to stay in the same line of business.

Small sales are also easier politically. Organized opposition has been weak. Services had been neglected under central planning, resulting in shortages, queuing, drab stores, and limited variety. Privatization has led to quick improvements in quantity and quality. Progress in this area can also provide an impetus for reforms elsewhere in the economy. Privatized small businesses can serve as schools for entrepreneurs and investors and can absorb labor being shed from large-scale enterprises.

The former Czechoslovakia, Hungary, and Poland were the first countries to achieve widespread ownership of small businesses, using very different approaches. The Czechs implemented a centrally conceived but locally administered system of open, competitive auctions. Poland's program, like its large-scale privatization program, was somewhat ad hoc and gave large concessions to employees. Hungary had a reasonably sized trade and services sector even under central planning, with strong, decentralized managerial control through leasehold. This sector grew less through widespread privatization than through the entry of private competitors. Following these leaders, most other transition economies have carried out substantial small-scale privatization, and Albania, the Baltic states, Croatia, Russia, and Slovenia have caught up with the early starters in terms of the percentage of small firms divested.

Russia has divested most of its small units, but as was true of large-scale privatization, insiders have ended up with much of the ownership. This is worrisome. Studies of small privatization in Central Europe, Russia, and Ukraine show the need to bring in outsiders, who tend to invest more and supply services better. Czech-style auctions result in a more competitive structure of ownership than other privatization methods and bring in the largest number of outside investors. But political realities cannot be ignored. Where insiders are strong enough to block outsider participation, privatization to insiders is still better than keeping the assets under state ownership, especially in the case of small firms, where competition can quite easily force subsequent restructuring and reshuffling of ownership.

Privatizing and restructuring farms

Chinese agriculture was collectivized in the 1950s, effectively stifling individual incentive. Agriculture was then heavily taxed through price and marketing controls until 1978, when the household responsibility system was introduced. This broke up collective farms and vested households with use rights over the land they worked. It also relaxed discriminatory price policies and controls over marketing. The result was a dramatic increase in agricultural production. Higher rural incomes followed, raising local demand for food, while the government continued to subsidize food in urban areas. The boom in agriculture helped propel growth throughout the economy. Vietnam went through a similar process in the mid-1980s, passing from importing to exporting rice in a very few years. In both countries market forces now mainly determine agricultural prices and production.

Agricultural reform has been harder in CEE and especially the NIS. In contrast to China, agriculture in these countries was both highly mechanized and heavily subsidized under central planning. Collective and state farms were too large to be managed effectively. Like large state-owned industrial firms, they were kept alive through easy access to bank credit and extensive subsidies to both farms and consumers. Coexisting with these large farms was a stunted private sector of small, individually owned farms and household plots. This dual structure deprived the state sector of efficient labor and the private sector of efficient technology. Reforms in the early 1990s cut consumer subsidies and other transfers to agriculture. The demise of the protected markets of the CMEA was an additional severe blow. Demand plummeted, particularly for meat and milk, and overall agricultural output fell by a quarter to a third. Some governments then squeezed agriculture even harder by retaining partial price controls on output while easing controls on inputs. Agriculture suffered a sharp fall in profitability.

Clear property rights, assigned to people rather than collectives, are as important in agriculture as in industry. Much of China's success can be attributed to its move toward more individualized land rights through explicit or implicit long-term leases. Commitment to full private ownership of agricultural land has been strong in Central Europe but partial in Belarus, Moldova, Russia, Ukraine, and the Transcaucasus. In Central Asia Turkmenistan allows private land ownership—with no right of transfer. (The constitutions of some other Central Asian republics forbid private landholding.) Where memory and documentation of prior ownership are strong, as in much of CEE and the Baltics, restitution of land has prevailed (Box 3.7). Elsewhere land rights have been distributed to employees of state farms and other rural residents through in-kind transfers, as in Albania and Armenia, or through paper entitlements (legal recognition that the holder owns a part of a cooperatively farmed unit), as in Belarus, Moldova, Russia, and Ukraine.

Privatizing farms is different from privatizing industries. For two reasons, reorganizing—or restructuring—has to be an integral part of the privatization program. The first relates to economies of scale: these are limited in farming, and supervising large numbers of workers is costly. Yet central planning left farms that are gigantic by world standards. Russian farms still average 6,000 hectares; in 1987 only 3 percent of U.S. farms exceeded 840 hectares. Russia has corporatized many former collective farms and divided ownership shares among members, but this does little to improve labor incentives. On the other hand, restitution and distribution in kind have in some cases gone too far in the other direction, creating many new owners of small holdings (often less than 2 hectares) that may be too fragmented to take full advantage of the limited economies of scale that do exist.

The second reason why reorganization needs to accompany privatization is that farms are poorly suited to the

Box 3.7 The pros and cons of restitution

Most communist regimes seized large amounts of private property. Restitution of this property to precommunist owners or their heirs is appealing—but fraught with difficulties. The Baltic countries and most of the CEE countries have taken steps to reverse earlier confiscations by paying compensation or returning property to former owners. Among the most aggressive efforts (besides those in the former East Germany) have been those of Bulgaria, the former Czechoslovakia, and Slovenia. All three passed laws providing for extensive restitution of land, housing, and enterprises, either in kind (if possible) or through substitute property, securities, or money. Estonia, Latvia, and Lithuania passed laws providing for restitution of urban and rural land; about 1 million people have filed claims in the three countries. Romania has aggressively pursued in-kind restitution of agricultural land, through which about 2.4 million private farms have been created. Hungary is one of the few holdouts: it has opted against in-kind restitution in favor of coupons that can be used to purchase privatized property (including land).

Restitution in kind can certainly contribute to private sector development, particularly in retail trade and services. However, it can be complex and sometimes arbitrary, creating uncertainty that may interfere with other privatization methods and clog the judicial system. In the Czech Republic, for example, tenants in restituted apartments have clashed with new owners over rights and responsibilities. Some interested private parties have been afraid to purchase businesses for fear of restitution claims. In Romania land often could not be returned to its former owners because it had been converted to nonagricultural uses; the allocation of alternative plots resulted in more than 300,000 court actions. Restitution of agricultural land was complicated and slowed in the Czech Republic by lack of proper title documentation.

Hungary's program of compensation coupons has been less disruptive but also less far-reaching. Privatization transactions have not been burdened by the uncertainty of potential compensation claims, and conflicts between competing claimants have not overburdened the courts. Compensation coupons are traded on the Budapest Stock Exchange and provide a useful source of domestic capital to purchase privatized firms. From an economic perspective Hungary's approach appears sensible, although some see it as less fair, and it contributes less to privatization and private sector development in the short run.

corporate form. Most corporate farms in North America, for example, are family farms incorporated for tax purposes, not companies with many shareholders. Secondary markets in shares of farm corporations are virtually unheard of. Corporatizing collective and state farms therefore creates farm structures with no counterpart in market economies and no ready mechanism for their evolution and reorganization, since share trading on secondary markets is unlikely to develop.

The reorganization of farmholdings should concentrate on establishing and documenting individual ownership of land and nonland assets and on creating markets through which owners can adjust farm size and capital intensity. Where owners choose to farm jointly, they should retain individual ownership of their parcels and not be required to transfer title to the group or enterprise in common. Nonetheless, over sixty years of nonprivate farming in parts of the NIS has instilled a view that land is not a commodity like any other, and that land markets should be highly constrained. This has created considerable resistance to change.

Varying share systems for farmland and other farm assets have been adopted in much of the NIS. But reorganization through share allotment brings little or no change to traditional farms. Shareholders need a mechanism for converting their stock into real assets such as land, farm equipment, and buildings. One of the few specific mechanisms that has been implemented (on a pilot scale in Nizhniy Novgorod, Russia) is the internal auction. After an initial period of share distribution, public education, and asset valuation, participants bid their shares in auctions against the farm's real assets. The farm is then liquidated, and the new enterprises created through the auction are registered. By mid-1995 sixty-eight farm enterprises had gone through this process. Out of five farms in the earliest stage of the program (1993–94), twenty collective enterprises, seventeen family farms, and six individual businesses were created. This is a promising beginning.

Whatever mechanism of initial privatization is adopted, the critical need is for freely functioning land markets. Such markets provide flexible mechanisms for reorganization, preventing resources from being locked into the forms created in the early stages of reform. Until late 1992, for example, Hungary allowed shareholders to propose a package of assets to trade for their shares and then to withdraw to form a new unit. If the remaining shareholders did not agree, the entire farm underwent an internal auction against shares. Although a natural tension exists between the stability needed for operation and the ease of exit needed for flexible evolution, the latter is critical in the transition environment.

Privatizing commercial real estate

Commercial real estate was considered to have no productive value under central planning. In market economies, however, commercial real estate is a vast store of wealth, often larger than industrial plant and equipment. Real estate is also a critical factor in new business entry; start-ups need access to premises or, equally important (given the poor state of many existing buildings), access to vacant land and permits to construct new buildings. Both are hard to come by in many cities in transition economies; the result is a severe shortage of commercial space, which is blocking private sector development.

Reformers had have meager success in privatizing commercial real estate: no transition economy has yet embarked on a systematic program. What progress some countries and cities have achieved has come as a side effect of other privatization initiatives. Bulgaria, the Czech and Slovak Republics, and Slovenia included substantial amounts of commercial real estate in their restitution programs (see Box 3.7). Many countries have transferred rights to commercial real estate—but often only lease rights—to occupants or to the highest bidders through small privatization programs. In both restitutions and small privatizations new owners have had to deal with the strong tenancy rights of current occupants. For example, one external investor gave up efforts to purchase a hotel site in Prague in 1994 when it could not reach agreement with the site's three tenants. In Bulgaria owners by restitution must continue to rent to the current tenants for three years. These conflicts between former occupiers and new owners are unavoidable. The key is to establish clear rules so that transactions can proceed and markets can develop. Some countries have included the real estate occupied by large state firms in enterprise privatization programs. (Poland and Russia are notable exceptions.) Furthermore, state enterprises in almost all transition economies have leased or otherwise transferred unneeded land and buildings when squeezed by hardening budget constraints or when tempted by opportunities for "spontaneous" privatization. However, because state enterprises typically hold only use rights, such transfers are often not legally valid.

The result of these partial efforts to privatize commercial real estate in most transition economies is a patchwork of confused property rights and continued widespread public ownership. Even in Bulgaria, the Czech and Slovak Republics, and Slovenia local governments still own large amounts of retail and office space and vacant land. Hungary has managed to free up the commercial rental market even though it has neither privatized extensively nor raised rents to market-clearing levels. Occupants (generally with long-term lease rights at below-market rents) are assured the right to sublet, provided they pay 20 percent of the "profit" (the difference between the rent they charge and the rent they pay) to local authorities. A large part of the market for commercial space operates in this manner. The Baltic countries and Poland, despite advances in adopting commercial management practices, have not transferred much commercial real estate to private hands. Other NIS and Romania have made little progress on paper or in practice, although some cities and regions are clearly ahead of others.

A major reason for the slow pace of privatization and new private construction is the conflicting incentives of local governments that control most commercial real estate. The more progressive and honest local governments realize that allocating this real estate efficiently can spur rapid private sector growth and increase their revenues. But other local governments hold on to their monopoly power to allocate scarce space (often at below-market rents) and to develop new space, to some extent because of the irregular income that can be derived. Ownership is not their only source of power. Local governments also provide the services that make commercial space usable, including power, water, sanitation, and fire protection. They also regulate development. Some governments enter into direct competition with private businesses by developing land themselves or by setting up joint ventures in commercial activities, using real estate as their contribution. The conflicts of interest among these many public roles lead to the creation and maintenance of artificial monopolies, complex regulations, arbitrary enforcement, and high costs for new private firms. Struggles among municipal agencies to play the lucrative role of owner-manager are commonplace. Some districts of Warsaw have been very progressive in making land and commercial real estate available to private investors, while others have been slow. The difference is clearly evident in the distribution of commercial activity in the city today.

These deficiencies of commercial real estate markets are a major barrier to private sector development. The problems will not solve themselves, and they invite corruption. Local governments must act forcefully (or be prodded into action by reformers at other levels of government) to privatize, loosen regulatory and zoning constraints on new development, and open up infrastructure and service provision to private competition. For buildings that remain in state hands, local governments should promote commercial management practices, including leasing with transparent rules and at market rents, and respect for contractual obligations. National governments may be able to spur the reform of local governments by financially rewarding those that make the most efficient and transparent use of their assets.

Privatizing housing

Patterns of housing ownership differed greatly among the centrally planned economies (Figure 3.1). In China and Vietnam most urban housing was and is still owned by enterprises, whereas rural residents were responsible for their own housing and had informal property rights—but no formal title. In CEE private ownership of housing was never entirely eliminated, and it expanded considerably during the reform initiatives of the 1970s and 1980s. More than half the housing stock in most CEE countries (even more in rural areas) was already privately owned at the start of transition; local governments owned most of the rest. In the NIS local governments or enterprises owned most urban housing, although private housing was not uncommon, particularly in rural areas.

Privatizing housing is a high priority in transition economies, for social and economic reasons. Housing accounts for about 30 percent of wealth in market economies. Transferring housing to individuals and households and developing housing markets to realize its value can help compensate citizens for the loss of savings many have suffered due to hyperinflation. Because housing was relatively equally distributed under central planning (more so in terms of space than with regard to quality or location), converting tenancy rights into ownership rights is a simple and equitable way to privatize. Nearly all housing privatization to date has taken the form of giveaways or low-cost sales to current tenants, often subject to space limits. The Baltic states have issued vouchers to all citizens (the amount varying with age), one use of which is to purchase their apartments. Belarus gives away a set square footage.

Privatization can relieve governments and enterprises of the costly burden of subsidies, but only if responsibilities for utilities and maintenance are also shifted to the new owners. Giving away housing and the costs associated with it actually improves the fiscal position of governments. Rents for public housing were extremely low under central planning, and governments and enterprises bore most of the costs of construction, maintenance, and utilities. Soviet local governments typically spent up to 15 percent of their budgets maintaining the municipal housing stock. By 1993 this had risen to 25 percent. From 1927 to 1992 the basic monthly rent charged to households in the Soviet Union was frozen at 0.132 ruble per square meter. By the end of the Soviet era, households devoted just 2.4 percent of their cash income to housing (rent plus utilities)—less than they spent on liquor and cigarettes. This underpricing encouraged waste of energy and much else, discouraged proper maintenance, and led to high demand, long waiting lists, and a flourishing shadow economy.

The other high economic cost of these housing policies was the crushing effect on interregional labor mobility. Workers had little hope of finding housing if they took a job in another city. Developing housing markets is an essential adjunct to enterprise restructuring in transition economies, both to free firms to focus on productive activities and to facilitate labor mobility. This is particularly true in countries such as China, where enterprises own much urban housing.

Several NIS have been at the forefront of housing privatization. Lithuania, the most successful, has reduced state ownership of housing from two-thirds of the total to less than one-tenth through a combination of voucher sales and restitution. Estonia started more slowly, but its program picked up speed as the end-1995 deadline for using vouchers approached. Seventy percent of its housing is now in private hands. Armenia and Moldova have been privatizing rapidly, too. Most CEE countries, initially in the vanguard, have moved more slowly since 1990, in part because they had much less public housing left to privatize—only Albania has matched the dramatic ownership changes of the leading NIS privatizers (Figure 3.1). Slovenia's program of low-cost sales in 1992 was instrumental in drawing foreign exchange from under the mattress (or from foreign bank accounts) and into the central bank's coffers. These growing foreign exchange reserves helped support the introduction of Slovenia's new currency, the tolar. On this score China and Vietnam are lagging; they have done little to separate housing from enterprises. In China enterprises own and manage about 75 percent of urban housing, and this share has actually increased in recent years as local governments have transferred housing to enterprises. It may be possible in the future to swap some of these assets against pension liabilities (see Box 4.6).

Building a strong housing market requires numerous reforms in addition to changing ownership. Tenant charges for rents, utilities, and maintenance in remaining state housing must be steadily increased. Tenancy rights inherited from central planning are much stronger than lease rights in some established market economies, and are de facto inheritable property rights. Moving from these to full ownership may have no meaning whatsoever unless the previous allocation of subsidies and responsibilities is altered as well.

Shifting the full economic costs of housing to households may not be possible overnight, particularly in economies that have suffered sharp drops in GDP and employment and sharp increases in poverty. To offset the short-term impact of higher rents in public housing and

Transition economies have contrasting patterns of housing ownership.

Figure 3.1 Housing ownership in urban areas in six transition economies

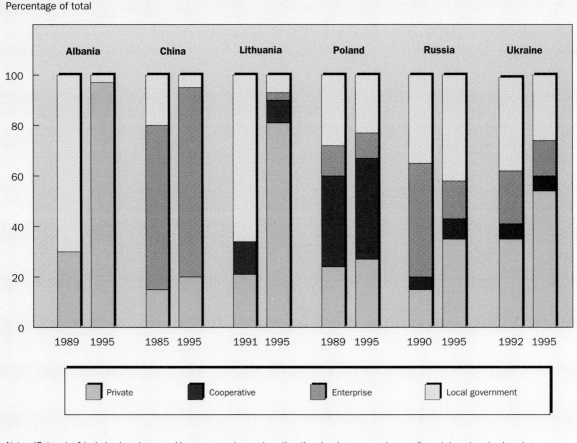

Note: "Enterprise" includes housing owned by government agencies other than local government, as well as state enterprise housing.
Source: Official data; World Bank 1995n; World Bank data.

higher maintenance and utility costs in all housing, governments might consider offering housing allowances to those hurt most by reforms, while at the same time raising cash wages to replace forgone subsidies. The critical point is that the true costs of housing—once hidden in repressed wages, budget deficits, inflation, and undersupply—need to be made explicit. Furthermore, new modes of finance are needed to help new private owners pay for housing as governments withdraw from housing construction and maintenance.

Local governments must also clarify property rights and zoning rules, improve real estate registries, and de-

velop efficient property tax regimes and condominium-type laws, needed to allocate responsibility for common areas of buildings. New owners will not appreciate the value of their homes without active housing markets through which to measure and realize that value. And these markets will not develop unless owners have clear and readily tradable rights to both structures and underlying land. Finally, an often overlooked issue in housing privatization is the distribution of ownership rights within households. Ensuring that husbands and wives have equal rights to privatized housing is an important step toward gender equality in transition.

Properly privatized housing opens the way to a host of new products and services, including property insurance, real estate brokerage, housing maintenance, mortgage finance, and property development. These create new jobs and make private housing markets work by spreading risk, supplying information to buyers and sellers, and providing needed financing.

New firms and foreign investment

Privatizing state enterprises is crucial to the long-term development of transition economies. But just as important is promoting the entry of new firms. Given the delays in divesting larger firms, the quickest returns have come from new private entrants. The return to growth of Poland and Romania in 1993 and 1994, for example, cannot be attributed to their formal privatization programs, which have been slow, but rather to their strong record on new entry. Owners and investors in new firms bring new ideas and techniques, and they are less constrained by established routines and personnel. Throughout history more technical progress and improvements in productivity have come from new firms replacing old firms—from "creative destruction"—than from reforms in old firms. Most new firms in CEE and the NIS are privately owned; in the planned East Asian economies new entrants have been both private and "nonstate" in nature (see Box 3.4).

New entry and privatization are not entirely separable. Privatized small enterprises can be almost indistinguishable from new entrants, particularly when the privatized firm's only "asset" of any value is its access to commercial real estate. New private firms are often built on assets or labor released from downsizing state enterprises. Indeed, "asset privatization" has proceeded much faster than enterprise privatization in most transition economies. This helps explain, for example, why Poland's private sector now produces some 60 percent of GDP (up from 30 percent in 1990) despite the slow official privatization program. Economic reforms lead to rapid growth in legal private businesses. But even where reforms are slow, informal shadow economies of private firms will emerge—with help from spontaneous privatization. The shadow economy in Ukraine may account for as much as 40 percent of economic output, despite the slow pace of economic reform and privatization. Certainly, formal private sector growth is preferable to the growth of shadow economies, but either is preferable to no growth at all (see Chapter 2).

What does the new formal private sector need to succeed and grow? Macroeconomic stability is vital. Countries with large budget deficits have trouble resisting the confiscatory taxation that tends to quash an emerging private sector, and firms find it hard to set prices, negotiate contracts, and estimate investment needs in an environment of high inflation. Price and market liberalization is another

must, along with freedom from overregulation. New private firms must be able to set prices for outputs, search for the best prices for inputs, change product lines, hire and fire workers, and get the foreign exchange they need if they are to adjust efficiently to changing market conditions. And they need clear and stable rules of the game that can be enforced at reasonable cost, as well as freedom from crime and corruption (see Chapter 5).

These preconditions have generally been met in Central Europe and to a somewhat lesser extent in Eastern Europe and the Baltics, where new private firms are free to operate in response to market forces (although they remain subject to high taxes, which many evade, and have some difficulty getting access to premises, as discussed above). Entrepreneurial freedom and access to inputs are more restricted in Russia and other non-Baltic NIS, yet many private firms manage to thrive in previously repressed sectors, such as trade and services, where pent-up demand is high. Entrepreneurs' biggest complaint in Poland in a 1992 survey was lack of financing, whereas in St. Petersburg and throughout Ukraine macroeconomic uncertainty, legal instability, and in many cases crime and corruption troubled entrepreneurs most, followed by high taxes and lack of finance.

Although domestic firms drive growth in all market economies, foreign investment also makes a highly valuable contribution. Foreigners bring capital, technology, management expertise, and access to markets—all critical to enterprise restructuring in transition economies. The less tangible effects of foreign investment, including the importation of new ideas and practices both through improved performance and support of policy change, are particularly important in transition settings. China has enjoyed rapid growth and has been a leader in foreign investment inflows, although much of this is thought to be domestic money recycled through Hong Kong, to take advantage of incentives offered only to foreign investors. Hungary shares the leadership title with China in foreign investment as a share of GDP (Figure 3.2).

Foreign investors can make an enormous difference. Consider the case of a Polish lighting company purchased by a Dutch businessman in 1991. The new owner invested heavily in technical and managerial training in such areas as cost accounting, computers, marketing, total quality management, and English-language training. He provided the Polish firm with technical know-how and state-of-the-art equipment that not only increased productivity but also reduced environmentally harmful emissions. He then modernized the company's offices and facilities. The results were startling. In three years the struggling company became a profitable and internationally competitive enterprise. Sales per employee almost doubled from 1991 to 1994 and are expected to double again by 2000. Polish

Some transition economies have proved much more attractive to foreign investment.

Figure 3.2 Cumulative foreign direct investment inflows

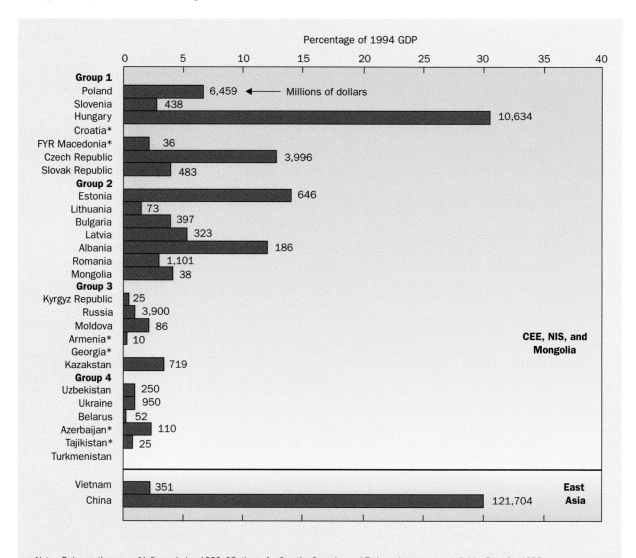

Note: Data are the sum of inflows during 1989–95; those for Croatia, Georgia, and Turkmenistan are unavailable. Data for 1995 are preliminary. Countries are ranked as in Figure 1.2. Asterisks indicate economies severely affected by regional tensions between 1989 and 1995. Source: World Bank 1996b; IMF and World Bank staff estimates.

consumers are paying 25 percent less for standard lighting products. Employment is stable at about 3,000, and salaries have risen by 10 percent a year. The company's operations have stimulated additional private employment within the community, engaged in transporting finished goods to domestic and foreign markets.

All foreign investors have the same concerns: political and economic stability and openness, laws and regulations that are fairly and transparently enforced, ready access to inputs at reasonable prices. All of these are heavily influenced by policy choices. Investors also look to the size and growth of domestic markets, which economic policy can influence, and closeness to major international markets, which it cannot. Foreign investment in natural resources is dictated by location—hence the interest of foreign energy companies in Kazakstan and Russia. Unique historical and cultural factors, such as the presence of a large diaspora, are also influential: Estonia has benefited from close ties with Finland and other Scandinavian countries, and most "foreign" investment in China has been made by overseas Chinese. But strong overseas ties are not enough. Armenia, Poland, Russia, and Vietnam have large émigré communities but have attracted relatively little investment from them, in part because of policies or privatization programs that are less than friendly to foreign investors (and in Armenia's case, because of blockade). The design of privatization programs heavily influences the amount of foreign involvement in privatized firms. Hungary and Estonia have both attracted foreign investment through sales of state enterprises, whereas Russia's insider privatization approach has kept foreign participation to just 2 percent of privatized equity.

Special foreign investment regimes create enclaves that benefit the rest of the economy little. These may be useful at the beginning of transition if they send the message that the country is serious about reform. But special tax breaks, exemptions from customs duties, and other incentives for foreigners can put domestic investors at a disadvantage and cost governments much-needed revenue. As quickly as possible, transition economies should dismantle these enclaves and put domestic and foreign investors on an equal footing. The Czech Republic took this step in 1992, for example, when it abolished specific foreign investment legislation in favor of a broad commercial code covering all investors.

The agenda

The lessons of experience from enterprise reform are quite clear and applicable across the range of transition economies, from the Czech Republic to China. Firms and farms surviving from central planning need major restructuring of their production and reorientation of their incentives. Entities that face strict financial discipline and competition and have clear owners are most likely to undertake the needed restructuring or to exit, leaving room for new and better firms. In the short run financial discipline can be fostered through the stabilization and liberalization measures outlined in Chapter 2. But in the longer run decentralized—preferably private—property rights and supporting institutions are needed to sustain financial discipline, to respond to market-oriented incentives, and to provide alternative forms of corporate finance and governance.

The patterns of ownership immediately resulting either from a shift to "nonstate" forms of enterprises or from privatization are unlikely to be optimal. This is particularly true for large firms and farms, but it may also apply to smaller firms, commercial real estate, and housing. Initial ownership may be too dispersed, as it was in Lithuania's mass privatization programs, or too entrenched in the hands of insiders, as in Russia's first-phase privatizations. Winners in the asset allocation process may try to construct barriers to secondary trading. Ownership can end up concentrated in entities that are either too large, like Russia's corporate farms, or too small, like Romania's fragmented landholdings. Ownership may be vested in entities, such as investment funds or absentee landlords, that are unable or unwilling to exercise efficient monitoring. A critical determinant of the longer-run success of any reform program is the extent to which ownership rights can evolve into more efficient forms. Programs that spur the growth of capital and asset markets, such as the Czech Republic's privatization program, have a distinct advantage. In all transition environments the evolution of ownership will also depend on tight macroeconomic policies, which force firms not only to restructure internally but also to turn to capital markets to raise needed finance.

But restructuring of the economy goes well beyond reform of existing enterprises. Entry and investment by new firms, both domestic and foreign, are at least as important for growth. Here the reformers in East Asia, CEE, and the NIS can learn from each other. China is increasingly concerned with the need to reform its state enterprises, which lag nonstate firms in financial performance and productivity growth but still consume the lion's share of investment resources. Reformers in CEE and the NIS have shown the importance of, and effective methods for, imposing financial discipline on state firms, allowing their downsizing and exit, developing debt workout mechanisms, and divesting housing, commercial real estate, and assets or shares of enterprises that the state no longer needs to own. In turn, some governments in CEE and the NIS can learn from China about the importance for growth and productivity of unrestricted new entry, the unleashing of competitive forces, and farm restructuring. In all transition economies the continued growth of new nonstate sectors, as well as the continued reform of enterprises that will stay in state hands, will depend on the development of institutions that sustain and deepen the reforms achieved to date. These include, among others, reforms in legal, financial, and government institutions. These are the subject of Part Two.

CHAPTER 4

People and Transition

In the end what matters is people. In the end a country's transition will be judged by whether its citizens live better than they did before. Equity—how people share the benefits and the pains of transition—is important. But how people fare during transition is not just an equity issue. Labor productivity, critical for economic growth, depends on workers' knowledge, skills, motivation, and health. Therefore relieving extreme poverty, maintaining human capital, and adapting it to the needs of a market system support growth as well as social justice and political sustainability. This is especially true in transition countries, where policymakers may be unable to sustain vital, growth-enhancing reforms if large parts of the population feel that transition has left them behind.

How has transition affected living standards, and what do these changes mean for employment and for redesigning income transfers? (The corresponding questions relating to investment in skills and health are taken up in Chapter 8.) The answers vary by country and depend on the interplay of four factors: the widening distribution of income and wealth, economic growth or the lack of it, the mobility of labor, and age.

Greater disparity of wages, income, and wealth is—up to a point—a necessary part of transition, because allowing wages to be determined by the market creates incentives for efficiency that are essential for successful reform. More-efficient workers must be rewarded for their contribution to growth. But increased inequality can raise poverty in the short run, because some people or (especially in China and Russia) some regions inevitably benefit more than others. But the "losers" will not necessarily be forced into poverty; it depends on whether the economy is growing—the second factor—and on whether governments restructure social safety nets to provide effective poverty relief.

Negative growth, especially when as severe as that in CEE and the NIS, contributes to rising poverty and aggra-

vates the uncertainty associated with a dramatic change of system. As tax revenues fall sharply with the decline in output, governments face fiscal pressures to spend less and, simultaneously, political pressures to spend more. To escape this dilemma, policymakers must restore growth through effective reforms (Chapter 2). They must also ensure that losses early in transition are indeed transitional and not transmitted from one generation to the next. By contrast—and this is central to the East Asian story—where growth has been rapid and broadly based, poverty has declined sharply. As China and Vietnam show, some transitions can reduce poverty even in the short run.

Mobility—the freedom of individuals to seek better options elsewhere—is the third factor. As Chapter 2 showed, moving to a market system involves a vast reallocation of labor across firms, sectors, and regions. Yet the labor markets inherited from central planning, at least for movement between different skills, effectively sacrificed labor mobility for greater individual security. For working people, security largely took the form of a guaranteed job or, in rural China, guaranteed land. In a market system employees move between employers, between types of work, and between places—and they may experience unemployment. Income transfers (for example, unemployment benefits) in transition countries therefore need reform, not only to reduce poverty and contain costs but also to assist mobility. This means, in particular, supporting the unemployed and getting enterprises out of the business of delivering social benefits. Otherwise labor will remain immobile, raising the costs of transition by creating pockets of poverty in declining regions, and by pressuring enterprises and governments to defer necessary restructuring.

Older people have also been affected by the fall in output in CEE and the NIS. Like the rest of the population, they have experienced a fall in their average living standard. Unlike the young, they will reap few of the long-term gains of reform, and many have also lost savings because of inflation. This poses important questions for pensions. There is a case for being generous to today's elderly, and in many countries they have been relatively well protected. But the cost of pensions can create major problems at a time when government revenues are falling sharply.

How does transition affect people's well-being?

People's well-being depends on their income, on their wealth—possession of a house or land, for example—and on less tangible factors, such as a fair degree of security. It also depends on access to public goods and social services. This section looks at the well-being of different groups, focusing mainly on changes in income.

Poverty, growth, and inequality—the unfolding story
Although many of their people have experienced material and nonmaterial gains (some of which are hard to quantify; see below), the CEE countries and the NIS have experienced an increase in poverty. Comparisons across countries and over time are very approximate (Box 4.1), but some

clear patterns emerge. As the CEE countries and the NIS went through a simultaneous decline in output and increase in inequality, poverty rose sharply. Inequality has risen throughout the region: because of wage liberalization; because of increasing income earned in the private sector, where incomes vary greatly; and because of increased individual wealth. Evidence from Poland shows that, as growth resumed, poverty rates tended to stabilize; however, it is too early to assess how rapidly they will decline. In contrast, in later reformers in the NIS (such as Belarus) output continues to fall and poverty to rise. As Figure 4.1 shows, income inequality is not out of line with that in comparator market economies and therefore may not fall significantly. The key to containing and reducing poverty, therefore, is resumed growth. However, for some people, such as those with outdated skills, the elderly, or children in large families, growth is not a complete solution. For such groups explicit remedial programs are needed. Even for the rest of the population, growth will need to be sustained to have a major impact on living standards.

In China the interactions between growth, inequality, and poverty produced very different results. The initial

Box 4.1 Why poverty and inequality are hard to measure

Measuring poverty is difficult because of conceptual problems and data deficiencies and because *all* definitions of poverty involve social judgments. Measuring inequality involves parallel difficulties.

How is poverty defined? *Absolute* poverty is defined by comparing personal or household income (or expenditure) with the cost of buying a given quantity of goods and services, *relative* poverty by comparing that income with the incomes of others, and *subjective* poverty by comparing actual income against the income earner's expectations and perceptions. There is no scientific, unequivocal definition of who is and is not poor.

Measuring poverty is difficult enough even in a stable economy with regular and continuous statistics. Transition economies pose additional major measurement problems. Many data on income and consumption are highly questionable, not least because of serious deficiencies in the conduct of household surveys and because of growing informal activity, which goes unrecorded. Interpretation is further complicated by huge changes in relative prices and by the increased availability of goods that accompanies a shift to the market. Improving the quality of data can itself create problems. Just as better reporting of crimes may result in a rising measured crime rate, so efforts to improve the collection of poverty and income data may lead

observers to exaggerate the effects of transition, if they are comparing the latest data with highly incomplete figures from prereform years. For all these reasons, comparisons of living standards before and after transition will be very approximate—at best.

Even where a definition of poverty has been agreed, measurement is problematic because poverty has several dimensions. Policymakers are interested in *how many* people are poor (the head count), *how far* below the poverty line their incomes fall (the poverty gap), and for *how long* they are poor—in other words, whether their poverty is transient or long run.

These are not just technical issues but inescapably involve social judgments. The figures in Table 4.1, except those for Estonia, are based on income per capita. If instead children were given a lower weight, the poverty line for a household of five, three of whom are children, might be (say) three times that for a single person. Investigation using income per capita will find more poor children and fewer old people than with a poverty line in which children receive a lower weight. Similarly, the choice of a household definition of income assumes that older people share the resources of younger family members and thus finds fewer poor old people. The findings on poverty in this chapter should be interpreted with these issues in mind.

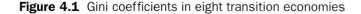

Inequality in transition economies is rising toward market economy levels.

Figure 4.1 Gini coefficients in eight transition economies

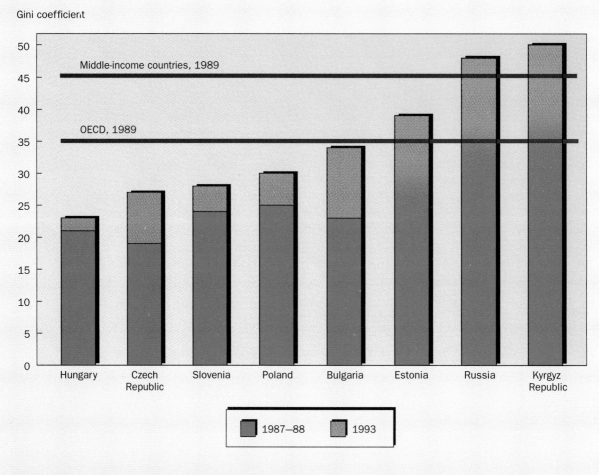

Gini coefficient

Note: For the NIS no reliable data exist for 1987–88 that would allow consistent comparison of income distributions over transition. Levels for middle-income and OECD countries are simple averages. Source: Milanovic, forthcoming.

phase of rural reform led to both increased growth and reduced inequality, lifting 200 million people out of poverty. But after 1985, as reforms centered on the industrial sector, inequality rose markedly, mainly because of increased urban-rural disparity (see below), and the number of poor stopped falling. Rural poverty is a continuing problem. In Vietnam strong growth, due to the combined effects of land reform, stabilization, and liberalization, helped reduce the poor from 75 to 55 percent of the population between 1984 and 1993.

How does transition increase inequality—and why?

The most frequently used measure of income inequality is the Gini coefficient, which ranges from zero (meaning that everyone has the same income) to 100 (one person receives all the income). By this measure, inequality has increased in Bulgaria, the Baltic countries, and the Slavic countries of the former Soviet Union, to levels broadly similar to those in the less-equal industrial market economies, such as the United States (Table 4.1 and Figure 4.1). Russia's Gini now appears similar to the average

Table 4.1 Inequality and poverty in selected transition economies

Country	Gini coefficient		Poverty head count[a]		
	1993	Change from 1987–88	1987–88	Income[b] (1993)	Expenditure (1993)
Central and Eastern Europe					
Bulgaria	34	11	2	33	..
Czech Republic	27	8	0	1	1
Hungary	23	2	1	2	6
Poland	30	5	6	12	12
Slovenia	28	4	0	1	1
Newly independent states[c]					
Estonia	39[d]	16[d,e]	..	23[d,f]	21[d,f]
Kyrgyz Republic	about 50	9–33[g]	..	76	57
Russia	48	14–24[g]	..	38	35

			Change in poverty head count (percentage points)	
			1978–85	1985–93
East Asia				
China	38[h]		−24	+1[i]
Vietnam	34		..	−20[j]

.. Not available.

Note: All data, and especially those for the NIS, are subject to major statistical difficulties; changes in Gini coefficients and poverty head counts should be regarded as only indicative. Any differences in Gini coefficients between this table and Table 5 in the World Development Indicators are due to differences in samples, time periods, definitions, or other technical assumptions.

a. Percentage of population below the poverty line. Poverty estimates for CEE and the NIS are based on a common poverty line of $120 at 1990 international prices per capita per month for CEE and the NIS. This is high for the poorer NIS, such as the Kyrgyz Republic. Estimates for the East Asian countries use much lower, country-specific poverty lines: $18 per capita per month for China, and for Vietnam a World Bank–determined poverty line based on a daily diet of 2,100 calories plus nonfood essentials.

b. Calculated from household survey data, adjusted upward where necessary to ensure compatibility with national income data.

c. For the NIS, no data exist that allow consistent comparison of income distributions over transition, and pretransition estimates of poverty head counts are unreliable because of data deficiencies.

d. Data are for 1995.

e. Based on Goskomstat data for the beginning and household survey data for the end of the period (Goskomstat end-of-period data are not available).

f. Calculated from 1993 PPP data for household size adjusted for equivalent adults.

g. The lower figure is based on Goskomstat data for both beginning and end of the period; the higher figure is based on Goskomstat data for the beginning and household survey data for the end of the period.

h. Figure is for 1992.

i. Datum is for 1985 to 1990.

j. Based on backward extrapolation from a 1993 household survey.

Source: Dollar, Glewwe, and Litvack, forthcoming; Milanovic, forthcoming; World Bank 1992; World Bank data.

for middle-income countries, although data for Russia (as for many other countries) probably do not take adequate account of the highest incomes. Inequality has increased less dramatically in some CEE countries, to levels similar to those in many Western European countries.

What have these overall changes in inequality meant for people of different incomes? Hungary made strenuous—and costly—efforts to offset rising inequality and has seen little change in income shares by population quintile, from that of the poorest 20 percent to that of the richest (Figure 4.2). The change was greater in Slovenia and greater still in Bulgaria and Ukraine. In Russia, where inequality rose sharply, the top quintile in 1993 received fully 20 percentage points more of total income than the top quintile in 1988, mainly because of an explosive

increase in the relative share of the very richest but also because of increasing wage dispersion. Income dispersion between sectors in Russia has also risen. The energy, banking, and related sectors all made major gains, with the biggest losers being agricultural workers, followed by workers in culture, education, and health.

China's rise in inequality has largely been driven by a different mechanism, one that has also been important in Russia, namely, differences in growth between regions and (critically in the case of China) between urban and rural areas. Income disparities within regions and cities in China remain relatively low. But the southeastern coastal area, for example, has been growing at an annual rate of over 13 percent, compared with the national average of 8.5 percent; meanwhile growth in populous central

Increasing income inequality is mostly at the upper end.

Figure 4.2 Changes in income by income quintile in four transition economies

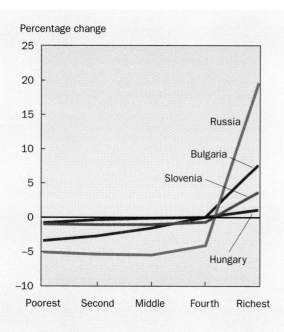

Note: Data represent the percentage change in the share of each income quintile in total income from 1988 to 1993.
Source: Milanovic, forthcoming.

has reinforced its central revenue capacity with the 1994 tax reforms, opening up the possibility of increased transfers to poor areas. But given China's outward-oriented economic strategy, the natural advantages of the south remain, and unofficial migration has already responded.

Regional inequality, significant even before the reforms, increased in Russia, with poverty rates of 70 percent in the Altai territory of Russian Central Asia but less than 10 percent in Moscow, St. Petersburg, and Murmansk. In June 1995 the richest 20 percent of territories (predominantly areas rich in natural resources, plus Moscow) received 44 percent of total income, compared with only 5 percent for the poorest 20 percent (largely ethnic republics in the North Caucasus and the Volga region). Regional inequality is almost inevitable in a country as large as Russia, but it has been exacerbated by the economically irrational siting of industries prior to reform and by constraints on mobility, which are less a matter of legal restrictions than of deficient housing markets. Limited mobility will remain a major source of inequality for the foreseeable future.

How does transition affect poverty?

The poverty estimates in Table 4.1 are based on a common poverty line for CEE and the NIS. This approach allows comparison across countries—although results are sensitive to a range of factors such as exchange rate fluctuations—but means that fewer people will be counted as poor in better-off countries like Slovenia than in poorer countries like the Kyrgyz Republic. The Visegrad countries, apart from Poland, experienced the smallest rise in poverty, but this does not mean that nobody in the Czech Republic has become poorer—merely that few Czechs fall below the common poverty line. Nor does it mean that there are no poor people; there are pockets of deep poverty in Hungary, for example. The Balkan countries, except Slovenia, experienced larger increases in poverty, and the NIS larger still. In the Kyrgyz Republic poverty is less high when measured in terms of expenditure; if one uses a lower, country-specific poverty line, its poverty head count is in the 30 to 45 percent range. Although all these results are subject to the strong cautions in Box 4.1, in the early transition poverty undoubtedly increased—in many countries substantially; however, as mentioned earlier, poverty levels have tended to stabilize in countries where growth has resumed.

In China and Vietnam the story is very different. They are much poorer countries, and their poverty line is therefore much lower. Both countries embarked on reform with large numbers of poor but experienced significant reductions in poverty over the course of reform. In both, the improvements resulted from rapid growth and a shift in policy favoring agriculture. Most people in China and

China has been around 6 percent. By 1992, household expenditure by urban families in the south was 75 percent higher than that in the north. A similar picture has emerged in Vietnam, where the area around Ho Chi Minh City, whose market memory helps it respond to reforms, is growing about 40 percent faster than the national average.

In addition to the emergence of previously suppressed comparative advantage, trade and investment policies have overwhelmingly favored China's coastal provinces, and the radical decentralization of the budget has reduced transfers from wealthier to poorer areas. The smaller transfers, higher foreign investment, and faster TVE development (Box 3.4) in the coastal provinces have all contributed to investment rates four times higher than in poorer regions. In response, the Chinese government has moved to equalize the treatment of different regions and

Vietnam are farmers, who were taxed under the old system but now benefit from price liberalization.

How deep is poverty in transition, and is it transient or enduring? Most poverty in CEE and the NIS is shallow. In 1993 the average income of those below the common poverty line fell roughly 25 to 30 percent below that level; relative to country-specific poverty lines the poverty gap was smaller, perhaps 10 to 15 percent. Even the higher figure is less than the average shortfall in many Latin American countries, relative to the same poverty line. Much poverty in CEE and the NIS is also transient: people often move repeatedly into and out of poverty. The same is true in rural China.

Which groups are most likely to be poor? In CEE and the NIS the risk factors include:

- *Belonging to a large or single-parent family.* In 1993 about 60 percent of families with three or more children were poor in Russia, and a similar proportion of single-parent families were poor in Belarus. As elsewhere, single parents are predominantly women.
- *Being out of work.* In Russia in 1993, 63 percent of households headed by an unemployed person were poor. In Hungary, with higher unemployment benefits, only 17.5 percent of such households are poor.
- *Lacking education.* The effect of education is striking. A person with little formal education in Poland is nine times (and one in Romania fifty times) as likely to be poor as someone with a college education.
- *Being old.* Here experience has differed. Because of political pressures, governments have tried to minimize the decline in real pensions. In some countries, such as Poland, pensioners have been relatively protected. Nevertheless, in most their living standards have declined sharply. Poverty in old age disproportionately affects women—in 1990 four out of five Russians over 80 were women. Very old people living alone are particularly at risk.
- *Lacking access to assets.* In particular, access to plots of land has been a critical safety net for many households, for example in Armenia and Ukraine.

The number of poor in a country depends also on how many people are in each high-risk group. Although only a modest fraction of pensioners are poor, there are many pensioners and thus many poor pensioners. For the same reason, in the Kyrgyz Republic and Russia about 65 percent of the poor are workers, and in Poland 60 percent. Children stand out as a group that is both at high risk *and* large, and they constitute an increasing share of the poor in transition economies. Rising child poverty is manifest, for example, in a decline in infants' nutritional status in Russia between 1992 and 1993.

In China and Vietnam, both predominantly rural, the risk factors are very different. Most of the poor (about 9 percent of the rural population in China) are concentrated in remote, resource-deficient areas, primarily in upland regions of interior provinces, where they typically make up entire communities. Although poor people in these regions—often populated by minorities—have land use rights, the land is of such low quality that even subsistence production is generally impossible. Furthermore, since the land is some of China's most ecologically fragile, the poor are often both the perpetrators and the victims of upland environmental destruction. In the face of these problems, provision of social services has stagnated in China's poorest regions. For example, about half the children of households at or below the absolute poverty line are at least mildly malnourished.

Nonmonetary gains and losses
Transition's effects on well-being go far beyond those measured by income. People now have a vastly wider array of goods to choose from, especially imports and high-quality consumer durables, and no longer must wait hours in line to buy them. In Poland, for example, between 1990 and 1993, ownership of videocassette recorders rose from 5 to 53 percent of working households, and ownership of durables has risen throughout the region. Liberalization has created individual wealth in the form of vouchers, enterprise shares, small businesses, land, and housing—although capital, credit, and other markets are needed to realize their value. Private land has been particularly important to well-being during transition. Survey evidence suggests that home food production has increased in many countries, boosting household consumption and sometimes income as well.

Political reforms have brought dramatic social liberalization in many transition economies. New laws and revised constitutions grant wide-ranging civil liberties, a fact that people clearly recognize. In fourteen European transition economies an overwhelming majority of survey respondents believe that their country's current system is better than the old regime at allowing people to choose their religion, and a similarly high share perceive greater freedom to join organizations, to say what they think, and to choose their political affiliation. Large majorities also say that their country's current system is better at allowing people to travel and live where they want (68 percent) and in ending fear of unlawful arrest (59 percent).

But drastic change, wherever it occurs, also brings stress and insecurity. It is well known that major upheavals in people's lives—even happy events such as marriage or a new job—are stressful. The stress is much greater when the entire structure of society is in flux, when attitudes and values are changing, and when people in great numbers face actual or potential poverty and great uncertainty.

A study of displaced U.S. steelworkers in the 1980s shows that four years after the first plant closures, many steelworkers—still without a new job—reported continuing depression and anger and a growing sense of futility; these problems led to alcoholism, deteriorating family relations, and domestic violence. In many transition economies the uncertainty of life after central planning is associated with an even broader range of ill effects. There is increased familial stress as incomes fall and food prices rise. Women are especially affected (Box 4.2), working long hours in paid employment and performing the bulk of domestic chores. Partly as a result, divorce rates have risen (in Belarus, for example, from 35 percent of marriages in 1990 to 55 percent in 1994). Birthrates fell in all the European transition economies, including eastern Germany, and birthrates and marriage rates declined in every region in Russia between 1990 and 1993. Alcoholism and illegal drug use are also on the rise. As discussed in Chapter 8, health deteriorated in many of the NIS, although not in the Visegrad countries, and poor health is itself a source of stress for the families affected. Crime and corruption have increased, as discussed in Chapter 5, further reducing peo-

ple's security. Finally, there has been the stress of adapting to a new culture. Women in the Kyrgyz Republic report that selling home-grown produce is stressful: in their culture a household with extra food always gave—not sold— food to neighbors in need.

As reforms take hold, poverty, uncertainty, and stress will decline, but in many countries neither quickly nor easily. Progress for most people—as the rest of this chapter discusses—will come through growth or better-targeted transfers.

Reforming labor markets: Helping people help themselves

Although people were both hired and paid wages under central planning, labor markets did not work anything like those in market economies. In CEE and the Soviet Union, firms faced incentives to employ as many as possible, so labor shortage, rather than unemployment, was the norm. Wages bore little relation to individual performance: "Work was somewhere we *went,* not something we *did.*" Wage structures were rigid and varied little from top to bottom; as much as half the compensation package

---

Box 4.2 Women and work: Has transition helped?

Transition affects women much differently in some ways than it does men. In considering whether transition has increased welfare for women, the real test is whether it has left them freer than before, or more constrained. So far, at least, the answer in many transition countries appears to be the latter.

Under the previous regime women were expected to work full-time, but the state provided day care and health care. Women are no longer seen as having a social duty to work, but reform has also brought a dramatic decline in affordable child care facilities and a deterioration in health care systems. In addition, economic hardship and uncertainty during transition make it more difficult to feed and clothe the family— responsibilities that have always fallen predominantly to women in these countries—although women have clearly gained from having to spend less time standing in shopping lines. These changes can constrain women's choices in two ways: women who would choose to work may be forced to stay at home because they cannot afford child care, whereas women who would choose not to work may have to because their families need the income. Moreover, women's employment choices may be constrained by increased labor market discrimination, as evidenced by layoffs

of women before men and open discrimination in job advertisements.

Many women have dropped out of the labor force. Nevertheless, in most transition economies women account for a disproportionate share of the unemployed. Part of the drop in labor force participation reflects women's free choice. But much of the decline represents women being forced to stay home by more burdensome domestic responsibilities or becoming discouraged workers. Survey data for several CEE countries show that the vast majority of women prefer to work outside the home. Besides the personal satisfaction and social interaction it provides, work gives them connections to the informal economy, vital for coping during transition. In some countries the social pressures restricting women's choices have merely changed direction: previously expected to work, women are now expected to stay at home. Russia's labor minister made this clear by asking, "Why should we employ women when men are out of work? It's better that men work and women take care of children and do housework." Policy should focus on increasing choices for women so that they can contribute to productivity growth. It should also increase choices for men—for example, by allowing paternity leave.

came in the form of benefits, including housing. To move toward well-functioning labor markets requires that people be paid at least broadly in line with efficiency. And it requires that people be free to move across types of work and, at least to some extent, geographically. How far have wages and employment adjusted to the requirements of a market system, and what policies can assist labor mobility while offering workers some protection against falling wages, exploitation, and job loss?

Adjusting to market forces

At the start of transition many doubted the ability of labor in CEE and the NIS to adjust rapidly to the enormous structural and macroeconomic changes. But labor *has* responded, in a variety of ways. Labor market adjustment has had three elements: changing wage levels and structures, changing sectoral and regional employment patterns (including increased work in the informal sector), and adjustment through unemployment.

WAGE ADJUSTMENT. Wages are starting to assist reform by creating incentives to work hard and acquire skills. Almost everywhere in CEE and the NIS in the early years of transition, wages fell relative to official consumer prices, often substantially. Initially there was little change in relative wages. But in CEE the distribution of wages is beginning to resemble that of a market economy. Evidence from Poland and the Czech Republic suggests an increase in the wage premium for white-collar skills and a significant increase in returns to education. In Russia, too, differentials based on skills have increased. In urban China wages are moving toward market patterns, with a shift from basic wages plus benefits (often in kind) to wages plus bonuses related to productivity or profitability. Relatively higher wages are also making jobs in joint ventures more attractive than those in Chinese state enterprises.

Transition has affected women's wages differently across countries. In Russia greater wage dispersion has meant that women, always disproportionately employed in low-wage jobs, now earn even less relative to men than before transition. In contrast, the earnings gap between men and women has narrowed in several countries, including Poland and Slovenia.

ADJUSTMENT THROUGH CHANGES IN EMPLOYMENT AND UNEMPLOYMENT. As earlier chapters have shown, the inherited distortions and the steep output decline in CEE and the NIS made labor shedding from the state sector unavoidable. Workers face four potential outcomes: staying in the state sector, moving to the new private sector, becoming unemployed (and possibly undergoing training), or dropping out of the labor force altogether (for example, through early retirement). But the employment story is complicated, particularly in the NIS, by the tendency toward informal activity. Where a household works

in several sectors, adjusting is less a simple choice between employment and unemployment than a matter of changing the mix of household members' activities (Box 4.3).

Transition labor markets show three broad patterns of adjustment. In the first, that typical of the CEE countries, employment in the state sector declined sharply. In the leading reformers labor shedding continued through the turnaround in output, leading to a recovery of labor productivity (see Figure 1.6). In Poland, Hungary, and the Czech Republic the private sector expanded strongly, whereas in Bulgaria and the Slovak Republic the state sector's decline was sharp and private sector growth weaker. In almost all the CEE countries registered unemployment rose sharply very early. It later declined, partly because of resumed growth and, more important, because people took early retirement or stopped registering as unemployed once their unemployment benefits expired. By the end of 1994 registered unemployment exceeded 10 percent in all of CEE except the Czech Republic.

Female employment has been hit particularly hard in CEE (and many of the NIS). Women were laid off in much larger numbers than men in the early transition, because their tasks were considered nonessential, because inherited social legislation like generous maternity leave made women more costly to employ, and sometimes because of outright discrimination see (see Box 4.2).

Long-term unemployment (that persisting for a year or more) increased rapidly in CEE with transition, as did youth unemployment. Geographical mismatches between jobs and workers produced large and persistent regional differences in unemployment. All three problems derive from the inherited industrial structure, the mismatch between workers' skills and those demanded in a market economy, inadequate housing markets, and inadequate job information. Although wages in areas with high unemployment have fallen relative to the average, the decline has been insufficient to stimulate much movement of labor. For all these reasons the pool of the unemployed shows little turnover. The private sector draws most new employees directly from the state sector rather than from the mass of unemployed. A key conclusion for policymakers is that unemployment, by itself, has not been a major contributor to restructuring.

The second pattern of adjustment—that in Russia, Ukraine, and many other NIS—is very different. There employment has so far fallen much less than output; instead wages have borne the burden of adjustment (Figure 4.3). Because firms were reluctant to resort to mass layoffs, workers remained formally attached to their firms, receiving low or zero wages but continuing to enjoy some enterprise benefits while working increasingly in the informal sector. At least in their formal sector activities these workers are only marginally employed. Would it

Box 4.3 Household coping mechanisms

Households have a variety of ways of coping with the hardships of transition. Many produce food; others sell family possessions through personal contacts or at bazaars (in Hungary such sales doubled between 1989 and 1995). Car owners often supplement their incomes by giving taxi rides. And some families rent out their summer homes or extra rooms in their apartments.

Households also cope by relying on private income transfers. In Poland and Vietnam about two-thirds of households either give or receive transfers (see table). The amounts can be large: in the Kyrgyz Republic and Vietnam private transfers were 7 percent

and 12 percent of total income, respectively, and more than 25 percent of the incomes of recipients.

Private transfers are most likely to go to households that are poor, have experienced a debilitating event such as illness or job loss, or are headed by the young, the very old, or women—in short, the very households that are the main target of safety nets. Could these private transfers reliably substitute in part for some public transfers? Simulations for Russia indicate that if public pensions were eliminated, private transfers would replace about 19 percent of their amount. The converse is also true: increasing pensions would not cause a ruble-for-ruble reduction in private support.

Private transfers in selected transition economies and the United States
(percentages of total)

	Kyrgyz Rep. (1993)	Poland (1992)	Russia (1993)	Vietnam (1993)	United States (1979)
Households giving or receiving	21.0	65.0	36.0	68.0	30
Transfers as a share of total income	7.4	3.2	4.4	11.9	2
Transfers as a share of recipient income	41.1	7.2	20.1	27.0	6

Source: Cox, Eser, and Jimenez, forthcoming; Cox, Fetzer, and Jimenez, forthcoming; Cox, Jimenez, and Jordan 1994; Cox, Jimenez, and Okrasa 1995; Cox and Raines 1985; Gale and Scholz 1994.

speed transition in the NIS if such workers became explicitly unemployed, as in the CEE countries? Keeping people on the payroll may reduce pressures to restructure. But if labor is immobile, as in Russia, increased unemployment does little to help match workers with jobs. Thus the argument that the NIS should follow the CEE pattern is not entirely clear-cut.

In the third pattern, that of China, state sector employment continued to grow until 1993, declining very slightly thereafter. During the first phase of urban reform, in 1985–90, the state sector provided about 70 percent of all new jobs, but by 1993 it provided only 9 percent of new urban employment. The engine of employment growth is the TVEs, where employment grew ten times faster than in the public sector (Figure 4.4). But growing nonstate employment will not be enough to pull labor out of the state sector. Including benefits, pay in the state sector is about 60 percent higher than in the nonstate sector, and because of continued migration from poor (particularly rural) regions into nonstate employment, the gap is unlikely to narrow. Policymakers will therefore have to find ways to deal with redundant state labor, estimated at some 20 percent of state sector employment.

Employment adjustment in Vietnam has followed the CEE pattern, although state sector employment never

exceeded about 15 percent of total employment. The key to creating additional employment will be continued trade liberalization and other policies to encourage labor-intensive industries.

Policy directions

An important lesson of reform to date, both economic and political, is that market forces alone cannot always drive the restructuring process forward. Greater market determination of wages and employment must be supported by policies to minimize adverse incentives, improve occupational and geographical mobility, and protect workers, both through labor market regulation and through policies to combat unemployment.

MINIMIZING ADVERSE INCENTIVES. As discussed in the next section, income transfers have an important redistributive role. But their structure, in terms both of benefits and of contributions, has important implications for the efficient operation of labor markets. In the early transition unemployment benefits were a large fraction of the recipient's previous wage (often up to 75 percent, and in Ukraine and Belarus 100 percent), and some countries set no time limit on benefits. Not surprisingly, this reduced incentives to find work. By 1995 benefits in all countries were low, largely for fiscal reasons, and some countries,

Wages have fallen further in the NIS than in CEE, but more workers have kept their jobs.

Figure 4.3 Unemployment and wages in CEE and the NIS

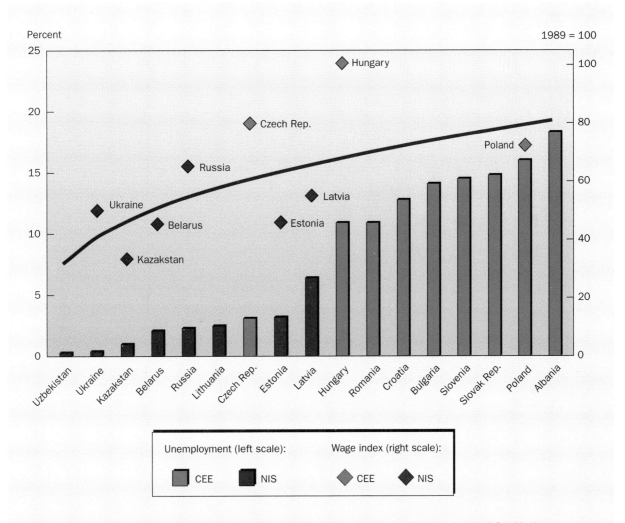

Note: Data are for 1994. Unemployment is measured by the registered unemployment rate; nominal wage data are deflated by the country's consumer price index. Because of the ending of shortages and improvements in the quality of goods, changes in deflated wages may not be a good index of changes in real purchasing power. The regression line is that for the regression of the wage index on countries' rank by unemployment level. Source: Official data.

including Hungary and Poland, paid benefits at the same flat rate to all recipients. Such an approach simultaneously improves work incentives, minimizes costs, and eases administration. All countries now limit the period for which unemployment benefits are paid, generally to a year or less. Once their entitlement has expired, unemployed workers must rely on poverty relief. The result is a high incidence of poverty among the unemployed in countries where poverty relief is patchy.

Incentives on the contributions side are also important. In CEE and the NIS payroll contributions that finance income transfers (including unemployment bene-

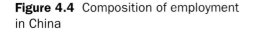

China's TVEs have produced most of the new jobs.

Figure 4.4 Composition of employment in China

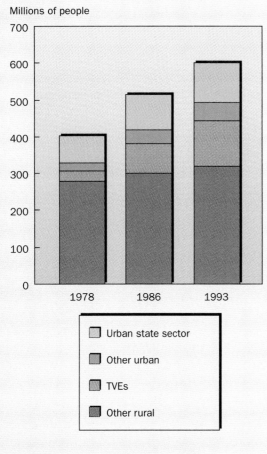

Millions of people

Urban state sector
Other urban
TVEs
Other rural

Source: China Statistical Publishing House 1995.

to who actually ends up paying it. But it has the great advantage that workers immediately see a larger deduction on their pay slip if benefits increase; this helps reduce pressure for higher benefits. Separately, governments also need to spread the tax net to include new private firms; otherwise the burden on larger firms increases and, with increased evasion, the tax base shrinks further. In all these areas progress has been scant.

IMPROVING LABOR MOBILITY. Many of the ingredients of a more mobile labor market in transition countries are more or less universal: well-designed unemployment benefits, improved job information, labor exchange services, adequate transport systems, and—even more important—an active housing market. But transition countries face a unique challenge in creating a labor market that frees workers to move from job to job and place to place, namely, how to dismantle structures of social support that tie workers to a single enterprise while simultaneously building a new system to replace them.

Decoupling delivery of a wide range of services from enterprises—housing and day care are particular problems—will be vital to allow workers to move readily. But the pitfalls are many, and progress has varied. If divesting of services is slow, reform is impeded; if rapid, it can lead to a breakdown in service provision. In the short run, therefore, municipalities have an important role in ensuring continued provision of key services, perhaps through underwriting part of enterprises' cost of provision. A longer-term approach has three steps. First, require enterprises to separate their general accounts from those for social services. Second, for tax purposes allow enterprises to offset the costs of social services against the income those services generate, but not against income earned from the enterprises' main activities. This gives enterprises strong incentives to charge for services and might encourage the spinoff of new service firms. Third, help families meet those charges through higher wages (in place of nonmonetary compensation) and through targeted income transfers such as family allowances. Over time, service-providing entities could become freestanding providers, could be taken over by the municipality, or could disappear. With finance decoupled from the enterprise, the last outcome would not be a problem, at least in urban areas with multiple providers, because provision would no longer be exclusively for enterprise employees. Indeed, providers would face incentives to attract new customers.

Migration, another aspect of mobility, is an important issue, particularly in China where enterprises provide pensions and health care on the assumption that people keep the same job for life. Legal controls on where people can live have been eased, and price reform, market development, and high urban demand for labor have led to enormous migration in search of employment. This "floating

fits) are high, hindering new employment, encouraging workers and employers to collude in fraud, and creating incentives for unofficial employment (Chapter 7). The employer contribution can be reduced in three ways: by reducing benefits, by financing through general taxation benefits that do not relate to any insurable risk (such as benefits for children), and by dividing the contribution between worker and employer (under the old system the employer paid the entire contribution, a fact regarded as one of the victories of socialism). "Sharing" contributions between worker and employer may make little difference population," mostly single men and young women, makes up 20 to 25 percent of the population in most cities. But this migration remains temporary, in large part because migrants are not eligible for education, health care, or subsidized housing. Both restricted mobility and completely free movement have costs: the former in lost opportunities for beneficial migration, the latter in strains on urban infrastructure, the breakdown of rural communities, and the risk of creating an urban underclass. But the present situation in China is unambiguously bad: mobility exists in practice, but institutions are based on the assumption that it does not.

PROTECTING WORKERS THROUGH REGULATION. Governments have a distinct role in setting the legal and regulatory frameworks within which trade unions and firms can operate and in ensuring that those frameworks encourage their positive contributions to growth. Governments also need to define minimum standards and prevent exploitation and discrimination. Successful labor policies are those that work in harmony with the market and avoid providing special protection and privileges to some labor groups at the expense of the poorest.

CEE and the NIS have inherited heavily unionized labor markets. Under the old regime, trade unions were in essence part of the government apparatus (as they are still in China and Vietnam). Their role needs to change if they are to support a market system in the ways explained in *World Development Report 1995*. Encouraging the beneficial side of trade unions in transition countries will be no easy matter, and the precise policies needed will vary considerably across countries. But there are two constants. The first is free competition in product markets, so that unions cannot capture economic rents. The second is ensuring that parties engaged in bargaining face the costs of its outcome. In Poland, for example, legislation in the early 1990s required that workers be paid even when on strike—a clear disincentive to compromise.

Another thorny issue is whether to have a minimum wage. This is a hotly debated question worldwide. But whatever the balance of general arguments for or against, a minimum wage could be particularly problematic for transition economies. Limited government capacity, aggravated by the tendency toward undeclared employment, makes it very difficult to enforce. Moreover, the difference between subsistence and the average wage is much smaller than in rich countries, creating a tension between a minimum wage high enough to avert poverty but low enough not to reduce employment. In Russia, where the minimum wage is the basis of the entire public sector wage structure, the government, to reduce inflationary pressures, has exerted downward pressure on the minimum wage. As a result it no longer protects the lowest-paid workers. To the extent that poverty among

the working poor disproportionately affects families with children, a family allowance (discussed in the next section) might be a more effective way of combining employment opportunities with poverty relief.

ADDRESSING UNEMPLOYMENT. Two questions are of particular relevance to CEE and the NIS regarding unemployment. Should governments continue to assist enterprises? And what should be the role of active labor market policies (policies aimed at improving work opportunities)? The speed and effectiveness of transition depend on the pace of restructuring in state and privatized firms. Where local unemployment is high and labor mobility severely constrained, a case can be made for temporary employment subsidies for firms that may survive in the long run or whose closure would devastate a region. But governments should ensure that such support is phased down on an established schedule (Chapter 3) and that financing is concentrated on employment. Finally, where explicit employment subsidies are provided, governments should also work to increase labor mobility and give workers information on job opportunities elsewhere.

Active labor market policies are of three broad types: employment services (placement, counseling) to "recycle" existing skills more effectively, training to increase human capital, and direct job creation. The usefulness of such policies during a general collapse in output is severely circumscribed, however. Except on a small scale and very selectively, they are likely to be beyond the means of CEE countries and the NIS, even though they can be an effective response to industrial decline and the corrosive effects of long-run unemployment. The Czech government instituted a package of labor market reforms in 1990–92 with three elements: a computerized job information system, reduced unemployment benefits, and job creation programs. The reduced unemployment benefits and the country's low initial level of unemployment made the job creation programs financially feasible, and the evidence suggests that they helped reduce the spread of long-term unemployment. However, the main driving force behind continuing low unemployment in the Czech Republic has not been specific labor policies but strong private sector growth.

Reforming income transfers: What redistributive role for the state?

In all middle- and high-income countries the state has an important role in organizing income transfers. These have several purposes: to redistribute income, to maintain political stability, to promote efficient labor markets, and to insure against important risks where private markets cannot.

The specific objectives of income transfers include *insurance,* protecting people against risks such as unemployment; *income smoothing,* allowing people to protect their living standards in old age by redistributing income from their younger years; and *poverty relief,* ensuring at least a minimum standard of living. The changes in labor markets that transition brings require a fundamental reform in the old system of income transfers: a widening wage and income distribution means that transfers must be targeted in ways that take more account of differences in circumstances; the loss of job security makes developing unemployment benefits urgent and means that transfers can no longer be administered by enterprises. Both these changes call for strengthening the administration of income transfers.

Inherited transfer systems

Inherited systems of income transfers in transition economies differ greatly but share some common tendencies: support is poorly targeted, much administration is devolved to enterprises, and some rural populations are neglected.

CEE AND THE NIS. Although relatively well adapted to the old regime, the system of income transfers in these countries failed in important ways to accord with the needs of a market economy. It distributed roughly equal benefits to all in the urban population rather than focusing them on the poor. In most countries poverty relief was rudimentary, and because officially unemployment did not exist, neither did unemployment benefits. Enterprises had a major role in benefit administration (for example, paying contributions en bloc for their workers, with the result that governments have no individual records), and no distinction existed between risk-related benefits (such as unemployment benefits) and others (for example, family allowances). A single social insurance contribution financed the whole gamut. Administrative capabilities, moreover, were limited. Pensions, for example, were paid in cash through the postal system.

There has been some progress. All the CEE countries and the NIS now have working systems of unemployment benefits, and many have established a broadly based, income-tested benefit of last resort, usually at low levels. Benefits, nevertheless, remain badly targeted. In Russia in 1992 only about 19 percent of transfers served to reduce poverty directly, compared with an average of 35 percent in the OECD countries and 50 percent in Australia.

High spending on benefits, particularly pensions, has been a central issue. The core of the problem is that pensioners are numerous. Pensionable age in CEE and the NIS is generally five years lower than in the West, and large groups such as miners and teachers were able to retire even earlier. As a result, the typical woman pensioner in the Czech Republic enjoys five more years of retirement than her American counterpart, and seven years more than her German counterpart. For men the difference is closer to one year. The comparison for Hungary, Poland, and Russia is broadly similar.

The multitude of pensioners can create a vicious circle in which high pension spending (16 percent of GDP in Poland in 1994) leads to high payroll contributions, to incentives not to declare employment, and thus to still higher contribution rates (Box 4.4). Yet pensions in most countries remain low because there are so many pensioners. The combined effects of unemployment, widespread informal activity, low pensionable age, and, in some countries, lack of rural coverage have led to low ratios of contributors to pensioners (Table 4.2). Poland, for example, has 4.6 people of working age for each person aged sixty or more, but only 1.9 of them contribute. Bulgaria has little more than one contributor per pensioner. Medium-term projections in many countries show that present arrangements are not sustainable.

Breaking this vicious circle is one of social policy's main challenges. So far there has been much debate but little change in policy (the Czech Republic and Latvia are among the few exceptions). In fact, the average age at which a pension is first paid has *declined* in most countries. Making the political economy of pension reform more difficult is the fact that employers pay the bulk of pension contributions, whereas pensioners as a group have the power to swing elections.

CHINA. Social protection in China differs from that in CEE and the NIS in several important ways: the country's population is still young (although the average age will rise rapidly over the next thirty years), its urban system of social protection is a series of enterprise-based islands rather than a unified system, and it has a large rural population (80 percent of the total population) with very limited social protection.

The urban system of income transfers (labor insurance) faces many problems parallel to those of the CEE countries and the NIS. Pensionable age, for example, is low and the social insurance system excessively fragmented. Workers in government agencies and state enterprises enjoy comprehensive benefits, while a parallel, less generous system serves employees in collective enterprises. By contrast with CEE and the NIS, Chinese enterprises have been responsible for administering *and* financing benefits. This arrangement ties workers—and pensioners—even more closely to the enterprise and slows enterprise reform. Furthermore, the generosity of benefits depends on the enterprise's financial capacity and on its age (newer enterprises have fewer pensioners). Some income pooling between enterprises has been introduced at the municipal level, but this is only a partial solution.

China's rural labor force remains outside the system of labor insurance, creating two sets of problems. First, more than 100 million people working in rural industry have only patchy access to health care and no pension rights unless they buy them privately. The huge rural population has relied on the extended family for old age support and

Box 4.4 Reforming income transfers in Hungary and Latvia

Hungary illustrates the potential vicious circle in financing income transfers. In 1992 about 90 percent of households received some sort of transfer, and transfers made up over 40 percent of household income. The problem arises in part because pensionable age is low and because registered employment fell by 20 percent between 1990 and 1995. High social spending may have helped prevent change in the income distribution (Figure 4.2), but it led to high contribution rates. These, coupled with limited enforcement capacity, increase incentives for evasion and informalization, thus reducing the number of contributors. Despite high spending, benefits are often inadequate, and additional, undeclared earning is becoming the norm. Reform is politically contentious, but the potential payoff to reduced informalization is huge: if 100,000 workers (about 1.9 percent of the labor force in 1990) moved from registered unemployment to registered employment, the fiscal balance would improve by about 0.5 percent of GDP.

Latvia has introduced major reform intended to break the vicious circle. State pension spending is to be reduced by abolishing favorable treatment for special groups and by paying lower benefits to people who retire earlier and higher benefits to people who defer retirement and continue to contribute. It is estimated that, if the reforms are successfully followed through, the savings by 2000 will equal roughly a quarter of expected contributions. Those savings will be channeled to a second, funded system in which the contributions will be held in reserve or invested by private managers. In essence, Latvia's older and younger generations have made a deal. Pensioners have agreed not to press for larger benefits, and workers have accepted the burden of higher contributions in the hope of greater security for themselves in old age.

If successfully followed through, the reforms will bring major benefits. They will reduce public pension spending. They will do away with arguments about the age of retirement, because workers can choose when to retire. And because pensions bear a direct relation to contributions, they will encourage people to come out of the informal economy.

---

poverty relief, but with a trend to smaller families and increasing labor mobility, these ties are weakening. The 30 million to 40 million absolute rural poor are on the margin of subsistence. Many would face starvation were it not for China's highly effective grain relief system, which provides them with just enough grain to live on. It is essential that this system survive transition. Beyond this, sustained economic growth should continue to aid poverty reduction. And because the poor make up a relatively small share of the rural population, the government should be able to target relief to the very poorest communities.

The second set of problems relates to a blurring of the distinction between urban and rural workers and the emergence of a growing migrant rural labor force. The social insurance system, still based on the assumption of low labor mobility, has yet to recognize that workers move between types of employment and between locations. One quarter of rural workers are now wage earners, yet still lack the labor insurance coverage of their urban counterparts. Likewise the growing "floating population" of migrant workers remains largely without coverage. Although most migrants do well, some do not, and they may represent the first of an emerging group of poor in areas that have not traditionally had large poor populations.

Table 4.2 Population structure and contributors per pensioner in selected transition economies

Country	Persons of working age per person over 60	Contributors per pensioner
Central and Eastern Europe		
Albania	7.9	1.0
Bulgaria	2.9	1.2
Czech Republic	3.5	2.0
Hungary	3.2	1.5
Poland	4.6	1.9
Romania	3.6	2.0
Newly independent states		
Russia	2.9	1.9
Kyrgyz Republic	5.0	2.6
Turkmenistan	6.6	3.6
Uzbekistan	6.3	3.0
Memorandum:		
OECD average, 1990	3.6	2.6

Note: Data are for 1993.
Source: World Bank Social Challenges of Transition data base; World Bank 1995k.

Policy directions

Broadly, social safety nets can take two forms: transfers, whether in cash or in kind; and programs that give people earning opportunities. There is a strong presumption that, where transfers are paid, they should be in cash wherever possible: cash payments leave buying decisions to the recipient, they are more transparent in budgeting, and they do not interfere with market prices. In some circumstances, however, benefits in kind have advantages: they usually maintain their value during inflation, and in specific cases—some of which are discussed below—they may be well targeted. Transition economies have very different incomes, administrative capacities, family structures, and social priorities. Some have much larger informal sectors than others, and some remain substantially rural. Their systems of income transfers will therefore differ widely.

PRIVATE INSURANCE. Many people are poor only for particular periods in their lives—for example, while unemployed. Should the state leave coverage of such risks to private insurance? The answer, as discussed in Chapter 7, is usually no. Private insurance deals badly, if at all, with certain risks, including unemployment. It may be an option for some risks (such as health-related absence from work) and for some people (the urban middle class). But even in the West, where the institutional framework is stronger, private insurance is no more than a supplemental source of income support.

SOCIAL INSURANCE. Social insurance benefits are paid on the basis of a worker's contributions (usually a fraction of his or her wages) and on the occurrence of a specified event, such as becoming unemployed or reaching a given age. Because participation is compulsory, social insurance can protect against risks that the private market cannot cover and can redistribute from rich to poor. Although all the CEE countries and the NIS have well-established systems that would be politically difficult to withdraw, social insurance may not be the way forward for all countries. Whether it is depends on the answers to several questions. Are the causes of income loss relatively clear-cut and in principle insurable? Is administrative capacity adequate? Can income be accurately measured for purposes of calculating contributions? And is it possible to enforce contributions and calculate benefits? In countries such as the Czech Republic, Hungary, and Poland the answer to these questions is yes. In some of the NIS, particularly the poorer Central Asian economies, it is probably no. Because much employment is informal, enforcing contributions is virtually impossible, and low administrative capacity makes enforcement problematic even in the formal sector.

Pensions pose special and difficult problems. Should members of the current older generation receive special treatment? In much of CEE and the NIS inflation destroyed the financial savings of the elderly. Unlike the young, they will not have the opportunity to recoup their losses in the market economy. A case can therefore be made on equity grounds for special treatment. In part this has already happened: many people have been allowed to retire early, and pensioners in many countries have held their ground relative to wage earners. Another possibility is to favor the elderly in distributing such assets as shares, vouchers, and housing. Wealth can empower the older generation: an elderly pensioner who owns her house can leave it to her children, trade it for regular income transfers from her children, or use her house as security for a loan or an annuity.

However, the inherited pension systems in CEE and the NIS need major reform. Benefit spending, like public spending generally, must be made compatible with a smaller public sector, to create room for private sector–led growth. In many countries spending on pensions has to be cut, either by reducing individual benefits or by reducing the number of pensioners—for instance, by raising pensionable age and stemming abuse of disability pensions. In the short run poverty relief should take precedence over other objectives; in some countries this may mean paying flat-rate benefits. This cuts spending but may create discontent. As always, policymakers have to strike a balance between what they cannot afford to do—and what they cannot afford not to do.

In the medium term, as fiscal and administrative constraints start to relax, the system can evolve toward one that more explicitly relates contributions to benefits. This will strengthen incentives to contribute—indeed, to the extent that it reduces perceptions that the contributions are a tax, it may also improve the incentive to work in the formal sector. Special arrangements for the current elderly should not be carried over to the younger generation, who have time to build up pension entitlements and other forms of wealth. Political difficulties notwithstanding, gradually raising the retirement age is inescapable, and this has started in a number of countries. Reform of state pensions should be accompanied by development of a complementary system of private pensions (discussed below).

In China there is broad agreement that a unified system, including rules for adjusting benefits for inflation, should cover all urban enterprises, state and private. For the same reasons as in CEE and the NIS, benefit administration and delivery should be shifted away from enterprises, and the retirement age should be raised. Contributions by employers and the different levels of government should be clearly delineated and, for the same reasons as elsewhere, worker contributions introduced.

Countries will need additional ways to relieve poverty, but that requires first identifying who is poor. There are three broad ways to do so: by measuring income (that is, by using an income test); by using an indicator of poverty, such as age or illness; or by devising programs with incentive properties that induce only poor people to participate.

INCOME-TESTED SOCIAL ASSISTANCE. Assistance to individuals or families with incomes below a specified level is appropriate for the lifetime poor and where contributions cannot be calculated or enforced. But broadly based, income-tested social assistance presents several problems: it creates important disincentives against work, the necessary tax rates are unsustainable for poor countries, determining eligibility is administratively demanding and costly even in wealthier countries, and income testing can be stigmatizing and intrusive and thus politically contentious. These problems are serious for many transition economies, especially where poverty is transient and often shallow, so that many people move into and out of poverty.

One alternative is to organize poverty relief locally and allow local officials some discretion in administering it. Uzbekistan has introduced a scheme of this sort. The smaller the locality, the better the information on applicants, which assists targeting. Localities can be given a fixed budget, so that spending can be controlled. Discretion, however, is administratively demanding at both the central and the local level. A mechanism is needed to ensure that the neediest localities receive greater resources than less needy ones. This requires both the technical capacity to make informed decisions and the ability to avoid discrimination and corruption.

TARGETED RELIEF USING POVERTY INDICATORS. It is sometimes possible to identify the poor through an indicator of poverty that is easier to measure than income. With services such as child care being withdrawn, family allowances are likely to be particularly well targeted in the European transition economies. An income test for all families with children is administratively costly, and the larger the informal sector, the less accurate it would be. Family allowances—a fixed amount per child per month—are paid without income tests throughout Western Europe and in several Latin American countries. Other uses of indicator targeting include help for pregnant women and infants through nutrition programs and medical checkups, and for schoolchildren through free meals and health checks. Old age, particularly in single-person households, is another good indicator of poverty and is administratively relatively undemanding (Box 4.5).

SELF-TARGETED POVERTY RELIEF. Some countries try to subsidize goods consumed mainly by the poor. But such commodities are few, and the list of subsidized commodities can be "hijacked" by the middle class. Another approach is to offer subsistence cash payments in return for work. In Estonia able-bodied people are eligible for

Box 4.5 Innovative pension delivery in South Africa

Each month on pension day in Kangwane, a former black homeland in South Africa, a thin line of grandparents walk across the rural wilderness clutching banknotes dispensed by some of the most sophisticated cash machines in the world. The cash machines arrive mounted on unmarked trucks and escorted by armed guards. Under makeshift awnings, each pensioner swipes a plastic card through the machine, then rolls a finger across a tiny scanner that checks the fingerprint against a digital template and then dispenses the monthly pension. The service now pays pensions to about 400,000 South African senior citizens.

The system works well in both social and administrative terms. It empowers the elderly, usually women, and it can be a good way, through a grandmother's discretion, of offering family support. And when a person dies and is therefore unable to collect the pension, payments cease automatically.

unemployment benefits only if they perform eighty hours of public service a month. Such "workfare" has advantages: the only people who participate are those for whom it is genuinely the least-bad option, and it may allow recipients to preserve their dignity by working. Broader benefits may accrue where the work creates useful infrastructure such as roads. But the approach is hard to implement, and it may face political opposition.

CONCLUSION. The experience even of the advanced reformers highlights the difficulties of targeting poverty relief effectively and shows the importance of devising simple eligibility criteria, of devolving initiatives to the community level, and of engaging a wide range of interested parties, including disadvantaged groups and community leaders in partnership. In this context nongovernmental organizations (NGOs) can have a valuable role, for example by providing shelter for the homeless. To encourage these activities, however, governments must first make them explicitly legal where they are not already, and possibly provide them with tax advantages or some explicit funding. NGOs can often relieve poverty and provide services more efficiently than state institutions, as well as encourage local participation and generally promote the development of civil society.

Pension reform—and the role of private schemes
State pensions, as discussed earlier, require fundamental reform in every transition country. Many of the less

advanced reformers should probably focus solely on getting their state systems in order. But some transition economies are developing private pensions or considering their introduction. Most state pensions operate on a pay-as-you-go basis (current pensions are paid out of current contributions), whereas most private schemes (whether compulsory or voluntary) are funded by the savings people accumulate during their working lives. Some elements are essential to any pension reform. Beyond these, policymakers in each country face a range of options. These, however, will be subject to the interplay between choice and initial circumstances highlighted in Chapter 1.

ESSENTIAL COMPONENTS OF REFORM. The first and central element of pension reform in transition economies is ensuring that public pension spending is compatible with economic growth. Problems with public spending must be addressed directly; private pensions are no solution to excessive state spending, especially when the public schemes are as overextended as they are in most transition countries. Second, any pension reform needs to be financed in some way. Adding a funded scheme to an existing scheme requires building up capital to pay future pensions while continuing to pay current pensions. This is rather like asking people to pay mortgages on two houses—their own and their parents'—at the same time. If the parents' home is small and the children's income rising (as in Chile and China), the added payment is not a major problem. But if the parents' home is large—and mortgaged to the hilt—and the children's income low or shrinking (as in CEE and the NIS), the parents' home will have to be financed in some other way. Alternative ways of funding pensions include taxation, asset sales, or borrowing. Introducing private pensions therefore needs to be part of a strategy that also embraces public pension spending (see the discussion of Latvia in Box 4.4). Indeed, as noted above, controlling public pension spending ought to be the driving priority for many less advanced reformers for the time being, since they are still some way from acquiring either the economic or the institutional basis for more ambitious, long-term reforms.

A third essential element is regulation and enforcement to protect contributors and pensioners; this in turn requires effective government. In many transition economies the necessary financial market regulation, including agreed and enforced accounting standards, is not yet in place. Putting it in place is a large task, but an essential first step in building private pensions. Especially where there are large pension funds, government also must be barred from trying to politicize the allocation of investment. Finally, funded pensions need time to mature; it takes up to forty years for workers to accumulate enough to support themselves in old age, although

this might in some cases be speeded by endowing pension funds with privatized assets (Box 4.6).

POLICY OPTIONS. Eventually, transition governments are likely to settle on a pension system that combines three elements: a state component, normally pay-as-you-go; a funded component, normally private; and, where the funded component is compulsory, a third component consisting of funded schemes to which individuals can make voluntary additional contributions. Within this framework, every country will have some strategic choices to make about the relative size of the three components and the design of each.

How large and how redistributive should the state pension be? Poor countries cannot afford to spend much on pensions. The cheapest way to maximize poverty relief in such cases is through flat-rate pensions. As fiscal constraints relax, other policy options become possible, including a higher flat-rate pension (as in the Netherlands) or a pension that is at least partly related to previous contributions (as in the United Kingdom and the United States).

How should private, funded pensions be organized: through individual accounts (as in Argentina and Chile), or should it also be possible for employers to organize schemes, as in many European countries? The choice depends in part on how broadly policymakers want risks to be shared. As a separate issue, how and how far should pensioners be protected against loss and high inflation—particularly salient risks in an economy undergoing major reform? The state might underwrite at least some of the inflation risk—pensioners should not face substantially more risk than wage earners, and the collapse of private pension schemes during the infancy of a market economy could undermine the political consensus underpinning economic reform.

Should membership be compulsory? Pay-as-you-go schemes are so by their nature. Some experts argue for small public pensions and compulsory membership in private schemes. But requiring membership raises tricky issues. The Czech Republic has an above-subsistence public pension and is bringing spending under control, in part through funded schemes, with tax advantages to encourage contributions. But the Czechs did not consider it politically feasible to take the further step of mandating contributions to the new private schemes. Many other transition countries will also find this difficult, given that inflation has so recently all but wiped out private savings.

PENSION PACKAGES. How should transition countries choose which mix of pension schemes is right for them? A typical system in Europe and North America has a state pay-as-you-go pension covering more than subsistence, complemented by a variety of regulated, privately managed, funded pensions. Where these are compulsory, individuals

Box 4.6 Can state property be used to fund pensions?

Governments enter transition with large obligations—but also with considerable property. In market economies the total value of wealth is roughly four times GDP: land, housing, and other structures (including commercial buildings) are each about equal to GDP; equipment, inventories, consumer durables, and livestock make up the remainder. Can transition governments use some of this wealth to fund obligations such as pensions?

Experience elsewhere suggests that it is possible. In Bolivia government shares in majority privatized companies will be placed in privately managed pension funds. In theory governments in transition economies could do the same. And enterprise shares are not the only asset they could use. Bonds placed on the books of some enterprises (with the government as beneficiary) are another available asset. Bonds have a steady payback, are more secure than equity shares, and may subject firms to creditor monitoring. Real estate could also be used to fund pensions. For example, some Chinese enterprises unable to pay pensions have considered transferring the housing they own to a property management subsidiary, which could borrow against the housing to pay the pensions. On the death of the pensioners the housing would be auctioned.

Although attractive in principle, these schemes are not easy to implement. The first problem is that not all state wealth is controlled by central governments. Subnational or municipal governments control much commercial real estate. Tenants often have strong presumptive rights to their homes, even if they are owned by government or state enterprises. A second problem is that funded pension schemes require regulatory oversight, liquid asset markets, and a pool of independent professional managers, and all take time to develop. But the alternatives are not necessarily easier. Governments could instead sell the property for revenue, but this is difficult if buyers with capital are scarce (see Chapter 3). Governments may sell property quickly and cheaply, hoping to collect property or capital gains taxes from the new owners; in practice, however, tax administration also takes time to develop, particularly for these complex taxes. Given the difficulties of any course of action, using state assets to fund pensions may be worth considering, but any scheme requires careful attention to both design and implementation.

---

may also make voluntary additional contributions to funded schemes. The three components address different purposes: the state scheme is concerned mainly with poverty relief and (often imperfectly) with redistribution, the second tier helps people redistribute their income across their lifetimes, and the third allows for differences in individual preferences. This approach accords a significant role to social solidarity and shares risks fairly broadly, but it can come under severe financial pressure from the twin threat of a slowly growing economy and a rapidly aging population. An alternative approach, used in Chile and Singapore, has a smaller public component. In Chile the state pension is a minimum guarantee for private pensions; people whose benefits are above the minimum receive no state pension. For most, pensions are provided by one or more funded, regulated, individual schemes. Individuals can make voluntary additional contributions. This approach does not redistribute from rich to poor or between generations other than through the minimum pension guarantee. Recent reforms in Latin America (Argentina, Colombia, and Peru) adopt something of a middle ground between the European–North American and the Chilean approaches.

The precise choice depends on a country's objectives and its constraints. Chile and several of the high-performing Asian economies gave priority to economic growth and therefore adopted more individualistic systems that encouraged high saving. Some transition economies face tighter constraints—economic, political, and social—than these countries, which have long-established market systems, relatively sophisticated banking systems and capital markets, and relatively stable prices (and Chile introduced its reform at a time of budgetary surplus). Moreover, government capacity in those countries is high. Social constraints also differ. The extended family is still important in the high-performing Asian economies, and strong family support structures also exist in the Central Asian republics; they are weaker in CEE and the other NIS. In the Kyrgyz Republic, for example, elderly ethnic Russians are worse off than elderly Kyrgyz, for whom the extended family support network still exists. Most of these constraints, and others elsewhere in the economy, can be overcome through consistent reform—indeed, that is one of the major purposes of reform. But they cannot be ignored in the short run.

The agenda

Some widening of the gap between rich and poor is an inescapable part of transition. Especially where rising inequality has also involved rising poverty, governments have come under pressure to narrow the gap once again. Over the long haul the only way to reduce poverty is to foster economic growth, largely by pursuing the pro-market policies—including lower public spending—described in Chapter 2. Tackling chronic labor immobility would encourage growth and reduce poverty at the same time. But freeing workers to respond to market signals will be tougher than freeing the markets themselves. It will involve not merely market-determined wages, but governments taking on the other hindrances that keep workers from freely changing jobs—in particular, the coupling of social benefits to enterprises and the lack of a functioning housing market. Growth and greater mobility would help most of the present losers from reform to make up their recent losses. However, policy must recog-

nize the true extent to which large numbers of people are suffering from poverty, insecurity, or both. Policymakers have to find a meeting ground between fiscal pressures and political and social imperatives. People left behind even after growth rebounds and labor markets become more flexible should be able to count on continued government support, including well-targeted social benefits. The elderly in transition countries stand much less chance of recovering their losses, and this generation presents a strong case for special treatment. But runaway spending on pensions in transition countries cannot be allowed to continue. Governments can address the problem now, by raising the age at which the next generations can retire, and over the long term, by building a pension system that can sustainably support the many generations to come.

PART TWO

The Challenge of Consolidation

LIBERALIZATION, STABILIZATION, PRIVATIZATION, and poverty relief are intrinsic to transition. But they are not enough to create vibrant market economies. Building on the early gains of transition will require major consolidating reforms, to develop strong market-supporting institutions, a skilled and adaptable work force, and full integration into the global economy.

The many institutions that support market exchange and shape ownership in advanced market economies—both concrete organizations and abstract rules of the game—largely disappeared under central planning. As Part One showed, even in this weak institutional setting, favorable policy reforms have been able to spur economic growth. But a growing body of evidence on market economies suggests that, for the longer term, if transition economies are to join the ranks of the advanced market economies, they will need not just good economic policies but strong and accountable institutions to support and implement them.

Which institutions are most critical? First are good laws and effective means for their enforcement (Chapter 5). These establish and apply the rules of the game, lower transaction costs, increase commercial certainty, create incentives for efficiency, and control crime and corruption so that businesses can focus on productive activities. Second are strong financial institutions (Chapter 6), to encourage saving and channel it to its most productive uses. Financial institutions also play an important role in corporate governance, complementing that of enterprise owners, by imposing financial discipline and overseeing the activities of borrowers. A third essential institution is government (Chapter 7), but the all-powerful, all-encompassing governments of the planning era need to be completely reoriented toward a smaller, more selective set of activities that support and complement, rather than stifle, private enterprise.

Institutions do not develop in a vacuum. Reformers' top-down efforts to develop strong legal and financial institutions and to change government behavior must be complemented by bottom-up demand for such reform. This demand will not spring up overnight, and it will often require deep changes in incentives, attitudes, and experience. But it will emerge faster if policymakers are vigilant in pursuing macroeconomic stability, open markets, and private sector development.

An extensive body of research shows the importance of human capital for the sustained growth and adaptation of market economies. Many countries enter transition with a strong human capital base, and their rising returns to education already show the importance of skills in the new economy. Nevertheless, thorough reform of education and health systems is needed, both to preserve past achievements and to adapt to the needs of the market (Chapter 8).

Finally, openness to trade and foreign investment has proved an equally robust predictor of strong economic performance across countries. Indeed, both have already had a large positive impact in transition economies. Deeper integration into the institutions of the global economy carries obligations as well as rights, and these can help integration serve a broader purpose: that of locking in reforms against the emergence of pressure groups (Chapter 9).

CHAPTER 5

Legal Institutions and the Rule of Law

Under central planning, law was first and foremost an instrument of state control. Law in market economies is fundamentally different; it defines the rules of the game and gives individuals the rights and tools to enforce them. Where the rule of law is in force, laws are applied fairly, transparently, and evenhandedly to all; individuals can assert and defend their rights; and the state's powers are defined and limited by law. People in countries with a well-established rule of law rarely stop to wonder where it comes from. But transition economies need to start over, to replace arbitrary rule by powerful individuals or institutions with a rule of law that inspires the public trust and respect that will enable it to endure.

Developing the rule of law

The rule of law requires good laws, demand for those laws, and institutions to bring them to life. Good laws are not easy to design or to enact even in the best of circumstances; the task is harder still in transition economies, where policy debates still rage over fundamentals, political pressures are intense, and experience with market mechanisms remains scant. Yet failure to pass good laws imposes costs that go beyond the mistakes in individual laws to the integrity of the legal system itself. Laws passed with major inconsistencies and uncertainties, or with clear avenues for abuse, simply deepen public cynicism and mistrust.

Where do new laws come from? Transition economies can turn to two sources: "home-grown" law, drawn up either from scratch or from legislation enacted before central planning, or law transplanted from established market economies. The CEE and Baltic countries, with their shorter history of central planning, have tended to draw from prewar legislation where possible, but this source is largely unavailable to most of the NIS or to China. The alternative, imported laws, has the advantage of experience, but importing is risky. Differing histories and cultural traditions shape the way legal systems work. If laws do not take local legal culture into account, they may be inappropriate or may not take root. An intermediate approach—borrowing ideas from best-practice models abroad, then adapting them through indigenous legal drafting and political debate—usually works best.

Many countries have good laws that are ignored, but the centrally planned economies brought this dichotomy between law and its application to an extreme. Many laws were put on the books—such as constitutional provisions guaranteeing basic freedoms—that were never meant to be applied in practice. Transition economies thus need to develop effective supporting institutions to move their new laws from theory to practice. One obvious example is the court system. Although, as discussed below, most contract enforcement is and should be informal, countries still need formal enforcement mechanisms at the margin. For these to work, however, litigants must be confident that courts have the power and the capacity to judge objectively and to get their judgments enforced.

The administrative-command system of central planning marginalized law within the economy, and all formal judicial institutions atrophied in the economic sphere. In most of CEE and the NIS, economic disputes between enterprises were removed from the courts' jurisdiction altogether and instead decided by special arbitration bodies. Even then, if a trading partner reneged, managers would generally turn to ministerial or party officials for redress rather than pursue administrative remedies. Ministries could order delivery of key inputs, whereas administrative bodies might only award money damages or impose fines—cold comfort to enterprise managers seeking to fulfill the plan.

With transition, independent courts and alternative dispute resolution and enforcement mechanisms need to play the remedial role formerly assigned to the bureaucracy. But to say that the state must withdraw from administrative control is not to say it should give up enforcing the law.

Transition economies struggle with a constant tension between, on the one hand, the need for a strong state to enforce laws and impose order and, on the other, the need for constraints on state power to make room for individual rights. Sorting out where state power is legitimate and where it is not is a constant task of governments everywhere. But whereas established market economies argue these questions at the margin, transition governments are completely refiguring the enforcement functions of public institutions.

Formal legal systems place judges, prosecutors, arbitrators, court functionaries (for example, bailiffs and bankruptcy trustees), and the private legal profession in the role of primary interpreters and enforcers of laws. But the full cast of characters underpinning the rule of law in any country runs much longer. Equally important are those who produce and distribute information and monitor market participants: among these "watchdog" institutions are accounting firms, credit rating services, securities regulators, investigators, and other elements of civil society—including a free press. Like the courts themselves, these institutions were neglected under central planning and must now be rebuilt, essentially from the ground up. And of course none of them can work well if people do not know what the law is, because it is constantly changing and they have no definitive and accessible compilation to turn to. Transition governments need to make sure that laws, decrees, and important court decisions are quickly published in an official and widely circulated text.

Finally, the rule of law can take hold only if good laws and competent institutions are supplemented by demand for them. This will vary across countries, depending on their history and culture, but economics also plays a role. Individuals and companies have strong economic incentives to claim their legal rights and abide by legal responsibilities only to the extent that they depend on the market—and their reputation in it. Banks and other creditors, for example, will not take seriously their new rights under collateral, debt collection, and bankruptcy laws unless convinced that state bailouts are unavailable. They have to see that aggressive debt collection is necessary for survival. Similarly, when managers require a law-abiding reputation to purchase supplies or raise capital, they will think twice about violating the sanctity of contract or abusing minority shareholders. If managers can instead turn to the government or the state banking system for subsidies, or if they enjoy a monopoly position, they will have no reason to worry about their market reputation. Market-oriented incentives therefore complement market-oriented laws and institutions. One cannot proceed far without the others, and all three are essential to developing the rule of law.

As noted in Chapter 9, a strong commitment to international integration can also stimulate demand for law and provide market-friendly models of legislation. The desire of many European transition economies to join the European Union has motivated them to adopt economic laws that meet EU requirements in such areas as taxation, trade, and competition policy. Trade agreements with the United States and eventual membership in the WTO and other international bodies can also encourage legal reform, as can a strong commitment to foreign direct investment. The point here is not that integration will push transition countries into precisely replicating foreign laws, but that it will fuel demand for certain types of law and help policymakers design laws that foster links with the outside world.

Creating legal frameworks for private sector development

Economic laws in market economies have at least four functions: defining and protecting property rights; setting rules for exchanging those rights; establishing rules for entry into and exit out of productive activities; and promoting competition by overseeing market structure and behavior and correcting market failures. Many transition economies are well along in drafting and enacting legislation in the fundamental areas of property, contracts, company organization, bankruptcy, and competition, as well as other, more specialized topics. Inconsistencies and omissions remain, however, and many laws are only now beginning to be implemented. Governments are often hesitant to relinquish control, citizens are slow to assert their new rights, judicial and other enforcement institutions are still severely underdeveloped, and a body of legal interpretation to help guide practice in specific areas must be created, largely from scratch.

Property rights
Property rights in successful market economies are complex things. They form a rich, intricately defined array extending from full ownership through partial use rights (such as leaseholds and easements) to rights contingent on specific events (such as inheritance rights and collateral rights to debtors' property). Countless types of property are defined and protected, from real estate and movable property to new ideas and inventions. Under central planning, concepts of property were based not on the scope of individual rights or the nature of the property, but on the identity of the owner. Laws established a hierarchy, with state property at the top, cooperative property in the middle, and individual property (generally restricted to housing and personal items) at the bottom.

At the start of transition most of the NIS and the CEE countries moved to expand the scope for private property and to put it on an equal footing with state property. China and Vietnam still hold to the supremacy of state ownership, but they do allow private property and have provided wide scope for long-term leases of property by individuals and small businesses. Chinese farmers, for example, typically lease their land for twenty to seventy years. Most transition economies, including those in Asia, have also adopted intellectual property laws, often at the urging of trading partners, although these laws are proving notoriously difficult to enforce.

Yet many of these new rights are limited by heavy restrictions on use, pledge, and ownership. Land use is often subject to strict controls, with prohibitions or high fees for the conversion of agricultural land to industrial use or of housing to commercial use. Both domestic and foreign lessees of state-owned commercial property may be subjected to arbitrary changes in lease terms or rental rates; rent controls often prevent owners from covering even maintenance costs. Although the letter of the law may permit the pledging of assets, the lack of a third-party notice system and of simple foreclosure procedures may preclude it in practice (Box 5.1). In sum, although property rights are now recognized on paper and to a growing extent in practice, they are still not free from extensive arbitrary interference. All societies preserve some role for government regulation over the use of private property (for example, through environmental or nuisance laws), but many transition economies still go well beyond what is normal in market settings.

Box 5.1 No loans for movable property?

Businesses in established market economies rely on movable capital: it accounts for about half of the private nonresidential capital stock and about three-quarters of corresponding gross investment. Yet private lenders in most transition economies are reluctant to make loans when the only collateral offered is movable property held by the borrower—tractors, livestock, inventory, machinery, or, in extreme cases, cars and trucks. Rather, lenders require that the movable properties be placed under their direct control—as if they were valuables in a bank vault or goods in a bonded warehouse—or that the borrower offer other types of collateral, such as real estate. This difficulty in using movable property as collateral results in much presumably desirable investment going unfinanced. Capital formation is slowed, resulting in lower output and growth. Why is real estate or merchandise in a vault acceptable as collateral, but not livestock, machinery, and inventories? The answer lies in the process of creating, prioritizing, and enforcing security interests in movable property—the underlying contracts necessary for loans and credit sales to work.

Creation. Legal systems should ideally permit the inexpensive creation of security interests for any person over any thing. Yet many transition economies restrict the development of such interests. Bulgaria and Estonia forbid the pledging of goods not currently held by the borrower, making it difficult to finance crops and livestock. In Hungary and Poland only banks may formally lend for property that remains in the borrower's hands; this limits development of nonbank lending. Vietnam forbids the sale of pledge items, making it difficult to finance inventory.

Determining priority. For pledging to work, lenders need a cheap and easy way to determine whether a prior security interest exists against the property offered as collateral. Some advanced legal systems do this by maintaining a publicly accessible registry; others do it less formally. Lenders in transition economies, however, cannot easily determine whether such security interests exist. In Bulgaria the priority of a security interest is determined by the date it is agreed to; without a central registry, this can only be uncovered by searching through hundreds of scattered notarial records. The pledge registry in Poland is open only to banks. In China and Lithuania a security interest in movable property can only be registered if the underlying asset requires registration—fine for cars, trucks, ships, and airplanes but useless for tractors, drill presses, and grain silos. In Latvia and Poland state taxes take automatic priority over secured private claims, so private lenders without intimate knowledge of the status of a borrower's tax payments cannot know if a loan is safe.

Enforcement. In the event of nonpayment, lenders also need a quick and inexpensive way to recover and sell pledged and mortgaged assets. In transition economies the time required for repossession and sale of a pledged asset ranges from six months to three years and can extend even longer. This is too long for most collateral to retain its economic value. Inventories of food, clothing, and even machinery will depreciate so much during this period that they cannot effectively guarantee a loan. Recent Russian and Chinese laws take some promising steps to address this problem, but it is too early to tell how well they are working.

Contracts

Freedom of contract is one of the great virtues of market-oriented legal systems, providing a decentralized way of allocating resources to their best uses. Parties are free to negotiate performance requirements and prices, to allocate risks of loss if conditions change, and to specify how disputes will be handled. And during the course of the contract, if the bargain ceases to make economic sense to one party, contract law generally allows that party to withdraw and pay monetary compensation rather than continue to perform under the contract.

In centrally planned systems, by contrast, parties had no freedom either to enter into or to exit from commercial contracts. Interenterprise contracts were mere instruments of the plan, and full performance was generally required. The collapse of central planning put an end to these notions of contract, to be replaced by new, amended, or revived civil and commercial codes. Although these codes generally follow Western European norms, tendencies toward control and paternalism sometimes remain. The new Russian civil code, for example, contains several provisions aimed at controlling the activities of firms perceived as economically strong. Many of the controls arise from a legitimate desire to protect consumers and debtors who are unfamiliar with markets, in situations of unequal bargaining power and inadequate judicial protection. But they can also reflect an older tradition of trying to dictate economic relations and outcomes. In a market setting some of these controls could end up hurting the very people they are meant to protect, by constraining their freedom to allocate risk or by preventing some transactions altogether.

The impact of these new contract laws will depend on their enforcement. Most day-to-day contracts in market economies do not require formal enforcement. Both parties fulfill their legal obligations because they benefit from the transaction or because neither party is willing to risk its reputation by reneging. But an economy still needs credible, low-cost formal enforcement mechanisms to which aggrieved parties can turn when all else fails.

The shortage of institutions to enforce contracts limits the scope of transactions, makes contracting more costly, and prohibits some contracts altogether. A recent study of contracting in Bulgaria, for example, found that private firms have little confidence in the courts (although they still use them from time to time) and instead rely heavily on trust when choosing business partners. They find suppliers who ship quickly and customers who pay quickly, and work with them on a continuing basis. They are suspicious of new customers, who are carefully screened and often required to pay up front. Lack of confidence in formal enforcement mechanisms, and thus in dealings with strangers, limits firms' activities and hinders new firms

from entering the market. Long-term interfirm contracts are almost nonexistent, because such contracts are particularly difficult to police and maintain. Limits on the scope of contracting are only some of the costs of inadequate formal enforcement. A more menacing cost is the vacuum opened for more violent enforcement mechanisms—such as the mafia—that corrode trust even further, as discussed below.

Company and foreign investment law

Well-designed and well-enforced company law is essential if private companies want to tap into capital markets. In 1995 financial markets valued a typical Russian firm at only about one-twentieth of its likely value in a mature market economy. This low valuation all but prevents firms from raising new capital by issuing shares. Why are share prices so low? A survey of foreign investors suggests that one important reason is the weakness of company law as an instrument for overseeing managers and protecting shareholders, particularly minority ones.

The need for comprehensive company law emerges in full force only when large-scale private activities are fully legalized. Transition economies have typically emulated the models in established market economies, particularly the company forms and related rules found in Western Europe. Most new company codes in transition economies provide for joint-stock companies, limited-liability companies (smaller entities often limited to fifty or so investors), and limited and general partnerships. The most popular form among smaller new firms has been the simpler and more flexible limited-liability company. The more formal joint-stock company predominates among large privatized firms and publicly traded companies.

Like most of the important legal changes discussed in this chapter, the move to modern forms of company law represents a radical shift for transition country governments, from controlling to merely facilitating economic activity. Company law has to walk a fine line between two often-conflicting goals: flexibility and protection. Company owners and managers need to be as free as possible to arrange their own activities, yet the public, including investors, employees, and other stakeholders, also needs protection from insider fraud and mismanagement. Western rules regarding joint-stock companies may not give adequate protection to investors in transition economies, which lack the highly developed market, legal, and government institutions on which such rules depend (Box 5.2).

The tension between flexibility and protection is particularly problematic in transition economies. In the name of protecting investors, creditors, or the public, many countries have erected high-cost barriers to entry. Two of the most conspicuous are high minimum capital requirements and complex registration requirements. Minimum capital requirements for joint-stock companies, for example, typically range from $20,000 to $40,000 and sometimes (as in Hungary) exceed $100,000. And in Moscow, for example, it takes an average of six to eight weeks to fulfill the ten steps typically required to register a new company (not including the additional licenses required for many activities). Supposedly designed to protect the public, these requirements are burdensome for new entrants—particularly small entrepreneurs who may therefore choose to remain in the informal sector—and are obvious sources of corruption. Many could be reduced or eliminated. Fraud is indeed a crucial issue in transition environments, but these are inefficient tools to combat it. Countries should work to develop more sophisticated legal devices, such as criminal prosecutions, class action suits for

aggrieved shareholders, and doctrines that look behind the corporate veil to make individuals personally liable in cases of fraud.

Bankruptcy law
A well-designed bankruptcy law—generally including procedures for both liquidation and reorganization of problem firms—plays several important roles in market economies. It provides failing firms with an orderly means of exit. It spurs ailing but potentially viable firms to restructure. And it promotes the flow of credit by protecting creditors. Ideally, bankruptcy shifts control over financially distressed firms to their creditors before all the assets have been misused or dissipated, and it gives creditors the information and power to direct the use of the remaining assets to recover debts. Without this safeguard, creditors

---

Box 5.2 Protecting investors: Corporate law from scratch

Transition economies have weak and sometimes corrupt courts and regulators, undeveloped capital markets, and a shortage of trained lawyers and accountants. It is difficult for potential investors to get information on companies and to enforce laws against managers, who may also be large shareholders. Hence the risk of insider opportunism is high, which discourages much-needed outside investment. Transition economies need a corporate law that can work even in this setting.

Two broad Western models for protecting investors through corporate law are available. So-called prohibitive corporate laws bar many kinds of behavior that are open to abuse, such as self-dealing transactions and cash mergers. This model was followed in nineteenth-century U.S. and British codes and is to some extent followed in European codes today. By contrast, the so-called enabling corporate laws that prevail in the United Kingdom and the United States today allow companies greater freedom and depend more on market constraints and other civil and criminal laws (such as antifraud statutes) to discipline managers and protect investors. The enabling model is almost certainly unsuitable for transition economies because of the weakness of these other constraints on insider opportunism. But the prohibitive model also has its costs. Not only can its inflexibility inhibit legitimate business behavior, but strong courts or administrative agencies are needed to enforce its many rules.

An alternative approach, followed to a large extent in the new Russian companies law, is a self-enforcing corporate law. This model focuses on structural and procedural rather than substantive requirements. Its goal is to give significant minority shareholders the power to protect themselves against opportunism by controlling insiders. At the shareholder level the model focuses on voting rules. For example, it puts more types of decisions up for shareholder approval, and it requires supermajority approval for important business decisions such as mergers or major sales of assets. At the governing level the model requires that a certain proportion of directors be independent, and it gives "disinterested" directors (those without a direct stake) sole power to approve certain types of transactions, such as those between related parties. It mandates "cumulative voting" for directors, a rule that ensures that large minority shareholders are represented on the board. By imposing these and other procedural requirements, the self-enforcing model tries to create self-policing mechanisms and to reduce reliance on courts and administrative agencies for enforcement.

Of course, the self-enforcing model also works better when judicial enforcement mechanisms can serve as a backdrop. But even without official enforcement, the introduction of procedural safeguards may slowly change norms of behavior as more and more companies adopt them to develop a good reputation for honest behavior, to emulate their peers, or simply because they are available and reasonable. No one knows whether this model will succeed in Russia or elsewhere, but it stands out as a pragmatic attempt to tailor long-term institutional reforms to the limitations of the transition environment.

will either refuse to make loans or turn to the state for support when loans turn bad. Bankruptcy is an important complement to—not a substitute for—disciplined macroeconomic policies and privatization.

Many transition economies have adopted new bankruptcy laws. Those in Bulgaria, Estonia, Hungary, and Slovenia are among the best designed. They provide, for example, clear criteria for determining insolvency and delineating claims, efficiency-enhancing priority rules (most important, giving preference to secured creditors over government claims), broad scope for debt forgiveness and workable voting rules (generally requiring one-half to two-thirds majorities to bind dissenting minorities) if creditors want to reorganize the firm, and flexibility as to the method of asset sale in cases of liquidation.

Design is only half the issue, however; bankruptcy laws are not yet effectively enforced in any transition economy. Hungary perhaps comes the closest (see Box 3.1), although creditor involvement remains inadequate to ensure efficient economic outcomes and guard against fraud. In some countries, such as the Czech and Slovak Republics, the government has deliberately slowed the implementation of bankruptcy law, and the number of cases (although increasing rapidly) is still relatively small. In others, such as Albania, Bulgaria, and Romania, laws are of recent vintage, and it remains uncertain whether creditors will have the incentive to use them effectively. Finally, China and most NIS (other than the Baltics) have not yet implemented a package of reforms, including subsidy reductions, privatization, and banking reforms, that will force hard budget constraints on creditors (whether banks or firms) and thereby create the widespread demand that brings bankruptcy laws to life.

Competition law

As discussed in Chapter 3, transition economies, particularly in CEE and the NIS, inherited an industrial structure with many monopolistic or oligopolistic firms, dominant state ownership, and a strong tradition of state control. Many governments continue to erect barriers to trade, whether through tariffs and quotas on imports, taxes on exports, or local government curbs on products entering other provinces. These anticompetitive legacies and practices need to be dismantled if markets are to function effectively. Experience in CEE confirms that reducing tariffs and removing other trade barriers can go a long way toward promoting competition, particularly in small countries, by imposing world prices (adjusted for transport costs) as an effective ceiling on domestic prices. Improving market infrastructure, both physical facilities and services, is also critical.

But these efforts need to be complemented by regulation of natural monopolies and by antimonopoly law to ensure efficiency and protect the public from the abuse of monopoly power. Both are difficult areas and further examples of the tension between the need for a strong state and the need for constraints on state power. Some transition economies, in their push to free up markets, have underestimated the need for active government involvement. Others have maintained overzealous and anticompetitive controls.

The case for regulation is not always clear-cut; electric power generation, for example, and natural gas production are potentially competitive, although the distribution side of both industries is a true natural monopoly (in which a single firm most efficiently supplies the market). In cases of natural monopoly, governments need to develop clear and effective regulation that is stable over time. This is especially important when countries want to exploit new opportunities for private sector involvement in infrastructure industries (see Box 3.6). To be credible, natural monopoly regulators must be independent, operating at arm's length from the regulated firm, other government agencies, and other vested interests. They must guard against both "capture" by the regulated firm and popular and political pressures to let prices fall below cost. Some transition economies, such as Ukraine and Albania, are already setting up autonomous regulatory bodies (in electric power and other industries) similar to models in the United States, the United Kingdom, and Latin America. Central European regulators in telecommunications—another industry that tends toward monopoly—are less independent, and formal tariff authority and other regulatory powers remain largely with ministers.

The CEE and Baltic countries, Kazakstan, Mongolia, and Russia have adopted antimonopoly laws that generally follow Western European models (in most cases to reflect the harmonization requirements of the European Union). These laws typically restrict horizontal and vertical restraints on trade and the abuse of a "dominant" market position (usually defined as 30 to 40 percent of the relevant market and the unilateral ability to restrict competition). Horizontal restraints are agreements among competitors to fix prices or divide markets; vertical restraints include a wide range of restrictive agreements between producers and distributors. These laws also empower the government to block anticompetitive mergers and in some cases to break up monopolies.

The European Union and several member and nonmember countries (particularly Germany, the United Kingdom, and the United States) have played important roles in helping design these competition laws, pushing for their adoption, and training staff for and otherwise assisting antimonopoly offices. Because transition economies inherited such a legacy of state dominance and are short on administrative capacity, however, antimonopoly offices face somewhat different priorities than their EU and U.S. counterparts. They must focus their scarce resources on big issues and big problems, becoming first and foremost strong and vocal advocates of competition and free trade. Of the offices established so far, those in Central Europe (most notably Poland and the Czech and Slovak Republics) have been among the most forceful and effective, although even their voices are sometimes difficult to hear. Offices also need to concentrate on dismantling regulatory and other barriers to the entry of new firms, because entry is a key source of competition in these economies. For example, exclusive supply or distribution agreements imposed by dominant firms may act as barriers to entry and may be challenged under competition laws. The Ukrainian antimonopoly office, established in 1994, has devoted much attention to preserving a level playing field for new firms by combating discrimination against them, particularly by state actors. With regard to horizontal restraints, offices should combat overt price fixing (and similar cartel agreements) among big producers and address structural concerns by maintaining veto power over anticompetitive mergers and by breaking up the most egregious state-owned monopolies before or during privatization. The Czech and Slovak antimonopoly offices, for example, have focused on dismantling monopolies prior to privatization. Russia could be more aggressive in confronting monopolistic structures, including some of the emerging financial-industrial groups.

Judicial institutions

As this chapter has stressed throughout, laws are only as good as the institutions that enforce them. And it is competent and reliable courts and specialized enforcement agencies such as securities commissions and antimonopoly offices that provide the foundation on which all enforcement activity—formal or informal—ultimately depends. Courts not only enforce laws and resolve disputes; their interpretations also fill in the many inevitable gaps in legislation. CEE and the NIS have followed different paths in re-creating judicial institutions for dispute resolution and enforcement. In most of the NIS the state arbitration system that used to mediate disputes between state enterprises was transformed into a formal court system— the *arbitrazh* courts—to supplement existing civil courts. In CEE, by contrast, the arbitration system was abolished, and civil courts were expanded to include separate commercial sections. Although the latter might be the better approach if it fosters more unified standards and a more professional judiciary, either route can work given the right incentives, training, and experience. The notorious powers of the pretransition "procuracy" to supervise courts and intervene in individual decisions has been reduced, and in CEE the procuracy has been transformed into an institution more akin to a Western public prosecutor's office. Most transition economies have also tried to reform appointment and oversight mechanisms and

give courts more independence by appointing judges for life. China, the Kyrgyz Republic, and Ukraine are among the few countries that maintain elections and shorter terms for judges. Private arbitration, always used in international trade disputes, is now also allowed for domestic disputes in most transition economies. This is extremely important because it can save scarce judicial resources by privatizing dispute resolution and can provide helpful competition to spur court reform.

Despite these important reforms, courts in transition economies will need time to overcome the legacies of the past and regain public confidence. Judges, particularly in the NIS, have limited experience with markets, earn low salaries, and as a profession enjoy little prestige or public trust. Clear notions of professional ethics are not yet well developed. Court fees are high and waits can be long. The newness and lack of clarity of many laws make for unpredictable decisions. And even when judgments have been reached, the winners can find them difficult to enforce. In Vietnam, for example, fewer than 40 percent of court rulings in 1993 and 1994 were actually enforced, and up to half the judgments of Russian courts go unenforced. These factors, combined with engrained cultural attitudes toward the law, help to explain why so few private businesses want to use the courts to settle disputes, particularly in the NIS and East Asia.

The private legal profession is another institution that must develop if people are to become familiar with the law and use it effectively. As markets grow and law becomes more complex, societies need independent lawyers to counsel clients, structure and formalize transactions, and help resolve disputes. In centrally planned economies lawyers were employees of the state. Their role in the commercial sphere was primarily administrative, and they had little independence and few of the skills needed in a market economy. Transition has brought a dramatic rise in the number of lawyers and the training opportunities open to them. In China, for example, the number of licensed lawyers rose from only 3,000 over the entire 1957–80 period to more than 60,000 in 1995. Law school enrollments today exceed 30,000, and the government has announced a target of 150,000 lawyers by 2000. But standards of competence and professional ethics will take longer to develop and enforce. Many transition economies are beginning to require bar examinations, but the recognition of conflicts of interest—and other ethical dilemmas—is still in its infancy.

Increasing the level of trust in the state

Defining and enforcing the laws governing private sector activity require a strong and competent state. Yet well-functioning markets also need a clear sense of where the state's role ends. The government must itself be ruled by law and trusted by private entities not to intervene arbitrarily in their affairs, to follow its announced policy statements, and to deliver on its obligations. Recent cross-country research suggests that citizens' level of trust in government to carry out its declared policies and to meet its obligations is positively associated with long-term economic growth (Figure 5.1). Separate surveys of private firms in 1995 suggest that the Czech Republic has achieved a high level of government credibility, whereas in Russia credibility is much lower. Countries with levels of credibility as different as in these two countries typically have widely differing economic growth rates. Trust in government depends partly on citizens knowing that they can seek recourse against arbitrary or illegal state acts, on limits on official corruption, and on the state's ability to control crime.

Constraining state power

Formal constraints on arbitrary state power in established market economies derive partly from constitutional and administrative law. These bodies of law ensure that all legislation is consistent with the national constitution and that regulations, in turn, are consistent with the law. They delineate the rulemaking authority of various state bodies, lay out the procedures for enacting laws and promulgating regulations, and provide individuals recourse against unlawful or capricious state action. Of course, these formal constraints are not created in a vacuum but are spurred by deep historical, cultural, and political forces. Unsurprisingly, there were very few legal or social constraints on state power in centrally planned systems. Sev-

Government credibility and faster growth usually go together.

Figure 5.1 Economic growth per capita and government credibility

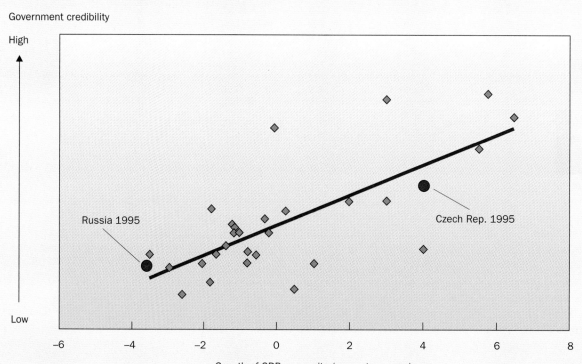

Note: The sample consists of twenty-eight economies plus Czech Republic and Russia. Growth data are annual averages for 1981–90, and data on government credibility are based on public opinion surveys taken in late 1992 (which included retrospective questions), except that data for Czech Republic and Russia are for 1995 on both measures. Source: Borner, Brunetti, and Weder 1994; World Bank data.

eral planned economies did establish administrative courts or empower regular courts with administrative oversight, beginning with Yugoslavia in 1952 and followed by other CEE countries in the 1960s and 1970s and eventually the Soviet Union (1987) and China (1989). But their power was tightly circumscribed, and the reforms had little practical impact.

Democratic reforms have led many transition economies to broaden the scope of judicial review to cover all administrative acts and to give civil or commercial courts clear oversight jurisdiction. In addition, all CEE countries and some NIS have established constitutional courts with the power to overturn laws and regulations that they find unconstitutional. Thus, the procedural means to oversee state actions is beginning to emerge. There is still, however, profound confusion about the division of authority among various state actors, particularly in the NIS. The distinction between the legislative authority of the parliament and the rulemaking authority of the executive is vague at best, as is the allocation of authority among national, provincial, and local governments. Different state bodies often issue laws or regulations on the same topics, producing a quagmire of conflicting rules. This struggle for rulemaking power often reflects a deep struggle over the speed and direction of reform. For example, reform-minded executives or ministries often try to push through reforms against defensive or undecided parliaments or local governments. Although this may speed reform in the short run, in the long run it could undermine the rule of law.

The emerging role of constitutional courts in transition economies offers an interesting example of the struggle to establish checks and balances in government and their interaction with economic reform. Hungary's and Poland's constitutional courts have been active in overturning economic reform initiatives. In Poland, for example, the court invalidated most of the government's efforts to cut public spending on pensions. The Hungarian court struck down provisions of the government's March 1995 stabilization package aimed at cutting spending on family allowances and education. This tension between competing authorities may slow some necessary economic adjustment, but it is a healthy indicator of democracy and is likely to ease through continued political debate and legal development.

Controlling corruption

The use of public office for private gain is hardly new to transition economies. Before reform, items as important as housing and as trivial as choice cuts of meat were often allocated through the back door in exchange for favors or bribes. Transition-style corruption, however, is different: it is more visible and more money-based. Corruption has emerged as a major concern in China. And most busi-

nesses in Lithuania, Russia, and Ukraine (to cite just three examples) acknowledge paying fees to various officials as well as to organized crime. These bribes are large by international standards: in Ukraine, for example, they can represent up to two months' gross sales per year. Some officials have used their positions to give special privileges to private businesses in which they have personal stakes. In many transition economies the public's perception of widespread corruption—including the misappropriation of public property—is undermining support for governments and for reform.

Why is corruption thriving? Evidence from other countries shows that corruption thrives when both public officials and private agents have much to gain and little to lose, precisely the situation in most transition settings. Traditional controls weaken before new legal restraints—not least, rules regarding conflicts of interest—become effective. In addition, the state retains enormous wealth—enterprises, properties, natural resources—and regulatory power, even as private property, business, and wealth are being legitimized. Uncertain rules, heavy regulation, and pervasive controls give officials exceptional power, many opportunities to seek bribes, and wide scope for appropriating public wealth. The weakness of civil society—political parties, interest groups, social organizations, and the like—in some transition environments means that this important countervailing force is largely absent.

The low official pay of public servants makes corruption particularly enticing. Indeed, in some countries it now represents the main incentive to remain in public service. Despite periodic anticorruption efforts, the risks of engaging in corrupt behavior have fallen dramatically. Not only is government oversight weak, but the legacy of personalized economic relationships and more recently of financial scandals undermine standards for official and private conduct alike. It is hard to punish one person for misconduct if the public perceives that everyone else—including high officials—is doing the same thing. This raises the danger that transition economies may experience an extended period of pervasive corruption.

Corruption is by no means costless. Recent cross-country analysis suggests a significant association with both lower private investment and slower economic growth. Bribes may help businesses avoid burdensome regulations, but they also create incentives to make regulations even more complex and costly. Officials may block further reforms to entrench their power and maintain their illicit income. State enterprise managers may realize that they can purchase or divert enterprise assets cheaply if they delay privatization and make their companies underperform. Corruption can divert public resources away from vital areas, such as education, where the potential for bribes is smaller. It also undercuts governments' ability to enforce legitimate regulations and collect public revenues, as activities shift into the shadow economy to avoid government altogether. Equally serious, corruption weakens public confidence in government and can help extremist politicians who promise order.

What can governments do to combat corruption? Having made the move to the market, they cannot turn back the clock and resurrect the old constraints. Instead, they must both reduce the opportunities for corruption and raise the attendant risks. Rapid and transparent privatization, liberalization, and demonopolization of the economy can do much to reduce the scope for corruption and restructure incentives. Higher salaries for public officials reduce the attraction of bribes and raise the cost of dismissal. Simplifying taxes and regulations—the most important concern, for example, of businesses surveyed in Lithuania—and clarifying property rights reduce opportunities for bribery and help firms survive without resorting to corruption. Where regulations are still needed, governments must strengthen oversight and appeal mechanisms and, where possible, provide alternative proce-

dures so as to reduce the monopoly power of officials in granting approvals. Finally, public education campaigns and serious attempts to publicize and punish high-level corruption can send a message that the rules of the game are changing. These approaches reinforce one another, as many countries, including the United States (Box 5.3), have found.

Stopping organized crime

Private organized crime antedated transition but has grown dramatically in recent years. It has become both more visible and, especially in Russia (where it ranks as a main concern in both household and business surveys), more violent. Crime is closely intertwined with corruption. With a private economy opening new avenues for private criminality, current and former public officials (including police officers and former secret police agents) often facilitate or participate in organized crime. Private security groups—including groups that are themselves criminal—have arisen in part to fill the void left by corrupt police or courts that are unable or unwilling to pro-

---

Box 5.3 Controlling corruption through overlapping jurisdictions: Examples from the United States

Corruption exists in all countries, albeit to different extents. How governments organize their activities affects the opportunities and incentives for corruption. One way to reduce the monopoly power of public officials is to give them overlapping domains. Corruption in passport issuance is kept low in the United States, for example, by letting people apply at any of numerous passport offices. (A national system of records prevents repeat issuance.) To avoid the payment of bribes for expedited service, the passport agency itself sells such a service. For tasks that impose costs instead of benefits, overlapping jurisdictions can reduce the gains from bribing any one official. For example, some observers claim that the coexistence of federal, state, and local narcotics enforcement authorities in the United States has reduced the level of official corruption.

Where possible, it helps to decriminalize or deregulate an activity that is a major source of crime and corruption. The Eighteenth Amendment to the U.S. Constitution, ratified in 1919, prohibited the manufacture and sale of alcohol. The amendment was repealed in 1933 after a period of widespread illegal activity and corruption of law enforcement officials. The U.S. experiment with prohibition is a case study of the risks and costs of introducing regulatory and

legal regimes that lack legitimacy in the eyes of a large segment of the public.

Even after all feasible structural and regulatory reforms have been implemented, strong leadership and law enforcement capacity are needed to fight corruption. The experience with reform in major U.S. cities as diverse as Toledo, Ohio, in 1900 and New York City in the 1980s shows the importance of a committed leader at the top, strong independent inspectors to pursue investigations and prosecutions, and grassroots citizen involvement. In New York, for example, widespread corruption and racketeering in the construction industry imposed billions of dollars in costs on the school system through waste and poor-quality construction and maintenance. In 1988 the city created an Office of Inspector General as a quasi-independent body within the school district with the power to pursue criminal investigations, civil prosecutions, administrative sanctions, and institutional reform. The office put heavy emphasis on prequalifying bidders and refused to do business with any company that lacked a reputation for honesty and integrity. In its first five years the office conducted more than 3,500 investigations, debarred 180 firms, and generated more than $20 million in savings, paying for itself and reducing corruption at the same time.

tect public safety and enforce contracts. Like corruption, economic crime thrives when property rights are poorly defined, when monopolies exist that mafias can tap, and when legal procedures are ineffective and thus the risk of punishment is low. It also thrives when widespread poverty and lack of economic opportunity leave potential young recruits susceptible to the lure of mafia wealth. New financial sectors offer a fruitful arena for crime, and in many NIS and CEE countries crime has been further spurred by the lucrative rewards of drug trafficking. The region is well located to be a conduit for drug transport between poppy-growing regions in South Asia (particularly Afghanistan) and markets in Western Europe.

Russia's mafia is not a single organization but a collection of perhaps 3,000 to 4,000 groups employing more than 25,000 people; several hundred of these groups now span the NIS and CEE and sometimes reach into the West. Some fill market gaps created by inadequate government institutions, providing security services for new private businesses or helping to enforce contracts (for example by collecting debts for banks, a significant number of which maintain close links with organized crime). But the value of these services is dwarfed by the sums these powerful criminal groups extort from private businesses. They force "loans" out of banks, demand protection money from new firms, and use banks and other businesses to gain access to wealthy clients. They disseminate counterfeit money and launder illicit income. Like their Sicilian namesakes, they adopt ruthless enforcement methods, as shown by the numerous murders of leading Russian bankers and businesspeople in recent years. And these are only the visible costs. What cannot be seen are the investments forgone for fear of extortion and the legitimate businesses that have failed because they could not compete with mafia-run enterprises.

Both corruption and organized crime are deep, long-term problems without easy solutions, particularly given the scale on which they are now emerging in some transition economies. Strong and internationally coordinated law enforcement efforts are needed. These in turn require an efficient and law-abiding security apparatus and dispute resolution mechanisms that ensure due process. Governments at both the national and the local level must therefore tackle internal corruption if they hope to control organized crime. Italy's recent success in combating the Sicilian mafia shows that dedicated, honest prosecutors and judges can make inroads against corruption and organized crime, but only if given strong political and logistical support from the top levels of government.

The agenda

It is a hard fact of transition that the features of a market economy that many of these countries need most are the very ones that will take the longest to build. As this chapter has emphasized, moving from plan to market requires a new way of thinking about the entire legal system. Partners to contracts, the lawyers who help draft them, and the courts that enforce them all must stop behaving as if they were still the instruments of a single central planner, and start working in the interests of the countless private individuals whose activities make up a market. People have to know—and respect—the law and the institutions charged with enforcing it. Just as important, they must have some faith that the government will apply the law consistently and will itself abide by certain constraints, refraining from arbitrary intervention and corruption. None of these ingredients will spring up overnight. But the message is not necessarily to proceed slowly toward a market economy, to allow these institutions and laws to develop at their own pace. Many of the countries now without an adequate rule of law are already market economies; governments cannot reassert control through the old mechanisms but must instead develop new policies and institutions to suit a new relationship between state and citizens. And as noted above, many market reforms—such as liberalization and demonopolization of industry—can actually speed the development of the rule of law, both by fueling demand for new laws and, just as important, by reducing the number and influence of groups who profit from their absence.

CHAPTER 6

Building a Financial System

Markets spur economic efficiency by allocating resources to their best uses, in response to supply and demand. A good system of financial markets and institutions is integral to this process, allocating savings to high-return investments. Worldwide experience confirms that countries with well-developed financial systems grow faster and more consistently than those with weaker systems and are better able to adjust to economic shocks. Transition implies vast reallocations of resources and ownership, a task at which effective financial systems could help enormously. Yet financial systems in transition economies start out in no fit state to help, with passive state-owned banks, often distressed, with limited capacity to assess credit risk, and an absence of financial regulation, key supporting institutions, and capital markets.

Reformers seeking to address these failings face a particularly thorny version of a common transition problem. The success of other market reforms depends on the health of the financial system; yet efforts to reform it cannot proceed independently of those other reforms, especially macroeconomic stabilization, enterprise reform, and the development of supporting legal institutions. Often transition countries respond to this dilemma with inaction, with the result that financial reforms lag behind.

The challenge for reformers is to find ways to help the financial system overcome the legacy of central planning, while at the same time sowing the seeds of a new system in which banks and other financial institutions will have to stand on their own two feet. The choice of approaches to banking reform brings this problem into stark relief. Should reformers use government funds to rehabilitate heavily overindebted state banks, and run the risk of their always coming to expect government bailouts? Or should reformers start afresh, encouraging the rapid entry of new banks and possibly the liquidation of old ones? Experience in transition economies to date provides evidence with which to assess both strategies and draw some tentative

lessons for future reform. Whichever approach—or combination of the two—countries follow, one clear lesson is that governments have a vital role in promoting the development of a stable financial sector and regulating it over time. That role does not necessarily extend to the direct allocation of financial resources, even though governments in transition economies can face strong pressure to intervene, particularly in the rural sector. Another lesson is that developing a financial system takes time. Reform must seek ways to nurture a system of banks, nonbank intermediaries, and capital markets that will evolve not in response to government dictate but to the changing needs of the market.

The legacy

Under central planning, banks were mere accounting agencies, passively taking in household deposits (which were often the only asset households could hold) and keeping track of the financial transactions that corresponded to allocations under the plan. Indeed, in China the credit plan still covers a large part of investment and remains an important lever of government policy. Normal banking skills, including risk management, project screening and selection, and a diversified menu of instruments to attract savers, were unknown. The other components of a financial system—including the payments system itself—were rudimentary; in most countries nonbank finance simply did not exist. Initially, one bank performed all lending. Early attempts at market reform in most countries replaced this monobank with a two-tiered system, comprising one central bank and a number of commercial banks, often specialized by sector. But this reorganization had little effect on banks' behavior.

Transition has shown up the tremendous weaknesses of the inherited banks. In CEE and the NIS many bank loans turned bad, as their traditional clients, the state enterprises, were exposed to competition. During the early stages of reform many banks continued to extend new loans to unprofitable enterprises. Unpaid interest and principal were rolled over, increasing dramatically the banks' stock of nonperforming loans—which sometimes amounted to most of their portfolios—and crowding out good borrowers. Even in China, where economic growth has been rapid and lending rates are below inflation, 20 percent of loans are officially recognized as nonperforming. Eventually these financial flows from banks to enterprises dried up, as stabilization took hold in almost all CEE countries and many NIS. In some countries high real lending rates caused net transfers (net new lending minus real interest payments) from enterprises to banks, instead of vice versa. In many NIS the flow of resources to enterprises simply stagnated: old loans continued to be rolled over but few new ones were made, so that net transfers in either direction were small. In China, by contrast, high household savings deposited with the banks have allowed substantial net transfers to enterprises to continue (see Chapter 2).

Many banks in CEE and the NIS currently limit their role to financing trade and some working capital, making negative contributions, or none, to enterprises' aggregate investment. The near-universal reluctance to lend for investment reflects in part the strains of stabilization, but also the banks' increased perception of both the risk of lending and the absence of effective means of recovering debts. Although bank lending has started to rebound and maturities have lengthened in some of the more advanced reformers, in most countries good firms have little access to bank financing, and that at very short maturities. The privileged access to financing that large state enterprises in many countries continue to enjoy is yet another financial barrier to the emergence of new private firms.

As already noted, the evolution of financial systems has also been heavily affected by the pace of legal and enterprise reforms. Banks rely on the legal system, including procedures for collateral recovery and bankruptcy, to enforce their claims and perform their role as monitors of firms. Capital markets require company laws to define the rights of shareholders of joint-stock and limited-liability enterprises and allow them to exert their influence on management. More progress in these and other economic laws is needed to make financial systems more effective (Chapter 5). Enterprise reform, including privatization and the entry of new private firms, is needed to resolve the bad loan problem and create new lending opportunities. Better firms also generate demand for better banking services and so advance institutional progress. Demand forces are strong in CEE and some NIS and have led to considerable improvements in the quality of banks. China's limited state enterprise reform, on the other hand, has delayed commercialization of its state banks. In the Baltics and the NIS, state enterprises have established

new or acquired parts of old banks. This carries risks, but governance of these banks has tended to improve with the privatization of the parent enterprises, greater diversification of ownership, and the introduction of prudential controls to limit lending to owners.

Approaches to banking reform

Transition countries have two main tasks in approaching banking reform. The first is for each country to develop its central bank into an institution that independently formulates and conducts monetary policy. Evidence from transition economies confirms the worldwide finding that greater central bank independence, including the right not to finance the government and to set interest rates without government interference, is associated with lower inflation and more effective monetary policy. All transition economies have established basic instruments and procedures of monetary policy, although their effectiveness varies across countries, in part because interbank payments systems are often still poorly developed. Building them up is essential to creating a market-based financial system. Central banks have often also played a constructive role in formulating general macroeconomic and fiscal policies. In China, however, more reforms will be needed to make the central bank an effective player in monetary and supervisory policy.

A much larger and more complicated task is to address the weaknesses of the commercial banks. Responding both to initial conditions and to developments early in transition, countries' approaches to banking reform have been based on either entry of new banks, rehabilitation of existing banks, or (usually) some combination of the two. Some countries, however, have yet to choose a consistent financial reform strategy. The new entry approach involves the entry of a relatively large number of new banks, the breakup and privatization of state banks, and in some cases the liquidation of old banks. Estonia and Russia have both taken this path, although not always as a strictly deliberate policy choice. In many of the NIS, the confusion surrounding the breakup of the Soviet Union created an environment in which many new banks emerged spontaneously (Box 6.1). The alternative, rehabilitation approach, adopted by Hungary and Poland among others, stresses recapitalization of existing banks, together with extensive programs to develop them institutionally and to privatize them as soon as possible.

Two factors largely determine each country's approach to banking reform: the depth of the financial system (the ratio of financial liabilities to GDP) and the institutional legacy. During the late 1980s, financial depth was similar across the transition economies. But their different experiences with inflation—and the collapse in confidence in financial assets in the high-inflation countries—have since caused an equally wide divergence. Money holdings

Box 6.1 Russia's radical banking reform

Following the creation of a two-tier banking system in 1987, Russia's approach to banking reform rapidly—and partly unintentionally—diverged from that of other transition economies. In 1988 a new law permitted the creation of cooperative banks to serve the nascent private sector. Establishment of joint-stock banks became possible with the 1990 banking law, with licensing subject to only minimal requirements. Competition between a reformist Russian government and a more conservative Soviet government led to a separation of Russian banks from Soviet banks and, in Russia, to the breakup of several state banks into independent regional banks. Together these events fueled an explosion in the number of Russian banks: from 5 in 1989 to 1,500 in 1992 and 2,500 in 1995.

Macroeconomic developments during this period created a competitive advantage for these new banks over the old state banks. Lack of fiscal and monetary control led to rampant inflation, and loan balances soon shrank to only a few weeks of production. This provided the new banks with an opportunity to gain market share quickly by providing higher-quality banking services to the newly emerging private sector. The voucher privatization program provided another new business opportunity, as many banks invested in enterprises directly or lent to other investors buying shares. As a result the share of the new banks in total banking system assets has risen sharply, to more than two-thirds as of early 1996, with the three remaining state banks holding the rest. Some of the larger new banks have rapidly become the country's leading commercial banks, with balance sheets of $1 billion to $3 billion. They move quickly into new business lines and

financial products, and quite a few are at the center of emerging financial-industrial conglomerates.

The banking industry's main problems are the large number of poorly capitalized and badly managed banks and an associated severe lack of transparency. As stabilization has taken hold in Russia, the environment for banking has become more difficult. A third of Russia's banks reported losses in 1995, almost immediately after real interest rates turned positive. Although Russia has started to address its bad banks problem by withdrawing licenses and restricting operations, many troubled banks remain. The authorities will need to deal with these banks quickly, in many cases through liquidation, to restore confidence and prevent a major crisis, and to allow resources to be intermediated by the better banks instead.

Increased transparency is another must. Accounting and disclosure standards are still rudimentary, a well-developed auditing profession does not yet exist, and banking supervision remains embryonic. These limitations open the door to fraud and imprudent investment and undermine confidence in the financial system. To address this problem the Russian government, with assistance from the World Bank and the European Bank for Reconstruction and Development (EBRD), has introduced an international banking standards project. Some of the best banks have been selected to on-lend World Bank and EBRD funds to the private sector. In return, the banks must submit to annual audits by international accounting firms and adhere to prudential norms with respect to capital adequacy, portfolio diversification, asset and liability management, and so on. It is estimated that some twenty to forty banks will eventually participate in this bottom-up approach to banking reform.

---

presently equal 89 percent of GDP in China but average only 42 percent in CEE countries and a mere 20 percent in the NIS (Figure 6.1). With inflation having wiped out bad loans and savings, leaving depositors with little confidence in the financial system, most NIS countries have little to lose by starting afresh. Countries in CEE started out with stronger institutional bases than did the NIS or the East Asian transition economies. This advantage, together with their deeper financial systems and generally better fiscal positions, led most CEE countries to opt for a more phased approach. China's very deep financial system has prompted its government to choose a phased approach for its banking reforms, even though banking skills are relatively undeveloped.

Financial reform with a stress on entry, including entry by foreign banks, can be a good approach for less advanced

countries. Comparison of countries according to the institutional capacity of the better segment of their banks shows that, while the reformers with more entry generally had much worse starting conditions, some have now caught up with the other countries. Progress has been particularly rapid in Estonia and Russia, despite an unfavorable starting point. A period of relatively free entry can thus stimulate decentralized institution building. But confidence can be undermined while the sector undergoes convulsive restructuring and as poor-quality banks spring up. Complementary policies are therefore needed to better screen new bank applicants, to weed out weak banks, and to improve the infrastructure for banking, including through enterprise and legal reform.

The rehabilitation approach has the advantage that it maintains a higher degree of confidence in the financial

Banking systems in transition economies vary greatly in size.

Figure 6.1 Money in circulation

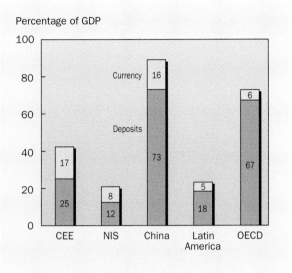

Percentage of GDP

Note: Regional and group data are simple averages of quarterly ratios for 1994 for ten CEE countries, thirteen NIS, twelve Latin American countries, and eighteen OECD countries. Source: IMF and World Bank staff estimates.

system and thus limits financial disintermediation (the tendency for financial transactions to bypass the banking system altogether). The downside is that it maintains a large role for existing state banks. Rehabilitation can also severely undermine banks' incentives to adopt prudent investment criteria, by fostering the expectation that, having bailed out troubled banks once, governments will do so again. In Hungary, for example, some banks have been recapitalized as many as five times. Thus, like the entry approach, a consistent rehabilitation policy requires a good many complementary reforms. These should focus on improving the interim governance of state banks, ensuring a strong commitment to privatization, and, perhaps, imposing certain restrictions on the state banks' activities. Poland started out with just such an approach (Box 6.2), although the privatization side of the program has slowed recently.

Where government should lead . . .

As we have seen, initial conditions are an important consideration in striking the balance between an entry and a rehabilitation approach to banking reform. Some coun-

tries may adopt a mixed strategy, limiting the activities of state banks while a new, private sector banking system develops in parallel. Whichever approach is followed, the crucial factor is the incentives it creates, and these depend significantly on government policies and how they are perceived. Experience to date yields several policy lessons.

Deal with problem banks quickly
Transition creates a difficult banking environment in which sizable loan losses are unavoidable, especially when

---

Box 6.2 Poland's rehabilitation approach to banking reform

Poland's commercial banking reforms accelerated after 1990. In 1991 the government advised its banks not to make new loans to enterprises that were in arrears on past loans; that restriction became law with the passage of the Enterprise and Bank Restructuring Program in February 1993. The Ministry of Finance required regular audits of all banks according to international standards, thus encouraging transparency and exposing the magnitude of the bad loan problem. The restructuring program further required banks to set up debt workout units and take actions to resolve loans that had been classified as nonperforming at the end of 1991. The program also provided for a new bank-led workout process (see Box 3.1).

Indirect incentives were also used. In 1992 bank employees were given the opportunity to purchase up to 20 percent of their bank's shares at half-price upon privatization. This strengthened incentives to adopt prudent policies with respect to both the workout of existing loans and new lending. Seven banks entered into intensive technical assistance programs with foreign banks to accelerate their institutional development. Experience in Poland and other countries shows that such technical assistance can be a valuable complement to a bank's desire for institutional change but is no substitute for a clear, commercially viable strategy on the part of owners and managers.

Bank recapitalization was implemented in September 1993. The aim was to determine the amount of the recapitalization on the basis of loans that were nonperforming at the end of 1991. This was intended to avoid penalizing banks that had already taken action to deal with their problems, and to maintain incentives for managers to try to keep other loans in their portfolios performing. The program was accompanied by a plan for privatization of the nine treasury-owned commercial banks.

real interest rates rise and firms have trouble servicing their loans. Unless governments act decisively, many transition economies can expect major financial crises to originate from troubled banks and from spillovers of problems at other financial intermediaries. Resolving financially distressed institutions requires three steps. First, financial flows to insolvent banks, whether from the government or from deposits attracted by high interest rates, must be stopped. Too often, troubled banks continue to receive normal or even preferential treatment. In Poland, for example, two state-owned banks specializing in housing and rural finance have poor performance records yet are covered by higher explicit deposit insurance than other banks, allowing them to attract funds at relatively low cost. Second, management, often a primary source of the problem, must almost always be changed. Third, to reduce incentives for excessive risk taking, private shareholders should completely lose their stakes in liquidated or restructured banks. Depositors may also have to bear part of the losses. Countries that have moved decisively in this way have incurred lower costs and restored household confidence faster, even when households have suffered some losses, and have had fewer subsequent problem banks. Estonia approached these problems forcefully in late 1992, and Croatia, Kazakstan, the Kyrgyz Republic, and FYR Macedonia are taking steps to liquidate or drastically restructure weak banks. Many other transition economies, however, still have to come to grips with their problem banks, often because the authority to intervene is missing, or because ad hoc and often damaging forms of intervention are attempted.

Develop effective supervision, screen new entry, and improve disclosure

All transition countries need improved prudential regulation and supervision of commercial banks and other financial intermediaries, including financial-industrial groups and investment funds. Establishing such mechanisms demands a fully independent and market-oriented supervisory agency. Every transition economy now has a supervisory structure in place, either as a part of the central bank or as a self-standing body, and has issued laws and regulations aimed at improving the functioning of the financial system. Much less progress, however, has been made in translating these reforms into effective regulation and supervision. It takes time to train bank examiners and for them to acquire adequate experience; therefore supervision is likely to remain weak in many transition countries for an extended period and will not be able to prevent every banking failure. Supervisors should focus their limited resources on addressing problem banks and nonbanks, screening entrants, and improving incentives for banks to adopt prudent practices.

Countries that allow relatively free entry of domestic banks have benefited from increased competition and fast institutional progress; for many, a period of market-driven consolidation of banks and closure of weak banks should reinforce this progress. But these countries also need to introduce high minimum capital requirements, checks on the suitability and integrity of owners and managers, and other formal guidelines to keep out applicants with poor prospects or fraudulent ventures. Even then, supervision will prevent only a few cases of fraud—a cause of many financial crises—and supervisors may lack the political support to intervene. Many warning signals were ignored, for example, prior to the fraud-induced failures of some large banks in the Baltics. Banks also need incentives to act prudently in the absence of adequate supervision. Greater transparency, through better disclosure of bank balance sheets and profitability, will help by allowing depositors, other investors, and bank supervisors to better assess banks' quality. In most transition economies accounting and information disclosure standards for banks—and other enterprises—are far below those in market economies. Supervisors and international agencies need to set mandatory standards, especially on improved classification of nonperforming loans and more realistic provisioning for losses, and require annual audits.

Beware of recapitalizing banks

Large numbers of nonperforming loans and undercapitalized banks can undermine macroeconomic stability, lead to high interest rates, and forestall a decentralized, case-by-case restructuring of enterprises. Some observers have argued for early, comprehensive loan forgiveness to make a clean break with the past. Canceling the nonperforming debt of state enterprises to state banks has no impact on either national or government wealth, or on bank profits or fiscal revenues, but it raises a serious danger that money-losing firms will fail to restructure once freed from the burden of servicing their old loans, and it sends a perverse signal to other borrowers. No country has simply forgiven debts across the board, and in those that forgave debt on a large scale (such as Bulgaria and Romania) unprofitable enterprises continued to borrow rather than adjust. Forgiveness also creates no incentives for banks to develop skills in debt workout and recovery.

A decentralized, case-by-case approach, such as that adopted in Hungary and Poland (see Box 3.1), can be more useful. Banks are held accountable for their problem loans and must take the lead in resolving them. As part of the operational restructuring of individual enterprises and farms, banks can limit new loans and restructure old ones. The strategy works, however, only if banks and the enterprises concerned are properly governed and managed and if banks have enough capital to recognize and make provisions against problem loans. This may mean increasing their capital. As noted above, recapitalizing banks—by injecting cash or bonds, taking over bad loans, and providing other forms of fiscal support—has been an important component of a rehabilitation strategy. But recapitalization is a wise use of taxpayers' money only if it quickly restores the health of the financial system and improves the prospects for bank privatization. Experience elsewhere with recapitalization is mixed. Banks often continue their bad lending policies, resources are frequently squandered or used fraudulently, and recapitalizations often are repeated again and again. Argentina, Chile, and the United States have all undertaken repeated recapitalizations of their banking systems. Recapitalization poses particularly large risks in transition countries. The adverse incentives it gives to already poorly governed state banks tend to be exacerbated by the fact that their privatization—a necessary complement to the rehabilitation approach—has proved difficult, making the endpoint unclear (Box 6.3).

Instead of relying on recapitalizations and other forms of government support, policies should promote self-help for banks to encourage them to build up their capital base. Relative to their large volumes of bad loans, banks in most transition economies make smaller provisions for loan losses than is usual in high- and middle-income countries. Almost all the transition economies tax banks heavily, both through profit taxes and indirectly through high reserve requirements, which yield little interest. In some countries, banks are still saddled with quasi-fiscal responsibilities, which deplete their capital. In China, for example, the profitability of state banks is depressed in part because interest rates on loans to enterprises are kept below household deposit rates, and the credit plan dictates a large part of their lending. To allow banks to grow out of their bad debt problems, governments need to pay higher interest rates on required reserves, eliminate quasi-fiscal demands on banks, raise or liberalize lending interest rates, and encourage banks to make more realistic provisions for loan losses.

Establish at least a few reliable banks early on

A combination of low confidence in the financial sector and sizable unofficial economies has meant that cash represents a large share of the money stock in CEE and the NIS, even compared with other countries with poor payments systems (see Figure 6.1). (In China, the limited payments system rather than lack of confidence explains the high level of cash.) To restore confidence, governments should aim to certify a few reliable institutions and try to protect the payments system from bank failures. Entry by foreign banks is one quick way to increase the quality of banking. In Armenia, for example, the entry of the Midland Armenia Bank promises to enhance the financial system greatly. But in almost all transition countries regulation or other barriers have impeded foreign entry. Another approach, adopted in a number of CEE countries and NIS, is to single out a few select banks for financial and technical assistance. This approach signals to enterprises and households which banks may be most deserving of their trust (see Box 6.1). Still another route, most relevant

Box 6.3 Privatizing banks is essential, but difficult

Enterprises in many NIS have acquired parts of the state banks and established new banks in the early transition. These enterprise-owned banks were then privatized when their owners were privatized. As their ownership diversifies, and provided that strict limits on lending to owners are applied, such banks are generally no worse managed than others. The privately owned banks in these countries typically are the most dynamic and dominate new lending to private firms.

In many CEE countries state banks still dominate; as elsewhere, privatizing these banks has been difficult for both economic and political reasons. Privatization of large state banks through cash sales has been rare. Hungary and Poland have had some success, privatizing a total of six large banks (two in Hungary, four in Poland), but such divestitures have become progressively more difficult, in part because local stock markets lack depth and are already dominated by bank shares.

Even when state banks are strengthened through capital injections, foreign commercial banks have shown little interest in acquiring them because of difficulties in evaluating their loan portfolios and integrating them with their own systems. Most foreign banks prefer to establish new banks. The potential for cash sales to domestic investors is limited in transition economies because of lack of capital markets and expertise. Political concerns have often complicated the pricing and methods of sales, particularly to foreign buyers. Transferring ownership through vouchers has been somewhat more successful. Large stakes in five banks in the Czech and Slovak Republics were transferred in this way. It has also proved difficult for the state to withdraw credibly from ownership. Like their privatized counterparts in Chile and Mexico, several banks in transition economies returned to state ownership when they ran into problems.

for the NIS, is to establish "safe" banks in the meantime, possibly built on the national savings banks. These banks would primarily collect household deposits and be allowed to invest only in safe assets such as government obligations or engage in limited interbank lending. Their presence can help restore households' confidence in the banking system and allow authorities to remove, or at least reduce, the (implicit) deposit insurance now provided to state banks and sometimes to other financial institutions.

The measures just described would be more useful and far less costly than large-scale formal deposit insurance. Deposit insurance is often proposed for two reasons: to contain the risk of an individual bank's failure spreading through the payments system to other banks, and to increase households' confidence. Experience suggests, however, that deposit insurance is not essential to contain the contagion effects of bank failure. Especially where banking supervision is weak, banks and other investors will discriminate on their own—often better than regulators—between insolvent banks and banks with temporary liquidity problems. Insuring deposits, by contrast, can create significant moral hazard problems because insured banks are able to attract low-cost funds regardless of how risky their loans are. The U.S. savings and loan debacle, which led to losses of more than $100 billion, was largely due to generous deposit insurance combined with weak supervision. Policymakers might decide to introduce a modest form of deposit insurance, for banks meeting tough eligibility criteria, to foster depositor confidence. But any such scheme would have to be accompanied by much-improved banking supervision, with strong powers to intervene in weak banks, to counter the moral hazard problem.

Provided households have access to reliable banks, conditions in many transition economies make the more liberal, universal banking model, common in continental Western Europe, more attractive than the U.S. practice of separating commercial and investment banks. Allowing banks to own shares in enterprises (subject to reasonable limits) and to engage in a variety of financial activities (including, for example, securities trading and insurance) exploits banks' advantages at collecting and analyzing financial information, which are at a premium in the high-risk, limited-information environment of many transition economies. The bank-centered financial systems of Germany and Japan, for example, are generally considered to have led to better monitoring of firms.

Most transition economies have, in fact, opted for some type of universal banking model. This model has its risks, however, especially given the generally weak supervision in transition economies. In the Czech Republic and Russia, for example, conflicts of interest may arise from substantial cross-holdings between banks, investment funds, and enterprises. Exposure guidelines, which limit

individual investments to a certain fraction of assets or capital, and disclosure standards will need to be strictly enforced for banks as well as financial-industrial groups, especially for lending to managers and affiliated enterprises. In addition, some activities will need to be capitalized separately to protect depositors.

. . . And where government should fear to tread

Some governments in transition countries still intervene in the financial sector to allocate resources, typically to unprofitable enterprises or sectors. In Belarus, for example, the six largest commercial banks have been brought under state control by presidential decree, and the functioning of the central bank is now monitored by a council chaired by the prime minister. In other countries enterprises and ministries are directed to hold deposits in distressed banks. Schemes where the government directs credit to certain sectors have been proposed in many transition economies. These types of administrative measures and pressures to direct resources inhibit the development of a strong, market-based financial system. They weaken the better banks, undermine the efficient functioning of the financial system, and reduce the credibility of financial regulation. China's credit plan, for example, is increasingly circumvented and has led to new avenues of rent seeking through an informal market as well as nonbank financial intermediaries that profit from low, controlled interest rates. Any government financial support to private and privatized firms should be on commercial principles and encourage, not impede, institution building in the financial sector through technical assistance and training programs.

Limit state ownership

Keeping state-owned banks that specialize in financing certain sectors or activities risks carrying on the legacy of poor resource allocation under central planning. Specialized banks have disappeared in many countries. State-owned development banks have generally performed poorly and cannot be expected to do better in the weak institutional environment of most transition economies. Where government-owned banks have been effective, lending has been tightly circumscribed. The government financial institutions in Japan, for example, employ well-designed, focused credit programs of relatively limited duration. It remains to be seen whether the new policy banks in China, which attempt to combine directed lending for infrastructure with commercial lending, will have the same success (Box 6.4).

Rural and housing finance: Should government fill the institutional void?

Most governments face strong pressure to provide credit for rural finance, which is in crisis in many transition

Box 6.4 China's new policy banks

Most bank lending in China has been directed by the government, rather than by commercial need, and undertaken by four banks, specialized by sector. As part of its financial sector reform China decided to free the banks of this policy-based lending, leaving them to transform themselves into true commercial banks. To facilitate this, three new policy banks were created in 1994. The State Development Bank makes loans for infrastructure and key industrial developments. The Agricultural Development Bank finances crop purchases and food reserves and lends for poverty alleviation and rural infrastructure. The Export and Import Bank focuses its support on machinery and electronics exports, mainly through suppliers' credits. The banks are funded by a combination of bonds (administratively placed with commercial banks), capital contributions from the government budget, and central bank lending. The three banks' operations are already significant: all bank-financed government investment is expected to flow through them, and their lending is expected to be about 9 percent of all investment, or 3 percent of GDP in 1995.

The new banks have removed the burden of one type of policy lending from the specialized banks. This move also makes the cost of subsidizing such policy lending more explicit. If professional banking standards are applied, it could also generate efficiency gains in the management of public investment. The signals are mixed, however: most of the new banks' staff come from the Planning Commission or its subsidiaries; on the other hand, the State Development Bank did refuse to finance some 10 percent of proposed projects in 1994.

The policy banks represent only one aspect of policy lending, however. The Chinese government sets many interest rates according to industrial or broader policy objectives rather than commercial ones, and the commercial banks are still obliged to carry the loans. Moreover, the commercial banks' biggest burden is working capital loans to cover public enterprise losses. The policy banks have no role in financing these, and there is no sign yet whether these loans will be transferred to the already strained government budget. The creation of the policy banks is therefore just one step toward a comprehensive reform of China's financial sector. If applied with rigor, it could prove a significant step. On the other hand, the policy banks may just as easily turn out to be merely another layer of government, and one that perpetuates market segmentation and the role of planning.

---

economies, especially among the NIS. Agricultural banks, like most specialized banks, are illiquid and often bankrupt and are likely to emerge from reform much smaller—if they survive at all. New banks are usually reluctant to serve agriculture, because the risks are high, profitability is low, credit histories are short or absent, and land is poorly registered and difficult to collateralize. Some countries, including Croatia and Poland, have made progress toward a legal framework that allows other farm assets, such as agricultural stockpiles and farm equipment, to be used as security for loans, but these are still the exceptions (see Box 5.1). In addition, farmers are usually heavy savers, so rural areas need access to reliable and competitive savings instruments as well as commercial credit.

Creating cooperative financial institutions, in some cases out of the remains of the agricultural bank, can be a constructive approach to self-sustaining rural finance. Credit cooperatives—which already exist in Hungary, China, and Vietnam—have many strengths: active peer monitoring of borrowers, close links with clients, and an emphasis on mobilization of savings. These benefits can be undermined, however, if the cooperatives depend on government as the source of finance. Modest initial injections

of budgetary funds can help capitalize the new institutions, but, as with other financial intermediaries, the key objectives must be to foster self-help and the long-term development of healthy institutions. One temporary solution might be the approach used in Latvia, where a specially created institution operates on commercial banking principles but has a limited life span, after which it will be closed or merged with a commercial bank. Alternatively, working capital finance could be used to capitalize a cooperative lending structure: in the Kyrgyz Republic, for example, temporary financial support for working capital will be made available to farmer cooperatives. In other parts of the world, commercial suppliers of inputs and providers of marketing services often offer credit to farmers. These entities can generally evaluate the credit risks of individual farmers as well as banks can, if not better. But in the initial stages suppliers may need some coaxing to enter these markets: the Moldovan government, for example, is providing insurance against certain policy changes that would adversely affect repayment, to encourage foreign suppliers to provide inputs on credit.

Housing construction has dropped sharply in many transition countries, partly for lack of finance. In most countries housing finance is constrained by low saving and a weak institutional framework. Sometimes, unfair competition from state-owned banks has also inhibited the development of market-based housing finance. Various specialized financial institutions and government-funded schemes have been proposed to revitalize the housing market. But these schemes do not address the fundamental constraints on housing finance in many countries: the poor legal environment for mortgages, controlled rents that discourage home ownership, the lack of institutional investors, and macroeconomic instability and high inflation. Indeed, such schemes may distract attention from what is really required to develop a good housing finance system, and they can have heavy fiscal costs.

The role of nonbank financial intermediaries

Many nonbank financial institutions, such as portfolio capital funds (mutual funds), venture capital funds, and leasing and factoring companies, are well suited to the needs of transition economies. They can fill the disintermediation gap now prevalent in many transition economies. They also tend to finance small and medium-size enterprises, which are important to overall growth, and they can require less in the way of legal infrastructure than other types of intermediary. Portfolio and venture capital funds have indeed grown rapidly in transition economies. By early 1995, just six years after the first venture capital fund was set up in CEE, there were more than eighty such funds, managing assets valued at $4.4 billion. These funds have proved an attractive way for one or a few large foreign investors to meet the equity needs of small firms. The venture capital funds in which the International Finance Corporation (IFC) participates, for example, have an average investment per firm of only $500,000. Such funds can be particularly useful in transition economies, not simply because equity investments offer some hedge against inflation, but also by providing for considerable control over management, with fund managers able to help inexperienced managers develop business plans and upgrade standards. They can also make for better audits and build up contacts with foreign firms. The IFC's venture capital manager, for example, helped a Ukrainian manufacturer of surgical needles by providing the company with U.S. equipment and training, enabling it to meet U.S. medical regulations. Demanding venture capital fund managers can also help spur the development of local capital and financial markets.

As noted elsewhere in this Report, entry of new firms has been the driving force behind private sector development in transition economies. But new small and medium-size enterprises have often found it particularly difficult to attract external finance. In this context, leasing—of machinery, say, or vehicles—offers many advantages over traditional bank loans, not least that it can work well even where collateral laws are still extremely weak. In Romania the existing civil law, although a century old, was used to draft watertight leasing arrangements, enabling leasing companies to operate effectively without a special leasing law. Furthermore, it is usually easier to assess the value of a leased asset than the credit of a firm, particularly one with a short credit history. Unsurprisingly, perhaps, leasing has come to finance a large share of new investment in transition economies: nearly a third in the case of Slovenia, and about one-sixth in some other countries. With most leases awarded to smaller enterprises, the average lease has likewise tended to be small. In Slovenia, for example, the leases extended by an operating company in which the IFC participates average $13,000. Leasing has also complemented the development of other forms of finance, including bond and commercial paper markets, as well as supported a more general improvement in the regulatory and legal frameworks in place for lending. The development of other nonbank financial institutions, such as insurance companies, will be slower, but over time they too can become important institutions for intermediating savings. Nurturing them, however, will require further improvements in countries' legal frameworks, particularly in the areas of property rights and contract law (see Chapter 5).

Developing capital markets

Capital markets are, at their most basic, easy to define and almost as easy to create. In a sense, a capital market exists wherever financial securities—vouchers, stocks, or bonds—change hands, whether on a formal securities exchange, within a less structured but established medium such as an over-the-counter market, or informally between any buyer and any seller. Yet as with so many of the institutions outlined in this part of the Report, the trick to capital markets is not bringing them into being but nurturing them so that they play their proper supporting role in the broader process of transition. For capital markets, especially the more formal kind, that role is largely one of facilitating the reallocation of property rights. Capital markets are especially needed after the initial distribution of vouchers and shareholdings in a mass privatization program, but also for the sale of state assets through direct share offerings. Some of the standard benefits of capital markets in a market economy can often be even more valuable for transition countries: capital markets improve corporate governance by monitoring managers and trading shares actively; they allow cash-strapped governments to issue bonds, and firms to make share and bond offerings; and they support long-term housing finance and pension reform. But even healthy capital markets are not self-sufficient; they rely heavily on well-functioning banks, to process payments and act as custodians, and money markets, to provide benchmarks for pricing securities. Both are sorely lacking in many transition economies. In addition, property rights are often poorly defined, there is a lack of necessary market skills and experience, and minority shareholder protection is extremely limited (see Chapters 3 and 5).

The more formal, centralized type of securities exchange is not particularly difficult to set up. At least nineteen transition economies have done so. And almost all countries in CEE, several NIS, and China and Vietnam have adopted (or are adopting) supporting, comprehensive securities laws. Yet both market capitalization and share turnover in these formal markets have tended to be low by both developing and industrial country standards (Figure 6.2). Accordingly, the new markets have raised only limited funding. In CEE and the NIS only the best firms have been able to raise any financing, altogether less than $1 billion from 1991 to 1995. In China new equity offerings have been comparatively large, amounting to more than $1 billion in 1993 alone. They still, however, account for only a small portion of total enterprise investment. In Russia and the Czech Republic, capital markets—including informal markets—are mostly used to build up controlling stakes, which investors then tend to hold; turnover on formal markets is consequently low. In very few countries has equity trading been active and had a disciplinary effect on managers.

Bringing capital markets to life in transition countries will mean raising both the supply of securities and, naturally, the demand for them, as well as improving the institutional background for transactions. On the supply side, bond markets, which often precede stock markets, have tended to develop because governments need to raise non-inflationary finance. Similarly, rapid privatizers among developing countries have experienced much faster growth in stock market capitalization than have slow privatizers. This is also true among transition economies: stock market capitalization is greater in relation to GDP in mass privatizers such as Russia and the Czech and Slovak Republics (see Figure 6.2). Yet trading activity and individual share prices are generally much lower among mass privatizers than in other countries, largely because demand is low and institutions are weak. China, with its limited privatization, is a notable exception, with high turnover due in part to speculation.

Boosting domestic demand for securities, and boosting securities trading, will require stable macroeconomic policies to raise saving, as well as the emergence of institutional investors such as private pension funds (see Chapter 4) and insurance companies. Policymakers will also need to improve the protection of creditors and investors, especially minority shareholders, and vigorously punish fraud and other white-collar crimes. Enhanced disclosure

requirements could help capital markets develop, just as the disclosure provisions of the Companies Act of 1900 promoted markets in the United Kingdom. Although many transition economies have made significant progress in enacting modern securities laws, few have succeeded in enforcing them, since supervisory institutions are often still lacking. There have been many cases of outright fraud, such as the Caritas scheme in Romania. And many transition economies still lack effective trading frameworks and supporting financial services.

In developing and improving rules and institutions, countries need to strike a balance between a top-down approach, where the government takes the initiative, and one that is more bottom-up, in that supply and demand create pressures for the types of markets countries need and the rules and institutions to govern them. Top-down strategies can deliver higher standards but risk overregulation and may fail to meet markets' true needs. Standards in several CEE countries, for example, are relatively high, but only government bonds and several dozen stocks are actively traded. This is especially likely when infrastructure is developed well in advance of demand or supply. Albania, for example, enacted a well-designed capital markets law, but its capital markets are not yet functioning for lack of strong banks, institutional investors, functioning courts, qualified lawyers, and a well-staffed regulatory commission. Top-down approaches are especially problematic since most countries need rapid change in the way firms are managed—through mass privatization and other programs—and this can be slowed by overregulation.

A bottom-up approach can have advantages. Experience in transition economies and elsewhere shows that more-effective rules and institutions tend to develop when they advance in step with demand and supply, rather than behind or well in front of them. There is also evidence that market participants, seeking to protect their own interests, tend to self-regulate through cross-monitoring, especially when trading in large volumes. In Russia, a system for over-the-counter trading in stocks and rules governing trades were introduced because brokers realized that it was in their own interest to share information with others and agree on common standards. The bottom-up approach still requires a supportive role for the government, especially in promoting the necessary institutions and in vetting the rules of the game, but it does not risk stifling a nascent market. China is an example of bottom-up regulatory development: the emergence of regional exchanges prompted regional regulators to formulate their own rules first, which were later absorbed into an overarching national regulatory framework.

Foreign demand can be particularly helpful in lifting standards and increasing confidence. Foreign portfolio investors stimulate infrastructure improvements because

Stock markets in most transition economies remain small and illiquid.

Figure 6.2 Stock market capitalization and turnover in selected countries

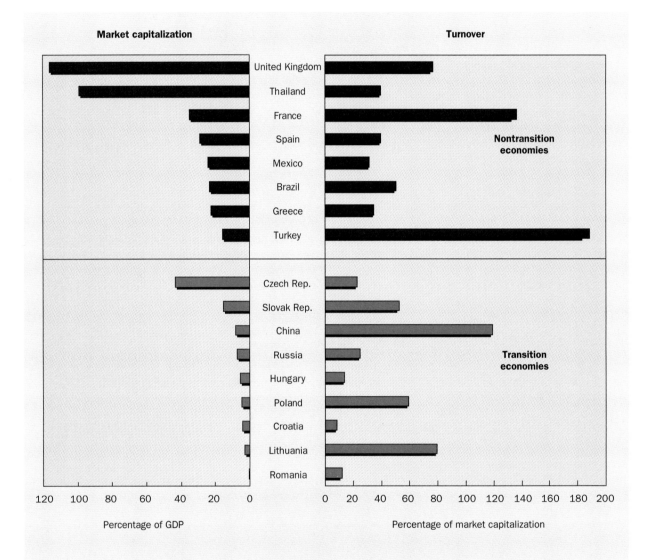

Note: Capitalization is the market value of shares outstanding at the end of 1995. Turnover is the market value of shares traded during 1995. Some economies with short histories of operating stock exchanges are not shown, as complete data are unavailable. Data do not cover all stock exchanges or over-the-counter trading, and only the most liquid stocks are included. Source: International Finance Corporation and World Bank staff estimates.

they demand good custody, trustee, audit, and bank payments systems—fiduciary functions missing in many transition economies. In Russia, for example, a British company acquired 20 percent of the shares of an aluminum company, but its share ownership was later annulled by the

company's management. The resulting international outcry spotlighted the deficiencies of Russia's regulatory process, leading to pressures for third-party registry facilities and a national registry company. A joint venture between Russian and several foreign institutions (the International Finance Corporation, the European Bank for Reconstruction and Development, and the Bank of New York) now handles custodian arrangements for shares, making purchases much easier and more attractive. Capital market development can also be accelerated through "demonstration" projects, such as portfolio and venture capital funds.

Capital markets in their various forms have played an important role in the transfer and initial reallocation of company ownership (vouchers and shares), particularly in mass-privatizing countries. Individual shareholders (including insiders) have sold their shares, often through informal markets, and strategic investors have sought to establish controlling ownership stakes. There are historical precedents for this process. In post–World War II Japan corporate ownership structure changed rapidly from one of wide distribution among individuals to one of institution-centered ownership with extensive cross-holdings. But increasing ownership concentration leads to illiquidity, especially in formal markets. In many transition economies with mass privatization programs, investors have held on to their stakes after the initial round of trading. Trading often occurs in blocks off the formal exchanges—such is the case with 80 to 90 percent of shares exchanged in the Czech Republic—as investors try to build up controlling stakes. Other countries show a similar tradeoff between concentration of ownership and market liquidity. Given the lack of sound corporate governance and scarcity of financial skills, concentrated outside ownership (combined with monitoring by banks) has its advantages in most transition economies. At least in the short run it is probably preferable to highly liquid and speculative capital markets that may impose little or no discipline on managers (see Chapter 3).

The agenda

All transition economies face similar obstacles in building strong, active financial systems, but they have approached them in very different ways. One lesson of the past few years is that reforming existing banks can be less efficient than decentralized institution building that stresses new entry. The best approach to banking reform for many countries, particularly the less advanced ones, might be to restrict the activities of state banks while a new or parallel private banking system develops. But the inherited weaknesses of the financial system and the way these tend to play out during transition demand a series of determined complementary reforms, no matter which approach governments take. Likewise, all transition governments should aim to minimize their direct and indirect role in the allocation of resources. Premature bailouts in particular have often undermined the credibility of reforms. Governments should instead encourage banks to be more self-reliant in building capital—for example, through more generous loan-loss provision rules—and improve the general framework for debt collection.

Accelerating the development of nonbank financial institutions—an essential part of any financial system—is important in all transition economies, because such institutions often finance the small, dynamic new firms that are proving central to economic growth. Capital markets are essential for raising financing and improving the governance of firms, and here transition economies may prefer to rely on demand and supply pressures when developing the supporting framework. In the long run, as evidence from other countries shows, the roles of banks, capital markets, and other intermediaries are complementary, and all have a positive influence on development and growth.

CHAPTER 7

Toward Better and Slimmer Government

The transition from plan to market calls for a wholesale reinvention of government. The state has to move from doing many things badly to doing its fewer core tasks well. This means government must at once shrink and change its nature. No longer the prime economic agent in most areas, it must instead facilitate private activity. This chapter steps back from the many demands on governments undergoing transition—the array of economic and institutional reforms outlined in other chapters—to analyze the more fundamental issue of the role of the state itself in the economy and how it should evolve during transition. It goes on to analyze how the reinvention of government should proceed in practice, focusing on the need to overhaul all aspects of the public finances. In most transition economies reforms have sapped power and revenue away from governments. Continuing to finance even a shrunken government without inflationary money creation or overborrowing, while at the same time reordering spending priorities, is proving a major challenge for almost all countries. Getting the government's own house in order—achieving tighter control on expenditure, better budget management, and tax administration, while reforming fiscal relations between levels of government—is a high priority for advanced and lagging reformers alike.

Achieving fundamental change in government

Voters and policymakers around the world increasingly ask what government is for, and whether some of its tasks might be better done by private agents. In transition countries the job of redefining government is at once more urgent and more daunting. First, the role of government in producing and distributing goods and services must shrink dramatically. Public provision must become the exception rather than the rule. State intervention is justified only where markets fail—in such areas as defense, primary education, rural roads, and some social insurance—and then only to the extent that it improves upon the market. Second, government must stop restricting and directly controlling private commercial activity and extricate itself from intimate involvement in the financial sector, focusing instead on promoting macroeconomic stability and providing a legal and institutional environment that supports private sector development and competition (Chapters 2, 5, and 6). Finally, instead of providing generous guarantees to secure adequate living standards for all, governments need to foster greater personal responsibility for income and welfare. Providing social protection is a key function of government in all economies, but in a market economy it should—in principle, at least—be mainly targeted at those vulnerable groups who need it most (Chapter 4).

These shifts are guided by the mix between private and public activity in a stylized market economy. They provide a general framework, not a rigid blueprint, for changes in the role of government during transition. Deciding, for example, exactly where market failures justify government intervention is a contentious business. But four groups of goods and services have features that tend to make private markets fail, or function inefficiently, creating a potential rationale for government intervention (although not necessarily government provision):

- Pure public goods such as defense, law and order, and environmental protection cannot be provided by private markets alone. Because everybody shares their benefits automatically, no one is willing to pay for them individually. But governments can provide them and impose their cost on taxpayers.

- Goods with positive externalities, or spillover benefits, are worth more to society than to any one consumer. Public health and education, for example, reduce infection rates, add to society's knowledge base, and raise productivity. Markets tend to undersupply these goods, and complementary public funding or provision can therefore improve efficiency. Similarly, markets ignore negative externalities, such as industrial pollution; regulation to curb or clean up the activity causing the pollution can improve social welfare.
- Natural monopolies such as gas pipelines, local transport networks, and other infrastructure services are most efficiently provided by a single firm. Unconstrained, monopoly producers tend to overprice and undersupply these services. But public provision or regulation can in principle be efficient.
- Imperfect information, on the part of either consumers or providers, may make markets fail. Private commercial insurance, for example, cannot efficiently insure against risks like unemployment, longevity, and deteriorating health in old age, because these risks are influenced by characteristics and behavior of the insured that the insurer cannot observe, along with government policy, and they affect large parts of the population equally and simultaneously. Governments can regulate private pensions and insurance and complement them with basic public pensions and insurance to improve efficiency and fill gaps in coverage. Governments also inspect food, set standards for airline safety, approve new drugs, and regulate banks and securities markets to protect consumers who have insufficient information about the quality of these goods.

Where markets fail, a case-by-case judgment is needed on whether government provision—or the regulation or funding of private provision—can do better. Governments, too, may fail: interventions may be guided by political objectives, be poorly implemented, create vested interests, or give rise to rents and corruption. Well-intentioned government intervention to correct market failures may prove even worse than suboptimal private provision. In a market economy the burden of proof regarding public intervention lies with the government.

Not surprisingly, market economies in the real world differ in how much education, health, and infrastructure the state provides for free; in the degree to which higher taxes on the rich are used to redistribute income; and in the scope and design of social welfare systems, among other things. Countries make these fundamental choices depending on their circumstances—a mountainous country spends more on roads than a flat one—and on their

national objectives. In the early stages of transition the state clearly needs to shrink and move toward less economic involvement, allowing more room for markets and the private sector. But as transition proceeds, policymakers increasingly confront tradeoffs between a somewhat more laissez-faire market economy (as in the United States) and a somewhat more "social" market economy (as in Germany or Sweden). However governments resolve these tradeoffs, they urgently need to improve the efficiency and quality of the services they provide, by focusing on the outcomes of government programs and their costs rather than only their inputs (see Chapter 8). An especially important task of governments during transition is that of educating the public about the necessity and process of reforms, including reform of government itself, and thoroughly explaining policy options and government decisions. This is crucial to building consensus and mobilizing support for reform.

Governments everywhere have found it extremely difficult to reorient and reduce their own involvement in the economy, not least for political reasons. Only a few countries have succeeded with large-scale government reforms, Australia and New Zealand being leading examples. Typically, as in New Zealand, such reforms have followed economic crises, which helped bring about the broad consensus needed for far-reaching change. Transition countries have a unique opportunity to achieve fundamental government reform in the course of their economic transformation; the political as well as economic breakthrough in many CEE countries and NIS gives them doubly good reasons for pushing ahead with government reforms. By acting decisively, transition countries can avoid some of the major fiscal and structural problems that have long plagued developing countries and have recently emerged in many industrial countries.

Making government more market-friendly and efficient entails improving public sector management. Country comparisons show that the two usually advance together (Figure 7.1). In both areas, progress with reforms has been greater where liberalization is more advanced. The reason is that some government reforms—the retreat from production and the removal of restrictive regulations—are essentially the institutional counterpart of liberalization. Others, such as targeting social assistance and improving tax administration, require long-term institution building and tend to lag behind market liberalization.

Changes in the role and management of government also entail the development of a professional civil service. Civil servants in transition economies tend to be concentrated in the wrong parts of government, given its changing functions. They frequently have the wrong skills for their jobs and face insufficient pay differentials and other poor incentives. Contrary to general belief, however,

As governments liberalize the economy, they usually reform themselves.

Figure 7.1 Government reform and liberalization by country group

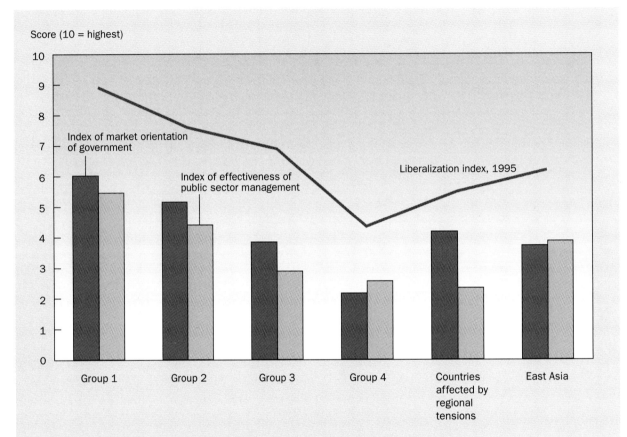

Note: The market orientation index is a composite measure of how much governments have imposed hard budgets on banks and enterprises, shifted public spending away from the productive sector and toward social services and infrastructure, withdrawn from commercial decisionmaking, divested enterprise social assets, and moved toward a targeted social security system. The index of management effectiveness combines measures of the consistency of fiscal policy and overall economic strategy; the quality of public investment planning, budget management, and tax administration; and the transparency of intergovernmental relations. Both indexes are constructed from relative country rankings, estimated based on comparative information and consultations with country specialists. See Figure 1.2 for details of the liberalization index and the grouping of countries. Source: De Melo, Denizer, and Gelb, background paper; World Bank staff estimates.

government as a whole is not vastly overstaffed or underpaid in most of these countries, and where total spending remains high, this has little to do with excessive wage bills. Data from selected CEE countries and NIS show that overall government employment and wages are broadly in line with those in industrial and middle-income developing countries—notwithstanding economy-wide declines in real wages, a rising gap between public and private wages, and often woefully inadequate staffing and pay in a few key areas such as customs, tax administration, and the police. The problem lies rather in the distribution of labor: the core central and local administrations in transition economies tend to be too small, whereas education, health, and other public services are overstaffed. Yet on balance there are too few professional and too many clerical staff. Even where average education and skill levels are high, government workers lack the accounting, tax, regulatory, and other public administration skills a market economy needs. Moreover, public sector pay is severely compressed, in both European and East Asian transition countries, and extensive and opaque systems of fringe benefits distort incentives further. Performance has little bearing on pay and promotions. Instead, personal loyalties and political considerations are still overemphasized in routine professional and career decisions. Not surprisingly, public administrations in many transition economies have been plagued by poor morale, absenteeism and moonlighting, low productivity, petty corruption, and loss of good staff to the private sector.

These problems have no quick fix, but the direction of needed reforms is clear. Pay, recruitment, promotions, and layoffs must become more flexible and merit-based. Most fringe benefits and in-kind payments need to be replaced with cash. Salary differentials must rise substantially. And, of special importance in transition economies, governments need to depoliticize the civil service, introduce systematic career development and link it to training in market economy skills, and integrate civil service staffing with wage bill and budget planning.

Rightsizing government

Governments in transition countries vary greatly in size. Most have shrunk during transition, by necessity or design, but many remain large in comparison with governments in market economies at similar levels of income (Figure 7.2). In CEE and the NIS, total government spending through central and local budgets and so-called extrabudgetary funds accounted for around half of GDP on average in 1989, about the same as in much richer countries. By 1994 average spending had fallen to 45 percent of GDP among CEE countries and 35 percent in the NIS. In the Baltics and some other NIS, nominal government spending adjusted for inflation now stands at half or less of prereform levels. Government has also shrunk dramatically in China; total spending now accounts for less than 20 percent of GDP. But in Vietnam its share in GDP has grown and now exceeds that in countries of similar income.

There is no systematic relationship between changes in government size and economic reforms. Both large and small governments are found among countries where liberalization and government reforms are advanced. In the Visegrad countries, for example, government spending exceeded half of GDP in 1994, compared with just above 20 percent of GDP (on average) in Chile, Colombia, the Republic of Korea, Thailand, and Turkey—countries whose incomes per capita were comparable or slightly

higher. By contrast, government spending in the Baltics and Romania was around one-third of GDP in 1994, almost 20 percentage points down from 1989 levels. Turkmenistan, where market reforms are the least advanced, now has the smallest government of all transition economies, with total spending below 10 percent of GDP in 1994. But government spending in Azerbaijan and Ukraine, where reforms are also lagging, still accounted for half or more of GDP in 1994.

What explains this diversity? Levels of income and development, sectoral structure, demographics, and politics are known to influence the level and trend of government spending in all countries. In transition economies three additional economic factors also seem to explain much of the change and variation in government size: pressures for social spending, financial constraints, and the degree of commitment to stabilization. In CEE and the NIS social spending pressures have risen because of output declines. In the Visegrad countries these new pressures, along with the prospects for integration with the European Union, have reinforced strong traditions of high spending for education, health, and social services. A few countries have been able to accommodate spending pressures and sustain large or growing governments with stable or rising tax revenues (the Visegrad countries, Vietnam), income from natural resources (Uzbekistan), or external financing (Albania, Hungary). But most governments have lacked access to such noninflationary funding. Some of them, such as Azerbaijan and Ukraine, delayed fiscal adjustment until 1994–95, after keeping up spending and suffering high inflation in the interim. Others reduced spending earlier in line with declining revenues—either in connection with stabilization (the Baltics, China, Romania) or because weak stabilization combined with slow market reforms led to growing informalization, spiraling inflation, and ever steeper declines in revenues and expenditures (Kazakstan, Turkmenistan). Walking a fine line between these outcomes are countries such as Belarus, Bulgaria, and Russia, which have kept expenditures high despite slowly declining revenues, but have usually—although not always—cut them by just enough at the right time to avoid a dangerous surge in inflation.

Are governments in the Visegrad and other high-spending countries too large? The size of government in all economies depends directly on the role and functions assigned to it. This, once again, is ultimately a matter of social choice. General empirical studies relating levels of government spending to economic growth yield few robust conclusions. In transition economies, however, there are stronger grounds for thinking that large governments will hurt economic performance: government spending, especially at high levels, tends to be quite inefficient and, as a result, to contribute less to growth than

Governments in most transition economies are shrinking, but many in Europe are still too big.

Figure 7.2 GDP per capita and ratios of government expenditure to GDP in selected transition economies

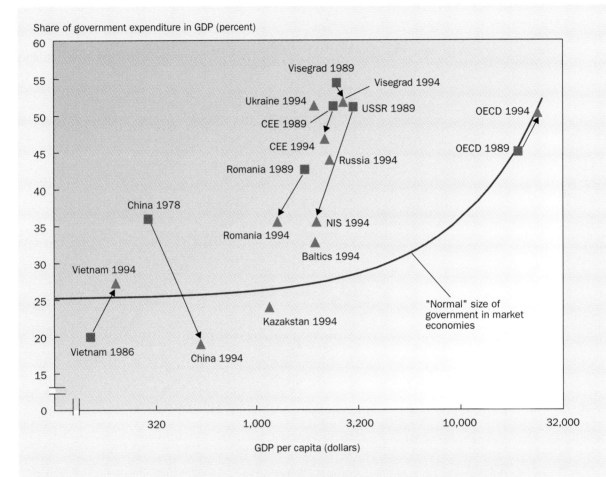

Note: GDP per capita is at market exchange rates and plotted on a logarithmic scale. Government expenditure is all expenditure for central and local government plus extrabudgetary operations (quasi-fiscal and state enterprise operations are excluded). The regression line is based on a separate sample of forty-seven developing and industrial market economies. Data for country groups are simple averages. Source: IMF, various years (c); official data; IMF and World Bank staff calculations and estimates.

in market economies; also, financing government programs is costlier and poses a greater risk of inflation.

Public spending is inefficient for several reasons. First, most large governments in transition economies spend a disproportionate share of public funds on programs with little if any impact on productivity and economic growth, such as subsidies and social transfers (see below). Since these programs create entitlements or vested interests,

there are strong pressures for them to expand. Second, government saving—revenues net of current spending—and public investment tend to be unusually low in CEE and the NIS. If government accounts for close to half of GDP but its saving is negligible (as currently in the Visegrad countries), even an impressive private saving rate of 30 to 35 percent of GDP can generate investment of only 15 to 20 percent of GDP, well below levels associated with rapid growth (Chapter 2). Third, the efficiency of government services such as health and education in many transition economies is undermined by entrenched spending allocations within sectors, weak implementation capacities, and high staffing ratios (see Chapter 8). Increased private participation and cost recovery are urgent priorities.

Financing government spending in transition economies tends to be costly. Only a few, such as the Visegrad countries, have been able to finance high spending out of taxes, in part because of significant tax reform. But tax systems even there remain relatively inefficient, so that the collection of a given level of revenues imposes a large economic burden on taxpayers, especially the emerging private sector. Indeed, tax revenues of nearly half of GDP in the Visegrad countries may well be unsustainable in the long run. In most transition economies revenues have been declining, so high government spending has tended to translate into large budget deficits. Around the world, large deficits often lead to high inflation and slow growth. This is an even greater danger in the many transition economies where the scope for domestic and external borrowing is limited and a large share of deficits can only be financed by printing money (Chapter 2).

Setting new spending priorities

Changes in the role of government during transition trigger shifts in spending priorities. The aim is to make the composition of expenditures consistent with the tasks of government in a market economy and conducive to long-run growth. Indeed, robust empirical evidence supports the view that government spending tends to be productive and to promote economic growth where it corrects proven market failures and truly complements private activity—as do some infrastructure investments, preventive health care, and basic education—but rarely otherwise.

The specific effects of public expenditures on growth in transition economies will vary according to initial conditions and the past composition of spending. In many CEE countries and the NIS, for example, the marginal return on general public education spending is likely to be relatively low because of historically high spending and educational attainment. But spending specifically on education in newly relevant market economy skills will have higher returns. The quality of spending also matters a great deal; the colossal capital investments under central planning were often ineffective. Finally, government spending serves multiple objectives, of which economic growth is only one. The resulting tradeoffs greatly complicate assessments of the benefits and costs of alternative compositions of spending. That said, the composition of public expenditure is at least open to economic analysis and, much more than the overall size of government, to public debate. Focusing spending decisions on the composition and effectiveness of expenditure, rather than simply their level, can help introduce economic considerations into the politics of budgeting, force a prioritization of expenditures, and facilitate reform.

The restructuring of government expenditures toward market economy patterns is well under way in most transition economies. The biggest changes—which are furthest advanced in the leading reformers—relate to spending on subsidies, social transfers, and capital investment (Figure 7.3).

Subsidies to enterprises and consumers have generally declined during transition, as has support to industry, agriculture, construction, and other "private commercial" sectors. As usual, the extent and pace of the decline mirror progress with liberalization. Total budgetary subsidies in CEE and the Baltic countries averaged 3 to 4 percent of GDP in 1994. In Russia they still accounted for an estimated 9 percent and in Ukraine for 17 percent. Ukraine cut subsidies sharply in 1995, but total government spending on activities that market economies tend to leave to the private sector still accounted for around 15 percent of GDP.

Where subsidies remain high, they are usually used to reduce consumer prices or cushion enterprises from the competitive and financial pressures of transition. Such subsidies are inefficient and should be replaced with direct income transfers, which can provide targeted, more effective transitional relief to vulnerable workers and households and do not delay necessary enterprise restructuring. Several CEE and Baltic countries have demonstrated that many subsidies can indeed be phased out abruptly. Where subsidies have already come down, the main challenges are to reduce any remaining subsidies—often concentrated in agriculture, energy, and housing—and recover a greater share of the costs of some education, health, and local transport services. Phasing out remaining subsidies becomes easier if governments commit to a credible schedule for reducing them, carefully monitor their costs, and regularly reassess the need for them. Governments should explicitly include all subsidies in the budget to enable both policymakers and the public to evaluate their true costs, and to facilitate the management of expenditures and macroeconomic stabilization. At one time or another most transition countries have bypassed the formal budget to channel large volumes of credit subsidies through the banking system. Although there is now a trend toward bringing them back into the budget, this practice remains a serious concern in countries such as China and Ukraine (see Chapter 2).

Social expenditures have risen across the board during transition. Part of the increase is desirable: new energy and housing allowances replace subsidies being phased out; rising social assistance and unemployment benefits

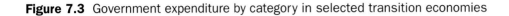

Governments' changing spending patterns reflect their increase in market orientation.

Figure 7.3 Government expenditure by category in selected transition economies

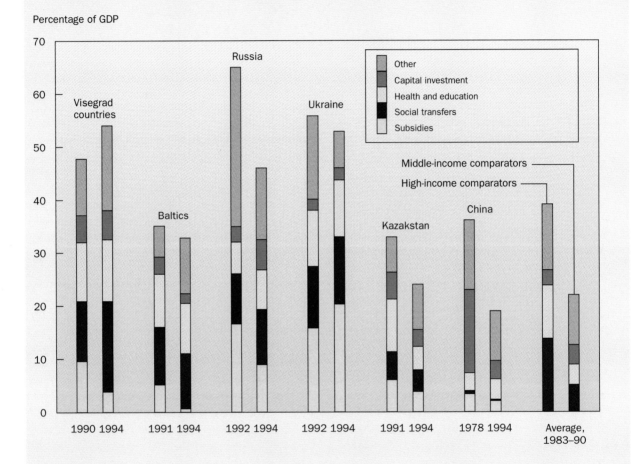

Percentage of GDP

Note: Data include central and local government plus extrabudgetary expenditures (quasi-fiscal and state enterprise expenditures are excluded). For the high-income comparators (Australia, Canada, Germany, Israel, Luxembourg, United Kingdom, and United States) and the middle-income comparators (Argentina, Chile, Malaysia, Panama, Republic of Korea, Swaziland, Turkey, and Zimbabwe), data are weighted averages, and the bottom segment represents subsidies plus social transfers. Source: IMF, various years (a); official data; World Bank staff estimates.

protect vulnerable households hit by income declines and layoffs resulting from enterprise restructuring; education and health expenditures increase as governments take over day care, schools, and hospitals from state enterprises. Yet the increase in social expenditures has varied enormously across countries, mostly because of diverging trends in pension costs. Sharply rising pension payments are the main reason social and total spending have remained high

in the Visegrad countries. In Poland, for example, payments rose from 7 percent of GDP in the late 1980s to 16 percent in 1993–94. Permitting this cost explosion to continue not only would further crowd out other expenditures but could jeopardize stabilization. Thus, pension reform is a top fiscal as well as social priority for the Visegrad countries (see Chapter 4). Indeed, Leszek Balcerowicz, the main architect of Poland's economic reform program, has cited the failure to take on pension reform as the biggest mistake of Poland's first reform government.

Finally, public investment has fallen sharply in many CEE countries and the NIS, often to less than 3 percent of GDP by 1994, because wages and other current expenditures were protected when total spending had to be cut. Capital repairs and upgrades have typically suffered, too, and many infrastructure facilities are deteriorating fast. In addition, the move to a market economy has rendered parts of the existing capital stock obsolete. So, is it possible that, after a period of correction of past investment excesses, public investment is now too low? Recent reviews by the World Bank of investment and expenditure in selected CEE countries and NIS propose target levels for public investment of around 5 percent of GDP. Another study, relating the composition of public expenditures in low- and middle-income countries to long-run growth, suggests that growth is highest when around one-fifth of total government spending is allocated to public investment. A small increase in those transition economies where public investment now is extremely low—such as the Baltics and several Central Asian states—would be consistent with both these findings.

Yet after decades of public overinvestment and misinvestment, any increase in public investment in the CEE countries and NIS must be contingent on fundamental improvements in the way such investments are made. First, public investment decisions must be integrated with the budget process, to ensure consistency with macroeconomic spending targets. Second, public investment needs to be depoliticized, and it should not substitute for private investment or for maintenance of existing facilities, but rather complement them. For example, investments in public roads should focus on highways rather than roadside services, and to the extent that maintaining roads is more cost-effective than upgrading or rebuilding them later, it should get priority. New construction would also be wasteful in sectors with excess capacity, such as hospitals or power generation in many CEE countries and NIS. Third, to make public investment more effective and efficient, projects should be systematically screened using economic and financial criteria, including cost-benefit analysis where feasible. Public investment policy in the Baltics now broadly follows these principles.

Toward better expenditure control and budget management

Under central planning the budget was driven by two factors: politics and accounting. Preparing the budget was essentially automatic and incremental, a matter of topping off the previous year's budget. This practice is still followed in China and some other countries. During transition the budget becomes an instrument of economic policy. Its effectiveness in maintaining macroeconomic stability, implementing new spending priorities, and promoting efficient use of public resources hinges on improved budget management and expenditure control. This requires many complex institutional and organizational changes over and beyond the civil service reforms outlined above.

To begin, the budget needs to be put on a sound legal footing. The executive will usually remain the primary arbiter between competing expenditures but becomes accountable to parliament. During budget preparation line agencies will need to submit more detailed spending proposals to the ministry of finance, using a common methodology open to careful analysis. The finance ministry then needs to assess these proposals against the government's agreed policy priorities and available financing. Its capacity to carry out economic analysis and forecast revenue should also be improved to reduce the likelihood of revenue shortfalls.

Finally, many governments have initially relied on sequestration to control cash flows, imposing ad hoc spending cuts on line agencies by releasing funds in accordance with incoming revenues rather than spending commitments. This crude and inefficient practice has often led to arrears on suppliers' payments, wages of civil servants or state enterprise employees, pensions, and so on. Government arrears bring a raft of problems: not only do they typically worsen an economy-wide arrears problem (see Chapter 2), but they impede private sector development, impose high social costs, and breed cynicism about government and market reforms overall. Instead, governments need to move quickly to develop working cash-management and treasury systems—a process now under way in the Baltics, Croatia, and Kazakstan.

Poland shows the progress that can be achieved in budget management. First, constitutional amendments defined the budgetary powers of government agencies, and an "organic" budget law set out the principles for budget formulation, execution, and control. Starting in 1992, instructions to budgetary units were modified to include uniform assumptions on key economic variables such as GDP growth and inflation. Current and capital expenditures were more clearly separated, and the overall resources available to individual budget units were better specified. The Ministry of Finance has refined its economic models and strengthened its collaboration with the central bank. These steps have dramatically increased government accountability and helped focus budget discussions on the substance of proposals rather than the politics.

Improving tax policy and administration: The key to closing the revenue gap

In the midst of transition some reforming countries have to confront an alarming revenue gap. The sharp drop in output, together with the serious limitations of current tax administrations, has constrained the capacity of countries in CEE and the NIS to raise revenues. This has created pressure to increase tax rates and introduce new taxes or, as in the Kyrgyz Republic, to seize bank deposits for tax payments. These methods of raising revenues are particularly costly. Yet it is politically difficult to cut expenditures in countries where spending has been high and the population has come to expect a broad range of services from government. Until the economy recovers and tax administration becomes effective, some temporary

external financing of the budget deficit may be warranted—in the context of policy measures to reform the tax system and reduce spending (Chapter 9).

Revenues have fallen in most transition economies (Figure 7.4). In the Visegrad countries and Slovenia, the ratio of revenues to GDP fell on average by 4 percentage points during 1989–94, although at one-half of GDP it was still high for middle-income countries. By contrast, the share of revenues in GDP dropped by an average of 16 percentage points in most of the other CEE countries and NIS (Ukraine, Uzbekistan, and the countries affected by

Tax revenues have fallen sharply in many transition economies.

Figure 7.4 Government revenue by source in selected transition economies

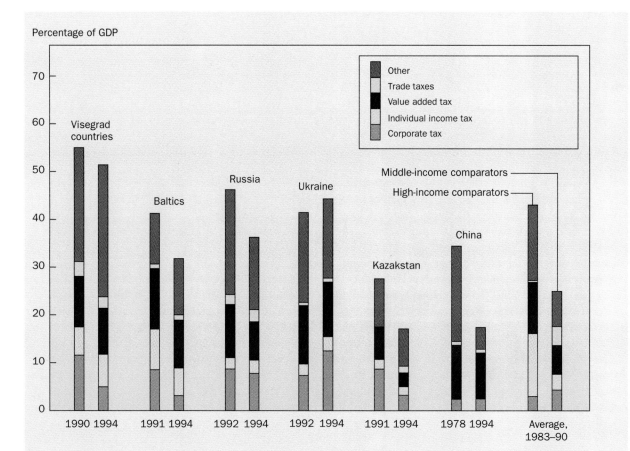

Note: Data include central and local government plus extrabudgetary revenues (revenues from quasi-fiscal and state enterprise operations are excluded). Data for the high-income and middle-income comparators are weighted averages (see Figure 7.3 for the countries in each group). Source: IMF, various years (a); official data; World Bank staff estimates.

regional tensions are excluded from this comparison), before stabilizing at about 29 percent of GDP in 1994. Russia's modest revenues partly reflect the political difficulties involved in taxing large and powerful state enterprises, such as the enormous natural gas monopoly Gazprom (Box 7.1). Despite rapid economic growth in China, its decline in revenues over the reform period was equally dramatic: from 34 percent of gross national product (GNP) in 1978 to 17 percent in 1994. By contrast, the share of revenues in GDP in Vietnam increased by 10 percentage points between 1989 and 1994, thanks to the greater profitability of state enterprises and the introduction of import taxes.

No one expected tax revenues to fall quite so dramatically during transition. Countries started out with high levels of taxation by international standards, and the fall in revenues was partly a consequence of market-oriented reforms and reducing the role of government. But the severe contraction in the state enterprise sector in CEE and the NIS added insult to injury, cutting revenues further by shrinking the main tax bases in these countries, namely, profits, wages, and consumption. Hardest hit have been slower reformers whose incomplete structural adjustment hurt profits and reduced tax payments by enterprises. Yet a fair part of the decline in revenues was self-inflicted. Most important, the use of taxation for economic and social "engineering" has generated pressures for exemptions and reduced rates. In Ukraine many goods, including

food and consumer items, are exempt from value added tax (VAT). And excise rates on alcohol and cigarettes in the NIS are about 20 percentage points lower than in OECD countries. Meanwhile in nearly all transition countries agriculture is exempt from profit taxes, and foreign investors continue to enjoy preferential tax rates. Finally, tax administrations have generally failed to collect taxes due from the traditionally dominant state sectors or to bring the rapidly growing private sector into the tax net, and tax arrears are generally on the rise (see Chapter 2).

China's sharp decline in government revenues, despite rapid economic growth, highlights the need for a coherent tax strategy in the pursuit of market reforms. Most of the revenue decline was due to smaller contributions by state enterprises. This partly reflected government intentions. In the interest of promoting enterprise autonomy, the authorities allowed state enterprises to retain a portion of their profits, and in 1984 introduced a corporate income tax that lowered their tax burden. Revenue collection was further undermined in 1988 by the new tax contract system, which officially sanctioned "tax payment by negotiation" for state enterprises, and again in the early 1990s, when this system was extended to turnover (sales) taxes. But not all of the revenue impact of the reforms was anticipated. Greater competition from collectives eroded the monopoly profits of state enterprises. Moreover, as local governments gained economic and political strength, they began reducing their efforts to collect those taxes that were to be shared

Box 7.1 Into the lion's den: Taxing Gazprom

Gazprom, the successor to the Soviet Ministry of the Gas Industry, is the largest company in Russia and one of the largest in the world. It is a highly profitable monopoly, with estimated revalued assets of some $150 billion ($400 billion or more if gas reserves are included). Its annual gas production is 600 billion cubic meters—twice the consumption of Western Europe. After-tax profits in 1995 were about $6 billion, which would put it second (after Royal Dutch/Shell) in net profits on the Fortune Global 500 list. Debt obligations are probably the lowest of any company of its size in the world: its debt-equity ratio is below 5 percent.

In 1994 half the company's shares were exchanged for vouchers in closed privatization auctions, going in large part to managers, employees, and residents in gas-producing regions. The company itself purchased an additional 10 percent of shares at par value from the government, which owns the remaining 40 percent. Shares cannot be registered in new owners' names without management approval.

Gazprom's tremendous wealth is a source of great power. The company, which is extremely secretive, has become a "state within a state." Its tax compliance is low, and it is allowed to retain billions in a tax-free "stabilization fund" for investment. Gazprom paid taxes in 1995 of about $4 billion. Had Gazprom not benefited from tax privileges, and had it complied with all tax obligations, its tax payments would have been more than twice as large. Equivalent to 2 to 3 percent of GDP, these payments would have gone quite some way in shrinking Russia's budget deficit. Gazprom has strong links with government, and in return for its special tax status is thought to allocate some of its spending to government priorities (such as support to industry or the military). Some critics argue that the company should pay higher taxes and be pushed to seek capital on world markets, which would force it to be more open. Others argue that it should be broken up, as was Standard Oil in the United States early in this century.

with the central government and granting tax relief to "their" enterprises. At the same time they managed to appropriate considerable resources for local purposes, by channeling local surcharges on taxes into their own extra-budgetary funds and letting local enterprises "donate" funds to local schools and build local bridges. Until 1994 China lacked an effective tax administration. Reversing the resulting decline in revenues will be crucial as China proceeds with reform, and as government takes on its full set of social obligations from enterprises.

Transition economies have made considerable progress in adjusting the mix of their taxes toward patterns common in market economies. VATs have generally replaced complex turnover taxes. Corporate income taxes are beginning to substitute for profit taxes and transfers. And systems of personal income taxation are being developed. Nevertheless, the tax systems that have emerged—often in an ad hoc manner—still fall well short of what might be considered best practice. The efficiency costs of taxation (the reduction in the real income of society due to the imposition of taxes) in a number of transition economies are probably as high as in some developing countries. A study for India, for example, suggests that every rupee of extra sales or import tax revenue raised by increasing tax rates has an efficiency cost of 0.85 and 0.77 rupee, respectively.

Heavy tax distortions in transition economies come from various sources. First, base rates are often high. In transition economies with many fledgling small enterprises and weak tax administration, high rates are likely to encourage already widespread tax evasion and informalization. Second, many countries still rely heavily on payroll taxes to finance social expenditures. In Hungary more than half of every forint in additional wage income is taxed away by the payroll tax and the individual income tax combined. As many market economies are discovering, payroll taxes, levied mainly on employers, can stifle entrepreneurial effort, discourage formal hiring, and push economic activity underground. The payroll tax base has indeed shrunk a great deal in some transition countries. Third, and perhaps most important, the many tax exemptions and special tax rates described above often coexist with higher tax rates on other activities, such as banking and insurance, and on the private sector generally. Such variations in tax treatment undermine revenue performance, complicate tax administration, and distort resource allocation.

Improving tax revenues in transition countries entails reforming the structure and composition of taxes as well as the collection of revenues. The first pillar, better tax design, will be essential for delivering higher, fairly predictable revenues, minimizing distortions, and avoiding large increases in tax rates and frequent changes in legislation. The key task is to strictly limit tax exemptions and eliminate sectoral differences in tax treatment. This will mean extending the VAT to all but a few goods and ser-

vices (notably exports, which should be zero-rated, and banking and insurance services, where it may be difficult to determine the amount of value added to be taxed). Major commodities such as gas and oil should be subject to the full tax regime, including not insignificant excise rates. Deductions from profit and personal income taxes need to be limited. The tax status of agriculture, especially in the NIS, will also have to be overhauled, first by lifting exemptions on major taxes and, over time, through introduction of a land tax. Small private businesses can be taxed through presumptive methods (based on selected indicators rather than actual profits), as is done in Vietnam and several other transition economies. Finally, when broadening tax bases, countries need to contain marginal tax rates and the overall tax burden of the private sector. In the Visegrad countries and Russia, for example, improving tax efficiency and reducing tax evasion will almost certainly require lowering combined corporate, personal income, payroll, and value added tax rates.

Improved tax administration is the second pillar of an effective revenue strategy. Effective tax administration in a market economy is based on voluntary compliance by a large number of decentralized taxpayers. Most transition economies have only recently started to address compliance issues and build up a modern tax administration with better overall revenue performance. China's new National Tax Service, established in 1994 with authority to collect the bulk of taxes, has helped increase the central government's share in total revenues.

A first step is to restructure how the work is organized. Tax administrations should develop around activities (such as recording or auditing), as in Hungary, rather than according to type of tax and taxpayer. More generally, tax payments need to be assessed, collected, and recorded more efficiently. Current procedures are rarely up to the job of dealing with a growing number of taxpayers, many of which—particularly private businesses and service enterprises—are tricky to tax at the best of times. Government might start by assigning identification numbers to all taxpayers, focusing its efforts on the large taxpayers who generate the bulk of revenue, and withholding wage taxes at the source. Next in line should be improved monitoring and follow-up action against those who fail to file returns or make payments. Latvia, for example, has issued regulations for an improved taxpayers' register: every taxpayer must register with the State Revenue Service; financial institutions will not be allowed to open accounts for any business or individual without a taxpayer code.

The nature of audits and enforcement must also change with the move to a compliance-based tax system. Audits need to be conducted selectively. Hungary is adopting this approach, but many NIS still conduct a full audit of every taxpayer every two years. Tax administrators in most transition countries will need to be given greater powers to enforce payment (in some NIS they are limited to calling banks for information on late taxpayers). Efforts are under way in Bulgaria and Poland to change the law so that the authorities can seize the assets of delinquent taxpayers. The new tax law in Latvia imposes various penalties on defaulting taxpayers, extending to closing their businesses.

Fiscal decentralization: Blessing or curse?

Facing political pressure to maintain or increase spending at a time of declining revenues, central governments in transition countries have shifted several spending responsibilities down to the local level. Consequently, local governments handle a large and increasing share of total public spending, including spending on some services—such as education, health, and social welfare—that have national as well as local benefits. In China and Russia, for example, subnational spending was just under 40 percent of total spending before 1989; now it is closer to 50 percent. As state enterprises are privatized, their spending on social services and infrastructure is also being shifted to subnational budgets.

The same trend toward decentralization has not taken place with regard to revenues, which remain centralized in almost all transition economies, largely for stabilization reasons. In countries as diverse as Hungary and Ukraine the center still keeps all revenues from corporate, value added, excise, and customs taxes. In Russia, revenues from all four main taxes—profit, personal income, value added, and excise taxes—are shared with local governments, but the underlying arrangements are opaque and the regional equalization mechanisms complementing them are ineffective. Meanwhile local governments' independently collected revenues are inadequate in most transition countries. Property taxes raise little revenue, and minor taxes such as those levied in Russia on dogs, used computers, logos, and horse racing are little more than a nuisance. A number of NIS inherited a tax on beards dating back to the Russian Empire.

Decentralizing expenditures while holding onto revenues has allowed central governments to meet deficit targets. This shift of spending responsibilities, without corresponding revenues, to subnational levels in the hope that they would do the cost cutting has severely squeezed local budgets. Localities have accumulated expenditure arrears and, in the case of Russia's oblasts, delayed their contribution to the federal budget. They have also borrowed from the financial sector, both directly and indirectly through "their" enterprises, and have established extrabudgetary funds. In effect, focusing stabilization policy on the federal deficit alone is leading to actions that can destabilize the economy and reduce the transparency of the budget. It can also impede privatization when local governments obtain significant resources from enterprises they own. Decentralizing spending responsibilities without decen-

tralizing revenue authority has fueled the trend toward greater regional inequality mentioned in Chapter 4. Russia's richest oblast, for example, now spends sixteen times more per capita than the poorest.

Yet decentralization has sometimes yielded benefits. In Poland, for example, the quality of local services appears to have improved: the fact that beneficiaries play a more active part in local decisionmaking and that local officials have greater accountability may have increased the user-friendliness of service provision. Local governments have not generated deficits and have thus supported macroeconomic stabilization. In China decentralization has been important in promoting an experimental approach to reforms, with the more successful regions setting an example to the rest.

There is no single "right" system of intergovernmental relations and no "best" country experience to serve as a model for transition economies in assigning revenues and expenditures between levels of government. Revenue assignments and basic tax systems need to be relatively stable so as not to disrupt incentives for investment and growth, and to ensure that the country remains a unified economic space. This can be particularly important in transition economies where liberalization implies a trend toward decentralization and regional differentiation. Thus, national uniformity is generally deemed preferable for profit and personal income taxes, the VAT, and taxes on natural resources and international trade. Revenues that can be assigned to subnational governments include excises, supplementary rates on the national personal income tax ("piggybacking," as has been recommended for Hungary, Poland, Russia, and Ukraine), and various property taxes and fees. The assignment of expenditures is even more complex and varies across countries. Whereas the central government retains such responsibilities as national public services and defense, subnational governments can be responsible for outlays ranging from education and intermunicipal infrastructure to purely local services. Subnational governments account for 15 percent of total spending in Argentina but more than 50 percent in Canada.

Imbalances between own revenues and expenditures at lower levels of government create a need for intergovernmental transfers—both to close the fiscal gap at local levels and to ensure minimum levels of public services across local governments (equalization). Worldwide experience in tackling this issue yields four broad lessons for transition economies. First, a cooperative approach (whereby transfers are made available to all subnational governments at a given level rather than to a selected few) can help engage subnational governments in the equalization process and ensure that central government revenues are not simply appropriated by powerful subnational governments. Second, the evolving role of the state and continuing refinements of price and enterprise reforms require some flexibility in the size and design of local transfers. Third, where possible, transfers should provide incentives for subnational governments to raise their own revenues and manage their expenditures efficiently; lump-sum general purpose transfers, for example, achieve this, but automatic "gap-filling" transfers from the central government to meet local deficits do not. Fourth, any equalization system should be tailored to suit the needs and constraints of the country in question. Economies with data problems—such as China—could start, for example, with a scheme that takes into account only a limited number of factors and redistributes only part of the central government's revenue surplus.

Without effective control over subnational borrowing, even the most elaborate transfer mechanisms could fail to establish the desired incentives for efficient management of local government finances. In transition economies local borrowing independent of the central authorities should be allowed only in the presence of strong institutional safeguards.

In short, a well-designed system of intergovernmental fiscal relations, based on these guidelines, can result in more responsive, better-quality local services, which can promote private sector development and poverty reduction. Failure to design the system carefully, however, has led to macroeconomic instability in several countries and impeded the reform agenda in some.

The agenda

Most transition economies are in the midst of a comprehensive reform of their governments. Crucial laws have been passed, new taxes have replaced old ones, and subsidies have generally been cut sharply. But progress at fiscal stabilization has been mixed, spending reallocations that hinge on deep sectoral reforms are difficult and slow, and tax collection and budget management remain weak in most countries. In the short term, some top priorities in fiscal reform will be to continue improving the design of the tax system (above all by eliminating widespread exemptions and cutting high marginal rates), put in place mandatory taxpayer registration, revamp budget preparation procedures, eliminate sequestration, initiate pension reform, and reduce the often large, hidden financial burdens on government in the form of tax arrears, government guarantees, state bank losses, or rolling directed credits. Other fiscal reforms—such as overhauling the civil service and clarifying and rebalancing central-local fiscal relations—may be equally important. But because they are ambitious in their demand on scarce institutional capacities, they cannot be accomplished by today's government alone. These are priorities for the long term. Finally, governments in transition also have a more outward-looking—and probably more important—challenge. Political reforms, economic liberalization and stabilization, and new private sector opportunities all help create a demand for the many legal, financial, and social institutions discussed in this part of the Report. They will not arise out of thin air. Establishing these institutions and nurturing them over time may be the single greatest contribution to the long-term success of transition that governments can make.

CHAPTER 8

Investing in People and Growth

A well-educated, healthy work force is essential for economic growth. Here the transition economies have a strong foundation on which to build. As the Introduction noted, high quality of and good access to basic education and health care were two of the proudest achievements of central planning. Yet the health care and education systems that transition governments inherited were built to fit the rigid environment of a command economy, not the more flexible and ever-changing demands of freely competitive markets. Reform of education is therefore needed, both to give workers more transferable, marketable skills and to develop informed citizens, capable of participating actively in civil society. Reform of the health care system is needed to raise life expectancy and to reduce the burden of disease and injury, contributing both to productivity and the quality of life. The trick for governments will be to reshape health care and education to meet the demands of a new economic system without throwing away the achievements of the old.

Reshaping skills

The primary purpose of the education system is to impart knowledge and skills and, just as important, to transmit certain values. The resulting education package will vary enormously across countries and cultures. Achieving the primary objective involves a number of subsidiary ones: equitable access to education and training; producing the types of educational activities that equip individuals—economically, socially, and politically—for the societies in which they live (external efficiency); running schools and other institutions as efficiently as possible (internal efficiency); and financing education in ways that are both fair and efficient.

Initial conditions

Under central planning the CEE countries and the Soviet Union were well-educated societies, with almost universal primary and lower secondary enrollment, high levels of literacy compared with countries at similar incomes (and sometimes with those with much higher income), and impressive levels of basic numeracy and engineering skills. Access was relatively equitable, for girls as well as for boys—a major achievement given the powerful effect of equal education on overall health and productivity. In China, too, levels of educational attainment were—and are—impressive by developing country standards.

Given these successes, and given the many other demands on policymakers during transition, one might think that education reform is one policy that governments could afford to put on hold. But reform of education is needed, and urgently. First, the inherited education system was highly inefficient even in the context of central planning. The state financed education on the basis of rigid formulas, allocating resources without regard to student or employer demand. And although the provision of education was for the most part a public monopoly, it was poorly coordinated. Programs for professional development were fragmented, and scarce resources were often wasted on duplication of facilities, as each enterprise and ministry developed its own. Nor did administrators or teachers have any incentive to use resources efficiently. The result was gross overstaffing and high unit costs. In many ways the education system—like the health system, as we shall see below—had problems similar to those of state enterprises. The solution, although not the same, will involve some of the same elements—for example, incentives to efficiency and greater responsiveness to consumer demand. As explained below, the second reason why reform is needed is that the inherited system has major deficiencies in terms of supporting a market system.

Education reform is urgent because the erosion of a country's human capital imposes high downstream costs. Ill-educated people make up a large proportion of the unemployed and the poor. Fortunately, there is good evidence that higher enrollments and a rapid response of the education system to changing labor markets pay dividends: such factors explain a significant part of the higher growth rates of the high-performing East Asian economies in recent decades. In transition economies a shortage of necessary skills hampers enterprise restructuring and privatization.

In China a serious problem is provision of social services, which has stagnated in China's poorest regions. Educational achievement in these areas is deplorable, and, as discussed below, so is health status. In the poorest towns and villages half the boys, and in some minority areas nearly all the girls, do not attend school and will not attain literacy. Only thirty of the seventy school-age children in a poor village in Tongxin County attend elementary school; in another village in the same county none of the fifty children have attended school in the four years since the local elementary school collapsed.

Adapting education and training to the market economy
Education systems under central planning focused, on the one hand, on teaching all students a uniform interpretation of history and national purpose, and on the other, on mastery of fixed, specialized bodies of knowledge to be applied in narrowly defined jobs. Education therefore emphasized conformity for all and specialist expertise for each. This philosophy rendered socialist education systems inadequate to the needs of a market economy in at least three ways. First, although basic education was in many ways superior to that in many Western countries, subsequent training was too specialized from too early an age. Poland's secondary technical schools taught about 300 occupational skills to meet the specific and fairly static demands of the central plan. In Germany, by contrast, about sixteen broad apprenticeship programs are available to sixteen- to eighteen-year-olds. Second, adult education and training, essential for job mobility in a market economy, was neglected because workers were expected to remain in their first occupation throughout their working lives. Third, subjects such as economics, management sciences, law, and psychology—all of which feature prominently in market economies—were deemed irrelevant and ignored or underemphasized.

Liberal market economies also use education to transmit cultural, political, and national values as well as knowledge and skills. In sharp contrast with education under central planning, however, their systems emphasize personal responsibility, intellectual freedom, and problem-solving skills.

The skills that students acquire through their education can be assessed along three dimensions: the ability to solve a known class of problem; the ability to apply a given technique to a new problem; and the ability to

choose which technique to use to solve a new problem. Although this hierarchy of skills was recognized throughout the centrally planned economies, in many the upper end—that involving independent, critical thought—was regarded as seditious. Figure 8.1 illustrates, in terms of these three dimensions, both the strengths of the old system and the need for change. Mathematics and science scores of children in the NIS, Hungary, and Slovenia are considerably above the international average. Clearly these countries have successful education systems. However, children in these countries, in comparison with their counterparts in Canada, France, Israel, and the United Kingdom, do better on tests of how much they know than on tests that ask them to apply that knowledge in new circumstances. These results suggest that the education systems of centrally planned and market economies were both effective in achieving their different objectives. They also indicate the direction in which change is needed in the systems of CEE and the NIS, both to help them convert human capital to meet the demands of a market system and to fill in gaps in knowledge. Higher education policy in China is increasingly facing similar problems.

Adapting the education package will not be easy (Table 8.1). The gaps in the curriculum have led to missing concepts and hence to missing words. "Efficiency," for example, means something very different to a manager seeking only to comply with a central plan than to one seeking to boost profit and market share in a competitive system. Although language adapts rapidly, missing concepts and, as a result, missing words can still impede speedy and effective transfer of knowledge and skills.

Policy directions
Priorities for reform lie in three principal areas: finance, content, and delivery. The financing of education should provide incentives for efficiency. One way is to allocate public funds for training and higher education on the basis of enrollment, to make the system more responsive to demand—although such a policy needs to be accompanied by improved accountability, as discussed below. Training vouchers would allow workers to choose what kind of training to seek and where; this would improve both occupational and geographical mobility. Reform of education financing is important not simply because it supports more efficient management of schools (internal efficiency) but also because it can improve the content of education (external efficiency) by empowering consumers to demand the education and training they need. A separate issue is to ensure that funding improves access—a major problem in rural China. Government must accept responsibility for guaranteeing access to quality education; this may require interregional transfers to help offset widening regional disparities (see Chapters 4 and 7).

Socialist education emphasized accumulating knowledge rather than applying it.

Figure 8.1 Science and mathematics test performance of children in selected transition and established market economies

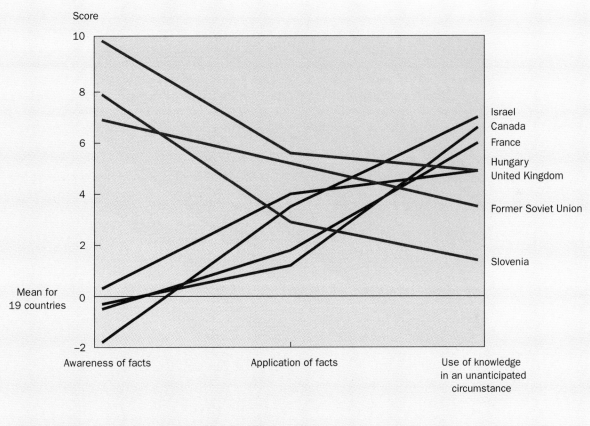

Note: Data are deviations from the overall mean, for a sample of nineteen countries, of test results of nine- and thirteen-year-olds on the second International Assessment of Educational Progress, conducted in 1991. The countries shown are those whose performance was above the sample mean. Source: Kovalyova 1994; for technical details see Education and Testing Service 1992a, 1992b.

New curricula are central to the reform of content, especially in such subjects as economics and history, both to produce a more critical type of learning and to adjust schooling to changing needs and values. New textbooks will be needed, and reform should encourage the development of a competitive commercial publishing industry. This would allow replacing the selection of textbooks from a centrally determined list with a pluralist model that allows schools, teachers, and pupils to choose for themselves. But perhaps most important to improving quality will be raising the accountability of educators. This must start with training new teachers and retraining

existing ones. Performance incentives for teachers and local administrators should be strengthened, as should the assessment of teachers. Finally, examinations need to be reformed so that they test the capacity to use knowledge as well as to accumulate it.

Improving the delivery of education is a complex process. It generally implies decentralization, to make education more responsive to local needs; diversification of supply, including private suppliers, to promote competition and thus efficiency; and diversification of educational practice, to enhance individual choice. These initiatives, however, require a major change in the role of the

Table 8.1 Examples of needed changes in the education package

Component of the education package	Objective
Knowledge	Preserve the achievements of the old system but rectify the earlier underemphasis on social sciences and law.
Skills	Assist the movement from specific skills to broader and more flexible skills better able to meet the continually changing demands of a market economy. Strengthen the ability to apply knowledge in new and unforeseen circumstances.
Attitudes	Strengthen the idea that the initiatives of workers and of others are rewarded. Assist the understanding that employing workers (subject to suitable regulation) is not exploiting them but giving them an opportunity to earn a living. Assist the understanding that business has its place in society and hence that profits are needed to provide an engine of growth.
Values	In line with the changed relationship between the citizen and the state, encourage the understanding that citizens need to take responsibility for their actions, including their choices about education, work, and lifestyle. Foster the understanding that freedom of expression is an essential and a constructive component of a pluralist society governed by consent.

state, which has to establish a framework that includes methods of funding, accreditation of providers, and monitoring of quality, particularly in poor areas.

Progress to date

Transition countries have made some progress toward these goals, but much remains to be done. During the early stages of transition education reform in CEE and the NIS, understandably perhaps, was not a high priority. As Chapter 7 noted, fiscal and political pressures prompted central governments to decentralize much of the financing of education. But local governments generally had even fewer resources than central government. Real spending on education fell, yet little effort was made to reduce overstaffing, with the result that a growing share of education spending now goes toward teachers' salaries. There has been both a tremendous decline regionwide in the provision of preschool education, with potentially devastating consequences for the learning ability of large numbers of children, and a decline in access to compulsory education in the less affluent countries, particularly for minorities.

The state sector, and its secondary vocational and technical training programs in particular, responded slowly to the arrival of a market economy. As a consequence many graduates now feed the lines of unemployed. On the positive side, new institutions have sprung up (many of them private), especially in the teaching of social sciences and business administration, partly because of rising returns to these disciplines. Most of the CEE countries and NIS have revised their curricula, especially in history and the social sciences. Decentralization has also occurred: in Russia, for example, the centrally determined part of the primary and secondary curriculum was reduced from 100

percent to about 80 percent. And schools can now choose their textbooks, although shortages make it difficult for teachers to follow the new curricula.

Yet although the content of lessons may have changed, the manner in which they are taught has not. Old methods persist throughout the region and will doubtless take time to change. The challenge is daunting. But no education system can hope to foster choice, autonomy, and accountability in society as a whole without first acquiring these characteristics itself.

Improving health

Health care consumes a significant share of resources in all countries, and the debate over access to and the cost of quality care inspires strong emotions everywhere. The primary objective of health policy is to improve citizens' health, within a budget constraint. Several subsidiary objectives follow from this twofold obligation: equitable access to health care; producing the quantity, quality, and mix of health interventions (including preventive care and health education) that bring about the greatest improvement in health (external efficiency); running medical institutions as efficiently as possible (internal efficiency); and financing health interventions in ways that are efficient and equitable.

Initial conditions and progress to date

Many of the CEE countries and the NIS face a health problem associated with transition itself, superimposed on a longer-term problem. By the mid-1960s life expectancy in the CEE countries was only one to two years shorter than that in the industrial market economies, and the gap seemed to be closing. Thereafter, however, the gap started to increase, strikingly so for middle-aged adults, as health outcomes increasingly lagged behind progress elsewhere. By the late 1980s Hungarian men aged fifteen to fifty-nine stood a greater risk of dying than their counterparts in Zimbabwe, and the risk of death in Czechoslovakia was higher than in Vietnam. By the mid-1980s mortality rates from heart disease among forty-five- to fifty-four-year-old men in Czechoslovakia were double those in Austria; thirty years earlier the rates had been much the same.

What has happened to health during transition? Two conclusions emerge: rapid reform is not necessarily detrimental to health indicators, but slow reform or the absence of reform does little to impede a long-run deterioration. In many of the NIS the long-run trend toward worsening mortality has accelerated since transition began, particularly for men. The sharp decline in men's life expectancy in Russia between 1990 and 1994 was the most dramatic shift of all (Box 8.1). By contrast, infant mortality and life expectancy improved in the advanced reformers (Table 1.1). In Poland between 1989 and 1995, infant mortality fell from 19.1 to 13.4 per 1,000 live births, and life expectancy increased by one year for men and six months for women. The picture is mixed in the other reform groups. The number of low-birthweight babies has risen sharply in Bulgaria, Romania, and the Slovak Republic from a combination of poor diet, stress, smoking, and excess alcohol consumption during pregnancy—all risk factors that have increased during transition. In FYR Macedonia declining levels of basic immunization in 1991 led to a striking increase in the incidence of measles during 1992 and 1993.

Maternal mortality improved dramatically in CEE between 1990 and 1995 but worsened slightly in the NIS, where mortality rates are now about four times above the European average. The Central Asian republics experienced a dramatic deterioration between 1988 and 1991. Some of the apparent worsening may simply be the result of improved data collection (see Box 4.1). The major causes, however, include the lack of contraception, high rates of abortion, deteriorating socioeconomic conditions, inadequate health services, and the indiscriminate use of pesticides and chemical fertilizers in agriculture. Of these, abortions are a particularly severe problem, and illegal abortions an even greater one. The most obvious remedies include improved education, especially for girls and young women, a greater emphasis on preventive measures—such as contraception, screening for cervical and breast cancer, and updated obstetrical practices—healthier lifestyles, and the promotion of breastfeeding.

The story in China has generally been very different, although parallels are now beginning to emerge. The health status of the Chinese people by the end of the 1970s was remarkably good for a country at China's income level. These gains, although partly the result of sound health policies, were largely due to rising income and what that means for diet, education, access to clean water and sanitation, and the like. Recent analysis, however, suggests that these gains, at least as indicated by mortality rates for children under age five, tailed off sometime in the early 1980s. By the late 1980s China had actually fallen behind countries at similar income levels. In addition, the incidence of noncommunicable diseases is rising rapidly. The death rate from lung cancer (70 percent of Chinese males smoke) is rising by 4.5 percent a year and that of deaths related to hypertension by 8.7 percent a year.

In rural China a share of communal production used to be set aside to finance collective needs, including primary health care, vaccination, birth control, and maternal health care. The downturn in China's health performance relative to its income level coincided with agricultural reforms that reduced the ability of the village to tax peasants. A system of cost recovery rapidly replaced tax funding, creating general problems of access. Infant and maternal mortality rates in rural areas are 50 to 100 percent greater than the national average. Problems are particularly severe for the rural poor (more than one in four referred to hospitals by village doctors never go because of high cost), and greater still in the poorest townships and villages—among the poorest quarter of the population, for example, the infant mortality rate is 3.5 times greater than among city dwellers.

Policy options

HOW CAN HEALTH BE IMPROVED? Four groups of factors influence a person's health: income, lifestyle, environmental pollution and occupational risks, and the quality of available health care. Experts agree that income and lifestyle are by far the most important; thus the causes of health outcomes go well beyond the health sector.

Lifestyle choices are clearly the key to improving health. The single largest contributor to the health gap between Eastern and Western Europe is cardiovascular and cerebrovascular disease—heart attacks and strokes—for which the main risk factors include excessive alcohol consumption, smoking, obesity, unhealthy diet, and lack of exercise. All these factors are more prevalent in CEE and the NIS than in industrial market economies. And the single most important factor, smoking, is far more prevalent: in the third quarter of 1995 Lithuanians spent 4 percent of GDP on alcohol and tobacco, compared with 2.1 percent on health care. As elsewhere, policies to reduce these risk factors in transition countries include taxation to discourage consumption of alcohol, tobacco, and unhealthy foods; removal of food subsidies that distort food prices in favor of unhealthy diets; and legislation on alcohol, tobacco advertising, and food labeling. Also important are public education programs to inform the population about diet (specifically, the benefits of reduced consumption of alcohol and fat, and of increased

Box 8.1 Is transition a killer?

More Russians are dying during transition. Male life expectancy fell by six years between 1990 and 1994 (from sixty-four to fifty-eight; see figure) and that of women by three years (from seventy-four to seventy-one). Early evidence suggests that the decline may now have stabilized: in 1995 men's life expectancy was unchanged, while women's actually rose by a year. The largest increase in mortality (about 50 percent) was among men aged twenty-five to fifty-four; the rise for the older men in that group was mainly due to an increase in cardiovascular disease, and that for younger men mainly to accidents, suicide, substance abuse, and murder. Russian adult mortality is now 10 percent higher than that in India. Similar if less dramatic increases in mortality have occurred in the other European NIS. In contrast, life expectancy has increased in the advanced reformers in CEE (Table 1.1).

Defective data are unlikely to be a major explanation. A second explanation—that transition itself is a direct cause—is the subject of continuing investigation. But increasing indirect evidence links economic hardship with declining health. Early results from a Hungarian study suggest that poor regions and those going through the greatest socioeconomic shock are starting to see mortality rates rise. These results are consistent with those from studies of equity and health in the United Kingdom over the past thirty years.

Two factors can be suggested as at least partial contributors. The first is substance abuse—alcohol and illicit drugs. Alcohol consumption was significantly reduced during President Mikhail Gorbachev's campaign to curb abuse during 1985–88, but the relaxation of that campaign in the late 1980s coincided with rising mortality, including through accidents, alcohol poisoning, and increased fatalities among those already suffering from cardiovascular disease. The second factor, less well documented but supported by extensive observation, is a decline in the quality of and access to medical care over the past five years, which has increased mortality among those with serious injuries and cardiovascular emergencies. Transition may have aggravated both sets of influences. It is not difficult to imagine a causal link between declining living conditions, stress, and alcohol consumption. Deterioration in law enforcement, particularly with respect to alcohol production and road safety, further increases the risk of injury.

Male life expectancy and death rates from injury and cardiovascular disease in Russia

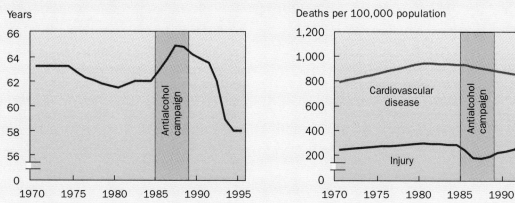

Note: "Injury" includes deaths caused by accident, assault, poisoning, and suicide. Source: World Bank data.

consumption of fruit and vegetables), exercise, and the risks of smoking and other dangerous behavior.

Pollution and occupational risks are also widespread in CEE and the NIS. Severe environmental pollution, in particular air pollution, is largely the result of these countries' heavy use of hydrocarbon energy sources. In the "Black Triangle," where Germany, the Czech Republic, and Poland meet, about 6.5 million people are exposed to extremely polluted air. Air pollution may explain around 9 percent of the Czech Republic's health gap with Austria. Cleanup will be neither easy nor cheap. On the other hand, health is damaged more by cigarette smoke than by smokestacks; individual behavior is crucial. Unhealthy living environments and behavioral risk factors both afflict the poor and the undereducated disproportionately. It is the poorest—because they have the fewest choices— who live in the shadow of belching chimneys and in cold, damp homes. As with other social policies, closing the gap in health will mean focusing on the most disadvantaged groups, disseminating information to them and maintaining their access to health care.

Health services under the old regime in CEE and the NIS were strong on preventive health care, especially in providing immunizations. Maintaining and building on this impressive record have received too little attention. Preventive health efforts need to focus on control of communicable diseases but are threatened in some countries by problems in vaccine production, purchase, and delivery. Improving education and preventive services for women and their babies is an effective way to improve overall health and avoid unnecessary medical expenditure. This is not to say that curative health services—primary health care and hospitals—should be neglected. Although they have a smaller direct impact on life expectancy than public health measures, well-being should be assessed not only in terms of length of life, but also in terms of its quality: a hip replacement or the removal of a cataract does little to increase life expectancy but can make a huge difference to one's enjoyment of life.

HOW TO IMPROVE HEALTH CARE DELIVERY. Curative health services in CEE and the NIS retain most of the inefficiencies inherited from central planning. In the NIS people can admit themselves to hospitals, and many enter for long stays for nonclinical reasons (in Russia 21 percent of the population spent time in the hospital in 1993, compared with 16 percent in the industrial market economies and around 10 percent in middle-income countries). Hospitals have too many doctors, who are poorly paid and often poorly trained. Rigid budgeting systems give managers neither the incentive nor the freedom to use resources efficiently. For example, funding of hospitals is related to inputs, such as the number of beds, rather than to treatment given or—best of all—to health outcomes; hospital

managers therefore have an incentive to keep a large number of beds, preferably empty ones. Public health programs are poorly structured, and modern methods of quality control are absent. There is little consumer choice and little accountability. Citizens are still considered the passive recipients of state-run health services rather than active participants in efforts to improve their lifestyle.

Addressing these problems means reforming the quantity, mix, and quality of health services. When national income is declining—as it did in every CEE country and the NIS in the early stages of reform—the health sector will almost inevitably shrink. This makes it all the more important to adjust the mix of health spending away from highly specialized care toward more basic and outpatient care and toward public, occupational, and environmental health services; this will require closure of unnecessary facilities or their conversion to other uses. Hungary, for example, is planning to eliminate 20,000 hospital beds during 1995 and 1996. Countries also need to make major efforts to boost the quality of care, including by upgrading and modernizing skills. Self-regulation of the medical profession—an important component of civil society—can increase quality. So too can greater competition between providers, and in particular private, nonprofit providers, often organized by NGOs.

As the economy starts growing again, policymakers have to devise a strategy to allow the health sector to grow in a controlled way, both to prevent an explosion in health spending and to ease efforts to adjust the overall mix of medical activities toward preventive and basic health care. Several countries are already experiencing pressures to increase medical spending sharply, particularly that on high-technology care. This is a common problem for health policy worldwide. Even though the best way to improve health is through improved lifestyles, preventive measures, and basic health care, the medical profession tends to be more interested in the hospital sector and state-of-the-art techniques. The medical lobby is well placed to steer policy in the CEE countries and the NIS because, in contrast with most market economies, the health minister is often a physician, as are many parliamentarians. As a result, the ministry of health can easily become the ministry of the health profession. Here, as elsewhere, policymakers ignore at their peril the politics of reform.

FINANCING HEALTH CARE. How should transition countries pay for their health care? Market economies choose among four approaches. Out-of-pocket payment, the main form of health finance until this century, remains so today in the very poorest countries, which have neither the tax revenues for public funding nor the institutional capacity for insurance. Private, for-profit insurance is important in many developing countries but among the industrial countries only in the United States.

Social insurance is the main source of health finance in many countries, including Argentina, Chile, Germany, the Republic of Korea, and Uruguay, whereas tax funding is the principal source in many others, including Denmark, Norway, Sweden, the United Kingdom, and many countries in Latin America, the Middle East, and North Africa. Reliance on public funding is not accidental. Technical advances have made much medical care too costly for most people to pay for out of pocket; this implies the need for some form of insurance. A purely private insurance system, however, can lead to gaps in coverage (because of uninsurable risks) and to exploding costs. The United States exemplifies both problems: despite high *public* medical spending about 17 percent of U.S. citizens below retirement age were uninsured in 1994, yet total medical spending that year absorbed over 14 percent of GDP, a much higher fraction than in any comparable country (the figure for the United Kingdom is 7 percent). To contain costs and promote access, the industrial market economies have increasingly financed health care through taxation, social insurance, or a mixture of the two.

Many of the transition economies, including Croatia, the Czech Republic, Estonia, Hungary, the Kyrgyz Republic, Latvia, FYR Macedonia, Russia, the Slovak Republic, and Slovenia, have already switched from taxes to social insurance to pay for health care, and many others are considering doing so. This shift has caused problems, not least because the same prerequisites for sustainable social insurance outlined in Chapter 4 apply when it is being used to fund health care. First, structural deficits arise because workers' contributions subsidize the nonactive population, including pensioners (who consume large amounts of health care). Second, substantial reliance on payroll taxes has increased labor costs and aggravated incentives to work in the informal sector (in Hungary, for example, as described in Box 4.4). Third, some governments have lost control of spending, because contributions and expenditure are determined separately by a more or less autonomous health insurance fund.

Alongside the question of how to raise resources is a second and separate issue: how to pay doctors, hospitals, and other providers. A number of approaches are used, none of them perfect. Payment on a fee-for-service basis creates an incentive to oversupply: the doctor has an incentive to prescribe more treatment, and if the insurance company pays most of the costs, the patient has no incentive to refuse. The resulting cost explosion has been a problem in almost all countries where fee-for-service is a significant part of health finance. However, carefully designed and regulated fee-for-service, together with a global budget cap for medical spending, can help raise efficiency and contain costs at the same time. For precisely this reason, many countries (Canada is an example) have adopted annual spending caps. An alternative approach, capitation, pays providers a fixed amount per patient per year. This method is excellent at containing costs but less good at maintaining service quality: doctors have an incentive to accept as many healthy patients as possible and then to see each as little as possible. The primary care systems of some countries (Romania is an example) pay doctors through a mix of capitation and fee-for-service, encouraging cost containment across most services but rewarding particular activities.

Paying medical providers has triggered a series of problems in CEE and the NIS, not the least of which is runaway expenditures. In 1992 the Czech Republic introduced fee-for-service payment without the necessary regulatory structure to cap medical spending, resulting in an entirely predictable—and entirely predicted—spending overrun. Most countries have yet to sort out the proper relationship between the public and the private sector. The private sector will supply health services only for a profit, and this raises questions about the extent to which public funding should be a source of private profit.

Future reforms of provider payment ought to have three central components. First, it is necessary to develop new payment systems that create incentives for efficient service delivery, for example by basing reimbursement as far as possible on health outcomes rather than the amount of diagnostic activity or treatment administered. Second, a framework is needed for monitoring quality and access and for tight control of spending. Third, policymakers must seek financing mechanisms that stimulate competition among providers, both public and private.

China faces difficult problems of health finance in both urban and rural areas. Like income transfers, urban health finance is based on the enterprise; the Anshan Iron and Steel Works, with 400,000 employees, has not only its own hospital but its own medical school. This ties workers to enterprises. In rural areas, as discussed earlier, the major problem is to finance health care in a way that assists access to medical care.

Health finance in Vietnam also faces severe problems. Household spending on health care is high, but there is no system to assist the poorest. Without a clearly defined government role, the private sector has remained largely unregulated. Ill effects include health care of variable quality and pharmaceuticals available without prescription. For both reasons, spending on private pharmaceuticals has exploded.

The big picture: How to make funding and delivery compatible

Experience from a cross-section of countries yields some clear lessons for transition countries on how to ensure that the means used to finance health care do not clash with the means of delivery. First, access and cost containment are both assisted by a substantial reliance on public rather than private funding. Second, health services can be delivered effectively by private providers for profit, by private nonprofit providers (often NGOs), by the public sector, or by a combination of these. Third, different approaches to funding and the different types of delivery cannot be mixed indiscriminately. One compatible package is tax funding of health care produced, often on a decentralized basis, by the state. Another is mainly public funding plus private, fee-for-service production plus regulation to contain expenditure. The last element is critical.

The agenda

Like the economy-wide production apparatus they were built to support, health and education systems under central planning were strong on accumulation but highly inefficient and unresponsive to changes in people's needs.

Ensuring that all citizens are able to enjoy and contribute to long-term economic growth will require coming to grips with these failings. In the health sector, policymakers must focus first on better allocation of resources: expenditures should be shifted from specialized services toward preventive care and encouraging healthier lifestyles. Another priority, particularly in rural China and Vietnam, must be to ensure universal access to basic health services. Better allocation of existing inputs will also be critical to upgrading education, although here the need to develop a demand-led system of provision is even stronger than in health. The ingredients for a healthy population are much the same under any economic system, but what counts as good education changes radically with the move from plan to market. Reformers must focus on developing an education system that is more responsive to demand, and that teaches people to think for themselves and to adapt to changing market circumstances.

CHAPTER 9

Transition and the World Economy

The global market that transition economies are reentering is an increasingly integrated one. World trade has grown far faster than global output in the past fifteen years, while total inflows of foreign direct investment (FDI) to developing countries have increased sixfold in just ten. Meanwhile a common set of overarching rules and institutions, including most prominently the new, 110-member World Trade Organization (WTO), has evolved to support even faster integration and to resolve disputes. Developing countries, many of which have recently made their own highly successful, if less comprehensive transitions toward more outward-looking economic policies, play an increasingly active part in this globalized economy. Exports and imports now account for 43 percent of developing countries' GDP, compared with 33 percent ten years ago. After years of isolation, transition economies may stand to gain even more from international integration than these other reformers. As Chapter 2 described, the economic benefits of moving into the world market are the benefits of internal market liberalization—writ enormous. Capital, goods, and ideas cross borders in response to demand and supply—rather than at the behest of a central planner—fueling faster growth in productivity, trade volumes, and national income. At the same time integration helps lock countries onto the path toward more-open trade, while membership in international institutions spurs domestic institution building.

Chapters 2 and 3, respectively, discussed the domestic importance of opening trade and of foreign investment. This chapter looks at transition economies' interactions with the rest of the world: trade flows to and from these countries and the consequences thereof for world trade; rapid and full-fledged membership in the WTO and relevant regional trade arrangements; and external capital flows to transition economies and the impact on other developing countries. The successful integration of transi-

tion countries brings benefits for the world economy—above all, by opening up almost a third of the world's population and a quarter of its land mass. A recurring concern, however, is that the transition countries' gains from this integration will come directly at other countries' expense. Such fears are understandable. Certainly, integration holds risks, as well as opportunities, for both sides. So far, however, the most commonly predicted global side effects of transition have not, by and large, been observed. As transition proceeds, many countries may indeed face adjustment costs. But the evidence suggests that these will be far outweighed by the benefits, for all countries, of being part of a larger and more competitive global marketplace.

The realignment of trade flows

Transition countries' potential trade growth . . .
Between 1978 and 1994 China went from being the world's thirty-second-largest exporter to its tenth-largest. Today the CEE countries and the NIS are similarly seeking to buy and sell in international markets. But how much will they trade—and with whom? Several estimates and projections based on economic models—and admittedly highly imperfect official statistics—broadly indicate the likely changes in trade patterns when the trade of the transition economies starts has adjusted to market economy patterns.

These calculations suggest that the CEE countries have a large untapped potential for trade with established market economies, not simply those in nearby Western Europe but industrial countries further afield as well. In the mid-1980s the CEE countries were on average fulfilling just one-quarter of this potential. Since then, trade shifts away from former CMEA markets and toward OECD markets have closed the gap and produced a pattern of trade that is better attuned to market forces. For example, based on its 1985 income level, Hungary would have been expected to send 43 percent of its exports to the

European Union; the actual share was 14 percent. By 1994, however, the share going to the EU countries was 49 percent. As Chapter 2 described, those countries that have liberalized and stabilized furthest have made the greatest strides in reorienting their trade toward patterns that would be predicted for market economies.

Although the Soviet Union itself was a very closed economy, Soviet planners fostered specialization rather than diversification within each republic. The result was very little trade with the rest of the world and very large amounts of trade between republics. In 1989, for example, more than 90 percent of Belarus' trade was with other Soviet republics; that share would have been about 32 percent had all the Soviet republics been market economies. Nearly 70 percent of Russia's exports went to other Soviet republics, compared with a predicted level of only 16 percent. Overall, trade among the former Soviet republics accounted for more than four-fifths of their total trade in 1989. This pattern seems likely to be reversed when trade is determined by market forces. The same estimates suggest that, as market economies, the NIS would send fully three-quarters of their exports to non-NIS partners, mostly in Western Europe. By 1994 the Baltics had made substantial progress in reorienting their trade toward market economies, but most of the other NIS had done very little. As Chapter 2 pointed out, the slow pace of price liberalization and maintenance of extensive export controls to keep goods at home resulted in slow progress in reorienting trade in many of the NIS. Lacking the institutional and physical infrastructure and expertise to support new patterns of trade, some transition economies face a daunting task in exploiting their trade potential as market economies; this is especially true for the Central Asian republics, most of whose transport and communications routes run through Russia.

Since the collapse of the Soviet Union, several largely unsuccessful attempts have been made to restore trade among the NIS and reduce adjustment costs through regional trade arrangements. Several "free trade" agreements have been concluded, but these were free in name only, because most of the countries preserved export controls on key products. Establishing a sound interstate payments system and convertibility of currencies is vital to market-based trade among the NIS. Removing trade barriers among the NIS alone is not the answer, especially because, as we saw above, under market-determined trade patterns much of their trade would be with countries outside the NIS. If agreements create barriers to reorienting trade and reintroduce the substantial diversion of trade that occurred under the Soviet Union, they will be counterproductive. Trade barriers should instead be removed on a nondiscriminatory basis, to deepen the integration of the NIS into the world trading system.

... And the implications for other countries

Transition economies offer the world great opportunities. Producers can look to new markets, and consumers can benefit from new products. Increased efficiency and resource mobilization in transition economies will expand the global supply of goods and services. The expected growth in inter- and intraindustry trade from integration—already evident in the CEE countries—will also increase world welfare by expanding the variety of products and encouraging gains from rationalization in industries subject to economies of scale. China's imports and exports have doubled in the past five years, while CEE's imports from OECD countries increased 216 percent and its exports to them 159 percent in the same period. Market economies, particularly the established industrial ones, have a strong interest in encouraging growth in these new markets by keeping their doors open. But reintegration will inevitably imply some adjustment costs. Some developing countries will face fiercer competition, particularly in labor-intensive products, while industrial countries' comparative advantage will also shift further away from these industries. However, where it has been possible to estimate the costs, they appear to be modest. Transition economies will not exhaust the world's appetite for variety, but only spur producers to invent and supply many more goods and services, for the benefit of many more people.

Should any countries fear the effects of transition economies' trade integration with the European Union? As noted above, the EU countries are already the CEE countries' main trading partners, trade between these regions having more than doubled since 1989. The CEE countries have proved exceptionally good export markets for the European Union, and the Europe Agreements (discussed below) between the Union and CEE countries provide free access to EU markets for most CEE manufactures. But there are still some restrictions on imports of sensitive products, agriculture remains protected, and the threat of contingent protection (antidumping and safeguard measures) limits the practical effect of liberalization measures on steel and chemical exports. Nevertheless, the Europe Agreements help to lock the CEE countries into open trade policies, thereby enhancing the credibility of their trade reforms. The evolving pattern of trade between the two regions is one of increasing intraindustry trade and of increasing processing and assembly activity by CEE firms. The Europe Agreements create incentives for EU companies to engage in outsourcing, where they provide designs and materials, monitor quality, and take care of marketing. Encouraging this form of trade helps EU firms exploit relatively skilled and cheap labor, while reducing the costs and risks that CEE partners face in developing new export markets.

There has been some concern in the European Union that a further opening of trade in sensitive products would impose heavy adjustment costs on EU producers. The evidence suggests, however, that complete liberalization of trade in these products would have only a marginal effect on EU imports, production, and employment because the CEE countries are only minor suppliers. Admittedly, long-term trade integration with the NIS could involve vastly greater trade flows. But even here the new flows would largely consist of the NIS sending increased supplies of energy—most notably, oil and natural gas—to Western Europe in return for a large volume of capital- and technology-intensive goods (machinery and equipment) and high-quality consumer durables.

Many Mediterranean and African countries, currently enjoying preferential trade with EU countries, also worry that they will lose from trade liberalization between the EU and CEE countries. Several Mediterranean countries have enjoyed duty-free access to EU markets for industrial goods and preferential access for agricultural commodities since the 1970s. None of these preferences will be seriously eroded by the emergence of the CEE countries as EU trade partners. It is fair to say that their arrival on the scene may have deprived Mediterranean exporters of whatever geographical advantage in EU markets they previously enjoyed. But in fact the market share of nonoil exports of Mediterranean countries in the EU market has been stable. Mediterranean nations and CEE countries naturally have very different relative strengths—revealed comparative advantages—in world trade. Indeed, the export structures of the two regions hardly overlap at all. Longstanding restrictions on exports to EU agricultural markets are a much more important issue for a number of Mediterranean countries that cannot fully exploit their agricultural export potential. The countries of Africa that are signatories to the Lomé Convention also continue to enjoy preferential access to EU markets. For most, head-to-head competition with the CEE countries is relatively rare, again because the comparative advantage of the two groups of countries does not generally lie in the same goods or industries. In agriculture, too, these countries compete directly with CEE in only a few products. To be balanced against any adverse effect on the export side is the fact that rapidly growing CEE countries are themselves another potential market for the exports of the Mediterranean and African countries.

The CEE countries enter the international arena with relatively highly skilled labor, although some reorientation in educational priorities is needed, as discussed in Chapter 8. Because FDI brings not only capital and equipment but also managerial skills and ties to a trade network, in the longer run the CEE countries would be expected to compete in medium- or high-skill-intensive products rather than in simple, labor-intensive products. This structural transformation would further reduce CEE countries' direct competition with low-income developing countries.

China's triumphant return to international markets has so far had the greatest impact on global trade of any transition country. As one would expect, given China's vast supply of unskilled labor, its export mix has been increasingly labor-intensive. With growth in China's exports in these types of products averaging 23 percent a year in the 1980s, labor-intensive exports rose from one-third of China's total exports in 1975 to three-quarters in 1990. Clothing, toys, sporting goods, and footwear together accounted for 30 percent of China's exports in 1994. Has China's rapid growth in labor-intensive products crowded out labor-intensive exporters from other developing countries in world markets? The answer appears to be no, for two reasons. First, and more important, China's export growth turns out to have replaced the exports of soon-to-be-high-income economies rather than other developing ones. And second, there is almost certainly more than enough demand for labor-intensive exports to go around.

China's dramatic growth in labor-intensive exports has been more than matched by a sharp decline in the export shares of East Asia's "four tigers"—Hong Kong, the Republic of Korea, Singapore, and Taiwan (China)—from 55 percent in 1984 to 24 percent in 1994. China's exports have simply replaced those of the tigers, so that their combined world market share has fallen for clothing, toys, and sporting goods (while remaining unchanged for footwear). The Chinese eclipse of the tigers has been fueled by FDI by the tigers themselves, whose firms in many cases simply moved their production lines to China. For example, about 25,000 factories in the Pearl River Delta region of Guangdong, directly or indirectly employing 3 million to 4 million workers, are engaged in subcontracting for Hong Kong companies. The tigers, meanwhile, have moved up the development ladder to produce more capital- and skill-intensive products.

Without the emergence of China, would other developing countries have captured larger markets as the tigers developed away from simple manufactures? Perhaps to some extent, but arguably the tigers vacated these markets precisely because of China's emergence. China's opening changed their comparative advantage in world trade, and instead of resisting, the tigers seized the opportunity, moving resources out of simple manufactures into more sophisticated lines of production and using their expertise to expand production in China.

There is a second reason why China's emergence as a force in labor-intensive exports has probably not affected other developing countries as much as many feared. That is the fact that world demand for these commodities from developing countries has grown threefold over the past decade.

In addition, developing countries are sizable markets for each other. Substantial trade among developing countries, including considerable intraindustry trade, makes it possible for them to be simultaneously importers and exporters of a wide range of manufactured goods. Developing countries sent more than one-quarter of their exports of labor-intensive goods to each other in 1994. They can therefore benefit directly from each other's export expansion, even when they are exporting similar goods.

Integration into world trading institutions

The OECD countries have taken significant steps to normalize trade relations with transition economies. They have granted transition economies most-favored-nation status and eliminated quantitative restrictions that applied only to "state trading countries," and some have granted trade preferences that put the transition economies on a par with developing countries already enjoying such preferences. But normalization is not yet complete. Transition economies still face certain quantitative restrictions and differential treatment in antidumping actions in OECD countries, and only a few are formally protected by WTO rules and procedures. Six transition countries—the Czech Republic, Hungary, Poland, Romania, the Slovak Republic, and Slovenia—are members of the WTO.

WTO membership is an important step for transition countries, and virtually all have applied to join. The WTO provides a firm institutional basis for the application and enforcement of multilaterally agreed trade rules on goods and services and on the protection of intellectual property rights. Each WTO member undertakes commitments to cap (bind) tariffs on imports and enjoys corresponding rights for its exports to member countries. No member may normally increase tariffs above bound levels without at least providing compensation. The WTO constrains various trade procedures to acceptable standards. For a country assuming obligations negotiated under WTO auspices, the requirement to maintain access to its market or pay compensation provides an effective constraint on internal pressures for increased trade protection.

Transition economies will benefit greatly from the rights attached to WTO membership. Participation will consolidate their access to international markets, providing some insurance against the arbitrary imposition of barriers by others. But transition economies will also benefit from accepting the corresponding obligations. Prompt and firm commitment to abide by WTO rules will greatly enhance the political feasibility of achieving and maintaining liberal trade regimes at home, in the face of the strong sectoral interests that are inevitably emerging.

Transition economies should therefore view WTO membership as an opportunity to further the reform of their trade regimes, not only to meet WTO requirements but also to increase economic efficiency through reducing distortions in trade policy. Relatively strict terms of accession—including comprehensive tariff bindings—can help reduce the payoff to domestic rent seeking. At the same time, without undermining the pressure on applicants to adopt liberal trade regimes, WTO members should do all they can to accelerate the process of admission. For some transition economies, technical assistance in meeting the extensive information requirements of accession would be helpful.

Integration into the European Union has profound implications for the transition economies concerned. The process began with the Europe Agreements and has entered a new phase with the preaccession strategy. The Europe Agreements signed between the European Union and six CEE countries (Bulgaria, the Czech Republic, Hungary, Poland, Romania, and the Slovak Republic; the agreement with Slovenia is not yet signed) and the Baltic states are the deepest and broadest of the EU Association Agreements. Like the association agreements signed with other countries, these agreements not only cover trade relations between the EU and CEE and Baltic countries but go on to deal with financial cooperation, commercial practices and law, and political dialogue at various levels. They also encourage these countries to liberalize trade among themselves, for example, through the newly created Central European Free Trade Association.

It has been more than four years since the first Europe Agreements were signed in early 1992. At the Copenhagen Summit in 1993 the European Union made its first clear commitment to CEE countries' accession. The so-called White Paper, published in June 1995, forms part of the preaccession strategy. It identifies the key measures required in each sector of the internal market, suggests an approximate sequence for legislation, and details the measures necessary for effective implementation and enforcement. Partly with this in mind, the European Union has been providing various types of assistance. Accession negotiations with some of the CEE and Baltic countries are expected to start soon after the conclusion of the EU Inter-Governmental Conference. Prompt accession should not be taken for granted, however: negotiations for the Union's most recent enlargement (with Austria, Finland, and Sweden) took less than two years, but negotiations with Spain took almost nine years. The benefits of accession are clear: political stability, free trade and capital flows, access to common funds, and locking into reasonably market-friendly policies.

Rapid EU accession would do much to sustain and deepen reforms in these transition economies. So what

Transition economies have absorbed only a modest share of global capital flows.

Figure 9.1 Capital flows to developing and transition countries by region

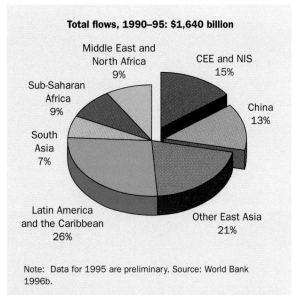

Total flows, 1990–95: $1,640 billion

- Middle East and North Africa 9%
- CEE and NIS 15%
- Sub-Saharan Africa 9%
- China 13%
- South Asia 7%
- Latin America and the Caribbean 26%
- Other East Asia 21%

Note: Data for 1995 are preliminary. Source: World Bank 1996b.

stands in the way? One obstacle is the need to develop administrative and organizational structures in the CEE and Baltic countries to implement and enforce the rules of the Union. The biggest barrier, however, is the EU budget, some 80 percent of which goes to finance the structural funds, which offer aid to poorer EU regions, and the Common Agricultural Policy (CAP), which subsidizes farmers in member countries. Extending these policies, unreformed, to CEE countries would be expensive. Elements of the CAP were reformed in 1992, but further reforms are needed. Integration is therefore likely to involve a phased process that advances certain elements of EU membership—free trade in particular—faster than others, while at the same time possibly stimulating some helpful reforms in the Union itself. As far as the transition economies are concerned, the faster accession proceeds, the better.

Capital flows and transition

One might have expected huge imports of capital, both private and official, to participate in financing the costly economic and political transformation required in countries undergoing transition. At the beginning of the transition in Europe there were concerns that large capital flows to CEE and the NIS would raise world interest rates at the expense of developing countries. However, except for the

former East Germany (see Box 1.1), CEE and the NIS have not absorbed a great deal of foreign capital—either private investment flows or official external assistance.

Has transition caused a major diversion of private capital flows . . .

Between them the countries of CEE and the NIS absorbed 15 percent of total capital flows to developing and transition countries in the period 1990–95 (Figure 9.1). Net resource inflows are much lower and even negative to some countries, once debt service and capital flight are taken into account. Capital flight from Russia alone has been estimated at some $50 billion for 1992–95, although part of this represented capital exported through Russia from other NIS.

Private capital flows to developing countries increased dramatically during the 1990s, with a surge in FDI and portfolio equity investment. CEE and the NIS, however, between them attracted just 13 percent of total private capital flows to developing and transition countries in 1990–95. In 1994, FDI to CEE and the NIS was only $6.5 billion, equivalent to the total received by Malaysia and Thailand. The distribution of these limited FDI flows among them has also been highly uneven. The Visegrad countries received fully three-quarters of the total, whereas many other countries in the region are still all but untouched by foreign investment (see Chapter 3). Capital flows to China more closely followed the trend for developing countries, with private sources accounting for the lion's share. FDI to China was $33.8 billion in 1994, second only to flows to the United States. However, a substantial portion consisted of domestic funds recycled as foreign investment to take advantage of fiscal concessions.

. . . Or of foreign assistance?

Given the relative failure of many CEE countries and NIS to capitalize on the growth of investment in emerging markets, a key goal of foreign official assistance must be to help them create a more attractive environment for private inflows and thus help them restructure toward international competitiveness. Annual net flows of official development finance—including official development assistance (grants and official concessional loans) and official nonconcessional loans—to CEE and the NIS averaged $8.8 billion in 1990–95. This has not, however, diverted official assistance from the world's poorest regions (Figure 9.2). For example, grants to the transition economies rose dramatically, from $641 million in 1990 to $4.7 billion in 1995, but grants to Sub-Saharan Africa increased in this period as well. Former Soviet clients have, however, lost aid—these countries received an estimated $4.5 billion from the Soviet Union in 1987, for example, and $554 million from Eastern Europe in 1985, but these flows have now virtually ceased.

Official assistance for transition economies has not been at Africa's expense.

Figure 9.2 Official development finance to developing and transition economies

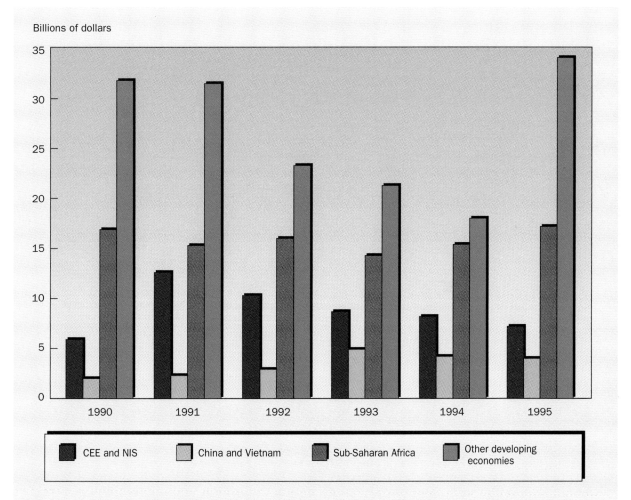

Billions of dollars

Note: Official development finance consists of official development assistance (grants and concessional lending) plus nonconcessional lending. Data for 1995 are preliminary. Source: World Bank 1996b.

All in all, then, transition has not absorbed a large slice of global capital flows. As transition economies recover, demand for investment in infrastructure, economic reconstruction, and private sector development will rise. As their creditworthiness improves, they could absorb a larger share of world capital flows and could increase total global demand for capital, raising world interest rates. But as noted in Chapter 2, in the long run all countries tend to finance the bulk of their investment from domestic rather than foreign savings. Moreover, any impact on world inter-est rates of rising demand for foreign capital from transition economies would be small compared with that already exerted by the combined budget deficits of the OECD countries, now running at some $700 billion a year.

How can external assistance help transition?
Through the early years of reform in CEE and the NIS, a major share of official assistance has taken the form of balance of payments and budgetary support and of debt relief. Official support from the international financial institu-

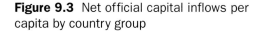

Reforming governments receive the most external assistance.

Figure 9.3 Net official capital inflows per capita by country group

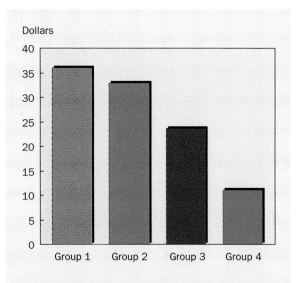

Note: Data are annual averages for 1990–95 (CEE) or 1992–95 (NIS); 1995 data are preliminary. See Figure 1.2 for the countries in each group. Countries severely affected by regional tensions are excluded. Source: World Bank 1996b.

tions and individual country donors has typically been much larger, relative to population or GDP, for those countries that have advanced further with reforms (Figure 9.3). For example, by the end of 1993 the Visegrad countries, in the first of the reform groups in Figure 1.2, had received more than half of disbursements by the international financial institutions to the region. In 1994 official lending shifted to the NIS, which had previously obtained little funding, as reforms advanced there. Among the NIS the Baltic states, which have undertaken substantial reforms, received more official assistance in relation to their population as well as to GDP than, for example, did Belarus.

Has external financial assistance been adequate? This controversial question can be answered in a number of different ways. Aid under the Marshall Plan after World War II averaged 2.5 percent of the incomes of the recipient countries at the time. Total official disbursements to the CEE economies, which have generally progressed furthest in their reforms, accounted on average for about 2.7

percent of their combined GDP in 1991–93. Under-recording of GDP in these economies may bias this ratio upward, but on this measure Marshall Plan disbursements were not materially larger than official flows to CEE. The Marshall Plan did, however, embody a larger grant element, and it was much more generous relative to the donor economy's income, at 1.5 percent of U.S. GDP.

Has the timing of external financial assistance been appropriate? This is another hotly debated issue. External finance has supported a number of stabilization programs, creating confidence (as was true of the Polish stabilization fund) or reducing the need for monetary financing to cover budget deficits (Chapter 2). However, one of the main findings of this Report is that liberalization, stabilization, and structural and institutional reforms have been highly complementary. Macroeconomic pressure often underpins the incentives for microeconomic change, so that external assistance programs in transition economies must be developed carefully—walking the narrow path between facilitating reform and diminishing its urgency—and must lock in reforms through conditionality. Indeed, ill-conceived or premature lending can create large external debts that complicate subsequent reforms—as shown by the experience of certain lines of credit awarded by export credit agencies.

Even after inflation has been brought down to moderate levels, external assistance may be needed—within limits—to help some countries bridge a transitional fiscal gap. Whereas government spending as a share of GDP still exceeds reasonable limits in some countries, other transition governments are small relative to their core functions. Some governments have been forced to cut social protection and public investment, probably to levels below those needed to sustain reforms. Some, with limited capacity for administering taxes, end up imposing distortionary taxes to meet their spending needs, at huge cost to economic efficiency (Chapter 7). Meanwhile a number of governments are themselves in arrears, undermining hard budget constraints elsewhere in the economy (Chapter 2). These problems merit close attention by assistance agencies. However, budget support should always be conditional on policy reforms, notably in the areas of tax policy and administration, budget management, targeted poverty programs, and human resource development.

As this Report has described, adjusting to a market economy involves sharp economic declines in some regions and social costs that may have political implications. In these areas assistance can speed recovery, for example through funding severance pay and extraordinary demands on local governments in distressed regions, as well as possible environmental costs associated with plant shutdowns. It may be necessary—and desirable—to cushion the impact of transition on certain regionally concentrated and overbuilt industries, such as Ukraine's coal sector (see Box 3.2). Here again, support needs to carefully target temporary losses and to address them without undermining the longer-run credibility of reforms and labor market incentives.

Yet, as ever, the development of market-supporting institutions is fundamental to transition. Postwar Western Europe already had long experience with markets, and the associated institutions—property rights, information, and legal systems and courts, as well as skills in using them, honed over generations of experience—were all well in place, so foreign aid could readily promote reconstruction and recovery. Even now, many developing countries have a stronger institutional base for a market economy than do most transition economies at similar levels of income. Foreign support therefore needs to embody a large component of technical assistance and institution building in areas that constitute critical reform bottlenecks. This involves helping create institutions such as independent central banks and property arrangements that make reforms more effective and harder to reverse. Bilateral assistance, including that provided by the European Union, has had a large component of technical assistance. The international financial institutions have also engaged heavily in this kind of institution building, across a wide range of areas, in addition to transferring financial resources.

Building institutions takes time and sometimes involves restoring entire professions in areas essential to a well-functioning market economy. For example, although considerable support has been given to privatization and the drafting of new legislation, more needs to be allocated for the training of judges and other legal professionals and for the upgrading of judicial facilities (Chapter 5). Technical assistance should encourage local capacity building through, among other things, more involvement of local participants. Far greater stress is needed on economic education in the broad sense as well as hands-on training in key marketable skills (Chapter 8).

Box 9.1 Business skills training is good for business—for trainers and trainees

Efforts to teach market-related skills and business know-how in transition countries have had a somewhat mixed record. But two programs show how to overcome the pitfalls and create valuable follow-on effects.

In early 1992 the World Bank's Economic Development Institute launched a training program to support enterprise restructuring and privatization in transition economies, based on learning by doing and helping local talent and stakeholders to help themselves. The 180 trainees recruited since the program began—including enterprise and bank managers, consultants, government officials, and parliamentarians—have worked with over forty local partner institutions and trained over 4,000 other participants. Evaluations by independent consultants concluded that the program has been highly cost-effective and has had a great impact on enterprise reform and private sector development. Dozens of enterprises have successfully restructured and privatized as a direct result.

The career of Mrs. Smirnova, a deputy director of the textile conglomerate Mayak in Nizhniy Novgorod, Russia, illustrates the potential benefits. Fresh out of the program, she had Mayak introduce international accounting standards before they were required by law, and retrained its accountants. She then initiated the firm's breakup into thirteen independent companies. Her business plan for Mayak won an international award, and around 70 percent of Mayak's production is now exported to the British market. A conference on business planning for Russian textile enterprises, which Mrs. Smirnova organized, led to the creation of various business associations, and working together with other graduates she has advised companies throughout Russia, in Kazakstan, and in Uzbekistan. All this has created momentum for similar restructuring activities by many other companies.

The East/West Enterprise Exchange Program at York University in Toronto puts a great emphasis on building personal business links in the program it has been running since 1989. It has brought over 450 business delegates from CEE and the NIS to Canada. Selection of delegates is based on the criteria of sponsoring Canadian firms, which fund the program in partnership with government, other donors, and the delegates themselves, who pay fees to participate. Delegates first take classes in business practices, accounting, marketing, and a range of associated topics. They then work with their sponsors to develop business plans to serve as the basis for future deals. An independent evaluation of the program concluded that it was having a significant impact on delegates' knowledge and attitudes and contributing positively to their careers. It was also contributing to business cooperation: preliminary estimates put the volume of technology transfers, trade deals, and joint ventures resulting from the program at many times the program's cost.

Because of the importance of new business entry for growth, assistance should also be strongly conditioned on reforms to reduce regulatory and other barriers, including access to premises. Carefully designed programs can combine commercial and educational objectives, and some may return more than their cost (Box 9.1). Business advice and financial support to the private sector should come mainly from the private sector itself, that is, from private business support services, equity investors, and private lenders of working and investment capital. These services and suppliers exist in embryo in some transition economies, not at all in many others. Does this justify a role for assistance agencies? Yes, if that role is assisting financial system reforms to speed the emergence of prudent and capable lenders and investors; and yes, if it means providing training and technical assistance to managers and entrepreneurs to overcome years of isolation from market forces. But no, if it means simply financing investment through government restructuring agencies.

As already noted, some countries face more of a transition problem, while others face more of a development problem. For the first group, heavy dependence on external assistance should be considered a temporary phase until reforms create an environment that can attract private capital. A key purpose of official financial assistance must be to bring down, decisively and sustainably, the barriers to committing external and domestic private capital, especially private equity investments. Some countries have passed through this phase very quickly. The Czech Republic, for example, drew on International Monetary Fund (IMF) credits and other official loans relatively heavily in 1991 and 1992 but started to repay the IMF earlier than planned (as did Poland in 1995). Equally encouraging, private capital flows picked up, rising to $2.85 billion in 1994 from $585 million two years earlier.

Some transition economies, however, may require longer-term development assistance. These include the Central Asian countries and a number of others whose economies have been severely disrupted by regional tensions. Yet even in these cases donors need to ensure that assistance strengthens rather than undermines reform. It might be tempting to think that the ability to replace official capital flows with private capital flows is a function of the level of income. In fact, it owes much to government policies. China, one of the poorest transition economies, relies mostly on private capital.

The agenda

The rapid integration of the global economy in recent decades springs from the widespread recognition that economies invariably achieve more working with each other—exchanging goods, capital, and ideas—than acting alone. The failure of the Soviet ideal of "socialism in one country" is further confirmation, if any were needed, of this simple truth. But ensuring that the transition economies realize their potential as members of the global trading system will not be easy—for them or their supporters. For the new entrants, the first step is to adopt the economic, social, and institutional policy reforms outlined in this Report, in order to attract foreign investors and foster growth. For those outside, particularly international bodies such as the European Union and the international financial institutions, it will mean careful consideration of how to help transition countries in ways that support rather than delay long-term reform. Speeding the removal of existing trade barriers, along with further direct efforts toward integration, will bring perhaps the largest and most immediate benefits for transition countries. But more-direct forms of support, such as short-term financial assistance and, critically, helping countries acquire much-needed skills and institutions, are also important. Finally, the integration process must be buttressed, on both sides, by determined efforts to allay fears about the costs of greater global competition and to persuade those diffident of integration that, in the long term, all they stand to lose is their isolation.

PART THREE

Conclusions

CHAPTER 10

Conclusions—and the Unfinished Agenda

Transition economies have made great strides in liberalizing their domestic markets and foreign trade regimes and in freeing up entry into private business. Many are trying to define property rights more clearly and to privatize, to create or renew essential institutions to support efficient markets, and to reshape social services and the social safety net to conform to the needs of a market system. Taken together, these measures constitute the economics of transition, but transition has had profound social, political, and strategic implications as well.

This chapter draws out the key messages from the analysis of the preceding chapters. What can these countries learn from each other? What does the experience of transition to date suggest for the many other countries grappling with similar issues of economic reform? What are the implications for external assistance—and for the reform priorities in the countries themselves?

Lessons of experience

Consistent policies, combining liberalization of markets, trade, and new business entry with reasonable price stability, can achieve a great deal—even in countries lacking clear property rights and strong market institutions.

Policies of liberalization and stabilization have been the major factor shaping the adjustment process in CEE and the NIS and have been vital to China's and Vietnam's rapid growth. In the first two regions there has been a strong link between consistent and credible reform and economic recovery: growth has typically resumed about three years after the determined application of such reforms, including stabilization programs. Less consistent reformers have recovered more slowly and, on average, have performed less well. Recovery has involved rapid

growth in previously repressed sectors (services in particular) and the penetration of new export markets.

The turnaround in the more successful reformers has included substantial adjustment, even by state enterprises. Governments have succeeded in imposing tight budget constraints on enterprises, spurring a highly decentralized process of deep cost cutting and restructuring by firms themselves, the breakup of some, the introduction of new products, and the acquisition of new capabilities, including marketing and financial management, not required under the old system. Just saying no to enterprises' requests for more resources produces positive results—at least for a time. The next stage of China's reforms will also involve redirecting savings away from unprofitable state firms and exposing them to greater competition.

A striking lesson from the experience of all transition economies is the importance of new entry in response to the lifting of restrictions on business. In China the new entrants were at first primarily the new township and village enterprises (TVEs); more recently new private firms and joint ventures constitute China's most dynamic sources of growth, employment, and exports. In Vietnam the protected state sector continues to generate growth, but it is the private sector that is producing new jobs. In CEE and the NIS new private firms, often using old assets carved out from the state sector—a process greatly encouraged by harder budgets—have clearly led the recovery. If it is to be widespread and effective, entry must be cheap and administratively easy. And new firms cannot flourish without access to broad markets for their products and inputs.

Market economies perform very poorly when inflation rises above a moderate level. The same appears to hold for transition economies. Liberalization at first causes prices to rise. This is painful, but in CEE and the NIS the freeing of prices was needed to sever the link between governments and enterprises and allow subsidies to be cut, thereby making stabilization possible.

Differences between countries are very important, both in setting the feasible range of policy choice and in determining the response to reforms.

Which works best, rapid or gradual reform? This question, the one most often asked in the study of transition, has no single or simple answer. Economic reform in CEE and the NIS was begun in the context of a fundamental dismantling of repressive political systems that had been, in many cases, propped up from without. These countries set out with severe macroeconomic imbalances and structural distortions created by central planning, as well as huge declines in trade as the previous system was dismantled. They have not been able to generate the savings necessary to sustain gradual adjustment of the greatly overbuilt state sectors. They therefore face a choice between rapid systemic reforms, entailing deep and often painful structural adjustment, and efforts aimed at prolonging the status quo. Although the latter course may appear less painful at the outset, its result is persisting inflation and economic disarray.

The differences between leading and lagging reformers have largely reflected how they approached this very difficult choice. Dedicated and audacious leaders have mattered a great deal, but transition is not just a matter of intelligent leaders choosing the right policy package or seizing the moment. Countries' characteristics—their unique advantages and disadvantages—influence what policies can be chosen and what leaders can accomplish. Important advantages include strong government administrative capacity, proximity to market economies, greater societal memory of market processes, and a strong desire to integrate into Western Europe. All of these have helped sustain the pace and scope of reform in the advanced reformers. Differences in the abruptness and timing of political change have also been reflected in the thrust of economic reform. Nevertheless, for the bulk of these economies, the answer to the question is now clear: faster and more consistent reform is better.

China, on the other hand, is both a successful reformer and a gradual one, although its first major reform, the shift from collective to household farming, involved a sharp change from the previous regime of agricultural collectivism. China embarked on its transition with a large, repressed rural economy. This allowed rapid productivity gains and growth of a nonstate sector using rural labor. Effective macroeconomic management encouraged a high rate of saving. With a reform program that skillfully took advantage of China's initial conditions, including strong government capacity and the ability to impose direct controls, the Chinese government was able to liberalize along a dual-track process without seriously undermining macroeconomic balance. The political fundamentals were

also quite different from those in CEE and the NIS, as China's transition has involved progressively greater weight on economic performance as a legitimating factor for an ongoing government.

Hungary and Vietnam offer another contrast illustrating the importance of initial conditions for the outcome of reform. Despite embarking on transition with a relatively liberalized economy, and despite postponing sharp macroeconomic adjustment until 1995, Hungary has not been able to avoid a deep transformational recession. Vietnam, on the other hand, had a large rural sector and a smaller state sector, and it sustained strong growth through a period of relatively rapid reform. Its restrictive macroeconomic policies included layoffs of a full third of state enterprise employees, but they were absorbed by the resurgent rural sector and the newly unleashed private sector.

An efficient response to market processes requires clearly defined property rights—and this will eventually require widespread private ownership.

The political economy of privatization plays out differently in different countries, and differently for each of the major types of asset (industrial firms, farms, real estate). Experience everywhere reveals a severe and politically charged tension between promoting efficiency and rewarding existing stakeholders. None of the methods used to privatize large firms—sales, management-employee buyouts, or equal-access voucher privatization—is without drawbacks in a transition setting, in terms of either the effectiveness of corporate governance, speed, fiscal impact, access to investment capital, or fairness.

Nevertheless, privatization is important. Initial privatization helps depoliticize economic restructuring and creates incentives to support change required at the firm level. Governments cannot manage and finance such restructuring on a wide scale. Privatization also frees government to focus on those few key areas of the economy—such as infrastructure and, perhaps, key natural resources—where its regulatory and ownership roles are most essential.

Is there an alternative to formal privatization? In theory, yes. But the experience of many CEE countries and the NIS suggests that in practice the alternative is often an ownership vacuum with fuzzy property rights, leading to informal and nontransparent privatization, either of the assets themselves or of the income streams they generate. China and Vietnam have so far been able to prevent wholesale and egregious asset stripping, but there are signs of similar processes at work there also. Informal privatization often precedes the legitimization of a private economy, but it accelerates thereafter. An ownership vacuum delays the restructuring of drifting firms, for which nobody is fully responsible and which cannot tap external resources. It can create or prolong macroeconomic problems, because it produces strong incentives for enterprise managers to show poor financial performance and then snap up their firms (or additional shares) at an artificially low price. It can also be inequitable and induce corruption, which can undermine the authority of government.

An initial assignment of property rights is only the first step. The broader goal is to develop an efficient secondary trading process in which ownership claims can be reorganized smoothly. All transition economies need such a process, particularly because many of the governance structures emerging during transition are themselves likely to be transitional. For example, in CEE and the NIS control of many firms will need to shift from insiders to outsiders if they are to attract the investments and skills needed to survive in a market economy. Agricultural reorganization will require moving from corporate to individual property rights to enable new, viable farms to emerge. Further clarification of property rights in China's TVEs is essential for their further development, including the ability to raise finance from outside the community. Countries need to beware of dead ends in the evolution of ownership: some transitional arrangements, such as the closed joint-stock corporations in Ukraine or the highly dispersed individual ownership seen in Mongolia, promise to become obstacles to reorganization, essentially because they entrench incumbent workers and managers. In contrast, besides sales (where feasible), the Czech approach, which creates strong external institutional investors and stimulates trading among them, appears to have many advantages.

Major changes in social policies must complement the move to the market—to focus on relieving poverty, to cope with increased mobility, and to counter the adverse intergenerational effects of reform.

Transition sets in motion vast social change. Much of this change is positive: it increases individual liberties and choice and gives broad access to information formerly available only to a privileged few. The negatives include greater economic uncertainty and, in some countries, a dramatic growth in crime.

Transition requires a major reorientation in the social role of the state, away from paternalistic, poorly targeted benefits conveyed largely through extensive cross-subsidies, and toward addressing poverty. Market-determined wages and employment are vital to achieving deep restructuring, but initial conditions in transition economies make increased income inequality an inevitable consequence of reform. Until this impact is offset by renewed growth—the indispensable element in any antipoverty policy—an increase in poverty is unavoidable.

How to target benefits to the poor—whether through income-tested assistance, locally organized relief, targeting based on indicators of poverty (one rationale behind, for example, child allowances), or self-targeting (such as in public works employment)—is a complex matter that depends on the administrative capacity of government agencies. The large informal sectors and limited capacity of many transition economies suggest that targeting by poverty indicators is perhaps the most realistic option in the short run. In urban China and much of the NIS, delinking of social services from enterprises will eliminate a serious impediment to restructuring.

In many countries the largest problem, both politically and in terms of demand on public resources, is state pensions. Generous access to pensions is one way of cushioning the impact of transition on a generation that was prevented from accumulating wealth in the previous system and has no opportunity to save in the new market system. But it is important to distinguish such transitional issues from longer-run policies. Retirement ages need to be raised and equalized for men and women. Private pensions are desirable for a variety of reasons but are no substitute for directly addressing the problem of excessive spending in the state sector. In China pensions need to be delinked from enterprise finances, and the continued expansion of the nonstate sector and rising labor mobility argue for extension of a formal social safety net beyond the state sector.

Institutions that support markets arise both by design and from demand.

Institutional development—of legal and financial systems and of a retooled government—normally takes years, if not decades. It therefore trails early macroeconomic reforms and formal ownership changes. Institutional reform is now high on the reform agenda in all transition economies. Reform is particularly badly needed because existing institutions were adapted to the needs of a very different economic system and because inadequate institutions impose high economic costs.

■ To be effective, legislation must be well designed and well implemented. In addition, the state must itself be ruled by law and trusted by the private sector to do what it says it will do. Yet governments are particularly susceptible to corruption during the phase when the state retains both vast assets and extensive powers to intervene in a growing private economy. Liberalization, demonopolization, and—if transparent—rapid privatization are key steps to reducing these two sources of huge economic rents and to strengthen demand for the rule of law. So are serious efforts to publicize and punish high-level corruption. Like corruption, organized crime thrives when property rights are unclear, legal procedures ineffective, and risks low. Effective action against organized crime also requires that the state be reasonably free of internal corruption.

- Financial sector reforms cannot proceed in isolation from macroeconomic and enterprise reform. For many countries the best approach involves a mixed strategy, restricting the scope of state banks while a new financial system develops. Both the entry of new institutions and the rehabilitation of old ones pose risks, requiring strong complementary policies.

- Transition means less government involvement in the economy, but where it remains involved—in setting the rules of the game, assisting the development of institutions, and providing social protection—it must become more effective. Far-reaching reforms are needed, especially to strengthen tax systems (reduce exemptions, lower rates, and tighten administration), improve expenditure control (eliminate government arrears), and build transparent intergovernmental relations.

In all these areas and many others, governments need to take an active, central role. However, the degree of institutional change is also closely related to the comprehensiveness and duration of macroeconomic and ownership reforms. Market-oriented reforms create demand for market-supporting institutions and for their associated skills. Experience shows that institutional development cannot proceed far in a vacuum or when the economic system makes it irrelevant or unwanted. Parties will have a strong incentive to abide by legal responsibilities only to the extent that they depend on the market—and their reputations in it—for survival. For example, manager-owners in private firms will be tempted to ignore minority shareholders' rights unless their access to capital depends on their reputation, and banks will not develop the capabilities necessary to function in a market system if they expect to be bailed out by government whenever crises occur.

Sustaining the human capital base for economic growth requires considerable reengineering of education and health delivery systems.

Relative to other countries at comparable income levels, people in centrally planned economies were often healthy and well educated. Today, broad access to health and education services needs to be protected in China. Such systems in CEE and the NIS require extensive restructuring to improve their effectiveness. In many respects these systems share the weaknesses of industrial enterprises under central planning, being input-intensive rather than responsive to changing needs. The decline in health status in this region relative to Western Europe, observable even before transition, emphasizes that the objective ought to be improved health, not simply more health care. This argues for a shift to include health promotion programs—including encouragement of healthy lifestyles—that maintain previous achievements while improving incentives for efficiency.

Transition requires major reforms of education and training, particularly in the NIS and parts of CEE, to enable it to provide the skills needed in a changing market economy. Incorporating private provision of education services, particularly in higher and adult education, and providing education vouchers as part of retraining assistance could help introduce demand-led restructuring.

International integration can help lock in successful reforms.

International integration is vital for successful reform in transition countries, especially considering their history of autarky. Imports help make their markets competitive. Exports provide a source of growth and learning. In some areas foreign direct investment is the only way of acquiring vital skills, markets, and finance. Institutional integration is also vital. Joining the World Trade Organization (WTO) would enhance market access and provide some protection against the arbitrary imposition of trade barriers. Equally important, quick access to the WTO will strengthen the political feasibility of maintaining a liberal trade regime in transition economies themselves.

The integration of transition economies into the global trading system will benefit the world economy. The countries of the Organization for Economic Cooperation and Development, especially, have a strong interest in encouraging transition by keeping their doors open. The costs of absorbing the transition economies into world trade are manageable. Enlargement of the European Union to include some of the transition economics may involve more concentrated adjustment costs, but even there the adjustment to trade flows is a less important issue than the budgetary effects.

The agenda for donors . . .

What should be the timing and composition of foreign assistance to transition economies? A first observation is that although only the poorer transition economies require long-term financial assistance, all but a very few could benefit from extended technical assistance to support the building of institutions. This process can take decades, as some aspects of institutional reform involve rebuilding entire professions and require massive training programs. Many countries will also require long-term support, from official sources, nongovernmental organizations, and the private sector, to help build the institutions of civil society.

Second, macroeconomic stress often strengthens incentives for reform. Aid programs in transition economies therefore require particular care in their design—to walk the narrow path between facilitating reform and diminishing its urgency—and should lock in reforms through setting strict conditions on aid provided. This involves creating the critical institutions, such as independent central banks and property rights, that make reforms more effective and harder to reverse. Because of the great importance of new entry for growth, assistance should also be conditioned on reforms to reduce barriers to new businesses.

Third, in addition to short-term support for stabilization programs, a case can sometimes be made for temporarily plugging a public finance gap while tax systems and budget management are overhauled. Marginal tax rates are high in many countries, encouraging informalization of the economy. Some governments now exceed reasonable size limits, but others lack revenues for essential functions. Public investment has virtually disappeared in many countries, and the maintenance backlog is large and growing. Transition involves costs, with economic decline in some regions and large losses for the banking sector, and it may be necessary—and desirable—to cushion the impact on certain groups. However, support needs to target these transitional issues and losses carefully.

Finally, business advice and financial support to the private (and privatized) sector should mainly come from the private sector itself, that is, from private business services, investors in equity, and private lenders of working and investment capital. These services and suppliers exist in embryo in some transition countries, but not at all in many others. Donor agencies can assist reform in the financial system to speed the creation of prudent and capable lenders and investors and can usefully provide hands-on training and technical assistance to managers and entrepreneurs to overcome the effects of years of isolation from market forces. Simply financing investment through government restructuring agencies should be avoided.

. . . And for the reformers

What reforms are most urgently needed to sustain transition? The answer differs for each country according to the stage it has reached.

With macroeconomic stabilization and liberalization largely accomplished, institutional reform and managing the realignment of the state are now priority areas for the leading reformers in CEE. Public finance has emerged as a critical focus. On the spending side this involves, in particular, reforming costly social programs, especially pensions and health. Action here will assist reform of currently very distortionary tax systems; in particular it should allow high

payroll taxes to be cut. More broadly, improving public accountability and strengthening the influence of civil, democratic society as a counterweight to government are also important. Another priority is continuing reform in the legal and regulatory systems, especially in areas relating to the financial sector, property rights and competition, better enforcement of contracts and regulations, and harmonization with EU standards in anticipation of accession. Addressing the problems associated with residual state ownership is a third important task. For these countries external financial assistance is progressively less important than technical assistance and institution building, which are important roles for bilateral and multilateral agencies.

Fiscal reforms are vital in the less advanced reformers as well. Improved tax administration is essential. So is the need to reduce subsidies through improved cost recovery, to gain fiscal elbow room for maintenance of and modest additions to public investments, and for clearing government's own arrears. But these countries also need to consolidate financial discipline both in banks and in large enterprises and to restore confidence in financial institutions. Tighter discipline, together with privatization, is also necessary to sustain pressure for more effective ownership. Some of these countries also face serious problems of crime, both economic and general. Addressing this and the associated issue of corruption is another very high priority, and indeed is essential for rapid growth. In most of these countries, including Russia, little progress has been made in the overhaul of social programs. Reforms are urgent if deep, intergenerational poverty is not to become institutionalized. Foreign assistance to these countries can usefully include transitional budgetary support, especially for maintenance and to buffer the human cost of transition. Extensive technical assistance, massive specialized training, and broad economic education are all desperately needed.

The next stage of reforms in the East Asian countries will be more complex and difficult than their past efforts, as they tackle reform of the core of their state sectors and the institutional underpinnings of their economies. Maintaining growth and improving the distribution of its rewards are central goals, because these are still poor countries, and also to sustain support for reform. This requires improving the efficiency with which savings are allocated and, in parallel, developing better indirect tools of macroeconomic management. Continuing fiscal reform, including recentralization of the budget in China, is one priority. So are raising capacity in the banking and legal systems and anticipating the need to deal with the many problem clients that will emerge as banks become more commercial and policies shift away from subsidizing credit. A clear definition of the role and scope of the state sector is called for, and this will almost certainly involve reducing its size. Also important are mechanisms to encourage effective corporate governance and accountability in state, nonstate, and private firms and to avoid an ownership vacuum. Social policy reforms should focus on sustaining broad access to key social services and improving their quality, both for increasingly mobile populations and in poor areas. Disentangling of social benefits from state enterprises is needed to unlock the door to further reforms.

With sustained reforms, transition countries have the potential to achieve strong growth. CEE can exploit the catch-up effect from its favorable location close to large, high-income markets. The NIS can look to major gains from far more efficient use of its natural resource and human capital endowments, and the East Asian reformers combine abundant labor, a tradition of high rates of saving, and large opportunities to increase the efficiency with which these resources are allocated. A successful transition therefore promises long-term growth rates considerably above world averages.

And what of the risk of failure? The chances of a return to the planned economy may be small, but long-term stagnation and rising poverty—likely outcomes of inconsistent and unstable policies—cannot be ruled out for some countries. In the last analysis, transition's reforms will not bear fruit unless they are underpinned by a broad political and social consensus. Developing this is perhaps the highest priority of all.

Bibliographical Note

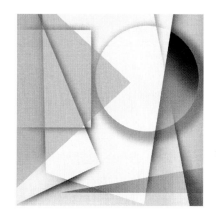

This Report has drawn on a wide range of World Bank reports and on numerous outside sources. World Bank sources include ongoing research as well as country economic, sector, and project work. These and other materials are listed alphabetically by author in the bibliography. The background papers, some of which will become available through the Policy Research Working Paper series, synthesize relevant literature and Bank work. The views they express are not necessarily those of the World Bank or of this Report.

In addition to the principal authors listed, many people, both inside and outside the World Bank, helped with the Report. The core team wishes to thank, in particular, Leszek Balcerowicz, Saul Estrin, Nicholas Lardy, Justin Yifu Lin, Peter Murrell, Mario Nuti, Andrei Poletayev, Jeffrey Sachs, Marcelo Selowsky, Lyn Squire, and Michael Walton for their extensive comments and suggestions. Bruce Ross-Larson and Meta de Coquereaumont provided valuable editorial advice and assistance at various stages. The core team wishes to thank Judith Hegedus for her excellent work as intern.

Recent and ongoing research underlying the Report has involved a wide range of institutions, particularly in CEE and parts of the NIS. They include CASE, Warsaw; CEEPN, Ljubljana; Central European University, Budapest; CMC, Prague; CEMI, Moscow; and the Leontief Center, St. Petersburg. We are grateful for having had the opportunity to discuss parts of the Report at meetings with some of these institutions. Several participants from this region attended the Paris meeting, and continuous regional consultation throughout the process was also provided by Laszlo Urban and Ardo Hansson.

Thanks also go to the participants at consultation meetings in Beijing, Hanoi, London, and Paris, and at the International Monetary Fund (IMF) in Washington. These include: *Beijing*—Pieter Bottelier, Weili Guan, Shuqing Guo, E. C. Hwa, Justin Yifu Lin, He Liu, Feng Lu, Guo-

qing Song, Jinglian Wu, Ping Xie, Gang Yi, Weiying Zhang, and Renwei Zha; *Hanoi*—Le Xuan Ba, Tran Tien Cuong, Dang Duc Dam, Le Dang Doanh, Vo Dai Luoc, Tran Duc Nguyen, Viet Phoung, Ha Huy Thanh, Vu Thieu, and Nguyen Minh Tu; *London:* nongovernmental organization consultation—Richard Blewitt, Matthew Bullard, Caroline Harper, Antony Mahony, Ruth Mayne, Angela Penrose, Paul Spray, Martin Summers, and David Wright; *Paris*—Wladimir Andreff, Leszek Balcerowicz, Roberta Benini, Peter Conze, Saul Estrin, Erich Geis, Gian Maria Gros-Pietro, Maurice Guyader, Karsten Hinrichs, Vincent Koen, Marie Lavigne, Sten Luthman, Hans-Joachim Maak, Satish Mishra, Alberto Moreno, Joaquin Muns, Alena Nesporova, Mario Nuti, Joan Pearce, Martin Raiser, Mark Schankerman, Dieter Schulze-Vornhagen, Pekka Sutela, and Pavel Tepulukhin. A meeting in Toronto provided a valued opportunity to share views with members of Canada's business community who have ethnic roots as well as business interests in transition countries. Participants included Tonu Altosaar, Charles Bassett, John Coleman, James L. Darroch, Dezso J. Horvath, Joseph Kairys, Kenneth E. Loucks, Gene Luczkiw, Hy Van Luong, Bohdan S. Onyschuk, Alina Pekarsky, Frank Potter, Andrew Sarlos, Andrew J. Szonyi, Ping Tan, Nguyen H. Trung, Paul C. White, John P. Wleugel, and D. M. Zakreski.

Those at the IMF who commented include Ehtisham Ahmad, William A. Allan, Mark Allen, Gerard Belanger, Eduardo Borensztein, Eduard Brau, Christopher Browne, Wayne Camard, Adrienne Cheasty, Ajai Chopra, John Crotty, J. M. Davis, Michael Deppler, P. V. Desai, J. R. Dodsworth, Allan Firestone, James Haley, M. Koch, Ashok Lahiri, Henri Lorie, G. A. Mackenzie, Donald Mathieson, John Odling-Smee, Alan Pearson, Peter Quirk, Ratna Sahay, Susan Schadler, Ludger Schuknecht, Gerd Schwartz, Teresa Ter-Minassian, and Konrad von den Heed. We are grateful to the IMF for having seconded Françoise Le Gall to the core team.

The Report also acknowleges the collaboration of Russell Pittman of the U.S. Department of Justice, Mark Schankerman of the EBRD, the U.N. International Drug Control Program, Christian Aid, and Save the Children (U.K.). Other contributors include Anthony Atkinson, David Begg, Willem Buiter, Athar Hussain, and Richard Rose.

Many at the World Bank—including consultants and visiting academics—provided substantial inputs or comments, often on many chapters. They include Wafa Abdelati, Arvil Adams, Harold Alderman, Ritu Anand, Robert E. Anderson, Paul Armington, Mark Baird, Ian Bannon, Luca Barbone, Paul Beckerman, Halsey Beemer, Brian Berman, Charles Blitzer, José-Luis Bobadilla, Zeljko Bogetic, Eduard Bos, Pieter Bottelier, Loup Brefort, Harry Broadman, Karen Brooks, Jonathan Brown, Robert Buckley, Richard Burcroff, Mary Canning, Gerard Caprio, Laurence Carter, Carlos Cavalcanti, Sandeep Chawla, Shaohua Chen, Simon Commander, Csaba Csaki, Peter Dean, Martha De Melo, Cevdet Denizer, Shantayanan Devarajan, John Dixon, David Dollar, David Donaldson, Donna Dowsett-Coirolo, William Easterly, Andrew Ewing, Nissim Ezekiel, Qimiao Fan, Richard Feachem, Carlos Ferreira, Bruce Fitzgerald, Heywood Fleisig, Monica Fong, Louise Fox, Lev Freinkman, Michael Fuchs, Hafez Ghanem, Daniela Gressani, Ardo Hansson, Ralph W. Harbison, April Harding, James R. Harrison, Stephen Heyneman, Bernard Hoekman, Bert Hofman, Malcolm Holmes, Nicholas Hope, Gordon Hughes, Ishrat Husain, Gregory Ingram, Estelle James, Dean Jamison, Emmanuel Jimenez, Olga Jonas, Bart Kaminski, Philip Keefer, Albert Keidel, Christine Kessides, Timothy King, Jeni Klugman, Paul Knotter, Ulrich Koester, Mihaly Kopanyi, Aart Kraay, Kathie Krumm, Arvo Kuddo, Anjali Kumar, Ulrich Lachler, Bruno Laporte, Barbara Lee, Philippe Le Houerou, Natalie Lichtenstein, Jennie Litvack, Norman Loayza, Millard Long, Laszlo Lovei, Nariman Mannapbekov, Tamar Manuelyan, Albert Martinez, Katarina Mathernova, William McCleary, William McGreevey, Oey Meesook, Costas Michalopoulos, Branko Milanovic, Pradeep Mitra, Fernando Montes-Negret, Claudia Morgenstern, Paul Murgatroyd, Vikram Nehru, Richard Newfarmer, Ian Newport, Erik Nielsen, Mick Nightingale, Barbara Nunberg, Daniel Oks, Robert Palacios, Shilpa Patel, Jo Ann Paulson, Kyle Peters, Djordjija Petkoski, Guy Pfeffermann, Alan Piazza, Brian Pinto, Gerhard Pohl, Hana Polackova, Richard Polard, Michael Pomerleano, Sanjay Pradhan, Alexander Preker, Lant Pritchett, Martin Ravallion, Bertrand Renaud, Alan Roe, Susan Rose-Ackerman, Jan Rutkowski, Michal Rutkowski, Randi Ryterman, George Schieber, Sabine Schlemmer-Schulte, Martin Schrenk, Ibrahim Shihata, John Shilling, Mary Shirley, I. J. Singh, Shamsher Singh, Warrick Smith, Renganaden Soopramanien, Mike Stevens, Mark Sundberg, Andres Rigo Sureda, Nok Suthiwart-Sethaput, Patrick Tardy, David Tarr, Margaret Thalwitz, Pham Van Thuyet, Anne Tinker, Mariana Todorova, Laura Tuck, Yoshine Uchimura, Laszlo Urban, Panos Varangis, Jaime Vazquez, Scott Vicary, Paulo Vieira da Cunha, Dimitri Vittas, Christine Wallich, Jonathan Walters, Yan Wang, Hugo Waszink, Douglas Webb, Dennis Whittle, Alan Winters, Holger Wolf, and Shahid Yusuf.

Introduction and Chapter 1
The many excellent treatments of socialist systems include Berliner 1952, Brus and Laski 1989, Chavance 1994, Held 1992, Hobsbawm 1994, Kornaï 1992, Lavigne 1995, Lin, Fang, and Zhou 1996, Sapir 1990, and White 1995. The most detailed appraisal of the Soviet economy prior to its dissolution is from the IMF and others 1991. Easterly and Fischer 1995a and 1995b review estimates of Soviet growth and productivity. Lin, Fang, and Zhou 1996 discuss total factor productivity growth in China before 1978. Poznanski 1985 provides a detailed discussion of quality problems in CEE manufactures. Roberts 1993 carries out detailed hedonic price comparisons for Russian and other cars sold in Finland between 1950 and 1990. Hughes 1995 and OECD 1993 consider environmental issues in the context of Eastern European reforms. Gordon Hughes provided Box 2.

The topic of systemic transformation has involved enormous debate on the speed and sequencing of reforms; see, for example, Aghion and Blanchard 1993, Balcerowicz 1995, Bosworth and Ofer 1995, Chaba 1995, Lipton and Sachs 1990a, OECF 1995, Portes 1993 and 1994, and Sachs 1990a, as well as *Transition* 1988–96. Much of this literature is reviewed by Murrell 1995. The background paper by Siebert, Raiser, and Langhammer surveys German research on this topic. For analyses of Poland's reforms see Lipton and Sachs 1990a, 1990b, and 1990c, and Sachs 1993 and 1994. Portes 1993 reviews progress in Eastern Europe, and Dornbusch and Wolf 1994, Sinn and Sinn 1992, and Welfens 1996 the economic aspects of German unification. Holger Wolf contributed Box 1.1. Reviews of China's reforms include Cao, Gang, and Woo 1995, Gelb, Jefferson, and Singh 1993, Harrold 1992, and Lin, Fang, and Zhou 1996. The growth of macroeconomic imbalances in the Soviet economy and Russia's reforms are treated in Åslund 1994a and 1995b, Dunlop 1993, IMF and others 1991, and Sachs 1995b and 1995c. Michalopoulos and Tarr 1994 provide estimates of intra-NIS trade volume declines. Kornaï 1996 provides a recent perspective on the macroeconomics of Hungary's reforms.

Attitudes to political change and economic reform in several CEE countries and the NIS are treated in the

Åslund background paper, Evans 1995, Nelson 1994, Rose 1995b, and Rose and Haerpfer 1994 and 1996. Åslund 1995a considers the case of Ukraine; Lubin 1994 provides information on social attitudes in Uzbekistan and Kazakstan. USIA 1995a and 1995b and VCIOM 1995 present assessments of political attitudes in Russia and other NIS; the *Russian Economic Barometer* various years presents assessments of business opinion. Perotti 1995 presents an econometric analysis of the relationship between economic growth, democracy, and income inequality; see also Persson and Tambellini 1994. For detailed reporting on reforms by category in CEE and the NIS, see EBRD 1994 and 1995. On data difficulties in transition and the underestimating of growth, see Berg 1993, Berg and Sachs 1992, Bratkowski 1993, and Goskomstat–World Bank 1995. Roberts 1995 estimates the impact on welfare of eliminating rationing. Murray and Bobadilla 1995 estimate adjustments to infant mortality from adopting WHO standards. EBRD 1995 notes also that the experience of the Visegrad countries shows that reforms have not necessarily meant a deterioration of social indicators.

The major analysis of the implications of China's structural features for its reform process relative to the NIS is in Sachs and Woo 1994; for more discussion see OECF 1995. McKinnon 1994 considers the implications of China's financial deepening for its macroeconomic stability. Brown, Ickes, and Ryterman 1994 consider concentration and regional specialization in Russian industry; the Ickes and Ryterman background paper discusses the organization of markets and their role in transition.

The discussion of separating out the effects of initial conditions from reforms also draws on ongoing research by Martha De Melo, Cevdet Denizer, Alan Gelb, and Stoyan Tenev. In this study, two composite initial conditions are constructed using factor analysis and a set of twelve country characteristics. They are then used as explanatory variables in panel regressions. Preliminary results suggest that both initial conditions—one relating to the degree of urbanization and industrialization, the other to initial macroeconomic imbalance and distance from market institutions—do influence country performance. The more difficult conditions of the NIS relative to CEE may result in growth rates two percentage points lower, on average. Policy reform is still, however, a major determinant of performance.

Chapter 2

Recent overviews of liberalization, stabilization, and growth issues in transition economies include Citrin and Lahiri 1995, Dervis and others 1995, EBRD 1994 and 1995, Fischer, Sahay, and Vegh 1995, Gros and Steinherr 1995, IMF 1994c, Lavigne 1995, Murrell 1991, Sachs 1996, and

Sahay and Vegh 1995b. These works have provided much of the backdrop and offer a range of interesting approaches to the topics of this chapter. The chapter draws from many individual country studies, including Banerjee and others 1995, Blanchard, Froot, and Sachs 1994, Cao, Gang, and Woo 1995, Dollar, Glewwe, and Litvack forthcoming, Ebrill and others 1994, IMF 1995b, the Kornaï background paper, Lin, Fang, and Zhou 1996, Lipton and Sachs 1990a, Reidel and Comer 1995, Sachs 1994, and World Bank 1995e, 1995k, 1995o, 1995q, and 1996a. The chapter also draws on a written survey of World Bank and IMF country staff to assess reform progress and economic performance in the twenty-eight transition economies covered by the report. Other main sources of data are the World Bank's data base and World Bank 1995s.

The different liberalization and stabilization strategies of various transition economies are examined in Balcerowicz and Gelb 1995, Dabrowski 1995a, the De Melo, Denizer, and Gelb background paper, and OECF 1995. Price reform issues in selected transition economies are examined in De Broeck, De Masi, and Koen 1995, De Masi and Koen 1995, Koen 1995, Rajaram 1992, Richards and Tersman 1995, and Roberts 1995. The treatment of energy pricing in Box 2.1 draws from Gray 1995, and lifeline pricing has been proposed for Poland by Freund and Wallich 1995. China's dual-track price reforms (Box 2.2) are discussed by, among others, Gang 1994, and World Bank 1993b. Murphy, Shleifer, and Vishny 1992 present the theoretical case against partial price reforms. The data on China's long-run productivity and growth patterns are from Kraay 1995 and World Bank 1996b. The output decline across CEE and the NIS has been the subject of a lively and controversial debate in the literature. The discussion here draws mainly on the articles in Blejer and others 1993, Borensztein, Demekas, and Ostry 1993, Christensen 1994, Gavrilenko and Koen 1994, Holzmann, Gacs, and Winckler 1995, and Kornaï 1994b. See also the references on measurement problems noted for Chapter 1. The treatment of unofficial economies in transition (Box 2.3) draws on Kaufmann and Kaliberda 1995 and Loayza forthcoming.

Much of the analysis of the relationship between liberalization and growth in CEE and the NIS draws from the De Melo, Denizer, and Gelb background paper. Trade policy reforms and performance across transition economies are discussed in Asselain 1994, de Menil 1995, Gacs 1993, IMF 1994b, Kaminski, Wang, and Winters 1996, and Michalopoulos and Tarr 1994 and 1996. China's trade regime and performance are analyzed in Lardy 1995, Wei 1993, and World Bank 1994b. The general phasing and design of trade liberalization are discussed by, among others, Dean, Desai, and Reidel 1994, who provide an overview of the extensive literature. Evidence in support of early, far-reaching trade liberalization in transition economies is provided by, among others, Åslund 1994b and 1995b, Berg and Sachs 1992, Djankov and Hoekman 1995, the Kaminski and Wang background paper, and Sachs and Warner 1996. De Melo and Ofer 1994 and Easterly, De Melo, and Ofer 1994 have analyzed the growth of services in transition economies. Output and labor restructuring in transition economies and the impact of liberalization and stabilization on such restructuring and, thereby, on growth are discussed in Alfandari, Fan, and Freinkman forthcoming, Anderson, Djankov, and Pohl 1995, Berg 1994, Brada, Singh, and Torok 1994, Claessens, Hunt, and Peters 1995, Commander and Coricelli 1995, Rutkowski 1995, and Rutkowski and Sinha 1995, in addition to many of the country studies. Box 2.6 was drafted by Gordon Hughes.

Inflation and stabilization in China are treated in Harrold, Hwa, and Jiwei 1993, Hofman 1995a and 1995b, Lin 1995, Montes-Negret 1995, and World Bank 1995e and 1996a. The first stage of inflation and early experiences with stabilization in CEE and the NIS are discussed in Åslund 1994a and 1994b, Bruno 1992, Calvo and Coricelli 1992, Dabrowski 1995c, Hardy and Lahiri 1994, Kolodko, Gotz-Kozierkiewicz, and Skrzeszewska-Paczek 1991, and Sachs 1995b. Many works document the essentially monetary nature of inflation in transition economies and examine the fiscal and quasi-fiscal pressures underlying it and implications for stabilization policy. These include Aghevli, Borensztein, and van der Willigen 1992, Citrin and Lahiri 1995, Fischer, Sahay, and Vegh 1995, Gaidar 1995, Hansson and Sachs 1994, Illarionov 1995a and 1995b, Koen and Marrese 1995, Sachs 1995c, Sachs and Lipton 1992, and Willet and others 1995. Box 2.7 draws on Easterly and Vieira da Cunha 1994. Recent studies of the empirical relationship between stabilization and growth for the transition economies include Bruno and Easterly 1995, Easterly forthcoming, and Fischer, Sahay, and Vegh 1995.

Regarding the specific design of stabilization policies in transition economies, Bredenkamp 1993 and Hilbers 1993 deal with the mix of direct and indirect instruments of monetary policy. Banerjee and others 1995, Calvo and others 1993, Calvo, Sahay, and Vegh 1995, Gomulka 1995, and Sahay and Vegh 1995a discuss exchange rate policy, capital inflows, and their impact on inflation, competitiveness, and growth in transition economies. *Russian and East European Finance and Trade* 1994 is devoted entirely to this subject. Coricelli and Lane 1993, Coricelli and Revenga 1992, Morsink 1995, and Tait and Erbas 1995 examine the role of incomes policies for stabilization in transition. Enterprise arrears and their causes, inflation implications, and remedies are discussed in Afanasief, Kuznetsov, and Isaev 1995, Alfan-

dari and Schaffer forthcoming, Fan and Lee 1995, Raiser 1993, Rostowski 1994, Rostowski and Nikolic 1995, and Schaffer 1995.

Dornbusch, Noelling, and Layard 1993 include a fascinating collection of papers on postwar economic reconstruction and growth and lessons for the transition economies. Wolf 1993 looks at the specific case of Germany, and the East Asian miracle is examined in World Bank 1993a. Schmidt-Hebbel, Serven, and Solimano 1995 and IMF 1995c provide recent overviews of the determinants of saving and investment and the relationship between them and economic growth. Dervis and others 1995 and *European Economy* 1995 discuss saving and investment in transition economies. Dervis and others 1995 and Sachs and Warner 1996 examine the medium- and long-term growth potential of transition economies and the speed of their catch-up with middle- and high-income market economies. Erdoas 1994 and Kornaï 1994a and 1995 examine the same issue from a transition economy perspective.

Chapter 3
The socialist legacy draws on Gelb and Gray 1991. Further references are found in the note to Chapter 1 above. The discussion of financial discipline and enterprise restructuring in CEE and NIS draws on Balcerowicz, Gray, and Hashi 1995, Belka and others 1994, Commander, Fan, and Schaffer forthcoming, *Cuadernos del Este* 1995, Dolgopyatova and Yevseyeva 1994a and 1994b, Estrin, Gelb, and Singh forthcoming, and Grosfeld and Roland 1995. Box 3.1 summarizes the findings in Gray and Holle forthcoming and Gray, Schlorke, and Szanyi forthcoming. For further analysis of Poland's bank-led restructuring, see Pawlowicz 1994. The discussion of enterprise reforms in Vietnam and China draws on Broadman 1995, Cao, Gang, and Woo 1995, Gelb, Jefferson, and Singh 1993, and Reidel and Comer 1995. Ideas on government intervention and isolation exercises draw in part on Selowsky and Vogel 1995 and World Bank 1993a and 1995b. The 1995 study of 400 to 500 firms is described in Pohl, Djankov, and Anderson forthcoming. Box 3.2 draws from a World Bank project being developed in Ukraine.

The discussion of private versus public enterprise performance in market economies draws on Galal and others 1994, Kikeri, Nellis, and Shirley 1992, Megginson, Nash, and van Randenborgn 1994, Millwood 1982, Vickers and Yarrow 1988, and Yarrow 1986. Surveys in transition economies are described in Barberis and others 1995, Belka and others 1994, Claessens, Hunt, and Peters 1995, Commander, Fan, and Schaffer forthcoming, Earle, Estrin, and Leshchenko forthcoming, Köllő 1995, and Dubey and Vodopivec 1995. The discussion of Poland follows Pinto, Belka, and Krajewski 1993 and Pinto and van Wijnbergen 1994. Box 3.4 draws on Byrd and Lin 1990, Findlay, Watson, and Wu 1994, Nolan and Dong 1990, Ody 1992, and Zweig 1991. The discussion on Bulgaria summarizes Bogetic and Hillman 1995.

There is a vast literature on privatization of medium-size and large enterprises in transition economies, summarized in the Gray background paper. For more on this, see Donaldson and Wagle 1995, Earle, Frydman, and Rapaczynski 1993, Estrin 1994b, Frydman, Gray, and Rapaczynski 1996, Lieberman and Nellis 1995, and Radygin 1995a. Gordon Hughes prepared Box 3.5. Data on Russian privatization are from Blasi 1996, Blasi and Shleifer 1996, and Earle, Estrin, and Leshchenko forthcoming. For more on Russian privatization, see Boycko, Shleifer, and Vishny 1995, Grigoriev 1995, and Shatalov 1991. The Ukraine-Russia comparison is from Buck and others 1995. The discussion of small-firm privatization draws on Barberis and others 1995 and Earle and others 1994. The section on farm privatization and restructuring was prepared with the help of Karen Brooks and draws on Csaki and Lerman forthcoming. The discussion of commercial real estate draws on the Harding background paper. The housing discussion tracks current World Bank assistance in CEE and the NIS.

Surveys on private sector development in transition economies include De Melo and Ofer 1994, Stone and Novitzky 1993 and 1995, and Webster 1994. The case of foreign investment in Poland was supplied by the International Finance Corporation. The discussion on conditions and incentives for foreign investors draws on Gray and Jarosz 1995.

Chapter 4
Box 4.4 draws on Fox 1995, Kornaï 1996, and Urban 1996. Emmanuel Jimenez, Timothy King, Jeni Klugman and Alan Piazza helped with various of the other boxes. The World Bank Social Challenges of Transition data base provided additional background data on the CEE countries, as did various chapters in Barr 1994.

The inheritance, especially as it affects human resources, is discussed by Estrin 1994a. The general problems of measuring poverty are discussed by Atkinson 1989, data issues in the CEE countries by Atkinson and Micklewright 1992, and methodology and OECD outcomes by Atkinson, Rainwater, and Smeeding 1995.

The first part of the chapter drew heavily on advice from Branko Milanovic and from Milanovic forthcoming and on various other World Bank studies, including Klugman forthcoming, Patil and Krumm 1995, van de Walle, Ravallion, and Gautam 1994, and World Bank 1990b. Poverty in China is discussed by Jalan and Ravallion

1996. On broader dimensions of well-being, see Moser 1996 and Zippay 1991.

The impact of the transition on women is discussed by Einhorn 1993, Fong 1996, Funk and Mueller 1993, and Human Rights Watch 1995a and 1995b. Box 4.2 draws on those sources and also on Chase 1995 and Rouse-Foley 1995.

The discussion of labor markets draws on Commander and Coricelli 1995, Jackman 1994, Jackman and Rutkowski 1994, Orazem, Vodopivec, and Wu 1995, M. Rutkowski 1995, J. Rutkowski forthcoming, and World Bank 1995r. Active labor market policies are discussed by Burda and Lubyova 1995 and in OECD 1995a and 1995b, and regional unemployment by Scarpetta and Wörgötter 1995. The Western backdrop is surveyed by Atkinson and Micklewright 1991 and Layard, Nickell, and Jackman 1991. Evidence of widening wage dispersion in Russia is presented in Brainerd 1995.

The issues surrounding the rationale for and construction of social safety nets are discussed in Atkinson 1996, Barr 1992, and Barr 1993a (in Polish 1993b). Reform in the CEE countries is discussed in the chapters by Barr and by Sipos in Barr 1994 (in Hungarian and Romanian, 1995a and 1995b, respectively, and forthcoming in Russian), Toth 1994 (Hungary) and World Bank 1995p (Poland). Reform in the NIS is discussed by Klugman forthcoming, Kosmarskii and Maleva 1995, and Mozhina 1994 (Russia), Mabbett forthcoming (Moldova), World Bank 1993c (Kyrgyz Republic), and Falkingham and others forthcoming (Central Asian republics). For reform in Asia see World Bank 1992 (China) and Dollar, Glewwe, and Litvack forthcoming (Vietnam).

Enterprise restructuring and the provision of social benefits is discussed in the Commander and Schankerman background paper. Rural issues are discussed by O'Brien and others 1993 and Patriorkovsky and others 1991. On methods of targeting, see Foley and Klugman forthcoming and Grosh 1994.

There is a huge literature on pension reform, including Barr 1992 and 1994, Queisser 1995, U.K. Department of Social Security 1993, Vittas 1993, Vittas and Michelitsch 1996, and World Bank 1994a. On the political economy of reform see Sachs 1995a, and on pensions and savings in Eastern Europe see Sachs and Warner 1996.

The role of politics and administration in reform is discussed by Crawford and Thompson 1994.

Introduction to Part Two and Chapter 5
Evidence on the relationship between institutions and growth is in Keefer and Knack 1995 and Knack and Keefer 1995. The discussion on developing the rule of law draws on Gray and Hendley forthcoming. The discussions of

legal frameworks for private sector development and judicial institutions are based primarily on Gray and Associates 1993 and on the Pistor background paper. Box 5.1 was prepared by Heywood Fleisig. For further discussion, see the Fleisig, Simpson, and Röver background paper. The study on contracting in Bulgaria is in Koford and Miller 1995. Box 5.2 is drawn from Black, Kraakman, and Hay 1996. CEE and NIS experiences in developing bankruptcy legislation are described in Balcerowicz, Gray, and Hashi forthcoming, Coates and Mirsky 1995, and Gray, Schlorke, and Szanyi forthcoming. For further discussion of market infrastructure see the background paper by Ickes and Ryterman. The discussion of the Chinese legal profession is from Alford 1995; for Vietnam, see Pham Van Thuyet 1995.

The cross-country research on economic growth and government credibility is described in Borner, Brunetti, and Weder 1994. The sections on crime and corruption in transition economies draw on studies of private firms cited in De Melo and Ofer 1995, Stone and Novitzky 1993 and 1995, and Webster 1994, as well as Keh 1994 and information provided by the United Nations Drug Control Programme. Mauro 1995 explores the relationship between corruption and growth. For more on the Russian mafia, see Handleman 1995. The workings of the Sicilian mafia are described in Stille 1995. Susan Rose-Ackerman helped prepare Box 5.3, which draws on Rose-Ackerman 1978 and Thacher 1995.

Chapter 6
The discussion on the legacies in the financial system in centrally planned economies is based on many sources but draws in particular on Bonin and Mizsei 1995, Gorton and Wilton 1996, Kornaï 1992, and McKinnon 1991. General references on financial reform in transition economies, used in various places throughout the chapter, are Bonin and Székely 1994, Borish, Long, and Noël 1995, Calari and Pinto 1995, Caprio 1995, Caprio, Folkerts-Landau, and Lane 1994, Dittus 1994a and 1994b, Pohl and Claessens 1994, Saunders and Walter 1991, and Varhegyi 1995. General macroeconomic developments affecting the financial system are discussed in the De Melo, Denizer, and Gelb background paper.

General background on the importance and role of the financial system is provided in World Bank 1989. Evidence on the relationships between financial system development and economic growth and adjustment comes from King and Levine 1993a and 1993b. Evidence on the importance of central bank independence is provided in Alesina and Summers 1993 and Fischer 1995. The complementary relationships between banks, nonbank financial intermediaries, and capital markets—at the macroeconomic level and at the individual firm level—is discussed and evidence provided in Demirgüç-Kunt and Levine forthcoming, Demirgüç-Kunt and Maksimovic forthcoming, and Singh 1995.

The typology of approaches to banking reform in transition economies draws on the general references mentioned above. Box 6.1 draws on Pohl 1995a and 1995b and Pohl and Claessens 1994. Box 6.2 draws on Baer and Gray 1996, Bakker 1993, and the Gray background paper. The Claessens background paper compares the progress in institutional capacity building in transition economies and the relationship between bank quality and the structural characteristics of these economies. The paper was based on a survey of experts in the World Bank on the quality of banks in twenty-five transition economies and five comparator countries, dividing banking systems into "better" and "worse" segments. The background paper also provides evidence about the effects on bank quality in transition economies of more liberal entry, the role of banking regulation, and intervention in troubled banks.

The discussion of problem banks and the occurrence and resolution of banking crises is based on Baer and Klingebiel 1994, Caprio and Klingebiel forthcoming, Caprio and Vittas forthcoming, Delyagin 1995, Hansson 1995, and Hausmann and Gavin 1995. Principles for restructuring problem banks are further discussed in Sheng 1996 and World Bank 1995a. The role of banking supervision is further discussed in World Bank 1989.

The discussion on the different models of debt restructuring draws on Begg and Portes 1993, Caprio and Levine 1994, Levine and Scott 1993, and van Wijnbergen 1992 and 1994. The evidence on bank recapitalization is reviewed in Baer and Gray 1996, Caprio and Klingebiel forthcoming, and World Bank 1995a. The section on deposit insurance draws on Caprio and Vittas forthcoming and Glaessner and Mas 1995. The discussion of the issues of universal banks and banks owning shares in enterprises is based on Coffee 1995, Caprio, Folkerts-Landau, and Lane 1994, Dittus and Prowse 1996, and Walter 1993.

Lessons on the benefits and costs of development banks and directed credit were derived from Vittas and Cho 1995, World Bank 1989, and World Bank 1995f. The discussion of creating rural finance is based on the Brooks, Burcroff, and Lerman background paper and Laura Tuck's research on best practices. The example and discussions of housing finance draw on Lea and Renaud 1995 and Renaud 1996.

The discussion of nonbank finance is in part based on Calari and Pinto 1995. The section on leasing and venture funds draws on Kuczynski, Barger, and Carter forthcoming (a) and forthcoming (b). The capital markets section draws on Aoki and Kim 1995, Calari and Pinto 1995, Morgenstern and Hay 1995, and Pohl, Jedrzejczak, and Anderson 1995. Data come from IFC 1996 and IMF various years.

Chapter 7
Recent overviews of public finance issues across transition economies, especially the widening deficits in many countries and their causes, include Barbone and Marchetti 1995, Barbone and Polackova forthcoming, Dabrowski 1995b, Fakin and de Crombrugghe 1996, and IMF various years (c).

The role of the state in market economies is an extensively discussed issue. Works that synthesize some of the literature include Barr 1994 (Chapter 2), Krueger 1990, Stiglitz 1986, World Bank 1988, World Bank 1991 (Chapter 7), and World Bank 1995b. The treatment of market failures also draws from Annex B of World Bank 1994c. The indices of government market orientation and of the effectiveness of public sector management are based on a survey of World Bank and IMF country staff to assess reform progress and economic performance in the twenty-eight transition economies covered by this Report. Civil service issues in transition countries are discussed in Ridley 1995, Schiavo-Campo 1994, World Bank 1994c, and various internal World Bank documents. Their treatment in this section has benefited from consultations with Barbara Nunberg. Hewitt and van Rijckeghem 1995 contains comparator data on civil service pay and employment in market economies.

Since Wagner 1883, which first examined the relationship of national income and government expenditures, the size of government and its determinants have been extensively discussed in the literature, including by Heller and Diamond 1990 and for transition economies by Barbone and Polackova forthcoming. Many works examine the empirical relationship between the size of government and economic growth, including Barro 1989 and 1991, Easterly and Rebelo 1993, Fischer 1993, Levine and Renelt 1992, and Slemrod 1995. Dervis and others 1995 and Sachs and Warner 1996, among others, examine this relationship for transition economies. The composition and effectiveness of government expenditures in general are analyzed and implications for expenditure prioritization drawn in Aschauer 1989, Bandyopadhyay and Devarajan 1994, Devarajan, Swaroop, and Zou 1995, Devarajan, Xie, and Zou 1994, Munnell 1992, Pradhan forthcoming, and Chu and others 1995; the latter two sources also provide an overview of the literature. For transition economies, the same issues are analyzed in many of the papers collected in Mizsei 1994 and Tanzi 1992 and 1993. Budget management issues in transition economies are discussed in, among others, Allan 1994, Le Houerou, Gold, and Katash 1994, World Bank 1995h, and various internal World Bank documents.

Revenue trends in transition economies and their causes are discussed in EBRD 1994, IMF 1994a, McLure and others 1995, and Shome and Escolano 1993. These works also discuss tax policy reforms in transition economies, as do the papers in Bogetic and Hillman 1995, Newbury 1995, some of those in Tanzi 1992 and 1993, and a number of World Bank country studies. Karnite and Dovladbekova 1995, World Bank 1990a and 1996a, and World Bank 1995q discuss tax administration issues in Latvia, China, and Vietnam, respectively. Tanzi and Pellechio 1995 is a recent overview of general tax administration issues. The section on fiscal decentralization has benefited from inputs and comments by Christine Wallich and draws from various works on intergovernmental relations in transition economies, including Ahmad 1995, Bird, Ebel, and Wallich 1995, Ma 1995, and Wallich 1994a and 1994b. Shah 1994 provides a recent overview of fiscal decentralization issues in developing countries.

Chapter 8
Additional background data on the health and education sectors in the CEE countries were provided by the World Bank Social Challenges of Transition data base. Figure 8.1 is based on Kovalyova 1994.

The section on education draws on Heyneman 1994 and Laporte and Schweitzer 1994. Marer and Mabert 1996 discuss the extent to which narrow, inflexible skills impede restructuring. For discussion of education in China, see Leung 1991 and Lewin and Wang 1994 on school education, Chunling 1995, Lee and Li 1994, and West 1995 on disparities in education, and Hertling 1996 on higher education.

José-Luis Bobadilla and Alexander Preker helped to draft Box 8.1. The section on health draws on Bobak and Feachem 1992, Preker 1994, Preker and Feachem 1994, and World Bank 1993e. On health developments in the CEE countries see Bobak and Feachem 1995 and Feachem 1994, and for Russia, see Shapiro 1993, Tulchinsky and Varavikova 1996, and Vella forthcoming. Rising health spending in the Czech Republic is discussed by Veprek, Papes, and Veprek 1994. Women's health is discussed in WHO 1994, and women's reproductive health by Jepsen and Brandrup-Lukanow 1995, Johnson and Andronache 1993, Popov 1991, and Weinstein, Oliveras, and McIntosh 1993.

Chapter 9
The discussion of trade and its realignment in CEE and the NIS is based on Collins and Rodrik 1991, Havrylyshyn and Pritchett 1991, Kaminski, Wang, and Winters 1996, Michalopoulos and Tarr 1994, Rosati 1992, and Winters and Wang 1994. The section on adjusting trade integra-

tion with the European Union draws on Faini and Portes 1995, Hoekman and Djankov 1995, and Winters and Wang 1994. The discussion on integration into the European Union draws on Baldwin 1994, Bofinger 1995, and CEPR 1992. The discussion on capital flows draws from Brau 1995, Eichengreen and Uzan 1992, and the Kaminski and Wang background paper, which also gives net official capital inflows by country. The information on integration into the European Union is provided by the Commission of the European Communities 1995a, 1995b, and 1995c. Data on trade are from Eurostat data bases such as EEC External Trade and from the IMF's *Direction of Trade Statistics 1995*, and the United Nations COMTRADE data base. Data on capital flows come from, among others, World Bank 1994d and 1996b.

Background papers

Åslund, Anders. "The Political Economy of Post-Communist Transformation."

Brooks, Karen, Richard Burcroff, and Zvi Lerman. "Agriculture in the Transition."

Chawla, Sandeep. "The Vulnerability of Transition Countries to Drug Trafficking, Drug Abuse, and Organized Crime." United Nations Drug Control Programme, Vienna.

Claessens, Stijn. "Banking Reform in Transition Economies."

Commander, Simon, and Mark Schankerman. "Enterprise Restructuring and the Efficient Provision of Social Benefits."

De Melo, Martha, Judith Brandsma, and Leila Webster. "Private Sector Development in Transition Countries: an Overview."

De Melo, Martha, and Cevdet Denizer. "Monetary Policy and Financial Developments in Transition."

De Melo, Martha, Cevdet Denizer, and Alan Gelb. "From Plan to Market: Patterns of Transition."

Fleisig, Heywood, John Simpson, and Jan-Hendrik Röver. "Security Interests in Moveable Property in Transition Economies: Issues and Options for Reform."

Gelb, Alan, Arye L. Hillman, and Heinrich W. Ursprung. "Rents and the Transition."

Gray, Cheryl. "In Search of Owners: Lessons of Experience with Privatization and Corporate Governance in Transition Economies."

Harding, April. "Markets for Non-residential Real Estate; Private Rights to Real Property: Are They Emerging in Transition Economies?"

Ickes, Barry W., and Randi Ryterman. "The Organization of Markets and Its Role in Macroeconomic Stabilization During Transition."

Kaminski, Bartlomiej, and Zhen Kun Wang. "External Assistance and Progress in Transition."

Kornaï, János. "The Hungarian Road. A Historical Case Study of the Political Economy of the Reform and Post-Socialist Transition."

Milanovic, Branko. "Poverty in Transition."

Pistor, Katharina. "Law Meets the Market: Matches and Mismatches in Transition Economies."

Siebert, Horst, Martin Raiser, and Rolf J. Langhammer. "The Transition in Central and Eastern Europe."

Wing Thye Woo. "Enterprise Reform in Europe and Asia."

Selected bibliography

Afanasief, M., P. Kuznetzov, and P. Isaev. 1995. "Krisis platejei v Rossii: Chto proishodit na samom dele? " ("Arrears Crisis in Russia—What is Happening in Fact?"). *Voprosi Economiki* 8: 52–72.

Agency for Economic Coordination and Development (ACED). 1993. *Bulgarian Economy in 1993,* Annual Report. Sofia.

Aghevli, Bijan, Eduardo Borensztein, and Tessa van der Willigen. 1992. *Stabilization and Structural Reform in the Czech and Slovak Republics: First Stage.* Occasional Paper No. 92. Washington, D.C.: International Monetary Fund.

Aghion, Phillippe, and Olivier Blanchard. 1993. "On the Speed of Transition in Central Europe." Working Paper No. 6. European Bank for Reconstruction and Development (EBRD), London.

Ahmad, Etisham, ed. 1995. *Financing Decentralized Expenditures: Intergovernmental Grants.* Aldershot, U.K.: Edward Elgar Publishing Limited.

Alam, A. S. "A Theory of Limits on Corruption and Some Applications." *Kyklos* 48: 419–35.

Alesina, Alberto, and Lawrence H. Summers. 1993. "Central Bank Independence and Macroeconomic Performance: Some Comparative Evidence." *Journal of Money, Credit and Banking* 25(2): 151–62.

Alexander, William E., Tomas J. T. Balino, and Charles Enoch. 1995. *The Adoption of Indirect Instruments of Monetary Policy.* Occasional Paper No. 126. Washington, D.C.: International Monetary Fund.

Alfandari, Gilles, and Mark Schaffer. Forthcoming. "On Arrears in Russia." In Simon Commander, Qimiao Fan, and Mark E. Schaffer, eds., *Enterprise Restructuring and Economic Policy in Russia.* EDI Development Studies. Washington, D.C.: World Bank.

Alfandari, Gilles, Qimiao Fan, and Lev Freinkman. Forthcoming. "Government Financial Transfers to Industrial Enterprises and Restructuring." In Simon Commander, Qimiao Fan, and Mark E. Schaffer, eds., *Enterprise Restructuring and Economic Policy in Russia.* EDI Development Studies, Washington, D.C.: World Bank.

Alford, William P. 1995. "Tasselled Loafers for Barefoot Lawyers: Transformation and Tension in the World of Chinese Legal Workers." *The China Quarterly.*

Allan, Bill. 1994. "Toward a Framework for a Budget Law for Economies in Transition." IMF Working Paper No. 94/149. International Monetary Fund, Washington, D.C.

Anderson, Robert E., Simeon Djankov, and Gerhard Pohl. 1995. "Restructuring of Large Industrial Firms in Central and Eastern Europe, 1992–94." World Bank, Washington, D.C.

Aoki, Masahiko, and Hyung-Ki Kim, eds., 1995. *Corporate Governance in Transitional Economies: Insider Control and the Role of Banks.* EDI Development Studies. Washington, D.C.: World Bank.

Artemiev, Igor, Gary Fine, Enna Karlova, and Ira Lieberman. 1996. "Russia: The Rush for State Shares in the 'Klondyke' of Wild East Capitalism." Paper presented to the Second Annual Institute Conference on Current Issues in International Trade at the U.S. Department of Commerce, Washington, D.C., March 28–29.

Aschauer, David A. 1989. "Is Public Expenditure Productive?" *Journal of Monetary Economics* 23 (March): 177–200.

Asian Development Bank. 1995. *Annual Report.* Manila.

Åslund, Anders, ed. 1994a. *Economic Transformation in Russia.* New York: St. Martin's Press.

_____. 1994b. "Lessons of the First Four Years of Systemic Change in Eastern Europe." *Journal of Comparative Economics* 19: 22–38.

_____. 1995a. "Eurasia Letter: Ukraine's Turnaround." *Foreign Policy* 100: 125-43

_____. 1995b. *How Russia Became a Market Economy.* Washington, D.C.: The Brookings Institution

Asselain, Jean-Charles. 1994. "Convertibilité précoce et protection par le change: un premier bilan de la réinsertion internationale des pays de l'Est." *Revue Economique* 45 (May): 833–44.

Atkinson, Anthony B. 1989. *Poverty and Social Security.* London: Harvester Wheatsheaf.

_____. 1991. "Poverty, Economic Performance and Income Transfer Policy in OECD Countries." *World Bank Economic Review* 5(1): 3–21.

_____. 1996. *Incomes and the Welfare State: Essays on Britain and Europe.* Cambridge, U.K.: Cambridge University Press.

Atkinson, Anthony B., and John Micklewright. 1991. "Unemployment Compensation and Labor Market Transitions: A Critical Review." *Journal of Economic Literature* 29(4): 1679-727.

_____. 1992. *Economic Transformation in Eastern Europe and the Distribution of Income.* Cambridge, U.K.: Cambridge University Press.

Atkinson, Anthony B., Lee Rainwater, and Timothy M. Smeeding. 1995. *Income Distribution in OECD Countries.* Social Policy Studies No. 18. Paris: OECD.

Avramov, Roumen, and Kamen Guenov. 1994. "The Rebirth of Capitalism in Bulgaria." *Bank Review* 4: 3–25, Bulgarian National Bank, Sofia.

Baer, Herbert L., and Cheryl W. Gray. 1996. "Debt as a Control Device in Transitional Economies: The Experience of Hungary and Poland." In Roman Frydman, Cheryl W. Gray, and Andrzej Rapaczynski, eds., *Corporate Governance in Central Europe and Russia. Volume 1: Banks, Funds, and Foreign Investors.* Budapest, London, and New York: Central European University Press.

Baer, Herbert, and Daniela Klingebiel. 1994. "Systemic Risk When Depositors Bear Losses: Five Case Studies." Policy Research Department, World Bank, Washington, D.C.

Bakker, Marie-Renée. 1993. "Twinning as a Tool for Institutional Development of Banks: The World Bank's Experience in Poland and Lessons to Be Learned for the Former Soviet Union." Europe and Central Asia Department, World Bank, Washington, D.C.

Balcerowicz, Leszek. 1995. *Socialism Capitalism Transformation.* Budapest: Central European University Press.

Balcerowicz, Leszek, and Alan Gelb. 1995. "Macropolicies in Transition to a Market Economy: A Three-Year Perspective." In Michael Bruno and Boris Pleskovic, eds. *Proceedings of the World Bank Annual Conference on Development Economics 1994*, Washington, D.C.

Balcerowicz, Leszek, Cheryl W. Gray, and Iraj Hashi, eds. 1995. "Enterprise Exit Processes in Transition Economies: Downsizing, Workouts, and Liquidation." Policy Research Department, World Bank, Washington, D.C.

Baldwin, Richard. 1994. *Towards an Integrated Europe.* London: Centre for Economic Policy Research.

Bandyopadhyay, Sushenjit, and Shantayanan Devarajan. 1994. "Using Project Rates of Return to Inform Sector Allocation Decisions?" World Bank, Washington, D.C.

Banerjee, Biswajit, Vincent Koen, Thomas Krueger, Mark S. Lutz, Michael Marrese, and Tapio O. Saavalainen. 1995. *Road Maps of the Transition: The Baltics, the Czech Republic, Hungary, and Russia.* Occasional Paper No. 127. Washington, D.C.: International Monetary Fund.

Barberis, Nicholas, Maxim Boycko, Andrei Schleifer, and Natalia Tsukanova. 1995. "How Does Privatization Work? Evidence from the Russian Shops." Working Paper No. 5136. National Bureau of Economic Research, Cambridge, Mass.

Barbone, Luca, and Domenico Marchetti, Jr. 1995. "Transition and the Fiscal Crisis in Central Europe." *Economics of Transition* 3(1): 59–74.

Barbone, Luca, and Hana Polackova. Forthcoming. "Public Finances and Economic Transition." Policy Research Working Paper. Central Europe Department, World Bank, Washington, D.C.

Barr, Nicholas. 1992. "Economic Theory and the Welfare State: A Survey and Interpretation." *Journal of Economic Literature* 30(2): 741–803.

_____. 1993a. *The Economics of the Welfare State,* 2d ed. Stanford, Calif.: Stanford University Press; Oxford: Oxford University Press.

_____. 1993b. *Ekonomika Panstwa Opiekunczego (The Economics of the Welfare State).* Poznan: Wydawnictwo Akademii Ekonomicznej w Poznaniu.

_____, ed. 1994. *Labor Markets and Social Policy in Central and Eastern Europe: The Transition and Beyond.* New York and Oxford: Oxford University Press.

_____, ed. 1995a. *Munkaeröpiac és Szociálpolitika közep-és Kelet-Európában: Az átalakulás, és ami utána jön (Labor Markets and Social Policy in Central and Eastern Europe: The Transition and Beyond. 1994).* Budapest: Hilscher Rezsö Szociálpolitikai Egyesület.

_____, ed. 1995b. *Pieţele Forţei de Muncă şi Politica Socială in Europa Centrală şi de Est. Volumul I. (Labor Markets and Social Policy in Central and Eastern Europe: The Transition and Beyond. 1994).* Bucharest: World Bank.

_____, ed. Forthcoming. *Rynki Truda i Sotsial'naya Politika v Stranakh Tsentral'noi i Vostochnoi Evropy (Labor Markets and Social Policy in Central and Eastern Europe: The Transition and Beyond. 1994).* Institut ekonomicheskogo razvitiia Vsemirnogo banka (EDI). Moskovskii gosudarstvennyi universitet im. M.V. Lomonosova. Moscow: Infra-M.

Barro, Robert J. 1991. "Economic Growth in a Cross Section of Countries." *Quarterly Journal of Economics* 106: 407–43.

_____. 1989. "A Cross-Country Study of Growth, Saving, and Government." NBER Working Paper No. 2855. National Bureau of Economic Research, Cambridge, Mass.

Begg, David, and Richard Portes. 1993. "Enterprise Debt and Financial Restructuring in Central and Eastern Europe." *European Economic Review* 37: 396–407.

Belka, Marek, Saul Estrin, Mark E. Schaffer, and Inderjit Singh. 1994. "Enterprise Adjustment in Poland: Evidence from a Survey of 200 Private, Privatized, and State-Owned Firms." Working Paper No. 658. CEP-LSE, London.

Berg, Andrew. 1993. "Measurement and Mismeasurement of Economic Activity During Transition to the Market." In Mario I. Blejer, Guillermo A. Calvo, Fabrizio Coricelli, and Alan H. Gelb, eds. *Eastern Europe in Transition: From Recession to Growth?* World Bank Discussion Paper No. 196. Washington, D.C.

_____. 1994. "Does Macroeconomic Reform Cause Structural Adjustment?" International Monetary Fund, Washington, D.C.

Berg, Andrew, and Jeffrey Sachs. 1992. "Structural Adjustment and International Trade in Eastern Europe: the Case of Poland." *Economic Policy: A European Forum* 14: 117–73.

Berliner, J. 1952. "The Informal Organization of the Soviet Firm." *The Quarterly Journal of Economics* 66: 342–65.

Bird, Richard M., Robert D. Ebel, and Christine I. Wallich, eds. 1995. *Decentralization of the Socialist State: Intergovernmental Finance in Transition Economies..* World Bank Regional and Sectoral Studies. Washington, D.C.

Black, Bernard, Reinier Kraakman, and Jonathan Hay. 1996. "Corporate Law from Scratch." In Roman Frydman, Cheryl W. Gray, and Andrzej Rapaczynski, eds., *Corporate Governance in Central Europe and Russia, Volume 2: Insiders and the State.* Budapest, London, and New York: Central European University Press.

Blanchard, Olivier Jean, Kenneth A. Froot, and Jeffrey D. Sachs, eds. 1994. *The Transition in Eastern Europe—A NBER Project Report.* Chicago, Ill.: University of Chicago.

Blasi, Joseph R. 1996. "Russian Enterprises After Privatization." Paper presented at the ASSA meeting in San Francisco, Calif., January.

Blasi, Joseph R., and Andrei Shleifer. 1996. "Corporate Governance in Russia: An Initial Look." In Roman Frydman, Cheryl W. Gray, and Andrzej Rapaczynski, eds. *Corporate Governance in Central Europe and Russia, Volume 2: Insiders and the State.* Budapest, London, and New York: Central European University Press.

Blejer, Mario I., Guillermo A. Calvo, Fabrizio Coricelli, and Alan H. Gelb, eds. 1993. *Eastern Europe in Transition: From Recession to Growth?* World Bank Discussion Paper No. 196. Washington, D.C.

Bloom, Benjamin S., ed. 1956. *Taxonomy of Educational Objective—Book 1, Cognitive Domain.* New York: Longman.

Bobak, Martin, and Richard Feachem. 1992. "Health Status in the Czech and Slovak Federal Republic." *Health Policy and Planning* 7(3): 234–42.

_____. 1995. "Air Pollution and Mortality in Central and Eastern Europe: An Estimate of the Impact." *European Journal of Public Health* 5: 82–86.

Boeri, Tito, and Burda, Michael C. 1995. "Active Labor Market Policies, Job Matching, and the Czech Miracle." Discussion Paper Series No. 1302. Centre for Economic Policy Research, London.

Bofinger, Peter. 1995. "The Political Economy of the Eastern Enlargement of the EU." Discussion Paper No. 1234. Centre for Economic Policy Research, London.

Bogetic, Zeljko, and Arye L. Hillman, eds. 1995. *Financing Government in the Transition—Bulgaria: The Political Economy of Tax Policies, Tax Bases, and Tax Evasion.* World Bank Regional and Sectoral Study. Washington, D.C.

Bonin, John P., and Kalman Mizsei. 1995. "State Withdrawal from the Banking Sector in Central and Eastern Europe." Institute for East-West Studies Working Paper. New York.

Bonin, John P., and István P. Székely, eds. 1994. *The Development and Reform of Financial Systems in Central and Eastern Europe.* Aldershot, U.K.: Edward Elgar Publishing Limited.

Borensztein, Eduardo, Dimitri G. Demekas, and Jonathan D. Ostry. 1993. "An Empricial Analysis of the Output Declines in Three Eastern European Countries." *IMF Staff Papers* 40 (1): 1–31.

Borish, Michael S., Millard F. Long, and Michel Noël. 1995. *Restructuring Banks and Enterprises: Recent Lessons from Transition Countries.* World Bank Discussion Paper No. 279. Washington, D.C.

Borner, Silvio, Aymo Brunetti, and Beatrice Weder. 1994. *Political Credibility and Economic Development.* New York: St. Martin's Press.

Bosworth, Barry P., and Gur Ofer. 1995. *Reforming Planned Economies in an Integrating World Economy.* Integrating National Economies Series. Washington, D.C.: The Brookings Institution.

Boycko, Maxim, Andrei Shleifer, and Robert Vishny. 1994a. "Politicians and Firms." *Quarterly Journal of Economics.* November.

_____. 1994b. "A Theory of Privatization." Department of Economics, Harvard University, Cambridge, Mass.

_____. 1995. *Privatizing Russia.* Cambridge, Mass.: MIT Press.

Brada, Joseph, I. J. Singh, and Adam Torok. 1994. *Firms Afloat and Firms Adrift: Hungarian Industry and the Economic Transition.* London: M.E. Sharpe.

Brainerd, Elizabeth. 1995. "Winners and Losers in Russia's Economic Transition." Department of Economics, Harvard University, Cambridge, Mass.

Bratkowski, Andrzej. 1993. "The Shock of Transformation or the Transformation of the Shock? The Big Bang in Poland and Official Statistics." *Communist Economies and Economic Transformation* 5(1).

Brau, Eduard. 1995. "External Financial Assistance: The Record and Issues." In Daniel A. Citrin and Ashok K. Lahiri, eds.,*Policy Experiences and Issues in the Baltics, Russia, and Other Countries of the Former Soviet Union.* Occasional Paper No. 133. Washington, D.C.: International Monetary Fund.

Bredenkamp, Hugh. 1993. "Conducting Monetary and Credit Policy in Countries of the Former Soviet Union: Some Issues and Options." IMF Working Paper No. 93/23. International Monetary Fund, Washington, D.C.

Broadman, Harry G. 1995. *Meeting the Challenge of Chinese Enterprise Reform.* World Bank Discussion Paper No. 283. Washington, D.C.

Brown, Annette N., Barry W. Ickes, and Randi Ryterman. 1994. "The Myth of Monopoly: A New View of Industrial Structure in Russia." Policy Research Working Paper No. 1331. World Bank, Washington, D.C.

Bruno, Michael. 1992. "Stabilization and Reform in Eastern Europe." *IMF Staff Papers* 39(4). Washington, D.C.: International Monetary Fund.

Bruno, Michael, and William Easterly. 1995. "Inflation Crises and Long-Run Growth." Policy Research Working Paper No. 1517. World Bank, Washington, D.C.

Brus, W., and K. Laski. 1989. *From Marx to the Market.* Oxford: Clarendon Press.

Buck, Trevor, Igor Filatochev, Mike Wright, and Yves van Frausum. 1995. "The Process and Impact of Privatization in Russia and Ukraine." Centre for Management Buy-Out Research Occasional Paper No. 59. University of Nottingham, United Kingdom.

Burda, Michael C., and Martina Lubyova. 1995. "The Impact of Active Labor Market Policies: A Closer Look at the Czech and Slovak Republics." Discussion Paper Series No. 1102. Centre for Economic Policy Research, London.

Byrd, William A., and Lin Qingsong, eds. 1990. *China's Rural Industry: Structure, Development, and Reform.* New York: Oxford University Press.

Cadot, Olivier, and Jaime De Melo. 1995. "France and the CEECs: Adjusting to Another Enlargement." In Riccardo Faini and Richard Portes, eds. *European Union Trade with Eastern Europe: Adjustment and Opportunities.* London: Centre for Economic Policy Reserach.

Calari, Cesare, and Brian Pinto. 1995. "Capital Markets: Lessons From Transition Economies." International Finance Corporation, Europe Department, Washington, D.C.

Calvo, Guillermo, and Fabrizio Coricelli. 1992. "Stabilizing a Previously Centrally Planned Economy: Poland 1990." *Economic Policy* 14: 176–226.

Calvo, Guillermo, Manmohan S. Kumar, Eduardo Borensztein, and Paul R. Masson. 1993. "Financial Sector Reforms and Exchange Arrangements in Eastern Europe." Occasional Paper No. 102. International Monetary Fund, Washington, D.C.

Calvo, Guillermo, Ratna Sahay, and Carlos A. Vegh. 1995. "Capital Flows in Central and Eastern Europe: Evidence and Policy Options." Working Paper No. 95/57. International Monetary Fund, Washington, D.C.

Cao, Yuan Zheng, Gang Fan, and Wing Thye Woo. 1995. "Chinese Economic Reforms: Past Successes and Future Challenges." In Wing Thye Woo, Stephen Parker, and Jeffrey Sachs, eds., *Key Issues and National Experience in the Transition to the Market Economy.* Cambridge, Mass.: MIT Press.

Caprio, Gerard, Jr. 1995. "The Role of Financial Intermediaries in Transitional Economies." *Carnegie-Rochester Conference Series on Public Policy* 42: 257–302.

Caprio, Gerard, Jr., David Folkerts-Landau, and Timothy D. Lane, eds. 1994. *Building Sound Finance in Emerging Market Economies.* Washington, D.C.: International Monetary Fund.

Caprio, Gerard, Jr., and Daniela Klingebiel. Forthcoming. "Bank Insolvency: Bad Luck, Bad Policy, or Bad Banking?" In Michael Bruno and Boris Pleskovic, eds., *Proceedings of the World Bank Annual Conference on Development Economics 1996.* Washington, D.C.

Caprio, Gerard, Jr., and Ross Levine. 1994. "Reforming Finance in Transitional Socialist Economies." *World Bank Research Observer* 9(1): 1–24.

Caprio, Gerard, Jr., and Dimitri Vittas. Forthcoming. *Reforming Finance: Lessons from History.* New York: Cambridge University Press.

CEPR (Centre for Economic Policy Research). 1992. *Monitoring European Integration: The Impact of Eastern Europe.* London.

Chaba, Laszlo. 1995. "Politico-economicheskie osnovi strategii reform: sravnenie opita Kitaia I stran Tzentralnoi I Vostochnoi Evropi" ("Political and economic foundations of reform strategies: comparison between Chinese and Eastern European experience"). *Voprosi Economiki* 12: 45–75.

Chase, Robert S. 1995. "Women's Labor Force Participation During and After Communism: A Case Study of the Czech Republic and Slovakia." Department of Economics, Yale University, New Haven, Conn.

Chavance, Bernard. 1994. *Les réformes économiques à l'Est: de 1950 aux années 1990. (The Transformation of the Communist System: Economic Reform since the 1950s.* Boulder, Colo.: Westview Press.) Paris: Nathan.

China Statistical Publishing House. 1995. *Statistical Yearbook of China.* Beijing.

Christensen, Benedikte Vibe. 1994. *The Russian Federation in Transition—External Developments.* IMF Occasional Paper No. 111. International Monetary Fund, Washington, D.C.

Chu, Ke-young, Sanjeev Gupta, Benedict Clemens, Daniel Hewitt, Sergio Lugaresi, Jerald Schiff, Ludger Schuknecht, and Gerd Schwartz. 1995. "Unproductive Public Expenditures: A Pragmatic Approach to Policy Analysis." Fiscal Affairs Department, Pamphlet Series No. 48. International Monetary Fund, Washington, D.C.

Chunling, Li. 1995. "An Educational System Grappling with Poverty: Primary Education in the Poor Areas of China." *China Perspectives* 1 (September/October): 30–35.

Citrin, Daniel A., and Ashok K. Lahiri, eds. 1995. *Policy Experiences and Issues in the Baltics, Russia, and Other Countries of the Former Soviet Union.* Occasional Paper No. 133. Washington, D.C.: International Monetary Fund.

Claessens, Stijn, Julie Hunt, and Kyle Peters. 1995. "Bulgaria: State Enterprise Adjustment." Europe and Central Asia Department, World Bank, Washington, D.C.

Coates, Richard D., and Arlene Elgart Mirsky. 1995. "Restructuring and Bankruptcy in Central and Eastern Europe." London: Deloitte Touche Tomatsu International.

Coffee, John C., Jr. 1995. "Corporate Governance in Central Europe and Russia: Institutional Investors in Transitional Economies—Lessons from the Czech Experience." Policy Research Paper No. 14850. Policy Research Department, World Bank, Washington, D.C.

Collins, Susan M., and Dani Rodrik. 1991. "Eastern Europe and the Soviet Union in the World Economy." *Policy Analyses in International Economics* 32. Institute for International Economics, Washington, D.C.

Commander, Simon, and Fabrizio Coricelli, eds. 1995. *Unemployment, Restructuring, and the Labor Market in Eastern Europe and Russia.* EDI Development Studies. Washington, D.C.: World Bank.

Commander, Simon, Qimiao Fan, and Mark E. Schaffer, eds. Forthcoming. *Enterprise Restructuring and Economic Policy in Russia.* EDI Development Studies. Washington, D.C.: World Bank

Commission of the European Communities. 1995a. "Interim Report from the Commission to the European Council on the Effects on the Policies of the European Union of Enlargement to the Associated Countries of Central and Eastern Europe." CSE (95) 605. Brussels.

_____. 1995b. "Preparation of the Associated Countries of Central and Eastern Europe for Integration into the Internal Market of the Union: White Paper." Office for Official Publications of the European Communities, Luxembourg.

_____. 1995c. "Progress Report on the Pre-Accession Strategy with the Associated Countries of Central and Eastern Europe." CSE (95) 606. Brussels.

Conway, Patrick. 1995. " Saving in Transition Economies: The Summary Report." Policy Research Working Paper No. 1509. World Bank, Europe and Central Asia Department, Washington, D.C.

Coricelli, Fabrizio, and Timothy D. Lane. 1993. "Wage Controls during the Transition from Central Planning to a Market Economy." *World Bank Research Observer* 8 (2, July): 195–210.

Coricelli, Fabrizio, and Ana Revenga, eds. 1992. *Wage Policy During the Transition to a Market Economy: Poland 1990-91.* World Bank Discussion Paper No. 158. Washington, D.C.

Cox, Donald, Zekeriya Eser, and Emmanuel Jimenez. Forthcoming. "Family Safety Nets During Economic Transition: A Study of Interhousehold Transfers in Russia." In Jeni Klugman, ed., *Poverty in Russia During the Transition.* World Bank Regional and Sectoral Studies. Washington, D.C.

Cox, Donald, James Fetzer, and Emmanuel Jimenez. Forthcoming. "The Role and Magnitude of the Private Safety Net During Transition: Private Interhousehold Transfers in Vietnam." In David Dollar, Peter Glewwe, and Jennie Litvack, eds., *Household Welfare and Vietnam's Transition to a Market Economy.* Washington, D.C.: World Bank.

Cox, Donald, Emmanuel Jimenez, and John Jordan. 1994. "Family Safety Nets and Economic Transition: A Study of Private Transfers in Kyrgyzstan." World Bank, Policy Research Department, Washington, D.C.

Cox, Donald, Emmanuel Jimenez, and Wlodek Okrasa. 1995. "Family Safety Nets and Economic Transition: A Case Study of Poland." Paper presented at the Northeast Universities Development Economics Conference, Harvard University, Cambridge, Mass., November.

Cox, Donald, and Fredric Raines. 1985 "Interfamily Transfers and Income Redistribution." In Martin David and Timothy Smeeding, eds., *Horizontal Equity, Uncertainty and Measures of Well Being.* Chicago, Ill.: University of Chicago Press.

Crawford, Iain, and Alan Thompson. 1994. "Driving Change: Politics and Administration." In Nicholas Barr, ed., *Labor Markets and Social Policy in Central and Eastern Europe: The Transition and Beyond.* New York and Oxford: Oxford University Press. (Available in Hungarian and Romanian; Russian forthcoming.)

Csaba, Laszlo. 1995: "Gazdasagstrategia helyett konjunktura-politika" ("Trade-Cycle Policy Instead of Economic Strategy"). *Kulgazdasag* 39(3): 36–46.

Csaki, Csaba, and Zvi Lerman. Forthcoming. "Agricultural Transition Revisited: Issues of Land Reform and Farm Restructuring in Central and Eastern Europe and the Former USSR." World Bank Discussion Paper. World Bank, Washington, D.C.

Cuadernos del Este 14. 1995. "Reestructuración industrial." Special issue on industrial restructuring in transition economies. Madrid.

Dabrowski, Marek. 1995a. "Different Strategies of Transition to a Market Economy: How Do They Work in Practice?" World Bank, Washington, D.C.

_____. 1995b. "Fiscal Crisis in the Transformation Period: Trends, Stylized Facts and Some Conceptual Problems." Center for Social and Economic Research, Warsaw, Poland.

_____. 1995c. "Why Did the Ruble Area Have to Collapse?" Center for Social and Economic Research, Warsaw, Poland.

Dean, Judith M., Seema Desai, and James Reidel. 1994. *Trade Policy Reforms in Developing Countries Since 1985—A Review of the Evidence.* World Bank Discussion Paper No. 267, Washington, D.C.

De Broeck, Mark, Paula De Masi, and Vincent Koen. 1995. "Inflation Dynamics in Kazakstan." IMF Working Paper No. 95/140. European II Department. International Monetary Fund, Washington, D.C.

Delyagin, M. 1995. "Bankovskiy crisis v svete osnovnyrh tendentziy ekonomicheskogo razvitiya Rossii" ("The Banking Crisis in the Light of the General Tendencies in Russia's Economic Development"). *Voprosi Ekonomiki* 10: 4–11.

De Masi, Paula, and Vincent Koen. 1995. "Relative Price Convergence in Russia." International Monetary Fund Working Paper No. 95/54. Washington, D.C.

De Melo, Martha, and Gur Ofer. 1994. *Private Service Firms in a Transitional Economy: Findings of a Survey in St. Petersburg.* Studies of Economies in Transition Paper No. 11. Washington, D.C.: World Bank.

de Menil, Georges. 1995. "Trade Policies in Transition Economies: a Comparison of European and Asian Experiences." Prepared for the Asia Foundation Project on Economies in Transition: Comparing Asia and Eastern Europe. DELTA, Paris, May 22.

Demirgüç-Kunt, Asli, and Ross Levine. Forthcoming. "Stock Market Development and Financial Intermediaries: Stylized Facts." *World Bank Economic Review.* Washington, D.C.

Demirgüç-Kunt, Asli, and Vojislav Maksimovic. Forthcoming. "Stock Market Development and Financing Choices for Firms." *World Bank Economic Review.* Washington, D.C.

Dervis, Kemal, Luca Barbone, Hana Polackova, and Pedro Rodriguez. 1995. "Macroeconomic Policies and the Transition." Europe and Central Asia Country Department, World Bank, Washington, D.C.

Devarajan, Shantayanan, Vinaya Swaroop, and Heng-Fu Zou. 1995. "The Composition of Public Expenditure and Economic Growth." Policy Research Department, World Bank, Washington, D.C.

Devarajan, Shantayanan, Danyang Xie, and Heng-fu Zou. 1994. "Does Public Capital Promote Economic Growth?" Policy Research Department, World Bank, Washington, D.C.

Dimelis, Sophia, and Konstantine Gatsios. 1995. "Trade with Central and Eastern Europe: The Case of Greece." In Riccardo Faini and Richard Portes, eds., *European Union Trade with Eastern Europe: Adjustment and Opportunities.* Centre for Economic Policy Research, London.

Dittus, Peter. 1994a. "Bank Reform and Behavior in Central Europe." *Journal of Comparative Economics* 19: 335–61.

———. 1994b. "Corporate Governance in Central Europe: The Role of Banks." *BIS Economic Papers* 42: 1021–2515. Monetary and Economic Department, Bank for International Settlements, Basel, Switzerland.

Dittus, Peter, and Stephen Prowse. 1996. "Corporate Control in Central Europe and Russia: Should Banks Own Shares?" In Roman Frydman, Cheryl Gray, and Andrzej Rapaczynski, eds., *Corporate Governance in Central Europe and Russia. Volume 1: Banks, Funds, and Foreign Investors.* Budapest, London, and New York: Central European University Press.

Djankov, Simeon, and Bernard Hoekman. 1995. "Trade Liberalization and Enterprise Restructuring in Bulgaria, 1992–94." Europe/Middle East and North Africa Technical Department, World Bank, Washington, D.C.

Dolgopyatova, T., and I. Yevseyeva. 1994a. *The Survival Strategy of State and Privatized Industrial Enterprises in the Transition Period.* Moscow: Vyshaya shkola.

———. 1994b. *Ekonomichskoye povedeniye promychlennyh predpriyatiy v perehodnoy ekonomike. (Economic Behaviour of Industrial Enterprises in the Transitional Economy.)*

Dollar, David, Peter Glewwe, and Jennie Litvack, eds. Forthcoming. *Household Welfare and Vietnam's Transition to a Market Economy.* Washington, D.C.: World Bank.

Donaldson, David J., and Dileep M. Wagle. 1995. *Privatization: Principles and Practice.* IFC Lessons of Experience Series. Washington, D.C.: World Bank.

Dornbusch, Rudiger, Wilhelm Noelling, and Richard Layard, eds. 1993. *Postwar Economic Reconstruction and Lessons for the East Today.* Cambridge, Mass.: MIT Press.

Dornbusch, Rudiger, and Holger C. Wolf. 1994. "East German Economic Reconstruction." In Olivier Jean Blanchard, Kenneth A. Froot, and Jeffrey D. Sachs, eds., *The Transition in Eastern Europe—A NBER Project Report.* Chicago, Ill.: University of Chicago Press.

Dubey, Ashutosh, and Milan Vodopivec. 1995. "Privatization and Efficiency During Slovenia's Transition: A Frontier Production Analysis." University of Maryland, College Park.

Duncan, Ian, and Alan Bollard. 1992. *Corporatization and Privatization: Lessons from New Zealand.* Auckland: Oxford University Press.

Dunlop, John B. 1993. *The Rise of Russia and the Fall of the Soviet Empire.* Princeton, N.J.: Princeton University Press.

Earle, John E., Saul Estrin, and Larisa L. Leshchenko. Forthcoming. "Ownership Structures, Patterns of Control and Enterprise Behavior in Russia." In Simon Commander, Qimiao Fan, and Mark E. Schaffer, eds., *Enterprise Restructuring and Economic Policy in Russia.* EDI Development Studies. Washington, D.C.: World Bank.

Earle, John E., Roman Frydman, and Andrzej Rapaczynski. 1993. *The Privatization Process in Central Europe.* Budapest: Central European University Press.

Earle, John E., Roman Frydman, Andrzej Rapaczynski, and Joel Turkewitz. 1994. *Small Privatization: The Transformation of Retail Trade and Consumer Services in the Czech Republic, Hungary and Poland.* Budapest: Central European University Press.

Easterly, William. Forthcoming. "When is Stabilization Expansionary?" *Economic Policy.*

Easterly, William, Martha De Melo, and Gur Ofer. 1994. "Services as a Major Source of Growth in Russia and Other Former Soviet States." World Bank Policy Research Working Paper No. 1292. Washington, D.C.

Easterly, William, and Stanley D. Fischer. 1995a. "The Soviet Economic Decline." *The World Bank Economic Review* 9(3): 341–71.

———. 1995b. "The Soviet Economic Decline: Historical and Republican Data." Working Paper Series No. 4735: 1–56. National Bureau of Economic Research, Cambridge, Mass.

Easterly, William, and Sergio Rebelo. 1993. "Fiscal Policy and Economic Growth: An Empirical Investigation." *Journal of Monetary Economics* 32: 417-58.

Easterly, William R., and Paulo Vieira da Cunha. 1994. "Financing the Storm: Russia's Macroeconomic Crisis." *Economics of Transition* 2(4): 443–66.

EBRD (European Bank for Reconstruction and Development). 1994. *Transition Report.* London.

———. 1995. *Transition Report 1995: Investment and Enterprise Development.* London.

———. 1996. *Transition Report Update.* London.

Ebrill, Liam P., Ajai Chopra, Charalambos Christofides, Paul Mylonas, Inci Otker, and Gerd Schwartz. 1994. *Poland: The Path to a Market Economy.* Occasional Paper No. 113. International Monetary Fund, Washington, D.C.

Education and Testing Service. 1992a. *Learning Mathematics.* Princeton, N.J.

Education and Testing Service. 1992b. *Learning Science.* Princeton, N.J.

Eichengreen, Barry, and Marc Uzan. 1992. "The Marshall Plan: Economic Effects and Implication for Eastern Europe and the Former USSR." *Economic Policy* 14 (April): 14–75.

Einhorn, Barbara. 1993. *Cinderella Goes To Market: Citizenship, Gender and Women's Movements in East Central Europe.* London: Verso.

Erdoas, Tibor. 1994: "A tartos novekedes realitasai es akadalyai" ("The Realities of Lasting Economic Growth and Obstacles to It"). *Kozgazdasagi Szemle* 41(6): 463–77.

Estrin, Saul. 1994a. "The Inheritance." In Nicholas Barr, ed., *Labor Markets and Social Policy in Central and Eastern Europe: The Transition and Beyond.* New York: Oxford University Press.

_____. ed. 1994b. *Privatization in Central and Eastern Europe.* London: Longman.

Estrin, Saul, Alan Gelb, and Inderjit Singh. Forthcoming. "Shocks and Adjustment by Firms in Transition: A Comparative Study." In Saul Estrin, Joe Brada, and Inderjit Singh, eds., *Firms in Transition: Cases from Poland, Czechoslovakia and Hungary.* Armonk, N.Y.: M. E. Sharpe.

European Economy. 1995. "Savings and Investment in Transition Countries: Recent Trends, Prospects, and Policy Issues." Supplement A: Economic Trends. No. 7 (July). European Commission, Directorate-General for Economic and Financial Affairs, Brussels.

Evans, Geoffrey. 1995. "Mass Political Attitudes and the Development of Market Democracy in Eastern Europe." Discussion Paper No. 39. Centre for European Studies, Nuffield College, Oxford.

Faini, Riccardo, and Richard Portes, eds. 1995. *European Union Trade with Eastern Europe: Adjustment and Opportunities.* London: Centre for Economic Policy Research.

Fakin, Barbara, and Alain de Crombrugghe. 1996. *Patterns of Government Expenditure and Taxation in Transition vs. OECD Economies.* Cahiers de la Faculté des Sciences Economiques et Sociales No. 162. Namur, France: Facultés Universitaires Notre-Dame de la Paix.

Falkingham, Jane, Jeni Klugman, Sheila Marnie, and John Micklewright. Forthcoming. *Household Welfare in Central Asia.* London: Macmillan.

Fan, Qimiao, and Une Lee. 1995. "Arrears in the Russia Economy: Basic Facts and Policy Implications." Europe and Central Asia Country Department, World Bank, Washington, D.C.

Feachem, Richard. 1994. "Health Decline in Eastern Europe." *Nature* 367(6461): 313–14.

Feachem, Richard G. A., Tord Kjellstrom, Christopher J. L. Murray, Mead Over, and Margaret A. Phillips, eds. 1992. *The Health of Adults in the Developing World.* New York: Oxford University Press.

Findlay, Christopher, Andrew Watson, and Harry X. Wu. 1994. *Rural Industry in China.* London: St. Martin's Press.

Fischer, Stanley. 1993. "The Role of Macroeconomic Factors in Growth." *Journal of Monetary Economics* 32: 458-512.

_____. 1995. "Modern Approaches to Central Banking." Paper presented at the Tercentenary Celebration of the Bank of England, June 9, 1995. NBER Working Paper No. 5064. National Bureau of Economic Research, Cambridge, Mass.

Fischer, Stanley, Ratna Sahay, and Carlos A. Vegh. 1995. "Stabilization and Growth in Transition Economies: Early Experiences." International Monetary Fund, Washington, D.C.

Foley, Mark C., and Jeni Klugman. Forthcoming. "The Impact of Social Support—Errors of Leakage and Exclusion." In Jeni Klugman, ed., *Poverty in Russia during the Transition.* World Bank Regional and Sectoral Studies. Washington, D.C.

Fong, Monica S. 1996. "Gender Barriers in the Transition to a Market Economy." World Bank, Poverty and Social Policy Department, Discussion Paper No. 87. Washington, D.C.

Fox, Louise. 1995. "Can Eastern Europe's Old-Age Crisis Be Fixed?" *Finance and Development* 32(4): 34–37.

Freedom Review. 1995.

Freund, Caroline L., and Christine I. Wallich. 1995. *Raising Household Energy Prices in Poland: Who Gains? Who Loses?* World Bank Policy Research Working Paper 1495. Washington, D.C.

Frydman, Roman, Cheryl W. Gray, and Andrzej Rapaczynski, eds. 1996. *Corporate Governance in Central Europe and Russia. Volume 1: Banks, Funds, and Foreign Investors. Volume 2: Insiders and the State.* Budapest, London, and New York: Central European University Press.

Fung, K. C. Forthcoming. "Accounting for Chinese Trade: Some National and Regional Considerations." In R. Baldwin, J. D. Richardson, and R. Lipsey, eds., *Geography and Ownership as a Basis for Economic Accounting.* Chicago, Ill.: University of Chicago Press.

Funk, Nanette, and Magda Mueller. 1993. *Gender Politics and Post-Communism: Reflections from Eastern Europe and the Former Soviet Union.* New York: Routledge.

Gacs, Janos. 1993: "A kulkereskedelem liberalizalasa Kelet-Europaban: gyors reformok es ujraertekeles. Csehszlovakia, Lengyelorszag es Magyarorszag tapasztalatai" ("Foreign Trade Liberalization in Eastern Europe: Fast Reforms and Re-evaluation. The Experience of Czechoslovakia, Poland and Hungary"). *Kulgazdasag* 37(12): 12–33.

Gaidar, Egor. 1995. "Postcomunistichiskie economicheskie reformi: proshlo piat let" ("Postcommunist economic reforms—five years have passed."). *Voprosi Economiki* 12: 4–11.

Galal, Ahmed, Leroy Jones, Pankaj Tandon, and Ingo Vogelsang. 1994. *Welfare Consequences of Selling Public Enterprises.* New York: Oxford University Press.

Gale, William G., and John Karl Scholz. 1994. "Intergenerational Transfers and the Accumulation of Wealth." *Journal of Economic Perspectives* 8 (Fall/4): 145–60.

Gang, Fan. 1994. "Incremental Changes and Dual-Track Transition: Understanding the Case of China. " Paper presented at the conference on Societies in Transformation: Experience of Market Reform for Ukraine, Kiev, May 19–21.

Gavrilenko, Evgeny, and Vincent Koen. 1994. "How Large Was the Output Collapse in Russia? Alternative Estimates and Welfare Implications." International Monetary Fund Working Paper No. 94/154. Washington, D.C.

Gelb, Alan H., and Cheryl W. Gray. 1991. *The Transformation of Economies in Central and Eastern Europe: Issues, Progress, and Prospects.* Policy and Research Series No. 17. Washington, D.C.: World Bank.

Gelb, Alan, Gary Jefferson, and Inderjit Singh. 1993. "Can Communist Economies Transform Incrementally? The Experience of China." In Olivier Jean Blanchard and Stanley Fischer, eds., *NBER Macroeconomics Annual 1993.* Cambridge, Mass.: MIT Press.

Glaessner, Thomas, and Ignacio Mas. 1995. "Incentives and the Resolution of Bank Distress." *World Bank Research Observer* 10(1): 53–73.

Gomulka, Stanislaw. 1995. "The IMF-Supported Programs of Poland and Russia, 1990-94: Principles, Errors, and Results." *Journal of Comparative Economics* 20:316–46.

Gorton, Gary, and Andrew Wilton. 1996. "Banking in Transition Economies: Does Efficiency Require Instability?" Wharton School of Business Working Paper, University of Pennsylvania, Philadelphia.

Goskomstat–World Bank. 1995. "Russian Federation: Report on the National Accounts." Government of the Russian Federation, State Statistics Committee, and World Bank ECA Country Department III. Washington, D.C.

Gray, Cheryl W., and Associates. 1993. "Evolving Legal Frameworks for Private Sector Development in Central and Eastern Europe." World Bank Discussion Paper No. 209. Washington, D.C.: World Bank.

Gray, Cheryl W., and Kathryn Hendley. Forthcoming. "Developing Commercial Law in Transition Economies: Examples from Hungary and Russia." In Jeffrey D. Sachs and Katharina Pistor, eds., *The Rule of Law and Economic Reform in Russia*. John M. Olin Critical Issues Series. Boulder, Colo.: Westview Press.

Gray, Cheryl W., and Arnold Holle. Forthcoming. "Bank-led Restructuring in Poland: Living Up to its Promises?" Policy Research Working Paper. World Bank, Washington, D.C.

Gray, Cheryl W., and W. Jarosz. 1995. "Law and the Regulation of Foreign Direct Investment: The Evidence from Central and Eastern Europe." *Columbia Journal of Transnational Law.* June.

Gray, Cheryl W., Sabine Schlorke, and Miklós Szanyi. Forthcoming. "Hungary's Bankruptcy Experience, 1992–93." *World Bank Economic Review.*

Gray, Dale. 1995. *Reforming the Energy Sector in Transition Economies: Selected Experience and Lessons.* World Bank Discussion Paper No. 296. Washington, D.C.

Grigoriev, L. 1995. "Ownership and Control Distribution in the Privatization Process." In A. Astapovich, ed., *Foreign Investment in Russia—Trends and Prospects.* Moscow.

Gros, Daniel, and Alfred Steinherr. 1995. *Winds of Change: Economic Transition in Central and Eastern Europe.* London: Longman.

Grosfeld, Irena, and Gérard Roland. 1995. "Defensive and Strategic Restructuring in Central European Enterprises." Centre for Economic Policy Research Discussion Paper No. 1135. London.

Grosh, Margaret. 1994. *Administering Targeted Social Programs in Latin America: From Platitudes to Practice.* World Bank Regional and Sectoral Studies. Washington, D.C.

Halpern, László. 1995. "Comparative Advantage and Likely Trade Pattern of the CEECs." In Riccardo Faini and Richard Portes, eds., *European Union Trade with Eastern Europe: Adjustment and Opportunities.* London: Centre for Economic Policy Research.

Handleman, Stephen. 1995. *Comrade Criminal.* New Haven, Conn.: Yale University Press.

Hansson, Ardo H. 1995. "Reforming the Banking System in Estonia." In Jacek Rostowski, ed., *Banking Reform in Central Europe and the Former Soviet Union.* Budapest: Central European University Press.

Hansson, Ardo H., and Jeffrey D. Sachs. 1994. "Monetary Institutions and Credible Stabilization: A Comparison of Experiences in the Baltics." Department of Economics, Harvard University, Cambridge, Mass.

Hardy, Daniel C., and Ashok K. Lahiri. 1994. "Cash Shortage in the Former Soviet Union." IMF Working Paper No. 94/67. International Monetary Fund, Washington, D.C.

Harrold, Peter. 1992. *China's Reform Experience to Date.* World Bank Discussion Paper No. 180. Washington, D.C.

Harrold, Peter, E. C. Hwa, and Lou Jiwei, eds. 1993. *Macroeconomic Management in China: Proceedings of a Conference in Dalian, June 1993.* World Bank Discussion Paper No. 220. Washington, D.C.

Hausmann, Ricardo, and Michael Gavin. 1995. "The Roots of Banking Crises: The Macroeconomic Context." Paper prepared for the Conference on Banking Crises in Latin America, Washington, D.C., October 6–7.

Havrylyshyn, Oleh, and Lance Pritchett. 1991. "European Trade Patterns After Transition." Policy Research and External Affairs Working Paper No. 748. World Bank, Washington, D.C.

Held, Joseph. 1992. *The Columbia History of Eastern Europe in the Twentieth Century.* New York: Columbia University Press.

Heller, Peter S., and Jack Diamond. 1990. *International Comparisons of Government Expenditure Revisited.* Occasional Paper No. 69. International Monetary Fund, Washington, D.C.

Hertling, James. 1996. "Critics Fear China Cannot Prepare Students for Future." *The Chronicle of Higher Education* 5 January.

Hewitt, Daniel, and Caroline van Rijckeghem. 1995. "Wage Expenditures of Central Governments." International Monetary Fund Working Paper No. 95/11.Washington, D.C.

Hexter, David. 1993. "Round Table in Banking: The Bad Debt Problem in Eastern Europe." *Economics of Transition* 1(1): 111–21.

Heyneman, Stephen P., ed. 1994. "Education in the Europe and Central Asia Region: Policies of Adjustment and Excellence." Report No. IDP–145. ECA Region, World Bank, Washington, D.C.

Hilbers, Paul. 1993. "Monetary Instruments and Their Use During the Transition from a Centrally Planned to a Market Economy." International Monetary Fund Working Paper No. 93/87. Washington, D.C.

Hobsbawm, Eric. 1994. *The Age of Extremes: A History of the World, 1914–1991.* New York: Pantheon Books.

Hoekman, Bernard, and Simeon Djankov. 1995. "Catching Up With Eastern Europe? The European Union's Mediterranean Free Trade Initiative." CEPR Discussion Paper No. 1300. Centre for Economic Policy Research, London.

Hofman, Bert. 1995a. "Fiscal Decline and Quasi-fiscal Response: China's Fiscal Policy and Fiscal System 1978–1994." Paper delivered at the CEPR/CEPII/OECD conference, Different Approaches to Market Reforms: A Comparison Between China and the CEECs, Budapest, October 6.

_____. 1995b. "Key Issues in China's Fiscal Policy." World Bank, China and Mongolia Department, Washington, D.C.

Holzmann, Robert, Janos Gacs, and Georg Winckler, eds. 1995. *Output Decline in Eastern Europe: Unavoidable, External Influence or Homemade.* Dordrecht, Netherlands: Kluwer Academic Publishers.

Hughes, Gordon. 1995. "Is the Environment Getting Cleaner in Central and Eastern Europe? Selected Evidence for Air Pollution and Drinking Water Contamination." Implementing the Environmental Action Program for Eastern Europe. Environment Department Work in Progress. World Bank, Washington, D.C.

Human Rights Watch. 1995a. "Abuses Against Women Workers." *The Human Rights Watch Global Report on Women's Human Rights.* New York.

_____. 1995b. "Russia: Neither Jobs Nor Justice: State Discrimination Against Women in Russia." *Human Rights Watch Women's Rights Project.* 7(5): 1–30.

Illarionov, A. 1995a. "Popyitki provedenia politiki finansovyi stabilizatcii v SSSR i Rossii" ("Attempts to Implement the Policy of Fiscal Stabilization in the USSR and Russia"). *Voprosi Economiki* 7: 4–37.

_____. 1995b. "Priroda rossiiskoi inflatcii" ("The Nature of Russia's Inflation"). *Voprosi Economiki* 3: 4–21.

IFC (International Finance Corporation). 1996. *Emerging Stock Markets Factbook 1996.* Washington, D.C.

IMF (International Monetary Fund). 1994a. "Eastern Europe—Factors Underlying the Weakening Performance of Tax Revenues." IMF Working Paper No. 94/104. Washington, D.C.

_____. 1994b. "Trade Policy Reform in the Countries of the Former Soviet Union." *IMF Economic Reviews 2/1994.* Washington, D.C.

_____. 1994c. *World Economic Outlook* (October). Washington, D.C.

_____. 1995a. *Direction of Trade Statistics 1995.* Washington, D.C.

_____. 1995b. "Russian Federation." *IMF Economic Reviews 16/1994.* Washington, D.C.

_____. 1995c. *World Economic Outlook* (May). Washington, D.C.

_____. Various years—a. *Government Statistics Yearbook.* Washington, D.C.

_____. Various years—b. *International Financial Statistics.* Washington, D.C.

_____. Various years—c. *World Economic Outlook.* Washington, D.C.

IMF, World Bank, Organisation for Economic Co-operation and Development, European Bank for Reconstruction and Development. 1991. *A Study of the Soviet Economy.* Paris: OECD.

Interstate Statistical Committee of the Commonwealth of Independent States. 1995. *Demographic Yearbook 1993.* Moscow: Goskomstat.

Jackman, Richard. 1994. "Economic Policy and Employment in the Transition Economies of Central and Eastern Europe: What Have We Learned?" *International Labour Review* 133(3): 327–45.

Jackman, Richard, and Michal Rutkowski. 1994. "Labor Markets: Wages and Employment." In Nicholas Barr, ed., *Labor Markets and Social Policy in Central and Eastern Europe: The Transition and Beyond.* New York: Oxford University Press.

Jalan, Jyotsna, and Martin Ravallion. 1996. "Transient Poverty in Rural China." Policy Research Department. World Bank, Washington, D.C.

Jepsen, Dorte, and Assia Brandrup-Lukanow. 1995. *Family Planning and Reproductive Health in CCEE/NIS.* Copenhagen: UNFPA and WHO.

Johnson, B. R., M. Horga, and L. Andronache. 1993. "Contraception and Abortion in Romania." *Lancet* 341: 875–80.

Jones, Derek C. 1996. "The Nature and Effects of Employee Ownership and Control: Evidence from the Baltics, Russia, and Bulgaria." Paper presented at the ASSA meeting in San Francisco, Calif., January.

Joskow, Paul, Richard Schmalensee, and Natalia Tsukanova. 1994. "Competition Policy in Russia During and After Privatization." *Brookings Papers on Economic Activity. Microeconomics* 301–81.

Kaminski, Bart, Zhen Kun Wang, and L. Alan Winters. 1996. "Foreign Trade in the Transition: the International Environment and Domestic Policy." In Studies of Economies in Transformation 20. Washington, D.C.: World Bank.

Karnite, Raita, and Inna Dovladbekova. 1995. *Institutions of Public Finance in Latvia.* San Francisco, Calif.: International Center for Economic Growth.

Kaufmann, Daniel, and Aleksander Kaliberda. 1995. "Integrating the Unofficial Economy into the Dynamics of Post-Socialist Economies: A Framework of Analysis and Evidence." Paper prepared for a conference on Economic Transition in the Newly Independent States, Kiev, August 16.

Keefer, Philip and Stephen Knack. 1995. "Why Don't Poor Countries Catch Up? A Cross-national Test of an Institutional Explanation." IRIS Working Paper. University of Maryland, College Park.

Keh, Douglas. 1994. "Economic Reform and the Implications of Criminal Finance." *UNDP Study Series.* U.N. International Drug Control Programme, Vienna.

Kikeri, Sunita, John Nellis, and Mary Shirley. 1992. *Privatization. The Lessons of Experience.* Washington, D.C.: World Bank.

King, Robert G., and Ross Levine. 1993a. "Finance, Entrepreneurship, and Growth: Theory and Evidence." *Journal of Monetary Economics* 32: 513–542.

_____. 1993b. "Finance and Growth: Schumpeter Might Be Right." *Quarterly Journal of Economics* 108: 717–38.

Klavens, Jonathan, and Anthony Zamparutti. 1995. *Foreign Direct Investment and Environment in Central and Eastern Europe: A Survey.* Washington, D.C: World Bank.

Klugman, Jeni, ed. Forthcoming. *Poverty in Russia during the Transition.* World Bank Regional and Sectoral Studies. Washington, D.C.

Knack, Stephen, and Philip Keefer. 1995. "Institutions and Economic Performance: Cross-country Tests Using Alternative Institutional Measures." *Economics and Politics* 7(3): 207–27.

Koen, Vincent. 1995. "Price Measurement and Mismeasurement in Central Asia." IMF Working Paper No. 95/82. International Monetary Fund, Washington, D.C.

Koen, Vincent, and Michael Marrese. 1995. "Stabilization and Structural Change in Russia, 1992–94." IMF Working Paper No. 95/13. International Monetary Fund, Washington, D.C.

Koford, Kenneth, and Jeffrey B. Miller. 1995. "Contracts in Bulgaria: How Firms Cope when Property Rights are Incomplete." IRIS Working Paper 166. University of Maryland, College Park.

Köllő, János. 1995. "Short-term Response of Employment to Sales in State-Owned and Private Firms in Hungary 1990–94." Paper presented at the World Bank/EDI Project on Employment, Unemployment and Restructuring in Eastern Europe and Russia, Washington, D.C., September.

Kolodko, Grzegorz W., Danuta Gotz-Kozierkiewicz, and Elzbieta Skrzeszewska-Paczek. 1991. *Hiperinflacja in stabilizacja w gospodarce postscocjalistycznej.* Warsaw: Instytut Finansow (*Hyperinflation and Stabilization in Postsocialist Economies.* Dordrecht: Kluwer Academic Publishers).

Koparanova, Malinka S. 1995. "Efficiency of State Firms in Bulgarian Industry: Microeconomic Evidence of an Empirical Study." Paper presented at the 70th Western Economic Association International Conference, San Diego, Calif., July.

Kornaï, János. 1986. "The Soft Budget Constraint." *Kyklos* 39(1), Budapest.

_____. 1992. *The Socialist System: The Political Economy of Communism.* Princeton, N.J.: Princeton University Press.

_____. 1994a. "Lasting Growth as the Top Priority. Macroeconomic Tensions and Government Economic Policy in Hungary" ("A legfontosabb: A tartos novekedes" *Nepszabadsa* Aug. 29–Sept. 2). Discussion Paper No. 1697, Harvard Institute of Economic Research, Cambridge, Mass.

_____. 1994b. "Transformational Recession: The Main Causes." *Journal of Comparative Economics* 19: 39–63.

_____. 1995. "A magyar gazdasagpolitika dilemmai" ("The Dilemmas of Hungarian Economic Policy"). *Kozgazdasagi Szemle* 42(7-8): 633–49.

_____. 1996. "Paying the Bill for Goulash-Communism: Hungarian Development and Macro Stabilization in a Political-Economy Context." Harvard Institute for Economics Research, Discussion Paper No. 1748. Cambridge, Mass.

Kosmarskii, B., and T. Maleva. 1995. "Sotzialnaya politika v Rossii v kontexte makroekonomicheskoy reformy" ("Russia's Social Policy in the Context of Macroeconomic Reforms"). *Voprosi Economiki* 9: 4–16.

Kovalyova, Galina. 1994. "Comparative Assessment of Students in Science and Math." In Stephen P. Heyneman, ed., "Education in the Europe and Central Asia Region: Policies of Adjustment and Excellence." Europe and Central Asia Region, Report No. IDP-145. World Bank, Washington, D.C.

Kraay, Aart. 1995. "Factor Accumulation, Factor Reallocation, and Growth in China." China and Mongolia Department, World Bank, Washington, D.C.

Krueger, Anne O. 1990. "Economists' Changing Perceptions of Government." Speech at the Kiel Institute, Germany, June 23.

Kuczynski, Irving, Teresa Barger, and Laurence Carter. Forthcoming—a. "IFC's Experience with Promoting Emerging Market Investment Funds." In IFC, ed., *Financial Sector: Lessons from Experience.* Washington, D.C.: International Finance Corporation.

_____. Forthcoming—b. "IFC's Experience with Promoting Leasing in Developing Countries." In IFC, ed., *Financial Sector: Lessons from Experience.* Washington, D.C.: International Finance Corporation.

Laporte, Bruno, and Julian Schweitzer. 1994. "Education and Training." In Nicholas Barr, ed., *Labor Markets and Social Policy in Central and Eastern Europe: The Transition and Beyond.* New York: Oxford University Press. (Available in Hungarian and Romanian; Russian forthcoming.)

Lardy, Nicholas. 1995. "Economic Engine? Foreign Trade and Investment in China." *The Brookings Review* 14(21): 10–15.

Lavigne, Marie. 1995. *The Economics of Transition From Socialist Economy to Market Economy.* New York: St. Martin's Press.

Layard, Richard, Stephen Nickell, and Richard Jackman. 1991. *Unemployment: Macroeconomic Performance and the Labour Market.* Oxford: Oxford University Press.

Lea, Michael J., and Bertrand Renaud. 1995. "Contractual Savings for Housing: How Suitable Are They for Transitional Economies?" Policy Research Working Paper No. 1516. World Bank, Financial Sector Development Department, Washington, D.C.

Lee, Wing On, and Zibiao Li. 1994. "Disparities in Educational Development in a Fast Developing Chinese City—Guangzhou." In Nelly P. Stromquist, ed., *Education in the Urban Areas: Cross-National Dimensions.* Westport, Conn.: Praeger.

Le Houerou, Philippe. 1994. "Decentralization and Fiscal Disparities among Regions in the Russian Federation." Report No. IDP 138. Europe and Central Asia Region, World Bank, Washington, D.C.

Le Houerou, Philippe, Elana Gold, and Stanislav Katash. 1994. "Budget Coverage and Government Finance in the Russian Federation." Report No. IDP 137. Europe and Central Asia Region, World Bank, Washington, D.C.

Leung, Y. M. 1991. "Curriculum Development in the People's Republic of China." In C. Marsh and P. Morris, eds., *Curriculum Development in East Asia.* London: Falmer Press.

Levine, Ross, and David Renelt. 1992. "A Sensitivity Analysis of Cross Country Growth Regressions." *American Economic Review* 82: 942–63.

Levine, Ross, and David Scott. 1993. "Old Debts and New Beginnings: A Policy Choice in Transitional Socialist Economies." *World Development* 21(3): 319–30.

Lewin, Keith M., and Wang Ying Jie. 1994. *Implementing Basic Education in China: Progress and Prospects in Rich, Poor and National Minority Areas.* Paris: International Institute for Educational Planning–UNESCO.

Lieberman, Ira, and John Nellis. 1995. *Russia: Creating Private Enterprises and Efficient Markets.* Studies of Economies in Transition 15. Washington, D.C.: World Bank.

Lin, Justin Yifu. 1995. "Inflation and Growth in China's Transition: An Analysis and Comparison with EE/FSO." China Center for Economic Research, Peking University, Beijing.

Lin, Justin Yifu, Fang Cai, and Zhou Li. 1996. *The China Miracle: Development Strategy and Economic Reform.* Chinese University of Hong Kong Press and Institute for Contemporary Studies, San Francisco, Calif.

Lipton, David, and Jeffrey Sachs. 1990a. "Creating a Market Economy in Eastern Europe: The Case of Poland." In David Lipton and Jeffrey Sachs, eds., *Brookings Papers on Economic Activity* 1: 75–147.

_____. 1990b. "Poland's Economic Reform." *Foreign Affairs* 69(3): 47–66.

_____. 1990c. "Privatization in Eastern Europe: The Case of Poland." In David Lipton and Jeffrey Sachs, eds., *Brookings Papers on Economic Activity* 2: 293–341.

Loayza, Norman V. Forthcoming. *The Economies of the Informal Sector: A Simple Model and Some Evidence from Latin America.* Carnegie-Rochester Series on Public Policy.

Lovei, Magda, and Barry S. Levy, eds. 1995. "Lead Exposure and Health in Central and Eastern Europe: The Impact on Children—Evidence from Hungary, Poland, and Bulgaria. World Bank, Washington, D.C.

Lubin, Nancy. 1994. "Leadership in Uzbekistan and Kazakhstan: The Views of the Led." The National Council for Soviet and Eastern Research, Title VIII Program. Washington, D.C.

Ma, Jin. 1995. "Macroeconomic Management and Intergovernmental Relations in China." Policy Research Working Paper No. 1408. World Bank, Washington, D.C.

Mabbett, Deborah. Forthcoming. "Social Insurance in the Transition to a Market Economy: Theoretical Issues with Application to Moldova." Policy Research Department Discussion Paper No. 1146. World Bank, Washington, D.C.

Marer, Paul, and Vincent Mabert. 1996. "GE Acquires and Restructures TUNGSRAM: The First Six Years (1990–95)." In *Performance of Privatised Enterprises: Corporate Governance, Restructuring, and Profitability.* Paris: OECD.

Martin, Will, and L. Alan Winters. 1995. *The Uruguay Round: Widening and Deepening the World Trading System.* Directions in Development Series. Washington, D.C.: World Bank.

Mauro, Paolo. 1995. "Corruption and Growth." *Quarterly Journal of Economics* August 110: 681–721.

McKinnon, Ronald I. 1991. "Financial Control in the Transition from Classical Socialism to a Market Economy." *Journal of Economic Perspectives* 5(4): 107–22.

McKinnon, Ronald I. 1994. "Gradual Versus Rapid Liberalization in Socialist Economies: The Problem of Macroeconomic Control." In Michael Bruno and Boris Pleskovic, eds., *Proceedings of the World Bank, Annual Conference on Development Economics* 1993. Washington, D.C.

McLure, Charles E., Jr., Andras Semjen, Tadeusz Baczko, Janusz Fiszer, and Ladislav Venys. 1995 *Tax Policy in Central Europe.* San Francisco, Calif.: International Center for Economic Growth.

Megginson, William L., Robert C. Nash, and Matthias van Randenborgh. 1994. "The Financial and Operating Performance of Newly Privatized Firms: An International Empirical Analysis." *Journal of Finance* 49(2): 403–52.

Michalopoulos, Constantine, and David G. Tarr. 1994. *Trade in the New Independent States.* Studies of Economies in Transformation No. 13. Washington, D.C.: World Bank.

_____. 1996. *Trade Policy in the New Independent States.* Directions in Development. Washington, D.C.: World Bank.

Milanovic, Branko. Forthcoming. *Income, Inequality and Poverty during the Transition.* Washington, D.C.: World Bank.

Millwood, R. 1982. "The Comparative Performance of Public and Private Ownership." In Lord E. Roll, ed., *The Mixed Economy.* New York: Macmillan.

Mizsei, Kalman, ed. 1994. *Developing Public Finance in Emerging Market Economies.* Boulder, Colo.: Westview Press.

Montes-Negret, Fernando. 1995. "China's Credit Plan: An Overview." *Oxford Review of Economic Policy* 11(4).

Morgenstern, Claudia, and Jonathan Hay. 1995. "The Regulatory Framework for Russia's Securities Markets: Challenges of Institution-Building in a Transition Economy." Paper presented at the Conference on Stock Markets, Corporate Finance, and Economic Growth, World Bank, Washington, D.C., February 16–17.

Morsink, James H. J. 1995. "Wage Controls During IMF Arrangements in Central Europe." In Susan Schadler, ed., *IMF Conditionality: Experience Under Stand-By and Extended Arrangements.* IMF Occasional Paper No. 129. Washington, D.C.: International Monetary Fund.

Moser, Caroline. 1996. *Confronting Crisis: A Summary of Household Responses to Poverty and Vulnerability in Four Poor Urban Communities.* Environmentally Sustainable Development Studies and Monographs Series No. 7. Washington, D.C: World Bank.

Mozhina, Marina, ed. 1994. "Bednost: Vzglyad uchenykh na problemu" ("Poverty: Point of View of Scientists"). *Demografiya i sotsiologiya.* Vypysk 10. Moscow: Institute sotsial'no-ekonomicheskikh problem narodnonaseleniya.

Munnell, Alicia H. 1992. "Policy Watch: Infrastructure Investment and Economic Growth." *The Journal of Economic Perspectives* 6(4): 189–98.

Murphy, Kevin M., Andrei Shleifer, and Robert W. Vishny. 1992. "Transition to a Market Economy: Pitfalls of Partial Reform." *Quarterly Journal of Economics* 107: 889–906.

Murray, Christopher J. L., and José-Luis Bobadilla. 1995. "Epidemiological Transitions in the Formerly Socialist Economies: Divergent Patterns of Mortality and Causes of Death." Harvard Center for Population and Development Studies, Cambridge, Mass.

Murrell, Peter. 1991. "Can Neoclassical Economics Underpin the Reform of Centrally Planned Economies?" *Journal of Economic Perspectives* 5(4): 59–76.

———. 1992. "Evolution in Economics and in the Economic Reform of the Centrally Planned Economies." In Christopher Clague and Gordon C. Rausser, eds., *Emergence of Market Economies in Eastern Europe*. London: Basil Blackwell.

———. 1995. "The Transition According to Cambridge, Massachusetts." *Journal of Economic Literature* 33 (March): 164–78.

Nelson, Joan M., ed. 1994. *A Precarious Balance: Democracy and Economic Reforms in Eastern Europe Vol. 1*. San Francisco, Calif.: International Center for Economic Growth.

Neven, Damien. 1995. "Trade Liberalization with Eastern Nations: How Sensitive." In Riccardo Faini and Richard Portes, eds., *European Union Trade with Eastern Europe*. London: Centre for Economic Policy Research.

Newbury, David M. G., ed. 1995. *Tax and Benefit Reform in Central and Eastern Europe*. London: Centre for Economic Policy Research.

Nolan, Peter, and Fureng Dong. 1990. *Market Forces in China*. London: Zed Books.

O'Brien, D., V. Patrorkovsky, I. Korkhova, and L. Dershem. 1993. "The Future of the Village in a Restructured Food and Agricultural Sector in the former Soviet Union." *Agriculture and Human Values* 10(1): 11–21.

Ody, Anthony. 1992. "Rural Enterprise Development in China." World Bank Discussion Paper No. 162. World Bank, Washington, D.C.

OECD (Organisation for Economic Co-operation and Development). 1993. "Survey of Active Labour Market Policies." *Employment Outlook*. Paris.

———. 1995a. *OECD Economic Outlook*. Paris.

———. 1995b. *The Regional Dimension of Unemployment in Transition Countries: A Challenge for Labor Market and Social Policies*. Paris.

———. 1995c. *Review of the Labour Market in the Czech Republic*. Paris.

OECF (Overseas Economic Cooperation Fund). 1995. *Transition Strategies and Economic Performance: "Gradualism" Revisited*. OECF Discussion Paper No. 8. Tokyo.

Orazem, Peter, Milan Vodopivec, and Ruth Wu. 1995. "Worker Displacement during the Transition: Experience from Slovenia." Policy Research Working Paper No. 1449. World Bank, Washington, D.C.

Patil, Pawan G., and Kathie Krumm. 1995. "Poverty and Social Transfers in Europe & Central Asia: A Survey of the Evidence." World Bank, Europe and Central Asia Department. Washington, D.C.

Patriorkovsky, V., A. Bonnanno, J. Chinn, and D. O'Brien. 1991. "Selected Rural Issues in the USA and the USSR: A Comparative Agenda." *The Rural Sociologist* 11 (Summer) 21–31.

Pawlowicz, Leszek, ed. 1994. *Restrukturyzacja Finansowa Przedsiebiorstw i Bankow*. I raport z badan. Gdansk, Poland: Instytut Badan nad Gospodarka.

Perotti, Roberto. 1995. "Growth, Income Distribution, and Democracy: What the Data Say." Department of Economics, Columbia University, New York.

Persson, Torsten, and Guido Tambellini. 1994. "Is Inequality Harmful for Growth?" *American Economic Review* 84 (3/June): 600–21.

Pham Van Thuyet. 1995. "The Emerging Legal Framework for Private Sector Development in Viet Nam's Transitional Economy." Policy Research Working Paper No. 1486. Washington, D.C.: World Bank.

Pinto, Brian, and Sweder van Wijnbergen. 1994. "Ownership and Corporate Control in Poland. Why State Firms Defied the Odds." Policy Research Working Paper No. 1308. World Bank, Washington, D.C.

Pinto, Brian, Marek Belka, and Stefan Krajewski. 1993. "Transforming State Enterprises in Poland. Evidence on Adjustment by Manufacturing Firms." *Brookings Papers on Economic Activity* 1. Washington, D.C.

Pohl, Gerhard. 1995a. "Banking Reforms in Russia and Eastern Europe." *Butterworth's Journal of International Banking and Financial Law* 10(9): 432–36.

———. 1995b. "Russian Banking, An Unexpected Revolution." *Leaders Magazine* 18(4): 215.

Pohl, Gerhard, and Stijn Claessens. 1994. "Banks, Capital Markets, and Corporate Governance: Lessons from Russia for Eastern Europe." Policy Research Working Paper No. 1326. World Bank, Europe and Central Asia, and Middle East and North Africa Regions Technical Department, Washington, D.C.

Pohl, Gerhard, Gregory T. Jedrzejczak, and Robert E. Anderson. 1995. *Creating Capital Markets in Central and Eastern Europe*. World Bank Technical Paper No. 295. Washington, D.C.

Pohl, Gerhard, Simeon Djankov, and Robert E. Anderson. Forthcoming. "Restructuring of Large Industrial Firms in Central and Eastern Europe, 1992–94." World Bank, Europe and Central Asia, and Middle East and North Africa Regions Technical Department, Washington, D.C.

Popov, A. A. 1991. "Family Planning and Induced Abortion in the USSR: Basic Health and Demographic Characteristics." *Studies in Family Planning* 22(6): 368–77.

Portes, Richard A., ed. 1993. *Economic Transformation in Central Europe: A Progress Report*. London: Centre for Economic Policy Research.

———. 1994. "Transformation Traps." *Economic Journal* 104 (September): 1178–89.

Poznanski, Kazimierz Z. 1985. *Technology, Competition, and the Soviet Bloc in the World Market*. Berkeley: University of California Press.

Pradhan, Sanjay. Forthcoming. *Evaluating Public Spending: A Framework for Public Expenditure*. World Bank Discussion Paper No. 323. Washington, D.C.

Preker, Alexander. 1994. "Meeting the Challenge: Policymaking and Management During Economic Transition." *Journal of Health Administration Education* 12(4): 433–47.

Preker, Alexander, and Richard Feachem. 1994. "Health and Health Care." In Nicholas Barr, ed., *Labor Markets and Social Policy in Central and Eastern Europe: The Transition and Beyond*. New York: Oxford University Press. (Available in Hungarian and Romanian; Russian forthcoming.)

Queisser, Monika. 1995. "Chile and Beyond: The Second-Generation Pension Reforms in Latin America." *International Social Security Review* 38(3–4): 23–39.

Radke, Detlef. 1995. *The German Social Market Economy: An Option for Transforming and Developing Countries?* Published in association with the German Development Institute, Berlin. GDI Book Series 4. London: Frank Cass.

Radygin, A. 1995a. "On the Theory of Privatization in the Transition Economy." *Voprosy economiki* 12: 54–67.

_____. 1995b. "Russian Privatization and Foreign Investment." In A. Astapovich, ed. *Foreign Investment in Russia—Trends and Prospects*. Moscow.

Raiser, Martin. 1993. "Searching for the Hole in the Public Pocket: The Institutional Legacy of Soft Budget Constraints and the Polish Transformation Process." *Economic Systems* 17(4): 251–78.

Rajaram, Anand. 1992. *Reforming Prices: The Experience of China, Hungary, and Poland*. World Bank Discussion Paper No. 144. Washington, D.C.

Reidel, James, and Bruce Comer. 1995. "Transition to Market Economy in Viet Nam." Prepared for the Asia Foundation Project on Economies in Transition: Comparing Asia and Eastern Europe. DELTA, Paris, May 22.

Renaud, Bertrand M. 1996. "Housing Finance in Transition Economies: The Early Years in Eastern Europe and the Former Soviet Union." World Bank, Policy Research Working Paper No. 1565, Financial Sector Development Department, Washington, D.C.

Richards, Anthony, and Gunnar Tersman. 1995. "Growth, Tradables, and Price Convergence in the Baltics." IMF Working Paper No. 95/45. International Monetary Fund, Washington, D.C.

Ridley, F. F. 1995. "Civil Service and Democracy: Questions in Reforming the Civil Service in Eastern and Central Europe." *Public Administration and Development* 15: 11–20.

Roberts, Bryan. 1993. "What Happened to Soviet Product Quality? Evidence from the Finnish Auto Market." University of Miami, Miami, Fla.

_____. 1995. "Price Liberalization, Market Power and Social Welfare in Transition Economies." University of Miami, Miami, Fla.

Rollo, Jim, and Alasdair Smith. 1993. "The Political Economy of Eastern European Trade with the European Community: Why So Sensitive?" *Economic Policy* 16 (April): 139–81.

Rosati, Dariusz K. 1992. "Problems of Post-CMEA Trade and Payments." Discussion Paper No. 650. Centre for Economic Policy Research, London.

Rose, Richard. 1995a. "Freedom as a Fundamental Value." *International Social Science Journal* 145: 457–71.

_____. 1995b. "New Russia Barometer IV—Survey Results." Studies in Public Policy No. 250. Centre for the Study of Public Policy, Strathclyde, Scotland.

Rose, Richard, and Christian Haerpfer. 1994. *New Democracies Barometer III*. Vienna: Paul Lazarsfeld Society.

_____. 1996. "Support for Democracy and Market System Rising in Central and Eastern Europe." Research report. Paul Lazarsfeld Society, Vienna.

Rose-Ackerman, Susan. 1978. *Corruption: A Study in Political Economy*. New York: Free Press.

Rostowski, Jacek. 1994. "Interenterprise Arrears in Post-Communist Economies." WP/94/43. International Monetary Fund, Washington, D.C.

Rostowski, Jacek, and Milan Nikolic. 1995. "Exit in the Framework of Macro-economic Shocks and Policy Responses during Transition: A Cross-Country Comparison." School of Slavonic and East European Studies, University of London.

Rouse-Foley, Mark C. 1995. "Labor Market Dynamics in Russia." Department of Economics, Yale University, New Haven, Conn.

The Russian Economic Barometer. Various years.

Russian & East European Finance and Trade: A Journal of Translations. 1994. *Exchange-Rate Regimes in Transitional Economies*. November–December 1994.

Rutkowski, Jan. 1996. "High Skills Pay Off: The Changing Wage Structure during Economic Transition in Poland." *Economics of Transition* 4(4): 89–111.

Rutkowski, Michal. 1995. "Workers in Transition." Working Paper No. 1556. Policy Research Department. World Bank, Washington, D.C.

Rutkowski, Michal, and Sarbajit Sinha. 1995. "Employment Flows and Sectoral Shifts During the Transition Shock in Post-Socialist Countries." Paper presented at the European Economic Association meeting, Prague.

Sachs, Jeffrey D. 1990. "Eastern Europe's Economies: What Is To Be Done?" *The Economist* 21–26.

_____. 1993. *Poland's Jump to the Market Economy*. Cambridge, Mass.: MIT Press.

_____. 1994. "Shock Therapy in Poland: Perspectives of Five Years." Paper delivered at conference, University of Utah, April 6–7.

_____. 1995a. "Postcommunist Parties and the Politics of Entitlements." *Transition Newsletter* 6(3). Washington, D.C.: World Bank.

_____. 1995b. "Russia's Struggle with Stabilization: Conceptual Issues and Evidence." *Proceedings of the World Bank Annual Conference on Development Economics 1994*. Washington, D.C.

_____. 1995c. "Why Russia Has Failed to Stabilize." In Anders Åslund, ed., *Russian Economic Reform at Risk*. London and New York: St. Martin's Press.

_____. 1996. "Reforms in Eastern Europe and the Former Soviet Union in Light of the East Asian Experiences." NBER Working Paper Series No. 5404: 1–71. National Bureau of Economic Research, Cambridge, Mass.

Sachs, Jeffrey D., and David Lipton. 1992. "Russia: Towards a Market-Based Monetary System." *Central Banking* III(1).

Sachs, Jeffery D., and Andrew M. Warner. 1995. "Economic Reform and the Process of Global Integration." *Brookings Papers on Economic Activity 1*. Washington, D.C.

_____. 1996. "Achieving Rapid Growth in the Transition Economies of Central Europe." Harvard Institute of International Development, Cambridge, Mass.

Sachs, Jeffrey D., and Wing Thye Woo. 1994. "Reform in China and Russia." *Economic Policy* April: 101–45.

Sahay, Ratna, and Carlos Vegh. 1995a. "Dollarization in Transition Economies: Evidence and Policy Implications." International Monetary Fund Working Paper No. 95/96. Washington, D.C.

_____. 1995b. "Inflation and Stabilization in Transition Economies: A Comparison with Market Economies." Working Paper No. WP/95/8. International Monetary Fund, Washington, D.C.

Sapir, André. 1994. "The Europe Agreements: Implications for Trade Laws and Institutions. Lessons from Hungary." Discussion Paper No. 1024. Centre for Economic Policy Research, London.

Sapir, Jacques. 1990. *L'Economie Mobilisée: Essai sur les Economies de Type Soviétique.* Paris: La Découverte.

Saunders, Anthony, and Ingo Walter. 1991. "The Reconfiguration of Banking and Capital Markets in Eastern Europe." *Journal of International Securities Markets* Autumn: 221–38.

Scarpetta, S., and A. Wörgötter, eds. 1995. *The Regional Dimension of Unemployment in Transition Countries.* Paris: OECD.

Schaffer, Mark. 1995. "Government Subsidies to Enterprises in Central and Eastern Europe—Budgetary Subsidies and Tax Arrears." In David M. G. Newbury, ed., *Tax and Benefit Reform in Central and Eastern Europe.* London: Centre for Economic Policy Research.

Schiavo-Campo, Salvatore, ed. 1994. *Institutional Change and the Public Sector in Transitional Economies.* World Bank Discussion Paper No. 241. Washington, D.C.

Schmidt-Hebbel, Klaus, Luis Serven, and Andres Solimano. 1995. "Saving and Investment: Paradigms, Puzzles, Policies." World Bank, Washington, D.C.

Selowsky, Marcelo, and Matthew Vogel. 1995. "Enterprise Credit and Stabilization in Transition Economies. Present Experiences with Enterprise 'Isolation' Programs." Paper presented at the First Dubrovnik Conference on Transition Economies, June.

Shah, Anwar. 1994. *The Reform of Intergovernmental Fiscal Relations in Developing and Emerging Market Economies.* Policy and Research Series 23. Washington, D.C.: World Bank.

Shapiro, Judith. 1993. "The Russian Mortality Crisis and Its Causes." In Anders Åslund, ed., *Russian Economic Reform at Risk.* London and New York: Pinter.

Shatalov, Sergei. 1991. *Privatization in the Soviet Union: The Beginnings of a Transition.* World Bank Discussion Paper No. 805. Washington, D.C.

Sheng, Andrew, ed. 1996. *Bank Restructuring: Lessons from the 1980s.* Washington, D.C.: World Bank.

Shome, Parthasarathi, and Julio Escolano. 1993. "The State of Tax Policy in the Central Asian and Transcaucasian Newly Independent States (NIS)." IMF Paper on Policy Analysis and Assessment PPAA/93/8. International Monetary Fund, Washington, D.C.

Singh, Ajit. 1995. *Corporate Financial Patterns in Industrializing Economies: A Comparative International Study.* IFC Technical Paper No. 2. Washington, D.C: World Bank.

Sinn, G., and H.-W. Sinn. 1992. *Kaltstart: Volkswirtschaftliche Aspekte der deutschen Vereinigungspolitik.* Tübingen: J.C.B. Mohr.

Sipos, Sándor. 1994. "Income Transfers: Family Support and Poverty Relief." In Nicholas Barr, ed., *Labor Markets and Social Policy in Central and Eastern Europe: The Transition and Beyond.* New York: Oxford University Press. (Available in Hungarian and Romanian; Russian forthcoming.)

Slemrod, Joel. 1995. "What Can be Learned from Cross-Country Studies about Taxes, Prosperity, and Economic Growth." National Bureau of Economic Research, Cambridge, Mass.

State Committee for Antimonopoly Policy and Support for New Economic Structures. 1995. "Razvitie konkurentzii na rinkah Rossiiskoi Federatzii, doklad podgotovlennoi Gosudarstvennim Komitom Rossiiskoi Federatzii po antimonopolnui polotoke i podderjke novuih economicheskih structur" ("The Evolution of Competition in the Russian Federation"). *Voprosi Economiki* 11: 4–48.

Stiglitz, Joseph E. 1986. *The Economics of the Public Sector.* New York: Norton.

Stille, Alexander. 1995. *Excellent Cadavers.* New York: Pantheon Press.

Stone, Andrew, and Irina Novitzky. 1993. "Ukrainian Private Enterprise: Profiting Against the Odds." Unpublished Private Sector Development Department Background Paper. Washington, D.C.: World Bank.

Stone, Andrew, and Irina and Victor Novitzky. 1995. "Private Enterprise in Ukraine: Getting Down to Business—Results of a Private Enterprise Survey." Unpublished Private Sector Development Department Background Paper. Washington, D.C.: World Bank.

Sylla, Richard. 1995. "The Rise of Securities Markets: What Can Government Do?" Policy Research Working Paper No. 1539. World Bank, Policy Research Department, Washington, D.C.

Syrquin, Moshe, and Hollis B. Chenery. 1989. Patterns of Development, 1950 to 1983. World Bank Discussion Paper No. 41. Washington, D.C.

Tait, Alan A., and S. Nuri Erbas. 1995. "Fiscal Affairs and Middle East Departments." IMF Working Paper No. 95/17. International Monetary Fund, Washington, D.C.

Tanzi, Vito, ed. 1992. *Fiscal Policies in Economies in Transition.* Washington, D.C.: International Monetary Fund.

_____, ed. 1993. *Transition to Market: Studies in Fiscal Reform.* Washington, D.C.: International Monetary Fund.

Tanzi, Vito, and Anthony Pellechio. 1995. "The Reform of Tax Administration." IMF Working Paper No. 95/22. International Monetary Fund, Washington, D.C.

Thacher, Thomas D., III. 1995. "The New York City School Construction Authority's Office of the Inspector-General: A Successful New Strategy for Reforming Public Contracting in the Construction Industry. "

Toth, Istvan Gyorgy. 1994: "A joleti rendszer az atmenet idoszakaban" ("The Welfare System During the Transition"). *Kozgazdasagi Szemle* 49(3): 313–40.

Transition: The Newsletter of Reforming Economies. 1988–96. Policy Research Department. Washington, D.C.: World Bank.

Tulchinsky, T. H., and E. A. Varavikova. 1996. "Addressing the Epidemiological Transition in the Former Soviet Union: Strategies for Health System and Public Health Reform in Russia." *American Journal of Public Health* 86(3): 313–20.

U. K. Department of Social Security. 1993. *Containing the Costs of Social Security—the International Context.* London: Her Majesty's Stationery Office.

United Nations Economic and Social Council. 1994. "Economic and Social Consequences of Drug Abuse and Illicit Trafficking: An Interim Report." Vienna.

USIA (United States Information Agency). 1995a. "In Ukraine, 'Mafia' Seen Active in Politics, Economics, Banking." Opinion Analysis M-1-95. Washington, D.C.

———. 1995b. "Russians' Disillusion Deepens: Confidence in Yeltsin Falling to New Lows." Opinion Analysis M-105-95. Washington, D.C.

Universalia. 1993. "East/West Enterprise Exchange Program Evaluation." Bureau of Assistance for Central and Eastern Europe. Universalia, Montreal.

Urban, Laszlo. 1996. "Hungary: Employment Trends, Wage Policies, and Macro-Implication." Europe and Central Asia Department, World Bank, Washington, D.C.

van de Walle, Dominique, Martin Ravallion, and Madhur Gautam. 1994. *How Well Does the Social Safety Net Work? The Incidence of Cash Benefits in Hungary, 1987–89.* Living Standards Measurement Study Working Paper No. 102. Washington, D.C.: World Bank.

van Wijnbergen, Sweder. 1992. "Enterprise Reform in Eastern Europe." In Richard O'Brian and Sarah Hewin, eds., *Finance and the International Economy: 5. The AMEX Bank Review Prize Essays.* New York: Oxford University Press.

———. 1994. "On the Role of Banks in Enterprise Restructuring: The Polish Example." In Andreja Böhm and Uroš Korže, eds., *Privatization Through Restructuring.* Ljubljana: Central and Eastern Europe Privatization Network.

Varhegyi, Eva. 1995. *Bankok Versenyben (Banks in Competition).* Budapest: Penzugykutato Rt.

VCIOM. 1995. *Economic and Social Change: The Monitoring of Public Opinion.* Moscow: Aspect Press.

Vella, Venanzio. Forthcoming. "Health and Nutritional Aspects of Well-Being." In Jeni Klugman, ed., *Poverty in Russia during the Transition.* World Bank Regional and Sectoral Studies. Washington, D.C.

Vepřek, Jaromír, Zdenřêk Papeš, and Pavel Vepřek. 1994. "Czech Health Care in Economic Transformation." Working Paper No. 63. Center for Economic Research and Graduate Education and Economics Institute of the Academy of Sciences of the Czech Republic, Prague, Czech Republic.

Vickers, J., and G. Yarrow. 1988. *Privatization: An Economic Analysis.* Cambridge, Mass.: MIT Press.

Vienna Institute for Comparative Economic Studies (Wiener Institut fur Internationale Wirtschaftsvergleiche), ed. 1995. *Countries in Transition 1995: WIIW Handbook of Statistics.* Vienna.

Vittas, Dimitri. 1993. "Swiss Chilanpore: The Way Forward for Pension Reform." World Bank Policy Research Working Paper No. 1093. Washington, D.C.

———. 1995. "Thrift Deposit Institutions in Europe and the United States." Policy Research Working Paper No. 1540. World Bank, Policy Research Department, Washington, D.C.

Vittas, Dimitri, and Joon Je Cho. 1995. "Credit Policies: Lessons from East Asia." Policy Research Working Paper No. 1458. World Bank, Financial Sector Development Department, Washington, D.C.

Vittas, Dimitri, and Roland Michelitsch. 1996. "The Potential Role of Pension Funds: Lessons from OECD and Developing Countries." In Roman Frydman, Cheryl W. Gray, and Andrzej Rapaczynski, eds., *Corporate Governance in Central Europe and Russia. Volume 1: Banks, Funds, and Foreign Investors.* Budapest, London, and New York: Central European University Press.

Wagner, Adolph. 1883. *Finanzwissenschaft.* Leipzig. Extracted in R. A. Musgrave and A. T. Peacock, eds. 1958. *Classics in the Theory of Public Finance.* London and New York: MacMillan.

Wallich, Christine I., ed. 1994a. *Russia and the Challenge of Fiscal Federalism.* World Bank Regional and Sectoral Studies. Washington, D.C.

———. 1994b. "Russia's Dilemma of Fiscal Federalism." Paper prepared for Conference on Intergovernmental Finances, Dalian, China, September 12–17.

Walter, Ingo. 1993. "The Battle of the Systems: Control of Enterprises and the Global Economy." *Kieler Vortrage* 122. Kiel, Germany: Institut fur Weltwirtschaft an der Universität.

Webster, Leila M. 1994. *Newly Privatized Russian Enterprises.* Studies of Economies in Transition No. 13. Washington, D.C.: World Bank.

Wei, Shang-Jin. 1993. *Open Door Policy and China's Rapid Growth: Evidence from City-Level Data.* NBER Working Paper Series No. 4602. Cambridge, Mass.: National Bureau of Economic Research.

Weinstein, Judith, Elizabeth Oliveras, and Noel McIntosh. 1993. "Women's Reproductive Health in the Central Asian Republics." World Bank, Population Health and Nutrition Department, Washington, D.C.

Welfens, Paul J. J., ed. 1996. *Economic Aspects of German Unification: Expectations, Transition Dynamics and International Perspectives.* 2d ed. Hamburg: Springer-Verlag.

West, L. A. 1995. "Regional Economic Variation and Basic Education in Rural China." Economic Development Institute, World Bank, Washington, D.C.

White, Eugene. 1995. "Deposit Insurance." Policy Research Working Paper No. 1541. World Bank, Policy Research Department, Washington, D.C.

Willett, Thomas D., Richard C. K. Burdekin, Richard J. Sweeney, and Clas Wihlborg. 1995. *Establishing Monetary Stability in Emerging Market Economies.* Boulder, Colo.: Westview Press.

Winters, L. Alan, and Zhen Kun Wang. 1994. *Eastern Europe's International Trade.* Manchester, U.K.: Manchester University Press.

Wolf, Holger. 1993. "The Lucky Miracle: Germany 1945–51." In Rudiger Dornbusch, ed., *Postwar Economic Reconstruction and Lessons for the East Today*. Cambridge, Mass.: MIT Press.

World Bank. 1988. *World Development Report 1988: Public Finance in Development*. New York: Oxford University Press.

_____. 1989. *World Development Report 1989: Financial Systems and Development*. New York: Oxford University Press.

_____. 1990a. *China: Revenue Mobilization and Tax Policy*. World Bank Country Studies. Washington, D.C.

_____. 1990b. *World Development Report 1990: Poverty*. New York: Oxford University Press.

_____. 1991. *World Development Report 1991: The Challenge of Development*. New York: Oxford University Press.

_____. 1992. *China: Strategies for Reducing Poverty in the 1990s*. Washington, D.C.

_____. 1993a. *The East Asian Miracle: Economic Growth and Public Policy*. A World Bank Policy Research Report. New York: Oxford University Press.

_____. 1993b. *China: The Achievement and Challenge of Price Reform*. World Bank Country Studies. Washington, D.C.

_____. 1993c. *Kyrgyzstan: The Transition to a Market Economy*. World Bank Country Study. Washington, D.C.

_____. 1993d. *Poverty Reduction Handbook*. Washington, D.C.

_____. 1993e. *World Development Report 1993: Investing in Health*. New York: Oxford University Press.

_____. 1994a. *Averting the Old Age Crisis*. A World Bank Policy Research Report. New York: Oxford University Press.

_____. 1994b. *China: Foreign Trade Reform*. World Bank Country Studies. Washington, D.C.

_____. 1994c. "Lithuania—Public Expenditure Review." Report No. 12792-LT, Washington, D.C.

_____. 1994d. *World Debt Tables 1994-95: External Finance for Developing Countries*. Washington, D.C.

_____. 1995a. "Bank Recapitalization: If and When." DEC Policy Review Note No. 2, April. Washington, D.C.

_____. 1995b. *Bureaucrats in Business—The Economics and Politics of Public Ownership*. A World Bank Policy Research Report. New York: Oxford University Press.

_____. 1995c. "China: The Emerging Capital Market." Volume I: Main Report, Strategic Issues and Options. Volume II: Detailed Technical Analysis. East Asia and Pacific Region, Report No. 14501-CHA. Washington, D.C.

_____. 1995d. "China: Health Care Finance Study: Health Care Financing Reform 1996–2001." Human Development Department. Washington, D.C.

_____. 1995e. *China: Macroeconomic Stability in a Decentralized Economy*. A World Bank Country Study. Washington, D.C.

_____. 1995f. "Directed Credit." DEC Policy Review Note No. 1, April. Washington, D.C.

_____. 1995g. *The Emerging Asian Bond Market*. Washington, D.C.

_____. 1995h. "Fiscal Management in the Russian Federation." Report No. 14862-RU. Europe and Central Asia Department III. Washington, D.C.

_____. 1995i. *Global Economic Prospects and the Developing Countries*. Washington, D.C.

_____. 1995j. "Hungary: Poverty and Social Transfers in Hungary." Washington, D.C.

_____. 1995k. "Hungary: Structural Reforms for Sustainable Growth." Report No. 13577-HU. Washington, D.C.

_____. 1995l. *Lithuania: Private Sector Development*. Washington, D.C.

_____. 1995m. "Poverty in Russia: An Assessment." Europe and Central Asia Regional Office. Report No. 14110-RUS. Washington, D.C.

_____. 1995n. "Russia Housing Reform and Privatization: Strategy and Transition Issues. Volume 1: Main Report." Europe and Central Asia Region, Report No. 14929-RU. Washington, D.C.

_____. 1995o. "Russian Federation: Towards Medium-Term Viability." Report No. 14472-RU. Washington, D.C.

_____. 1995p. *Understanding Poverty in Poland*. A World Bank Country Study. Washington, D.C.

_____. 1995q. "Vietnam: Economic Report on Industralization and Industrial Policy." Report No. 14645-VN. Washington, D.C.

_____. 1995r. *World Development Report 1995: Workers in an Integrating World*. New York: Oxford University Press.

_____. 1995s. *Statistical Handbook 1995: States of the Former USSR*. Studies of Economies in Transition 19. Washington, D.C.

_____. 1996a. "The Chinese Economy: Fighting Inflation, Deepening Reforms." Report No. 15288-CHA. China and Mongolia Department, Washington, D.C.

_____. 1996b. *World Debt Tables 1996*. Washington, D.C.

World Bank and Organisation for Economic Co-Operation and Development (OECD). 1993. *Environmental Action Programme for Central and Eastern Europe—Setting Priorities*. Washington, D.C.: World Bank.

WHO (World Health Organization). 1994. "Highlights on Women's Health in CEE and NIS, Women's Health Profile: Comparative Analysis of the Country Reports." Women's Health Counts: Conference on the Health of Women in Central and Eastern Europe, February.

Yarrow, George. 1986. "Privatization in Theory and Practice." *Economic Policy* 2: 324–64.

Yusuf, Shahid. 1993. "The Rise of China's Nonstate Sector." China and Mongolia Department. World Bank. Washington, D.C.

Zippay, Allison. 1991. *From Middle Income to Poor: Downward Mobility among Displaced Steelworkers*. New York: Praeger Publishers

Zweig, David. 1991. "Internationalizing China's Countryside." *China Quarterly* December (128).

Selected Indicators for Economies in Transition

This appendix contains selected statistical indicators for twenty-eight transition economies in Central and Eastern Europe, the newly independent states, and Asia. These data, particularly for later years, are provisional and subject to revision. Data are taken from the World Bank statistical data base except where otherwise indicated. The sources and methods used in the calculation of these indicators may be found in the Technical Notes to the Selected World Development Indicators in this Report. Updates to these data will be made available in the annually published *World Development Indicators.*

Table A.1 Basic socioeconomic indicators

Country	Population (millions), mid-1994	GNP per capita (dollars), 1994	Infant mortality rate (per 1,000 live births)				Life expectancy at birth (years)				Secondary school enrollment (percent of age group)		
			1971–80	1981–90	1991–93	1994	1971–80	1981–90	1991–93	1994	1980	1990	1993
Albania	3.2	380	52.0	35.0	32.1	31.0	68.7	71.2	72.5	72.8	67	78	..
Bulgaria	8.4	1,250	23.7	15.8	16.1	15.3	71.3	71.4	71.0	71.2	84	73	68
Croatia	4.8	2,560	..	14.9	11.6	10.9	..	71.0	72.9	73.5	..	77	83
Czech Republic	10.3	3,200	18.2	12.8	9.6	7.9	70.3	71.1	72.4	73.0	..	..	86
Hungary	10.3	3,840	29.6	18.2	14.2	11.6	69.7	69.6	69.3	69.6	70	79	81
Macedonia, FYR	2.1	820	54.2	42.9	27.7	23.8	..	71.3	72.1	72.7	61	53	54
Poland	38.5	2,410	24.5	18.1	14.3	15.1	70.7	70.9	70.9	71.7	77	81	84
Romania	22.7	1,270	34.3	26.0	23.1	23.9	69.5	69.6	69.8	69.5	71	92	..
Slovak Republic	5.3	2,250	22.8	15.6	12.1	11.2	70.3	70.9	71.2	72.3	..	..	89
Slovenia	2.0	7,040	18.3	12.2	7.9	6.5	70.1	71.5	73.2	73.6	..	..	89
Armenia	3.7	680	26.2	23.4	17.8	15.1	71.8	70.5	70.5	71.1	..	..	85
Azerbaijan	7.5	500	30.4	28.2	26.3	25.2	68.4	69.6	69.8	69.4	..	..	88
Belarus	10.4	2,160	16.3	13.9	12.3	13.2	70.3	71.1	69.8	69.3	98	93	92
Estonia	1.5	2,820	18.2	14.4	15.0	14.5	69.5	70.0	69.6	70.1	..	..	92
Georgia	5.4	..	29.1	22.3	14.8	18.3	70.7	71.4	72.6	73.0	..	..	..
Kazakstan	16.8	1,160	32.7	29.2	27.3	27.4	66.6	68.2	69.0	68.3	..	..	90
Kyrgyz Republic	4.5	630	46.1	38.6	31.0	29.1	65.5	65.8	67.9	67.8	..	..	..
Latvia	2.5	2,320	21.7	15.7	16.5	15.5	69.2	69.8	68.8	68.1	..	..	87
Lithuania	3.7	1,350	21.5	15.8	15.6	14.1	70.7	71.4	70.0	68.7	..	..	78
Moldova	4.4	870	36.1	27.9	19.9	22.6	66.5	66.8	67.7	68.3	..	..	69
Russia	148.4	2,650	24.6	19.9	18.6	18.7	67.1	68.8	67.2	64.0	96	94	88
Tajikistan	5.8	360	58.1	47.5	44.5	40.6	64.8	69.0	68.1	66.6	..	..	..
Turkmenistan	4.4	..	53.6	52.5	45.5	46.4	61.9	64.9	65.8	66.3	..	..	..
Ukraine	51.9	1,910	21.2	14.9	14.3	14.3	69.1	70.0	69.8	67.9	94	93	80
Uzbekistan	22.4	960	47.0	42.7	35.0	28.2	67.3	68.1	69.3	69.8	..	..	94
China	1,190.9	530	48.8	37.6	31.0	29.9	65.2	68.3	69.0	69.3	46	48	55
Mongolia	2.4	300	90.0	71.2	58.9	53.0	55.7	60.5	63.6	64.5	91	86	78
Vietnam	72.0	200	70.1	49.2	43.9	42.0	61.0	65.2	67.0	67.5	42	33	35

.. Not available.

Table A.2 Indicators of economic growth

Country	GDP growth rate (percent)[a]								Gross domestic investment (percent of GDP)		
	1971–80 (average annual)	1981–89 (average annual)	1990	1991	1992	1993	1994	1995	1980	1990	1994
Albania	..	1.7	− 10.0	− 27.7	− 9.7	11.0	7.4	6.0	34.5	28.9	13.5
Bulgaria	..	4.9	− 9.1	− 11.7	− 6.0	− 4.2	0.0	3.0	34.0	25.6	20.8
Croatia	..	..	..	− 15.1	− 12.8	− 3.2	1.8	2.0	..	13.4	13.8
Czech Republic	..	1.8	− 1.2	− 14.2	− 6.4	− 0.5	2.6	5.0	..	28.6	20.4
Hungary	4.6	1.8	− 2.5	− 7.7	− 4.3	− 2.3	2.5	2.0	30.7	25.4	21.5
Macedonia, FYR	..	..	..	− 9.8	− 12.4	− 12.0	− 5.7	− 4.0	..	32.0	18.0
Poland	..	2.6	− 11.6	− 7.0	2.6	3.8	5.5	7.0	26.4	25.6	15.9
Romania	7.6	1.0	− 5.6	− 12.9	− 13.8	1.3	2.4	7.0	39.8	30.2	26.9
Slovak Republic	..	2.7	− 2.5	− 14.6	− 6.2	− 4.1	4.8	7.0	37.3	33.5	17.1
Slovenia	..	..	..	− 9.3	− 5.7	1.0	4.0	5.0	..	16.9	20.8
Armenia	14.5	3.5	− 7.2	− 8.8	− 52.3	− 14.8	3.0	7.0	28.5	47.1	10.2
Azerbaijan	21.5	2.9	− 11.7	− 0.7	− 35.2	− 23.1	− 21.9	− 17.0	23.3	27.8	22.5
Belarus	6.6	5.0	− 2.8	− 1.5	− 10.1	− 9.0	− 21.5	− 12.0	19.5	27.4	..
Estonia	5.1	0.2	− 7.1	− 22.1	− 21.6	− 6.6	6.0	4.0	28.5	30.2	..
Georgia	6.8	1.2	− 14.8	− 20.1	− 40.3	− 31.6	− 28.2	− 5.0	..	..	..
Kazakstan	4.4	2.0	− 4.6	− 6.8	− 13.0	− 15.6	− 25.0	− 9.0	37.6	42.6	24.0
Kyrgyz Republic	4.4	4.0	6.9	− 9.1	− 15.8	− 16.3	− 26.5	− 6.0	28.7	23.8	..
Latvia	4.7	3.7	− 1.2	− 8.1	− 35.0	− 14.9	0.0	1.0	25.7	40.1	..
Lithuania	4.6	1.8	− 3.3	− 13.1	− 39.3	− 16.2	2.0	3.0	31.2	34.3	..
Moldova	..	..	− 1.5	− 18.6	− 25.0	− 8.8	− 22.1	2.0	..	..	7.7
Russia	6.5	3.0	− 3.6	− 5.0	− 14.5	− 8.7	− 12.6	− 4.0	22.4	30.1	27.0
Tajikistan	4.9	3.3	− 2.4	− 8.7	− 30.0	− 27.6	− 15.0	− 12.0	30.0	23.4	..
Turkmenistan	4.0	4.0	0.8	− 5.0	− 5.4	..	..	− 5.0	28.5	40.0	..
Ukraine	..	..	− 3.8	− 12.0	− 12.5	− 7.2	− 24.3	− 12.0	..	27.5	..
Uzbekistan	6.2	3.4	2.0	− 0.5	− 11.1	− 2.4	− 4.5	− 2.0	31.6	32.2	23.3
China	5.5	11.1	3.9	8.0	13.6	13.4	11.8	10.2	35.2	34.8	42.1
Mongolia	..	5.7	− 2.0	− 9.9	− 7.6	− 1.3	3.3	6.3	46.2	42.3	20.9
Vietnam	..	4.4	4.5	6.0	8.6	8.1	8.6	9.5	..	13.0	24.2

.. Not available.
a. GDP growth rates for 1990–94 are from the IMF, and those for 1995 from EBRD 1995. Data may differ from those available at the time of writing of the main text of this Report.

Table A.3 Inflation

Country	Average annual inflation rates (percent)[a]					
	1990	1991	1992	1993	1994	1995
Albania	0.0	35.5	225.9	85.0	28.0	8.0
Bulgaria	22.0	333.5	82.0	72.8	89.0	62.0
Croatia	135.6	249.5	938.2	1,516.0	98.0	4.1
Czech Republic	10.8	56.7	11.1	20.8	10.2	9.1
Hungary	29.0	34.2	22.9	22.5	19.0	28.2
Macedonia, FYR	120.5	229.7	1,925.2	248.0	65.0	50.0
Poland	586.0	70.3	43.0	35.3	32.2	27.8
Romania	5.1	174.5	210.9	256.0	131.0	32.3
Slovak Republic	10.8	61.2	10.1	23.0	14.0	9.9
Slovenia	549.7	117.7	201.0	32.0	19.8	12.6
Armenia	10.3	100.0	825.0	3,732.0	5,458.0	175.0
Azerbaijan	7.8	105.6	616.0	833.0	1,500.0	412.0
Belarus	4.5	83.5	969.0	1,188.0	2,200.0	800.0
Estonia	23.1	210.6	1,069.0	89.0	48.0	29.0
Georgia	3.3	78.5	913.0	3,126.0	18,000.0	160.0
Kazakstan	4.2	91.0	1,610.0	1,760.0	1,980.0	180.0
Kyrgyz Republic	3.0	85.0	854.6	1,208.7	280.0	45.0
Latvia	10.5	124.4	951.2	109.0	36.0	25.0
Lithuania	8.4	224.7	1,020.3	390.2	72.0	35.0
Moldova	4.2	98.0	1,276.0	789.0	327.0	30.0
Russia	5.6	92.7	1,353.0	896.0	303.0	190.0
Tajikistan	4.0	111.6	1,157.0	2,195.0	452.0	635.0
Turkmenistan	4.6	102.5	492.9	3,102.0	2,400.0	1,800.0
Ukraine	4.0	91.2	1,210.0	4,735.0	842.0	375.0
Uzbekistan	3.1	82.2	645.0	534.0	746.0	315.0
China	1.6	3.0	5.4	13.0	21.7	17.0
Mongolia	0.0	208.6	321.0	183.0	145.0	75.0
Vietnam	67.5	67.6	17.5	5.2	8.0	17.0

a. Data are percentage increases in the consumer price index. Data for 1990–94 are from the IMF, and data for 1995 from EBRD 1995, except for Croatia and Tajikistan, which are from the World Bank. Data may differ from those available at the time of writing of the main text of this Report.

Table A.4 Selected demographic indicators

Country	Annual average population growth (percent)			Urban population (percent of total population)		
	1971–80	1981–90	1991–94	1980	1990	1994
Albania	2.2	2.1	− 0.6	33.8	36.6	37.0
Bulgaria	0.4	− 0.2	− 0.8	61.2	67.7	70.4
Croatia	0.4	0.4	0.0	50.1	59.8	63.5
Czech Republic	0.5	0.1	0.1	63.6	64.9	65.0
Hungary	0.4	− 0.3	− 0.3	57.0	62.1	64.0
Macedonia, FYR	1.5	0.7	0.9	53.5	57.8	59.0
Poland	0.9	0.7	0.3	58.2	62.5	64.2
Romania	0.9	0.4	− 0.5	49.0	53.3	55.1
Slovak Republic	0.9	0.6	0.3	51.6	56.6	58.0
Slovenia	1.0	0.5	− 0.1	48.1	59.0	63.0
Armenia	2.0	1.3	1.4	65.7	67.5	68.5
Azerbaijan	1.7	1.5	1.0	52.8	54.4	55.5
Belarus	0.6	0.6	0.2	56.5	66.9	70.3
Estonia	0.8	0.6	− 1.2	69.7	71.8	72.8
Georgia	..	0.7	− 0.2	51.7	56.0	58.0
Kazakstan	..	1.2	0.1	54.0	57.6	59.3
Kyrgyz Republic	..	1.9	0.4	38.3	38.2	38.8
Latvia	..	0.5	− 1.5	68.3	71.2	72.6
Lithuania	0.8	0.9	0.0	61.2	68.8	71.4
Moldova	..	0.9	− 0.1	39.9	47.8	50.9
Russia	..	0.6	0.0	69.8	73.8	73.2
Tajikistan	..	2.9	2.0	34.3	32.2	32.2
Turkmenistan	..	2.5	4.6	47.1	44.9	44.9
Ukraine	..	0.4	0.0	61.7	67.5	69.7
Uzbekistan	..	2.5	2.2	40.8	40.6	41.2
China	1.7	1.5	1.2	19.4	26.4	27.5
Mongolia	2.8	2.8	1.9	52.1	58.0	60.3
Vietnam	2.3	2.1	2.1	19.2	19.9	20.7

.. Not available.

Selected
World
Development
Indicators

Contents

Introduction to Selected World Development Indicators

The nearly two decades since the World Development Indicators (WDI) were first issued have seen dramatic changes not only in the global economy but in the way in which we assess and measure development. These changes are reflected in the increasing emphasis on poverty reduction through broad-based growth and human resource development and on environmental sustainability. The increasing importance of the private sector in development strategies is mirrored by profound changes in the role of the state. Over the years the WDI has tried to keep up with these changes, but it is now time for a major redesign.

New data publication

A new, freestanding, and more comprehensive *World Development Indicators* will appear in the autumn of 1996. The traditional annex to the *World Development Report* is being replaced in this edition by a set of Selected World Development Indicators drawn from the WDI data sets. The design of the new *World Development Indicators* will enhance its usefulness in examining the world's progress in three broad areas: people, the environment, and the economy. In addition it will provide indicators that describe progress in selected areas of national economic management, such as macroeconomic stability, structural reforms (including financial sector development, trade policy reforms, state enterprise reforms, etc.), and the evolving role of the state. Its companion CD-ROM product will reflect these changes and include time-series data and a more extensive guide to data sources and statistical issues.

Changes from previous editions of *World Development Report*

The indicators tables in this Report have been redesigned to provide a core set of standard indicators covering the same three development themes: people, the environment, and the economy. The layout of the seventeen tables retains the tradition of presenting comparative socioeconomic data for more than 130 economies for the most recent year for which data are available and for an earlier year. An additional table presents basic indicators for seventy-six economies with sparse data or with populations less than 1 million.

Because the World Bank's primary business is providing lending and policy advice to its low- and middle-income member countries, the issues covered in this publication focus mainly on these economies. Where available, information on the high-income economies is also provided for comparison. Readers may wish to refer to national statistical publications or publications from the Organisation for Economic Co-operation and Development and the European Union for more information on the high-income economies.

More about the Selected World Development Indicators

Tables 1 to 3, *Summary of socioeconomic development indicators*, offers an overview of key development issues: How rich or poor are the people? What is the life expectancy of newborns? What percentage of adults are illiterate? How has the economy performed in terms of growth and inflation? What kind of external economic environment do countries face?

Tables 4 to 7, *Human resources*, shows the rate of progress in social development during the past decade. A standard measure of income inequality, the Gini index, has been added. Measures of well-being, such as malnutrition and access to health care, school enrollment ratios, and gender differences of adult illiteracy, are also presented.

Tables 8 to 10, *Environmental sustainability*, brings together the key country-level indicators in this area. This section provides information on air, water, cities, and energy consumption.

Tables 11 to 17, *Economic performance*, presents information on the economic structure and growth of the world's economies, as well as information on foreign investment, external debt, and integration into the global economy that is providing new challenges and opportunities for both developed and developing economies.

Classification of economies

As in the Report itself, the main criterion used to classify economies and broadly distinguish different stages of economic development is GNP per capita. Countries are traditionally classified into three categories: low, middle, and high income. The GNP per capita cutoff levels are: low-income: $725 or less in 1994 (51 economies); middle-income: $726 to $8,955 (57 economies); and high-income: $8,956 or more (25 economies). Economies are further classified by region, exports, and indebtedness. For a list of economies in each group, see the tables on classification of economies at the back of the book.

Data sources and methodology

Socioeconomic data presented here are drawn from several sources: primary collection by the World Bank, member country statistical publications, research institutes such as the World Resources Institute, and international agencies such as the United Nations and its specialized agencies, the International Monetary Fund, and the Organisation for Economic Co-operation and Development (see Data Sources at the end of the Technical Notes for a complete listing of sources). Although international standards of coverage, definition, and classification apply to most statistics reported by countries and international agencies, there are inevitably differences in coverage, currentness, and the capabilities and resources devoted to basic data collection and compilation. In some cases, competing sources of data require review by World Bank staff to ensure that the most reliable data available on a given topic are presented. In some instances, where

available data are deemed to be too weak to provide reliable measures of levels and trends or do not adequately adhere to international standards, the data are not shown.

Differences between data presented in each edition reflect not only updates by the countries, but also revisions to historical series and changes in methodology. Thus data of different vintages may be published in different editions of Bank publications. Readers are advised not to compare data series between publications. Consistent time-series data are available in the *World*Data 1995 CD-ROM*.

All dollar figures are current U.S. dollars unless otherwise stated. The various methods used for converting from national currency figures are described in the Technical Notes.

Summary measures

The summary measures in the colored bands on each table are totals (indicated by *t*), weighted averages (*w*), or median values (*m*) calculated for groups of economies. Countries for which data in the summary measures are not shown in the main tables have been implicitly included on the assumption that they have followed the trend of reporting economies during such periods. The countries excluded from the main tables (those presented in Table 1a. Basic indicators for other economies) have been included in the summary measures when data are available or, if no data are available, by assuming that they follow the trend of reporting countries. This gives a more consistent aggregated measure by standardizing country coverage for each period shown. Where missing information accounts for a third or more of the overall estimate, however, the group measure is reported as not available. The weightings used for computing the summary measures are stated in each technical note.

Terminology and country coverage

In these notes and tables the term "country" does not imply political independence but may refer to any territory for which authorities report separate social or economic statistics.

Economic data reported for Germany before 1991 refer to the former Federal Republic, but demographic and social data generally refer to the unified Germany. Throughout the tables, exceptions are footnoted to explain coverage. The data for China do not include Taiwan, China, but footnotes to Tables 15 and 16 provide estimates of international transactions for Taiwan, China. Data reported for Ethiopia after 1991 exclude Eritrea unless otherwise stated.

Table layout

The table format of this edition generally follows the format used in previous editions. In each group, economies are listed in ascending order of GNP per capita, except that those for which no such figure can be calculated are italicized and listed in alphabetical order at the end of the group deemed appropriate. This order is used in all tables. Economies in the high-income group marked by the symbol † are those classified by the United Nations, or otherwise regarded by their authorities, as developing. Economies with a population of fewer than 1 million and those with sparse data are not shown separately in the main tables but are included in the aggregates. Basic indicators for these economies may be found in Table 1a. The alphabetical list in the Key shows the reference number for each economy; here, too, italics indicate economies with no current estimates of GNP per capita.

Technical notes

The Technical Notes, Key, country classification tables, and footnotes to the tables should be consulted for interpreting data. They outline the methods, concepts, definitions, and data sources used in compiling the tables. The Data Sources section at the end of the notes lists sources that contain more comprehensive definitions and descriptions of the concepts used.

Comments and questions relating to the Selected World Development Indicators should be addressed to: Development Data Group, International Economics Department, The World Bank, 1818 H St. N.W., Washington, D.C. 20433, by fax 202-522-1498, by e-mail to info@world-bank.org, or by calling 800-590-1906 or 202-473-7824.

To order World Bank publications, e-mail your request to books@worldbank.org, or write to World Bank Publications at the address above, or call 202-473-1155.

For more information, click on "publications" on the World Wide Web at www.worldbank.org.

Groups of economies

For this map, economies are classified by income group, as they are for the tables that follow.
Low-income economies are those with a GNP per capita of $725 or less in 1994; middle-income,
$726 – $8,955; high-income, $8,956 or more. Six middle-income economies—American Samoa (US),
Fiji, French Polynesia (Fr), Kiribati, Tonga, and Western Samoa—and Tuvalu, for which income data are
not available, are not shown on the map because of space constraints.

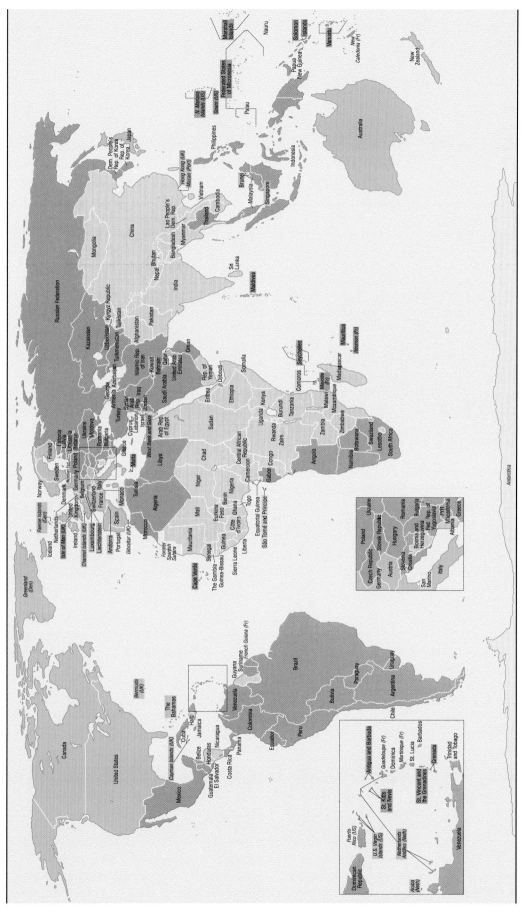

Low-income economies

Middle-income economies

High-income economies

Data not available

Key

The Key table, below, provides an index to the countries included in the Selected World Development Indicators and additional information on the sources of demographic data for the 133 countries included in the main statistical tables. In each statistical table of the Selected World Development Indicators, economies are listed in ascending order of GNP per capita, except those for which no GNP per capita can be calculated; the latter are italicized, in alphabetical order, at the end of the income group to which they belong. The ranking below by GNP per capita therefore indicates a country's place in the statistical tables.

Figures in colored bands in the tables are summary measures for groups of economies. The letter *w* means weighted average; *m*, median value; and *t*, total.

Except where noted in the Technical Notes, growth rates for economic data are in real terms.

Data cutoff date is April 30, 1996.

The symbol . . means not available.

A blank space means not applicable.

The figures 0 and 0.0 mean zero or less than half the unit shown.

Figures in italics indicate data that are for years or periods other than those specified.

The symbol † indicates high-income economies classified by the United Nations, or regarded by their own authorities, as developing.

Economy	GNP per capita ranking in tables	Population census	Sources of 1994 demographic data		
			Population	Total fertility rate	Infant mortality rate
Albania	32	1989	Official [1]	Official	Official
Algeria	71	1987	World Bank [3]	Survey 1992	Survey 1992
Argentina	107	1991	Official [2]	U.N. Pop. Div.	U.N. Pop. Div.
Armenia	46	1989	World Bank [3]	Official	Official
Australia	114	1991	Official [2]	Official	Official
Austria	126	1991	Official [2]	Official	Official
Azerbaijan	36	1989	Official [2]	Official	Official
Bangladesh	13	1991	World Bank [2]	Survey 1994	Survey 1994
Belarus	77	1989	Official [2]	Official	Official
Belgium	123	1991	Official [2]	Official	Official
Benin	30	1992	World Bank [2]	World Bank	World Bank
Bolivia	52	1992	Official [2]	U.N. Pop. Div.	U.N. Pop. Div.
Botswana	88	1991	World Bank [2]	Survey 1988	Survey 1988
Brazil	92	1991	World Bank [1]	U.N. Pop. Div.	U.N. Pop. Div.
Bulgaria	62	1992	Official [2]	Official	Official
Burkina Faso	21	1985	World Bank [3]	Survey 1992	World Bank
Burundi	5	1990	World Bank [3]	U.N. Pop. Div.	U.N. Pop. Div.
Cameroon	47	1987	World Bank [1]	Survey 1991	Survey 1991
Canada	119	1991	Official [2]	Official	Official
Central African Republic	31	1988	World Bank [1]	U.N. Pop. Div.	U.N. Pop. Div.

Economy	GNP per capita ranking in tables	Sources of 1994 demographic data			
		Population census	Population	Total fertility rate	Infant mortality rate
Chad	8	1993	World Bank [2]	U.N. Pop. Div.	U.N. Pop. Div.
Chile	97	1992	Official [2]	Official	Official
China	39	1990	World Bank [3]	Official	Survey 1991
Colombia	72	1993	World Bank [2]	Survey 1990	Survey 1990
Congo	43	1984	World Bank [2]	World Bank	World Bank
Costa Rica	80	1984	World Bank [3]	U.N. Pop. Div.	U.N. Pop. Div.
Côte d'Ivoire	42	1988	World Bank [3]	Survey 1994	Survey 1994
Croatia	84	1991	Official [2]	World Bank	World Bank
Czech Republic	95	1991	Official [2]	Official	Official
Denmark	130	1991	Official [2]	Official	Official
Dominican Republic	65	1993	World Bank [1]	U.N. Pop. Div.	U.N. Pop. Div.
Ecuador	64	1990	World Bank [3]	Survey 1994	Survey 1994
Egypt, Arab Rep.	48	1986	World Bank [2]	Survey 1992	Survey 1992
El Salvador	67	1992	World Bank [1]	U.N. Pop. Div.	U.N. Pop. Div.
Estonia	89	1989	Official [2]	Official	Official
Ethiopia[a]	3	1994	World Bank [3]	Survey 1990	U.N. Pop. Div.
Finland	116	1990	Official [2]	Official	Official
France	124	1990	Official [2]	Official	Official
Gabon	100	1993	World Bank [1]	U.N. Pop. Div.	U.N. Pop. Div.
Gambia, The	26	1993	World Bank [2]	World Bank	World Bank
Georgia	50	1989	World Bank [3]	Official	Official
Germany[b]	127	—	Official [2]	Official	Official
Ghana	33	1984	World Bank [3]	Survey 1993	Survey 1993
Greece	106	1991	Official [2]	Official	Official
Guatemala	60	1994	Official [2]	U.N. Pop. Div.	U.N. Pop. Div.
Guinea	38	1983	World Bank [1]	World Bank	World Bank
Guinea-Bissau	16	1991	World Bank [2]	World Bank	World Bank
Haiti	14	1982	World Bank [1]	U.N. Pop. Div.	U.N. Pop. Div.
Honduras	40	1988	World Bank [3]	Survey 1991–92	Survey 1991–92
† Hong Kong	120	1991	Official [1]	Official	Official
Hungary	99	1990	Official [2]	Official	Official
India	23	1991	World Bank [2]	Survey 1993	Survey 1993
Indonesia	55	1990	World Bank [2]	Survey 1994	Survey 1994
Iran, Islamic Rep.	90	1991	World Bank [2]	U.N. Pop. Div.	Official
Ireland	112	1991	Official [2]	Official	Official
† Israel	113	1983	Official [2]	Official	Official
Italy	117	1991	Official [2]	Official	Official
Jamaica	69	1991	World Bank [3]	World Bank	U.N. Pop. Div.
Japan	131	1990	Official [2]	Official	Official
Jordan	68	1994	World Bank [2]	Official	Survey 1990
Kazakstan	59	1989	World Bank [3]	Official	Official
Kenya	17	1989	World Bank [2]	Survey 1993	Survey 1993
Korea, Rep. of	108	1990	Official [1]	Official	Official
† Kuwait	118	1985	Official [2]	U.N. Pop. Div.	U.N. Pop. Div.
Kyrgyz Republic	44	1989	World Bank [3]	Official	Official
Lao PDR	24	1985	World Bank [1]	U.N. Pop. Div.	U.N. Pop. Div.
Latvia	79	1989	Official [2]	Official	Official

Economy	GNP per capita ranking in tables	Sources of 1994 demographic data			
		Population census	Population	Total fertility rate	Infant mortality rate
Lesotho	49	1986	World Bank [3]	Survey 1991	Survey 1991
Lithuania	66	1989	Official [2]	Official	Official
Macedonia, FYR	53	1991	World Bank [3]	Official	Official
Madagascar	10	1993	World Bank [2]	Survey 1992	Survey 1992
Malawi	7	1987	World Bank [2]	Survey 1992	Survey 1992
Malaysia	96	1991	World Bank [1]	U.N. Pop. Div.	U.N. Pop. Div.
Mali	18	1987	World Bank [2]	Survey 1987	Survey 1987
Mauritania	35	1988	World Bank [3]	U.N. Pop. Div.	U.N. Pop. Div.
Mauritius	94	1990	World Bank [3]	U.N. Pop. Div.	U.N. Pop. Div.
Mexico	101	1990	World Bank [2]	U.N. Pop. Div.	U.N. Pop. Div.
Moldova	54	1989	Official [2]	Official	Official
Mongolia	22	1989	World Bank [1]	U.N. Pop. Div.	U.N. Pop. Div.
Morocco	58	1994	World Bank [2]	Survey 1995	Survey 1995
Mozambique	2	1980	World Bank [1]	U.N. Pop. Div.	U.N. Pop. Div.
Myanmar	51	1983	World Bank [1]	U.N. Pop. Div.	U.N. Pop. Div.
Namibia	75	1991	World Bank [2]	Survey 1992	Survey 1992
Nepal	11	1991	World Bank [2]	U.N. Pop. Div.	U.N. Pop. Div.
Netherlands	121	1971	Official [1]	Official	Official
New Zealand	110	1991	Official [2]	Official	Official
Nicaragua	27	1971	World Bank [1]	Survey 1992–93	Survey 1992–93
Niger	15	1988	World Bank [2]	Survey 1992	Survey 1992
Nigeria	19	1991	World Bank [2]	Survey 1990	Survey 1990
Norway	129	1990	Official [2]	Official	Official
Oman	103	1993	World Bank [3]	Survey 1989	Survey 1989
Pakistan	34	1981	World Bank [2]	World Bank	World Bank
Panama	85	1990	World Bank [3]	U.N. Pop. Div.	U.N. Pop. Div.
Papua New Guinea	61	1989	World Bank [1]	U.N. Pop. Div.	U.N. Pop. Div.
Paraguay	70	1992	World Bank [3]	Survey 1990	Survey 1990
Peru	76	1993	World Bank [2]	Survey 1991–92	Survey 1991–92
Philippines	56	1990	Official [2]	Survey 1993	U.N. Pop. Div.
Poland	81	1988	Official [2]	Official	Official
Portugal	109	1991	Official [2]	Official	Official
Romania	63	1992	Official [2]	Official	Official
Russian Federation	86	1989	World Bank [3]	Official	Official
Rwanda	1	1991	World Bank [2]	Survey 1992	U.N. Pop. Div.
Saudi Arabia	105	1992	World Bank [2]	Survey 1990	Survey 1990
Senegal	41	1988	World Bank [2]	Survey 1992–93	Survey 1992–93
Sierra Leone	6	1985	World Bank [1]	U.N. Pop. Div.	U.N. Pop. Div.
† Singapore	122	1990	Official [1]	Official	Official
Slovak Republic	78	1991	Official [2]	Official	Official
Slovenia	104	1991	Official [2]	Official	Official
South Africa	93	1991	World Bank [1]	U.N. Pop. Div.	U.N. Pop. Div.
Spain	111	1991	Official [2]	Official	Official
Sri Lanka	45	1981	Official [2]	Survey 1987	Survey 1987
Sweden	125	1990	Official [2]	Official	Official
Switzerland	132	1990	Official [2]	Official	Official
Tajikistan	29	1989	Official [2]	Official	Official

	GNP per capita ranking in tables	Sources of 1994 demographic data			
Economy		Population census	Population	Total fertility rate	Infant mortality rate
Tanzania	4	1988	World Bank [1]	U.N. Pop. Div.	U.N. Pop. Div.
Thailand	82	1990	World Bank [1]	U.N. Pop. Div.	U.N. Pop. Div.
Togo	25	1981	World Bank [1]	U.N. Pop. Div.	U.N. Pop. Div.
Trinidad and Tobago	98	1990	World Bank [2]	Survey 1987	Survey 1987
Tunisia	73	1994	World Bank [2]	U.N. Pop. Div.	U.N. Pop. Div.
Turkey	83	1990	World Bank [1]	U.N. Pop. Div.	U.N. Pop. Div.
Turkmenistan	91	1989	World Bank [3]	Official	Official
Uganda	9	1991	World Bank [2]	Survey 1991	Survey 1991
Ukraine	74	1991	Official [2]	Official	Official
† *United Arab Emirates*	133	1980	World Bank [1]	U.N. Pop. Div.	Survey 1987
United Kingdom	115	1991	Official [1]	Official	Official
United States of America	128	1990	Official [2]	Official	Official
Uruguay	102	1985	World Bank [3]	U.N. Pop. Div.	U.N. Pop. Div.
Uzbekistan	57	1989	World Bank [3]	Official	Official
Venezuela	87	1990	Official [2]	U.N. Pop. Div.	U.N. Pop. Div.
Vietnam	12	1989	World Bank [3]	Survey 1995	Survey 1995
Yemen, Rep. of	20	1994	World Bank [2]	Survey 1991–92	Survey 1991–92
Zambia	28	1990	World Bank [1]	U.N. Pop. Div.	Survey 1987
Zimbabwe	37	1992	World Bank [2]	Survey 1994	Survey 1994

Note: Economies with sparse data or with populations of more than 30,000 and fewer than 1 million are shown separately only in Table 1a; however, they are included in the country group totals and weighted averages in the main tables. For data comparability and coverage, see the Technical Notes.

a. In all tables, data for Ethiopia after 1991 exclude Eritrea unless otherwise noted.

b. In all tables, data refer to the unified Germany unless otherwise noted.

Population

Official
  1. Published by a National Statistical Office, or another official country source, such as Central Bank, Ministry of Planning, etc.
  2. Reported as an official estimate by Eurostat, Council of Europe, U.N. Statistical Office, South Pacific Commission, or similar international organization.

World Bank
  1. Based on the U.N. Population Division's latest estimates and projections for 1990 and 1995.
  2. Based on a projection from the latest census.
  3. Based on a projection from the latest available official estimate.

Fertility and Mortality Rates

Official
  Estimate based on vital registration or other official data collection instrument.
U.N. Pop. Div.
  World Bank estimate based on the U.N. Population Division's estimates and projections for 1990–94 and 1995–99.
Survey
  World Bank estimate from the latest available Demographic and Health Survey, Contraceptive Prevalence Survey, or other survey or census module showing vital rates estimates.
World Bank
  Estimated from other sources, including Bank economic and sector reports, other country studies, and level and trends in other indicators.

Table 1. Basic indicators

		Population (millions) mid-1994	Area (thousands of sq. km)	GNP per capita[a] Dollars 1994	GNP per capita[a] Avg. ann. growth (%) 1985–94	PPP estimates of GNP per capita[b] US=100 1987	PPP estimates of GNP per capita[b] US=100 1994	PPP estimates of GNP per capita[b] Current int'l $ 1994	Life expectancy at birth (years) 1994	Adult illiteracy (%) 1995
	Low-income economies	3,182.2 t	40,391 t	380 w	3.4 w				63 w	34 w
	Excluding China and India	1,077.7 t	27,543 t	360 w	–1.1 w				56 w	46 w
1	Rwanda	7.8	26	80	–6.6	3.8	1.3	330[c]	. .	40
2	Mozambique	15.5	802	90	3.8	2.7	3.3	860[d]	46	60
3	Ethiopia	54.9	1,097	100	. .	2.0	1.7	430[c]	49	65
4	Tanzania[e]	28.8	945	140	0.8	2.6	2.4	620[c]	51	32
5	Burundi	6.2	28	160	–0.7	3.4	2.7	700[d]	50	65
6	Sierra Leone	4.4	72	160	–0.4	3.1	2.7	700[c]	40	69
7	Malawi	9.5	118	170	–0.7	3.1	2.5	650[c]	44	44
8	Chad	6.3	1,284	180	0.7	2.7	2.8	720[d]	48	52
9	Uganda	18.6	236	190	2.3	5.0	5.4	1,410[d]	42	38
10	Madagascar	13.1	587	200	–1.7	3.1	2.5	640[c]	52	. .
11	Nepal	20.9	141	200	2.3	4.4	4.8	1,230[d]	54	73
12	Vietnam	72.0	332	200	. .	. .	. .	. .	68	6
13	Bangladesh	117.9	144	220	2.0	4.9	5.1	1,330[c]	57	62
14	Haiti	7.0	28	230	–5.0	6.2	3.6	930[d]	57	55
15	Niger	8.7	1,267	230	–2.1	3.8	3.0	770[d]	46	86
16	Guinea-Bissau	1.0	36	240	2.2	2.9	3.2	820[d]	38	45
17	Kenya	26.0	580	250	0.0	5.7	5.1	1,310[c]	59	22
18	Mali	9.5	1,240	250	1.0	2.3	2.0	520[c]	49	69
19	Nigeria	108.0	924	280	1.2	4.3	4.6	1,190[c]	52	43
20	Yemen, Rep.	14.8	528	280	. .	. .	. .	. .	53	. .
21	Burkina Faso	10.1	274	300	–0.1	3.5	3.1	800[d]	49	81
22	Mongolia	2.4	1,566	300	–3.2	. .	. .	. .	64	. .
23	India	913.6	3,288	320	2.9	4.4	4.9	1,280[c]	62	48
24	Lao PDR	4.7	237	320	. .	. .	. .	. .	52	43
25	Togo	4.0	57	320	–2.7	6.0	4.4	1,130[d]	55	48
26	Gambia, The	1.1	11	330	0.5	4.8	4.3	1,100[d]	45	61
27	Nicaragua	4.2	130	340	–6.1	13	7	1,800[d]	67	34
28	Zambia	9.2	753	350	–1.4	4.1	3.3	860[c]	47	22
29	Tajikistan[f]	5.8	143	360	–11.4	12.1	3.7	970[g]	67	. .
30	Benin	5.3	113	370	–0.8	7.0	6.3	1,630[c]	50	63
31	Central African Republic	3.2	623	370	–2.7	5.4	4.5	1,160[d]	49	40
32	Albania	3.2	29	380	. .	. .	. .	. .	73	. .
33	Ghana	16.6	239	410	1.4	7.9	7.9	2,050[d]	58	36
34	Pakistan	126.3	796	430	1.3	8.5	8.2	2,130[c]	60	62
35	Mauritania	2.2	1,026	480	0.2	6.4	6.1	1,570[d]	51	62
36	Azerbaijan[f]	7.5	87	500	–12.2	21.7	5.8	1,510[g]	69	. .
37	Zimbabwe	10.8	391	500	–0.5	8.7	7.9	2,040[c]	58	15
38	Guinea	6.4	246	520	1.3	. .	. .	. .	44	64
39	China	1,190.9	9,561	530[h]	7.8	5.8	9.7	2,510[h]	69	19
40	Honduras	5.8	112	600	0.5	8.1	7.5	1,940[i]	66	27
41	Senegal	8.3	197	600	–0.7	7.3	6.1	1,580[c]	50	67
42	Côte d'Ivoire	13.8	322	610	–4.6	8.3	5.3	1,370[c]	56	60
43	Congo	2.6	342	620	–2.9	11.2	7.3	1,900[c]	51	25
44	Kyrgyz Republic[f]	4.5	198	630	–5.0	13.5	6.7	1,730[g]	68	. .
45	Sri Lanka	17.9	66	640	2.9	10.7	12.2	3,160[c]	72	10
46	Armenia[f]	3.7	30	680	–13.0	26.5	8.3	2,160[g]	71	. .
47	Cameroon	13.0	475	680	–6.9	15.0	7.5	1,950[c]	57	37
48	Egypt, Arab Rep.	56.8	1,001	720	1.3	14.4	14.4	3,720[c]	62	49
49	Lesotho	1.9	30	720	0.6	6.6	6.7	1,730[d]	61	29
50	*Georgia* [f]	5.4	70	. .	. .	. .	. .	. .	73	. .
51	*Myanmar*	45.6	677	. .	. .	. .	. .	. .	58	17
	Middle-income economies	1,569.9 t	61,263 t	2,520 w	–0.1 w				67 w	. .
	Lower-middle-income	1,096.9 t	40,594 t	1,590 w	–1.2 w				67 w	. .
52	Bolivia	7.2	1,099	770	1.7	8.9	9.3	2,400[i]	60	17
53	Macedonia, FYR	2.1	26	820	. .	. .	. .	. .	73	. .
54	Moldova[f]	4.3	34	870	. .	. .	. .	. .	68	. .
55	Indonesia	190.4	1,905	880	6.0	10.0	13.9	3,600[i]	63	16
56	Philippines	67.0	300	950	1.7	10.4	10.6	2,740[c]	65	5
57	Uzbekistan[f]	22.4	447	960	–2.3	12.5	9.2	2,370[g]	70	. .
58	Morocco	26.4	447	1,140	1.2	13.1	13.4	3,470[c]	65	56
59	Kazakstan[f]	16.8	2,717	1,160	–6.5	24.2	10.9	2,810[g]	68	. .
60	Guatemala	10.3	109	1,200	0.9	13.5	13.3	3,440[i]	65	44
61	Papua New Guinea	4.2	463	1,240	2.2	9.1	10.4	2,680[d]	57	28
62	Bulgaria	8.4	111	1,250	–2.7	23.5	16.9	4,380[j]	71	. .
63	Romania	22.7	238	1,270	–4.5	22.7	15.8	4,090[j]	70	. .
64	Ecuador	11.2	284	1,280	0.9	15.9	16.2	4,190[i]	69	10
65	Dominican Republic	7.6	49	1,330	2.2	13.9	14.5	3,760[i]	70	18
66	Lithuania[f]	3.7	65	1,350	–8.0	33.8	12.7	3,290[j]	69	. .
67	El Salvador	5.6	21	1,360	2.2	8.4	9.3	2,410[i]	67	29
68	Jordan	4.0	89	1,440	–5.6	25.4	15.8	4,100[i]	70	13
69	Jamaica	2.5	11	1,540	3.9	11.1	13.1	3,400[k]	74	15
70	Paraguay	4.8	407	1,580	1.0	13.7	13.7	3,550[i]	68	8
71	Algeria	27.4	2,382	1,650	–2.5	. .	. .	. .	69	38
72	Colombia	36.3	1,139	1,670	2.4	19.0	20.6	5,330[i]	70	9

Note: For other economies see Table 1a. For data comparability and coverage, see the technical notes.

		Population (millions) mid-1994	Area (thousands of sq. km)	GNP per capita[a] Dollars 1994	GNP per capita[a] Avg. ann. growth (%) 1985–94	PPP estimates of GNP per capita[b] US=100 1987	PPP estimates of GNP per capita[b] US=100 1994	PPP estimates of GNP per capita[b] Current int'l $ 1994	Life expectancy at birth (years) 1994	Adult illiteracy (%) 1995
73	Tunisia	8.8	164	1,790	2.1	18.5	19.4	5,020[c]	68	33
74	Ukraine[f]	51.9	604	1,910	–8.0	20.4	10.1	2,620[j]	68	..
75	Namibia	1.5	824	1,970	3.3	17.0	16.7	4,320[d]	59	..
76	Peru	23.2	1,285	2,110	–2.0	18.0	13.9	3,610[i]	65	11
77	Belarus[f]	10.4	208	2,160	–1.9	25.1	16.7	4,320[j]	69	..
78	Slovak Republic	5.3	49	2,250	–3.0	..	..	..	72	..
79	Latvia[f]	2.5	64	2,320	–6.0	24.1	12.4	3,220[j]	68	..
80	Costa Rica	3.3	51	2,400	2.8	..	..	..	77	5
81	Poland	38.5	313	2,410	0.8	21.4	21.2	5,480[j]	72	..
82	Thailand	58.0	513	2,410	8.6	16.4	26.9	6,970[c]	69	6
83	Turkey	60.8	779	2,500	1.4	20.9	18.2	4,710[j]	67	18
84	Croatia	4.8	57	2,560	..	..	..	..	73	..
85	Panama	2.6	76	2,580	–1.2	26.6	22.1	5,730[i]	73	9
86	Russian Federation[f]	148.3	17,075	2,650	–4.1	30.6	17.8	4,610[j]	64	..
87	Venezuela	21.2	912	2,760	0.7	33.7	30.0	7,770[i]	71	9
88	Botswana	1.4	582	2,800	6.6	15.4	20.1	5,210[c]	68	30
89	Estonia[f]	1.5	45	2,820	–6.1	29.9	17.4	4,510[j]	70	..
90	*Iran, Islamic Rep.*	62.5	1,648	..	..	..	..	..	68	28
91	*Turkmenistan[f]*	4.4	488	..	..	..	..	..	66	..
Upper-middle-income		**472.8 t**	**20,669 t**	**4,640 w**	**1.4 w**				**69 w**	**13 w**
92	Brazil	159.1	8,512	2,970	–0.4	24.2	20.9	5,400[i]	67	17
93	South Africa	40.5	1,221	3,040	–1.3	23.9	19.8	5,130[d]	64	18
94	Mauritius	1.1	2	3,150	5.8	39.4	49.1	12,720[c]	70	17
95	Czech Republic	10.3	79	3,200	–2.1	44.1	34.4	8,900[j]	73	..
96	Malaysia	19.7	330	3,480	5.6	23.5	32.6	8,440[k]	71	17
97	Chile	14.0	757	3,520	6.5	24.8	34.4	8,890[i]	72	5
98	Trinidad and Tobago	1.3	5	3,740	–2.3	40.9	33.5	8,670[d]	72	2
99	Hungary	10.3	93	3,840	–1.2	28.9	23.5	6,080[i]	70	..
100	Gabon	1.3	268	3,880	–3.7	..	..	..	54	37
101	Mexico	88.5	1,958	4,180	0.9	27.8	27.2	7,040[k]	71	10
102	Uruguay	3.2	177	4,660	2.9	28.1	29.8	7,710[i]	73	3
103	Oman	2.1	212	5,140	0.5	34.7	33.2	8,590[d]	70	..
104	Slovenia	2.0	20	7,040	..	33.3	24.1	6,230[j]	74	..
105	Saudi Arabia	17.8	2,150	7,050	–1.7	45.7	36.6	9,480[d]	70	37
106	Greece	10.4	132	7,700	1.3	42.1	42.2	10,930[i]	78	..
107	Argentina	34.2	2,767	8,110	2.0	32.1	33.7	8,720[i]	72	4
108	Korea, Rep.	44.5	99	8,260	7.8	27.3	39.9	10,330[c]	71	m
Low- and middle-income		**4,752.2 t**	**101,655 t**	**1,090 w**	**0.7 w**				**64 w**	**29 w**
Sub-Saharan Africa		**571.9 t**	**24,274 t**	**460 w**	**–1.2 w**				**52 w**	**43 w**
East Asia and Pacific		**1,734.7 t**	**16,367 t**	**860 w**	**6.9 w**				**68 w**	**17 w**
South Asia		**1,220.3 t**	**5,133 t**	**320 w**	**2.7 w**				**61 w**	**50 w**
Europe and Central Asia		**487.4 t**	**24,354 t**	**2,090 w**	**–3.2 w**				**68 w**	**.. **
Middle East and N. Africa		**266.7 t**	**11,021 t**	**1,580 w**	**–0.4 w**				**66 w**	**39 w**
Latin America and Caribbean		**470.9 t**	**20,505 t**	**3,340 w**	**0.6 w**				**68 w**	**13 w**
High-income economies		**849.9 t**	**31,824 t**	**23,420 w**	**1.9 w**				**77 w**	**.. **
109	Portugal	9.9	92	9,320	4.0	41.3	46.3	11,970[j]	75	..
110	New Zealand	3.5	271	13,350	0.7	63.2	61.3	15,870[j]	76	m
111	Spain	39.1	505	13,440	2.8	50.2	53.1	13,740[j]	77	..
112	Ireland	3.6	70	13,530	5.0	40.6	52.4	13,550[j]	76	m
113	†Israel	5.4	21	14,530	2.3	56.5	59.1	15,300[i]	77	..
114	Australia	17.8	7,713	18,000	1.2	69.9	70.0	18,120[j]	77	m
115	United Kingdom	58.4	245	18,340	1.3	70.7	69.4	17,970[j]	76	m
116	Finland	5.1	338	18,850	–0.3	72.1	62.4	16,150[j]	76	m
117	Italy	57.1	301	19,300	1.8	70.9	71.3	18,460[j]	78	m
118	†Kuwait	1.6	18	19,420	1.1	84.3	95.6	24,730[d]	76	21
119	Canada	29.2	9,976	19,510	0.3	83.2	77.1	19,960[j]	78	m
120	†Hong Kong	6.1	1	21,650[n]	5.3[n]	..	..	..	78	8
121	Netherlands	15.4	37	22,010	1.9	70.0	72.4	18,750[j]	78	m
122	†Singapore	2.9	1	22,500	6.1	60.2	84.6	21,900[d]	75	9
123	Belgium	10.1	31	22,870	2.3	74.6	78.3	20,270[j]	76	m
124	France	57.9	552	23,420	1.6	75.9	76.0	19,670[j]	78	m
125	Sweden	8.8	450	23,530	–0.1	76.1	66.2	17,130[j]	78	m
126	Austria	8.0	84	24,630	2.0	72.8	75.6	19,560[j]	77	m
127	Germany	81.5	357	25,580	..	..	75.3	19,480[j]	76	m
128	United States	260.6	9,364	25,880	1.3	100.0	100.0	25,880[j]	77	m
129	Norway	4.3	324	26,390	1.4	77.7	78.1	20,210[j]	78	m
130	Denmark	5.2	43	27,970	1.3	76.6	76.8	19,880[j]	75	m
131	Japan	125.0	378	34,630	3.2	74.7	81.7	21,140[j]	79	m
132	Switzerland	7.0	41	37,930	0.5	104.5	97.2	25,150[j]	78	m
133	† *United Arab Emirates*	2.4	84	..	0.4	..	..	..	75	21
World		**5,601.3 t**	**133,478 t**	**4,470 w**	**0.9 w**				**67 w**	**.. **

†Economies classified by the United Nations or otherwise regarded by their authorities as developing. a. *Atlas* method; see the technical notes. b. Purchasing power parity; see the technical notes. c. Extrapolated from 1985 ICP estimates. d. Based on regression estimates. e. In all tables, GDP and GNP cover mainland Tanzania. f. Estimates for economies of the former Soviet Union are preliminary; their classification will be kept under review. g. Extrapolated from 1990 ICP estimates. h. World Bank estimate. i. Extrapolated from 1980 ICP estimates. j. Extrapolated from 1993 ICP estimates. k. Extrapolated from 1975 ICP estimates. m. According to UNESCO, illiteracy is less than 5 percent. n. Data refer to GDP.

Table 2. Macroeconomic indicators

| | | Central gov't. curr. deficit/surplus[a] (% of GNP) | | Money, broadly defined | | | Nominal interest rates of banks (average annual %) | | | | Average annual inflation (%) (GDP deflator) | Current account balance before official transfers (% of GNP) | | Gross international reserves (months of import cov.) | | Net present value of external debt (% of GNP) |
| | | | | Avg. ann. nom. gr. rate (%) | Average outstanding as a % of GDP | | Deposit rate | | Lending rate | | | | | | | |
		1980	1994	1985–94	1980	1994	1980	1994	1980	1994	1984–94	1980	1994	1980	1994	1994
	Low-income economies															**32 w**
	Excluding China and India															**60 w**
1	Rwanda	3.5	−5.5	5.4	13.6	..	6.3	5.0	13.5	15.0	4.5	−13.3	−69.1	6.7	1.1	78
2	Mozambique	..	..	..	..	..	..	..	..	..	53.2	−20.7	−71.4	..	..	331
3	Ethiopia	..	..	..	..	44.4	..	11.5	..	14.3		−4.8[b]	−6.9	4.0[b]	5.9	68
4	Tanzania	−1.3	..	35.0	..	30.7	4.0	..	11.5	39.0	33.3	−9.7	..	..	..	167
5	Burundi	1.9	..	8.5	13.5	..	2.5	..	12.0	..	5.4	..	−16.6	..	8.5	50
6	Sierra Leone	−5.1[c]	−1.9[c]	56.4	20.6	11.0	9.2	11.6	11.0	27.3	67.3	−19.9	..	..	..	138
7	Malawi	1.2[c]	..	21.4	18.0	20.5	7.9	25.0	16.7	31.0	18.8	−27.4	−44.0	1.4	0.6	73
8	Chad	..	..	−2.7	20.0	10.9	5.5	8.1	11.0	17.5	1.7	−2.1	..	1.7	2.9	43
9	Uganda	−2.2	..	..	12.7	9.8	6.8	10.0	10.8	..	75.4	..	−6.7	..	..	48
10	Madagascar	..	−2.5	23.7	18.2	20.5	..	..	..	..	15.8	−15.5	−18.5	..	..	161
11	Nepal	7.6	..	21.2	21.9	33.7	4.0	..	14.0	..	12.1	−5.1	−6.1	8.9	6.8	27
12	Vietnam	..	..	..	..	..	..	..	..	..	102.6	..	..	..	..	135
13	Bangladesh	11.2[c]	..	14.2	18.4	35.0	8.2	6.4	11.3	14.4	6.6	−11.1	−1.4	1.5	7.9	32
14	Haiti	−3.3	..	15.3	24.0	43.0	10.0	..	..	..	13.2	−9.4	−6.8	0.6	..	25
15	Niger	5.1	..	1.0	13.3	14.6	6.2	7.8	14.5	16.8	0.2	−17.3	−7.1	1.6	3.9	58
16	Guinea-Bissau	..	..	62.9	..	14.1	..	28.7	..	36.3	65.7	−48.9	−15.6	..	..	222
17	Kenya	2.6[c]	−0.4	18.9	29.8	32.2	5.8	..	..	10.6	11.7	−13.7	−0.5	2.1	2.5	80
18	Mali	−1.4	..	5.3	17.9	20.0	6.2	7.8	14.5	16.8	3.4	−14.5	−10.6	0.6	3.4	84
19	Nigeria	..	..	23.3	23.8	..	5.3	13.1	8.4	20.5	29.6	5.7	−6.4	5.7	1.6	92
20	Yemen, Rep.	..	..	..	..	..	..	..	..	..	..	..	..	..	1.0	..
21	Burkina Faso	2.0	0.5	8.2	13.8	20.0	6.2	7.8	14.5	16.8	1.6	−15.5	−17.5	1.5	5.0	31
22	Mongolia	..	3.7	..	..	23.9	..	92.3	..	233.6	46.0	−24.9	−8.2	..	2.4	38
23	India	0.0	1.8	16.9	34.7	45.2	..	..	16.5	16.3	9.7	−1.7	−0.9	8.0	6.7	24
24	Lao PDR	..	..	38.4	..	13.2	7.2	12.0	4.8	24.0	24.2	..	−8.5	..	2.0	40
25	Togo	1.9	..	−1.2	29.0	25.3	6.2	7.8	14.5	17.5	3.3	−16.4	−3.1	1.4	3.5	98
26	Gambia, The	7.1	7.5	15.2	21.1	23.8	5.0	12.6	15.0	25.0	10.1	−51.4	−5.1	..	..	59
27	Nicaragua	−1.6	−0.9	..	24.5	23.2	..	11.7	..	20.1	1,311.2	−26.0	−67.7	0.9	1.2	707
28	Zambia	−8.7	−2.9	73.3	28.4	10.8	7.0	48.5	9.5	113.3	92.0	−14.5	..	1.3	..	157
29	Tajikistan	..	..	..	..	..	..	..	..	..	104.3	..	..	..	..	25
30	Benin	..	..	9.5	17.1	25.0	6.2	7.8	14.5	16.8	2.9	−7.9	..	0.4	6.1	56
31	Central African Republic	−2.0	..	4.2	18.9	18.6	5.5	8.1	10.5	17.5	2.6	−18.0	..	2.2	9.2	52
32	Albania	..	..	..	..	..	..	19.8	..	23.7	32.7	..	−12.9	6.7	..	45
33	Ghana	−2.9[c]	−0.9[c]	38.4	16.2	15.8	11.5	23.1	19.0	..	28.6	−1.4	−9.0	3.1	3.9	63
34	Pakistan	1.8	−2.1	15.3	38.7	42.3	..	..	..	..	8.8	−4.9	−3.9	3.1	3.5	42
35	Mauritania	..	..	8.7	20.5	21.7	5.5	5.0	12.0	10.0	7.2	−37.6	−14.4	3.6	0.9	162
36	Azerbaijan	..	..	..	..	..	..	..	..	..	122.8	..	..	..	..	3
37	Zimbabwe	−9.1	..	20.7	35.2	25.8	3.5	26.8	17.5	34.9	19.7	−4.8	−5.7	2.7	3.2	69
38	Guinea	..	3.1	..	..	9.4	..	18.0	..	22.0	18.6	..	..	..	..	60
39	China	..	..	23.7	33.2	85.5	5.4	11.0	5.0	11.0	8.4	−1.6	1.4	4.9	5.9	16
40	Honduras	..	..	18.2	21.1	25.3	10.6	11.6	16.5	24.7	13.0	−13.4	−9.7	1.5	1.2	97
41	Senegal	1.8	..	3.1	26.6	18.6	6.2	7.8	14.5	16.8	2.9	−18.1	−9.4	0.2	1.3	65
42	Côte d'Ivoire	4.0	..	0.2	26.7	24.6	6.2	7.8	14.5	16.8	0.2	−18.7	−13.3	0.1	0.7	282
43	Congo	..	..	1.1	14.8	16.2	6.5	8.1	11.0	17.5	−0.3	−15.2	..	0.9	0.5	382
44	Kyrgyz Republic	..	..	..	..	..	..	..	..	..	100.9	..	..	..	..	13
45	Sri Lanka	−4.6	−3.0	16.5	28.5	30.5	14.5	15.3	19.0	13.0	11.0	−18.7	−8.1	1.5	4.4	41
46	Armenia	..	..	..	..	..	..	..	..	..	138.6	..	..	..	..	8
47	Cameroon	5.7	0.2	−3.3	18.5	19.1	7.5	8.1	13.0	17.5	1.3	−5.8	−3.8	1.1	0.1	86
48	Egypt, Arab Rep.	9.6	6.5	19.9	52.2	97.2	8.3	11.8	13.3	16.5	16.4	−2.0	−1.3	3.1	10.7	52
49	Lesotho	0.7	..	14.1	..	31.4	9.6	8.4	11.0	14.3	14.0	−17.8	−26.6	..	..	26
50	*Georgia*	..	..	..	..	..	..	..	..	..	228.3	..	..	..	..	56
51	*Myanmar*	3.9	0.8	16.3	23.9	..	1.5	9.0	8.0	..	26.5	−5.3	−0.5	5.6	3.5	7
	Middle-income economies															**29 w**
	Lower-middle-income															**36 w**
52	Bolivia	..	−2.7	46.7	16.2	45.1	18.0	18.4	28.0	55.6	20.0	−1.8	−7.3	6.0	5.8	66
53	Macedonia, FYR	..	..	..	..	..	..	..	..	..	..	..	..	..	1.2	53
54	Moldova	..	..	..	..	7.2	..	..	..	..	..	..	−4.9	..	2.6	12
55	Indonesia	10.0	8.9	23.5	13.2	..	6.0	20.4	..	20.2	8.9	3.3	−1.6	4.1	3.2	50
56	Philippines	4.1[c]	1.9[c]	20.3	20.7	41.2	12.3	10.5	14.0	15.1	10.0	−6.2	−4.5	4.6	3.1	53
57	Uzbekistan	..	..	..	..	..	..	..	..	..	109.1	..	0.0	..	..	5
58	Morocco	0.5	5.7	13.8	38.5	58.4	4.9	..	7.0	10.0	5.0	−8.6	−2.5	1.7	5.6	64
59	Kazakstan	..	..	..	..	..	..	..	..	..	150.2	..	−4.0	..	..	14
60	Guatemala	2.1	0.8	23.3	20.5	23.4	9.0	9.7	11.0	22.9	19.5	−2.5	−6.0	4.2	3.0	19
61	Papua New Guinea	−6.4[c]	−4.6[c]	8.5	32.9	30.2	6.9	5.1	11.1	9.2	3.9	−22.6	8.5	3.6	0.6	46
62	Bulgaria	..	−4.7	..	..	..	..	54.5	..	64.1	42.2	5.1	1.9	..	..	100
63	Romania	15.9	2.2	44.7	33.4	15.2	..	..	..	..	62.0	..	−1.0	2.0	4.9	17
64	Ecuador	1.0[c]	3.6[c]	41.0	20.2	..	..	33.6	9.0	44.0	47.5	−5.6	−6.2	4.2	4.4	85
65	Dominican Republic	3.0	8.4	33.8	17.8	23.5	..	..	..	..	28.9	−11.0	−2.5	1.5	0.9	37
66	Lithuania	..	0.2	..	..	..	..	27.4	..	62.3	102.3	..	..	..	2.9	7
67	El Salvador	−0.4[c]	0.8[c]	21.2	28.0	36.4	..	13.6	..	19.0	15.5	0.1	−3.7	3.6	3.4	20
68	Jordan	..	3.5[c]	10.9	..	104.5	..	3.2	..	9.0	9.2	..	−12.5	6.3	5.0	87
69	Jamaica	..	..	32.3	32.8	40.0	9.5	36.4	15.6	49.5	27.6	−5.6	−0.4	0.8	1.5	94
70	Paraguay	3.2	3.0	37.8	19.8	24.7	..	23.1	..	32.5	26.2	..	..	6.7	3.1	22
71	Algeria	..	..	14.6	53.3	46.4	..	..	..	..	22.0	0.8	−4.5	5.8	4.5	61
72	Colombia	1.6	2.9	31.9	17.1	19.8	..	29.4	..	40.5	25.6	..	..	..	5.8	28

Note: For data comparability and coverage, see the technical notes. Figures in italics are for years other than those specified.

| | | Central gov't. curr. deficit/surplus[a] (% of GNP) | | Money, broadly defined | | | Nominal interest rates of banks (average annual %) | | | | Average annual inflation (%) (GDP deflator) | Current account balance before official transfers (% of GNP) | | Gross international reserves (months of import cov.) | | Net present value of external debt (% of GNP) |
| | | | | Avg. ann. nom. gr. rate (%) | Average outstanding as a % of GDP | | Deposit rate | | Lending rate | | | | | | | |
#		1980	1994	1985–94	1980	1994	1980	1994	1980	1994	1984–94	1980	1994	1980	1994	1994
73	Tunisia	9.4	3.5	10.2	37.6	44.3	2.5	..	7.2	..	6.3	–5.0	–2.7	2.1	2.3	52
74	Ukraine	..	..	..	..	..	..	208.6	..	250.3	297.0	..	..	..	..	6
75	Namibia	..	0.7	..	..	33.0	..	9.2	..	17.1	10.6	..	–0.6	..	1.3	..
76	Peru	2.1c	2.2c	469.4	16.5	15.3	..	22.3	..	53.6	492.2	–1.2	–6.0	6.6	9.7	41
77	Belarus	..	–0.5	..	..	..	..	..	..	..	136.7	..	..	..	..	5
78	Slovak Republic	..	..	..	..	69.3	..	9.3	..	14.6	9.8	..	5.8	..	3.1	30
79	Latvia	..	–0.9	..	..	30.4	..	31.7	..	55.9	69.8	..	..	..	5.3	6
80	Costa Rica	–3.7	–2.3	24.8	38.8	36.5	18.3	17.7	25.0	33.0	18.2	–14.8	–6.5	1.2	2.7	42
81	Poland	..	–1.0	94.8	57.0	31.7	..	30.6	8.0	32.8	97.8	–6.9	–3.1	0.3	2.8	37
82	Thailand	–0.1	6.6	20.1	34.5	74.2	12.0	8.5	18.0	14.4	5.0	–7.0	–5.9	3.3	5.3	42
83	Turkey	3.2	–2.1	70.2	17.2	21.9	8.0	87.8	..	..	65.8	–6.2	1.7	4.3	3.4	44
84	Croatia	..	4.6	..	..	18.3	..	6.5	..	22.9	..	..	0.0	..	2.5	15
85	Panama	0.3	6.0	10.5	32.8	64.8	..	6.1	..	10.2	1.6	–9.7	–2.6	..	..	104
86	Russian Federation	..	–5.7	..	..	13.7	..	..	..	..	124.3	..	..	..	1.5	23
87	Venezuela	7.4	2.7	35.0	28.7	24.0	..	39.0	..	46.6	36.4	6.7	..	9.3	9.3	59
88	Botswana	11.6c	23.3c	20.6	28.2	26.4	5.0	10.4	8.5	13.9	11.7	–22.5	4.4	..	..	13
89	Estonia	..	..	..	..	23.8	..	11.5	..	23.1	77.3	..	–1.7	..	3.8	4
90	*Iran, Islamic Rep.*	–6.1	8.6	23.6	54.4	37.2	..	..	..	..	23.4	–2.8	..	9.2	..	33
91	*Turkmenistan*	..	..	..	..	..	..	..	..	..	58.6	..	18.0	..	..	1
Upper-middle-income																..
92	Brazil	..	..	916.8	9.6	..	115.0	5,175.0	..	..	900.3	–5.6	–0.2	2.3	8.5	26
93	South Africa	4.6	–7.7	21.7	30.8	50.4	5.5	11.1	9.5	15.6	14.3	4.9	–0.2	3.7	1.3	..
94	Mauritius	–1.9	4.1	21.0	40.0	70.1	9.2	11.0	12.2	18.9	8.8	–11.1	–6.8	1.9	3.9	35
95	Czech Republic	..	3.4	..	..	74.1	..	7.1	..	13.1	11.8	..	–0.0	..	4.2	28
96	Malaysia	7.4	8.9	14.8	46.1	83.9	6.2	..	7.8	7.6	3.1	1.0	–6.6	4.7	4.5	33
97	Chile	6.9	4.9	26.2	21.0	34.9	37.7	15.1	47.1	20.3	18.5	–7.8	–2.4	5.9	10.3	41
98	Trinidad and Tobago	25.4	..	3.8	27.1	39.3	6.6	6.9	10.0	16.0	6.5	5.9	5.6	11.3	2.3	47
99	Hungary	4.9	..	18.2	..	43.4	3.0	20.3	..	27.4	19.4	–2.2	–9.4	..	5.1	66
100	Gabon	..	..	..	15.3	13.0	7.5	8.1	12.5	17.5	3.3	8.8	..	0.7	0.9	110
101	Mexico	3.9	..	49.3	25.2	30.2	20.6	13.3	28.1	..	40.0	–5.4	–8.1	1.5	1.0	32
102	Uruguay	2.2	–0.3	75.5	31.2	34.0	50.3	37.0	66.6	95.1	73.8	–7.7	–2.8	..	5.0	31
103	Oman	8.9	–6.0	5.6	13.8	30.4	..	4.3	..	8.6	0.1	15.4	–10.4	3.2	2.2	28
104	Slovenia	..	..	..	..	29.2	..	27.9	..	39.4	..	..	3.9	..	2.2	15
105	Saudi Arabia	..	..	5.3	13.8	52.4	..	..	..	..	2.8	30.2	–10.9	5.0	2.1	..
106	Greece	–0.4	–14.3	15.1	50.5	53.2	14.5	18.9	21.2	27.4	15.5	–5.5	–6.3	3.7	8.2	..
107	Argentina	..	..	311.1	19.0	16.1	79.6	8.1	..	10.1	317.2	–6.3	–3.6	7.0	6.1	25
108	Korea, Rep.	2.9	4.9	18.8	29.0	40.6	19.5	8.5	18.0	8.5	6.8	–9.5	–1.1	1.3	2.6	14
Low- and middle-income																30 w
Sub-Saharan Africa																50 w
East Asia and Pacific																28 w
South Asia																26 w
Europe and Central Asia																25 w
Middle East and N. Africa																32 w
Latin America and Caribbean																39 w
High-income economies																..
109	Portugal	–2.8	–2.1	16.5	69.9	77.1	19.0	8.4	18.8	15.0	12.0	–3.8	–1.9	..	8.8	..
110	New Zealand	–1.7	1.5	21.0	..	75.7	11.0	6.4	12.6	9.7	4.6	–4.2	–3.1	0.6	2.4	..
111	Spain	0.4	–1.4	11.8	75.4	79.2	13.1	6.7	16.9	8.9	6.5	–2.4	–1.5	6.0	4.7	..
112	Ireland	–5.9	–2.1	11.3	43.5	49.6	12.0	0.3	16.0	6.1	2.0	–14.2	2.3	2.8	1.9	..
113	†Israel	–17.4	–1.6	22.0	19.9	38.4	..	12.2	176.9	17.4	18.0	–11.3	–8.4	3.6	2.4	..
114	Australia	0.6	–2.6	12.6	36.5	58.2	8.6	..	10.6	12.0	4.1	–2.2	–3.7	2.5	2.5	..
115	United Kingdom	–1.2	–4.9	16.3	29.8	..	14.1	3.4	16.2	5.5	5.4	1.5	0.4	2.0	1.5	..
116	Finland	2.0	–11.0	7.2	39.8	58.5	9.0	3.3	9.8	7.9	4.2	–3.1	1.0	1.6	3.9	..
117	Italy	–6.3	–8.5	7.9	70.9	..	12.7	4.8	19.0	11.2	6.2	–2.2	2.5	6.4	2.7	..
118	†Kuwait	60.3	..	2.9	33.1	80.2	9.2	7.1	9.2	7.9	..	48.0	15.4	6.2	4.4	..
119	Canada	–2.4	..	9.2	45.1	58.3	12.9	5.6	14.3	6.9	3.1	–0.7	–3.3	2.3	0.8	..
120	†Hong Kong	..	..	..	60.7	..	..	..	..	..	9.0	–4.4	..	..	..	..
121	Netherlands	1.2	–2.2	5.8	67.1	84.2	6.0	3.0	13.5	8.3	1.6	–0.5	3.8	4.6	3.1	..
122	†Singapore	10.1	13.7	14.9	57.7	83.6	9.4	3.0	11.7	5.9	3.9	–10.2	3.5	2.2	..	..
123	Belgium	–3.0	–3.9	5.5	45.0	..	7.7	4.9	18.0	9.4	3.2	–2.9	7.0	3.6	1.2	..
124	France	2.2	–4.2	3.2	71.7	61.4	7.3	4.6	12.5	7.9	2.9	–0.2	1.8	5.3	1.7	..
125	Sweden	–2.6	–11.7	..	54.0	47.5	11.2	4.9	15.2	10.6	5.8	–2.8	1.2	2.0	3.8	..
126	Austria	0.6	–1.6	7.2	72.6	89.3	5.0	2.3	..	..	3.2	–5.5	–0.8	6.4	3.4	..
127	Germany	..	–0.3	8.3	..	62.5	7.9	4.5	12.0	11.5	..	..	0.3	5.5	2.5	..
128	United States	–0.4	–2.2	4.4	58.7	60.5	13.1d	4.6d	15.3	7.1	3.3	0.3	–2.1	6.2	2.0	..
129	Norway	4.5	–1.4	6.3	51.6	63.6	5.0	5.2	12.6	8.4	3.0	2.2	4.2	3.0	5.1	..
130	Denmark	–1.2	–4.7	4.7	42.6	61.5	10.8	3.8	17.2	8.3	2.9	–4.5	4.1	1.9	2.0	..
131	Japan	–3.2	..	6.4	83.4	112.1	5.5	1.7	8.3	4.1	1.3	–0.4	3.0	2.9	3.5	..
132	Switzerland	0.7	..	4.7	..	120.7	8.8	3.6	5.6	5.5	3.7	0.2	6.9	..	7.7	..
133	†*United Arab Emirates*	–10.5c	–8.9c	4.3	19.0	..	9.5	..	12.1	..	..	..	..	..	..	..
World																..

a. Refers to current budget balance excluding grants. b. Includes Eritrea. c. Data are for budgetary accounts only. d. Certificate of deposit rate.

Table 3. External economic indicators

		Terms of trade (1987=100)		Export concentration index		Aggregate net resource flows (% of GNP)		Net private capital flows (millions $)		Official development assistance (% of GNP)	
		1985	1994	1984	1992	1980	1994	1980	1994	1980	1994
	Low-income economies	90 m	..							2.1 w	2.7 w
	Excluding China and India	89 m	..							4.3 w	7.0 w
1	Rwanda	136	75	0.811	0.505	9.3	106.1	14	1	13.3	123.4
2	Mozambique	113	124	0.274	..	3.8	73.8	0	32	8.4	100.1
3	Ethiopia	119a	74	0.622a	0.557	8.2	18.2	26	−12	4.7	22.9
4	Tanzania	126	83	0.359	0.248	16.4	22.7	100	12	12.4	30.3
5	Burundi	133	52	0.776	..	8.1	28.1	−3	−1	12.8	32.2
6	Sierra Leone	109	89	0.391	0.586	5.5	21.5	−7	38	8.5	21.4
7	Malawi	99	87	0.530	0.704	15.7	24.3	30	−1	12.6	37.0
8	Chad	99	103	0.617	..	3.4	19.4	0	7	4.9	24.1
9	Uganda	149	58	0.932	0.561	9.7	12.9	54	−11	9.0	18.3
10	Madagascar	124	82	0.466	0.285	8.7	12.2	131	2	5.8	16.0
11	Nepal	98	85	0.237	0.519	6.5	8.0	0	−3	8.3	10.8
12	Vietnam	..	..	..	0.308	..	6.5	0	272	..	5.2
13	Bangladesh	126	94	0.326	0.246	13.5	5.9	11	47	9.9	6.9
14	Haiti	89	52	0.201	0.266	5.2	37.2	20	2	7.3	37.8
15	Niger	91	101	0.738	..	12.9	19.2	199	−22	6.8	25.5
16	Guinea-Bissau	91	92	0.557	..	98.4	29.3	18	1	56.6	74.2
17	Kenya	124	80	0.340	0.305	8.8	1.6	301	−272	5.6	10.2
18	Mali	100	103	0.578	..	12.1	16.5	10	44	16.6	22.0
19	Nigeria	167	86	0.943	0.934	0.9	5.7	694	1,885	0.0	0.6
20	Yemen, Rep.	131	84	0.663	..	..	..	97	12	..	..
21	Burkina Faso	103	103	0.541	0.623	8.4	15.9	4	1	12.5	22.3
22	Mongolia	..	..	..	..	0.0	14.4	0	−12	0.0	22.5
23	India	92	100	0.183	0.140	1.4	2.4	868	5,497	1.3	0.8
24	Lao PDR	..	..	0.345	..	..	13.0	0	60	..	13.4
25	Togo	139	90	0.461	0.491	12.7	11.3	83	0	8.3	12.2
26	Gambia, The	137	111	0.520	..	35.0	13.9	21	6	24.4	20.9
27	Nicaragua	111	95	0.454	0.289	13.8	27.4	−26	36	10.9	41.6
28	Zambia	89	85	0.844	0.787	14.6	14.8	175	−4	8.9	22.3
29	Tajikistan	..	..	..	..	..	11.5	0	10	..	3.2
30	Benin	111	110	0.428	..	7.2	12.9	4	5	6.4	15.7
31	Central African Republic	109	91	0.452	..	10.7	16.0	4	4	13.9	19.9
32	Albania	..	..	..	..	..	9.1	0	45	..	7.8
33	Ghana	93	64	0.544	0.465	4.1	24.2	−26	838	4.3	11.1
34	Pakistan	112	101	0.207	0.228	5.4	6.4	230	1,657	5.1	2.5
35	Mauritania	110	106	0.622	0.605	29.4	20.5	27	2	26.2	25.9
36	Azerbaijan	..	..	..	..	..	3.7	0	0	..	4.0
37	Zimbabwe	100	84	0.295	0.329	4.2	6.7	22	−70	3.1	10.1
38	Guinea	120	91	0.952	..	..	9.6	80	21	..	10.8
39	China	109	105	..	0.076	1.0	9.6	1,731	46,555	0.0	0.6
40	Honduras	118	73	0.401	0.457	11.7	14.7	136	66	4.2	9.8
41	Senegal	107	107	0.311	0.258	9.0	13.8	18	−9	9.0	17.4
42	Côte d'Ivoire	109	81	0.318	0.368	11.7	28.0	936	30	2.2	26.2
43	Congo	150	93	0.796	0.636	35.5	9.1	440	−130	6.0	31.2
44	Kyrgyz Republic	..	..	..	..	..	5.9	0	10	..	5.8
45	Sri Lanka	106	88	0.456	0.232	10.6	5.7	129	213	9.8	4.6
46	Armenia	..	..	..	..	..	7.0	0	0	..	6.9
47	Cameroon	113	79	0.479	..	9.6	9.5	409	59	3.9	10.7
48	Egypt, Arab Rep.	147	95	0.475	0.361	14.2	6.2	1,131	1,006	6.5	6.4
49	Lesotho	..	..	..	..	10.5	7.3	7	14	14.9	8.3
50	*Georgia*	..	..	..	..	..	9.0	0	10	..	8.4
51	*Myanmar*	128	107	..	0.282	4.7	0.2	29	34	5.4	0.2
	Middle-income economies	90 m	..							0.6 w	0.5 w
	Lower-middle-income	88 m	..							1.3 w	1.1 w
52	Bolivia	130	69	0.540	0.318	14.1	9.0	203	−5	5.9	10.3
53	Macedonia, FYR	..	..	..	..	..	−2.4	0	−15	..	..
54	Moldova	..	..	..	..	..	5.1	0	23	..	1.4
55	Indonesia	145	79	0.499	0.194	2.5	5.4	987	7,408	1.3	1.0
56	Philippines	99	114	0.298	0.293	3.9	6.9	840	4,107	0.9	1.6
57	Uzbekistan	..	..	..	..	..	0.2	0	52	..	0.1
58	Morocco	99	107	0.284	0.160	7.4	3.9	550	877	4.9	2.1
59	Kazakstan	..	..	..	..	..	4.4	0	394	..	0.3
60	Guatemala	114	93	0.310	0.219	2.8	1.9	91	84	0.9	1.7
61	Papua New Guinea	94	90	0.495	0.465	16.8	−0.5	105	−231	13.1	6.5
62	Bulgaria	..	..	..	..	1.7	0.1	0	−376	0.0	1.6
63	Romania	66	111	..	..	..	4.3	1,360	787	..	0.5
64	Ecuador	143	82	0.616	0.467	7.4	5.3	594	705	0.4	1.4
65	Dominican Republic	115	144	0.430	0.383	7.1	1.0	132	113	1.9	0.7
66	Lithuania	..	..	..	..	..	1.8	0	13	..	1.4
67	El Salvador	122	89	0.557	0.238	3.2	1.9	−17	−40	2.8	3.9
68	Jordan	127	118	0.335	0.331	..	4.4	28	−159	..	6.4
69	Jamaica	89	105	0.462	0.406	12.3	1.9	9	123	5.1	2.9
70	Paraguay	110	101	0.468	0.362	3.6	2.3	120	135	0.7	1.3
71	Algeria	173	83	0.534	0.546	3.1	3.4	896	424	0.4	1.0
72	Colombia	124	71	0.505	0.238	2.9	2.3	688	1,860	0.3	0.2

Note: For data comparability and coverage, see the technical notes. Figures in italics are for years other than those specified.

		Terms of trade (1987=100)		Export concentration index		Aggregate net resource flows (% of GNP)		Net private capital flows (millions $)		Official development assistance (% of GNP)	
		1985	1994	1984	1992	1980	1994	1980	1994	1980	1994
73	Tunisia	123	93	0.414	0.209	7.2	2.8	336	80	2.7	0.7
74	Ukraine	..	..	..	..	..	0.9	0	424	..	0.4
75	Namibia	..	..	..	..	..	..	..	..	0.0	5.9
76	Peru	111	86	0.247	0.260	1.8	7.7	−67	3,214	1.0	0.9
77	Belarus	..	..	..	..	..	1.6	0	105	..	0.6
78	Slovak Republic	..	..	..	..	0.0	6.6	0	577	0.0	0.6
79	Latvia	..	..	..	..	..	5.2	0	222	..	0.9
80	Costa Rica	111	92	0.352	0.303	9.2	0.3	248	29	1.4	0.9
81	Poland	95	109	..	..	5.5	3.8	10	1,244	0.0	2.0
82	Thailand	103	105	0.182	0.090	6.5	3.3	1,465	4,138	1.3	0.4
83	Turkey	82	109	0.159	0.119	3.7	1.0	660	1,530	1.7	0.1
84	Croatia	..	..	..	0.108	..	0.3	0	96	..	..
85	Panama	104	86	0.343	0.422	4.1	8.4	65	633	1.3	0.6
86	Russian Federation	..	..	..	..	..	0.8	0	658	..	0.5
87	Venezuela	166	82	0.652	0.555	2.6	0.9	1,825	70	0.0	0.1
88	Botswana	97	152	..	..	20.3	−0.5	114	−50	11.8	2.2
89	Estonia	..	..	..	..	..	5.5	0	211	..	0.9
90	*Iran, Islamic Rep.*	176	90	0.965	0.880	−0.3	−2.1	−178	−1,579	0.0	0.2
91	*Turkmenistan*	..	..	..	..	..	1.0	0	13	..	0.1
	Upper-middle-income	**93 m**	..							**0.1 w**	**0.2 w**
92	Brazil	101	101	0.126	0.089	2.8	1.8	5,655	11,871	0.0	0.1
93	South Africa	101	102	0.457	0.378	..	..	..	..	..	..
94	Mauritius	77	121	0.656	0.332	8.3	3.5	49	124	2.9	0.4
95	Czech Republic	..	..	..	..	0.0	7.8	0	2,642	0.0	0.4
96	Malaysia	114	92	0.276	0.156	8.7	10.2	1,913	6,661	0.6	0.1
97	Chile	91	94	0.324	0.308	8.7	8.2	2,447	4,300	0.0	0.3
98	Trinidad and Tobago	138	86	0.546	0.422	6.3	8.9	258	343	0.1	0.5
99	Hungary	103	99	..	..	3.3	7.3	596	2,717	0.0	0.5
100	Gabon	154	90	0.790	0.743	−1.9	2.5	−93	−128	1.4	5.6
101	Mexico	145	92	0.534	0.153	4.8	4.6	8,182	17,394	0.0	0.1
102	Uruguay	91	112	0.239	0.176	5.3	3.3	479	378	0.1	0.6
103	Oman	182	77	0.435	0.824	3.3	4.5	34	395	3.1	0.9
104	Slovenia	..	..	..	0.083	..	2.4	0	368	..	..
105	Saudi Arabia	175	92	0.887	0.776	..	..	..	..	0.0	0.0
106	Greece	96	99	0.127	0.118	..	..	..	..	0.1	0.1
107	Argentina	123	120	0.194	0.153	4.6	3.2	3,476	8,214	0.0	0.1
108	Korea, Rep.	94	102	0.193	0.109	4.0	2.1	1,782	8,132	0.2	0.0
	Low- and middle-income	**90 m**	..							**1.1 w**	**1.1 w**
	Sub-Saharan Africa	**92 m**	..							**3.4 w**	**12.4 w**
	East Asia and Pacific	**87 m**	..							**0.7 w**	**0.8 w**
	South Asia	**91 m**	..							**2.4 w**	**1.4 w**
	Europe and Central Asia	**97 m**	..							**1.0 w**	**0.3 w**
	Middle East and N. Africa	**83 m**	..							**1.1 w**	**1.6 w**
	Latin America and Caribbean	**84 m**	..							**0.3 w**	**0.3 w**
	High-income economies	**100 m**	..							..	..
109	Portugal	87	104	0.144	0.106					..	..
110	New Zealand	90	108	0.212	0.174					..	..
111	Spain	82	112	0.120	0.142					..	..
112	Ireland	96	92	0.161	0.125					..	..
113	† Israel	99	113	0.208	0.256					4.1	1.9
114	Australia	110	98	0.180	0.196					..	..
115	United Kingdom	104	105	0.152	0.063					..	..
116	Finland	88	94	0.210	0.230					..	..
117	Italy	84	104	0.100	0.056					..	..
118	† Kuwait	165	88	0.570	0.742					0.0	0.0
119	Canada	99	97	0.225	0.125					..	..
120	† Hong Kong	118	87	0.310	0.152					0.0	0.0
121	Netherlands	101	101	0.137	0.061					..	..
122	† Singapore	108	91	0.238	0.183					0.1	0.0
123	Belgium[b]	93	101	0.115	0.106					..	..
124	France	89	106	0.085	0.064					..	..
125	Sweden	92	105	0.151	0.110					..	..
126	Austria	92	93	0.078	0.061					..	..
127	Germany[c]	84	97	0.136	0.084					..	..
128	United States	101	101	0.110	0.080					..	..
129	Norway	141	97	0.345	0.366					..	..
130	Denmark	91	102	0.087	0.077					..	..
131	Japan	73	128	0.209	0.140					..	..
132	Switzerland	85	64	0.119	0.102					..	..
133	† *United Arab Emirates*	181	93	0.801	0.691					0.0	0.0
	World	**93 m**	..							..	..

a. Includes Eritrea. b. Includes Luxembourg. c. Data prior to 1990 refer to the Federal Republic of Germany before unification.

Table 4. Population and labor force

		Population						Labor force								
		Total (millions)		Avg. annual growth rate (%)		Age 15–64 (millions)		Total[a] (millions)		Avg. annual growth rate (%)		Female (%)		Agriculture (%)		Industry (%)
		1980	1994	1980–90	1990–94	1980	1994	1980	1994	1980–90	1990–94	1980	1994	1980	1990	1980	1990
	Low-income economies	2,412 t	3,182 t	2.1 w	1.8 w	1,357 t	1,925 t	1,165 t	1,575 t	2.3 w	1.9 w	41 w	42 w	73 w	69 w	13 w	15 w
	Excluding China and India	743 t	1,078 t	2.7 w	2.5 w	374 t	575 t	327 t	474 t	2.7 w	2.6 w	42 w	43 w	72 w	66 w	10 w	12 w
1	Rwanda	5	8	3.0	2.6	3	4	3	4	3.2	2.9	49	49	93	92	3	3
2	Mozambique	12	15	1.6	2.2	6	9	7	8	1.2	2.7	49	50	84	83	7	8
3	Ethiopia	38	55	3.1	1.7	19	27	16	23	2.5	2.8	41	40	89	86	2	2
4	Tanzania	19	29	3.2	3.0	9	15	10	15	3.3	2.8	50	49	86	84	4	5
5	Burundi	4	6	2.9	3.0	2	3	2	3	2.7	2.9	50	49	93	92	2	3
6	Sierra Leone	3	4	2.1	2.4	2	2	1	2	1.8	2.3	36	36	70	68	14	15
7	Malawi	6	10	3.3	2.8	3	5	3	5	3.9	2.4	51	54	87	87	5	5
8	Chad	4	6	2.4	2.5	2	3	2	3	1.9	2.7	43	44	88	83	3	4
9	Uganda	13	19	2.4	3.2	7	9	7	10	2.9	2.9	49	52	87	85	4	5
10	Madagascar	9	13	2.9	2.9	5	7	4	7	2.9	3.2	47	49	82	78	6	7
11	Nepal	15	21	2.6	2.5	8	11	7	10	2.4	2.5	39	40	94	94	1	0
12	Vietnam	54	72	2.1	2.1	28	41	26	37	2.8	2.1	48	50	73	71	13	14
13	Bangladesh	87	118	2.4	1.7	44	62	42	59	2.4	2.7	43	42	73	65	9	16
14	Haiti	5	7	1.9	1.9	3	4	3	3	1.3	1.9	45	43	71	68	8	9
15	Niger	6	9	3.3	3.2	3	4	3	4	3.0	3.0	45	45	91	90	3	4
16	Guinea-Bissau	1	1	1.8	2.0	0	1	0	1	1.5	1.9	39	41	87	85	2	2
17	Kenya	17	26	3.4	2.7	8	13	8	13	3.7	3.4	46	48	82	80	6	7
18	Mali	7	10	2.5	3.0	3	5	4	5	2.7	2.8	49	51	89	86	2	2
19	Nigeria	71	108	3.0	2.9	36	56	30	43	2.5	2.8	37	36	54	43	8	7
20	Yemen, Rep.	9	15	3.3	5.5	..	7	2	4	3.6	4.8	31	26	73	61	13	17
21	Burkina Faso	7	10	2.6	2.9	4	5	4	5	2.0	2.0	48	46	92	92	3	2
22	Mongolia	2	2	2.8	1.9	1	1	1	1	2.9	2.8	46	46	40	32	21	22
23	India	687	914	2.1	1.8	396	550	300	394	1.9	2.1	34	32	70	64	13	16
24	Lao PDR	3	5	2.7	3.1	2	2	2	2	2.3	2.6	45	47	80	78	6	6
25	Togo	3	4	3.0	3.2	1	2	1	2	2.6	3.0	39	40	69	66	10	10
26	Gambia, The	1	1	3.6	3.9	0	1	0	1	3.4	3.4	45	44	84	82	7	8
27	Nicaragua	3	4	2.7	3.1	1	2	1	2	2.7	4.5	28	36	39	28	24	26
28	Zambia	6	9	3.5	3.0	3	5	2	4	3.5	3.0	45	44	76	75	8	8
29	Tajikistan	4	6	2.9	2.0	..	3	2	2	2.0	3.3	47	44	45	41	23	23
30	Benin	3	5	3.1	2.9	2	3	2	2	2.5	2.7	47	47	67	63	7	8
31	Central African Republic	2	3	2.4	2.5	1	2	1	2	1.7	2.1	48	47	85	80	3	3
32	Albania	3	3	2.1	–0.6	2	2	1	2	2.6	1.4	39	43	57	55	23	23
33	Ghana	11	17	3.3	2.8	6	9	5	8	3.2	3.0	51	51	62	59	13	13
34	Pakistan	83	126	3.1	2.9	45	67	30	49	3.4	3.3	23	28	60	52	15	19
35	Mauritania	2	2	2.6	2.5	1	1	1	1	2.0	2.7	45	44	72	55	7	10
36	Azerbaijan	6	7	1.5	1.0	..	5	3	3	1.0	1.8	47	44	35	31	28	29
37	Zimbabwe	7	11	3.3	2.5	4	6	3	5	3.6	2.4	45	45	72	68	12	8
38	Guinea	4	6	2.5	2.8	2	3	2	3	2.1	2.7	47	48	91	87	1	2
39	China	981	1,191	1.5	1.2	587	800	548	715	2.2	1.1	44	46	74	72	14	15
40	Honduras	4	6	3.3	3.0	2	3	1	2	3.4	3.7	25	28	57	41	15	20
41	Senegal	6	8	2.9	2.7	3	4	3	4	2.5	2.6	42	42	81	77	6	8
42	Côte d'Ivoire	8	14	3.8	3.6	4	7	3	5	3.1	2.9	32	33	65	60	8	10
43	Congo	2	3	3.1	3.1	1	1	1	1	2.9	2.7	43	42	58	49	13	15
44	Kyrgyz Republic	4	4	1.9	0.4	..	3	2	2	1.5	2.0	47	48	34	32	29	27
45	Sri Lanka	15	18	1.4	1.3	9	11	5	7	2.4	2.0	27	35	52	48	18	21
46	Armenia	3	4	1.4	1.4	..	2	1	2	1.1	1.4	48	45	21	18	43	43
47	Cameroon	9	13	2.8	3.0	5	7	4	5	2.5	2.9	37	37	73	70	8	9
48	Egypt, Arab Rep.	41	57	2.5	2.0	23	33	15	22	2.5	2.9	28	30	57	40	16	22
49	Lesotho	1	2	2.8	2.3	1	1	1	1	2.5	2.9	38	38	41	40	34	28
50	*Georgia*	5	5	0.7	–0.2	..	4	3	3	0.4	0.2	49	47	32	26	27	31
51	*Myanmar*	34	46	2.1	2.2	19	27	17	23	2.2	2.1	44	43	76	73	8	10
	Middle-income economies	1,240 t	1,570 t	1.8 w	1.5 w	545 t	966 t	517 t	685 t	2.1 w	1.9 w	39 w	41 w	38 w	31 w	27 w	27 w
	Lower-middle-income	874 t	1,097 t	1.7 w	1.4 w	340 t	674 t	377 t	486 t	1.8 w	1.8 w	42 w	43 w	41 w	36 w	26 w	27 w
52	Bolivia	5	7	2.0	2.4	3	4	2	3	2.6	2.6	33	37	53	47	18	18
53	Macedonia, FYR	2	2	0.7	0.9	..	1	1	1	1.8	1.4	34	41	36	21	33	40
54	Moldova	4	4	0.9	–0.1	..	3	2	2	0.1	0.5	50	49	43	33	26	30
55	Indonesia	148	190	1.8	1.6	84	117	60	89	3.0	2.5	36	40	58	55	12	14
56	Philippines	48	67	2.4	2.2	26	38	19	27	2.6	2.6	35	36	52	46	15	15
57	Uzbekistan	16	22	2.5	2.2	..	12	6	9	2.2	2.9	48	46	38	34	25	25
58	Morocco	19	26	2.3	2.0	10	16	7	10	2.7	2.6	34	35	56	45	20	25
59	Kazakstan	15	17	1.2	0.1	..	10	7	8	1.1	0.9	48	47	24	22	32	32
60	Guatemala	7	10	2.8	2.9	4	5	2	4	2.9	3.5	22	25	54	52	19	17
61	Papua New Guinea	3	4	2.2	2.2	2	2	2	2	2.1	2.3	42	42	82	79	6	7
62	Bulgaria	9	8	–0.2	–0.8	6	6	5	4	0.0	–0.5	45	50	20	13	45	48
63	Romania	22	23	0.4	–0.5	14	15	11	11	–0.2	0.1	46	45	35	24	41	47
64	Ecuador	8	11	2.5	2.2	4	7	3	4	3.5	3.1	20	26	40	33	20	19
65	Dominican Republic	6	8	2.2	1.7	3	5	2	3	3.1	2.7	25	29	32	25	24	29
66	Lithuania	3	4	0.9	0.0	..	2	2	2	0.6	–0.1	50	48	28	18	38	41
67	El Salvador	5	6	1.3	2.1	2	3	2	2	2.1	3.3	27	33	43	36	19	21
68	Jordan	2	4	3.7	6.0	1	2	1	1	4.9	5.2	20	25	18	15	24	23
69	Jamaica	2	2	1.2	0.9	1	2	1	1	1.9	1.6	46	45	31	25	16	23
70	Paraguay	3	5	3.1	2.8	2	3	1	2	3.1	3.0	26	28	45	39	20	22
71	Algeria	19	27	2.9	2.3	9	16	5	8	3.7	4.2	22	23	36	26	27	31
72	Colombia	28	36	1.9	1.9	15	23	9	15	4.0	2.6	25	35	40	27	21	23

Note: For data comparability and coverage, see the key and technical notes.

		Population						Labor force									
		Total (millions)		Avg. annual growth rate (%)		Age 15–64 (millions)		Total[a] (millions)		Avg. annual growth rate (%)		Female (%)		Agriculture (%)		Industry (%)	
		1980	1994	1980–90	1990–94	1980	1994	1980	1994	1980–90	1990–94	1980	1994	1980	1990	1980	1990
73	Tunisia	6	9	2.5	1.9	3	5	2	3	2.6	3.0	29	30	39	28	30	33
74	Ukraine	50	52	0.4	0.0	..	34	26	26	−0.2	−0.1	50	48	25	20	39	40
75	Namibia	1	2	2.7	2.8	1	1	0	1	2.3	2.6	40	40	56	49	15	15
76	Peru	17	23	2.2	1.9	9	14	5	8	3.2	3.0	24	28	40	36	18	18
77	Belarus	10	10	0.6	0.2	..	7	5	5	0.4	−0.1	50	48	26	20	38	40
78	Slovak Republic	5	5	0.6	0.3	..	4	2	3	0.9	0.9	45	48	14	12	36	32
79	Latvia	3	3	0.5	−1.2	..	2	1	1	0.2	−0.8	51	51	16	16	42	40
80	Costa Rica	2	3	2.8	2.1	1	2	1	1	3.8	2.8	21	29	35	26	23	27
81	Poland	36	39	0.7	0.3	23	25	19	19	0.1	0.5	45	46	30	27	38	36
82	Thailand	47	58	1.8	1.0	26	39	24	34	2.6	1.5	47	47	71	64	10	14
83	Turkey	44	61	2.3	2.0	25	37	19	28	2.9	2.3	35	35	60	53	16	18
84	Croatia	5	5	0.4	0.0	..	3	2	2	0.2	−0.1	38	41	25	16	33	34
85	Panama	2	3	2.1	1.9	1	2	1	1	3.1	2.6	30	33	29	26	19	16
86	Russian Federation	139	148	0.6	0.0	..	99	76	77	0.2	0.0	49	48	16	14	44	42
87	Venezuela	15	21	2.6	2.3	8	13	5	8	3.4	3.1	27	33	15	12	28	27
88	Botswana	1	1	3.5	3.1	0	1	0	1	3.4	3.2	50	46	63	46	10	20
89	Estonia	1	1	0.6	−1.2	..	1	1	1	0.4	−0.4	51	51	15	14	43	41
90	*Iran, Islamic Rep.*	39	63	3.5	2.9	20	32	12	20	3.8	3.2	20	24	46	39	24	23
91	*Turkmenistan*	3	4	2.5	4.6	..	2	1	2	2.3	2.8	47	41	39	37	24	23
Upper-middle-income		366 t	473 t	1.9 w	1.7 w	206 t	293 t	140 t	199 t	2.7 w	2.2 w	32 w	36	31 w	21 w	28 w	27 w
92	Brazil	121	159	2.0	1.7	71	99	48	71	3.2	1.9	28	34	37	23	24	23
93	South Africa	29	41	2.4	2.2	17	24	11	16	2.7	2.5	35	37	17	14	35	32
94	Mauritius	1	1	0.9	1.3	1	1	0	0	2.3	1.6	26	31	27	17	28	43
95	Czech Republic	10	10	0.1	−0.1	..	7	5	6	0.1	0.5	47	47	13	11	56	45
96	Malaysia	14	20	2.6	2.4	8	11	5	8	2.8	2.7	34	36	41	27	19	23
97	Chile	11	14	1.7	1.5	7	9	4	5	2.7	2.2	26	31	21	19	25	25
98	Trinidad and Tobago	1	1	1.3	1.2	1	1	0	1	1.2	2.1	32	36	11	11	39	31
99	Hungary	11	10	−0.3	−0.3	7	7	5	5	−0.8	−0.1	43	44	18	15	43	38
100	Gabon	1	1	3.5	3.2	0	1	0	1	2.6	1.9	45	44	65	51	12	16
101	Mexico	67	89	2.0	2.0	35	53	22	35	3.5	2.9	27	32	36	28	29	24
102	Uruguay	3	3	0.6	0.6	2	2	1	1	1.6	1.0	31	40	17	14	28	27
103	Oman	1	2	4.6	4.5	1	1	0	1	4.1	4.0	7	13	50	44	22	24
104	Slovenia	2	2	0.5	−0.1	..	1	1	1	0.3	0.3	44	45	15	6	43	46
105	Saudi Arabia	9	18	5.2	3.2	5	10	3	6	6.5	2.5	8	12	43	19	16	20
106	Greece	10	10	0.5	0.6	6	7	4	4	1.2	0.7	28	36	31	23	29	27
107	Argentina	28	34	1.5	1.2	17	21	11	13	1.3	2.0	28	30	13	12	34	32
108	Korea, Rep.	38	44	1.2	1.0	24	31	16	21	2.3	1.9	39	40	37	18	27	35
Low- and middle-income		3,652 t	4,752 t	2.0 w	1.7 w	1,902 t	2,892 t	1,682 t	2,259 t	2.2 w	1.9 w	41 w	42 w	62 w	58 w	17 w	18 w
Sub-Saharan Africa		380 t	572 t	3.0 w	2.7 w	197 t	296 t	171 t	251 t	2.8 w	2.7 w	43 w	44 w	72 w	68 w	9 w	9 w
East Asia and Pacific		1,398 t	1,735 t	1.6 w	1.4 w	822 t	1,134 t	719 t	967 t	2.3 w	1.5 w	43 w	45 w	72 w	69 w	14 w	16 w
South Asia		903 t	1,220 t	2.2 w	1.9 w	511 t	715 t	389 t	525 t	2.1 w	2.3 w	35 w	33 w	70 w	64 w	13 w	16 w
Europe and Central Asia		437 t	487 t	0.9 w	0.4 w	83 t	315 t	219 t	238 t	0.6 w	0.6 w	47 w	46 w	27 w	23 w	37 w	37 w
Middle East and N. Africa		175 t	267 t	3.1 w	2.8 w	87 t	146 t	53 t	85 t	3.2 w	3.6 w	26 w	28 w	49 w	37 w	21 w	24 w
Latin America and Caribbean		359 t	471 t	2.0 w	1.8 w	202 t	286 t	130 t	194 t	3.0 w	2.5 w	28 w	33 w	34 w	26 w	25 w	24 w
High-income economies		776 t	850 t	0.6 w	0.7 w	497 t	569 t	352 t	408 t	1.1 w	0.9 w	39 w	43 w	7 w	5 w	35 w	31 w
109	Portugal	10	10	0.1	0.0	6	7	5	5	0.4	0.4	39	43	26	18	36	34
110	New Zealand	3	3	0.8	0.9	2	2	1	2	2.0	1.5	34	44	11	10	33	25
111	Spain	37	39	0.4	0.2	24	27	14	17	1.3	1.0	28	36	18	12	37	33
112	Ireland	3	4	0.3	0.5	2	2	1	1	0.4	1.5	28	33	19	14	34	29
113	† Israel	4	5	1.8	3.7	2	3	1	2	2.3	3.6	34	38	6	4	32	29
114	Australia	15	18	1.5	1.1	9	12	7	9	2.3	1.6	36	42	6	6	32	26
115	United Kingdom	56	58	0.2	0.4	36	38	27	29	0.6	0.3	39	43	3	2	38	29
116	Finland	5	5	0.4	0.5	3	3	2	3	0.6	0.2	46	47	12	8	35	31
117	Italy	56	57	0.1	0.2	36	39	23	25	0.8	0.4	33	37	13	9	38	31
118	† Kuwait	1	2	4.4	−6.8	1	1	0	1	5.9	−2.3	13	33	2	1	32	25
119	Canada	25	29	1.2	1.3	17	20	12	15	1.9	1.1	40	44	7	3	33	25
120	† Hong Kong	5	6	1.2	1.5	3	4	2	3	1.6	0.8	34	36	1	1	50	37
121	Netherlands	14	15	0.6	0.7	9	11	6	7	2.0	0.7	31	39	6	5	31	26
122	† Singapore	2	3	1.7	2.0	2	2	1	1	1.7	1.0	37	37	2	0	42	36
123	Belgium	10	10	0.1	0.4	6	7	4	4	0.2	0.5	34	40	3	3	35	28
124	France	54	58	0.5	0.5	34	38	24	26	0.3	0.8	40	44	8	5	35	29
125	Sweden	8	9	0.3	0.6	5	6	4	5	1.0	0.3	44	47	..	..	..	..
126	Austria	8	8	0.2	1.0	5	5	3	4	0.5	0.5	40	40	10	8	41	38
127	Germany	78	82	0.1	0.6	52	56	37	40	0.6	0.2	40	41	7	4	45	38
128	United States	228	261	0.9	1.0	151	171	110	131	1.3	1.1	42	45	3	3	31	28
129	Norway	4	4	0.4	0.6	3	3	2	2	0.9	0.7	40	45	8	6	29	25
130	Denmark	5	5	0.0	0.3	3	4	3	3	0.7	−0.1	44	46	7	6	31	28
131	Japan	117	125	0.6	0.3	79	87	57	66	1.1	0.6	38	40	11	7	35	34
132	Switzerland	6	7	0.6	1.0	4	5	3	4	1.7	1.0	37	40	6	6	39	35
133	† *United Arab Emirates*	1	2	4.7	2.9	1	1	1	1	4.4	1.8	5	13	5	8	38	27
World		4,428 t	5,601 t	1.7 w	1.5 w	2,400 t	3,461 t	2,034 t	2,667 t	2.0 w	1.7 w	41 w	42	53 w	49 w	20 w	20 w

a. Participation rates from ILO are applied to population estimates to derive labor force estimates.

Table 5. Distribution of income or consumption

				Percentage share of income or consumption						
		Survey year	Gini index	Lowest 10%	Lowest 20%	Second quintile	Third quintile	Fourth quintile	Highest 20%	Highest 10%
Low-income economies										
Excluding China and India										
1	Rwanda	1983/85[a,b]	28.9	4.2	9.7	13.2	16.5	21.6	39.1	24.2
2	Mozambique		..	..	..	..	..	..	..	..
3	Ethiopia		..	..	..	..	..	..	..	..
4	Tanzania	1993[a,b]	38.1	2.9	6.9	10.9	15.3	21.5	45.4	30.2
5	Burundi		..	..	..	..	..	..	..	..
6	Sierra Leone		..	..	..	..	..	..	..	..
7	Malawi		..	..	..	..	..	..	..	..
8	Chad		..	..	..	..	..	..	..	..
9	Uganda	1992[a,b]	40.8	3.0	6.8	10.3	14.4	20.4	48.1	33.4
10	Madagascar	1993[a,b]	43.4	2.3	5.8	9.9	14.0	20.3	50.0	34.9
11	Nepal	1984/85[c,d]	30.1	4.0	9.1	12.9	16.7	21.8	39.5	25.0
12	Vietnam	1993[a,b]	35.7	3.5	7.8	11.4	15.4	21.4	44.0	29.0
13	Bangladesh	1992[a,b]	28.3	4.1	9.4	13.5	17.2	22.0	37.9	23.7
14	Haiti		..	..	..	..	..	..	..	..
15	Niger	1992[a,b]	36.1	3.0	7.5	11.8	15.5	21.1	44.1	29.3
16	Guinea-Bissau	1991[a,b]	56.2	0.5	2.1	6.5	12.0	20.6	58.9	42.4
17	Kenya	1992[a,b]	57.5	1.2	3.4	6.7	10.7	17.0	62.1	47.7
18	Mali		..	..	..	..	..	..	..	..
19	Nigeria	1992/93[a,b]	37.5	1.3	4.0	8.9	14.4	23.4	49.3	31.3
20	Yemen, Rep.		..	..	..	..	..	..	..	..
21	Burkina Faso		..	..	..	..	..	..	..	..
22	Mongolia		..	..	..	..	..	..	..	..
23	India	1992[a,b]	33.8	3.7	8.5	12.1	15.8	21.1	42.6	28.4
24	Lao PDR	1992[a,b]	30.4	4.2	9.6	12.9	16.3	21.0	40.2	26.4
25	Togo		..	..	..	..	..	..	..	..
26	Gambia, The		..	..	..	..	..	..	..	..
27	Nicaragua	1993[a,b]	50.3	1.6	4.2	8.0	12.6	20.0	55.2	39.8
28	Zambia	1993[a,b]	46.2	1.5	3.9	8.0	13.8	23.8	50.4	31.3
29	Tajikistan		..	..	..	..	..	..	..	..
30	Benin		..	..	..	..	..	..	..	..
31	Central African Republic		..	..	..	..	..	..	..	..
32	Albania		..	..	..	..	..	..	..	..
33	Ghana	1992[a,b]	33.9	3.4	7.9	12.0	16.1	21.8	42.2	27.3
34	Pakistan	1991[a,b]	31.2	3.4	8.4	12.9	16.9	22.2	39.7	25.2
35	Mauritania	1988[a,b]	42.4	0.7	3.6	10.6	16.2	23.0	46.5	30.4
36	Azerbaijan		..	..	..	..	..	..	..	..
37	Zimbabwe	1990[a,b]	56.8	1.8	4.0	6.3	10.0	17.4	62.3	46.9
38	Guinea	1991[a,b]	46.8	0.9	3.0	8.3	14.6	23.9	50.2	31.7
39	China	1992[c,d]	37.6	2.6	6.2	10.5	15.8	23.6	43.9	26.8
40	Honduras	1992[c,d]	52.7	1.5	3.8	7.4	12.0	19.4	57.4	41.9
41	Senegal	1991[a,b]	54.1	1.4	3.5	7.0	11.6	19.3	58.6	42.8
42	Côte d'Ivoire	1988[a,b]	36.9	2.8	6.8	11.2	15.8	22.2	44.1	28.5
43	Congo		..	..	..	..	..	..	..	..
44	Kyrgyz Republic		..	..	..	..	..	..	..	..
45	Sri Lanka	1990[a,b]	30.1	3.8	8.9	13.1	16.9	21.7	39.3	25.2
46	Armenia		..	..	..	..	..	..	..	..
47	Cameroon		..	..	..	..	..	..	..	..
48	Egypt, Arab Rep.	1991[a,b]	32.0	3.9	8.7	12.5	16.3	21.4	41.1	26.7
49	Lesotho	1986/87[a,b]	56.0	0.9	2.8	6.5	11.2	19.4	60.1	43.4
50	*Georgia*		..	..	..	..	..	..	..	..
51	*Myanmar*		..	..	..	..	..	..	..	..
Middle-income economies										
Lower-middle-income										
52	Bolivia	1990[c,d]	42.0	2.3	5.6	9.7	14.5	22.0	48.2	31.7
53	Macedonia, FYR		..	..	..	..	..	..	..	..
54	Moldova	1992[c,d]	34.4	2.7	6.9	11.9	16.7	23.1	41.5	25.8
55	Indonesia	1993[a,b]	31.7	3.9	8.7	12.3	16.3	22.1	40.7	25.6
56	Philippines	1988[a,b]	40.7	2.8	6.5	10.1	14.4	21.2	47.8	32.1
57	Uzbekistan		..	..	..	..	..	..	..	..
58	Morocco	1990/91[a,b]	39.2	2.8	6.6	10.5	15.0	21.7	46.3	30.5
59	Kazakstan	1993[c,d]	32.7	3.1	7.5	12.3	16.9	22.9	40.4	24.9
60	Guatemala	1989[c,d]	59.6	0.6	2.1	5.8	10.5	18.6	63.0	46.6
61	Papua New Guinea		..	..	..	..	..	..	..	..
62	Bulgaria	1992[c,d]	30.8	3.3	8.3	13.0	17.0	22.3	39.3	24.7
63	Romania	1992[c,d]	25.5	3.8	9.2	14.4	18.4	23.2	34.8	20.2
64	Ecuador	1994[a,b]	46.6	2.3	5.4	8.9	13.2	19.9	52.6	37.6
65	Dominican Republic	1989[c,d]	50.5	1.6	4.2	7.9	12.5	19.7	55.7	39.6
66	Lithuania	1993[c,d]	33.6	3.4	8.1	12.3	16.2	21.3	42.1	28.0
67	El Salvador		..	..	..	..	..	..	..	..
68	Jordan	1991[a,b]	43.4	2.4	5.9	9.8	13.9	20.3	50.1	34.7
69	Jamaica	1991[a,b]	41.1	2.4	5.8	10.2	14.9	21.6	47.5	31.9
70	Paraguay		..	..	..	..	..	..	..	..
71	Algeria	1988[a,b]	38.7	2.8	6.9	11.0	15.1	20.9	46.1	31.5
72	Colombia	1991[c,d]	51.3	1.3	3.6	7.6	12.6	20.4	55.8	39.5

Note: For data comparability and coverage, see the technical notes.

		Survey year	Gini index	Percentage share of income or consumption						
				Lowest 10%	Lowest 20%	Second quintile	Third quintile	Fourth quintile	Highest 20%	Highest 10%
73	Tunisia	1990a,b	40.2	2.3	5.9	10.4	15.3	22.1	46.3	30.7
74	Ukraine	1992c,d	25.7	4.1	9.5	14.1	18.1	22.9	35.4	20.8
75	Namibia		..	..	..	..	..	..	..	..
76	Peru	1994a,b	44.9	1.9	4.9	9.2	14.1	21.4	50.4	34.3
77	Belarus	1993c,d	21.6	4.9	11.1	15.3	18.5	22.2	32.9	19.4
78	Slovak Republic	1992c,d	19.5	5.1	11.9	15.8	18.8	22.2	31.4	18.2
79	Latvia	1993c,d	27.0	4.3	9.6	13.6	17.5	22.6	36.7	22.1
80	Costa Rica	1989c,d	46.1	1.2	4.0	9.1	14.3	21.9	50.7	34.1
81	Poland	1992a,b	27.2	4.0	9.3	13.8	17.7	22.6	36.6	22.1
82	Thailand	1992a,b	46.2	2.5	5.6	8.7	13.0	20.0	52.7	37.1
83	Turkey		..	..	..	..	..	..	..	..
84	Croatia		..	..	..	..	..	..	..	..
85	Panama	1989c,d	56.6	0.5	2.0	6.3	11.6	20.3	59.8	42.2
86	Russian Federation	1993a,b	49.6	1.2	3.7	8.5	13.5	20.4	53.8	38.7
87	Venezuela	1990c,d	53.8	1.4	3.6	7.1	11.7	19.3	58.4	42.7
88	Botswana		..	..	..	..	..	..	..	..
89	Estonia	1993c,d	39.5	2.4	6.6	10.7	15.1	21.4	46.3	31.3
90	Iran, Islamic Rep.		..	..	..	..	..	..	..	..
91	Turkmenistan	1993c,d	35.8	2.7	6.7	11.4	16.3	22.8	42.8	26.9
Upper-middle-income										
92	Brazil	1989c,d	63.4	0.7	2.1	4.9	8.9	16.8	67.5	51.3
93	South Africa	1993a,b	58.4	1.4	3.3	5.8	9.8	17.7	63.3	47.3
94	Mauritius		..	..	..	..	..	..	..	..
95	Czech Republic	1993c,d	26.6	4.6	10.5	13.9	16.9	21.3	37.4	23.5
96	Malaysia	1989c,d	48.4	1.9	4.6	8.3	13.0	20.4	53.7	37.9
97	Chile	1994c,d	56.5	1.4	3.5	6.6	10.9	18.1	61.0	46.1
98	Trinidad and Tobago		..	..	..	..	..	..	..	..
99	Hungary	1993a,b	27.0	4.0	9.5	14.0	17.6	22.3	36.6	22.6
100	Gabon		..	..	..	..	..	..	..	..
101	Mexico	1992a,b	50.3	1.6	4.1	7.8	12.5	20.2	55.3	39.2
102	Uruguay		..	..	..	..	..	..	..	..
103	Oman		..	..	..	..	..	..	..	..
104	Slovenia	1993c,d	28.2	4.1	9.5	13.5	17.1	21.9	37.9	23.8
105	Saudi Arabia		..	..	..	..	..	..	..	..
106	Greece		..	..	..	..	..	..	..	..
107	Argentina		..	..	..	..	..	..	..	..
108	Korea, Rep.		..	..	..	..	..	..	..	..
Low- and middle-income										
Sub-Saharan Africa										
East Asia and Pacific										
South Asia										
Europe and Central Asia										
Middle East and N. Africa										
Latin America and Caribbean										
High-income economies										
109	Portugal		..	..	..	..	..	..	..	..
110	New Zealand	1981/82e,f	..	..	5.1	10.8	16.2	23.2	44.7	28.7
111	Spain	1988e,f			8.3	13.7	18.1	23.4	36.6	21.8
112	Ireland		..	..	..	..	..	..	..	..
113	† Israel	1979e,f	..		6.0	12.1	17.8	24.5	39.6	23.5
114	Australia	1985e,f	..	..	4.4	11.1	17.5	24.8	42.2	25.8
115	United Kingdom	1988e,f	..	..	4.6	10.0	16.8	24.3	44.3	27.8
116	Finland	1981e,f	..	..	6.3	12.1	18.4	25.5	37.6	21.7
117	Italy	1986e,f	..	..	6.8	12.0	16.7	23.5	41.0	25.3
118	† Kuwait		..	..	..	..	..	..	..	..
119	Canada	1987e,f	..	..	5.7	11.8	17.7	24.6	40.2	24.1
120	† Hong Kong	1980e,f	..	..	5.4	10.8	15.2	21.6	47.0	31.3
121	Netherlands	1988e,f	..	..	8.2	13.1	18.1	23.7	36.9	21.9
122	† Singapore	1982/83e,f	..	..	5.1	9.9	14.6	21.4	48.9	33.5
123	Belgium	1978/79e,f	..	..	7.9	13.7	18.6	23.8	36.0	21.5
124	France	1989e,f	..	..	5.6	11.8	17.2	23.5	41.9	26.1
125	Sweden	1981e,f	..	..	8.0	13.2	17.4	24.5	36.9	20.8
126	Austria		..	..	..	..	..	..	..	..
127	Germany	1988e,f	..	..	7.0	11.8	17.1	23.9	40.3	24.4
128	United States	1985e,f	..	..	4.7	11.0	17.4	25.0	41.9	25.0
129	Norway	1979e,f	..	..	6.2	12.8	18.9	25.3	36.7	21.2
130	Denmark	1981e,f	..	..	5.4	12.0	18.4	25.6	38.6	22.3
131	Japan	1979e,f	..	..	8.7	13.2	17.5	23.1	37.5	22.4
132	Switzerland	1982e,f	..	..	5.2	11.7	16.4	22.1	44.6	29.8
133	† United Arab Emirates		..	..	..	..	..	..	..	..
World										

a. Refers to expenditure shares by fractiles of persons. b. Ranked by expenditure per capita. c. Refers to income shares by fractiles of persons. d. Ranked by income per capita. e. Refers to income shares by fractiles of households. f. Ranked by household income.

Table 6. Health

		Percentage of total population with access to						Infant mortality rate (per 1,000 live births)		Prevalence of malnutrition (% under 5)	Contraceptive prevalence rate (%)	Total fertility rate		Maternal mortality ratio (per 100,000 live births)
		Health care		Safe water		Sanitation								
		1980	1993	1980	1993	1980	1993	1980	1994	1989–95	1989–95	1980	1994	1989–95
	Low-income economies							**87 w**	**58 w**			**4.4 w**	**3.3 w**	
	Excluding China and India							**118 w**	**86 w**			**6.2 w**	**5.1 w**	
1	Rwanda	..	..	60	64	51	..	128	..	28	21	8.3	..	..
2	Mozambique	..	..	..	22	10	21	157	146	..	..	6.5	6.6	1,512a
3	Ethiopia	..	55	..	18	..	10	155	120	47	4	6.6	7.5	1,528a
4	Tanzania	72	93	49	52	66	86	104	84	28	20	6.7	5.8	748a
5	Burundi	..	80	25	37	58	48	121	99	..	..	6.8	6.7	1,327a
6	Sierra Leone	26	..	20	43	12	..	190	163	23	..	6.5	6.5	800
7	Malawi	40	..	50	..	..	70	169	134	27	13	7.6	6.7	620b
8	Chad	..	26	29	..	..	27	147	119	..	..	5.9	5.9	1,594a
9	Uganda	..	..	..	..	..	67	116	122	23	..	7.2	7.1	550
10	Madagascar	..	..	21	..	..	3	138	90	32	17	6.5	6.0	660
11	Nepal	10	..	15	45	..	6	142	95	70	23	6.4	5.3	..
12	Vietnam	75	..	..	..	..	65	57	42	45	49	5.0	3.1	105
13	Bangladesh	80	74	41	78	3	35	132	81	84	40	6.1	3.6	887a
14	Haiti	..	..	33	42	19	24	113	86	27	18	5.2	4.8	600b
15	Niger	..	30	40	59	7	37	150	120	..	4	7.4	7.4	593b
16	Guinea-Bissau	30	..	..	25	15	29	168	138	..	..	6.0	6.0	..
17	Kenya	..	..	28	..	30	49	72	59	22	33	7.8	4.9	646a
18	Mali	20	..	15	49	..	..	184	125	..	..	6.6	7.1	1,249a
19	Nigeria	40	67	36	40	..	63	99	81	43	6	6.9	5.6	1,027
20	Yemen, Rep.	16	..	..	..	..	51	141	102	30	10	7.9	7.4	1,471a
21	Burkina Faso	..	..	..	67	5	..	154	128	..	8	6.5	6.9	939a
22	Mongolia	90	..	..	66	..	..	82	53	10	..	5.3	3.4	240
23	India	50	..	55	..	7	16	116	70	63	43	5.0	3.3	437
24	Lao PDR	..	..	..	28	5	4	127	92	40	..	6.1	6.6	660
25	Togo	..	..	10	71	13	..	110	81	..	..	6.6	6.5	626a
26	Gambia, The	90	..	40	55	..	73	159	128	..	12	6.5	5.4	1,050
27	Nicaragua	..	..	..	53	..	..	90	51	12	44	6.2	4.9	..
28	Zambia	..	..	46	59	..	55	90	108	27	15	7.0	6.0	229
29	Tajikistan	..	..	..	..	..	62	58	41	..	..	5.6	4.4	39
30	Benin	..	42	..	49	16	23	122	96	36	..	6.5	6.1	2,500
31	Central African Rep.	..	..	..	12	..	..	117	100	..	15	5.8	5.7	649a
32	Albania	100	..	..	..	..	..	47	31	..	..	3.6	2.7	..
33	Ghana	..	25	49	56	26	27	100	74	27	20	6.5	5.3	742a
34	Pakistan	65	85	39	..	13	28	124	92	40	12	7.0	5.4	..
35	Mauritania	..	..	..	66	..	64	120	98	..	4	6.3	5.2	800
36	Azerbaijan	..	..	..	..	..	..	30	25	..	..	3.2	2.5	29
37	Zimbabwe	55	..	..	5	..	58	82	54	16	48	6.8	4.0	80
38	Guinea	..	45	..	60	11	14	161	131	18	..	6.1	6.5	880
39	China	..	..	..	71	..	..	42	30	17	83	2.5	1.9	115c
40	Honduras	..	..	..	..	35	64	70	47	19	47	6.5	4.7	221
41	Senegal	..	40	43	49	36	34	103	64	20	7	6.7	5.8	510
42	Côte d'Ivoire	..	..	17	83	17	..	110	90	..	11	7.4	6.5	822a
43	Congo	..	..	20	..	..	9	124	112	..	..	6.0	6.7	887a
44	Kyrgyz Republic	..	..	..	..	..	53	43	29	..	..	4.1	3.3	43
45	Sri Lanka	90	..	37	60	67	61	34	16	38	..	3.5	2.4	30
46	Armenia	..	..	..	..	..	..	26	15	..	..	2.3	2.0	35
47	Cameroon	20	..	26	..	..	..	94	57	14	16	6.5	5.7	511
48	Egypt, Arab Rep.	100	99	75	86	70	..	120	52	9	47	5.1	3.5	..
49	Lesotho	..	..	17	46	12	..	84	44	21	23	5.6	4.7	598a
50	*Georgia*	..	..	..	..	..	..	25	18	..	..	2.2	2.2	55
51	*Myanmar*	30	..	25	33	20	40	109	80	31d	..	5.1	4.0	518a
	Middle-income economies							**63 w**	**40 w**			**3.8 w**	**2.8 w**	
	Lower-middle-income							**66 w**	**36 w**			**3.8 w**	**2.7 w**	
52	Bolivia	..	..	42	46	18	44	118	71	13	45	5.5	4.7	373b
53	Macedonia, FYR	..	..	..	..	..	..	54	24	..	..	2.5	2.2	..
54	Moldova	..	..	..	..	..	50	35	23	..	..	2.4	2.1	34
55	Indonesia	..	..	32	42	23	55	90	53	39	55	4.3	2.7	..
56	Philippines	..	..	54	81	75	72	52	40	30	40	4.8	3.8	208b
57	Uzbekistan	..	..	..	..	..	18	47	28	..	..	4.8	3.8	43
58	Morocco	..	62	..	..	..	63	99	56	9	50	5.4	3.5	..
59	Kazakstan	..	..	..	..	..	..	33	27	..	59	2.9	2.3	53
60	Guatemala	..	..	50	60	30	71	75	44	..	31	6.5	5.2	464a
61	Papua New Guinea	..	..	16	33	15	25	67	65	..	..	5.7	4.9	700
62	Bulgaria	..	..	..	100	..	..	20	15	..	..	2.0	1.5	..
63	Romania	..	..	..	100	50	49	29	24	..	57	2.4	1.4	..
64	Ecuador	..	..	58	58	43	54	67	37	45	57	5.0	3.3	..
65	Dominican Rep.	..	..	60	62	15	60	76	38	10	56	4.2	2.9	..
66	Lithuania	..	..	..	..	..	..	20	14	..	..	2.0	1.5	29
67	El Salvador	..	..	..	41	35	72	81	42	22	53	5.3	3.8	..
68	Jordan	..	90	86	99	70	70	41	32	17	35	6.8	4.8	132a
69	Jamaica	..	..	..	72	..	74	21	13	10	67	3.7	2.5	..
70	Paraguay	..	..	25	33	..	30	50	34	4	48	4.8	4.5	180
71	Algeria	..	..	..	..	..	..	98	35	9	51	6.7	3.7	140
72	Colombia	88	..	..	..	61	56	45	20	10	72	3.8	2.6	107a

Note: For data comparability and coverage, see the key and technical notes. Figures in italics are for years other than those specified.

		Percentage of total population with access to						Infant mortality rate (per 1,000 live births)		Prevalence of malnutrition (% under 5)	Contraceptive prevalence rate (%)	Total fertility rate		Maternal mortality ratio (per 100,000 live births)
		Health care		Safe water		Sanitation								
		1980	1993	1980	1993	1980	1993	1980	1994	1989–95	1989–95	1980	1994	1989–95
73	Tunisia	95	90	64	..	46	72	71	40	..	..	5.2	3.0	139a
74	Ukraine	..	..	..	..	50	49	17	14	..	..	2.0	1.5	33
75	Namibia	..	..	..	..	..	36	90	57	..	29	5.9	5.1	..
76	Peru	..	..	54	58	36	45	81	48	16	59	4.5	3.1	..
77	Belarus	..	..	..	..	50	..	16	13	..	..	2.0	1.6	25
78	Slovak Republic	..	..	..	77	..	51	21	11	..	..	2.3	1.7	..
79	Latvia	..	..	..	..	..	..	20	16	..	..	2.0	1.4	..
80	Costa Rica	..	..	90	94	91	..	20	13	2	75	3.7	2.9	..
81	Poland	100	..	..	100	50	..	21	15	..	..	2.2	1.8	..
82	Thailand	30	59	66	..	..	87	49	36	13	..	3.5	2.0	155a
83	Turkey	..	..	..	92	10	95	109	62	..	63	4.3	3.2	183e
84	Croatia	..	..	..	63	..	68	19	11	..	..	1.9	1.5	..
85	Panama	..	..	..	83	71	..	28	20	7	..	3.7	2.7	..
86	Russian Federation	..	..	..	..	..	..	22	19	..	..	1.9	1.4	52
87	Venezuela	..	..	..	89	52	55	41	32	6	..	4.1	3.2	200
88	Botswana	..	..	56	..	..	..	63	34	..	..	6.7	4.5	220a
89	Estonia	..	..	..	..	..	..	17	14	..	..	2.0	1.5	41
90	Iran, Islamic Rep.	50	..	52	89	60	..	92	47	16	..	6.1	4.7	..
91	Turkmenistan	..	..	..	..	..	60	54	46	..	..	4.9	3.9	55
Upper-middle-income								**54 w**	**36 w**			**3.9 w**	**2.8 w**	
92	Brazil	..	..	75	96	..	73	74	56	18	..	3.9	2.8	200
93	South Africa	..	..	..	..	..	..	67	50	..	..	4.9	3.9	404a
94	Mauritius	100	99	99	100	94	100	32	17	..	75	2.7	2.0	112
95	Czech Republic	..	..	..	..	..	..	16	8	..	69	2.0	1.4	..
96	Malaysia	..	88	80	78	70	94	30	12	23	..	4.2	3.4	34f
97	Chile	..	..	85	86	83	83	33	12	1	..	2.8	2.5	..
98	Trinidad and Tobago	..	..	98	96	..	56	35	14	..	..	3.3	2.5	..
99	Hungary	..	..	..	100	..	..	23	12	..	..	1.9	1.6	..
100	Gabon	..	..	50	58	..	76	116	89	..	..	4.5	5.5	438a
101	Mexico	51	..	74	78	55	66	53	35	..	..	4.5	3.2	..
102	Uruguay	..	..	80	..	51	82	37	19	..	..	2.7	2.2	36
103	Oman	75	89	15	57	..	79	41	18	..	9	9.9	7.1	184
104	Slovenia	..	..	..	..	..	90	15	6	..	..	2.1	1.3	..
105	Saudi Arabia	85	98	84	95	70	78	65	26	..	..	7.3	6.3	108a
106	Greece	..	..	..	100	..	..	18	8	..	..	2.2	1.4	..
107	Argentina	..	..	..	64	..	89	35	23	..	..	3.3	2.6	140
108	Korea, Rep.	..	100	..	78	100	100	32	12	..	79	2.6	1.8	30
Low- and middle-income								**87 w**	**58 w**			**4.2 w**	**3.1 w**	
Sub-Saharan Africa								**115 w**	**92 w**			**6.6 w**	**5.9 w**	
East Asia and Pacific								**51 w**	**35 w**			**3.1 w**	**2.2 w**	
South Asia								**119 w**	**73 w**			**5.3 w**	**3.6 w**	
Europe and Central Asia								**34 w**	**23 w**			**2.5 w**	**1.9 w**	
Middle East and N. Africa								**95 w**	**49 w**			**6.1 w**	**4.5 w**	
Latin America and Caribbean								**60 w**	**41 w**			**4.1 w**	**2.9 w**	
High-income economies								**12 w**	**7 w**			**1.9 w**	**1.7 w**	
109	Portugal	..	..	..	100	41	..	24	8	..	..	2.2	1.4	..
110	New Zealand	..	100	..	97	..	..	13	7	..	..	2.1	2.1	..
111	Spain	..	..	..	100	95	97	12	7	..	..	2.2	1.2	..
112	Ireland	..	..	..	100	..	..	11	6	..	60	3.2	1.9	..
113	†Israel	..	..	..	100	..	70	15	8	..	..	3.2	2.4	..
114	Australia	99	..	..	..	99	..	11	6	..	..	1.9	1.9	..
115	United Kingdom	..	..	..	100	..	96	12	6	..	..	1.9	1.8	..
116	Finland	..	..	..	100	..	100	8	5	..	..	1.6	1.9	..
117	Italy	..	..	..	100	99	..	15	7	..	..	1.6	1.3	..
118	†Kuwait	100	..	100	100	100	..	27	11	..	..	5.3	3.0	18
119	Canada	..	..	..	..	60	85	10	6	..	..	1.7	1.9	..
120	†Hong Kong	..	..	..	..	..	..	11	5	..	..	2.0	1.2	..
121	Netherlands	..	..	..	100	100	100	9	6	..	..	1.6	1.6	..
122	†Singapore	..	..	100	100	80	100	12	5	14	..	1.7	1.8	..
123	Belgium	..	..	..	100	99	..	12	8	..	..	1.7	1.6	..
124	France	..	..	..	100	85	..	10	6	..	..	1.9	1.6	..
125	Sweden	..	..	..	100	85	..	7	4	..	..	1.7	1.9	..
126	Austria	..	..	..	100	85	..	14	6	..	..	1.6	1.5	..
127	Germany	..	..	..	..	..	..	12	6	..	..	1.6	1.2	..
128	United States	..	..	..	..	98	85	13	8	..	..	1.8	2.0	..
129	Norway	..	..	..	100	..	..	8	5	..	..	1.7	1.9	..
130	Denmark	..	..	..	100	100	100	8	6	..	..	1.5	1.8	..
131	Japan	..	100	..	..	..	85	8	4	3	..	1.8	1.5	..
132	Switzerland	..	..	..	100	85	100	9	6	..	..	1.5	1.5	..
133	†United Arab Emirates	96	90	100	..	75	95	55	16	..	..	5.4	4.1	20a
World								**81 w**	**53 w**			**3.8 w**	**2.9 w**	

a. UNICEF/World Health Organization estimate. b. Based on indirect estimation using survey data. c. Based on a study covering thirty provinces. d. Refers to children three years of age and younger. e. Based on sample surveys. f. Based on civil registration.

Table 7. Education

	Percentage of age group enrolled in education										Percentage of cohort reaching grade 4				Adult illiteracy (%)	
	Primary				Secondary				Tertiary		Female		Male		Female	Male
	Female		Male		Female		Male									
	1980	1993	1980	1993	1980	1993	1980	1993	1980	1993	1980	1988	1980	1988	1995	1995
Low-income economies	80 w	98 w	103 w	112 w	26 w	42 w	42 w	55 w	3 w	..					45 w	24 w
Excluding China and India	64 w	67 w	85 w	82 w	15 w	21 w	27 w	30 w	4 w	..					55 w	37 w
1 Rwanda	60	50	66	50	3	9	4	11	0	..	74	75	73	73	48	30
2 Mozambique	84	51	114	69	3	6	8	9	0	0	..	60	..	67	77	42
3 Ethiopia[a]	23	*19*	44	*27*	6	*11*	11	*12*	0	*1*	48	..	42	..	75	55
4 Tanzania	86	69	99	71	2	5	4	6	..	..	89	87	90	87	43	21
5 Burundi	21	63	32	76	2	5	4	9	1	*1*	83	76	83	78	78	51
6 Sierra Leone	43	..	61	..	8	..	20	..	1	..	..	..	..	..	82	55
7 Malawi	48	*77*	72	*84*	2	*3*	5	*6*	1	*1*	55	*68*	62	*73*	58	28
8 Chad	..	*38*	..	*80*	..	..	..	..	..	*1*	..	66	..	74	65	38
9 Uganda	43	83	56	99	3	10	7	17	1	1	*74*	..	83	..	50	26
10 Madagascar	133	72	139	75	..	14	..	14	3	4	..	64	..	63	..	..
11 Nepal	49	85	117	129	9	*23*	33	46	6	3	..	..	..	..	86	59
12 Vietnam	106	..	111	..	40	..	44	..	2	2	67	..	71	..	9	4
13 Bangladesh	46	105	76	128	9	12	26	26	3	..	30	*46*	29	44	74	51
14 Haiti	70	..	82	..	13	..	14	..	1	..	64	*60*	63	60	58	52
15 Niger	18	*21*	33	*35*	3	*4*	7	*9*	0	*1*	79	..	82	..	93	79
16 Guinea-Bissau	43	..	94	..	2	2	10	10	..	..	47	..	63	..	58	32
17 Kenya	110	91	120	92	16	23	23	28	1	..	85	..	84	..	30	14
18 Mali	19	24	34	38	5	6	12	12	1	..	77	..	73	..	77	61
19 Nigeria	104	*82*	135	*105*	14	*27*	27	*32*	2	..	..	73	..	88	53	33
20 Yemen, Rep.	..	..	..	..	..	..	..	..	..	..	..	..	..	..	..	..
21 Burkina Faso	14	*30*	23	*47*	2	*6*	4	*11*	0	..	79	83	79	83	91	70
22 Mongolia	107	..	107	..	97	..	85	..	..	..	..	..	..	..	..	..
23 India	67	91	98	113	20	38	39	59	5	..	52	..	57	..	62	35
24 Lao PDR	104	92	123	123	16	19	25	31	0	2	31	..	31	..	56	31
25 Togo	91	81	146	122	16	12	51	34	2	3	84	*82*	90	87	63	33
26 Gambia, The	35	61	67	84	7	*13*	16	25	..	..	..	..	..	..	75	47
27 Nicaragua	102	105	96	101	45	44	39	39	13	9	55	..	51	..	33	35
28 Zambia	83	99	97	109	11	..	22	..	2	..	..	..	..	..	29	14
29 Tajikistan	..	88	..	91	..	101	..	98	24	25	..	..	..	..	..	..
30 Benin	41	*44*	87	*88*	9	*7*	24	*17*	2	..	73	..	77	..	74	51
31 Central African Republic	51	51	92	92	7	..	21	..	1	*2*	..	*81*	..	85	48	32
32 Albania	111	97	116	95	63	..	70	..	8	10	96	..	97	..	..	..
33 Ghana	71	*70*	89	*83*	31	*28*	51	*44*	2	..	82	..	87	..	47	24
34 Pakistan	27	49	51	80	8	..	20	..	..	..	41	*45*	53	55	76	50
35 Mauritania	26	62	47	76	4	11	17	19	..	4	86	83	96	82	74	50
36 Azerbaijan	..	87	..	91	..	88	..	89	25	26	..	..	..	..	..	..
37 Zimbabwe	*57*	114	65	123	*7*	40	*8*	51	1	*6*	64	80	67	81	20	10
38 Guinea	25	30	48	61	*10*	*6*	*24*	*17*	5	..	*57*	73	85	80	78	50
39 China	103	116	121	120	37	51	54	60	1	4	..	81	..	97	27	10
40 Honduras	99	112	98	111	31	*37*	29	*29*	8	9	*40*	..	35	..	27	27
41 Senegal	37	50	56	67	7	*11*	15	*21*	3	3	90	*90*	93	94	77	57
42 Côte d'Ivoire	63	58	95	80	12	*17*	27	*33*	3	..	91	83	94	85	70	50
43 Congo	..	..	..	..	..	..	..	..	..	..	91	*87*	91	88	33	17
44 Kyrgyz Republic	..	..	..	..	..	..	..	..	28	21	..	..	..	..	..	..
45 Sri Lanka	100	105	105	106	57	78	52	71	3	6	..	98	..	97	13	7
46 Armenia	..	93	..	87	..	90	..	80	30	49	..	..	..	..	..	..
47 Cameroon	89	..	107	..	13	..	24	..	2	2	81	..	81	..	48	25
48 Egypt, Arab Rep.	61	89	84	105	39	69	61	81	16	*17*	83	97	75	92	61	36
49 Lesotho	120	105	85	90	21	31	14	21	2	2	77	84	61	74	38	19
50 *Georgia*	..	..	..	..	..	..	..	..	30	..	..	..	..	..	..	..
51 *Myanmar*	89	..	93	..	..	..	..	..	..	..	..	..	..	..	22	11
Middle-income economies	101 w	102 w	107 w	105 w	48 w	63 w	53 w	65 w	20 w	23 w					..	..
Lower-middle-income	99 w	101 w	107 w	105 w	49 w	62 w	55 w	64 w	24 w	24 w					..	..
52 Bolivia	81	..	92	..	32	..	42	..	16	23	50	..	52	..	24	10
53 Macedonia, FYR	..	87	..	88	..	55	..	53	28	16	..	..	..	..	..	..
54 Moldova	..	77	..	78	..	72	..	67	29	35	..	..	..	..	..	..
55 Indonesia	100	*112*	115	*116*	23	*39*	35	48	..	10	65	82	88	97	22	10
56 Philippines	112	..	113	..	69	..	61	..	24	26	..	85	..	84	6	5
57 Uzbekistan	..	79	..	80	..	92	..	96	30	33	..	..	..	..	..	..
58 Morocco	63	*60*	102	*85*	20	*29*	32	*40*	6	10	89	85	90	85	69	43
59 Kazakhstan	..	86	..	86	..	91	..	89	34	42	..	..	..	..	..	..
60 Guatemala	65	78	77	89	17	23	20	25	8	..	56	..	66	..	51	38
61 Papua New Guinea	51	*67*	66	*80*	8	*10*	15	15	2	..	85	67	77	68	37	19
62 Bulgaria	98	84	98	87	84	70	85	66	16	32	95	90	98	93	..	..
63 Romania	101	*86*	102	*87*	69	*82*	73	83	12	*12*	..	94	..	93	..	..
64 Ecuador	116	*122*	119	*124*	53	*56*	53	*54*	35	..	76	..	78	..	12	8
65 Dominican Republic	..	99	..	95	..	43	..	30	..	..	..	..	..	..	18	18
66 Lithuania	..	90	..	95	..	79	..	76	49	39	..	..	..	..	..	..
67 El Salvador	75	80	75	79	23	30	26	27	4	15	55	..	52	..	30	27
68 Jordan	102	*95*	105	*94*	73	*54*	79	*52*	27	19	95	97	95	99	21	7
69 Jamaica	104	*108*	103	*109*	71	*70*	63	62	7	6	..	*100*	..	98	11	19
70 Paraguay	101	110	107	114	*24*	38	25	36	8	10	*74*	81	74	79	9	7
71 Algeria	81	*96*	108	*111*	26	55	40	66	6	*11*	91	96	92	97	51	26
72 Colombia	126	120	123	118	41	68	40	57	9	*16*	46	74	42	72	9	9

Note: For data comparability and coverage, see the technical notes. Figures in italics are for years other than those specified.

		Percentage of age group enrolled in education										Percentage of cohort reaching grade 4				Adult illiteracy (%)	
		Primary				Secondary				Tertiary		Female		Male		Female	Male
		Female		Male		Female		Male									
		1980	1993	1980	1993	1980	1993	1980	1993	1980	1993	1980	1988	1980	1988	1995	1995
73	Tunisia	88	113	118	123	20	49	34	55	5	11	90	93	94	93	45	21
74	Ukraine	..	87	..	87	..	95	..	65	42	46	..	..	..	..	..	..
75	Namibia	..	138	..	134	..	61	..	49	..	3	..	64	..	65	..	..
76	Peru	111	..	117	..	54	..	63	..	17	40	83	..	85	..	17	6
77	Belarus	..	95	..	96	..	96	..	89	39	44	..	..	..	..	..	..
78	Slovak Republic	..	101	..	101	..	90	..	87	..	17	..	..	..	..	..	..
79	Latvia	..	82	..	83	..	90	..	84	45	39	..	..	..	..	..	..
80	Costa Rica	104	105	106	106	51	49	44	45	21	30	84	90	80	92	5	5
81	Poland	99	97	100	98	80	87	75	82	18	26	..	97	..	98	..	..
82	Thailand	97	97	100	98	28	37	30	38	13	19	..	..	..	..	8	4
83	Turkey	90	98	102	107	24	48	44	74	5	16	..	98	..	99	28	8
84	Croatia	..	87	..	87	..	86	..	80	..	27	..	..	..	..	..	..
85	Panama	105	..	108	..	65	..	58	..	21	23	88	86	87	84	10	9
86	Russian Federation	102	107	102	107	97	91	95	84	46	45	..	..	..	..	..	..
87	Venezuela	104	97	104	95	25	41	18	29	21	29	83	..	84	..	10	8
88	Botswana	100	120	83	113	20	55	17	49	1	3	98	95	91	91	40	20
89	Estonia	..	83	..	84	..	96	..	87	43	38	..	..	..	..	..	..
90	Iran, Islamic Rep.	..	101	..	109	32	58	52	74	..	15	..	93	..	94	34	22
91	Turkmenistan	..	..	..	..	..	..	..	..	23	..	..	..	..	..	..	..
Upper-middle-income		103 w	..	106 w	..	47 w	..	48 w	..	13 w	20 w					14 w	12 w
92	Brazil	97	..	101	..	36	..	31	..	11	12	..	..	..	..	17	17
93	South Africa	..	110	..	111	..	84	..	71	..	13	..	..	..	..	18	18
94	Mauritius	91	106	94	107	49	60	51	58	1	4	97	99	97	99	21	13
95	Czech Republic	..	100	..	99	..	88	..	85	18	16	..	..	..	..	..	..
96	Malaysia	92	93	93	93	46	61	50	56	4	..	..	99	..	98	22	11
97	Chile	108	98	110	99	56	70	49	65	12	27	81	95	78	94	5	5
98	Trinidad and Tobago	100	94	98	94	62	78	60	74	4	8	89	97	83	96	3	1
99	Hungary	97	94	96	94	67	82	72	79	14	17	96	98	96	98	..	..
100	Gabon	..	136	..	132	..	..	..	..	..	3	79	..	82	..	47	26
101	Mexico	121	110	122	114	46	58	51	57	14	14	63	74	85	95	13	8
102	Uruguay	107	108	107	109	62	..	61	..	17	30	99	99	93	99	2	3
103	Oman	36	82	69	87	6	57	19	64	..	5	77	96	99	97	..	..
104	Slovenia	..	97	..	97	..	90	..	88	..	28	..	..	..	..	..	..
105	Saudi Arabia	49	73	74	78	23	43	36	54	7	14	90	93	90	93	50	29
106	Greece	103	..	103	..	77	..	85	..	17	..	98	99	98	98	..	..
107	Argentina	106	107	106	108	60	75	52	70	22	41	76	..	73	..	4	4
108	Korea, Rep.	111	102	109	100	74	92	82	93	15	48	96	100	96	100	b	b
Low- and middle-income		89 w	99 w	104 w	110 w	32 w	50 w	45 w	59 w	8 w	..					..	..
Sub-Saharan Africa		69 w	64 w	91 w	77 w	10 w	23 w	20 w	..	1 w	..					54 w	35 w
East Asia and Pacific		103 w	115 w	117 w	119 w	38 w	53 w	51 w	61 w	3 w	6 w					24 w	9 w
South Asia		60 w	87 w	91 w	110 w	18 w	35 w	36 w	55 w	5 w	..					64 w	37 w
Europe and Central Asia		..	97 w	..	97 w	..	90 w	..	81 w	31 w	..					..	..
Middle East and N. Africa		74 w	91 w	98 w	104 w	32 w	51 w	52 w	..	11 w	..					50 w	28 w
Latin America and Caribbean		105 w	..	108 w	..	41 w	..	40 w	..	14 w	15 w					14 w	12 w
High-income economies		102 w	104 w	103 w	104 w	..	98 w	..	97 w	37 w	53 w					..	..
109	Portugal	123	118	124	122	40	..	34	..	11	23	..	..	..	..	b	b
110	New Zealand	111	101	111	102	84	104	82	103	27	58	..	97	..	97	b	b
111	Spain	109	105	110	104	89	120	85	107	23	41	94	93	92	91	..	..
112	Ireland	100	103	100	103	95	110	85	101	18	34	100	99	100	99	b	b
113	† Israel	97	96	95	95	76	91	66	84	29	35	98	97	97	98	..	..
114	Australia	110	107	112	108	72	86	70	83	25	42	97	100	94	99	b	b
115	United Kingdom	103	113	103	112	85	94	82	91	19	37	..	..	..	..	b	b
116	Finland	96	100	97	100	105	130	94	110	32	63	99	98	99	98	b	b
117	Italy	100	99	100	98	70	82	73	81	27	37	..	..	..	..	b	b
118	† Kuwait	100	65	105	65	76	60	84	60	11	16	81	..	85	..	25	18
119	Canada	99	104	99	106	89	103	87	104	52	103	97	98	94	95	b	b
120	† Hong Kong	106	..	107	..	65	..	63	..	10	21	99	..	100	..	12	4
121	Netherlands	101	99	99	96	90	120	95	126	29	45	100	..	97	..	b	b
122	† Singapore	106	..	109	..	59	..	56	..	8	..	100	..	99	..	14	4
123	Belgium	103	100	104	99	92	104	90	103	26	..	81	..	78	..	b	b
124	France	110	105	112	107	92	107	77	104	25	50	95	95	93	100	b	b
125	Sweden	97	100	96	100	93	100	83	99	31	38	100	..	99	..	b	b
126	Austria	98	103	99	103	87	104	98	109	22	43	97	100	92	98	b	b
127	Germany c	99	98	99	97	92	100	96	101	26	36	98	99	96	97	b	b
128	United States	100	106	101	107	..	97	..	98	56	81	..	..	..	..	b	b
129	Norway	100	99	100	99	96	114	92	118	26	54	100	..	99	..	b	b
130	Denmark	95	98	96	97	104	115	105	112	28	41	..	98	..	98	b	b
131	Japan	101	102	101	102	94	97	92	95	31	30	100	100	100	100	b	b
132	Switzerland	..	102	..	100	..	89	..	93	18	31	94	..	92	..	b	b
133	† United Arab Emirates	88	108	90	112	49	94	55	84	3	11	..	93	..	94	20	21
World		89 w	100 w	104 w	109 w	38 w	57 w	49 w	65 w	13 w	18 w					..	..

a. Data for 1980 include Eritrea. b. According to UNESCO, illiteracy is less than 5 percent. c. Data before 1990 refer to the Federal Republic of Germany before unification.

Table 8. Commercial energy use

		Energy use (oil equivalent)								Net energy imports as % of energy consumption		CO2 emissions[a]			
		Total (thous. metric tons)		Per capita (kg)		Avg. annual growth rate (%)		GDP per kg. ($)				Total (mill. metric tons)		Per capita (metric tons)	
		1980	1994	1980	1994	1980–90	1990–94	1980	1994	1980	1994	1980	1992	1980	1992
	Low-income economies	652,586 t	1,222,928 t	271 w	384 w	5.5 w	3.7 w	..	1.0 w			2,195.1 t	4,012.9 t	0.91 w	1.30 w
	Excluding China and India	..	230,666 t	..	174 w	..	..	..	1.9 w			355.8 t	575.5 t	0.40 w	0.45 w
1	Rwanda	..	209	..	27	..	..	..	2.8	..	78	0.3	0.5	0.05	0.06
2	Mozambique	1,123	614	93	40	−5.8	5.8	1.8	2.4	−15	74	3.2	1.0	0.26	0.07
3	Ethiopia	624	1,156	17	21	6.4	0.9	..	4.1	91	86	1.8	2.9	0.05	0.05
4	Tanzania	1,023	975	55	34	−0.7	2.9	..	3.5	92	83	1.9	2.1	0.10	0.08
5	Burundi	..	143	..	23	..	..	..	7.0	..	97	0.1	0.2	0.03	0.03
6	Sierra Leone	..	323	..	73	..	..	..	2.6	..	100	0.6	0.4	0.18	0.10
7	Malawi	..	370	..	39	..	..	..	3.5	..	59	0.7	0.7	0.12	0.07
8	Chad	..	100	..	16	..	..	..	9.1	..	100	0.2	0.3	0.05	0.04
9	Uganda	..	425	..	23	..	..	..	9.4	..	58	0.6	1.0	0.05	0.05
10	Madagascar	..	479	..	37	..	..	..	4.0	..	83	1.6	0.9	0.18	0.08
11	Nepal	174	486	12	23	7.2	16.4	11.2	8.3	91	84	0.5	1.3	0.04	0.07
12	Vietnam	4,024	7,549	75	105	4.0	8.3	..	2.1	32	−55	17.0	21.5	0.32	0.31
13	Bangladesh	2,809	7,700	32	65	9.0	5.8	4.6	3.4	60	31	7.6	17.2	0.09	0.15
14	Haiti	..	326	..	47	..	..	..	5.0	..	70	0.8	0.8	0.14	0.12
15	Niger	..	327	..	37	..	..	..	4.7	..	83	0.6	1.1	0.10	0.13
16	Guinea-Bissau	..	39	..	37	..	..	..	6.2	..	100	0.1	0.2	0.17	0.21
17	Kenya	1,991	2,792	120	107	4.2	3.3	3.6	2.5	95	82	6.2	5.3	0.37	0.22
18	Mali	..	205	..	22	..	..	..	9.1	..	80	0.4	0.4	0.06	0.05
19	Nigeria	9,879	17,503	139	162	2.9	4.6	9.4	2.0	−968	−484	68.1	96.5	0.96	0.95
20	Yemen, Rep.	1,364	3,165	160	214	7.8	1.9	..	..	100	−406	3.3	10.1	0.39	0.73
21	Burkina Faso	..	160	..	16	..	..	..	11.6	..	100	0.4	0.6	0.06	0.06
22	Mongolia	..	2,550	..	1,079	..	..	..	0.3	..	15	6.7	9.3	4.03	4.08
23	India	93,907	222,262	137	243	6.9	4.8	1.8	1.3	21	20	350.1	769.4	0.51	0.87
24	Lao PDR	..	182	..	38	..	..	..	8.4	..	−19	0.2	0.3	0.06	0.06
25	Togo	..	183	..	46	..	..	..	5.4	..	100	0.6	0.7	0.23	0.19
26	Gambia, The	..	60	..	56	..	..	..	6.0	..	100	0.2	0.2	0.25	0.20
27	Nicaragua	..	1,001	..	241	..	..	..	1.8	..	84	2.0	2.5	0.72	0.64
28	Zambia	1,685	1,292	294	140	−3.0	2.3	2.3	2.7	32	29	3.5	2.5	0.62	0.29
29	Tajikistan	..	3,695	..	642	..	..	..	0.6	..	55	..	4.0	..	0.71
30	Benin	149	97	43	18	−1.4	−2.3	9.4	15.7	93	−239	0.5	0.6	0.14	0.12
31	Central African Republic	..	93	..	29	..	..	..	9.4	..	76	0.1	0.2	0.05	0.07
32	Albania	3,058	1,350	1,145	422	−1.0	−12.0	0.5	1.3	0	28	7.4	4.0	2.77	1.24
33	Ghana	1,303	1,511	121	91	1.6	0.5	3.4	3.6	57	64	2.4	3.8	0.23	0.24
34	Pakistan	11,698	32,247	142	255	8.0	6.4	2.0	1.6	38	38	31.7	71.9	0.38	0.60
35	Mauritania	..	229	..	103	..	..	..	4.5	..	100	0.6	2.9	0.39	1.36
36	Azerbaijan	15,001	10,545	2,433	1,414	5.2	−18.8	..	0.3	1	−41	..	63.9	..	8.71
37	Zimbabwe	2,797	4,654	399	432	5.5	0.7	1.9	1.2	28	26	9.7	18.7	1.39	1.82
38	Guinea	..	418	..	65	..	..	..	8.1	..	87	0.9	1.0	0.21	0.17
39	China	413,130	770,000	421	647	5.6	4.0	0.5	0.7	−4	−1	1,489.2	2,668.0	1.52	2.29
40	Honduras	..	969	..	169	..	..	..	3.4	..	71	2.1	3.1	0.56	0.56
41	Senegal	875	840	158	102	0.8	−1.5	3.4	4.6	100	100	2.8	2.8	0.50	0.36
42	Côte d'Ivoire	1,435	2,350	175	170	1.6	17.9	7.1	2.9	87	82	4.7	6.3	0.57	0.49
43	Congo	262	379	157	147	0.6	7.3	6.5	4.2	−1,193	−2,492	0.4	4.0	0.23	1.64
44	Kyrgyz Republic	1,938	3,197	534	715	0.9	2.9	..	0.9	−113	76	..	15.4	..	3.42
45	Sri Lanka	1,411	1,979	96	111	0.5	7.5	2.9	5.9	91	83	3.4	5.0	0.23	0.29
46	Armenia	..	2,500	..	667	..	..	..	1.0	..	87	..	4.2	..	1.14
47	Cameroon	774	1,077	89	83	3.5	−1.2	9.7	6.9	−269	−525	3.9	2.2	0.45	0.18
48	Egypt, Arab Rep.	15,176	34,538	371	608	7.2	3.0	1.5	1.2	−120	−67	45.2	84.0	1.11	1.54
49	Lesotho	..	..	..	..	..	..	..	..	..	..	..	..	..	..
50	*Georgia*	4,474	3,098	882	572	−1.7	−12.2	..	0.7	−5	81	..	13.8	..	2.54
51	*Myanmar*	..	..	..	..	..	..	..	..	..	..	4.8	4.4	0.14	0.10
	Middle-income economies	..	2,501,145 t	..	1,593 w	..	..	..	1.7 w			4,009.3 t	5,370.8 t	3.23 w	3.52 w
	Lower-middle-income	..	1,689,117 t	..	1,540 w	..	..	..	1.1 w			..	..	..	..
52	Bolivia	1,713	2,220	320	307	−0.6	4.4	1.8	2.5	−107	−90	4.5	6.6	0.84	0.96
53	Macedonia, FYR	..	..	..	..	..	..	..	..	..	..	..	4.1	..	1.99
54	Moldova	..	4,185	..	962	..	..	..	0.9	..	99	..	14.2	0.00	3.26
55	Indonesia	25,028	74,794	169	393	7.4	9.3	3.1	2.3	−275	−101	94.6	184.6	0.64	1.00
56	Philippines	13,406	24,428	277	364	2.6	8.3	2.4	2.6	79	70	36.5	49.7	0.76	0.77
57	Uzbekistan	..	42,209	..	1,886	..	..	..	0.5	..	3	..	123.3	..	5.74
58	Morocco	4,927	8,107	254	307	3.6	4.3	3.8	3.8	87	95	16.0	27.3	0.82	1.08
59	Kazakstan	76,799	62,368	5,153	3,710	3.6	−10.8	..	0.3	0	−16	..	298.0	..	17.55
60	Guatemala	1,443	1,921	209	186	0.3	9.2	5.5	6.7	84	70	4.5	5.7	0.65	0.58
61	Papua New Guinea	..	990	..	236	..	..	..	5.5	..	−150	1.8	2.3	0.60	0.56
62	Bulgaria	28,476	23,500	3,213	2,786	0.3	−2.6	0.7	0.4	74	63	74.9	54.4	8.45	6.37
63	Romania	63,846	39,782	2,876	1,750	0.3	−8.8	0.8	0.9	19	27	191.4	122.1	8.62	5.36
64	Ecuador	4,209	5,807	529	517	2.6	0.0	2.8	2.9	−156	−223	13.4	18.9	1.69	1.76
65	Dominican Republic	..	2,591	..	340	..	..	..	4.0	..	89	6.4	10.2	1.12	1.40
66	Lithuania	11,353	8,164	3,326	2,194	3.0	−19.6	..	0.6	−2	80	..	22.0	..	5.88
67	El Salvador	..	1,236	..	219	..	..	..	6.6	..	58	2.1	3.6	0.47	0.66
68	Jordan	1,710	4,024	784	997	5.8	5.0	..	1.5	100	97	4.7	11.3	2.17	3.03
69	Jamaica	2,169	2,776	1,017	1,112	−0.3	2.3	1.2	1.5	99	100	8.4	8.0	3.96	3.29
70	Paraguay	550	1,251	175	261	6.8	9.6	8.3	6.3	88	−141	1.5	2.6	0.47	0.58
71	Algeria	12,078	28,244	647	1,030	6.2	4.7	3.5	1.5	−452	−273	66.2	79.2	3.55	3.02
72	Colombia	13,972	22,271	501	613	3.7	1.3	2.4	3.0	7	−103	39.3	61.5	1.41	1.76

Note: For data comparability and coverage, see the technical notes.

		Energy use (oil equivalent)						GDP per kg. ($)		Net energy imports as % of energy consumption		CO2 emissions[a]			
		Total (thous. metric tons)		Per capita (kg)		Avg. annual growth rate (%)						Total (mill. metric tons)		Per capita (metric tons)	
		1980	1994	1980	1994	1980–90	1990–94	1980	1994	1980	1994	1980	1992	1980	1992
73	Tunisia	3,083	5,204	483	590	4.0	3.4	2.8	3.0	−99	−7	9.5	13.6	1.48	1.60
74	Ukraine	108,290	170,910	2,164	3,292	6.9	−9.8	..	0.5	−1	43	..	611.3	..	11.72
75	Namibia	..	..	..	..	..	..	..	..	..	..	..	..	..	..
76	Peru	8,139	8,159	471	351	−0.5	3.1	2.5	6.1	−36	1	23.5	22.3	1.36	1.00
77	Belarus	..	27,881	..	2,692	..	..	..	0.7	..	89	..	102.0	..	9.89
78	Slovak Republic	..	..	..	..	..	..	..	..	..	..	..	37.0	..	6.97
79	Latvia	..	4,469	..	1,755	..	..	..	1.3	..	88	..	14.8	..	5.62
80	Costa Rica	..	1,843	..	558	..	..	..	4.5	..	41	2.5	3.8	1.08	1.20
81	Poland	124,500	98,800	3,499	2,563	−0.4	0.2	0.5	5	3	5	459.6	341.9	12.92	8.91
82	Thailand	12,093	44,655	259	770	9.5	10.0	2.7	3.2	96	59	40.0	112.5	0.86	1.98
83	Turkey	31,314	58,100	705	955	5.8	2.7	1.8	2.3	45	56	76.0	145.5	1.71	2.49
84	Croatia	..	5,051	..	1,057	..	..	..	2.8	..	28	..	16.2	..	3.39
85	Panama	1,376	1,479	703	566	−1.7	6.6	2.6	4.7	97	83	3.6	4.2	1.86	1.68
86	Russian Federation	750,240	599,027	5,397	4,038	4.2	−8.9	..	0.6	0	−52	..	2,103.1	..	14.14
87	Venezuela	35,011	49,355	2,354	2,331	1.5	4.6	2.0	1.2	−280	−245	89.6	116.4	6.03	5.75
88	Botswana	..	549	..	380	..	..	..	7.3	..	55	1.0	2.2	1.10	1.60
89	Estonia	..	5,325	..	3,552	..	..	..	0.9	..	42	0.4	20.9	0.28	13.53
90	*Iran, Islamic Rep.*	38,347	97,891	980	1,565	7.5	8.9	2.4	0.7	−118	−127	116.1	235.5	2.97	3.97
91	*Turkmenistan*	7,948	14,090	2,778	3,198	25.0	−29.9	..	..	−101	−116	..	42.3	..	10.48
Upper-middle-income		**475,209 t**	**810,681 t**	**1,297 w**	**1,715 w**	**4.9 w**	**3.5 w**	**..**	**2.8 w**			**1,358.3 t**	**1,907.7 t**	**3.71 w**	**4.17 w**
92	Brazil	72,141	110,000	595	691	4.3	3.2	3.3	5.0	65	38	183.6	217.1	1.51	1.41
93	South Africa	60,511	91,349	2,074	2,253	3.6	0.0	1.3	1.3	−14	−33	213.4	290.3	7.31	7.49
94	Mauritius	..	431	..	387	..	..	..	7.9	..	92	0.6	1.4	0.61	1.26
95	Czech Republic	29,394	40,324	2,873	3,902	73.7	−4.5	1.0	0.9	−29	13	..	135.6	..	13.15
96	Malaysia	9,522	33,662	692	1,711	9.4	11.2	2.6	2.1	−58	−66	28.0	70.5	2.03	3.76
97	Chile	7,743	13,200	695	943	3.9	4.3	3.6	3.9	50	66	27.0	34.7	2.42	2.55
98	Trinidad and Tobago	3,863	5,891	3,570	4,549	3.9	−0.4	1.6	0.8	−240	−89	16.7	20.6	15.41	16.28
99	Hungary	28,322	25,191	2,645	2,455	0.8	−3.4	0.8	1.6	49	44	82.0	59.9	7.66	5.80
100	Gabon	759	676	942	520	−3.6	5.6	5.6	5.8	−1,106	−2,268	4.8	5.6	5.93	4.50
101	Mexico	97,434	139,600	1,453	1,577	2.3	2.0	2.0	2.7	−49	−55	260.1	332.9	3.88	3.92
102	Uruguay	2,208	1,971	758	623	−0.9	2.7	4.6	7.9	89	68	5.8	5.0	1.98	1.61
103	Oman	1,346	4,924	1,223	2,347	12.4	5.8	4.4	2.4	−1,024	−801	5.9	10.0	5.33	5.24
104	Slovenia	..	2,995	..	1,506	..	..	..	4.7	..	19	..	5.5	..	2.76
105	Saudi Arabia	35,496	85,326	3,787	4,744	5.8	6.1	4.4	1.4	−1,361	−435	130.8	220.6	13.95	13.11
106	Greece	15,973	23,300	1,656	2,235	3.6	1.2	2.5	3.3	77	63	51.4	73.9	5.33	7.16
107	Argentina	39,669	47,850	1,411	1,399	1.1	3.5	1.9	5.9	8	−21	107.5	117.0	3.82	3.50
108	Korea, Rep.	41,426	133,374	1,087	3,000	8.5	10.2	1.5	2.8	77	85	125.7	289.8	3.30	6.64
Low- and middle-income		**..**	**3,716,470 t**	**..**	**782 w**	**..**	**..**	**..**	**1.5 w**			**6,378.8 t**	**9,849.7 t**	**1.75 w**	**2.14 w**
Sub-Saharan Africa		**104,833 t**	**155,832 t**	**276 w**	**272 w**	**3.2 w**	**1.0 w**	**..**	**1.9 w**			**356.8 t**	**478.6 t**	**0.94 w**	**0.88 w**
East Asia and Pacific		**566,538 t**	**1,162,092 t**	**405 w**	**670 w**	**5.9 w**	**5.4 w**	**..**	**1.3 w**			**1,979.2 t**	**3,682.4 t**	**1.42 w**	**2.18 w**
South Asia		**112,057 t**	**269,625 t**	**124 w**	**221 w**	**7.0 w**	**5.1 w**	**..**	**1.5 w**			**395.2 t**	**866.5 t**	**0.44 w**	**0.74 w**
Europe and Central Asia		**..**	**1,329,092 t**	**..**	**2,727 w**	**..**	**..**	**..**	**0.8 w**			**..**	**..**	**..**	**..**
Middle East and N. Africa		**143,540 t**	**333,267 t**	**821 w**	**1,250 w**	**6.4 w**	**6.2 w**	**..**	**1.5 w**			**500.5 t**	**860.2 t**	**2.86 w**	**3.40 w**
Latin America and Caribbean		**322,214 t**	**453,021 t**	**898 w**	**962 w**	**2.5 w**	**2.7 w**	**..**	**3.7 w**			**857.6 t**	**1,047.0 t**	**2.39 w**	**2.31 w**
High-income economies		**3,743,415 t**	**4,392,058 t**	**4,822 w**	**5,168 w**	**1.5 w**	**1.4 w**	**..**	**4.7 w**			**9,835.0 t**	**10,087.4 t**	**12.67 w**	**12.03 w**
109	Portugal	10,291	18,100	1,054	1,828	4.7	2.6	2.8	4.8	86	90	27.1	47.2	2.77	4.78
110	New Zealand	9,202	15,200	2,956	4,352	4.5	2.2	2.4	3.3	39	5	17.6	26.2	5.65	7.60
111	Spain	68,692	94,500	1,837	2,414	2.6	1.3	3.1	5.1	77	69	200.0	223.2	5.35	5.72
112	Ireland	8,485	11,200	2,495	3,136	2.1	1.5	2.4	4.6	78	70	25.1	30.9	7.37	8.69
113	†Israel	8,616	15,151	2,222	2,815	4.5	6.7	2.6	5.1	98	96	21.1	41.6	5.45	8.13
114	Australia	70,399	92,300	4,792	5,173	2.1	1.5	2.3	3.6	−22	−91	202.8	267.9	13.80	15.33
115	United Kingdom	201,200	219,200	3,572	3,754	1.0	0.6	2.7	4.6	2	−9	588.3	566.2	10.44	9.76
116	Finland	24,998	30,300	5,230	5,954	2.3	1.3	2.1	3.2	72	62	55.1	41.2	11.53	8.17
117	Italy	139,190	154,800	2,466	2,710	1.4	−0.1	3.3	6.6	86	81	372.1	407.7	6.59	7.17
118	†Kuwait	9,500	12,337	6,909	7,615	4.1	11.7	3.0	2.0	−739	−711	24.7	16.0	17.99	11.42
119	Canada	193,170	228,000	7,854	7,795	1.6	2.2	1.4	2.4	−7	−46	430.2	409.9	17.49	14.36
120	†Hong Kong	5,628	13,822	1,117	2,280	7.0	7.7	5.1	9.5	100	100	16.4	29.1	3.26	5.01
121	Netherlands	65,106	70,100	4,601	4,558	1.0	1.2	2.6	4.7	−10	9	152.8	139.0	10.80	9.16
122	†Singapore	6,049	19,210	2,651	6,556	7.2	10.5	1.9	3.6	100	100	30.1	49.8	13.19	17.67
123	Belgium	46,122	51,500	4,684	5,091	1.3	1.2	2.6	4.4	83	77	127.7	101.8	12.97	10.13
124	France	190,660	222,400	3,539	3,839	1.9	0.2	3.5	6.0	75	47	484.1	362.1	8.99	6.31
125	Sweden	40,992	49,200	4,933	5,603	2.1	0.2	3.1	4.0	61	36	71.4	56.8	8.60	6.55
126	Austria	23,449	26,300	3,105	3,276	1.6	−0.4	3.3	7.5	67	65	52.2	56.6	6.91	7.15
127	Germany	359,170	334,000	4,587	4,097	0.5	−1.5	..	6.1	49	58	1,068.3	878.1	13.64	10.89
128	United States	1,801,000	2,060,400	7,908	7,905	1.3	1.8	1.5	3.2	14	19	4,623.2	4,881.3	20.30	19.11
129	Norway	18,865	23,100	4,611	5,326	1.9	1.5	3.1	4.7	−195	−636	40.0	60.2	9.78	14.06
130	Denmark	19,488	20,800	3,804	3,996	0.5	2.4	3.4	7.0	97	27	63.2	53.9	12.34	10.42
131	Japan	347,120	478,000	2,972	3,825	2.4	2.3	3.1	9.6	88	82	933.9	1,093.5	8.00	8.79
132	Switzerland	20,840	25,200	3,298	3,603	2.1	0.2	4.9	10.3	66	59	40.9	43.7	6.48	6.36
133	†*United Arab Emirates*	8,558	24,017	8,205	12,795	8.8	4.4	3.5	..	−996	−470	36.3	70.6	34.77	39.74
World		**6,711,356 t**	**8,035,058 t**	**1,516 w**	**1,434 w**	**2.7 w**	**0.3 w**	**..**	**3.3 w**			**15,659.9 t**	**18,821.8 t**	**3.54 w**	**3.46 w**

a. From industrial processes.

Table 9. Land use and urbanization

		Land use (% of total land area)						Urban population				Population in urban agglomerations of 1 million or more in 1990, as % of			
		Cropland		Permanent pasture		Other		As % of total population		Avg. annual growth rate (%)		Urban		Total	
		1980	1993	1980	1993	1980	1993	1980	1994	1980–90	1990–94	1980	1994	1980	1994
	Low-income economies	11 w	13 w	28 w	31 w	62 w	56 w	22 w	28 w	4.2 w	3.8 w	32 w	34 w	7 w	10 w
	Excluding China and India	6 w	8 w	27 w	30 w	68 w	61 w	23 w	29 w	4.4 w	4.4 w	29 w	31 w	7 w	9 w
1	Rwanda	54	47	29	18	17	34	5	6	4.9	4.4	0	0	0	0
2	Mozambique	4	4	62	56	33	40	13	33	9.1	7.4	48	41	6	13
3	Ethiopia	13	13	41	41	46	47	10	13	4.7	3.2	30	29	3	4
4	Tanzania	1	4	10	40	89	56	15	24	6.8	6.4	30	24	5	6
5	Burundi	8	53	6	36	86	12	4	7	6.9	6.7	0	0	0	0
6	Sierra Leone	3	8	13	31	84	62	24	35	5.0	4.9	0	0	0	0
7	Malawi	25	18	35	20	40	62	9	13	6.1	5.7	0	0	0	0
8	Chad	3	3	37	36	60	62	19	21	3.4	3.5	0	0	0	0
9	Uganda	41	34	13	9	46	57	9	12	4.9	5.6	0	0	0	0
10	Madagascar	7	5	79	41	14	53	18	26	5.7	5.7	0	0	0	0
11	Nepal	17	17	14	15	69	68	6	13	8.0	7.4	0	0	0	0
12	Vietnam	22	20	1	1	77	79	19	21	2.5	3.0	27	32	5	7
13	Bangladesh	79	75	5	5	15	21	11	18	5.9	4.9	46	46	5	8
14	Haiti	5	33	3	18	92	49	24	31	3.9	4.0	55	56	13	17
15	Niger	3	3	8	7	90	90	13	22	7.5	6.9	0	0	0	0
16	Guinea-Bissau	10	12	38	38	51	50	17	22	3.5	4.3	0	0	0	0
17	Kenya	3	8	48	37	49	55	16	27	7.5	6.1	32	28	5	8
18	Mali	2	2	22	25	76	74	18	26	5.1	5.7	0	0	0	0
19	Nigeria	33	36	44	44	23	21	27	38	5.8	5.3	23	27	6	10
20	Yemen, Rep.	3	3	28	30	70	67	20	33	7.0	8.4	0	0	0	0
21	Burkina Faso	13	13	48	22	39	65	9	25	10.0	11.5	0	0	0	0
22	Mongolia	1	1	65	80	34	19	52	60	3.9	2.9	0	0	0	0
23	India	73	57	5	4	22	39	23	27	3.2	2.9	25	35	6	9
24	Lao PDR	6	3	5	3	89	93	13	21	6.2	6.4	0	0	0	0
25	Togo	17	45	48	4	36	52	23	30	5.3	4.8	0	0	0	0
26	Gambia, The	1	18	0	9	99	73	18	25	6.0	6.5	0	0	0	0
27	Nicaragua	10	11	41	46	48	43	53	62	3.9	4.2	42	44	23	28
28	Zambia	7	7	40	40	53	53	40	43	4.2	3.6	23	32	9	14
29	Tajikistan	..	6	..	25	..	70	34	32	2.3	2.0	0	0	0	0
30	Benin	16	17	4	4	80	79	32	41	5.2	4.9	0	0	0	0
31	Central African Republic	7	3	11	5	82	92	35	39	3.0	3.5	0	0	0	0
32	Albania	26	26	15	15	59	59	34	37	2.9	-0.4	0	0	0	0
33	Ghana	13	19	23	22	63	59	31	36	4.3	4.2	30	27	9	10
34	Pakistan	26	30	6	6	67	64	28	34	4.5	4.7	39	52	11	18
35	Mauritania	0	0	40	38	60	62	29	52	7.6	5.5	0	0	0	0
36	Azerbaijan	..	23	..	26	..	51	53	56	1.9	1.6	48	44	26	25
37	Zimbabwe	7	7	14	13	78	80	22	31	6.0	5.0	0	0	0	0
38	Guinea	7	3	65	22	27	75	19	29	5.7	5.7	65	77	12	22
39	China	12	10	39	43	49	47	19	29	4.8	4.1	41	35	8	10
40	Honduras	7	17	10	14	82	69	36	47	5.4	4.9	0	0	0	0
41	Senegal	23	12	30	16	47	72	36	42	4.0	4.0	49	55	18	23
42	Côte d'Ivoire	14	12	59	41	27	47	35	43	5.4	5.3	44	45	15	19
43	Congo	0	0	5	29	95	70	41	58	5.9	5.1	0	0	0	0
44	Kyrgyz Republic	..	7	..	47	..	46	38	39	1.9	0.8	0	0	0	0
45	Sri Lanka	10	29	2	7	87	64	22	22	1.4	2.2	0	0	0	0
46	Armenia	..	20	..	24	..	55	66	69	1.6	1.8	51	50	34	34
47	Cameroon	2	15	2	4	96	81	31	44	5.4	5.3	19	36	6	16
48	Egypt, Arab Rep.	2	3	..	5	98	92	44	45	2.6	2.4	52	51	23	23
49	Lesotho	2	11	12	66	86	24	13	22	6.8	6.1	0	0	0	0
50	*Georgia*	..	14	..	29	..	57	52	58	1.6	0.7	42	43	22	25
51	*Myanmar*	30	15	1	1	69	84	24	26	2.5	3.3	27	32	7	8
	Middle-income economies	8 w	10 w	25 w	23 w	74 w	67 w	52 w	61 w	3.0 w	2.4 w	32 w	33 w	16 w	20 w
	Lower-middle-income	8 w	11 w	17 w	18 w	83 w	71 w	47 w	56 w	3.0 w	2.3 w	28 w	30 w	12 w	16 w
52	Bolivia	3	2	43	24	54	73	46	58	4.2	3.2	30	29	14	17
53	Macedonia, FYR	..	26	..	25	..	49	54	59	1.5	1.6	0	0	0	0
54	Moldova	..	67	..	11	..	22	40	51	2.7	1.5	0	0	0	0
55	Indonesia	31	17	19	7	50	76	22	34	5.3	3.8	33	38	7	13
56	Philippines	26	31	3	4	70	65	38	53	5.2	4.4	33	25	12	13
57	Uzbekistan	..	11	..	52	..	37	41	41	2.5	2.6	28	24	11	10
58	Morocco	15	22	40	47	44	31	41	48	3.5	3.0	26	37	11	18
59	Kazakstan	..	13	..	70	..	17	54	59	1.9	0.9	12	12	6	7
60	Guatemala	28	17	21	23	52	60	37	41	3.4	4.0	0	0	0	0
61	Papua New Guinea	1	1	0	0	99	99	13	16	3.6	3.7	0	0	0	0
62	Bulgaria	11	39	5	17	84	44	61	70	1.0	0.0	20	23	12	16
63	Romania	62	43	26	21	12	36	49	55	1.3	0.2	18	17	9	9
64	Ecuador	9	11	15	8	77	82	47	58	4.2	3.6	29	44	14	26
65	Dominican Republic	29	30	43	0	27	70	50	64	4.1	3.1	49	51	25	33
66	Lithuania	..	46	..	7	..	47	61	71	2.1	0.9	0	0	0	0
67	El Salvador	35	35	29	29	36	35	42	45	1.9	2.7	0	0	0	0
68	Jordan	4	5	9	9	88	87	60	71	5.1	7.0	49	40	29	28
69	Jamaica	4	20	3	24	94	56	47	55	2.3	2.1	0	0	0	0
70	Paraguay	4	6	40	54	56	40	42	52	4.8	4.4	0	0	0	0
71	Algeria	3	3	15	13	82	84	43	55	4.8	3.9	25	24	11	13
72	Colombia	10	5	75	39	14	56	64	72	2.8	2.7	34	38	22	28

Note: For data comparability and coverage, see the technical notes.

		Land use (% of total land area)						Urban population				Population in urban agglomerations of 1 million or more in 1990, as % of			
		Cropland		Permanent pasture		Other		As % of total population		Avg. annual growth rate (%)		Urban		Total	
		1980	1993	1980	1993	1980	1993	1980	1994	1980–90	1990–94	1980	1994	1980	1994
73	Tunisia	13	32	10	23	77	46	51	57	3.2	2.8	34	39	17	22
74	Ukraine	..	59	..	13	..	28	62	70	1.2	0.9	22	22	14	15
75	Namibia	1	1	46	46	53	53	23	36	6.2	6.2	0	0	0	0
76	Peru	3	3	21	21	76	76	65	72	3.0	2.6	40	43	26	31
77	Belarus	..	30	..	15	..	55	56	70	2.2	1.5	24	24	14	17
78	Slovak Republic	..	34	..	17	..	49	52	58	1.5	1.1	0	0	0	0
79	Latvia	..	28	..	13	..	59	68	73	1.0	-0.8	0	0	0	0
80	Costa Rica	15	10	61	46	23	44	43	49	3.8	3.3	0	0	0	0
81	Poland	49	48	13	13	38	38	58	64	1.4	1.0	31	28	18	18
82	Thailand	50	41	2	2	48	58	17	20	2.8	2.4	59	56	10	11
83	Turkey	45	36	15	16	39	48	44	67	5.8	4.6	39	34	17	23
84	Croatia	..	25	..	22	..	52	50	64	2.2	1.5	0	0	0	0
85	Panama	7	9	18	20	75	71	50	54	2.8	2.7	0	0	0	0
86	Russian Federation	..	8	..	5	..	88	70	73	1.2	-0.2	23	25	16	19
87	Venezuela	7	4	31	20	62	75	83	92	3.5	2.9	20	29	16	27
88	Botswana	0	1	6	45	94	54	15	30	8.9	7.6	0	0	0	0
89	Estonia	..	27	..	7	..	66	70	73	1.0	-0.9	0	0	0	0
90	Iran, Islamic Rep.	6	11	21	27	73	62	50	58	5.0	3.9	26	35	13	20
91	Turkmenistan	..	3	..	74	..	23	47	45	2.0	5.1	0	0	0	0
Upper-middle-income		**9 w**	**7 w**	**37 w**	**32 w**	**55 w**	**61 w**	**64 w**	**74 w**	**3.0 w**	**2.6 w**	**40 w**	**40 w**	**26 w**	**30 w**
92	Brazil	15	6	52	22	33	72	66	77	3.3	2.7	42	42	27	32
93	South Africa	10	11	59	67	31	23	48	50	2.7	2.9	23	37	11	19
94	Mauritius	2	52	0	3	98	44	42	41	0.4	1.4	0	0	0	0
95	Czech Republic	..	43	..	11	..	46	64	65	0.3	0.1	18	18	12	12
96	Malaysia	17	15	0	0	83	85	42	53	4.4	4.0	16	12	7	6
97	Chile	2	6	6	18	91	76	81	86	2.1	1.8	41	41	33	35
98	Trinidad and Tobago	41	24	4	2	56	74	63	66	1.6	1.7	0	0	0	0
99	Hungary	46	55	11	13	43	33	57	64	0.5	0.6	34	31	19	20
100	Gabon	8	2	82	18	10	80	36	49	6.0	5.1	0	0	0	0
101	Mexico	17	13	52	39	31	48	66	75	2.9	2.8	41	38	27	28
102	Uruguay	3	7	27	77	70	15	85	90	1.0	0.9	49	46	42	42
103	Oman	0	0	3	5	97	95	8	13	8.7	8.6	0	0	0	0
104	Slovenia	..	15	..	28	..	57	48	63	2.6	1.3	0	0	0	0
105	Saudi Arabia	1	2	40	56	59	42	67	80	6.9	4.1	28	27	19	21
106	Greece	38	27	51	41	11	32	58	65	1.3	1.5	54	54	31	35
107	Argentina	10	10	52	52	38	38	83	88	1.9	1.6	42	44	35	39
108	Korea, Rep.	38	21	1	1	62	78	57	80	3.8	2.9	65	64	37	51
Low- and middle-income		**10 w**	**11 w**	**27 w**	**26 w**	**68 w**	**63 w**	**32 w**	**39 w**	**3.6 w**	**3.1 w**	**32 w**	**34 w**	**10 w**	**13 w**
Sub-Saharan Africa		**4 w**	**7 w**	**24 w**	**33 w**	**72 w**	**60 w**	**24 w**	**31 w**	**4.9 w**	**4.8 w**	**21 w**	**24 w**	**5 w**	**8 w**
East Asia and Pacific		**13 w**	**12 w**	**35 w**	**34 w**	**52 w**	**54 w**	**22 w**	**32 w**	**4.6 w**	**3.9 w**	**40 w**	**36 w**	**9 w**	**11 w**
South Asia		**50 w**	**45 w**	**12 w**	**10 w**	**39 w**	**45 w**	**22 w**	**26 w**	**3.5 w**	**3.3 w**	**27 w**	**36 w**	**6 w**	**10 w**
Europe and Central Asia		**39 w**	**13 w**	**16 w**	**16 w**	**92 w**	**71 w**	**58 w**	**65 w**	**2.0 w**	**1.0 w**	**24 w**	**24 w**	**14 w**	**16 w**
Middle East and N. Africa		**4 w**	**6 w**	**19 w**	**24 w**	**78 w**	**70 w**	**48 w**	**56 w**	**4.4 w**	**3.7 w**	**32 w**	**35 w**	**15 w**	**18 w**
Latin America and Caribbean		**9 w**	**7 w**	**38 w**	**29 w**	**53 w**	**64 w**	**65 w**	**74 w**	**3.0 w**	**2.6 w**	**36 w**	**37 w**	**24 w**	**28 w**
High-income economies		**15 w**	**12 w**	**32 w**	**25 w**	**54 w**	**63 w**	**76 w**	**77 w**	**0.8 w**	**0.3 w**	**40 w**	**43 w**	**30 w**	**34 w**
109	Portugal	34	34	9	9	57	56	29	35	1.4	1.3	46	52	13	18
110	New Zealand	2	14	53	51	45	35	83	86	0.9	1.2	0	0	0	0
111	Spain	25	40	13	21	62	40	73	76	0.7	0.5	27	23	20	18
112	Ireland	5	13	19	68	77	18	55	57	0.6	0.7	0	0	0	0
113	† Israel	11	21	3	7	86	72	89	90	..	..	41	39	37	35
114	Australia	6	6	57	54	37	39	86	85	1.4	1.0	55	68	47	58
115	United Kingdom	11	27	18	46	71	27	89	89	0.3	0.4	28	26	25	23
116	Finland	8	8	1	0	91	91	60	63	0.7	1.1	0	0	0	0
117	Italy	53	41	22	15	25	45	67	67	0.1	0.2	39	31	26	20
118	† Kuwait	0	0	1	8	99	92	90	97	5.1	-5.4	67	70	60	67
119	Canada	8	5	5	3	87	92	76	77	1.4	1.3	38	45	29	35
120	† Hong Kong	5	..	1	..	94	..	92	95	1.6	1.7	100	100	91	95
121	Netherlands	24	27	35	31	41	41	88	89	0.6	0.8	8	16	7	14
122	† Singapore	14	2	0	0	86	98	100	100	1.7	2.0	100	100	100	100
123	Belgium	..	31	..	21	..	48	95	97	0.2	0.5	13	11	12	11
124	France	34	35	23	20	42	45	73	73	0.4	0.6	29	28	21	21
125	Sweden	21	7	5	1	74	92	83	83	0.3	0.6	20	21	17	17
126	Austria	20	18	25	24	56	58	55	55	0.3	1.0	49	46	27	26
127	Germany	..	34	..	15	..	51	83	86	0.4	1.0	46	47	38	40
128	United States	30	20	38	25	32	55	74	76	1.2	1.3	49	56	36	43
129	Norway	3	3	0	0	97	97	71	73	0.6	0.8	0	0	0	0
130	Denmark	63	60	6	5	31	35	84	85	0.2	0.4	32	30	27	26
131	Japan	22	12	3	2	76	86	76	78	0.7	0.4	44	48	34	37
132	Switzerland	12	11	47	32	40	56	57	61	1.0	1.4	0	0	0	0
133	† United Arab Emirates	0	0	2	2	97	97	72	83	6.1	3.7	0	0	0	0
World		**11 w**	**11 w**	**28 w**	**26 w**	**65 w**	**63 w**	**39 w**	**45 w**	**2.7 w**	**2.3 w**	**34 w**	**35 w**	**14 w**	**16 w**

Table 10. Forests and water resources

		Forest area			Nationally protected areas, 1994[a]			Annual freshwater withdrawal, 1970–94[b]			
		Total area (thousand sq. km) 1990	Ann. deforestation, 1981–90						As % of	Per capita (cu. m)	
			Thousand sq. km	As % of total area	Thousand sq. km	Number	As % of total surface area	Total (cu. km)	total water resources	Domestic	Other
Low-income economies					2,006.6 t	1,666 t	5.0 w				
Excluding China and India					1,282.4 t	829 t	4.7 w				
1	Rwanda	2	0.0	0.2	3.3	2	12.4	0.2	2.4	6	18
2	Mozambique	173	1.4	0.8	0.0	1	0.0	0.8	0.4c	13	42
3	Ethiopia	142	0.4	0.3	60.2	23	5.5	2.2	2.0	6	45
4	Tanzania	336	4.4	1.3	138.9	30	14.7	0.5	0.5c	7	28
5	Burundi	2	0.0	0.6	0.9	3	3.2	0.1	2.8	7	13
6	Sierra Leone	19	0.1	0.6	0.8	2	1.1	0.4	0.2	7	92
7	Malawi	35	0.5	1.5	10.6	9	8.9	0.2	0.9c	7	13
8	Chad	114	0.9	0.8	114.9	9	9.0	0.2	0.4c	6	29
9	Uganda	63	0.6	1.0	19.1	31	8.1	0.2	0.3c	7	14
10	Madagascar	158	1.3	0.9	11.1	37	1.9	16.3	4.8	16	1,568
11	Nepal	50	0.5	1.1	11.1	12	7.9	2.7	1.6	6	144
12	Vietnam	83	1.4	1.6	13.3	59	4.0	28.9	7.7	54	361
13	Bangladesh	8	0.4	4.9	1.0	8	0.7	22.5	1.0c	7	213
14	Haiti	0	0.0	6.5	0.1	3	0.4	0.0	0.4	2	5
15	Niger	24	0.1	0.4	84.2	5	6.6	0.3	0.9c	9	33
16	Guinea-Bissau	20	0.2	0.8	..	..	..	0.0	0.0c	3	8
17	Kenya	12	0.1	0.6	35.0	36	6.0	1.1	3.6c	14	37
18	Mali	121	1.1	0.9	40.1	11	3.2	1.4	1.4c	3	159
19	Nigeria	156	1.2	0.8	29.7	19	3.2	3.6	1.3c	13	28
20	Yemen, Rep.	41	0.0	0.0	..	..	..	3.4	136.0	17	318
21	Burkina Faso	44	0.3	0.7	26.6	12	9.7	0.2	0.5	5	13
22	Mongolia	139	1.3	0.9	61.7	15	3.9	0.6	2.2	30	243
23	India	517	3.4	0.7	143.5	374	4.4	380.0	18.2c	18	594
24	Lao PDR	132	1.3	1.0	24.4	17	10.3	1.0	0.4	21	239
25	Togo	14	0.2	1.6	6.5	11	11.4	0.1	0.8c	17	11
26	Gambia, The	1	0.0	0.8	0.2	5	2.0	0.0	0.3c	2	27
27	Nicaragua	60	1.2	2.1	9.0	59	6.9	0.9	0.5	92	275
28	Zambia	323	3.6	1.1	63.6	21	8.5	0.4	0.3c	54	32
29	Tajikistan	..	..	..	0.9	3	0.6	12.6	13.2c	123	2,332
30	Benin	49	0.7	1.4	7.8	2	6.9	0.1	0.4c	7	19
31	Central African Republic	306	1.3	0.4	61.1	13	9.8	0.1	0.0	5	20
32	Albania	14	0.0	0.0	0.3	11	1.2	0.2	0.9c	6	88
33	Ghana	96	1.4	1.4	11.0	9	4.6	0.3	0.6c	12	23
34	Pakistan	19	0.8	4.1	37.2	55	4.7	153.4	32.8c	21	2,032
35	Mauritania	6	0.0	0.0	17.5	4	1.7	0.7	6.4c	59	436
36	Azerbaijan	..	..	..	1.9	12	2.2	15.8	56.4c	90	2,158
37	Zimbabwe	89	0.6	0.7	30.7	25	7.9	1.2	6.1c	19	117
38	Guinea	67	0.9	1.3	1.6	3	0.7	0.7	0.3	14	126
39	China	1,246	8.8	0.7	580.7	463	6.1	460.0	16.4	28	433
40	Honduras	46	1.1	2.4	8.6	44	7.7	1.5	2.1c	12	282
41	Senegal	75	0.5	0.7	21.8	10	11.1	1.4	3.5c	10	191
42	Côte d'Ivoire	109	1.2	1.1	19.9	12	6.2	0.7	0.9	15	52
43	Congo	199	0.3	0.2	11.8	10	3.4	0.0	0.0c	12	7
44	Kyrgyz Republic	..	..	..	2.8	5	1.4	11.7	24.0	82	2,647
45	Sri Lanka	17	0.3	1.5	8.0	56	12.1	6.3	14.6	10	493
46	Armenia	..	..	..	2.1	4	7.2	3.8	45.8c	149	996
47	Cameroon	204	1.2	0.6	20.5	14	4.3	0.4	0.1	17	20
48	Egypt, Arab Rep.	0	0.0	0.0	7.9	12	0.8	56.4	97.1c	67	889
49	Lesotho	0	..	..	0.1	1	0.2	0.1	1.0	7	24
50	*Georgia*	..	..	..	1.9	15	2.7	4.0	6.5c	156	586
51	*Myanmar*	289	4.0	1.4	1.7	2	0.3	4.0	0.4	7	94
Middle-income economies					2,984.5 t	2,675 t	4.9 w				
Lower-middle-income					2,161.0 t	1,670 t	5.4 w				
52	Bolivia	493	6.3	1.3	92.3	25	8.4	1.2	0.4	20	181
53	Macedonia, FYR	9	0.0	0.1	2.2	16	8.4	..	..	..	..
54	Moldova	..	..	..	0.1	2	0.2	3.7	29.1c	60	793
55	Indonesia	1,095	12.1	1.1	185.6	175	9.7	16.6	0.7	12	83
56	Philippines	78	3.2	4.0	6.1	27	2.0	29.5	9.1	123	562
57	Uzbekistan	..	..	..	2.4	10	0.5	82.2	76.4c	165	3,956
58	Morocco	90	−1.2	−1.3	3.6	10	0.8	10.9	36.2	23	404
59	Kazakstan	..	..	..	8.9	9	0.3	37.9	30.2c	92	2,202
60	Guatemala	42	0.8	1.9	8.3	17	7.6	0.7	0.6	13	127
61	Papua New Guinea	360	1.1	0.3	0.8	5	0.2	0.1	0.0	8	20
62	Bulgaria	37	−0.1	−0.2	3.7	46	3.3	13.9	6.8c	43	1,501
63	Romania	63	0.0	0.0	10.9	39	4.6	26.0	12.5c	91	1,044
64	Ecuador	120	2.4	2.0	111.1	15	39.2	5.6	1.8	41	541
65	Dominican Republic	11	0.4	3.3	10.5	17	21.5	3.0	14.9	22	423
66	Lithuania	..	..	..	6.3	76	9.7	4.4	19.0c	83	1,107
67	El Salvador	1	0.0	2.6	0.1	2	0.2	1.0	5.3	17	228
68	Jordan	1	0.0	−1.0	2.9	10	3.3	0.4	32.1c	50	123
69	Jamaica	2	0.3	11.2	0.0	1	0.2	0.3	3.9	11	148
70	Paraguay	129	4.0	3.1	14.8	19	3.6	0.4	0.1c	16	93
71	Algeria	41	0.3	0.8	119.2	19	5.0	3.0	20.3c	35	125
72	Colombia	541	3.7	0.7	93.6	79	8.2	5.3	0.5	71	103

Note: For data comparability and coverage, see the technical notes.

		Forest area			Nationally protected areas, 1994[a]			Annual freshwater withdrawal, 1970–94[b]			
		Total area (thousand sq. km) 1990	Ann. deforestation, 1981–90						As % of total water resources	Per capita (cu. m)	
			Thousand sq. km	As % of total area	Thousand sq. km	Number	As % of total surface area	Total (cu. km)		Domestic	Other
73	Tunisia	7	−0.1	−1.8	0.4	7	0.3	2.3	60.5c	41	276
74	Ukraine	92	−0.2	−0.3	5.2	20	0.9	34.7	40.0c	108	565
75	Namibia	126	0.4	0.3	102.2	12	12.4	0.1	0.3c	7	103
76	Peru	679	2.7	0.4	41.8	22	3.2	6.1	15.3	57	243
77	Belarus	63	−0.3	−0.4	2.4	10	1.2	3.0	5.4c	94	200
78	Slovak Republic	18	0.0	0.1	10.2	40	20.7	1.8	5.8	..	..
79	Latvia	..	..	..	7.8	45	12.0	0.7	2.2c	110	152
80	Costa Rica	14	0.5	3.5	6.4	29	12.5	1.4	1.4	31	749
81	Poland	87	−0.1	−0.1	30.6	111	9.8	12.3	21.9c	42	279
82	Thailand	127	5.2	4.0	70.2	111	13.7	31.9	17.8c	24	578
83	Turkey	202	0.0	0.0	8.2	44	1.1	33.5	17.3c	140	445
84	Croatia	20	0.0	0.1	3.8	29	6.8	..	..	..	..
85	Panama	31	0.6	2.1	13.3	15	17.6	1.3	0.9	91	664
86	Russian Federation	..	..	..	655.4	199	3.8	117.0	2.7c	134	656
87	Venezuela	457	6.0	1.3	263.2	100	28.9	4.1	0.3c	164	218
88	Botswana	143	0.8	0.5	106.6	9	18.3	0.1	0.6c	5	94
89	Estonia	..	..	..	4.4	39	9.8	3.3	21.2c	105	1,992
90	*Iran, Islamic Rep.*	180	0.0	0.0	83.0	68	5.0	45.4	38.6	54	1,307
91	*Turkmenistan*	..	..	..	11.1	8	2.3	22.8	32.6c	64	6,326
Upper-middle-income					**823.5 t**	**1,005 t**	**4.0 w**				
92	Brazil	5,611	36.7	0.7	321.9	273	3.8	36.5	0.5c	54	191
93	South Africa	45	−0.4	−0.8	69.3	237	5.7	14.7	29.3c	47	348
94	Mauritius	1	0.0	0.2	0.0	3	2.0	0.4	16.4	66	344
95	Czech Republic	26	0.0	0.0	10.7	34	13.5	2.7	4.7	109	157
96	Malaysia	176	4.0	2.3	14.9	54	4.5	9.4	2.1	177	592
97	Chile	88	−0.1	−0.1	137.2	66	18.1	16.8	3.6	98	1,528
98	Trinidad and Tobago	2	0.0	−1.9	0.2	6	3.1	0.2	2.9	40	108
99	Hungary	17	−0.1	−0.5	5.7	53	6.2	6.8	5.7c	59	601
100	Gabon	182	1.2	0.6	10.4	6	3.9	0.1	0.0	41	16
101	Mexico	486	6.8	1.4	97.3	65	5.0	77.6	21.7	54	845
102	Uruguay	7	0.0	−0.6	0.3	8	0.2	0.6	0.5c	14	227
103	Oman	41	0.0	0.0	37.4	29	17.6	0.5	24.0	17	547
104	Slovenia	10	0.0	0.0	1.1	10	5.3	..	..	..	..
105	Saudi Arabia	12	0.0	0.0	62.0	10	2.9	3.6	163.6	224	273
106	Greece	60	0.0	0.0	2.2	24	1.7	5.0	8.6c	42	481
107	Argentina	592	0.9	0.1	43.7	86	1.6	27.6	2.8c	94	949
108	Korea, Rep.	65	0.1	0.1	6.9	28	7.0	27.6	41.8	117	515
Low- and middle-income					**4,991.1 t**	**4,341 t**	**5.0 w**				
Sub-Saharan Africa					**1,361.7 t**	**677 t**	**5.7 w**				
East Asia and Pacific					**997.4 t**	**993 t**	**6.1 w**				
South Asia					**212.6 t**	**520 t**	**4.1 w**				
Europe and Central Asia					**807.0 t**	**940 t**	**3.3 w**				
Middle East and N. Africa					**318.2 t**	**172 t**	**3.2 w**				
Latin America and Caribbean					**1,294.2 t**	**1,039 t**	**6.3 w**				
High-income economies					**4,324.5 t**	**5,508 t**	**13.6 w**				
109	Portugal	31	−0.1	−0.4	5.8	25	6.3	7.3	10.5c	111	628
110	New Zealand	75	..	..	61.5	206	22.7	2.0	0.6	271	318
111	Spain	256	0.0	0.0	42.5	215	8.4	30.8	27.6c	94	687
112	Ireland	4	0.0	−1.1	0.5	12	0.7	0.8	1.6c	37	196
113	†Israel	1	0.0	−0.3	3.1	15	14.6	1.9	84.1c	65	343
114	Australia	1,456	0.0	0.0	935.5	892	12.1	14.6	4.3	607	327
115	United Kingdom	24	−0.2	−1.0	51.3	191	20.9	11.8	16.6	41	164
116	Finland	234	−0.1	0.0	27.3	82	8.1	2.2	1.9c	53	387
117	Italy	86	..	..	22.8	172	7.6	56.2	33.7c	138	848
118	†Kuwait	0	0.0	0.0	0.3	2	1.5	0.5	..	336	189
119	Canada	4,533	..	..	825.5	640	8.3	45.1	1.6	288	1,314
120	†Hong Kong	0	0.0	−0.5	..	..	..	..	..	..	..
121	Netherlands	3	0.0	−0.3	3.9	79	10.4	7.8	8.7c	26	492
122	†Singapore	0	0.0	2.5	0.0	1	4.8	0.2	31.7	38	46
123	Belgium	6	0.0	−0.3	0.8	3	2.5	9.0	72.2 c	101	816
124	France	135	−0.1	−0.1	56.0	110	10.2	37.7	19.1c	106	559
125	Sweden	280	−0.1	0.0	29.9	214	6.6	2.9	1.6c	123	218
126	Austria	39	−0.1	−0.4	20.0	170	23.9	2.4	2.6c	101	203
127	Germany	107	−0.5	−0.4	92.0	504	25.8	46.3	27.1c	64	518
128	United States	2,960	3.2	0.1	1,042.4	1,494	11.1	467.3	18.9c	244	1,626
129	Norway	96	..	..	55.4	114	17.1	2.0	0.5c	98	390
130	Denmark	5	0.0	0.0	13.9	113	32.2	1.2	9.2c	70	163
131	Japan	238	0.0	0.0	27.6	80	7.3	90.8	16.6	125	610
132	Switzerland	12	−0.1	−0.6	7.3	109	17.7	1.2	2.4c	40	133
133	†*United Arab Emirates*	0	0.0	0.0	..	..	..	0.9	300.0	97	787
World					**9,315.5 t**	**9,849 t**	**7.1 w**				

a. Data may refer to earlier years and are the most recent reported by the World Conservation Monitoring Centre in 1994. b. Refers to any year from 1970 to 1994.
c. Total water resources include river flows from other countries.

Table 11. Growth of the economy

		GDP		GDP deflator		Agriculture		Industry		Services[a]		Exports of goods and nonfactor services		Gross domestic investment	
		1980–90	1990–94	1980–90	1990–94	1980–90	1990–94	1980–90	1990–94	1980–90	1990–94	1980–90	1990–94	1980–90	1990–94
	Low-income economies	5.8 w	6.2 w	13.0 w	59.0 w	3.5 w	2.8 w	7.4 w	11.0 w	6.8 w	5.2 w	5.7 w	10.4 w	6.1 w	7.9 w
	Excluding China and India	2.9 w	1.4 w	24.8 w	150.2 w	2.0 w	1.5 w	2.7 w	–0.7 w	3.7 w	2.1 w	2.5 w	3.0 w	–0.4 w	–1.8 w
1	Rwanda	2.3	–15.5	3.3	9.7	0.7	–13.8	1.7	–23.4	4.3	–14.2	4.4	1.2	3.7	–12.3
2	Mozambique	–0.2	7.3	38.4	49.3	1.6	2.4	–9.8	–2.4	2.8	12.7	–5.0	7.2	–2.5	8.6
3	Ethiopia	2.3[b]	..	3.4[b]	..	1.1[b]	..	0.1[b]	..	4.4[b]	..	..	..	..	..
4	Tanzania	3.8	3.1	35.7	20.4	4.9	5.8	3.4	9.7	2.8	–3.1	..	..	..	..
5	Burundi	4.4	–1.4	4.4	7.1	3.1	–3.1	4.5	–3.4	6.3	1.5	4.5	–2.5	4.5	–4.0
6	Sierra Leone	0.9	0.6	56.0	55.9	2.9	0.6	–2.0	7.4	0.7	–2.7	–7.6	5.4	–4.0	1.1
7	Malawi	2.7	–0.7	14.6	22.8	2.0	–0.6	2.9	–0.4	3.0	–1.0	2.5	0.4	–3.9	–14.5
8	Chad[c]	6.3	1.3	1.1	6.6	b	6.9	8.0	–9.9	9.9	1.2	7.7	–15.8	19.0	–2.9
9	Uganda	3.1	5.6	125.6	28.8	2.3	3.3	6.0	9.3	3.5	7.7	2.3	5.3	9.3	2.6
10	Madagascar	1.1	–0.2	17.1	16.8	2.5	1.5	0.9	–0.7	0.5	–1.1	–2.0	4.4	4.9	–7.4
11	Nepal	4.6	4.9	11.1	12.6	4.0	1.3	6.0	10.5	4.8	6.8	0.9	26.8	2.2	6.3
12	Vietnam[c]	..	8.0	..	29.8	..	4.5	..	..	..	..	..	..	..	..
13	Bangladesh[c]	4.3	4.2	9.5	4.1	2.7	1.9	4.9	7.1	5.7	5.0	6.6	11.7	1.4	4.7
14	Haiti	–0.2	–8.1	7.5	20.9	..	..	..	..	..	..	1.2	–19.0	–0.6	–45.7
15	Niger[c]	–1.1	–0.3	2.9	4.7	1.8	–3.5	–3.3	–1.3	–5.2	–2.2	–4.6	–6.7	–5.9	–6.9
16	Guinea-Bissau	4.5	3.6	56.1	53.4	6.7	4.7	0.4	2.3	3.3	2.3	–1.6	–6.2	5.8	0.7
17	Kenya	4.2	0.9	9.0	17.7	3.3	–1.5	3.9	0.9	4.8	2.0	4.3	0.4	0.8	–2.2
18	Mali[c]	1.5	2.0	5.6	8.0	4.3	1.7	2.7	5.3	–1.4	1.1	5.2	3.0	5.4	5.0
19	Nigeria	1.6	2.4	16.6	37.4	3.3	2.2	–1.0	0.3	2.8	4.5	–0.3	1.7	–10.9	–4.6
20	Yemen, Rep.	..	..	..	..	..	..	..	..	..	..	..	..	..	..
21	Burkina Faso	3.7	2.5	3.1	4.0	3.1	4.6	3.7	1.4	4.2	1.6	–0.6	–2.4	8.6	–15.1
22	Mongolia[c]	5.5	–4.4	–1.2	157.7	2.9	–4.0	4.6	–7.0	18.5	–4.0	5.2	–13.0	1.7	–20.3
23	India	5.8	3.8	8.0	10.1	3.1	2.9	7.1	3.2	6.9	4.6	5.9	13.6	6.5	1.2
24	Lao PDR[c]	..	6.2	..	8.8	..	..	..	..	..	..	..	8.3	..	..
25	Togo[c]	1.8	–3.4	4.7	5.7	5.6	3.3	1.1	–6.0	–0.3	–8.6	0.6	–13.6	2.1	–34.3
26	Gambia, The	3.4	1.4	18.7	5.6	0.4	–0.5	6.0	–0.8	4.8	2.4	0.6	–5.6	0.8	3.0
27	Nicaragua[c]	–2.0	0.5	422.6	148.6	–2.2	0.3	–1.7	–4.4	–2.0	2.2	–3.8	3.8	–4.7	2.8
28	Zambia[c]	0.8	–0.1	42.4	124.2	3.6	2.1	1.0	–1.3	0.1	0.4	–3.3	13.7	–2.7	–16.9
29	Tajikistan	2.9	–22.5	0.5	522.3	–1.4	..	3.6	..	5.9	..	..	..	4.2	..
30	Benin[c]	2.6	4.1	1.6	7.9	5.1	4.9	2.1	3.5	1.2	3.5	–2.2	1.9	–6.2	12.1
31	Central African Republic	1.7	–0.1	5.6	6.2	2.7	1.5	3.1	–4.6	0.5	–2.9	–3.7	4.4	4.8	–8.7
32	Albania	1.5	–4.2	–0.4	101.6	2.4	6.4	3.2	–21.8	–2.4	4.3	–2.6	–6.6	–0.3	–11.3
33	Ghana[c]	3.0	4.3	42.4	20.7	1.0	1.8	3.3	4.3	6.4	7.3	2.5	7.5	4.5	–3.9
34	Pakistan	6.3	4.6	6.7	10.8	4.3	2.7	7.3	6.3	6.9	4.7	8.1	11.3	5.9	4.7
35	Mauritania	1.7	3.6	8.6	7.6	1.7	5.3	4.9	2.0	0.3	3.3	3.4	–3.8	–4.1	3.2
36	Azerbaijan[c]	2.1	–22.9	..	696.6	–1.4	..	2.8	..	4.2	..	..	..	0.4	..
37	Zimbabwe	3.5	1.1	11.5	27.0	2.4	1.6	3.6	–3.6	3.9	1.3	5.4	4.5	1.3	0.2
38	Guinea	..	3.5	..	11.7	..	4.3	..	1.9	..	4.3	..	0.5	..	–1.1
39	China[c]	10.2	12.9	5.8	10.8	5.9	4.1	11.1	18.8	13.6	9.9	11.5	16.0	11.0	15.4
40	Honduras	2.7	3.8	5.7	16.9	2.7	3.4	3.3	6.0	2.5	1.5	1.1	1.4	2.9	12.6
41	Senegal[c]	3.2	0.0	6.4	7.1	2.9	–4.9	3.8	1.1	3.1	1.2	2.8	1.4	3.6	–0.1
42	Côte d'Ivoire	–0.1	–0.2	3.1	6.8	–0.5	–0.9	4.4	0.2	–1.4	0.1	–1.0	–1.2	–10.8	1.4
43	Congo[c]	3.6	–0.1	0.3	2.1	3.4	–2.8	5.2	3.4	2.6	–2.6	4.8	5.7	–11.9	–6.7
44	Kyrgyz Republic	4.2	–16.9	0.1	454.9	2.2	..	..	..	..	..	..	..	2.5	16.0
45	Sri Lanka	4.2	5.4	10.9	9.5	2.2	2.0	4.6	7.5	5.0	5.8	3.7	10.7	1.7	10.8
46	Armenia	3.3	–27.8	0.3	967.0	–3.9	–1.9	5.1	–36.7	4.4	–28.7	..	..	6.2	–25.0
47	Cameroon[c]	1.9	–4.1	5.7	2.7	1.2	–1.2	3.7	–6.9	1.0	–3.9	9.1	–0.6	–0.8	–10.0
48	Egypt, Arab Rep.	5.0	1.1	11.7	14.9	1.5	1.8	2.6	0.1	7.5	1.2	6.1	–1.5	2.7	–2.7
49	Lesotho	4.3	6.1	13.6	11.9	2.6	–2.3	7.2	11.4	3.6	4.7	4.1	10.6	6.9	10.4
50	*Georgia*	0.5	–31.2	1.9	2,707.1	0.7	–31.5	1.8	–38.8	–1.3	–26.6	..	..	..	..
51	*Myanmar*	0.6	5.7	12.2	24.4	0.5	5.1	0.5	9.4	0.7	5.5	1.9	13.6	–4.1	9.4
	Middle-income economies	2.2 w	0.2 w	57.3 w	334.6 w	..	0.9 w	..	1.3 w	..	3.7 w	..	..	..	2.1 w
	Lower-middle-income	2.2 w	–2.3 w	15.5 w	326.4 w	..	..	..	..	..	..	..	..	..	..
52	Bolivia[c]	..	3.8	317.4	10.9	2.0	..	–2.9	..	–0.1	..	3.5	6.1	–9.9	5.8
53	Macedonia, FYR	..	..	..	..	..	..	..	..	..	..	..	..	..	..
54	Moldova	..	..	..	..	..	..	..	..	..	..	..	..	..	..
55	Indonesia[c]	6.1	7.6	8.5	7.4	3.4	3.0	6.9	9.8	7.0	7.6	2.9	10.8	7.0	7.5
56	Philippines[c]	1.0	1.6	14.9	9.6	1.0	1.6	–0.9	0.9	2.8	2.1	3.5	8.0	–2.1	2.3
57	Uzbekistan	3.4	–5.0	–0.7	628.7	–0.1	–0.7	4.3	–6.7	5.4	–6.3	..	..	0.4	–9.1
58	Morocco[c]	4.2	1.7	7.2	4.4	6.7	–1.5	3.0	0.3	4.2	3.4	5.6	2.1	2.5	–2.7
59	Kazakstan	1.5	–14.3	2.8	976.5	..	..	..	..	..	..	..	..	1.9	–26.0
60	Guatemala[c]	0.8	4.1	14.6	15.5	2.3	2.5	2.1	4.2	2.1	4.9	–2.1	5.2	–1.8	10.7
61	Papua New Guinea[c]	1.9	11.5	5.3	3.8	1.8	5.3	1.9	24.3	0.7	..	3.3	18.3	–0.9	–4.1
62	Bulgaria	4.0	–5.9	1.2	90.0	–2.1	–2.9	5.2	–9.3	4.8	–0.6	–3.5	–5.3	2.4	–10.1
63	Romania	0.6	–3.7	2.5	191.9	..	–2.3	..	–5.1	..	–3.1	..	..	..	–13.1
64	Ecuador[c]	2.0	3.5	36.4	41.0	4.4	2.0	1.2	5.2	1.8	2.9	5.4	7.5	–3.8	5.9
65	Dominican Republic[c]	2.7	4.2	21.5	13.6	0.4	3.0	2.2	3.7	3.7	4.6	2.8	5.2	3.7	7.0
66	Lithuania[c]	2.3	–20.3	3.5	390.6	..	..	..	..	..	..	..	..	..	..
67	El Salvador[c]	0.2	6.2	16.4	11.4	–1.1	1.0	0.1	4.2	0.7	8.8	–3.4	12.1	2.2	16.0
68	Jordan	–1.5	8.2	7.0	4.7	13.2	10.2	–1.3	7.9	–7.3	7.9	14.0	3.3	7.3	6.5
69	Jamaica[c]	2.0	3.5	18.6	42.8	0.6	8.3	2.4	–0.5	1.9	6.0	5.4	–1.0	–0.1	5.8
70	Paraguay[c]	2.5	2.9	24.4	19.3	3.6	1.4	–0.3	1.9	3.4	4.1	11.5	13.5	–0.8	1.2
71	Algeria	2.9	–0.6	7.8	27.1	4.5	–0.2	1.7	–0.8	3.3	–0.6	4.1	–0.4	–2.3	–6.8
72	Colombia	3.7	4.3	24.6	23.8	2.9	1.4	5.0	3.0	3.1	6.4	7.5	5.9	0.5	21.2

Note: For data comparability and coverage, see the technical notes.

		GDP		GDP deflator		Agriculture		Industry		Services[a]		Exports of goods and nonfactor services		Gross domestic investment	
		Average annual growth rate (%)													
		1980–90	1990–94	1980–90	1990–94	1980–90	1990–94	1980–90	1990–94	1980–90	1990–94	1980–90	1990–94	1980–90	1990–94
73	Tunisia	3.3	4.5	7.5	5.5	2.8	0.5	3.1	4.0	3.5	5.9	5.6	5.9	–1.8	2.3
74	Ukraine[c]	..	–14.4	..	1,169.1	..	–8.5	..	–19.4	..	–11.3	..	..	..	..
75	Namibia	1.1	4.1	13.6	9.5	1.8	6.8	–1.1	2.9	2.2	4.1	0.2	6.1	11.9	–2.8
76	Peru[c]	–0.2	4.2	229.6	83.0	..	..	..	..	..	..	–1.7	7.4	–4.2	10.7
77	Belarus	4.8	–10.5	0.6	905.5	1.8	–6.8	6.2	–5.3	4.9	–11.1	..	..	4.4	–5.3
78	Slovak Republic[c]	1.9	–5.4	1.8	17.0	0.6	–2.6	2.2	–11.8	1.7	3.4	..	..	4.4	–20.5
79	Latvia	3.5	–17.7	0.0	205.1	2.3	–19.1	4.3	–35.7	3.1	–8.0	..	..	..	..
80	Costa Rica[c]	3.0	5.6	23.5	18.8	3.1	3.8	2.8	6.1	3.1	6.0	6.1	10.7	5.3	10.6
81	Poland	1.7	1.6	53.9	36.9	0.7	–3.0	0.1	1.2	2.2	2.6	4.5	6.3	0.9	–3.3
82	Thailand[c]	7.6	8.2	3.9	4.4	4.0	3.1	9.9	10.9	7.3	7.4	14.0	14.6	9.4	9.3
83	Turkey	5.6	3.2	48.4	71.7	4.4	0.8	6.4	4.3	5.5	3.3	16.6	7.7	5.3	2.2
84	Croatia	..	..	..	..	..	..	..	..	..	..	..	..	..	..
85	Panama[c]	0.3	7.0	2.4	1.6	..	5.1	..	18.6	..	5.5	..	4.9	..	19.6
86	Russian Federation	1.9	–10.6	3.2	616.7	..	..	..	..	..	..	..	..	..	..
87	Venezuela[c]	1.1	3.2	19.3	34.2	3.0	2.3	0.5	4.1	1.1	2.6	2.8	5.0	–5.3	6.9
88	Botswana[c]	10.3	4.4	13.1	8.4	2.2	0.6	11.4	1.7	11.0	7.9	..	..	..	..
89	Estonia[c]	0.2	–11.6	4.4	208.4	–1.9	–9.3	1.6	–19.4	–0.5	–27.1	..	..	0.5	–33.8
90	*Iran, Islamic Rep.*	1.5	5.2	14.6	30.3	4.5	5.8	3.3	4.5	–0.3	5.4	6.9	9.0	–2.5	–7.8
91	*Turkmenistan*	3.6	–5.2	0.7	545.8	1.2	..	2.7	..	7.2	..	..	..	3.6	..
	Upper-middle-income	**2.2 w**	**3.4 w**	**121.5 w**	**347.1 w**	**2.5 w**	**0.9 w**	**2.1 w**	**2.6 w**	**2.7 w**	**4.4 w**	**7.1 w**	**7.8 w**	**0.7 w**	**5.7 w**
92	Brazil	2.7	2.2	284.5	1,231.5	2.8	3.2	2.0	0.8	3.5	3.2	7.5	9.0	0.2	1.8
93	South Africa	1.3	–0.1	14.8	11.9	3.0	–2.3	–1.1	–1.2	2.9	0.6	1.9	2.3	–4.8	2.4
94	Mauritius	6.5	5.3	8.7	7.2	2.6	–2.1	9.2	6.0	5.3	6.4	10.4	4.6	11.8	5.5
95	Czech Republic[c]	1.7	–4.7	1.5	21.3	..	..	..	..	..	..	..	..	2.3	–6.6
96	Malaysia[c]	5.2	8.4	1.7	3.7	3.8	2.8	7.2	9.8	4.3	9.1	10.9	12.9	2.6	14.9
97	Chile[c]	4.1	7.5	20.9	15.3	5.6	4.0	3.7	7.5	4.2	9.7	7.0	9.0	9.6	12.9
98	Trinidad and Tobago	–2.5	0.3	4.1	6.4	–5.8	0.9	–5.5	–0.5	1.3	0.9	8.9	12.1	–10.1	–0.6
99	Hungary[c]	1.6	–2.0	8.6	22.4	0.6	–9.4	–2.6	–1.1	4.8	–0.5	4.0	–5.9	–0.4	3.2
100	Gabon[c]	0.5	–2.1	1.9	10.5	1.7	–0.3	1.0	2.8	–0.3	–9.2	2.8	4.5	–4.6	–2.8
101	Mexico[c]	1.0	2.5	70.4	13.1	0.6	1.1	1.0	2.5	1.1	2.7	6.6	4.0	–3.1	6.5
102	Uruguay[c]	0.4	4.4	61.3	60.0	0.1	3.3	–0.2	–2.6	0.9	8.5	4.3	8.4	–7.8	11.6
103	Oman[c]	8.3	6.7	–3.6	–3.4	7.9	2.1	10.3	6.2	6.0	11.4	..	..	..	..
104	Slovenia	..	..	..	..	..	..	..	..	..	..	..	..	..	..
105	Saudi Arabia[c]	–1.2	1.9	–3.7	0.4	13.4	..	–2.3	..	–1.2	..	..	..	..	..
106	Greece	1.7	1.4	17.9	13.7	–0.1	3.3	1.3	–1.1	2.3	2.3	7.1	10.4	–0.9	1.2
107	Argentina	–0.3	7.6	389.1	27.6	0.9	1.2	–0.9	8.0	0.0	8.4	3.7	2.7	–4.7	22.0
108	Korea, Rep.[c]	9.4	6.6	5.9	6.3	2.8	1.8	13.1	6.1	8.2	7.5	12.0	10.6	11.9	4.3
	Low- and middle-income	**3.1 w**	**1.9 w**	**45.7 w**	**262.4 w**	**3.1 w**	**1.9 w**	**3.9 w**	**4.6 w**	**3.8 w**	**4.0 w**	**7.3 w**	..	**2.3 w**	..
	Sub-Saharan Africa	**1.7 w**	**0.9 w**	**18.8 w**	**39.2 w**	**1.8 w**	**0.7 w**	**0.5 w**	**–0.2 w**	**2.4 w**	**0.9 w**	**1.8 w**	**2.1 w**	**–4.1 w**	**–0.4 w**
	East Asia and Pacific	**7.9 w**	**9.4 w**	**9.3 w**	**9.9 w**	**4.4 w**	**3.6 w**	**9.7 w**	**13.4 w**	**8.6 w**	**8.0 w**	**9.7 w**	**12.7 w**	**9.1 w**	**10.6 w**
	South Asia	**5.7 w**	**3.9 w**	**8.0 w**	**9.9 w**	**3.2 w**	**2.7 w**	**6.9 w**	**3.8 w**	**6.8 w**	**4.6 w**	**6.1 w**	**13.1 w**	**6.1 w**	**1.8 w**
	Europe and Central Asia	**2.3 w**	**–7.5 w**	**9.8 w**	**528.9 w**	..	..	..	..	..	..	..	..	..	..
	Middle East and N. Africa	**0.2 w**	**2.3 w**	**8.2 w**	**15.9 w**	**4.5 w**	..	**1.0 w**	..	**1.3 w**	..	..	..	..	..
	Latin America and Caribbean	**1.7 w**	**3.6 w**	**179.4 w**	**482.8 w**	**2.0 w**	**2.3 w**	**1.3 w**	**2.9 w**	**2.1 w**	**4.4 w**	**5.4 w**	**6.3 w**	**–1.5 w**	**7.9 w**
	High-income economies	**3.2 w**	**1.7 w**	**4.7 w**	**2.5 w**	**2.3 w**	..	**3.2 w**	..	**3.2 w**	..	**5.1 w**	..	**4.1 w**	..
109	Portugal[c]	2.9	0.6	18.1	10.1	..	..	..	..	..	..	8.7	*1.0*	2.6	*2.7*
110	New Zealand[c]	1.9	3.0	10.8	1.2	4.1	..	1.3	..	1.8	..	4.1	*5.4*	4.4	*2.4*
111	Spain[c]	3.2	0.7	9.3	5.6	..	*–1.0*	..	..	..	..	5.7	*7.8*	5.7	*–5.4*
112	Ireland	3.3	4.5	6.3	2.0	..	..	..	..	..	..	8.9	*9.7*	–0.4	*–10.8*
113	† Israel	3.5	6.2	101.4	12.9	..	..	..	..	..	..	5.5	*9.2*	2.1	*12.2*
114	Australia[c]	3.5	3.4	7.3	1.2	3.3	*–0.1*	2.6	*–0.2*	4.0	*2.8*	7.0	*7.6*	2.6	*0.9*
115	United Kingdom	3.0	0.0	5.7	*1.0*	..	..	..	..	..	..	3.9	*1.9*	6.4	*–2.0*
116	Finland	3.3	–2.2	6.8	1.9	–0.2	*–2.6*	3.3	*–4.0*	3.7	*–4.2*	2.2	*6.6*	3.0	*–19.5*
117	Italy[c]	2.4	0.7	9.9	4.9	0.6	*2.1*	2.2	*–0.5*	2.7	*0.9*	4.1	*5.2*	2.1	*–5.9*
118	† Kuwait[c]	0.9	..	–2.4	..	14.7	..	1.0	..	0.9	..	–2.3	..	–4.5	..
119	Canada	3.4	1.4	4.4	1.4	1.5	*–1.2*	2.9	*–0.9*	3.6	*1.0*	6.0	*6.5*	5.2	*–1.3*
120	† Hong Kong	6.9	5.7	7.7	8.9	..	..	..	..	..	..	14.4	14.3	4.0	9.1
121	Netherlands[c]	2.1	1.5	1.7	2.2	..	*2.6*	..	*–0.4*	..	*1.9*	4.6	*3.0*	3.3	*–2.8*
122	† Singapore[c]	6.4	8.3	2.0	3.7	–6.2	*–1.3*	5.4	8.7	7.2	8.1	10.0	12.3	3.7	6.1
123	Belgium[c]	1.9	0.9	4.4	3.3	1.8	*7.7*	2.2	..	1.8	..	4.6	*2.8*	3.2	*–1.7*
124	France[c]	2.4	0.8	6.0	2.3	2.0	*0.4*	1.1	*–1.0*	3.0	*1.1*	3.7	*3.8*	2.8	*–6.3*
125	Sweden	2.3	–1.0	7.4	3.2	1.5	*–1.9*	2.8	*–2.7*	2.1	*–1.2*	4.3	*2.4*	4.3	*–13.3*
126	Austria[c]	2.1	1.6	3.7	3.8	1.1	*–2.8*	1.9	*0.9*	2.3	*2.2*	4.6	*2.6*	2.5	*0.9*
127	Germany[d]	2.2	1.1	2.6	3.8	1.7	..	1.2	..	2.9	..	4.4	*–3.0*	2.0	*–1.8*
128	United States[c]	3.0	2.5	4.1	2.4	4.0	..	2.8	..	3.1	..	5.2	6.7	3.4	*4.1*
129	Norway	2.9	3.3	5.5	0.5	0.9	..	3.5	..	2.6	..	5.0	7.2	0.6	–0.4
130	Denmark	2.4	1.8	5.5	1.7	3.1	*1.3*	2.9	*0.4*	2.1	*1.5*	4.4	*2.7*	4.0	*–6.9*
131	Japan[c]	4.1	1.2	1.5	1.1	1.1	*–2.8*	4.9	*0.7*	3.7	*2.6*	4.8	*4.0*	5.7	*–0.4*
132	Switzerland[c]	2.2	0.1	3.7	2.8	..	..	..	..	..	..	3.4	*1.5*	4.8	*–7.3*
133	† *United Arab Emirates*	–2.0	..	0.7	..	9.6	9.3	–4.2	–1.8	2.0	..	..	..	–8.7	..
	World	**3.1 w**	**1.8 w**	**14.8 w**	**66.2 w**	**2.8 w**	..	**3.4 w**	..	**3.3 w**	..	**5.3 w**	..	**3.7 w**	..

a. Services include unallocated items.   b. Includes Eritrea.   c. GDP components are at purchaser values.   d. Data prior to 1990 refer to the Federal Republic of Germany before unification.

Table 12. Structure of the economy: production

		GDP (million $)		Distribution of gross domestic product (%)							
				Agriculture		Industry		(Manufacturing[a])		Services[b]	
		1980	1994	1980	1994	1980	1994	1980	1994	1980	1994
	Low-income economies	751,872 t	1,208,422 t	34 w	28 w	32 w	34 w	21 w	25 w	32 w	36 w
	Excluding China and India	377,855 t	392,644 t	..	38 w	..	21 w	..	13 w	..	39 w
1	Rwanda	1,163	585	50	51	23	9	17	3	27	40
2	Mozambique	2,028	1,467	37	33	31	12	..	..	32	55
3	Ethiopia[c]	5,179	4,688	56	57	12	10	6	3	31	32
4	Tanzania	5,702	3,378	46	57	18	17	11	8	37	26
5	Burundi	920	1,001	62	53	13	18	7	12	25	29
6	Sierra Leone	1,100	843	33	47	22	18	6	2	45	35
7	Malawi	1,238	1,302	37	31	19	21	12	14	44	47
8	Chad[d]	727	910	54	44	12	22	..	16	34	35
9	Uganda	1,267	4,001	72	49	4	14	4	7	23	37
10	Madagascar	4,042	1,918	30	35	16	13	..	..	54	52
11	Nepal	1,946	4,048	62	44	12	21	4	9	26	35
12	Vietnam[d]	..	15,570	..	28	..	30	..	22	..	43
13	Bangladesh[d]	12,950	26,164	50	30	16	18	11	10	34	52
14	Haiti	1,462	1,623	..	44	..	12	..	9	..	44
15	Niger[d]	2,538	1,540	43	39	23	18	4	7	35	44
16	Guinea-Bissau	105	243	44	45	20	18	..	7	36	37
17	Kenya	7,265	6,860	33	29	21	17	13	11	47	54
18	Mali[d]	1,629	1,871	58	42	9	15	4	9	32	42
19	Nigeria	93,082	35,200	27	43	40	32	8	7	32	25
20	Yemen, Rep.	..	..	..	..	..	..	..	..	..	..
21	Burkina Faso	1,709	1,856	33	34	22	27	16	21	45	39
22	Mongolia[d]	2,329	741	14	21	28	45	..	..	57	34
23	India	172,321	293,606	38	30	26	28	18	18	36	42
24	Lao PDR[d]	..	1,534	..	51	..	18	..	13	..	31
25	Togo[d]	1,136	981	27	38	25	21	8	9	48	41
26	Gambia, The	233	363	30	28	16	15	7	7	53	58
27	Nicaragua[d]	2,144	1,833	23	33	31	20	26	16	45	46
28	Zambia[d]	3,884	3,481	14	31	41	35	18	23	44	34
29	Tajikistan	..	2,009	..	..	..	..	..	..	..	..
30	Benin[d]	1,405	1,522	35	34	12	12	8	7	52	53
31	Central African Republic	797	872	40	44	20	13	7	..	40	43
32	Albania	1,636	1,808	28	55	37	22	..	..	35	23
33	Ghana[d]	4,445	5,421	58	46	12	16	8	8	30	39
34	Pakistan	23,690	52,011	30	25	25	25	16	18	46	50
35	Mauritania	709	1,027	30	27	26	30	..	12	44	43
36	Azerbaijan[d]	..	3,541	22	27	47	32	39	44	31	41
37	Zimbabwe	5,355	5,432	14	15	34	36	25	30	52	48
38	Guinea	..	3,395	..	24	..	31	..	5	..	45
39	China[d]	201,696	522,172	30	21	49	47	41	37	21	32
40	Honduras	2,566	3,333	24	20	24	32	15	18	52	48
41	Senegal[d]	3,016	3,881	19	17	25	20	15	14	57	63
42	Côte d'Ivoire	10,175	6,716	31	41	24	26	15	26	45	32
43	Congo[d]	1,706	1,578	12	10	47	44	7	7	42	46
44	Kyrgyz Republic	..	2,666	..	37	..	30	..	..	..	33
45	Sri Lanka	4,024	11,712	28	24	30	25	18	16	43	51
46	Armenia	..	2,607	44	49	..	30	..	..	..	26
47	Cameroon[d]	7,499	7,470	28	32	26	28	8	12	46	41
48	Egypt, Arab Rep.	22,912	42,923	18	20	37	21	12	15	45	59
49	Lesotho	368	886	24	14	29	46	7	17	47	40
50	Georgia	..	2,063	..	61	..	23	..	17	..	16
51	Myanmar	..	..	47	63	13	9	10	7	41	28
	Middle-income economies	2,477,885 t	4,069,532 t	..	10 w	..	36 w	..	20 w	..	52 w
	Lower-middle-income	..	1,783,221 t	..	13 w	..	36 w	..	..	..	49 w
52	Bolivia[d]	3,074	5,506	18	..	35	..	15	..	47	..
53	Macedonia, FYR	..	1,678	..	..	..	..	..	..	..	..
54	Moldova	..	3,672	..	48	..	28	..	25	..	25
55	Indonesia[d]	78,013	174,640	24	17	42	41	13	24	34	42
56	Philippines[d]	32,500	64,162	25	22	39	33	26	23	36	45
57	Uzbekistan	..	21,508	28	33	37	34	27	18	35	34
58	Morocco[d]	18,821	30,803	18	21	31	30	17	17	51	49
59	Kazakstan	..	18,167	..	44	..	35	..	..	..	21
60	Guatemala[d]	7,879	12,919	..	25	..	19	..	..	..	56
61	Papua New Guinea[d]	2,548	5,403	33	28	27	38	10	8	40	33
62	Bulgaria	20,040	10,199	14	13	54	35	..	..	32	53
63	Romania	..	30,086	..	21	..	33	..	..	..	46
64	Ecuador[d]	11,733	16,556	12	12	38	38	18	21	50	50
65	Dominican Republic[d]	6,631	10,416	20	15	28	22	15	15	52	63
66	Lithuania[d]	..	5,224	19	21	53	41	..	..	29	38
67	El Salvador[d]	3,574	8,116	38	14	22	24	16	..	40	62
68	Jordan	..	6,105	..	8	..	27	..	14	..	65
69	Jamaica[d]	2,679	4,241	8	8	38	37	17	17	54	54
70	Paraguay[d]	4,579	7,826	29	24	27	22	16	16	44	54
71	Algeria	42,347	41,941	10	12	54	44	9	11	36	44
72	Colombia	33,399	67,266	19	14	32	32	23	18	49	54

Note: For data comparability and coverage, see the technical notes. Figures in italics are for years other than those specified.

		GDP (million $)		Agriculture		Industry		(Manufacturing[a])		Services[b]	
		1980	1994	1980	1994	1980	1994	1980	1994	1980	1994
73	Tunisia	8,743	15,770	16	15	36	32	14	20	48	53
74	Ukraine	..	91,307	..	19	..	50	..	38	..	31
75	Namibia	2,190	2,884	12	14	53	29	5	9	35	56
76	Peru[d]	20,661	50,077	10	7	42	37	20	23	48	56
77	Belarus[d]	..	20,287	18	17	53	54	45	44	29	29
78	Slovak Republic[d]	12,027	12,370	7	7	63	36	..	..	30	57
79	Latvia	..	5,817	..	9	..	34	..	20	..	57
80	Costa Rica[d]	4,831	8,281	18	15	27	24	19	19	55	61
81	Poland	57,068	92,580	..	6	..	40	..	..	..	54
82	Thailand[d]	32,354	143,209	23	10	29	39	22	29	48	50
83	Turkey	56,919	131,014	23	16	30	31	21	20	47	52
84	Croatia	..	14,017	..	13	..	25	..	20	..	62
85	Panama[d]	3,592	6,975	..	11	..	16	..	..	..	73
86	Russian Federation	..	376,555	9	7	54	38	..	31	37	55
87	Venezuela[d]	69,377	58,257	5	5	46	42	16	14	49	53
88	Botswana[d]	971	4,011	13	5	44	49	4	4	43	46
89	Estonia[d]	..	4,578	14	10	49	36	42	23	37	55
90	Iran, Islamic Rep.	92,664	63,716	18	21	32	37	9	14	50	42
91	Turkmenistan	..	5,156	..	..	..	..	..	..	..	..
	Upper-middle-income	**1,054,324 t**	**2,264,369 t**	**8 w**	**8 w**	**47 w**	**37 w**	**22 w**	**20 w**	**43 w**	**53 w**
92	Brazil	236,995	554,587	11	13	44	39	33	25	45	49
93	South Africa	78,743	121,888	7	5	50	31	23	23	43	65
94	Mauritius	1,132	3,385	12	9	26	33	15	22	62	58
95	Czech Republic[d]	29,123	36,024	7	6	63	39	..	..	30	55
96	Malaysia[d]	24,488	70,626	22	14	38	43	21	32	40	42
97	Chile[d]	27,572	51,957	7	..	37	..	21	..	55	..
98	Trinidad and Tobago	6,236	4,792	2	3	60	46	9	10	38	51
99	Hungary[d]	22,163	41,374	..	7	..	33	..	23	..	60
100	Gabon	4,279	3,945	7	8	60	52	5	11	33	40
101	Mexico[d]	194,905	377,115	8	8	33	28	22	20	59	64
102	Uruguay[d]	10,133	15,539	14	8	34	23	26	17	53	69
103	Oman[d]	5,982	11,628	3	3	69	53	1	4	28	44
104	Slovenia	..	14,037	..	5	..	38	..	29	..	57
105	Saudi Arabia[d]	156,487	117,236	1	..	81	..	5	..	18	..
106	Greece	40,147	77,721	20	16	35	31	22	18	44	53
107	Argentina	76,962	281,922	6	5	41	30	29	20	52	65
108	Korea, Rep.[d]	63,661	376,505	15	7	40	43	29	29	45	50
	Low- and middle-income	**3,222,247 t**	**5,276,483 t**	..	**14 w**	..	**36 w**	..	**21 w**	..	**48 w**
	Sub-Saharan Africa	**297,077 t**	**277,021 t**	**24 w**	**20 w**	**36 w**	**30 w**	**13 w**	**15 w**	**38 w**	**48 w**
	East Asia and Pacific	**524,972 t**	**1,520,558 t**	**27 w**	**18 w**	**39 w**	**42 w**	**28 w**	**30 w**	**32 w**	**41 w**
	South Asia	**219,283 t**	**394,958 t**	**39 w**	**29 w**	**24 w**	**26 w**	**16 w**	**15 w**	**35 w**	**43 w**
	Europe and Central Asia	..	**1,029,958 t**	..	..	..	..	..	..	..	..
	Middle East and N. Africa	**463,036 t**	**425,707 t**	**9 w**	..	**57 w**	..	**7 w**	**10 w**	**32 w**	..
	Latin America and Caribbean	**762,475 t**	**1,624,083 t**	**10 w**	**10 w**	**38 w**	**33 w**	**25 w**	**21 w**	**50 w**	**55 w**
	High-income economies	**7,685,574 t**	**20,120,240 t**	**3 w**	..	**36 w**	..	**23 w**	..	**59 w**	..
109	Portugal[d]	28,526	87,257	..	..	..	..	..	..	..	..
110	New Zealand[d]	22,469	50,777	11	..	31	..	22	..	58	..
111	Spain[d]	211,542	482,841	..	3	..	..	..	17	..	..
112	Ireland	20,231	52,060	..	8	..	9	..	3	..	83
113	† Israel	22,690	77,777	..	..	..	..	..	..	..	..
114	Australia[d]	159,728	331,990	5	3	36	30	19	15	58	67
115	United Kingdom	537,383	1,017,306	2	2	43	32	27	22	55	66
116	Finland	51,306	97,961	10	5	40	32	28	24	51	63
117	Italy[d]	452,648	1,024,634	6	3	39	31	28	20	55	66
118	† Kuwait[d]	28,639	24,289	0	0	75	53	6	11	25	47
119	Canada	263,192	542,954	4	..	36	..	20	..	60	..
120	† Hong Kong	28,496	131,881	1	0	31	18	23	11	68	82
121	Netherlands[d]	172,280	329,768	..	3	..	27	..	18	..	70
122	† Singapore[d]	11,718	68,949	1	0	38	36	29	27	61	64
123	Belgium[d]	118,021	227,550	2	2	34	..	24	..	64	..
124	France[d]	664,595	1,330,381	4	2	34	28	24	20	62	70
125	Sweden	125,557	196,441	4	2	34	30	23	20	62	68
126	Austria[d]	76,882	196,546	4	2	40	34	28	23	56	64
127	Germany	..	2,045,991	..	1	..	..	..	29	..	..
128	United States[d]	2,708,147	6,648,013	3	..	34	..	22	..	64	..
129	Norway	57,711	109,568	4	..	40	..	16	..	57	..
130	Denmark	66,322	146,076	6	4	30	27	20	19	65	69
131	Japan[d]	1,059,257	4,590,971	4	2	42	40	29	27	54	58
132	Switzerland[d]	101,646	260,352	..	..	..	..	..	..	..	..
133	† United Arab Emirates	29,625	35,405	1	2	77	57	4	8	22	40
	World	**10,759,322 t**	**25,223,462 t**	**8 w**	..	**37 w**	..	**22 w**	..	**53 w**	..

a. Because manufacturing is generally the most dynamic part of the industrial sector, its share is shown separately. b. Services, etc., include unallocated items. c. Data prior to 1992 include Eritrea. d. GDP components are at purchaser values.

Table 13. Structure of the economy: demand

		General govt. consumption		Private consumption, etc.		Gross domestic investment		Gross domestic saving		Exports of goods and nonfactor services		Resource balance	
		1980	1994	1980	1994	1980	1994	1980	1994	1980	1994	1980	1994
	Low-income economies	12 w	12 w	66 w	62 w	24 w	30 w	22 w	28 w	13 w	19 w	–3 w	–2 w
	Excluding China and India	11 w	10 w	71 w	79 w	20 w	17 w	18 w	11 w	20 w	17 w	–4 w	–6 w
1	Rwanda	12	11	83	158	16	6	4	–69	14	8	–12	–75
2	Mozambique	21	20	78	75	22	60	1	5	20	23	–22	–55
3	Ethiopia	14ᵃ	12	83ᵃ	85	9ᵃ	15	3ᵃ	3	11ᵃ	12	–6ᵃ	–12
4	Tanzania	12	8	69	88	29	31	19	3	14	24	–10	–28
5	Burundi	9	11	92	99	14	9	–1	–10	9	14	–15	–19
6	Sierra Leone	8	12	92	83	16	9	–1	4	24	17	–17	–5
7	Malawi	19	22	70	79	25	16	11	–1	25	29	–14	–16
8	Chad	8	17	99	93	4	9	–6	–10	9	13	–10	–19
9	Uganda	11	10	89	85	6	14	0	4	19	8	–6	–10
10	Madagascar	12	7	89	91	15	12	–1	2	13	22	–16	–10
11	Nepal	7	9	82	78	18	21	11	12	12	24	–7	–8
12	Vietnam	..	9	..	77	..	24	..	13	..	23	..	–11
13	Bangladesh	6	7	92	85	15	14	2	8	6	12	–13	–6
14	Haiti	10	6	82	101	17	2	8	–7	22	4	–9	–9
15	Niger	10	17	67	82	37	6	23	1	24	13	–14	–4
16	Guinea-Bissau	29	8	77	90	30	20	–6	2	8	19	–36	–18
17	Kenya	20	15	62	62	29	21	18	24	28	39	–11	3
18	Mali	10	12	91	82	17	26	–2	6	16	21	–19	–21
19	Nigeria	12	10	56	79	22	10	32	11	29	22	10	1
20	Yemen, Rep.	..	..	..	..	..	..	..	..	..	..	..	..
21	Burkina Faso	10	16	95	78	17	22	–6	6	10	14	–23	–16
22	Mongolia	b	14	73	71	46	21	27	15	19	56	–20	–6
23	India	10	11	73	68	21	23	17	21	7	12	–4	–2
24	Lao PDR	..	..	..	..	..	..	..	..	..	..	..	..
25	Togo	22	15	53	78	30	11	25	7	51	30	–5	–4
26	Gambia, The	20	18	79	76	26	21	1	5	47	44	–26	–16
27	Nicaragua	20	14	83	95	17	18	–2	–9	24	24	–19	–27
28	Zambia	26	13	55	84	23	7	19	4	41	34	–4	–3
29	Tajikistan	19	..	57	..	30	..	24	..	..	..	–6	..
30	Benin	9	9	96	82	15	20	–5	9	23	27	–20	–10
31	Central African Republic	15	15	94	78	7	14	–10	7	26	21	–17	–6
32	Albania	9	15	56	100	35	13	35	–15	23	12	0	–29
33	Ghana	11	12	84	84	6	16	5	4	8	25	–1	–12
34	Pakistan	10	12	83	71	18	20	7	17	12	16	–12	–3
35	Mauritania	25	10	68	80	36	17	7	10	37	43	–29	–8
36	Azerbaijan	19	b	40	96	23	23	41	4	..	55	18	–18
37	Zimbabwe	20	19	64	64	19	22	16	17	30	39	–3	–6
38	Guinea	..	9	..	82	..	14	..	9	..	20	..	–5
39	China	15	13	51	43	35	42	35	44	6	24	–0	2
40	Honduras	13	13	70	73	25	26	17	14	36	36	–8	–12
41	Senegal	22	12	78	79	15	16	0	10	28	36	–16	–6
42	Côte d'Ivoire	17	17	63	58	27	13	20	25	35	47	–6	13
43	Congo	18	23	47	54	36	16	36	23	60	44	0	8
44	Kyrgyz Republic	20	11	61	74	29	30	18	14	..	..	–10	–15
45	Sri Lanka	9	9	80	76	34	27	11	15	32	34	–23	–12
46	Armenia	16	18	47	101	29	10	37	–19	..	32	9	–29
47	Cameroon	9	8	69	73	25	14	22	20	24	29	–3	5
48	Egypt, Arab Rep.	16	14	69	81	28	18	15	6	31	22	–12	–12
49	Lesotho	36	28	124	86	42	86	–60	–14	20	15	–102	–99
50	Georgia	..	..	..	..	..	..	..	..	..	..	..	..
51	Myanmar	b	b	82	89	21	12	18	11	9	2	–4	–1
	Middle-income economies	..	14 w	..	59 w	..	26 w	..	25 w	..	23 w	..	–1 w
	Lower-middle-income	..	14 w	..	62 w	..	26 w	..	25 w	..	..	..	–1 w
52	Bolivia	14	13	67	79	15	15	19	8	21	20	4	–7
53	Macedonia, FYR	..	7	..	89	..	18	..	4	..	41	..	–14
54	Moldova	..	21	..	79	..	8	..	0	..	32	..	–8
55	Indonesia	11	8	52	61	24	29	37	30	33	25	13	1
56	Philippines	9	11	67	71	29	24	24	18	24	34	–5	–6
57	Uzbekistan	19	25	54	51	32	23	27	24	..	63	–5	1
58	Morocco	18	17	68	68	24	21	14	16	17	22	–10	–5
59	Kazakstan	20	20	55	60	38	24	25	20	..	28	–12	–4
60	Guatemala	8	6	79	86	16	17	13	8	22	19	–3	–9
61	Papua New Guinea	24	15	61	53	25	15	15	32	43	53	–10	17
62	Bulgaria	6	15	55	64	34	21	39	21	36	53	5	0
63	Romania	5	13	60	62	40	27	35	25	35	25	–5	–2
64	Ecuador	15	7	60	70	26	21	26	23	25	29	0	2
65	Dominican Republic	8	4	77	80	25	20	15	16	19	24	–10	–4
66	Lithuania	20	13	64	76	31	18	16	11	..	71	–15	–7
67	El Salvador	14	8	72	88	13	19	14	4	34	20	1	–15
68	Jordan	..	22	..	75	..	26	..	3	..	49	..	–23
69	Jamaica	20	12	64	69	16	22	16	19	51	60	0	–3
70	Paraguay	6	7	76	79	32	23	18	14	15	36	–13	–9
71	Algeria	14	17	43	57	39	32	43	27	34	24	4	–5
72	Colombia	10	9	70	75	19	20	20	15	16	15	1	–4

Note: For data comparability and coverage, see the technical notes. Figures in italics are for years other than those specified.

		Distribution of gross domestic product (%)											
		General govt. consumption		Private consumption, etc.		Gross domestic investment		Gross domestic saving		Exports of goods and nonfactor services		Resource balance	
		1980	1994	1980	1994	1980	1994	1980	1994	1980	1994	1980	1994
73	Tunisia	14	16	62	62	29	24	24	22	40	45	−5	−2
74	Ukraine	..	..	..	..	..	..	..	..	..	..	..	..
75	Namibia	17	31	44	52	29	20	39	17	76	53	10	−3
76	Peru	11	10	57	70	29	24	32	20	22	11	3	−4
77	Belarus	23	22	46	51	19	35	32	27	..	46	12	−8
78	Slovak Republic	b	24	70	53	37	17	31	23	..	72	−6	6
79	Latvia	10	22	58	53	26	9	32	25	..	72	7	16
80	Costa Rica	18	17	66	60	27	28	16	23	26	40	−10	−5
81	Poland	9	19	67	64	26	16	23	17	28	24	−3	1
82	Thailand	12	9	65	55	29	40	23	35	24	39	−6	−5
83	Turkey	13	11	73	67	22	22	14	23	6	21	−8	1
84	Croatia	..	28	..	60	..	14	..	12	..	47	..	−2
85	Panama	..	16	..	61	..	25	..	23	..	38	..	−2
86	Russian Federation	15	21	62	50	22	27	22	29	..	27	0	2
87	Venezuela	12	7	55	72	26	13	33	22	29	30	7	8
88	Botswana	19	32	53	44	38	25	28	25	53	52	−10	0
89	Estonia	12	24	63	48	28	32	25	28	..	70	−4	−4
90	*Iran, Islamic Rep.*	21	15	53	54	30	23	26	31	13	30	−3	8
91	*Turkmenistan*	18	..	50	..	28	..	32	..	..	..	3	..
Upper-middle-income		**12 w**	..	**56 w**	..	**25 w**	..	**32 w**	..	**28 w**	..	**6 w**	..
92	Brazil	9	17	70	61	23	21	21	22	9	8	−2	2
93	South Africa	13	21	50	59	28	18	36	20	36	24	8	2
94	Mauritius	14	13	75	64	21	32	10	23	51	59	−10	−9
95	Czech Republic	..	22	..	58	..	20	..	20	..	52	..	0
96	Malaysia	17	10	51	53	30	39	33	37	58	90	3	−2
97	Chile	12	9	67	63	25	27	20	28	23	28	−4	1
98	Trinidad and Tobago	12	12	46	63	31	14	42	24	50	40	11	10
99	Hungary	10	13	61	72	31	21	29	15	39	29	−2	−6
100	Gabon	13	13	26	40	28	25	61	47	65	62	33	22
101	Mexico	10	12	65	70	27	23	25	18	11	13	−2	−5
102	Uruguay	12	10	76	79	17	13	12	12	15	20	−6	−2
103	Oman	25	39	28	33	22	17	47	27	63	..	25	10
104	Slovenia	..	21	..	55	..	21	..	25	..	58	..	4
105	Saudi Arabia	16	29	22	44	22	24	62	28	71	40	41	3
106	Greece	16	19	60	73	29	18	23	8	21	22	−5	−10
107	Argentina	b	b	76	82	25	20	24	18	5	7	−1	−2
108	Korea, Rep.	12	10	64	53	32	38	25	39	34	36	−7	−1
Low- and middle-income		**14 w**	**14 w**	**57 w**	**60 w**	**26 w**	**27 w**	**28 w**	**26 w**	**23 w**	**22 w**	**2 w**	**−1 w**
Sub-Saharan Africa		**14 w**	**17 w**	**60 w**	**68 w**	**23 w**	**17 w**	**27 w**	**16 w**	**30 w**	**27 w**	**2 w**	**−2 w**
East Asia and Pacific		**12 w**	**11 w**	**58 w**	**54 w**	**29 w**	**36 w**	**28 w**	**37 w**	..	**28 w**	**0 w**	**0 w**
South Asia		**9 w**	**11 w**	**75 w**	**70 w**	**20 w**	**22 w**	**15 w**	**20 w**	**8 w**	**13 w**	**−6 w**	**−3 w**
Europe and Central Asia		..	**18 w**	..	**60 w**	..	**24 w**	..	**23 w**	..	..	..	**−4 w**
Middle East and N. Africa		..	..	..	..	..	..	..	..	..	..	..	..
Latin America and Caribbean		**11 w**	**12 w**	**67 w**	**67 w**	**25 w**	**21 w**	**23 w**	**20 w**	**16 w**	**15 w**	**−3 w**	**−2 w**
High-income economies		**17 w**	..	**60 w**	..	**23 w**	..	**23 w**	..	**22 w**	..	**1 w**	..
109	Portugal	14	17	65	66	34	26	22	17	24	26	−13	−9
110	New Zealand	18	15	62	60	21	21	20	24	30	31	−1	3
111	Spain	13	18	66	63	23	20	21	19	16	19	−2	−1
112	Ireland	19	16	67	56	27	14	14	28	47	68	−13	14
113	† Israel	38	26	51	61	22	23	11	13	40	31	−11	−10
114	Australia	18	18	59	63	25	20	24	19	16	19	−2	0
115	United Kingdom	22	22	59	64	17	15	19	14	27	25	2	−1
116	Finland	18	23	54	57	29	14	28	20	33	33	−1	5
117	Italy	15	18	61	62	27	17	24	20	22	23	−3	4
118	† Kuwait	11	37	31	41	14	11	58	22	78	55	44	12
119	Canada	19	22	55	61	24	18	25	18	28	30	2	−1
120	† Hong Kong	6	8	60	59	35	31	34	33	90	139	−1	2
121	Netherlands	17	15	61	61	22	19	21	24	50	51	0	5
122	† Singapore	10	8	53	40	46	32	38	51	207	177	−9	19
123	Belgium	18	15	63	62	22	18	19	23	63	69	−3	5
124	France	18	19	59	61	24	18	23	20	22	23	−1	2
125	Sweden	29	28	51	55	21	13	19	17	29	33	−2	4
126	Austria	18	19	56	55	28	25	26	26	37	38	−2	1
127	Germany	..	20	..	58	..	22	..	22	..	22	..	0
128	United States	18	17	63	68	20	16	19	15	10	10	−1	−1
129	Norway	19	22	47	52	28	20	34	26	47	43	6	7
130	Denmark	27	26	56	52	19	14	17	21	33	34	−1	7
131	Japan	10	10	59	58	32	30	31	32	14	9	−1	2
132	Switzerland	13	14	64	59	27	22	24	27	37	36	−4	5
133	† *United Arab Emirates*	11	18	17	49	28	25	72	33	78	68	43	9
World		**15 w**	..	**59 w**	..	**24 w**	..	**24 w**	..	**22 w**	..	**1 w**	..

a. Includes Eritrea. b. General government consumption figures are not available separately; they are included in private consumption, etc.

Table 14. Central government budget

		Percentage of GNP								Percentage of total expenditure[b]				Overall deficit/surplus[c] (% of GNP)	
		Total revenue[a]				Total expenditure				Defense		Social services[d]			
		Tax		Nontax		Current		Capital							
		1980	1994	1980	1994	1980	1994	1980	1994	1980	1994	1980	1994	1980	1994
Low-income economies															
Excluding China and India															
1	Rwanda	11.0	*11.6*	1.8	*1.6*	9.3	*18.7*	5.0	*6.5*	..	..	..	..	−1.7	−6.9
2	Mozambique	..	..	..	..	..	..	..	..	..	..	..	..	..	..
3	Ethiopia	*13.2*e	12.4	*3.5*e	2.4	..	..	..	..	..	..	..	..	..	..
4	Tanzania	17.2	..	0.7	..	*19.2*	..	10.4	..	9.2	..	21.9	..	−7.0	..
5	Burundi	13.3	..	0.8	..	11.6	..	11.0	..	..	..	..	..	−3.9	..
6	Sierra Leone[f]	15.2	15.2	1.7	0.6	22.6	17.6	5.8	7.8	..	..	..	..	−13.2	−6.1
7	Malawi[f]	18.1	..	2.7	..	19.6	..	18.0	..	11.3	..	14.2	..	−17.3	..
8	Chad	..	..	..	..	..	..	..	..	..	..	..	..	..	..
9	Uganda	3.0	..	0.1	..	5.3	..	0.8	..	24.4	..	23.5	..	−3.1	..
10	Madagascar	13.1	8.5	0.3	1.6	..	12.6	..	7.8	..	..	..	..	..	−5.0
11	Nepal	6.5	..	1.3	..	0.2	..	0.2	..	..	..	15.6	..	−3.0	..
12	Vietnam	..	..	..	..	..	..	..	..	..	..	..	..	..	..
13	Bangladesh[f]	7.7	..	3.6	..	..	..	..	..	..	..	15.8	..	2.5	..
14	Haiti	9.4	..	1.3	..	14.0	..	3.5	..	..	..	..	..	−4.7	..
15	Niger	12.4	..	2.2	..	9.6	..	9.1	..	3.6	..	24.8	..	−4.8	..
16	Guinea-Bissau	..	..	..	..	..	..	..	..	..	..	..	..	..	..
17	Kenya[f]	19.8	22.4	2.9	2.5	20.0	25.3	6.1	6.1	15.3	*6.1*	30.3	25.7	−4.6	−3.6
18	Mali	9.6	..	0.9	..	12.4	..	1.9	..	10.5	..	20.7	..	−4.7	..
19	Nigeria[f]	..	..	..	..	..	..	..	..	..	..	..	..	..	..
20	Yemen, Rep.	..	..	..	..	..	..	..	..	..	29.4	..	27.0	..	..
21	Burkina Faso	10.5	*8.7*	1.2	2.9	9.8	*11.3*	2.3	4.5	17.7	..	30.1	..	0.2	..
22	Mongolia	..	17.1	..	4.0	..	17.4	..	3.2	..	9.8	..	28.1	..	−1.8
23	India	9.7	9.6	1.9	3.2	11.7	14.6	1.6	2.0	14.1	12.8	5.5	9.3	−6.5	−6.0
24	Lao PDR	..	..	..	..	..	..	..	..	..	..	..	..	..	..
25	Togo	28.0	..	4.5	..	24.8	..	9.3	..	7.0	..	39.9	..	−2.0	..
26	Gambia, The	21.0	*22.1*	3.6	*1.4*	17.5	*16.0*	16.2	*4.7*	..	..	23.7	..	−4.7	*3.6*
27	Nicaragua	21.6	28.8	2.5	1.7	26.3	31.3	6.0	11.1	10.9	5.7	33.2	45.5	−7.3	−5.7
28	Zambia	25.0	10.6	2.0	0.4	35.7	13.9	4.3	7.1	..	..	17.4	29.3	−20.0	−7.3
29	Tajikistan	..	..	..	..	..	..	..	..	..	..	..	..	..	..
30	Benin	..	..	..	..	..	..	..	..	..	..	..	..	..	..
31	Central African Republic	*14.9*	..	*1.5*	..	*18.4*	..	*1.3*	..	9.6	..	28.6	..	−3.5	..
32	Albania	..	..	..	..	..	..	..	..	..	..	..	..	..	..
33	Ghana[f]	6.4	*13.1*	0.5	*3.8*	9.8	*17.9*	1.1	*3.1*	3.7	4.8	35.1	38.5	−4.2	−2.5
34	Pakistan	13.5	13.2	3.0	5.3	14.6	20.7	3.1	3.6	..	..	..	..	−5.8	−6.9
35	Mauritania	..	..	..	..	..	..	..	..	..	..	..	..	..	..
36	Azerbaijan	..	..	..	..	..	..	..	..	..	..	..	..	..	..
37	Zimbabwe	19.5	..	4.9	..	33.5	..	1.8	..	24.9	..	28.5	..	−11.1	..
38	Guinea	..	*12.6*	..	*1.4*	..	*10.9*	..	*11.0*	..	..	..	..	..	−3.3
39	China[f]	..	*2.6*	..	*0.5*	..	..	..	..	..	19.0	..	3.3	..	−2.1
40	Honduras	14.4	..	1.0	..	..	..	..	..	..	..	..	..	..	..
41	Senegal	21.5	..	1.6	..	23.1	..	2.0	..	16.7	..	36.8	..	0.9	..
42	Côte d'Ivoire	22.2	..	1.8	..	20.0	..	9.5	..	..	..	..	..	−11.4	..
43	Congo	29.9	..	9.2	..	*23.6*	..	*19.1*	..	..	..	7.0	..	−5.8	..
44	Kyrgyz Republic	..	..	..	..	..	..	..	..	..	..	..	..	..	..
45	Sri Lanka	19.3	17.4	1.1	1.9	24.9	22.3	16.7	5.3	1.6	11.6	23.6	33.0	−18.4	−8.7
46	Armenia	..	..	..	..	..	..	..	..	..	..	..	..	..	..
47	Cameroon	14.8	*10.9*	1.3	*4.9*	10.4	*16.1*	5.1	*1.7*	9.1	9.3	25.4	25.5	0.5	−2.0
48	Egypt, Arab Rep.	*31.1*	26.4	*17.9*	15.0	*39.4*	34.9	*9.7*	8.1	*11.6*	8.2	22.2	29.7	−6.8	2.1
49	Lesotho	*14.7*	..	2.4	..	16.5	..	..	..	..	..	..	..	..	..
50	*Georgia*	..	..	..	..	..	..	..	..	..	..	..	..	..	..
51	*Myanmar*	9.7	*4.9*	6.4	*2.6*	12.1	*6.7*	3.8	*3.5*	21.9	39.1	26.5	24.6	1.2	−2.2
Middle-income economies															
Lower-middle-income															
52	Bolivia	..	12.1	..	5.7	..	20.5	..	5.6	..	8.5	..	42.0	..	−3.7
53	Macedonia, FYR	..	..	..	..	..	..	..	..	..	..	..	..	..	..
54	Moldova	..	..	..	..	..	..	..	..	..	..	..	..	..	..
55	Indonesia	21.1	16.3	1.1	2.8	12.2	8.9	10.9	*8.1*	12.7	6.2	11.8	14.4	−2.3	0.6
56	Philippines[f]	12.5	*15.1*	1.5	*1.8*	9.9	*15.0*	3.5	*2.9*	13.5	10.2	20.8	*23.1*	−1.4	*−1.4*
57	Uzbekistan	..	..	..	..	..	..	..	..	..	..	..	..	..	..
58	Morocco	21.0	26.7	3.0	3.3	23.5	24.2	10.7	*7.2*	17.8	13.9	27.0	27.2	−10.0	−1.4
59	Kazakstan	..	..	..	..	..	..	..	..	..	..	..	..	..	..
60	Guatemala	8.8	6.8	0.7	0.8	7.4	6.9	5.1	2.3	10.0	15.2	29.8	29.5	−3.5	−1.2
61	Papua New Guinea[f]	21.1	20.8	2.5	3.4	29.9	28.8	5.4	3.6	4.3	3.3	27.2	30.7	−2.0	−4.5
62	Bulgaria	..	29.3	..	8.9	..	42.8	..	1.1	..	6.1	..	36.3	..	−4.5
63	Romania	10.3	26.5	36.0	3.5	30.5	27.8	15.3	4.3	3.8	7.3	18.8	46.9	0.5	−2.5
64	Ecuador[f]	12.9	14.9	0.6	2.0	12.5	13.3	2.4	3.5	12.5	..	43.9	..	−1.5	0.0
65	Dominican Republic[f]	11.4	*16.1*	3.3	*1.4*	11.7	*9.0*	5.3	*8.7*	7.8	4.7	35.5	39.8	−2.7	0.0
66	Lithuania	..	18.3	..	0.8	..	18.9	..	1.6	..	..	..	..	..	..
67	El Salvador[f]	11.3	10.7	0.5	1.3	12.0	11.2	2.9	3.7	8.8	8.7	34.3	39.4	−5.9	−0.8
68	Jordan[f]	..	22.2	..	8.4	..	27.1	..	6.7	*22.4*	21.3	23.0	40.7	..	1.9
69	Jamaica	30.4	..	1.3	..	..	..	..	..	..	..	..	..	−16.9	..
70	Paraguay	9.7	*9.0*	0.9	*5.0*	7.4	*11.0*	2.4	*1.9*	11.7	10.7	33.6	46.3	0.3	1.2
71	Algeria	..	..	..	..	..	..	..	..	..	..	..	..	..	..
72	Colombia	10.4	14.4	1.7	2.8	10.5	*12.2*	4.2	*2.6*	6.7	8.1	44.1	31.5	−1.8	−0.6

Note: For data comparability and coverage, see the technical notes. Figures in italics are for years other than those specified.

		Percentage of GNP								Percentage of total expenditure[b]				Overall deficit/surplus[c] (% of GNP)	
		Total revenue[a]				Total expenditure				Defense		Social services[d]			
		Tax		Nontax		Current		Capital							
		1980	1994	1980	1994	1980	1994	1980	1994	1980	1994	1980	1994	1980	1994
73	Tunisia	24.6	24.3	7.1	5.4	22.8	26.2	9.7	6.9	11.1	5.4	34.2	43.0	–2.9	–2.6
74	Ukraine	..	..	..	..	..	..	..	..	..	..	..	..	..	..
75	Namibia	..	30.7	..	3.8	..	33.8	..	6.0	..	..	..	..	..	–4.7
76	Peru[f]	16.5	13.7	1.4	1.3	15.8	12.9	4.6	2.9	21.0	..	21.2	..	–2.5	3.1
77	Belarus	..	30.8	..	0.6	..	31.9	..	5.9	..	4.1	..	57.2	..	–5.2
78	Slovak Republic	..	..	..	..	..	..	..	..	..	..	..	..	..	..
79	Latvia	..	25.3	..	1.6	..	27.8	..	1.3	..	3.1	..	52.8	..	–4.4
80	Costa Rica	17.6	22.8	1.1	3.0	22.4	28.1	5.4	3.5	2.6	0.0	62.4	61.3	–7.8	–5.9
81	Poland	..	37.9	..	4.2	..	43.1	..	1.6	..	..	..	..	..	–2.4
82	Thailand	13.3	17.0	1.2	1.8	14.6	11.4	4.4	3.9	20.9	17.0	28.0	35.4	–4.9	1.9
83	Turkey	17.7	15.4	4.6	4.1	19.1	21.6	7.2	2.0	15.2	9.5	23.8	21.7	–3.8	–4.0
84	Croatia	..	41.7	..	1.7	..	38.8	..	3.0	..	20.2	..	53.6	..	1.7
85	Panama	19.5	21.8	7.1	10.0	26.2	25.8	5.8	3.1	0.0	5.6	39.6	70.9	–5.4	4.6
86	Russian Federation	..	19.1	..	1.4	..	26.2	..	1.3	..	14.5	..	54.1	..	–10.7
87	Venezuela	18.9	15.4	3.4	4.2	14.9	16.9	4.0	2.6	4.9	..	..	32.0	0.0	–4.3
88	Botswana[f]	26.8	30.5	9.8	25.6	24.9	32.8	11.6	7.4	8.5	10.3	30.6	36.0	–0.2	11.2
89	Estonia	..	29.1	..	1.5	..	..	..	..	..	3.0	..	56.4	..	1.2
90	*Iran, Islamic Rep.*	6.8	8.3	14.6	16.9	27.5	16.6	7.9	8.9	16.1	6.5	36.7	37.4	–13.7	–0.1
91	*Turkmenistan*	..	..	..	..	..	..	..	..	..	..	..	..	..	..
Upper-middle-income															
92	Brazil	18.4	17.5	5.0	7.5	19.2	33.8	1.7	1.0	3.2	2.5	32.3	36.7	–2.5	–4.0
93	South Africa	21.4	24.7	3.1	2.0	20.0	34.4	3.2	1.6	..	..	..	..	–2.5	–9.2
94	Mauritius	18.5	20.0	2.4	3.0	22.8	18.9	4.6	4.5	0.7	1.4	40.7	48.6	–10.4	–0.3
95	Czech Republic	..	38.0	..	3.0	..	37.7	..	4.9	..	6.6	..	60.6	..	0.9
96	Malaysia	24.4	22.5	2.9	7.7	19.9	21.4	10.3	5.0	13.1	12.0	26.8	39.5	–6.2	4.1
97	Chile	26.6	19.1	6.6	2.6	26.3	17.8	2.8	3.4	12.1	8.8	57.6	64.9	5.6	1.7
98	Trinidad and Tobago	37.5	..	7.2	..	19.3	..	12.6	..	..	..	..	..	7.6	..
99	Hungary	*46.5*	..	8.9	..	*50.6*	..	7.7	..	4.3	..	26.7	..	–2.9	..
100	Gabon[f]	26.1	..	13.3	..	..	..	..	..	..	..	..	..	6.8	..
101	Mexico	14.8	..	0.8	..	11.7	..	5.7	..	2.1	..	36.1	..	–3.1	..
102	Uruguay	21.8	31.7	1.3	2.3	20.9	34.3	1.8	2.8	13.1	7.3	61.1	73.1	0.0	–3.0
103	Oman	12.1	9.1	30.8	26.5	34.0	41.7	9.1	7.8	49.6	36.7	9.4	30.0	0.5	–12.6
104	Slovenia	..	..	..	..	..	..	..	..	..	..	..	..	..	..
105	Saudi Arabia	..	..	..	..	..	..	..	..	..	..	..	..	..	..
106	Greece	26.5	25.8	3.1	2.1	30.1	*38.6*	5.4	*4.3*	12.5	8.9	51.2	30.6	–4.8	–15.6
107	Argentina	10.5	..	5.3	..	18.4	..	..	..	14.3	..	28.6	..	–2.6	..
108	Korea, Rep.	15.8	18.1	2.2	2.8	15.1	16.0	2.5	2.9	29.3	18.7	22.0	32.0	–2.3	0.3
Low- and middle-income															
Sub-Saharan Africa															
East Asia and Pacific															
South Asia															
Europe and Central Asia															
Middle East and N. Africa															
Latin America and Caribbean															
High-income economies															
109	Portugal	24.9	29.3	1.9	4.4	29.6	37.4	4.6	5.4	7.0	..	46.0	..	–8.7	–2.2
110	New Zealand	31.3	33.5	3.6	3.1	36.6	35.1	2.5	1.0	4.8	3.5	57.0	69.1	–6.8	0.8
111	Spain	22.4	30.1	1.9	2.5	24.0	34.0	3.0	2.5	4.1	3.4	64.8	48.6	–4.2	–4.8
112	Ireland	31.8	39.2	4.0	2.8	41.7	44.0	4.8	3.0	3.2	3.2	49.3	57.3	–12.9	–2.3
113	† Israel	44.6	33.5	7.3	4.8	69.3	39.8	2.9	4.4	36.8	19.2	25.7	49.1	–16.1	–3.0
114	Australia	19.9	21.2	2.2	3.2	21.5	27.0	1.6	1.2	9.1	7.8	45.5	57.5	–1.5	–2.9
115	United Kingdom	30.6	31.9	4.6	3.1	36.4	39.9	1.8	2.8	13.1	10.4	43.7	52.2	–4.6	–6.6
116	Finland	25.5	29.6	2.1	5.3	25.6	46.0	3.0	1.8	5.3	3.7	50.3	59.3	–2.2	–14.1
117	Italy	29.1	38.8	2.5	1.1	37.5	48.5	2.1	1.9	3.3	..	48.8	..	–10.7	–10.6
118	† Kuwait	2.3	1.3	74.1	..	16.1	43.6	7.6	6.3	11.0	..	24.0	..	50.2	..
119	Canada	16.6	19.5	2.6	2.5	21.6	..	0.3	..	7.4	6.9	43.8	51.4	–3.6	–4.5
120	† Hong Kong	..	..	..	..	..	..	..	..	..	..	..	..	..	..
121	Netherlands	44.0	44.7	5.2	3.8	48.1	50.7	4.6	2.2	5.5	4.3	62.9	69.3	–4.5	–0.5
122	† Singapore	18.2	17.1	8.1	10.0	16.2	13.4	4.6	4.2	20.8	21.4	24.1	35.9	2.2	15.7
123	Belgium	42.1	42.8	1.9	1.8	47.0	48.4	4.3	2.0	5.5	..	60.2	..	–8.2	–6.1
124	France	36.5	38.0	2.9	2.7	37.3	44.9	2.1	2.5	7.3	5.6	69.4	68.7	–0.1	–5.5
125	Sweden	30.2	31.7	4.9	6.9	37.7	50.3	1.8	0.7	7.0	5.3	58.2	56.8	–8.1	–13.4
126	Austria	32.2	33.7	2.7	3.1	34.3	38.4	3.4	3.2	3.0	2.2	70.0	70.1	–3.4	–5.1
127	Germany	..	29.6	..	2.0	..	31.9	..	1.7	9.0	..	68.8	..	..	–2.5
128	United States	18.3	18.5	1.6	1.5	20.3	22.2	1.4	0.8	20.3	18.1	48.8	52.1	–2.8	–3.0
129	Norway	38.6	37.0	3.8	9.5	37.9	47.9	1.3	1.9	6.8	6.5	47.4	55.5	–2.0	–7.5
130	Denmark	32.2	33.3	4.2	6.2	37.6	44.3	2.8	1.7	6.5	4.7	56.3	53.5	–2.7	–5.7
131	Japan	11.0	17.8	0.6	3.3	14.8	..	3.6	..	..	4.2	..	59.2	–7.0	–1.6
132	Switzerland	17.5	20.0	1.4	..	18.2	..	1.3	..	10.1	..	63.6	..	–0.2	..
133	† *United Arab Emirates*	0.0	0.5	0.2	1.7	10.7	11.0	0.9	0.4	41.4	37.1	20.5	29.9	2.0	–0.2
World															

a. Refers to current revenue. b. Includes lending minus repayments. c. Includes grants. d. Refers to education, health, social security, welfare, housing, and community amenities. e. Includes Eritrea. f. Data are for budgetary accounts only.

Table 15. Exports and imports of merchandise

		Exports Total (million $)		Exports Manufactures (% of total)		Imports Total (million $)		Imports Food (% of total)		Imports Fuels (% of total)		Average annual growth rate (%) Exports		Imports	
		1980	1994	1980	1993	1980	1994	1980	1993	1980	1993	1980–90	1990–94	1980–90	1990–94
	Low-income economies	85,945 t	202,239 t			102,726 t	218,960 t					5.7 w	9.1 w	1.6 w	13.0 w
	Excluding China and India	60,700 t	56,192 t			69,547 t	76,433 t					1.0 w	2.6 w	–4.0 w	3.9 w
1	Rwanda	112	..	0	..	243	..	12	..	13	..	5.6	–19.6	1.3	–1.9
2	Mozambique	281	..	2	20	800	1,000	..	..	..	..	–10.5	–0.3	–1.0	2.9
3	Ethiopia[a]	425	372	0	12	717	1,033	8	16	25	23	1.2	–9.4	3.3	–3.3
4	Tanzania	511	519	14	..	1,250	1,505	13	..	21	..	–1.8	10.0	–3.3	12.7
5	Burundi	65	106	3	10	168	224	13	..	19	..	7.4	–4.8	1.4	–14.6
6	Sierra Leone	224	115	40	29	427	150	24	..	2	..	–2.1	–4.3	–9.9	–1.1
7	Malawi	295	325	7	4	439	491	8	8	15	11	0.1	–1.8	1.3	–1.6
8	Chad	71	..	8	12	74	..	23	..	2	..	5.4	–10.0	10.5	–12.1
9	Uganda	345	421	3	1	293	870	11	..	23	..	–1.4	3.9	–0.6	28.7
10	Madagascar	401	277	6	20	600	434	9	14	15	19	–0.1	–6.8	–4.6	–5.6
11	Nepal	80	363	31	88	342	1,176	4	9	18	12	7.8	22.1	4.9	6.8
12	Vietnam	339	3,770	..	..	1,310	4,440	..	..	..	..	..	..	..	..
13	Bangladesh	793	2,661	69	83	2,600	4,701	24	16	10	10	7.5	12.7	1.8	5.3
14	Haiti	226	73	..	..	375	292	24	..	13	..	–2.9	–11.2	–4.4	–6.8
15	Niger	566	..	2	..	594	..	14	..	26	..	–6.4	–2.0	–4.5	2.5
16	Guinea-Bissau	11	32	..	..	55	63	20	..	6	..	–5.1	–18.3	1.3	–5.4
17	Kenya	1,250	1,609	12	29	2,120	2,156	8	14	34	15	2.6	16.6	1.1	–5.6
18	Mali	205	..	9	..	439	..	19	..	35	..	2.6	–3.7	1.2	–3.4
19	Nigeria	26,000	9,378	0	2	16,700	6,511	17	6	2	1	–2.4	–1.9	–17.5	7.6
20	Yemen, Rep.	802	..	51	4	2,510	..	28	..	7	..	1.5	7.2	–5.9	11.1
21	Burkina Faso	90	..	11	14	359	..	21	..	13	..	5.4	1.3	2.1	8.3
22	Mongolia	..	324	..	..	..	223	..	..	..	..	..	..	..	..
23	India	8,590	25,000	59	75	14,900	26,846	9	3	45	27	6.3	7.0	4.5	2.7
24	Lao PDR	31	300	8	..	29	564	..	..	..	..	..	..	..	..
25	Togo	338	..	11	9	551	..	17	22	23	10	4.9	9.0	1.1	–11.2
26	Gambia, The	31	35	9	36	165	209	23	..	11	..	2.3	26.9	1.0	9.0
27	Nicaragua	451	352	14	11	887	824	15	23	20	14	–4.4	–8.7	–4.1	7.3
28	Zambia	1,300	..	6	9	1,340	..	5	..	22	..	–3.5	26.9	–5.0	–6.2
29	Tajikistan	..	531	..	..	..	619	..	..	..	..	..	..	..	..
30	Benin	63	..	8	11	331	..	26	..	8	..	7.7	–0.3	–6.3	29.4
31	Central African Republic	116	..	29	47	81	..	21	..	2	..	2.5	3.5	6.0	–3.3
32	Albania	..	116	..	..	..	596	..	..	..	..	..	..	..	..
33	Ghana	1,260	..	1	24	1,130	..	10	11	27	17	3.9	9.1	1.6	12.8
34	Pakistan	2,620	7,370	49	85	5,350	8,890	13	14	27	17	9.5	8.8	2.1	10.3
35	Mauritania	194	..	2	1	286	..	30	..	14	..	7.8	3.5	1.1	4.4
36	Azerbaijan	..	682	..	..	..	791	..	..	..	..	..	..	..	..
37	Zimbabwe	1,410	..	38	38	1,450	..	3	11	39	15	2.2	–6.6	–2.2	–5.1
38	Guinea	401	..	..	..	270	..	..	..	..	..	–3.6	–8.6	–2.9	–2.8
39	China*	18,100	121,047	48	81	19,900	115,681	..	3	..	6	11.4	14.3	10.0	24.8
40	Honduras	830	843	13	13	1,010	1,056	10	13	16	14	1.3	10.7	–1.0	7.0
41	Senegal	477	..	15	22	1,050	..	25	29	25	11	2.6	3.6	1.0	6.1
42	Côte d'Ivoire	3,130	..	..	16	2,970	2,000	13	..	16	..	3.3	–7.5	–4.0	5.4
43	Congo	911	..	7	14	580	..	19	..	14	..	5.5	9.7	–2.0	2.5
44	Kyrgyz Republic	..	340	..	..	..	459	..	..	..	..	..	..	..	..
45	Sri Lanka	1,070	3,210	16	74	2,040	4,780	20	14	24	8	6.3	17.0	2.0	15.0
46	Armenia	..	209	..	..	..	401	..	..	..	..	..	..	..	..
47	Cameroon	1,380	..	4	14	1,600	1,100	9	16	12	3	4.5	–1.7	–1.4	–11.2
48	Egypt, Arab Rep.	3,050	3,463	11	33	4,860	10,185	32	24	1	2	–0.2	–0.1	–0.7	–2.9
49	Lesotho	58	..	..	..	464	..	..	..	..	..	..	..	..	..
50	*Georgia*	..	381	..	..	..	744	..	..	..	..	..	..	..	..
51	*Myanmar*	472	771	6	10	353	886	7	..	3	..	–7.0	27.2	–7.0	38.7
	Middle-income economies	606,399 t	826,822 t			453,101 t	890,818 t					3.5 w	7.0 w	1.0 w	9.8 w
	Lower-middle-income	..	..			..	..					..	..	..	..
52	Bolivia	942	1,032	3	19	665	1,209	19	9	1	5	1.7	–5.4	–2.8	18.9
53	Macedonia, FYR	..	1,120	..	..	..	1,260	..	..	..	..	..	..	..	..
54	Moldova	..	618	..	..	..	672	..	..	..	..	..	..	..	..
55	Indonesia	21,900	40,054	2	53	10,800	31,985	13	7	16	8	5.3	21.3	1.2	9.1
56	Philippines	5,740	13,304	37	76	8,300	22,546	8	8	28	12	2.9	10.2	2.4	15.2
57	Uzbekistan	..	3,543	..	..	..	3,243	..	..	..	..	..	..	..	..
58	Morocco	2,490	4,013	24	57	4,160	7,188	20	17	24	14	4.2	0.8	2.9	1.7
59	Kazakstan	..	3,285	..	..	..	4,205	..	..	..	..	..	..	..	..
60	Guatemala	1,520	1,522	24	30	1,600	2,604	8	11	24	12	–1.3	8.2	–0.6	19.3
61	Papua New Guinea	1,030	2,640	3	12	1,180	1,521	21	..	15	..	4.5	19.3	–0.2	2.1
62	Bulgaria	10,400	4,165	..	..	9,650	4,160	..	8	..	22	..	..	..	..
63	Romania	11,200	6,151	..	76	12,800	7,109	..	14	..	26	–6.8	–4.7	–0.9	–5.4
64	Ecuador	2,480	3,820	3	7	2,250	3,690	8	5	1	2	3.0	8.9	–3.9	10.0
65	Dominican Republic	962	633	24	52	1,640	2,630	17	..	25	..	–1.0	–10.2	2.6	8.9
66	Lithuania	..	1,892	..	64	..	2,210	..	11	..	44	..	..	..	..
67	El Salvador	967	844	35	46	966	2,250	18	13	18	11	–2.8	13.0	1.3	16.2
68	Jordan	574	1,424	34	51	2,400	3,382	18	20	17	13	7.4	7.1	–3.1	13.0
69	Jamaica	963	1,192	63	65	1,100	2,164	20	14	38	19	1.2	1.3	3.1	7.0
70	Paraguay	310	817	12	17	615	2,370	..	11	..	12	9.9	–1.9	3.2	7.3
71	Algeria	13,900	8,594	0	4	10,600	8,000	21	27	3	1	2.5	–0.8	–5.1	–5.7
72	Colombia	3,920	8,399	20	40	4,740	11,883	12	8	12	4	9.7	4.8	–1.9	22.3
*	Data for Taiwan, China	19,800	92,847	88	93	19,700	85,507	8	6	25	8	11.6	5.9	12.8	14.2

Note: For data comparability and coverage, see the technical notes. Figures in italics are for years other than those specified.

		Exports Total (million $)		Manufactures (% of total)		Imports Total (million $)		Food (% of total)		Fuels (% of total)		Average annual growth rate (%) Exports		Imports	
		1980	1994	1980	1993	1980	1994	1980	1993	1980	1993	1980–90	1990–94	1980–90	1990–94
73	Tunisia	2,200	4,660	36	75	3,540	6,580	14	8	21	8	6.2	7.7	1.3	6.4
74	Ukraine	..	11,818	..	..	..	14,177	..	..	..	..	..	..	..	..
75	Namibia	..	1,321	..	..	..	1,196	..	..	..	..	..	..	..	..
76	Peru	3,900	4,555	18	17	2,500	6,794	20	20	2	8	–1.9	11.0	–1.0	12.1
77	Belarus	..	3,134	..	..	..	3,857	..	..	..	..	..	..	..	..
78	Slovak Republic	..	6,587	..	..	..	6,823	..	..	..	..	..	..	..	..
79	Latvia	..	967	..	..	..	1,367	..	..	..	..	..	..	..	..
80	Costa Rica	1,000	2,215	34	33	1,540	3,025	9	8	15	9	4.9	10.1	2.8	15.1
81	Poland	14,200	17,000	71	68	16,700	21,400	14	11	18	12	4.8	3.9	1.5	26.3
82	Thailand	6,510	45,262	28	73	9,210	54,459	5	5	30	8	14.3	21.6	12.1	12.7
83	Turkey	2,910	18,106	27	72	7,910	23,270	4	6	48	14	12.0	8.8	11.3	11.2
84	Croatia	..	4,259	..	71	..	5,231	..	7	..	10	..	..	..	..
85	Panama	358	584	9	16	1,450	2,404	10	10	31	13	2.6	23.3	–4.1	14.3
86	Russian Federation[b]	..	53,000	..	..	..	41,000	..	..	..	..	..	..	..	..
87	Venezuela	19,900	15,480	2	14	10,700	7,710	15	11	2	1	1.6	–0.1	–6.1	19.3
88	Botswana	502	1,845	..	..	692	1,638	..	..	..	..	11.4	–0.8	7.7	–5.6
89	Estonia	..	1,329	..	..	..	1,690	..	..	..	..	..	..	..	..
90	*Iran, Islamic Rep.*	14,700	13,900	5	9	12,200	20,000	13	..	0	..	7.4	10.2	–4.0	15.7
91	*Turkmenistan*	..	2,176	..	..	..	1,690	..	..	..	..	..	..	..	..
Upper-middle-income		280,750 t	404,146 t			174,465 t	428,837 t					3.5 w	7.8 w	2.2 w	10.4 w
92	Brazil	20,100	43,600	39	60	25,000	36,000	10	10	43	16	6.1	6.6	–1.5	8.5
93	South Africa	25,500	25,000	39	94	19,600	23,400	3	6	0	1	0.9	2.8	–0.8	5.3
94	Mauritius	431	1,347	27	90	609	1,926	26	14	14	7	8.6	2.0	11.0	2.5
95	Czech Republic	..	14,252	..	..	..	15,636	..	..	..	..	..	..	..	..
96	Malaysia	13,000	58,756	19	70	10,800	59,581	12	6	15	4	11.5	17.8	6.0	15.7
97	Chile	4,710	11,539	10	18	5,800	11,800	15	6	18	10	5.7	10.5	1.4	14.5
98	Trinidad and Tobago	3,960	1,867	4	34	3,160	1,131	11	15	38	16	–4.3	4.9	–12.1	8.1
99	Hungary	8,670	10,733	66	68	9,220	14,438	8	6	16	13	3.0	–1.8	0.7	7.9
100	Gabon	2,170	..	0	3	674	..	19	..	1	..	0.6	5.7	–2.0	2.0
101	Mexico	15,600	61,964	12	75	19,500	80,100	16	8	2	2	12.2	14.7	5.7	18.7
102	Uruguay	1,060	1,913	38	43	1,680	2,770	8	8	29	9	2.9	–3.1	–2.0	21.7
103	Oman	2,390	5,418	3	15	1,730	3,915	15	19	11	3	13.1	9.8	–1.6	18.5
104	Slovenia	..	6,828	..	86	..	7,304	..	8	..	11	..	..	..	..
105	Saudi Arabia	109,000	38,600	1	7	30,200	22,796	14	..	1	..	–8.2	4.0	–8.4	5.9
106	Greece	5,150	9,384	47	53	10,500	21,466	9	14	23	11	5.1	11.9	5.8	12.8
107	Argentina	8,020	15,839	23	32	10,500	21,527	6	5	10	2	3.1	–1.0	–8.6	..
108	Korea, Rep.	17,500	96,000	90	93	22,300	102,348	10	6	30	18	13.7	7.4	11.2	7.7
Low- and middle-income		683,360 t	1,033,887 t			550,291 t	1,098,170 t					3.9 w	7.5 w	1.1 w	10.5 w
Sub-Saharan Africa		77,330 t	59,065 t			67,448 t	63,330 t					1.1 w	0.9 w	–3.7 w	1.8 w
East Asia and Pacific		87,323 t	388,383 t			88,303 t	404,292 t					10.7 w	14.4 w	8.3 w	14.5 w
South Asia		13,855 t	38,922 t			25,884 t	47,582 t					6.5 w	8.5 w	3.4 w	5.3 w
Europe and Central Asia		..	..			..	..					..	..	..	..
Middle East and N. Africa		203,874 t	96,741 t			104,130 t	107,306 t					–2.3 w	1.1 w	–5.9 w	6.1 w
Latin America and Caribbean		..	..			99,344 t	212,790 t					..	..	0.6 w	13.7 w
High-income economies		1,375,665 t	3,291,137 t			1,478,865 t	3,307,266 t					5.0 w	5.1 w	6.1 w	4.6 w
109	Portugal	4,640	17,540	72	84	9,310	26,680	14	14	24	9	12.2	0.5	9.8	2.4
110	New Zealand	5,420	12,200	20	27	5,470	11,900	6	8	23	7	3.6	5.4	4.6	5.5
111	Spain	20,700	73,300	72	78	34,100	92,500	13	14	39	11	6.9	11.2	10.1	5.3
112	Ireland	8,400	34,370	58	75	11,200	25,508	12	10	15	5	9.3	11.4	4.7	5.6
113	† Israel	5,540	16,881	82	91	9,780	25,237	11	7	27	7	5.9	10.0	4.6	12.3
114	Australia	21,900	47,538	20	42	22,400	53,400	5	5	14	6	5.8	8.1	4.9	5.1
115	United Kingdom	110,000	205,000	74	82	116,000	227,000	13	11	14	5	4.4	1.8	6.3	0.9
116	Finland	14,200	29,700	70	83	15,600	23,200	7	7	29	13	2.3	8.7	4.4	–1.9
117	Italy	78,100	189,805	85	89	101,000	167,685	13	13	28	9	4.4	6.0	5.3	–1.7
118	† Kuwait	19,700	11,614	10	84	6,530	21,716	15	15	1	1	–2.0	42.3	–6.3	23.0
119	Canada	67,700	166,000	49	66	62,500	155,072	8	6	12	4	5.7	8.4	6.2	6.2
120	† Hong Kong	19,800	151,395	92	95	22,400	162,000	12	6	6	2	15.4	15.3	11.0	15.8
121	Netherlands	74,000	155,554	51	63	76,600	139,795	15	15	24	9	4.5	5.8	4.6	4.3
122	† Singapore	19,400	96,800	50	80	24,000	103,000	9	6	29	11	12.1	16.1	8.6	12.1
123	Belgium[c]	64,500	137,394	74	81	71,900	125,762	11	11	17	8	4.4	2.4	4.0	0.3
124	France	116,000	235,905	74	78	135,000	230,203	10	11	27	9	4.1	2.3	5.0	0.8
125	Sweden	30,900	61,292	79	85	33,400	51,800	7	7	24	9	4.6	7.4	4.9	5.0
126	Austria	17,500	45,200	83	89	24,400	55,300	6	5	16	5	6.4	3.9	5.8	1.9
127	Germany[d]	193,000	427,219	86	90	188,000	381,890	12	10	23	8	4.6	2.2	4.9	2.8
128	United States	226,000	513,000	68	82	257,000	690,000	8	5	33	10	3.6	5.6	7.2	7.4
129	Norway	18,600	34,700	32	31	16,900	27,300	8	7	17	3	6.8	6.5	4.2	0.7
130	Denmark	16,700	41,417	56	66	19,300	34,800	12	14	22	5	4.4	5.4	3.6	3.4
131	Japan	130,000	397,000	96	97	141,000	275,000	12	18	50	21	5.0	0.4	6.5	4.0
132	Switzerland	29,600	66,200	91	94	36,300	64,100	8	7	11	4	6.0	3.3	4.9	–6.7
133	† *United Arab Emirates*	20,700	19,700	3	13	8,750	21,100	11	11	11	2	6.1	6.3	–1.3	21.0
World		2,003,736 t	4,326,096 t			2,007,961 t	4,391,660 t					4.8 w	5.7 w	5.0 w	5.7 w

a. Data prior to 1992 include Eritrea. b. Excludes trade with other members of the Commonwealth of Independent States. c. Includes Luxembourg. d. Data prior to 1990 refer to the Federal Republic of Germany before unification.

Table 16. Balance of payments

		Exports of goods and services[a] (million $)		Imports of goods and services[a] (million $)		Current transfers				Current account balance before official transfers (million $)		Gross international reserves (million $)	
						Net workers' remittances (million $)		Other net private transfers (million $)					
		1980	1994	1980	1994	1980	1994	1980	1994	1980	1994	1980	1994
	Low-income economies	105,529 t	237,848 t	136,812 t	285,936 t							42,943 t	119,140 t
	Excluding China and India	74,386 t	76,664 t	98,041 t	121,425 t							20,842 t	37,138 t
1	Rwanda	182	51	335	496	−14	0	11	45	−155	−400	187	39
2	Mozambique	452	341	875	1,403	0	55	0	138	−423	−870	..	..
3	Ethiopia[b]	590	563	797	1,189	22	247	58	61	−126	−317	262	588
4	Tanzania	762	855	1,412	2,067	0	0	22	450	−628	−762	..	..
5	Burundi	..	106	..	307	0	0	..	29	..	−171	105	211
6	Sierra Leone	276	..	494	..	−2	..	10	..	−209	..	..	..
7	Malawi	315	390	638	639	0	0	13	18	−310	−230	76	48
8	Chad	71	181	83	336	−4	..	0	−8	−16	−163	12	80
9	Uganda	331	333	450	901	−2	0	..	304	−121	−264	..	..
10	Madagascar	518	630	1,121	988	−30	−2	10	33	−623	−327	..	..
11	Nepal	239	1,004	368	1,320	0	70	29	−4	−100	−250	272	752
12	Vietnam	..	4,918	..	6,218	..	..	..	170	..	−1,130	..	..
13	Bangladesh	976	3,220	2,622	4,830	197	1,090	13	154	−1,436	−366	331	3,175
14	Haiti	309	64	498	216	52	0	0	43	−137	−109	27	..
15	Niger	644	245	1,016	351	−47	10	−9	−10	−429	−106	132	115
16	Guinea-Bissau	17	55	83	102	−14	0	0	9	−80	−37	..	..
17	Kenya	2,061	2,666	3,095	2,844	0	−3	27	151	−1,006	−30	539	588
18	Mali	263	392	537	817	40	85	0	146	−234	−194	26	229
19	Nigeria	27,749	9,879	22,044	12,504	−410	546	0	0	5,295	−2,079	10,640	1,649
20	Yemen, Rep.	..	2,010	..	3,178	..	1,059	..	−15	..	−124	..	274
21	Burkina Faso	225	343	596	933	100	71	12	26	−259	−493	75	241
22	Mongolia	443	421	934	481	0	0	0	−0	−491	−59	..	94
23	India	12,348	35,020	18,105	43,692	2,786	4,976	74	1,224	−2,897	−2,473	12,010	24,221
24	Lao PDR	..	259	..	400	..	0	..	10	−99	−131	..	68
25	Togo	570	305	752	341	1	5	−0	−0	−181	−31	85	99
26	Gambia, The	66	220	181	254	0	0	4	13	−112	−20	..	..
27	Nicaragua	514	459	1,049	1,429	0	30	2	0	−534	−940	75	146
28	Zambia	1,625	1,185	1,987	1,593	−61	..	−122	−19	−545	−427	206	..
29	Tajikistan	..	..	..	..	..	..	..	..	..	..	..	..
30	Benin	241	405	428	518	75	65	0	0	−112	−48	15	262
31	Central African Republic	205	186	329	280	−19	..	3	0	−141	−95	62	214
32	Albania	386	276	375	775	0	265	6	−4	16	−238	209	..
33	Ghana	1,213	1,386	1,264	2,123	−4	12	0	259	−54	−466	330	689
34	Pakistan	3,010	8,401	6,042	12,812	1,748	1,446	147	945	−1,137	−2,020	1,568	3,716
35	Mauritania	270	427	493	568	−27	24	−1	−23	−251	−140	146	44
36	Azerbaijan	..	637	..	852	..	..	..	36	..	−179	..	..
37	Zimbabwe	1,719	2,016	1,900	2,338	8	0	−129	26	−302	−295	419	585
38	Guinea	553	678	577	952	−8	9	5	−50	−26	−315	..	..
39	China	20,901	124,665	24,752	118,344	640	395	0	441	−3,211	7,157	10,091	57,781
40	Honduras	967	1,370	1,306	1,859	0	90	8	5	−331	−394	159	179
41	Senegal	830	1,349	1,337	1,740	−15	40	−4	1	−526	−350	25	191
42	Côte d'Ivoire	3,640	3,177	4,761	3,590	−716	−312	0	0	−1,836	−726	46	221
43	Congo	1,029	1,078	1,195	1,400	−38	..	−26	−25	−230	−346	93	55
44	Kyrgyz Republic	..	340	..	490	..	0	..	−52	..	−202	..	..
45	Sri Lanka	1,340	4,087	2,269	5,646	152	698	−16	−72	−793	−933	283	1,686
46	Armenia	..	258	..	525	..	0	..	36	..	−232	..	..
47	Cameroon	1,828	2,210	2,226	2,485	11	52	−8	−34	−395	−257	206	14
48	Egypt, Arab Rep.	6,516	10,511	9,745	16,121	2,696	5,073	95	0	−438	−536	2,480	14,413
49	Lesotho	363	551	482	914	0	0	2	3	−117	−360	..	..
50	Georgia	..	..	..	..	..	..	..	..	..	..	..	..
51	Myanmar	556	1,125	869	1,776	0	0	7	312	−307	−339	409	518
	Middle-income economies	662,723 t	1,047,195 t	670,749 t	1,214,187 t							173,363 t	316,491 t
	Lower-middle-income	..	..	..	..							78,989 t	136,901 t
52	Bolivia	1,046	1,226	1,112	1,670	0	−1	13	25	−53	−419	553	793
53	Macedonia, FYR	..	1,226	..	1,733	..	..	..	137	..	−370	..	166
54	Moldova	..	618	..	823	..	0	..	22	..	−183	..	180
55	Indonesia	22,241	46,295	19,432	49,704	0	449	0	0	2,810	−2,960	6,803	13,321
56	Philippines	7,997	24,051	10,348	27,809	202	367	97	93	−2,052	−3,316	3,978	7,126
57	Uzbekistan	..	3,561	..	3,569	..	0	..	0	..	−8	..	..
58	Morocco	3,270	7,035	5,807	9,901	989	2,061	15	55	−1,533	−750	814	4,622
59	Kazakstan	..	3,114	..	3,916	..	0	..	80	..	−722	..	..
60	Guatemala	1,834	2,586	2,107	3,734	0	0	109	378	−164	−770	753	943
61	Papua New Guinea	1,089	2,909	1,561	2,356	0	0	−106	−150	−578	402	458	120
62	Bulgaria	9,443	5,507	8,547	5,525	0	0	58	164	954	146	..	..
63	Romania	12,160	7,158	14,580	7,704	0	0	0	194	−2,420	−352	2,511	3,092
64	Ecuador	2,975	4,521	3,647	5,482	0	0	0	0	−672	−962	1,257	2,003
65	Dominican Republic	1,313	2,601	2,237	3,253	183	420	17	0	−725	−232	279	259
66	Lithuania	..	2,153	..	2,463	..	0	..	31	..	−279	..	597
67	El Salvador	1,271	1,675	1,289	2,982	11	967	6	37	−1	−303	382	829
68	Jordan	1,781	3,058	3,318	4,783	715	1,093	−120	−91	−942	−723	1,745	1,997
69	Jamaica	1,422	2,680	1,678	3,112	51	327	31	120	−175	−189	105	..
70	Paraguay	781	2,657	1,399	3,981	0	0	0	42	−618	−1,282	783	1,030
71	Algeria	14,500	9,698	14,552	12,919	241	0	36	1,400	225	−1,821	7,064	4,813
72	Colombia	5,860	12,428	6,231	16,283	68	211	96	651	−207	−2,993	6,474	7,862
*	Data for Taiwan, China	22,627	112,899	23,445	105,524	..	..	−92	−1,316	−910	6,059	4,055	97,653

Note: For data comparability and coverage, see the technical notes. Figures in italics are for years other than those specified.

		Exports of goods and services[a] (million $)		Imports of goods and services[a] (million $)		Current transfers				Current account balance before official transfers (million $)		Gross international reserves (million $)	
						Net workers' remittances (million $)		Other net private transfers (million $)					
		1980	1994	1980	1994	1980	1994	1980	1994	1980	1994	1980	1994
73	Tunisia	3,356	6,983	4,119	8,086	304	675	−2	8	−462	−419	700	1,544
74	Ukraine	..	14,426	..	15,837	..	0	..	−566	..	−1,977	..	..
75	Namibia	..	1,758	..	1,806	..	0	..	30	..	−19	..	203
76	Peru	4,832	5,996	5,080	9,197	0	280	0	−14	−248	−2,935	2,804	7,420
77	Belarus	..	2,770	..	3,345	..	..	..	70	..	−505	..	..
78	Slovak Republic	..	9,138	..	8,496	..	0	..	63	..	706	..	2,186
79	Latvia	..	1,263	..	1,446	..	..	..	..	..	−158	..	641
80	Costa Rica	1,219	3,399	1,897	4,004	0	0	20	89	−659	−516	197	906
81	Poland	16,200	22,189	20,338	25,898	0	0	593	991	−3,545	−2,718	574	6,023
82	Thailand	8,575	59,161	10,861	68,429	0	0	75	986	−2,212	−8,282	3,026	30,280
83	Turkey	3,672	30,084	9,251	30,589	2,071	2,627	82	126	−3,426	2,248	3,298	8,633
84	Croatia	..	6,654	..	6,872	..	340	..	−116	..	7	..	1,410
85	Panama	7,736	*7,647*	8,062	*7,756*	0	*0*	−52	−25	−378	*−136*	..	..
86	Russian Federation[c]	..	59,000	..	59,208	..	..	..	0	..	−202	..	7,206
87	Venezuela	22,232	19,170	17,065	15,993	−418	−746	0	436	4,749	2,450	13,360	12,459
88	Botswana	748	2,356	954	2,096	−17	..	15	−85	−207	174	..	..
89	Estonia	..	*1,173*	..	*1,240*	..	*0*	..	*0*	..	−68	..	446
90	*Iran, Islamic Rep.*	14,073	19,765	16,509	16,384	0	0	0	1,200	−2,436	4,581	12,783	..
91	*Turkmenistan*	..	..	..	..	..	..	..	..	..	..	..	..
Upper-middle-income		**305,516 t**	**488,002 t**	**286,289 t**	**569,204 t**							**94,374 t**	**179,589 t**
92	Brazil	23,275	50,674	36,250	54,474	1	0	126	2,597	−12,848	−1,203	6,875	38,492
93	South Africa	29,258	29,580	25,989	30,215	0	0	94	−19	3,363	−654	7,888	3,295
94	Mauritius	574	2,087	712	2,385	0	0	10	68	−129	−230	113	771
95	Czech Republic	..	19,602	..	19,744	..	0	..	126	..	−16	..	6,949
96	Malaysia	14,836	65,795	15,100	70,106	0	0	−43	48	−307	−4,262	5,755	26,339
97	Chile	6,276	14,881	8,360	15,978	0	0	64	52	−2,020	−1,045	4,128	13,802
98	Trinidad and Tobago	3,371	2,161	2,972	1,943	1	26	−44	−30	357	213	2,813	373
99	Hungary	*9,780*	11,441	*10,374*	16,404	*0*	*0*	63	896	−531	−4,067	..	6,853
100	Gabon	2,434	2,418	1,926	2,275	−143	..	−14	−72	350	71	115	180
101	Mexico	22,240	53,607	33,496	86,406	687	3,705	106	216	−10,463	−28,878	4,175	6,441
102	Uruguay	1,594	3,442	2,312	3,892	0	0	2	33	−716	−416	2,401	1,622
103	Oman	3,852	*5,800*	2,650	*5,558*	−362	*−1,329*	0	*0*	840	*−1,087*	704	1,090
104	Slovenia	..	8,628	..	8,185	..	56	..	33	..	532	..	1,499
105	Saudi Arabia	114,208	*54,598*	62,710	*52,159*	−4,094	*−15,717*	0	*0*	47,404	*−13,278*	26,129	9,139
106	Greece	8,374	15,650	11,670	22,732	1,066	2,576	21	53	−2,209	−4,453	3,607	15,809
107	Argentina	11,202	21,029	15,999	31,421	0	0	23	318	−4,774	−10,074	9,297	16,003
108	Korea, Rep.	22,577	116,228	28,347	121,364	0	0	399	832	−5,371	−4,304	3,101	25,764
Low- and middle-income		**763,625 t**	**1,290,939 t**	**797,322 t**	**1,484,372 t**							**216,306 t**	**435,631 t**
Sub-Saharan Africa		91,798 t	79,026 t	96,504 t	100,724 t							22,249 t	20,107 t
East Asia and Pacific		101,752 t	451,795 t	117,669 t	482,575 t							33,794 t	161,686 t
South Asia		18,792 t	52,585 t	30,493 t	69,750 t							15,403 t	31,901 t
Europe and Central Asia		..	..	..	..							11,445 t	63,580 t
Middle East and N. Africa		218,507 t	..	165,659 t	..							76,217 t	46,538 t
Latin America and Caribbean		132,434 t	233,334 t	178,545 t	319,456 t							57,197 t	111,820 t
High-income economies		**1,908,362 t**	**4,923,317 t**	**1,916,810 t**	**4,792,515 t**							**730,811 t**	**1,031,132 t**
109	Portugal	6,846	*24,586*	10,916	*30,354*	2,928	*3,844*	71	−3	−1,072	*−1,926*	13,863	21,671
110	New Zealand	6,561	16,011	7,630	18,116	143	177	−35	806	−961	−1,123	365	3,709
111	Spain	33,863	111,791	41,089	121,337	1,647	1,780	411	99	−5,168	−7,667	20,474	47,531
112	Ireland	10,418	40,446	13,754	39,483	0	0	123	−52	−3,213	911	3,071	6,253
113	† Israel	9,858	24,527	13,458	33,898	0	0	1,060	3,260	−2,540	−6,111	4,055	6,796
114	Australia	26,668	*58,062*	30,683	*68,755*	0	*0*	295	*738*	−3,720	−9,955	6,366	14,313
115	United Kingdom	201,137	386,474	189,683	380,663	0	0	−473	−398	10,980	5,414	31,755	48,079
116	Finland	17,332	36,490	18,621	34,992	0	0	−20	−96	−1,308	1,402	2,451	11,430
117	Italy	105,011	278,378	116,794	256,921	1,609	242	−155	−247	−10,329	21,453	62,428	57,817
118	† Kuwait	27,344	17,927	10,463	12,261	−692	−1,445	0	0	16,190	4,221	5,425	4,474
119	Canada	77,995	190,101	79,859	209,087	0	0	53	832	−1,811	−18,153	15,462	13,775
120	† Hong Kong	24,190	..	25,448	..	..	..	..	..	−1,258	..	..	..
121	Netherlands	97,922	197,115	97,610	180,466	−316	−395	−498	−1,547	−503	14,707	37,549	47,859
122	† Singapore	25,239	*101,929*	26,695	*99,194*	0	*0*	−104	*−482*	−1,560	*2,253*	..	..
123	Belgium[d]	88,925	*224,364*	92,625	*209,188*	−266	*−360*	−104	*−240*	−4,070	14,576	27,974	23,474
124	France	171,817	424,737	171,856	408,318	−2,591	−1,290	137	−87	−2,494	15,043	75,592	57,627
125	Sweden	39,388	83,406	42,495	80,711	0	91	−301	−273	−3,407	2,513	6,996	25,579
126	Austria	29,152	82,237	32,951	83,834	−67	33	9	−294	−3,857	−1,858	17,725	23,852
127	Germany[e]	233,971	565,307	235,078	554,118	−4,437	−4,634	−1,464	−4,228	−7,007	2,327	104,702	113,841
128	United States	344,440	836,415	333,830	957,209	−810	−7,680	−220	−8,010	9,580	−136,484	171,413	163,591
129	Norway	28,252	50,837	26,658	45,573	−23	−236	−32	−215	1,539	4,813	6,746	19,479
130	Denmark	24,152	*72,481*	26,642	*67,263*	0	*0*	−89	*−133*	−2,578	*5,086*	4,347	9,680
131	Japan	158,230	600,110	167,450	463,390	0	0	−240	−2,820	−9,460	133,900	38,919	135,145
132	Switzerland	59,462	*119,920*	58,524	*100,364*	−603	*−2,007*	−98	*−220*	238	*17,329*	64,748	66,645
133	† *United Arab Emirates*	..	..	..	..	..	..	..	..	11,800	..	2,355	6,964
World		**2,639,869 t**	**6,275,740 t**	**2,666,779 t**	**6,276,817 t**							**947,117 t**	**1,466,763 t**

a. Corresponds to the fourth edition of the IMF's *Balance of Payments Manual* definition. b. Data prior to 1992 include Eritrea. c. Excludes trade with other members of the Commonwealth of Independent States. d. Includes Luxembourg. e. Data prior to 1990 refer to the Federal Republic of Germany before unification.

Table 17. External debt

		Total external debt (million $)		External debt as percentage of GNP		External debt as percentage of Exports of goods and services		Debt service as % of exports of goods and services		Ratio of present value to nominal value of debt (%)	Multilateral debt as % of total external debt	
		1980	1994	1980	1994	1980	1994	1980	1994	1994	1980	1994
Low-income economies		..	..	..	..	..	..	..	..		..	..
Excluding China and India		..	..	..	..	..	..	..	..		..	..
1	Rwanda	190	954	16.3	164.8	113.7	2,163.9	4.6	14.7	47.3	47.8	78.5
2	Mozambique	..	5,491	..	450.4	..	1,388.7	..	23.0	73.5	0.0	19.2
3	Ethiopiaa	824	5,058	..	109.8	139.4	630.0	7.6	11.5	62.3	41.2	42.0
4	Tanzania	2,616	7,441	..	229.5	349.7	877.5	21.5	20.5	72.9	21.6	35.5
5	Burundi	166	1,125	18.2	113.8	..	1,144.9	..	41.7	43.7	35.7	78.3
6	Sierra Leone	435	1,392	40.7	187.3	158.3	..	23.3	..	73.7	14.2	23.9
7	Malawi	821	2,015	72.1	160.3	262.4	523.0	27.8	17.4	45.6	26.7	78.8
8	Chad	228	816	31.6	91.0	320.2	450.9	8.3	8.1	47.2	32.6	72.3
9	Uganda	702	3,473	55.7	88.1	213.2	1,042.7	17.4	45.6	54.9	11.6	58.4
10	Madagascar	1,241	4,134	31.1	225.3	240.7	652.1	20.5	9.5	71.6	14.7	38.6
11	Nepal	205	2,320	10.4	56.2	91.5	223.4	3.4	7.9	48.5	62.0	77.8
12	Vietnam	6	25,115	..	161.3	..	514.3	..	6.1	83.7	100.0	0.9
13	Bangladesh	4,327	16,569	33.4	63.4	399.8	400.7	25.6	15.8	50.7	29.0	55.9
14	Haiti	303	712	20.9	44.2	73.4	1,108.9	6.3	1.2	56.5	43.8	73.3
15	Niger	863	1,569	34.5	104.2	138.6	617.4	22.7	26.1	55.4	16.5	52.7
16	Guinea-Bissau	135	816	128.4	340.7	..	1,801.8	..	15.2	65.3	21.6	44.6
17	Kenya	3,383	7,273	48.1	112.4	168.6	275.0	21.6	33.6	70.9	18.6	37.9
18	Mali	732	2,781	45.4	151.8	227.2	589.2	5.1	27.5	55.3	23.7	44.3
19	Nigeria	8,921	33,485	10.1	102.5	33.0	322.6	4.3	18.5	89.4	6.4	14.4
20	Yemen, Rep.	1,684	5,959	..	..	..	196.3	..	4.8	80.1	14.9	20.3
21	Burkina Faso	330	1,125	19.5	61.1	91.8	..	6.2	..	50.0	42.9	78.1
22	Mongolia	..	443	..	61.3	..	106.5	..	9.6	62.1	..	25.5
23	India	20,582	98,990	11.9	34.2	146.5	253.7	10.0	26.9	71.4	29.5	31.8
24	Lao PDR	350	2,080	..	135.6	..	803.1	..	7.7	29.3	5.9	25.4
25	Togo	1,052	1,455	95.9	156.6	187.9	470.5	9.3	7.8	62.3	11.3	46.9
26	Gambia, The	137	419	61.5	117.3	206.5	194.6	6.3	14.4	50.6	29.9	71.5
27	Nicaragua	2,192	11,019	108.5	800.6	443.4	2,286.1	23.2	38.0	88.3	19.2	11.9
28	Zambia	3,261	6,573	90.7	204.3	202.3	560.1	25.5	31.5	77.0	12.2	30.3
29	Tajikistan	..	594	..	28.7	..	..	..	..	88.5	..	11.4
30	Benin	424	1,619	30.2	109.4	139.7	399.9	6.7	10.1	51.5	24.5	48.5
31	Central African Republic	195	891	24.3	104.0	96.9	490.6	5.0	12.9	50.2	27.4	66.3
32	Albania	..	925	..	50.8	..	190.7	..	2.5	88.4	..	7.1
33	Ghana	1,398	5,389	31.6	101.5	115.8	389.2	13.2	24.8	62.1	19.9	49.6
34	Pakistan	9,930	29,579	42.4	56.6	211.0	303.3	18.1	35.1	74.5	15.4	38.9
35	Mauritania	843	2,326	125.5	240.1	326.7	518.1	18.4	23.3	67.6	14.8	35.7
36	Azerbaijan	..	113	..	3.1	..	17.7	..	0.0	96.6	..	7.4
37	Zimbabwe	786	4,368	14.9	85.9	48.3	..	4.0	..	80.0	0.4	34.1
38	Guinea	1,117	3,104	..	94.7	202.0	455.7	19.8	14.2	63.2	11.6	42.0
39	China	4,504	100,536	2.2	19.3	21.4	84.3	4.4	9.3	85.2	0.0	13.5
40	Honduras	1,472	4,418	60.6	..	156.3	345.3	22.0	33.9	76.4	31.2	46.7
41	Senegal	1,473	3,678	50.5	99.1	167.0	277.6	29.4	14.9	65.7	17.8	48.3
42	Côte d'Ivoire	7,445	18,452	76.9	338.9	208.3	581.0	39.4	40.1	83.2	7.0	18.2
43	Congo	1,526	5,275	99.0	454.2	149.2	489.2	10.6	51.5	84.1	7.7	13.2
44	Kyrgyz Republic	..	441	..	16.2	..	129.8	..	4.8	79.3	..	21.9
45	Sri Lanka	1,841	7,811	46.1	67.6	127.6	168.3	12.4	8.7	61.2	11.7	34.0
46	Armenia	..	214	..	8.3	..	83.4	..	1.7	91.9	..	48.6
47	Cameroon	2,513	7,275	36.8	107.0	138.2	325.1	15.4	16.7	80.7	16.8	22.3
48	Egypt, Arab Rep.	19,131	33,358	89.2	78.9	213.9	231.8	13.8	15.8	65.7	13.7	12.5
49	Lesotho	72	600	11.4	44.4	79.5	331.9	6.1	16.9	58.3	56.1	68.6
50	*Georgia*	..	1,227	..	58.6	..	254.2	..	1.2	95.3	..	12.1
51	*Myanmar*	1,499	6,502	26.0	8.8	278.0	580.8	26.2	15.4	74.8	18.6	22.4
Middle-income economies		..	..	..	..	..	..	..	..		..	..
Lower-middle-income		..	..	..	..	..	..	..	..		..	..
52	Bolivia	2,702	4,749	93.4	89.4	262.4	390.1	35.5	28.2	74.0	16.5	47.9
53	Macedonia, FYR	..	924	..	56.9	..	75.4	..	12.7	93.5	..	23.6
54	Moldova	..	492	..	13.2	..	79.7	..	2.2	88.7	..	33.1
55	Indonesia	20,944	96,500	28.0	57.4	94.7	211.3	13.9	32.4	87.2	8.8	19.8
56	Philippines	17,417	39,302	53.7	59.7	233.9	189.7	29.3	21.9	89.1	7.5	21.2
57	Uzbekistan	..	1,156	..	5.4	..	33.0	..	3.2	91.2	..	0.4
58	Morocco	9,710	22,512	53.3	76.3	227.0	257.1	33.0	33.3	84.0	7.4	27.4
59	Kazakstan	..	2,704	..	14.9	..	88.1	..	1.9	91.0	..	8.0
60	Guatemala	1,166	3,017	14.9	23.4	67.4	121.4	8.4	11.4	80.6	30.0	28.3
61	Papua New Guinea	719	2,878	28.9	57.5	69.9	99.4	14.6	30.0	80.3	21.2	31.3
62	Bulgaria	392	10,468	2.0	104.8	4.2	193.1	0.5	14.0	95.6	0.0	13.3
63	Romania	9,762	5,492	..	18.3	80.9	78.0	12.7	8.4	92.0	8.3	25.2
64	Ecuador	5,997	14,955	53.8	96.6	207.7	335.3	34.9	22.1	87.6	5.4	16.1
65	Dominican Republic	2,002	4,293	31.2	41.8	137.7	144.8	26.1	17.0	87.9	10.2	21.8
66	Lithuania	..	438	..	8.4	..	20.3	..	2.8	82.9	..	27.2
67	El Salvador	911	2,188	26.1	26.9	74.0	84.0	7.8	13.1	74.6	28.3	57.2
68	Jordan	1,971	7,051	..	121.8	86.2	172.9	9.2	12.4	71.3	8.0	14.3
69	Jamaica	1,913	4,318	78.0	110.1	135.7	149.8	19.9	20.6	85.4	14.9	27.4
70	Paraguay	955	1,979	20.7	25.1	136.2	78.3	20.7	10.2	88.6	20.2	36.0
71	Algeria	19,365	29,898	47.1	74.3	132.8	312.1	28.0	56.0	81.9	1.5	11.1
72	Colombia	6,940	19,416	20.9	29.6	128.8	159.4	17.7	30.3	93.7	19.5	27.7

Note: For data comparability and coverage, see the technical notes.

		Total external debt (million $)		External debt as percentage of				Debt service as % of exports of goods and services		Ratio of present value to nominal value of debt (%)	Multilateral debt as % of total external debt	
				GNP		Exports of goods and services						
		1980	1994	1980	1994	1980	1994	1980	1994	1994	1980	1994
73	Tunisia	3,526	9,254	41.6	60.8	98.5	122.1	15.2	18.8	85.9	12.3	37.9
74	Ukraine	..	5,430	..	6.6	..	37.7	..	2.0	92.4	..	4.1
75	Namibia	..	..	..	..	..	..	..	..	..	..	..
76	Peru	9,386	22,623	47.6	46.2	202.5	379.6	46.4	17.7	88.5	5.5	14.8
77	Belarus	..	1,272	..	6.3	..	45.9	..	4.3	74.4	..	13.6
78	Slovak Republic	670	4,067	5.6	33.2	..	45.3	..	9.3	91.9	0.0	12.5
79	Latvia	..	364	..	6.3	..	28.8	..	2.1	89.6	..	31.5
80	Costa Rica	2,744	3,843	59.7	47.8	229.3	116.4	29.6	15.0	88.1	16.4	33.6
81	Poland	8,894	42,160	16.3	46.2	55.5	195.0	18.1	14.3	79.3	0.0	4.6
82	Thailand	8,297	60,991	25.9	43.1	104.5	107.9	20.4	16.3	98.4	12.0	5.1
83	Turkey	19,131	66,332	34.3	51.4	336.2	217.1	28.2	33.4	85.8	11.2	14.0
84	Croatia	..	2,304	..	16.4	..	33.4	..	4.2	93.8	..	22.9
85	Panama	2,975	7,107	81.8	107.2	88.0	..	14.4	..	96.6	11.0	8.2
86	Russian Federation	4,477	94,232	..	25.4	..	161.1	..	6.3	92.2	0.0	1.7
87	Venezuela	29,345	36,850	42.1	65.6	146.6	209.7	30.2	21.0	90.2	0.7	8.5
88	Botswana	147	691	16.3	17.4	22.7	32.3	2.4	4.3	75.9	57.5	72.6
89	Estonia	..	186	..	4.1	..	..	..	..	90.3	..	35.2
90	*Iran, Islamic Rep.*	4,500	22,712	4.8	36.6	34.5	118.6	7.4	22.5	90.9	13.8	1.3
91	*Turkmenistan*	..	418	..	..	..	17.2	..	4.2	90.6	..	13.2
Upper-middle-income		..	..	..	..	..	..	..	..		..	..
92	Brazil	72,920	151,104	31.8	27.9	334.0	336.0	67.7	35.8	92.6	4.2	6.1
93	South Africa	..	..	..	..	..	..	..	..		..	..
94	Mauritius	467	1,355	41.6	40.3	82.1	68.1	9.2	7.3	86.5	16.6	19.2
95	Czech Republic	3,789	10,694	13.0	29.7	..	56.8	..	13.1	94.3	0.0	8.8
96	Malaysia	6,611	24,767	28.0	36.9	46.8	39.0	6.6	7.9	89.3	11.3	6.9
97	Chile	12,081	22,939	45.5	45.5	202.4	160.0	45.3	20.3	90.2	2.9	19.0
98	Trinidad and Tobago	829	2,218	14.0	50.3	26.4	104.1	7.3	31.6	93.9	8.6	18.4
99	Hungary	9,764	28,016	44.8	70.1	..	260.9	..	53.0	94.2	0.0	12.4
100	Gabon	1,514	3,967	39.3	122.5	63.0	165.1	18.0	10.5	89.8	2.7	11.4
101	Mexico	57,378	128,302	30.5	35.2	266.4	238.4	50.9	35.4	91.4	5.6	13.3
102	Uruguay	1,660	5,099	17.0	33.2	108.6	161.4	19.6	16.1	93.3	11.0	23.9
103	Oman	599	3,084	11.2	30.7	15.8	..	6.6	..	90.6	5.8	5.2
104	Slovenia	..	2,290	..	16.4	..	26.8	..	5.4	93.1	..	21.6
105	Saudi Arabia	..	..	..	..	..	..	..	..		..	..
106	Greece	..	..	..	..	..	..	..	..		..	..
107	Argentina	27,157	77,388	35.6	27.8	274.6	405.4	42.3	35.1	88.5	4.0	9.9
108	Korea, Rep.	29,480	54,542	47.9	15.3	134.5	48.1	20.3	7.0	91.2	8.0	5.7
Low- and middle-income		647,308 t	1,921,450 t	26.5 w	37.6 w	88.3 w	162.8 w	13.2 w	16.6 w		7.6 w	14.6 w
Sub-Saharan Africa		84,049 t	212,416 t	30.6 w	78.7 w	90.9 w	265.7 w	9.7 w	14.0 w		9.0 w	23.9 w
East Asia and Pacific		94,307 t	421,329 t	21.5 w	30.9 w	93.6 w	93.3 w	13.4 w	12.0 w		8.3 w	12.5 w
South Asia		38,112 t	161,128 t	17.4 w	42.0 w	161.1 w	271.6 w	11.6 w	25.6 w		24.5 w	35.4 w
Europe and Central Asia		87,919 t	356,090 t	25.7 w	32.8 w	54.6 w	153.7 w	8.6 w	14.6 w		5.4 w	8.6 w
Middle East and N. Africa		84,257 t	207,669 t	18.6 w	41.7 w	36.8 w	148.5 w	5.0 w	15.4 w		6.7 w	10.1 w
Latin America and Caribbean		258,665 t	562,818 t	36.2 w	37.2 w	206.0 w	258.6 w	36.9 w	27.5 w		5.5 w	12.2 w
High-income economies												
109	Portugal											
110	New Zealand											
111	Spain											
112	Ireland											
113	† Israel											
114	Australia											
115	United Kingdom											
116	Finland											
117	Italy											
118	† Kuwait											
119	Canada											
120	† Hong Kong											
121	Netherlands											
122	† Singapore											
123	Belgium											
124	France											
125	Sweden											
126	Austria											
127	Germany											
128	United States											
129	Norway											
130	Denmark											
131	Japan											
132	Switzerland											
133	† *United Arab Emirates*											
World												

a. Includes Eritrea.

Table 1a. Basic indicators for other economies

		Population (thousands) mid-1994	Area (thousands of sq. km)	GNP per capita[a]		PPP estimates of GNP per capita[b]			Life expectancy at birth (years) 1994	Adult illiteracy (%) 1995
				Dollars 1994	Avg. ann. growth (%) 1985–94	US=100 1987	US=100 1994	Current int'l $ 1994		
1	Afghanistan	22,789	652.09	c	..	..	..	..	44	69
2	American Samoa	55	0.20	d	..	..	..	..	..	..
3	Andorra	65	0.45	e	..	..	..	..	79	..
4	Angola	10,442	1,246.70	f	−6.8	..	..	..	47	..
5	Antigua and Barbuda	67	0.44	6,770	2.5	..	..	..	75	..
6	Aruba	77	0.19	e	..	..	..	..	75	..
7	Bahamas, The	272	13.88	11,800	−0.8	73.1	59.8	15,470g	73	2
8	Bahrain	557	0.68	7,460	−0.7	57.7	51.1	13,220g	72	15
9	Barbados	260	0.43	6,560	−0.0	48.0	43.3	11,210g	..	3
10	Belize	211	22.96	2,530	5.0	18.0	21.6	5,600g	69	..
11	Bermuda	63	0.05	e	−1.2	..	..	..	..	..
12	Bhutan	675	47.00	400	4.4	4.8	4.9	1,270g	..	58
13	Bosnia and Herzegovina	4,383	51.13	c	..	..	..	..	..	..
14	Brunei	280	5.77	14,240	..	..	..	..	75	12
15	Cambodia	9,951	181.04	e	..	..	..	..	52	..
16	Cape Verde	372	4.03	930	2.0	7.1	7.4	1,920g	65	28
17	Cayman Islands	33	0.26	e	..	..	..	..	77	..
18	Channel Islands	143	0.19	e	..	..	..	..	78	..
19	Comoros	485	2.23	510	−1.4	6.8	5.5	1,430g	55	43
20	Cuba	10,978	110.86	f	..	..	..	..	76	4
21	Cyprus	726	9.25	10,260	4.6	47.2	57.2	14,800g	77	..
22	Djibouti	603	23.20	c	..	..	..	..	49	54
23	Dominica	72	0.75	2,800	4.3	..	..	..	73	..
24	Equatorial Guinea	386	28.05	430	2.2	..	..	..	48	..
25	Eritrea	3,482	125.00	c	..	..	..	..	48	..
26	Faeroe Islands	45	1.40	e	..	..	..	..	77	..
27	Fiji	767	18.27	2,250	2.4	20.4	23.0	5,940g	72	8
28	French Guiana	141	90.00	d	..	..	..	..	73	..
29	French Polynesia	219	4.00	d	..	..	..	..	69	..
30	Greenland	55	341.70	e	..	..	..	..	66	..
31	Grenada	92	0.34	2,630	..	..	..	..	..	..
32	Guadeloupe	421	1.71	d	..	..	..	..	75	..
33	Guam	146	0.55	d	..	..	..	..	73	..
34	Guyana	826	214.97	530	0.4	8.8	10.6	2,750g	66	2
35	Iceland	266	103.00	24,630	0.3	86.4	74.2	19,210h	79	..
36	Iraq	20,356	438.32	f	..	..	..	..	67	42
37	Isle of Man	72	0.57	d	..	..	..	..	..	..
38	Kiribati	78	0.73	740	..	..	..	..	61	..
39	Korea, Dem. Rep.	23,448	120.54	f	..	..	..	..	70	..
40	Lebanon	3,930	10.40	f	..	..	..	..	69	8
41	Liberia	2,719	97.75	c	..	..	..	..	53	..
42	Libya	5,218	1,759.54	d	..	..	..	..	64	..
43	Liechtenstein	31	0.16	e	..	..	..	..	72	..
44	Luxembourg	404	3.00	39,600	1.2	143.1	138.6	35,860h	76	i
45	Macao	444	0.02	e	..	..	..	..	..	..
46	Maldives	246	0.30	950	7.7	..	..	..	62	7
47	Malta	368	0.32	d	5.1	..	..	..	77	..
48	Marshall Islands	54	0.20	f	..	..	..	..	63	..
49	Martinique	383	1.10	d	..	..	..	..	76	..
50	Mayotte	89	0.37	d	..	..	..	..	60	..
51	Micronesia, Fed. Sts.	104	0.70	f	..	..	..	..	65	..
52	Monaco	33	..	e	..	..	..	..	78	..
53	Netherlands Antilles	198	0.80	e	..	..	..	..	77	..
54	New Caledonia	187	18.58	d	..	..	..	..	72	..
55	Northern Mariana Islands	47	0.48	f	..	..	..	..	..	..
56	Puerto Rico	3,651	8.90	d	1.6	..	..	..	75	..
57	Qatar	610	11.00	12,820	−2.4	90.4	73.8	19,100g	72	21
58	Reunion	640	2.51	d	..	..	..	..	74	..
59	São Tomé and Principe	125	0.96	250	−2.1	..	..	..	68	..
60	Seychelles	72	0.45	6,680	4.8	..	..	..	72	21
61	Solomon Islands	365	28.90	810	2.2	8.2	8.1	2,100g	62	..
62	Somalia	8,775	637.66	c	−2.3	..	..	..	49	..
63	St. Kitts and Nevis	41	0.36	4,760	4.7	30.4	36.0	9,310g	69	..
64	St. Lucia	160	0.62	3,130	4.0	..	..	..	71	..
65	St. Vincent and the Grenadines	110	0.39	2,140	4.5	..	..	..	72	..
66	Sudan	27,364	2,505.81	c	−0.2	8.8	..	..	54	54
67	Suriname	407	163.27	860	1.8	13.8	9.5	2,470g	69	7
68	Swaziland	906	17.36	1,100	−1.2	14.0	11.6	3,010j	58	23
69	Syrian Arab Republic	13,844	185.18	f	−2.1	..	..	..	68	..
70	Tonga	101	0.75	1,590	0.3	..	..	..	69	..
71	Vanuatu	165	12.19	1,150	−0.3	9.3	9.2	2,370g	60	..
72	Virgin Islands (U.S.)	100	0.34	e	..	..	..	..	75	..
73	West Bank & Gaza	1,951	0.38	f	..	..	..	..	..	..
74	Western Samoa	164	2.84	1,000	−0.3	9.5	8.0	2,060g	69	..
75	Yugoslavia, Fed. Rep.	10,520	102.17	f	..	..	..	..	72	..
76	Zaire	42,540	2,344.86	c	−1.0	..	..	..	..	33

a. *Atlas* method; see the technical notes. b. Purchasing power parity; see the technical notes. c. Estimated to be low income ($725 or less). d. Estimated to be upper middle income ($2,896 to $8,955). e. Estimated to be high income ($8,956 or more). f. Estimated to be lower middle income ($726 to $2,895). g. Based on regression estimates. h. Extrapolated from 1993 ICP estimates. i. According to UNESCO, illiteracy is less than 5 percent. j. Extrapolated from 1985 ICP estimates.

Technical Notes

T hese technical notes discuss the sources and methods used to compile the 120 indicators included in the 1996 Selected World Development Indicators. Notes on specific indicators are arranged by table heading and, within each table, by order of appearance of the indicator.

The 133 economies included in the main tables are listed in ascending order of GNP per capita. A separate table (Table 1a) shows basic indicators for seventy-six economies that have sparse data or have populations of fewer than 1 million.

Sources
Indicators published here are based on data compiled by the World Bank from a variety of sources. Data on external debt are reported directly to the World Bank, by developing member countries, through the Debtor Reporting System. Other data are drawn mainly from the United Nations (U.N.) and its specialized agencies, the International Monetary Fund (IMF), and country reports to the World Bank. Bank staff estimates are also used to improve currentness or consistency. For most countries, national accounts estimates are obtained from member governments through World Bank economic missions. In some instances these are adjusted by staff to ensure conformity with international definitions and concepts, consistency, and currentness. Most social data from national sources are drawn from regular administrative files, special surveys, or periodic census inquiries. Citations of specific sources are included in the Key table and with the indicator notes below.

Data consistency and reliability
Considerable effort has been made to standardize the data, but full comparability cannot be ensured, and care must be taken in interpreting the indicators. Many factors affect availability, comparability, and reliability: statistical systems in many developing economies are still weak; statistical methods, coverage, practices, and definitions differ widely among countries; and cross-country and cross-time comparisons involve complex technical and conceptual

problems that cannot be unequivocally resolved. For these reasons, although the data are drawn from the sources thought to be most authoritative, they should be construed only as indicating trends and characterizing major differences among economies rather than offering precise quantitative measures of those differences. Also, national statistical agencies tend to revise their historical data, particularly for recent years. Thus, data of different vintages may be published in different editions of World Bank publications. Readers are advised not to compare such data from different editions. Consistent time series are available from the *World*Data 1995 CD-ROM*. In addition, data issues have yet to be resolved for the fifteen economies of the former Soviet Union: coverage is sparse, and the data are subject to more than the normal range of uncertainty.

Ratios and growth rates
For ease of reference, only ratios and rates of growth are usually shown. Absolute values are generally available from other World Bank publications, notably the 1995 edition of the *World Tables* and *World*Data 1995 CD-ROM*. Most growth rates are calculated for two periods, 1980–90 and 1990–94, and are computed, unless otherwise noted, by using the least-squares regression method. (See notes on statistical methods below.) Because this method takes into account all available observations in a period, the resulting growth rates reflect general trends that are not unduly influenced by exceptional values. To exclude the effects of inflation, constant-price economic indicators are used in calculating growth rates. Data in italics are for years or periods other than those specified—up to two years on either side of the date shown for economic indicators and up to three years for social indicators, because the latter tend to be collected less regularly and change less dramatically over short periods of time.

Constant price series
To facilitate international comparisons and include the effects of changes in intersectoral relative prices for the national accounts aggregates, constant price data for most

economies are first partially rebased to three sequential base years and then "chain-linked" together and expressed in the prices of a common base year, 1987. The year 1970 is the base year for the period from 1960 to 1975, 1980 for 1976 to 1982, and 1987 for 1983 and beyond.

During the chain-linking procedure, components of gross domestic product (GDP) by industrial origin are individually rescaled and summed to provide the rescaled GDP. In this process a rescaling deviation may occur between the constant price GDP by industrial origin and the constant price GDP by expenditure. Such rescaling deviations are absorbed under the heading *private consumption, etc.* on the assumption that GDP by industrial origin is a more reliable estimate than GDP by expenditure. Independently of the rescaling, value added in the services sector also includes a statistical discrepancy as reported by the original source.

Summary measures

The summary measures across countries for regions and income groups, presented in the blue bands in the tables, are calculated by simple addition when they are expressed in levels. Growth rates and ratios are usually combined by a base-year, value-weighting scheme. The summary measures for social indicators are weighted by population or subgroups of population, except for infant mortality, which is weighted by the number of births. See notes on specific indicators for more information.

For summary measures that cover many years, the calculation is based on the same country composition over time. The methodology permits group measures to be compiled only if the country data available for a given year account for at least two-thirds of the full group, as defined by the 1987 benchmarks. As long as that criterion is met, missing reporters are assumed to behave like those that provide estimates. Readers should keep in mind that the goal of the summary measures is to provide representative aggregates for each topic, despite myriad problems with country data, and that nothing meaningful can be deduced about behavior at the country level by working back from group indicators. In addition, the weighting process may result in discrepancies between subgroup and overall totals.

Table 1. Basic indicators

Basic indicators for economies with sparse data or with populations of fewer than 1 million are shown in Table 1a.

Total population estimates are for mid-1994. See the Key table and notes to Table 4 for additional information on the definition and sources of population estimates.

Area data come from the Food and Agriculture Organization (FAO). Area is the total surface area, measured in square kilometers, comprising land area and inland waters.

GNP per capita: Gross national product (GNP) in U.S. dollars is calculated using the *World Bank Atlas* method, which is described in the section on statistical methods at the end of these notes.

GNP measures the total domestic and foreign value added claimed by residents. It comprises GDP (see Table 12) plus net factor income from abroad, which is the income residents receive from abroad for factor services (labor and capital) less similar payments made to nonresidents who contribute to the domestic economy. GNP per capita is calculated using the resident population in the corresponding year.

GNP per capita is a useful measure of average economic productivity but does not, by itself, measure welfare or success in development. It does not distinguish between the aims and ultimate uses of a given product, nor does it say whether a product merely offsets some natural or other obstacle, or harms or contributes to general welfare. More generally, GNP does not deal adequately with environmental costs and benefits, particularly those associated with natural resource use. The World Bank has joined with others to see how national accounts might provide insights into these issues. "Satellite" accounts that delve into practical and conceptual difficulties (such as assigning a meaningful economic value to resources that markets do not yet perceive as "scarce" and allocating costs that are essentially global within a framework that is national) have been included in the 1993 revision of the *System of National Accounts* (SNA). This will provide a framework within which national accountants can consider environmental factors in estimating alternative measures of income.

In estimating GNP per capita, the World Bank recognizes that perfect cross-country comparability of GNP per capita estimates cannot be achieved. Beyond the classic, strictly intractable, index number problem, two obstacles stand in the way. One concerns the GNP and population estimates themselves. There are differences in national accounting and demographic reporting systems and in the coverage and reliability of underlying statistical information among various countries. The other obstacle is the use of official exchange rates for converting GNP data expressed in different national currencies to a common denomination—conventionally the U.S. dollar—to compare them across countries.

Recognizing that these shortcomings affect the comparability of the GNP per capita estimates, the World Bank has introduced several improvements in the estimation procedures. Through its regular review of member countries' national accounts, the Bank systematically evaluates the GNP estimates, focusing on the coverage and concepts employed and, where appropriate, making adjustments to improve comparability. As part of the review process, World Bank staff make estimates of GNP (and sometimes of population).

The World Bank also systematically assesses the appropriateness of official exchange rates as conversion factors. An alternative conversion factor is used when the official exchange rate is judged to diverge by an exceptionally large margin from the rate effectively applied to domestic transactions of foreign currencies and traded products. This applies to only a small number of countries. Using either the official or the alternative conversion factor, GNP per capita is calculated using the *World Bank Atlas* method. Because of unresolved problems associated with the availability of comparable data and the determination of conversion factors, information on GNP per capita is not shown for some economies.

Some sixty low- and middle-income economies suffered declining real GNP per capita during the late 1980s and early 1990s. In addition, significant fluctuations in currency values and the terms of trade and the time lag between exchange rate movements and domestic price adjustments have affected relative income levels. For this reason, the levels and ranking of GNP per capita estimates, calculated by the *Atlas* method, have sometimes changed in ways not necessarily related to the relative domestic growth performance of the economies.

Purchasing power parity (PPP) estimates of GNP per capita: the U. N. International Comparison Programme (ICP) has developed measures of GDP on an internationally comparable scale, using purchasing power parities instead of exchange rates as conversion factors. The PPP conversion factor is defined as the number of units of a country's currency required to buy the same amounts of goods and services in the domestic market as one dollar would buy in the United States.

The ICP collects average domestic prices of representative products included in each participating country's national accounts through special price surveys and derives its PPP in relation to the average international prices that are implicitly derived from the prices of all participating countries. In Table 1, the most recent ICP estimates are expressed in GNP terms rather than in GDP terms to make them consistent with *World Bank Atlas*–based estimates.

Information on the ICP has been published in a number of other reports. The most recent report is for 1993, part of which has already been published by the Organisation for Economic Co-operation and Development (OECD). To obtain the estimates shown here, several sets of data were employed. The data include (a) results of the ICP for 1993 for OECD, Eastern Europe, and FSU countries extrapolated backward to 1987; (b) results for 1985 for non-OECD countries, extrapolated to 1987; (c) the latest available results for either 1980 or 1975 extrapo-

lated to 1987 for countries that participated in the earlier phases only; (d) World Bank estimates for China, and (e) ICP estimates obtained by regression for the remaining countries. These estimates are expressed as an index (U.S.=100 in column 5). Economies whose 1987 estimates are based on regressions are footnoted.

This blend of extrapolated and regression-based 1987 figures was extrapolated to 1994, using World Bank estimates of real GNP per capita growth rates, and scaled up by inflation rates measured by SDR deflators. These estimates are expressed as an index (U.S.=100) in columns 5 and 6. Economies whose 1987 figures are extrapolated from another year or imputed by regression are footnoted accordingly. The adjustments do not take account of changes in the terms of trade.

The estimates of GNP per capita shown in column 8 are stated in *international dollars* by applying the PPP conversion factor to local currency GNP and then dividing by the midyear population. The international dollar, used as the common currency, is the unit of account that equalizes price levels in all participating countries. It has the same purchasing power over total GNP as the U.S. dollar in a given year, but purchasing power over subaggregates is determined by average international prices at that level rather than by U.S. relative prices.

For further details on ICP procedures, readers may consult the ICP Phase IV report, *World Comparisons of Purchasing Power and Real Product for 1980* (New York: United Nations, 1986). Readers interested in detailed ICP survey data for 1975, 1980, 1985, and 1990 may refer to *Purchasing Power of Currencies: Comparing National Incomes Using ICP Data* (World Bank, 1993).

Life expectancy at birth indicates the number of years a newborn infant would live if prevailing patterns of mortality at the time of its birth were to stay the same throughout its life. The data are from a variety of sources, including national statistical offices, demographic and health surveys, censuses, the U.N. Population Division, and the World Bank.

Adult illiteracy: see Table 7.

The summary measures for GNP per capita, life expectancy, and adult illiteracy in Table 1 are weighted by population.

Table 2. Macroeconomic indicators

The principal sources of the data in Table 2 are the IMF's *Government Finance Statistics* (GFS) and *International Financial Statistics* (IFS). Data on GNP, GDP, and total external debt come from the World Bank's data files.

Central government current deficit/surplus is defined as current revenue of the central government less current expenditure. Note that grants are excluded. This is a useful measure of the government's own fiscal capacity. The overall deficit/surplus, including grants and the capital account, is shown in Table 14.

Money, broadly defined, comes from the IFS. Broadly defined money comprises most liabilities of a country's monetary institutions to residents other than the central government. For most countries, broadly defined money is the sum of money (IFS line 34) and quasi-money (IFS line 35). Money comprises the economy's means of payment: currency outside banks and demand deposits other than those of the central government. Quasi-money comprises time and savings deposits and similar bank accounts that the issuer can exchange for money with little, if any, delay or penalty and foreign currency deposits of resident sectors other than those of the central government. Where non-monetary financial institutions are important issuers of quasi-monetary liabilities, these are often included in the measure of broadly defined money. The *average annual nominal growth rate of broadly defined money* is calculated from year-end figures using the least-squares method. The average of the year-end figures for the specified year and the previous year is used to calculate the *average of broadly defined money outstanding as a percentage of GDP.*

The *nominal interest rates of banks* show the deposit rate paid by commercial or similar banks for demand, time, or savings deposits and the lending rate charged by the banks on loans to prime customers. The data are of limited international comparability, partly because coverage and definitions vary. Interest rates (and growth rates for broadly defined money) are expressed in nominal terms; therefore, much of the variation among countries stems from differences in inflation.

The *average annual rate of inflation* is measured by the rate of change in the GDP implicit deflator. The implicit deflator is calculated by dividing annual GDP at current prices by the corresponding value of GDP at constant prices, both in national currency. The least-squares method is then used to calculate the growth rate of the GDP deflator for the period. This measure of inflation, like any other, has limitations but is the most broadly based measure, showing annual price movements for all goods and services produced in an economy.

The *current account balance before official transfers* is the sum of net exports of goods, services, and private transfers. Net official transfers are excluded. See also Table 16.

Gross international reserves comprise holdings of monetary gold, special drawing rights (SDRs), the reserve position of members in the IMF, and holdings of foreign exchange under the control of monetary authorities. International reserves in U.S. dollars are shown in Table 16. Reserve holdings as *months of import coverage* are calculated as the ratio of gross international reserves to the current U.S. dollar value of imports of goods and services multiplied by 12.

The *net present value of total external debt* is the discounted sum of all debt service payments due over the life of existing loans in current prices. To estimate the ratio to GNP, the debt figures are converted into U.S. dollars from currencies of repayment at end-of-year official exchange rates, and GNP is converted from national currencies to U.S. dollars by applying the conversion procedure described in the technical note for Table 12.

The summary measures are computed from group aggregates for gross international reserves and total imports of goods and services in current dollars.

Table 3. External economic indicators

Data in this table reflect a country's openness to international markets and its potential vulnerability to changes in export prices, international interest rates, and the availability of private capital flows and official development assistance.

The *terms of trade,* or the net barter terms of trade, measure the relative movement of export prices against that of import prices. Calculated as the ratio of a country's index of average export prices to its average import price index, this indicator shows changes over a base year in the level of export prices as a percentage of import prices. The terms of trade index numbers are shown for 1985 and 1994, where 1987 = 100. The data come from the U.N. Conference on Trade and Development (UNCTAD) data base and the IMF's *International Financial Statistics.* See also Table 15.

The *export concentration index* is taken from UNCTAD's *Handbook of International Trade and Development Statistics.* The index measures the degree to which a country's exports are concentrated in, or diversified among, SITC (Revision 2) three-digit level commodities. The index is calculated using the Hirschman or Herfindahl methodology: the shares of exports in each commodity are squared summed; the index is the square root of the sum, normalized to a range of zero to one (maximum concentration). An interesting interpretation is that the inverse of the index represents the equivalent number of commodities, each having equal-sized shares, that the country trades. There are 239 commodities identified at the three-digit level in the SITC Revision 2.

Aggregate net resource flows are the sum of net flows on long-term debt (excluding use of IMF credit), plus official grants (excluding technical assistance), net foreign direct investment, and net portfolio equity flows. Total net flows on long-term debt are disbursements less the repayment of principal on public, publicly guaranteed, and private nonguaranteed long-term debt. Official grants are transfers made by an official agency in cash or in kind, in respect of which no legal debt is incurred by the recipient.

Net private capital flows consist of private debt and nondebt flows. Private debt flows include commercial bank lending, bonds, and other private credits; nondebt private flows are net foreign direct investment and portfolio investment.

Official development assistance (ODA) comprises loans and grants made on concessional financial terms by all bilateral official agencies and multilateral sources to promote economic development and welfare. Net disbursements equal gross disbursements less payments to the originators of aid for amortization of past aid receipts. In order to qualify as ODA, each transaction must meet the following tests: it is administered with the promotion of the economic development and welfare of developing countries as its main objective; and it is concessional in character and conveys a grant element of at least 25 percent.

Summary measures for ODA as a percentage of GNP are computed from group totals for ODA and GNP in current U.S. dollars.

Table 4. Population and labor force

Population and labor force data provide a basic profile of the demographic trends in a country.

Population estimates for mid-1994 are from a variety of sources, including the U.N. Population Division, national statistical offices, and World Bank country departments. (See also the notes in the Key table.) The World Bank uses the de facto definition of a country's population, which counts all residents regardless of legal status or citizenship. Note, however, that refugees not permanently settled in the country of asylum are generally considered to be part of the population of their country of origin.

The *average annual growth rate* of population is computed from end-point data using an exponential growth model. See the section on statistical methods for more information.

Age structure of the population shows the proportion of the total population between the ages of fifteen and sixty-four inclusively.

Total labor force estimates are derived by applying participation rates from the International Labour Office (ILO) to the population estimates. They cover the so-called economically active population, a restrictive concept that includes the armed forces and the unemployed but excludes homemakers and other unpaid caregivers.

Percentage of females in the total labor force is from ILO data. This indicator shows the extent to which women are "gainfully employed" in the formal sector. Labor force numbers in several developing countries reflect a significant underestimation of female participation rates.

The *structure of labor force* shows the share of the labor force engaged in agricultural and industrial activities. The agricultural labor force includes people engaged in farming, forestry, hunting, and fishing. The industrial labor force

includes people working in the mining, manufacturing, construction, and electricity, water, and gas industries.

All summary measures are country data weighted by population or population subgroup.

Table 5. Distribution of income or consumption

The table describes the distribution of income or consumption expenditures accruing to subgroups of the population in sixty-five low- and middle-income countries and twenty high-income countries. Because the subgroups are ranked by per capita income or expenditure or, in the case of high-income countries, by household income, the resulting shares indicate the extent to which the distribution of income or consumption expenditures in each country differs from strict equality.

Survey year is the year in which the underlying data were collected. The data sets refer to different years between 1985 and 1994 and are drawn from nationally representative household surveys.

The *Gini index* is a summary measure of the extent to which the actual distribution of income or consumption differs from a hypothetical uniform distribution in which each person or household receives an identical share. The Gini index has a maximum value of 100 percent, indicating that one person or household receives everything, and a minimum value of zero, indicating absolute equality. The Gini index is the most popular measure of inequality, but it is not a very discriminating indicator. For example, when the underlying Lorenz (income distribution) curves cross, countries with different income distributions may have the same index value. See the section on statistical methods for more information.

The following columns report the *percentage share of income or consumption* by quintiles and deciles of the population. Income distribution data for low- and middle-income countries have been compiled from two main sources: government statistical agencies and the World Bank. Where the original unit record data from the household survey were available, these have been used to calculate directly the income (or consumption) shares by quintile; otherwise, shares have been estimated from the best available grouped data. The distribution indicators for low- and middle-income countries have been adjusted for household size, thus providing a more consistent measure of income or consumption per capita. No adjustment has been made for spatial cost-of-living differences within countries, because the data needed for such calculations are not generally available. For further details on both the data and the estimation methodology for low- and middle-income countries, see Martin Ravallion and Shaohua Chen (1996).

The data for Australia, Canada, Israel, Italy, Norway, Sweden, Switzerland, and the United States are from the

Luxembourg Income Study data base (1990); those for France, Germany, Netherlands, Spain, and the United Kingdom are from the Statistical Office of the European Union. The data for Belgium, Denmark, Finland, Japan, and New Zealand come from the U.N., *National Accounts Statistics: Compendium of Income Distribution Statistics, 1985.* Data for other high-income countries come from national sources.

There are significant comparability problems across countries in the income distribution data presented here. The underlying household surveys are not fully comparable, although these problems are diminishing as survey methodologies both improve and become more standardized, particularly through the initiatives of the United Nations (under the Household Survey Capability Program) and the World Bank (under the Living Standard Measurement Study and the Social Dimensions of Adjustment Project for Sub-Saharan Africa). The following three sources of noncomparability ought to be noted. First, the surveys differ in the use of income or consumption expenditure as the living standard indicator. For thirty-nine of the sixty-five low- and middle-income countries, the data refer to consumption expenditure. Typically, income is more unequally distributed than consumption. Second, the surveys differ in the use of the household or the individual as their unit of observation. Further, household units differ in the number of household members and the extent of income sharing among members. Individuals differ in age and need for consumption. Where households are used as the observation unit, the quintiles refer to the percentage of households, rather than the percentage of persons. Third, the surveys differ according to whether the units of observation are ranked by household or income (or consumption) per capita. The footnotes to the table identify these differences for each country.

The international comparability of high-income country data is particularly limited, because the observation unit is a household unadjusted for size, and households are ranked according to total household income rather than income per household member. These data are presented pending the publication of improved data from the Luxembourg Income Study, where household members are ranked by the average disposable income per adult-equivalent person. The estimates in the table, therefore, should be treated with considerable caution.

Table 6. Health

This table provides selected indicators of the prevailing health infrastructure and the health status of the population.

Access to health care is measured by the percentage of the population that can reach local health services by the usual means of transportation in no more than one hour. Note that facilities tend to be concentrated in urban areas. In some cases, rural areas may have a much lower level of access.

Population with access to safe water is the percentage of the population with reasonable access to safe water supply (including treated surface waters or untreated but uncontaminated water, such as from springs, sanitary wells, and protected boreholes). In an urban area this may be a public fountain or standpost located not more than 200 meters away. In rural areas it implies that members of the household do not have to spend a disproportionate part of the day fetching water. The definition of safe water has changed over time.

Access to sanitation refers to the percentage of population with at least adequate excreta-disposal facilities that can effectively prevent human, animal, and insect contact with excreta.

The *infant mortality rate* is the number of deaths of infants under one year of age per thousand live births in a given year. The data are a combination of observed values and interpolated and projected estimates. A few countries, such as the economies of the former Soviet Union, employ an atypical definition of live births that reduces the reported infant mortality rate relative to the standard (World Health Organization) definition.

Prevalence of malnutrition measures the percentage of children under five with a deficiency or an excess of nutrients that interferes with their health and genetic potential for growth. Methods of assessment vary, but the most commonly used are the following: less than 80 percent of the standard weight for age; less than minus 2 standard deviations from the fiftieth percentile of the weight-for-age reference population; and the Gomez scale of malnutrition. Note that for a few countries the figures are for children three or four years of age and younger.

Contraceptive prevalence rate is the proportion of women who are practicing, or whose husbands are practicing, any form of contraception. Contraceptive usage is generally measured for married women age fifteen to forty-nine. A few countries use measures relating to other age groups, especially fifteen to forty-four. Data are mainly derived from demographic and health surveys, contraceptive prevalence surveys, and World Bank country data.

The *total fertility rate* represents the number of children that would be born to a woman were she to live to the end of her childbearing years and bear children at each age in accordance with prevailing age-specific fertility rates. The data are a combination of observed, interpolated, and projected estimates.

The *maternal mortality ratio* refers to the number of female deaths that occur during pregnancy and childbirth per 100,000 live births. Because deaths during childbirth are defined more widely in some countries to include complications of pregnancy or the period after childbirth or of abortion, and because many pregnant women die from lack of suitable health care, maternal mortality is difficult to measure consistently and reliably across countries. Clearly, many maternal deaths go unrecorded, particularly in countries with remote rural populations. This may account for some of the low estimates shown in the table, especially for several African countries. The data are drawn from diverse national sources. Where national administrative systems are weak, estimates are derived from demographic and health surveys using indirect estimation techniques or from other national sample surveys. For a number of developing countries, maternal mortality estimates are derived by the World Health Organization (WHO) and the United Nations Children's Fund (UNICEF) using modeling techniques.

All summary measures, except for infant mortality, are weighted by population or by subgroups of the population. Infant mortality is weighted by the number of births.

Table 7. Education

The data in this table refer to a variety of years, generally not more than two years distant from those specified. The data are from the U.N. Educational, Scientific, and Cultural Organization (UNESCO).

Primary school enrollment data are estimates of the ratio of children of all ages enrolled in primary school to the country's population of primary school–age children. Although many countries consider primary school age to be six to eleven years, others use different age groups. For countries with universal primary education, the gross enrollment ratios may exceed 100 percent because some pupils are younger or older than the country's standard primary school age.

Secondary school enrollments are calculated in the same manner, and again the definition of secondary school age differs among countries. It is most commonly considered to be twelve to seventeen years. Late entry of students as well as repetition and the phenomenon of "bunching" in final grades can influence these ratios.

The *tertiary enrollment ratio* is calculated by dividing the number of pupils enrolled in all postsecondary schools and universities by the population in the twenty to twenty-four age group. Pupils attending vocational schools, adult education programs, two-year community colleges, and distant education centers (primarily correspondence courses) are included. The distribution of pupils across these different types of institutions varies among countries. The youth population—that is, twenty to twenty-four years—has been adopted by UNESCO as

the denominator, because it represents an average tertiary level cohort, although people above and below this age group may be registered in tertiary institutions.

The percentage of cohort reaching grade 4 is the proportion of children starting primary school in 1980 and 1988 who continued to the fourth grade by 1983 and 1991, respectively. Figures in italics represent earlier or later cohorts. The data are based on enrollment records.

Adult illiteracy is defined here as the proportion of the population fifteen years and older who cannot, with understanding, read and write a short, simple statement on their everyday life. This is only one of three widely accepted definitions, and its application is subject to qualifiers in a number of countries. The data are from the illiteracy estimates and projections prepared in 1995 by UNESCO.

The summary enrollment measures in this table are computed from country enrollment rates weighted by population.

Table 8. Commercial energy use

The data on *commercial energy use* are primarily from International Energy Agency (IEA) and U.N. sources. They refer to commercial forms of primary energy— petroleum (crude oil, natural gas liquids, and oil from unconventional sources), natural gas, solid fuels (coal, lignite, and other derived fuels), and primary electricity (nuclear, hydroelectric, geothermal, and other)—all converted into oil equivalents. For converting nuclear electricity into oil equivalents, a notional thermal efficiency of 33 percent is assumed; hydroelectric power is represented at 100 percent efficiency.

Total energy use refers to domestic primary energy use before transformation to other end-use fuels (such as electricity or refined petroleum products) and is calculated as indigenous production plus imports and stock changes, minus exports and international marine bunkers. Energy consumption also includes products for nonenergy uses, mainly derived from petroleum. The use of firewood, dried animal excrement, and other traditional fuels, although substantial in some developing countries, is not taken into account, because reliable and comprehensive data are not available.

Energy use per capita is based upon total population estimates in the years shown.

GDP per kilogram of commercial energy use is the U.S. dollar estimate of GDP produced per kilogram of oil equivalent.

Net energy imports as a percent of consumption: both imports and consumption are measured in oil equivalents for the purpose of calculating their ratio. A negative sign indicates that the country is a net exporter.

The data on *carbon dioxide emissions* cover industrial contributions to the carbon dioxide flux from solid fuels, liquid fuels, gas fuels, gas flaring, and cement manufacture. They are based on several sources as reported by the World Resources Institute. They are mainly from the the Carbon Dioxide Information Analysis Center (CDIAC), Environmental Science Division, Oak Ridge National Laboratory.

CDIAC annually calculates emissions of CO_2 from the burning of fossil fuels and the manufacture of cement for most of the countries of the world. These calculations are based on data on the net apparent consumption of fossil fuels from the World Energy Data Set maintained by the United Nations Statistical Division and from data on world cement manufacture based on the Cement Manufacturing Data Set maintained by the United States Bureau of Mines. Emissions are calculated using global average fuel chemistry and usage. Estimates do not include bunker fuels used in international transport because of the difficulty of apportioning these fuels among the countries benefiting from that transport. Although the estimates of world emissions are probably within 10 percent of actual emissions, individual country estimates may have larger error bounds.

The summary measures of energy use are computed by aggregating the respective volumes for each of the years covered by the periods and applying the least-squares growth rate procedure. For energy consumption per capita, population weights are used to compute summary measures for the specified years.

The summary measures of CO_2 emissions are computed from group aggregates. For per capita estimates, aggregate emissions and population are used.

Table 9. Land use and urbanization

The data on *land use* are compiled by the World Resources Institute (WRI). The main source, however, is the Food and Agricultural Organization (FAO), which gathers these data from national agencies through annual questionnaires and national agricultural censuses. However, countries sometimes use different definitions of land use. The FAO often adjusts the definitions of land use categories and sometimes substantially revises earlier data. Because the data on land use reflect changes in data reporting procedures as well as actual land use changes, apparent trends should be interpreted with caution. Most land use data are from 1993.

Cropland includes land under temporary and permanent crops, temporary meadows, market and kitchen gardens, and land that is temporarily fallow. Permanent crops are those that do not need to be replanted after each harvest, but excludes land used to grow trees for wood or timber.

Permanent pasture is land used for five or more years for forage, including natural crops and cultivated crops. Only a few countries regularly report data on permanent pasture, as this category is difficult to assess because it includes wild land used for pasture.

Other land includes forest and woodland, which is the land under natural or planted stands of trees, as well as logged-over areas that will be forested in the near future. It also includes uncultivated land, grassland not used for pasture, wetlands, wastelands, and built-up areas. The latter refers to residential, recreational, and industrial lands and areas covered by roads and other fabricated infrastructure.

Urban population as a percentage of total population and estimates of the population in *urban agglomerations* come from the U.N.'s *World Urbanization Prospects: The 1994 Revision.* Urban agglomerations are metropolitan areas with populations of 1 million or more. To compute the *growth rate of the urban population,* the U.N.'s ratio of urban to total population is first applied to the World Bank's estimates of total population (see Table 4). The resulting series of urban population estimates are also used to compute the *population in urban agglomerations as a percentage of the urban population.* Because the estimates in this table are based on different national definitions of what is urban, cross-country comparisons should be made with caution.

The summary measures for urban population as a percentage of total population are calculated from country percentages weighted by each country's share in the aggregate population. The other summary measures are weighted in the same fashion, using urban population.

Table 10. Forests and water resources

This table provides information on the status of two important environmental resources. The data are drawn from sources cited in the the World Resources Institute's *World Resources 1994–95.* Perhaps even more than other data in this report, however, these data should be used with caution. Although they are indicative of major differences in resource endowments and uses among countries, true comparability is limited because of variation in data collection, statistical methods, definitions, and government resources. They have been chosen because they are available for most countries and reflect some general conditions of the environment.

Forest areas refer to natural stands of woody vegetation in which trees predominate. These estimates are derived from country statistics assembled by the FAO and the United Nations Economic Commission for Europe (UNECE). New assessments were published in 1993 for tropical countrie by FAO and for temperate zones by UNECE/FAO.

FAO and UNECE/FAO use different definitions in their assessments. The FAO defines natural forest in tropical countries as either a closed forest, where trees cover a high proportion of the ground with no continuous grass cover, or an open forest, which is defined as mixed forest and grasslands with at least 10 percent tree cover and a continuous grass layer on the forest floor. A tropical forest encompasses all stands, except plantations, and includes stands that have been degraded to some degree by agriculture, fire, logging, or acid precipitation. The UNECE/FAO defines a forest as land where tree crowns cover more than 20 percent of the area. Also included are open forest formations; forest roads and firebreaks, small, temporarily cleared areas, young stands expected to achieve at least 20 percent crown cover on maturity, and windbreaks and shelter belts. Plantation area is included under temperate country estimates of natural forest area. Some countries in this table also include other wooded land, defined as open woodland and scrub, shrub, and brushland.

Deforestation refers to the permanent conversion of forestland to other uses, including shifting cultivation, permanent agriculture, ranching, settlements, or infrastructure development. Deforested areas do not include areas logged but intended for regeneration or areas degraded by fuel wood gathering, acid precipitation, or forest fires. The extent and percentage of total area shown refer to the average annual deforestation of natural forest area.

Nationally protected areas are areas of at least 1,000 hectares that fall into one of five management categories: scientific reserves and strict nature reserves; national parks of national or international significance (not materially affected by human activity); natural monuments and natural landscapes with some unique aspects; managed nature reserves and wildlife sanctuaries; and protected landscapes and seascapes (which may include cultural landscapes). This table does not include sites protected under local or provincial law or areas where consumptive uses of wildlife are allowed. These data are subject to variations in definition and in reporting to the organizations, such as the World Conservation Monitoring Centre, that compile and disseminate them. Total surface area is used to calculate the percentage of total area protected. (See Table 1.)

Data on *annual freshwater withdrawal* are subject to variation in collection and estimation methods but are indicative of the magnitude of water use in both total and per capita terms. These data, however, also hide what can be significant variations in total renewable water resources from one year to another. They also fail to distinguish the seasonal and geographic variations in water availability within a country. Because freshwater resources are based

on long-term averages, their estimation explicitly excludes decade-long cycles of wet and dry. The Département Hydrogéologie in Orléans, France, compiles water resource and withdrawal data from published documents, including national, United Nations, and professional literature. The Institute of Geography at the National Academy of Sciences in Moscow also compiles global water data on the basis of published work and, where necessary, estimates water resources and consumption from models that use other data, such as area under irrigation, livestock populations, and precipitation. These and other sources have been combined by the World Resources Institute to generate data for this table. Withdrawal data are for single years and vary from country to country between 1970 and 1994. Data for small countries and countries in arid and semiarid zones are less reliable than those for larger countries and countries with higher rainfall.

Total water resources include both internal renewable resources and, where noted, river flows from other countries. Estimates are from 1992. Annual internal renewable water resources refer to the average annual flow of rivers and aquifers generated from rainfall within the country. Withdrawals include those from nonrenewable aquifers and desalting plants but do not include losses from evaporation. Withdrawals can exceed 100 percent of renewable supplies when extractions from nonrenewable aquifers or desalting plants are considerable or if there is significant water reuse.

Total per capita water withdrawal is calculated by dividing a country's total withdrawal by its population in the year for which withdrawal estimates are available. For most countries, sectoral per capita withdrawal data are calculated using sectoral withdrawal percentages estimated for 1987 to 1992. *Domestic use* includes drinking water, municipal use or supply, and use for public services, commercial establishments, and homes. *Other withdrawals* are those for direct industrial use, including withdrawals for cooling thermoelectric plants and withdrawals for agriculture (irrigation and livestock production).

Tables 11, 12, and 13. Growth and structure of the economy

Table 11 shows the growth of gross domestic product (GDP) and its components. Table 12 shows the structure of GDP by industrial origin. Table 13 shows the corresponding structure of GDP by its uses.

Most of the definitions used are those of the *U.N. System of National Accounts* (SNA), Series F, No. 2, Version 3. Version 4 of the SNA was completed only in 1993, and it is likely that many countries will continue to use the recommendations of version 3 for the next few years. Estimates are obtained from national sources, sometimes reaching the World Bank through other international agencies but more often collected by World Bank staff.

World Bank staff review the quality of national accounts data and, in some instances, help adjust national series. Because of the sometimes limited capabilities of statistical offices and basic data problems, strict international comparability cannot be achieved, especially in economic activities that are difficult to measure, such as parallel market transactions, the informal sector, or subsistence agriculture.

GDP measures the total output of goods and services for final use produced by residents and nonresidents, regardless of the allocation to domestic and foreign claims. It is calculated without making deductions for depreciation of fabricated assets or depletion and degradation of natural resources. International comparability of the estimates is affected by differing country practices in valuation systems for reporting value added by production sectors. The SNA envisages estimates of GDP by industrial origin to be at either basic or producer prices, but many countries report such details at purchaser prices. As a practical solution, GDP estimates are shown at purchaser prices in Table 11 if the components are on this basis, and such instances are footnoted. In Table 13, GDP is measured in purchaser values for all countries.

In Table 11, growth rates are computed from partially rebased, chain-linked, 1987 constant price series in domestic currencies.

The *growth rate of exports of goods and nonfactor services* is based on national accounts data in constant prices.

In Table 12, the figures for GDP are U.S. dollar values converted from domestic currencies using single-year official exchange rates. For a few countries where the official exchange rate does not reflect the rate effectively applied to actual foreign exchange transactions, an alternative conversion factor is used. Note that Table 12 does not use the three-year averaging technique applied to GNP per capita in Table 1.

Summary measures in Table 12 are computed from group aggregates of sectoral GDP in current U.S. dollars.

Agriculture covers forestry, hunting, and fishing, as well as cultivation of crops. In developing countries with high levels of subsistence farming, much agricultural production is either not exchanged or not exchanged for money. This increases the difficulty of measuring the contribution of agriculture to GDP and reduces the reliability and comparability of such numbers.

Industry comprises value added in mining, *manufacturing* (also reported as a separate subgroup in Table 12), construction, and electricity, water, and gas. Value added in all other branches of economic activity, such as wholesale and retail trade, transportation, government, and per-

sonal services and including imputed bank service charges, import duties, and any statistical discrepancies noted by national compilers, are included in *services*.

In Table 13, *general government consumption* includes all current expenditures for purchases of goods and services by all levels of government, but excluding most government enterprises. Capital expenditure on national defense and security is regarded as a general government consumption expenditure.

Private consumption is the market value of all goods and services, including durable products (such as cars, washing machines, and home computers) purchased or received as income in kind by households and nonprofit institutions. It excludes purchases of dwellings but includes imputed rent for owner-occupied dwellings. In practice, it may include any statistical discrepancy in the use of resources.

Gross domestic investment consists of outlays on additions to the fixed assets of the economy plus net changes in the level of inventories.

Gross domestic saving is calculated by deducting total consumption from GDP.

Exports of goods and nonfactor services represent the value of all goods and nonfactor services provided to the rest of the world. This includes the value of merchandise, freight, insurance, travel, and other nonfactor services. The value of factor services, such as investment income, interest, and labor income, is excluded. Current transfers are also excluded.

The *resource balance* is the difference between exports of goods and nonfactor services and imports of goods and nonfactor services.

In calculating the summary measures for each indicator in Table 11, partially rebased, constant 1987, U.S. dollar values for each economy are calculated for each year of the periods covered; the values are aggregated across countries for each year; and the least-squares procedure is used to compute the growth rates. The average sectoral percentage shares in Tables 12 and 13 are computed from group aggregates of sectoral GDP in current U.S. dollars.

Table 14. Central government budget

The data on central government revenues and expenditures are from the IMF's *Government Finance Statistics Yearbook* (1995), and IMF data files. The accounts of each country are reported using the system of common definitions and classifications found in the IMF's *A Manual on Government Finance Statistics* (1986). For complete and authoritative explanations of concepts, definitions, and data sources, see these IMF sources. The commentary that follows is intended mainly to place these data in the context of the broad range of indicators reported here.

Because of differences in coverage of available data, the individual components of central government expenditure and revenue shown may not be strictly comparable across all economies.

Inadequate statistical coverage of state, provincial, and local governments requires the use of central government data; this may seriously understate or distort the statistical portrayal of the allocation of resources for various purposes, especially in countries where lower levels of government have considerable autonomy and are responsible for many economic and social services. In addition, "central government" can mean either of two accounting concepts: consolidated or budgetary. For most countries, central government finance data have been consolidated into one overall account, but for others only the budgetary central government accounts are available. Because budgetary accounts do not always include all central government units, the overall picture of central government activities is usually incomplete. Countries reporting budgetary data are footnoted.

Consequently, the data presented, especially those for social services, are not comparable across countries. In many economies, private health and education services are substantial; in others, public services represent the major component of total expenditure but may be financed by lower levels of government. Caution should therefore be exercised in using the data for cross-country comparisons.

Total revenue is derived from tax and nontax sources. *Tax revenues* comprise compulsory, unrequited, nonrepayable receipts for public purposes. They include interest collected on tax arrears and penalties collected on nonpayment or late payment of taxes and are shown net of refunds and other corrective transactions.

Nontax revenue comprises receipts that are not compulsory, nonrepayable payments for public purposes, such as fines, administrative fees, or entrepreneurial income from government ownership of property. Proceeds of grants and borrowing, funds arising from the repayment of previous lending by governments, incurrence of liabilities, and proceeds from the sale of capital assets are not included.

Central government expenditure comprises the expenditure by all government offices, departments, establishments, and other bodies that are agencies or instruments of the central authority of a country. It includes both current and capital (development) expenditures.

Defense comprises all expenditures, whether by defense or other departments, on the maintenance of military forces, including the purchase of military supplies and equipment, construction, recruiting, and training. Also in this category are closely related items such as military aid programs. Defense does not include expenditure on public order and safety, which are classified separately. Defense is treated as a current expenditure.

Social services comprises expenditures on health, education, housing, welfare, social security, and community amenities. These categories also cover compensation for loss of income to the sick and temporarily disabled; payments to the elderly, the permanently disabled, and the unemployed; family, maternity, and child allowances; and the cost of welfare services, such as care of the aged, the disabled, and children. Many expenditures relevant to environmental defense, such as pollution abatement, water supply, sanitary affairs, and refuse collection, are included indistinguishably in this category.

Overall deficit/surplus is defined as current and capital revenue and official grants received, less total expenditure and lending minus repayments. This is a broader concept than the current government deficit/surplus shown in Table 2.

Table 15. Exports and imports of merchandise

The main source of current trade values is the U.N. Conference on Trade and Development (UNCTAD) trade data base, supplemented by the data from the IMF's *International Financial Statistics* (IFS), the U.N.'s Commodity Trade (COMTRADE) data base, and World Bank estimates. The shares in these tables are derived from trade values in current dollars reported in the UNCTAD trade data system, supplemented by data from the U.N. COMTRADE system.

Merchandise *exports* and *imports*, with some exceptions, cover international movements of goods across customs' borders; trade in services is not included. Exports are valued f.o.b. (free on board) and imports c.i.f. (cost, insurance, and freight) unless otherwise specified in the foregoing sources. These values are in current U.S. dollars.

The categorization of exports and imports follows the *Standard International Trade Classification* (SITC), Series M, No. 34, Revision 1. For some countries, data for certain commodity categories are unavailable. *Food* commodities are those in SITC Sections 0, 1, and 4 and Division 22 (food and live animals, beverages and tobacco, animal and vegetable oils and fats, oilseeds, oil nuts, and oil kernels). *Fuels* are the commodities in SITC Section 3 (mineral fuels, lubricants, and related materials).

Average annual growth rates of exports and imports are calculated from values in constant prices, which are derived from current values deflated by the relevant price index. The World Bank uses the price indexes produced by UNCTAD for low- and middle-income economies and those presented in the IMF's *International Financial Statistics* for high-income economies. These growth rates can differ from those derived from national sources because national price indexes may use different base years and weighting procedures from those used by UNCTAD or the IMF.

The summary measures for the growth rates are calculated by aggregating the 1987 constant U.S. dollar price series for each year and then applying the least-squares growth rate procedure for the periods shown.

Table 16. Balance of payments

The data for this table are based on IMF data files. World Bank staff also make estimates and, in rare instances, adjust coverage or classification to enhance international comparability. Definitions and concepts are based on the IMF's *Balance of Payments Manual, Fourth Edition* (1977). The IMF now uses the fifth edition to compile balance of payments data. As a result, some indicators shown here may differ from those published in recent IMF publications. Values are in U.S. dollars converted at official exchange rates.

Exports and imports of goods and services comprise all transactions involving a change of ownership of goods and services between residents of a country and the rest of the world, including merchandise, nonfactor services, and factor services.

Net workers' remittances cover payments and receipts of income by migrants who are employed or expect to be employed for more than a year in their new economy, where they are considered residents. These remittances are classified as private unrequited transfers, whereas those derived from shorter-term stays are included in services as labor income. The distinction accords with internationally agreed guidelines, but some developing countries classify workers' remittances as a factor income receipt (hence, a component of GNP). The World Bank adheres to international guidelines in defining GNP and therefore may differ from national practices.

Other net private transfers comprise net unrequited private transfers other than workers' remittances.

The *current account balance before official transfers* is the sum of net exports of goods and services and net private transfers, but excludes net official transfers.

Gross international reserves comprise holdings of monetary gold, special drawing rights (SDRs), the reserve position of members in the IMF, and holdings of foreign exchange under the control of monetary authorities. The data on holdings of international reserves are from IMF data files. The gold component of these reserves is valued at year-end (December 31) London prices: that is, $589.50 an ounce in 1980 and $383.25 an ounce in 1994. Because of differences in the definition of international reserves, in the valuation of gold, and in reserve management practices, the levels of reserve holdings published in national sources may not be strictly comparable. The reserve levels for 1980 and 1994 refer to the end of the year indicated and are in current U.S. dollars at pre-

vailing exchange rates. See Table 2 for reserve holdings expressed as months of import coverage.

The summary measures are computed from group aggregates for gross international reserves.

Table 17. External debt

The data on debt in this table come from the World Bank Debtor Reporting System, supplemented by World Bank estimates. The system is concerned solely with developing economies and does not collect data on external debt for other groups of borrowers or for economies that are not members of the World Bank. Debt is stated in U.S. dollars converted at official exchange rates. The data on debt include private nonguaranteed debt reported by thirty developing countries and complete or partial estimates for an additional twenty that do not report but for which this type of debt is known to be significant.

Total external debt is the sum of public, publicly guaranteed, and private nonguaranteed long-term debt, use of IMF credit, and short-term debt. Long-term debt has three components: public, publicly guaranteed, and private nonguaranteed loans. Public loans are external obligations of public debtors, including the national government, its agencies, and autonomous public bodies. Publicly guaranteed loans are external obligations of private debtors that are guaranteed for repayment by a public entity. Private nonguaranteed loans are external obligations of private debtors that are not guaranteed for repayment by a public entity. Use of IMF credit denotes repurchase obligations to the IMF for all uses of IMF resources, excluding those resulting from drawings in the reserve tranche. It comprises purchases outstanding under the credit tranches, including enlarged access resources, and all special facilities (the buffer stock, compensatory financing, extended fund, and oil facilities), trust fund loans, and operations under the enhanced structural adjustment facilities. Use of IMF credit outstanding at year-end (a stock) is converted to U.S. dollars at the dollar-SDR exchange rate in effect at year-end. Short-term debt is debt with an original maturity of one year or less. It includes interest arrears on long-term debt outstanding and disbursed that are due but not paid on a cumulative basis. Available data permit no distinctions between public and private nonguaranteed short-term debt.

Total external debt as a percentage of GNP and exports of goods and services (including workers' remittances) is calculated in U.S. dollars.

Total debt service as a percentage of exports of goods and services is the sum of principal repayments and interest payments on total external debt. It is one of several conventional measures used to assess a country's ability to service debt.

The *ratio of present value to nominal value* of debt is the discounted value of future debt service payments divided by the face value of total external debt. The present value of external debt is the discounted sum of all debt service payments due over the life of existing loans. The present value can be higher or lower than the nominal value of debt. The determining factors for the present value being above or below par are the interest rates of loans and the discount rate used in the present value calculation. A loan with an interest rate higher than the discount rate yields a present value that is larger than the nominal value of debt; the opposite holds for loans with an interest rate lower than the discount rate.

The discount rates used to calculate the present value are interest rates charged by Organisation of Economic Co-operation and Development (OECD) countries for officially supported export credits. The rates are specified for the Group of Seven (G7) currencies—British pounds, Canadian dollars, French francs, German marks, Italian lire, Japanese yen, and U.S. dollars. International Bank for Reconstruction and Development (IBRD) loans and International Development Association (IDA) credits are discounted by the most recent IBRD lending rate, and International Monetary Fund (IMF) loans are discounted by the Special Drawing Rights (SDR) lending rate. For debt denominated in other currencies, discount rates are the average of interest rates on export credits charged by other OECD countries. For variable rate loans, for which the future debt service payments cannot be precisely determined, debt service is calculated using the end-1994 rates for the base period specified for the loan.

Multilateral debt as a percentage of total external debt conveys information about the borrower's receipt of aid from the World Bank, regional development banks, and other multilateral and intergovernmental agencies. Excluded are loans from funds administered by an international organization on behalf of a single donor government.

The summary measures are taken from the *1996 World Debt Tables*, Volume 1.

Statistical methods

This section describes the calculation of the least-squares growth rate, the exponential (end-point) growth rate, the Gini index, and the World Bank's *Atlas* methodology for estimating the conversion factor used to estimate GNP and GNP per capita in U.S. dollars.

Least-squares growth rate

The least-squares growth rate, r, is estimated by fitting a least-squares linear regression trend line to the logarithmic annual values of the variable in the relevant period. More specifically, the regression equation takes the form

$$\log X_t = a + bt,$$

which is equivalent to the logarithmic transformation of the geometric growth rate equation,

$$X_t = X_o (1 + r)^t.$$

In these equations, X is the variable, t is time, and $a = \log X_o$ and $b = log (1 + r)$ are the parameters to be estimated. If b^* is the least-squares estimate of b, then the average annual growth rate, r, is obtained as [antilog $(b^*)-1$] and is multiplied by 100 to express it as a percentage.

The calculated growth rate is an average rate that is representative of the available observations over the period. It does not necessarily match the actual growth rate between any two periods. Assuming that geometric growth is the appropriate "model" for the data, the least-squares estimate of the growth rate is consistent and efficient.

Exponential growth rate

The growth rate between two points in time for certain demographic data, notably labor force and population, is calculated from the equation:

$$r = \ln(p_n / p_1) / n$$

where p_n and p_1 are the last and first observations in the period, n is the number of years in the period, and ln is the natural logarithm operator.

This growth rate is based on a model of continuous, exponential growth. To obtain a growth rate for discrete periods comparable to the least-squares growth rate, take the antilog of the calculated growth rate and subtract 1.

The Gini index

The Gini index measures the extent to which the distribution of income (or, in some cases, consumption expenditures) among individuals or households within an economy deviates from a perfectly equal distribution. A Lorenz curve plots the cumulative percentages of total income received against the cumulative percentage of recipients, starting with the poorest individual or household. The Gini index measures the area between the Lorenz curve and a hypothetical line of absolute equality, expressed as a percentage of the maximum area under the line. Thus a Gini index of zero presents perfect equality while an index of 100 percent implies maximum inequality.

The World Bank employs a numerical analysis program, POVCAL, to estimate values of the Gini index; see Chen, Datt, and Ravallion (1992).

World Bank Atlas method

The *Atlas* conversion factor for any year is the average of a country's exchange rate (or alternative conversion factor) for that year and its exchange rates for the two preceding years, after adjusting them for differences in rates of inflation between the country and the G-5 countries (France, Germany, Japan, the United Kingdom, and the United States.) The inflation rate for G-5 countries is represented by changes in the SDR deflators. This three-year averaging smooths annual fluctuations in prices and exchange rates for each country. The *Atlas* conversion factor is applied to the country's GNP. The resulting GNP in U.S. dollars is divided by the midyear population for the latest of the three years to derive GNP per capita.

The following formulas describe the procedures for computing the conversion factor for year *t*:

$$e_t^* = \frac{1}{3}\left[e_{t-2}\left(\frac{p_t}{p_{t-2}} \Big/ \frac{p_t^{S\$}}{p_{t-2}^{S\$}} \right) + e_{t-1}\left(\frac{p_t}{p_{t-1}} \Big/ \frac{p_t^{S\$}}{p_{t-1}^{S\$}} \right) + e_t \right]$$

and for calculating GNP per capita in U.S. dollars for year *t*:

$$Y_t^{\$} = (Y_t / N_t) / e_t^*$$

where

Y_t = current GNP (local currency) for year *t*;

p_t = GNP deflator for year *t*;

e_t = average annual exchange rate (national currency to the U.S. dollar) for year *t*;

N_t = midyear population for year *t*;

$p_t^{S\$}$ = SDR deflator in U.S. dollar terms for year *t*.

Data Sources

Summary of socioeconomic development indicators

International Monetary Fund. Various years. *Government Finance Statistics Yearbook.* Vol. 11. Washington, D.C.
——. Various years. *International Financial Statistics.* Washington, D.C.
U.N. International Comparison Programme Phases IV (1980), V (1985), and VI (1990) reports, and data from ECE, ESCAP, Eurostat, OECD, and U.N.
World Bank. 1993. *Purchasing Power of Currencies: Comparing National Incomes Using ICP Data.* Washington, D.C.
FAO, IMF, UNCTAD, World Bank data, and national sources.

Human resources

Atkinson, Anthony, Lee Rainwater, and Timothy Smeeding. 1995. *Income Distribution in Advanced Economies: The Evidence from the Luxembourg Income Study (LIS).* Paris: OECD.
Bos, Eduard, My T. Vu, Ernest Massiah, and Rodolfo A. Bulatao. 1994. *World Population Projections, 1994–95 Edition.* Baltimore, Md.: Johns Hopkins University Press.
Chen, Shaohua, Gaurav Datt, and Martin Ravallion. 1992. *POVCAL, A Program for Poverty Measurement for Grouped Data.* World Bank, Policy Research Department, Washington, D.C.
Council of Europe. 1995. *Recent Demographic Developments in Europe and North America.* Council of Europe Press.
Eurostat. Various years. *Demographic Statistics.* Luxembourg: Statistical Office of the European Community.
Institute for Resource Development/Westinghouse. 1987. *Child Survival: Risks and the Road to Health.* Columbia, Md.
International Labour Office. 1995. *Year Book of Labour Statistics.* Geneva.
——. 1995. *Labour Force Estimates and Projections, 1950–2010.* Geneva.
——. 1995. *Estimates of the Economically Active Population by Sex and Age Group and by Main Sectors of Economic Activity.* Geneva.
Ravallion, Martin, and Chen, Shaohua. 1996. "What can new survey data tell us about recent changes in living standards in developing and transitional economies?" World Bank, Policy Research Department, Washington, D.C.
Ross, John, and others. 1993. *Family Planning and Population: A Compendium of International Statistics.* New York: The Population Council.
U.N. Administrative Committee on Co-ordination, Subcommittee on Nutrition. Various years. *Update on the Nutrition Situation.* Geneva.
U.N. Department of Economic and Social Information and Policy Analysis (formerly U.N. Department of International Economic and Social Affairs). Various years. *Demographic Yearbook.* New York.
——. Various years. *Statistical Yearbook.* New York.
——. Various years. *Levels and Trends of Contraceptive Use.* New York.
——. 1988. *Mortality of Children under Age 5: Projections 1950–2025.* New York.
——. 1994. *World Population Prospects: The 1994 Edition.* New York.
——. Various years. *Population and Vital Statistics Report.* New York.
U.N. Educational Scientific and Cultural Organization. Various years. *Statistical Yearbook.* Paris.
UNICEF. 1996. *The State of the World's Children 1996.* Oxford: Oxford University Press.
United States Bureau of the Census. Various years. *World Population—Recent Estimates for the Countries and Regions of the World.* Washington, D.C.: U.S. Government Printing Office.
World Health Organization. Various years. *World Health Statistics Annual.* Geneva.
——. Various years. *The International Drinking Water Supply and Sanitation Decade.* Geneva.
——. 1986. *Maternal Mortality Rates: A Tabulation of Available Information,* 2nd edition. Geneva.
——. 1991. *Maternal Mortality: A Global Factbook.* Geneva.
——. Various years. *World Health Statistics Report.* Geneva.
—— and UNICEF. 1995. "Modeling maternal mortality in the developing world". Geneva.
FAO, ILO, U.N., and World Bank data; demographic and health surveys from national sources.

Environmentally sustainable development

International Energy Agency. 1995. *IEA Statistics: Energy statistics and balances.* Paris: OECD.
U.N. Department of Economic and Social Information and Policy Analysis (formerly U.N. Department of International Economic and Social Affairs). Various years. *World Energy Supplies.* Statistical Papers, series J. New York.
——. Various years. *Energy Statistics Yearbook.* Statistical Papers, series J. New York.
——. 1994. *World Urbanization Prospects, 1994 Revision.* New York.
World Resources Institute. 1994. *World Resources 1994–95.* New York.
——. 1996. *World Resources 1996–97.* New York.

Economic performance

International Monetary Fund. Various years. *Government Finance Statistics Yearbook.* Vol. 11. Washington, D.C.
——. Various years. *International Financial Statistics.* Washington, D.C.
Organisation for Economic Co-operation and Development. Various years. *Development Co-operation.* Paris.
——. 1988. *Geographical Distribution of Financial Flows to Developing Countries.* Paris.
U.N. Conference on Trade and Development. Various years. *Handbook of International Trade and Development Statistics.* Geneva.
U.N. Department of Economic and Social Information and Policy Analysis (formerly U.N. Department of International Economics and Social Affairs). Various years. *Monthly Bulletin of Statistics.* New York.
——. Various years. *Yearbook of International Trade Statistics.* New York.
FAO, IMF, OECD, UNIDO, and World Bank data; World Bank Debtor Reporting System; national sources.

Table 1. Classification of economies by income and region, 1996

Income group	Subgroup	Sub-Saharan Africa — East and Southern Africa	West Africa	Asia — East Asia and Pacific	South Asia	Europe and Central Asia — Eastern Europe and Central Asia	Rest of Europe	Middle East and North Africa — Middle East	North Africa	Americas
Low-income		Burundi Comoros Eritrea Ethiopia Kenya Lesotho Madagascar Malawi Mozambique Rwanda Somalia Sudan Tanzania Uganda Zaire Zambia Zimbabwe	Benin Burkina Faso Cameroon Central African Republic Chad Congo Côte d'Ivoire Equatorial Guinea Gambia, The Ghana Guinea Guinea-Bissau Liberia Mali Mauritania Niger Nigeria São Tomé and Principe Senegal Sierra Leone Togo	Cambodia China Lao PDR Mongolia Myanmar Vietnam	Afghanistan Bangladesh Bhutan India Nepal Pakistan Sri Lanka	Albania Armenia Azerbaijan Bosnia and Herzegovina Georgia Kyrgyz Republic Tajikistan Republic		Yemen, Rep.	Egypt, Arab Rep.	Guyana Haiti Honduras Nicaragua
Middle-income	Lower	Angola Botswana Djibouti Namibia Swaziland	Cape Verde	Fiji Indonesia Kiribati Korea, Dem. Rep. Marshall Islands Micronesia, Fed. Sts. N. Mariana Islands Papua New Guinea Philippines Solomon Islands Thailand Tonga Vanuatu Western Samoa	Maldives	Belarus Bulgaria Croatia Estonia Kazakstan Latvia Lithuania Macedonia, FYR[a] Moldova Poland Romania Russian Federation Slovak Republic Turkmenistan Ukraine Uzbekistan Yugoslavia, Fed. Rep.	Turkey	Iran, Islamic Rep. Iraq Jordan Lebanon Syrian Arab Republic West Bank and Gaza	Algeria Morocco Tunisia	Belize Bolivia Colombia Costa Rica Cuba Dominica Dominican Republic Ecuador El Salvador Grenada Guatemala Jamaica Panama Paraguay Peru St. Vincent and the Grenadines Suriname Venezuela
	Upper	Mauritius Mayotte Reunion Seychelles South Africa	Gabon	American Samoa Guam Korea, Rep. Malaysia New Caledonia		Czech Republic Hungary Slovenia	Greece Isle of Man Malta	Bahrain Oman Saudi Arabia	Libya	Antigua and Barbuda Argentina Barbados Brazil Chile French Guiana Guadeloupe Martinique Mexico Puerto Rico St. Kitts and Nevis St. Lucia Trinidad and Tobago Uruguay
Subtotal:	165	27	23	25	8	27	4	10	5	36

Table 1 *(continued)*

| Income group | Subgroup | Sub-Saharan Africa | | Asia | | Europe and Central Asia | | Middle East and North Africa | | Americas |
		East and Southern Africa	West Africa	East Asia and Pacific	South Asia	Eastern Europe and Central Asia	Rest of Europe	Middle East	North Africa	
High-income	OECD countries			Australia Japan New Zealand			Austria Belgium Denmark Finland France Germany Iceland Ireland Italy Luxembourg Netherlands Norway Portugal Spain Sweden Switzerland United Kingdom			Canada United States
	Non-OECD countries			Brunei French Polynesia Hong Kong Macao Singapore OAE[b]			Andorra Channel Islands Cyprus Faeroe Islands Greenland Liechtenstein Monaco	Israel Kuwait Qatar United Arab Emirates		Aruba Bahamas, The Bermuda Cayman Islands Netherlands Antilles Virgin Islands (U.S.)
Total: 210		27	23	34	8	27	28	14	5	44

a. Former Yugoslav Republic of Macedonia.
b. Other Asian economies—Taiwan, China.

For operational and analytical purposes, the World Bank's main criterion for classifying economies is gross national product (GNP) per capita. Every economy is classified as low income, middle income (subdivided into lower-middle and upper-middle), or high income. Other analytical groups, based on geographic regions, exports, and levels of external debt, are also used.

Low-income and middle-income economies are sometimes referred to as developing economies. The use of the term is convenient; it is not intended to imply that all economies in the group are experiencing similar development or that other economies have reached a preferred or final stage of development. Classification by income does not necessarily reflect development status.

Definitions of groups

These tables classify all World Bank member countries and all other economies with populations of more than 30,000.

Income group: Economies are divided according to 1994 GNP per capita, calculated using the *World Bank Atlas* method. The groups are: low income, $725 or less; lower-middle income, $726 to $2,895; upper-middle income, $2,896 to $8,955; and high income, $8,956 or more.

The estimates for the republics of the former Soviet Union are preliminary and their classification will be kept under review.

Table 2. Classification of economies by major export category and indebtedness, 1996

| | Low- and middle-income | | | | | | | High-income | |
| | Low-income | | | Middle-income | | | | | |
Group	Severely indebted	Moderately indebted	Less indebted	Severely indebted	Moderately indebted	Less indebted	Not classified by indebtedness	OECD	Non-OECD
Exporters of manufactures		India Pakistan	Armenia China Georgia Kyrgyz Republic	Bulgaria	Russian Federation	Belarus Czech Republic Estonia Korea, Dem. Rep. Korea, Rep. Latvia Lebanon Lithuania Malaysia Moldova Romania Thailand Ukraine Uzbekistan		Canada Finland Germany Ireland Italy Japan Sweden Switzerland	Hong Kong Israel Macao Singapore OAE[a]
Exporters of nonfuel primary products	Burundi Côte d'Ivoire Equatorial Guinea Ghana Guinea Guinea-Bissau Guyana Honduras Liberia Madagascar Mali Mauritania Myanmar Nicaragua Niger Rwanda São Tomé and Principe Somalia Sudan Tanzania Togo Uganda Vietnam Zaire Zambia	Albania Chad Malawi Zimbabwe	Mongolia	Bolivia Cuba Peru	Chile	Botswana Namibia Solomon Islands Suriname Swaziland Islands	American Samoa French Guiana Guadeloupe Reunion	Iceland New Zealand	Faeroe Islands Greenland
Exporters of fuels (mainly oil)	Congo Nigeria			Algeria Angola Gabon Iraq	Venezuela	Bahrain Iran, Islamic Republic Libya Oman Saudi Arabia Trinidad and Tobago Turkmenistan			Brunei Qatar United Arab Emirates
Exporters of services	Cambodia Ethiopia Mozambique Yemen, Rep.	Benin Comoros Egypt, Arab Rep. Gambia, The Haiti Nepal	Bhutan Burkina Faso Lesotho	Jamaica Jordan Panama	Cape Verde Dominican Republic Greece Morocco Western Samoa	Antigua and Barbuda Barbados Belize Djibouti El Salvador Fiji Grenada Kiribati Maldives Paraguay Seychelles St. Kitts and Nevis St. Lucia Tonga Vanuatu	Martinique	United Kingdom	Aruba Bahamas, The Bermuda Cayman Islands Cyprus French Polynesia Kuwait Monaco

240

Table 2 *(continued)*

Group	Low- and middle-income — Low-income — Severely indebted	Moderately indebted	Less indebted	Middle-income — Severely indebted	Moderately indebted	Less indebted	Not classified by indebtedness	High-income — OECD	Non-OECD
Diversified exporters[b]	Afghanistan Cameroon Central African Republic Kenya Sierra Leone	Bangladesh Lao PDR Senegal	Azerbaijan Sri Lanka Tajikistan	Argentina Brazil Ecuador Mexico Poland Syrian Arab Republic	Colombia Hungary Indonesia Papua New Guinea Philippines Tunisia Turkey Uruguay	Costa Rica Dominica Guatemala Kazakstan Malta Mauritius South Africa St. Vincent and the Grenadines Yugoslavia, Fed. Rep.		Australia Austria Belgium Denmark France Luxembourg Netherlands Norway Portugal Spain United States	Netherlands Antilles
Not classified by export category						Croatia Macedonia, FYR[c] New Caledonia Slovak Republic Slovenia	Bosnia and Herzegovina Eritrea Guam Isle of Man Marshall Islands Mayotte Micronesia, Fed. Sts. N. Mariana Islands Puerto Rico West Bank and Gaza		Andorra Channel Islands Liechtenstein Virgin Islands (U.S.)
Number of economies: 210	36	15	11	17	16	55	15	22	23

a. Other Asian economies—Taiwan, China.
b. Economies in which no single export category accounts for 50 percent or more of total exports.
c. Former Yugoslav Republic of Macedonia.

Definitions of groups

These tables classify all World Bank member economies plus all other economies with populations of more than 30,000.

Major export category: Major exports are those that account for 50 percent or more of total exports of goods and services from one category in the period 1990–93. The categories are: nonfuel primary (SITC 0, 1, 2, 4, plus 68); fuels (SITC 3); manufactures (SITC 5 to 9, less 68); and services (factor and nonfactor service receipts plus workers' remittances). If no single category accounts for 50 percent or more of total exports, the economy is classified as *diversified*.

Indebtedness: Standard World Bank definitions of severe and moderate indebtedness, averaged over three years (1992–94), are used to classify economies in this table.

Severely indebted means that either of the two key ratios is above critical levels: present value of debt service to GNP (80 percent) and present value of debt service to exports (220 percent). *Moderately indebted* means that either of the two key ratios exceeds 60 percent of, but does not reach, the critical levels. For economies that do not report detailed debt statistics to the World Bank Debtor Reporting System (DRS), present-value calculation is not possible. Instead, the following methodology is used to classify the non-DRS economies. *Severely indebted* means that three of four key ratios (averaged over 1992–94) are above critical levels: debt to GNP (50 percent); debt to exports (275 percent); debt service to exports (30 percent); and interest to exports (20 percent). *Moderately indebted* means that three of the four key ratios exceed 60 percent of, but do not reach, the critical levels. All other classified low- and middle-income economies are listed as *less-indebted*.

World Development Report 1996: From Plan to Market

World Development Report 1996: From Plan to Market steps back from the extraordinary array of recent events and policy changes in 28 former centrally planned economies—those in Central and Eastern Europe and the newly independent states of the former Soviet Union, along with China, Mongolia and Vietnam—to ask what we have learned about the key elements of any successful transition and how they should be pursued.

Available June 28, 1996. Published for the World Bank by Oxford University Press.

Full English text available in two formats:

English (Hardback) Stock no. 61108 (ISBN 0-19-521108-1) $45.95.
English (Paperback) Stock no. 61107 (ISBN 0-19-521107-3) $22.95.

Forthcoming in paperback; $22.95 each:

Arabic: Stock no. 13269 (ISBN 0-8213-3269-4) September 1996
Chinese: Stock no. 13268 (ISBN 0-8213-3268-6) September 1996
French: Stock no. 13264 (ISBN 0-8213-3264-3) August 1996
German: Stock no. 13266 (ISBN 0-8213-3266-X) September 1996
Japanese: Stock no. 13267 (ISBN 0-8213-3267-8) September 1996
Portuguese: Stock no. 13271 (ISBN 0-8213-3271-6) September 1996
Russian: Stock no. 13270 (ISBN 0-8213-3270-8) September 1996
Spanish: Stock no. 13265 (ISBN 0-8213-3265-1) August 1996

 World Bank Publications

Distributors of World Bank Publications

Prices and credit terms vary from country to country. Consult your local distributor before placing an order.

ALBANIA
Adrion Ltd.
Perlat Rexhepi Str.
Pall. 9, Shk. 1, Ap. 4
Tirana

ARGENTINA
Oficina del Libro Internacional
Av. Cordoba 1877
1120 Buenos Aires

AUSTRALIA, FIJI, PAPUA NEW GUINEA, SOLOMON ISLANDS, VANUATU, AND WESTERN SAMOA
D.A. Information Services
648 Whitehorse Road
Mitcham 3132
Victoria

AUSTRIA
Gerold and Co.
Graben 31
A-1011 Wien

BANGLADESH
Micro Industries Development Assistance Society (MIDAS)
House 5, Road 16
Dhanmondi R/Area
Dhaka 1209

BELGIUM
Jean De Lannoy
Av. du Roi 202
1060 Brussels

BRAZIL
Publicacões Tecnicas Internacionais Ltda.
Rua Peixoto Gomide, 209
01409 Sao Paulo, SP.

CANADA
Renouf Publishing Co. Ltd.
1294 Algoma Road
Ottawa
Ontario K1B 3W8

CHINA
China Financial & Economic Publishing
House 8, Da Fo Si Dong Jie,
Beijing

COLOMBIA
Infoenlace Ltda.
Apartado Aereo 34270
Bogotá D.E.

COTE D'IVOIRE
Centre d'Edition et de Diffusion Africaines (CEDA)
04 B.P. 541
Abidjan 04 Plateau

CYPRUS
Center of Applied Research
Cyprus College
6, Diogenes Street, Engomi
P.O. Box 2006
Nicosia

CZECH REPUBLIC
National Information Center
prodejna, Konviktska 5
CS – 113 57 Prague 1

DENMARK
SamfundsLitteratur
Rosenoerns Allé 11
DK-1970 Frederiksberg C

EGYPT, ARAB REPUBLIC OF
Al Ahram
Al Galaa Street
Cairo

The Middle East Observer
41, Sherif Street
Cairo

FINLAND
Akateeminen Kirjakauppa
P.O. Box 23
FIN-00371 Helsinki

FRANCE
World Bank Publications
66, avenue d'Iéna
75116 Paris

GERMANY
UNO-Verlag
Poppelsdorfer Allee 55
53115 Bonn

GREECE
Papasotiriou S.A.
35, Stournara Str., 106 82 Athens

HONG KONG, MACAO
Asia 2000 Ltd.
Sales & Circulation Department
Seabird House,
unit 1101-02
22-28 Wyndham Street, Central, Hong Kong

HUNGARY
Foundation for Market Economy
Dombovari Ut 17-19
H-1117 Budapest

INDIA
Allied Publishers Ltd.
751 Mount R
Madras - 600 002

INDONESIA
Pt. Indira Limited
Jalan Borobudur 20
P.O. Box 181
Jakarta 10320

IRAN
Kowkab Publishers
P.O. Box 19575-511 Tehran

Ketab Sara Co. Publishers
Khaled Eslamboli Ave., 6th St.
Kusheh Delafrooz No. 8
Tehran

IRELAND
Government Supplies Agency
Oifig an tSoláthair
4-5 Harcourt Road
Dublin 2

ISRAEL
Yozmot Literature Ltd.
P.O. Box 56055
Tel Aviv 61560

R.O.Y. International
PO Box 13056
Tel Aviv 61130

Palestinian Authority/Middle East
Index Information Services
P.O.B. 19502 Jerusalem

ITALY
Licosa Commissionaria Sansoni SPA
Via Duca Di Calabria, 1/1
Casella Postale 552
50125 Firenze

JAMAICA
Ian Randle Publishers Ltd.
206 Old Hope Road, Kingston 6

JAPAN
Eastern Book Service
Hongo 3-Chome,
Bunkyo-ku 113
Tokyo

KENYA
Africa Book Service (E.A.) Ltd.
Quaran House
Mfangano Street
P.O. Box 45245, Nairobi

KOREA, REPUBLIC OF
Daejon Trading Co. Ltd.
P.O. Box 34
Yeoeida, Seoul

MALAYSIA
University of Malaya
CooperativeBookshop, Limited, P.O. Box 1127
Jalan Pantai Baru
59700 Kuala Lumpur

MEXICO
INFOTEC
Apartado Postal 22-860
14060 Tlalpan
Mexico D.F.

NETHERLANDS
De Lindeboom/InOr-Publikaties
P.O. Box 202
7480 AE Haaksbergen

NEW ZEALAND
EBSCO NZ Ltd.
Private Mail Bag 99914
New Market, Auckland

NIGERIA
University Press Limited
Three Crowns Building Jericho
Private Mail Bag 50
Ibadan

NORWAY
Narvesen Information Center
Book Department
P.O. Box 6125 Etterstad
N-0602 Oslo 6

PAKISTAN
Mirza Book Agency
65, Shahrah-e-Quaid-e-Azam
P.O. Box No. 729
Lahore 54000

Oxford University Press
5 Bangalore Town
Sharae Faisal
PO Box 13033
Karachi-75350

PERU
Editorial Desarrollo SA
Apartado 3824
Lima 1

PHILIPPINES
International Booksource Center .Inc.
Suite 720, Cityland 10
Condominium Tower 2
H.V dela Costa, corner
Valero St., Makati, Metro Manila

POLAND
International Publishing Service
Ul. Piekna 31/37
00-577 Warzawa

PORTUGAL
Livraria Portugal
Rua Do Carmo 70-74
1200 Lisbon

ROMANIA
Compani De Librarii Bucuresti S.A.
Str. Lipscani no. 26
sector 3
Bucharest

RUSSIAN FEDERATION
Isdatelstvo <Ves Mir>
9a, Kolpachniy Pereulok
Moscow 101831

SAUDI ARABIA, QATAR
Jarir Book Store
P.O. Box 3196
Riyadh 11471

SINGAPORE, TAIWAN,
MYANMAR, BRUNEI
Asahgate Publishing Asia
    Pacific Pte. Ltd.
41 Kallang Pudding Road #04-03
Golden Wheel Building
Singapore 349316

SLOVAK REPUBLIC
Slovart G.T.G. Ltd.
Krupinska 4
PO Box 152
852 99 Bratislava 5

SOUTH AFRICA, BOTSWANA
For single titles:
Oxford University Press Southern Africa
P.O. Box 1141
Cape Town 8000

For subscription orders:
International Subscription Svc.
P.O. Box 41095
Craighall
Johannesburg 2024

SPAIN
Mundi-Prensa Libros, S.A.
Castello 37
28001 Madrid

Mundi-Prensa Barcelona
Consell de Cent, 391
08009 Barcelona

SRI LANKA
THE MALDIVES
Lake House Bookshop .
P.O. Box 244
100, Sir Chittampalam A.
Gardiner Mawatha
Colombo 2

SWEDEN
Fritzes Customer Service
Regeringsgaton 12
S-106 47
Stockholm

Wennergren-Williams AB
P. O. Box 1305
S-171 25
Solna

SWITZERLAND
Librairie Payot
Service Institutionnel
Côtes-de-Montbenon 30
1002 Lausanne

Van Diermen Editions Techniques
Ch. de Lacuez 41
CH1807 Blonay

TANZANIA
Oxford University Press
Maktaba Street
PO Box 5299
Dar es Salaam

THAILAND
Central Books Distribution
306 Silom Road
Bangkok

TRINIDAD & TOBAGO, JAMAICA
Systematics Studies Unit
#9 Watts Street
Curepe
Trinidad
West Indies

UGANDA
Gustro Ltd.
Madhvani Building
PO Box 9997
Plot 16/4 Jinja Rd.
Kampala

UNITED KINGDOM
Microinfo Ltd.
P.O. Box 3
Alton,
Hampshire GU34 2PG
England

ZAMBIA
University Bookshop
Great East Road Campus
P.O. Box 32379
Lusaka

ZIMBABWE
Longman Zimbabwe
(Pte.) Ltd.
Tourle Road, Ardbennie
P.O. Box ST125
Southerton

Order Form

To order *World Development Report 1996*, fill in quantity desired, shipping and handling costs, and total price. Thank you for your order.

Customers in the United States
Detach this form at the perforation and return to: The World Bank, P.O. Box 7247-8619, Philadelphia, PA 19170-8619, USA.

Customers outside the United States
Return your order to the authorized World Bank publications distributor whose name and address are indicated on the preceding pages.

> If no distributor has been noted for your country, return your order to: The World Bank, P.O. Box 7247-8619, Philadelphia, PA 19170-8619, USA. Payment may be made by credit card as noted, or by US dollar check drawn on a US bank.
>
> **Orders received by the World Bank from countries with authorized distributors will be returned to customer.**

Payment: Note that orders from individuals must be accompanied by payment or credit card information. Credit cards accepted only for orders addressed to the World Bank. Check with local distributor about acceptable credit cards. Please do not send cash.

❏ Enclosed is my check.
Make check payable to the World Bank in US dollars drawn on a US bank unless you are ordering from your local distributor.

❏ **Bill me. Institutional customers in the US only.**
(Please include purchase order)

❏ Charge my   ❏ **VISA**   ❏ **MasterCard**   ❏ AMERICAN EXPRESS

Account Number _____   Expiration Date _____   Signature (required to validate all orders) _____

Note: If you are paying by check or credit card, shipping and handling charges are US$5.00 per order. For air mail delivery outside North America, add US$8.00 for one item plus US$6.00 for each additional item. Prices may vary by country and are subject to change without notice.

Ship to:

Name and Title _____   Address _____

(___)

City _____   State ___   Postal Code ___   Country ___   Telephone _____

Please send the World Bank products listed below:

Quantity	Language	Title	Stock #	Price	Total Price
___	___	**World Development Report 1996**	___	___	___
___	___	___	___	___	___
___	___	___	___	___	___

Subtotal cost $ _____

Shipping and handling $ __5.00__

Airmail surcharge outside USA $ _____

Total $ _____

4088